Southern Living
2006 ANNUAL RECIPES

Oxmoor House

best recipes of 2006

Not all recipes are created equal. At *Southern Living,* only those that have passed muster with our Test Kitchens staff and Foods editors—not an easy crowd to please—make it onto the pages of our magazine. Members of our Foods Staff gather almost every day to taste-test recipes to ensure not only that they're reliable, but also that they taste as good as they possibly can. Here we share this year's favorites.

All of our winning recipes in Cook-off 2006 received our highest rating as well. These recipes begin on page 309.

Lemon Cheesecake Pies *(page 50)* ▶
The inspiration for this citrus favorite comes from a Lemon Chess Pie Filling that boasts a fresh lemon flavor.

▼ **Double Chocolate Cheesecake** *(page 48)*
The sweetness of this scrumptious dessert checks in at just the right level to let the chocolate flavor stand out.

▲ **Herbed Salad With Grilled Balsamic Vegetables** *(page 61)* Grilled vegetables flavored with a tangy balsamic dressing mingle with mixed baby greens, a variety of herbs, and two types of cheese for an unbelievable spring salad.

◀ **Baby Blue Salad** *(page 52)* The Balsamic Vinaigrette and Sweet-and-Spicy Pecans put this salad in a category of its own.

▲ **Chicken-fried Steak** *(page 39)* Because of its crunchy coating, tender inside, and peppery gravy, we have named this dish one of our best-ever recipes.

Beginner's Roast *(page 40)* Long, slow oven-cooking is the secret to this juicy, pull-apart tender entrée that contains just five ingredients and takes just five minutes to assemble.

Browned Butter-Pecan Shortbread *(page 86)* It's impossible to resist the rich and nutty taste of browned butter that flavors these delicate cookies.

Smoked Lemon-Chipotle Chickens *(page 109)* You can't beat the hickory-smoked flavor accented with a lemon-chipotle mixture of this crowd-pleasing recipe.

▲ **Pound Cake Banana Pudding** *(page 68)* Grab a whisk and saucepan for this fresh twist on a Southern classic that uses pound cake in place of vanilla wafers.

◄ **Classic Strawberry Shortcake** *(page 121)* Sweet biscuits, fresh berries, and a lavish crown of whipped cream make this Southern dessert irresistible.

Cranberry-Key Lime Sauce *(page 251)* Key limes (peel and all) provide the zesty flavor to this twist-on-traditional Thanksgiving dish.

▲ **Watermelon-Mint Margaritas** *(page 151)* Dip the rims of glasses in a lime-and-sugar coating to serve this slushy drink bursting with refreshing summer flavor.

Billie's Favorite Strawberry Milk Shake *(page 89)* Three simple ingredients and five minutes are all that you need to whip up this frosty beverage.

Hot Cross Buns *(page 104)* With the right combination of spices, dried fruit, and icing, these delicious treats melt in your mouth.

Traditional King Cake *(page 51)* This Mardi Gras classic is as rich in tradition and history as it is in color and taste. Bread flour makes this yeast bread light and airy.

▲ **Pan-fried Okra, Onion, and Tomatoes** *(page 155)* Showcase the freshest vegetables of the season in this colorful side dish.

Creamy Cheese Grits *(page 31)* ▶
The combination of tangy sharp Cheddar cheese and mild Monterey Jack cheese creates the perfect balance of creaminess and flavor in this old-fashioned Southern stick-to-your-ribs favorite.

Fresh Peach Salsa *(page 202)* Jalapeño pepper, cilantro, and sweet onion give a savory spin to juicy peaches in this hot and spicy condiment.

Bananas Foster Gratin *(page 207)* Crushed biscotti adds a crunchy twist to this showstopping dessert that also gets its great flavor from rum, brown sugar, butter, and bananas.

Cinnamon-Raisin Rolls *(page 212)* This variation of the Apricot-Pecan Cinnamon Rolls replaces the apricots with golden raisins for a melt-in-your-mouth treat.

Apricot-Pecan Cinnamon Rolls *(page 212)* No one would ever guess that this sweet and buttery homemade favorite begins with a package of frozen biscuits. ▼

Tres Leches Flan *(page 254)* A combination of three different milks gives this rich dessert its name.

Basil-Thyme Crème Brûlée *(page 255)* These make-ahead custards make a handsome presentation with their crackly topping.

Easy Homemade Biscuits
(page 276) ▶
It takes only four ingredients
and less than 30 minutes to
make these perfect biscuits.
Our **Easy Cheddar Biscuits**
boast a cup of Cheddar cheese
for a tangy variation.

Roasted Pecan Fudge
(page 263) Marshmallows,
roasted pecans, and chocolate
make every bite of this homemade treat heavenly.

▼ **Overnight Marinated
Shrimp** *(page 250)* A variety
of flavors that includes yellow
bell pepper, onion, sugar,
lemon, and hot sauce—just to
name a few—will have you
raving about this easy, make-
ahead recipe.

▲ **Chocolate-Mint Cake** *(page 286)* Dark and moist, with a velvety-rich texture, this dessert makes a dazzling finale to any meal.

◄ **Glazed Butternut Squash** *(page 242)* Apple cider and chopped pecans bring together the taste of fall in this hearty side dish.

Chocolate Sheet Cake *(page265)* This rich, single-layer dessert boasts a lush, a fudgelike frosting.

Pecan Pie *(page 267)* No one would guess that it takes just five minutes to make this Southern holiday staple.

Cream Cheese Pound Cake *(page 286)* It takes a few simple staples to whip up this moist and delicious Southern classic.

▲ **Spicy Braised Short Ribs With Peach Gravy and Green Rice** *(page 316)* Peach gelatin is the secret ingredient in this dish that won $10,000 and was the category winner for Super-Quick Family Favorites in our cook-off.

Eggnog With Coffee and Irish Cream *(page 287)* Brewed coffee and Irish cream liqueur add a tasty twist on a holiday favorite.

◄ **Sweet Potato Cinnamon Rolls** *(page 310)* With a buttery filling and sweet glaze, this melt-in-your-mouth homemade favorite was the $100,000 grand prize winner in our cook-off.

Pecan Pie Cake *(page 285)* Dusting buttered pans with finely chopped pecans instead of flour creates a crisp coating around each luscious layer of caramel-filled Pecan Pie Cake.

Caramel Cream Cake *(page 285)* Use our decadent Pecan Pie Cake Batter and Filling along with toasted pecans and coconut to make this sensational dessert.

▼ **Mexi-Texi Bistec Pedazos on Roasted Corn and Garlic Chipotle-Cilantro Mashers** *(page 311)* This deliciously seasoned beef pairs perfectly with a flavorful mashed potato dish.

Grilled Sweet Chili Chicken With Mango-Cucumber Slaw *(page 312)* ▶ A sweet chili sauce mixture flavors both the grilled chicken and the slaw in this $10,000 cook-off category winner for Healthy and Good for You.

Toffee-Apple Dip *(page 289)* Five minutes and five ingredients are all it takes to stir up this creamy mixture.

Brown Sugar-Pecan Coffee Cake *(page 290)* A crispy, buttery crust makes this the perfect party pick-me-up.

▼ **Chunky Tomato 'n' Grilled Corn Bisque** *(page 318)* The surprising tastes of tomato, basil, sugar, whipping cream, blue cheese, and fresh corn combine for a one-of-a-kind soup.

▲ **Baby Sweet Potato Cakes With Sticky Caramel-Pecan Sauce** *(page 314)* Muffin cups shape this elegant dessert that garnered $10,000 in the cook-off Southern Desserts category.

◄ **Shrimp Bruschetta With Guacamole** *(page 317)* Avocados, lime juice, cilantro, and salsa punch up the flavor of this favorite that won $10,000 in the cook-off Party Starters category.

Apple-Cinnamon Breakfast Cobbler *(page 289)* Apples and cinnamon baked in a sweet pastry crust taste incredible topped with ice cream.

meet the *Southern Living* foods staff

Dozens of recipes go through our Test Kitchens each day, where they are evaluated on taste, appearance, practicality, and ease of preparation. On these pages, we invite you to match the names and faces of the people who test, photograph, and write about our favorites (left to right unless otherwise noted).

▲ (standing) LYDA JONES BURNETTE, *Test Kitchens Director;* JAMES SCHEND, *Assistant Test Kitchens Director;* MARIAN COOPER CAIRNS, *Test Kitchens Professional;* (sitting) PAM LOLLEY, *Test Kitchens Professional;* VANESSA MCNEIL ROCCHIO, *Test Kitchens Specialist/Food Styling;* REBECCA KRACKE GORDON *and* ANGELA SELLERS, *Test Kitchens Professionals*

▲ (sitting) SCOTT JONES, *Executive Editor;* PAT YORK, *Editorial Assistant;* (standing) SHANNON SLITER SATTERWHITE, *Foods Editor;* SANDRA J. THOMAS, *Administrative Assistant*

(standing) SHIRLEY HARRINGTON, *Associate Foods Editor;* ▶ DONNA FLORIO, *Senior Writer;* KATE NICHOLSON, *Associate Foods Editor;* JOHN MCMILLAN, *Assistant Recipe Editor;* MARY ALLEN PERRY, *Associate Foods Editor;* ANDRIA SCOTT HURST, *Senior Writer;* (sitting) CHARLA DRAPER, VICKI A. POELLNITZ, *and* HOLLEY JOHNSON, *Associate Foods Editors*

our year at
Southern Living.

Dear Food Friends,

2006 has been exciting at *Southern Living.* Not only did the magazine turn 40 this year, but the special occasion allowed us to celebrate some of the most memorable recipes to have graced our pages. We also reflected on the unique connection we've established with generations of devoted readers. You've made us a part of your extended family, and we certainly think of each reader as part of ours. (Don't miss Cook's Chat beginning on page 24, a terrific example of this relationship and a way for readers to comment online about some of their favorite recipes.)

"You've made us a part of your extended family, and we certainly think of each reader as part of ours. "

As you flip through these pages and prepare the recipes, you're ultimately experiencing a month-to-month scrapbook of our year in food. Be sure to reference the Test Kitchens Notebook tips scattered throughout the chapters. You'll uncover our top secrets for success and learn everything you need to know to get these irresistible recipes just right. One of my favorite sections is the Menu Index on page 336, which supplies over 50 terrific menu ideas—it's the perfect companion for planning supper.

This coming year, please allow us to set the *Southern Living* table with you in mind.
• Is there a subject you'd like us to cover? Write us.
• Do you know someone who makes the "best something" you've ever tasted? Introduce us to them.
• Have you reinvented a favorite dish or made it healthier? Tell us about it.
• Do you see products in the grocery store that you'd like to know how to use in the kitchen? Ask us.

Thanks for inviting us into your homes. I look forward to hearing from you and seeing more of your recipes soon.

Sincerely,

Scott Jones
Executive Editor

ISBN-13: 978-0-8487-3104-2
ISBN-10: 0-8487-3104-2

Printed in the United States of America
First printing 2006

To order additional publications, call 1-800-765-6400.

Cover: Lemon-Coconut Cake, page 284

Page 1 (clockwise from front): Pear-Glazed Pork Roast, page 281; Sautéed Beans and Peppers, page 258; Cranberry-Apple Pie, page 282 garnished with a wreath of Pecan Pie-Glazed Pecans, page 281; Twice-Baked Sweet Potatoes, page 282; Rice Timbales, page 282

Southern Living®
Executive Editor: Scott Jones
Foods Editor: Shannon Sliter Satterwhite
Senior Writers: Donna Florio, Andria Scott Hurst
Associate Foods Editors: Natalie Brown, Charla Draper,
    Shirley Harrington, Holley Johnson, Kate Nicholson,
    Mary Allen Perry, Vicki A. Poellnitz
Assistant Recipe Editor: Ashley Leath
Test Kitchens Director: Lyda Jones Burnette
Assistant Test Kitchens Director: James Schend
Test Kitchens Specialist/Food Styling: Vanessa McNeil Rocchio
Test Kitchens Professionals: Marian Cooper Cairns,
    Rebecca Kracke Gordon, Pam Lolley, Angela Sellers
Administrative Assistant: Sandra J. Thomas
Production and Color Quality Manager: Katie Terrell Morrow
Photography and Cover Art Director: Jon Thompson
Copy Chief: Paula Hunt Hughes
Copy Editor: Cindy Riegle
Senior Foods Photographers: Ralph Anderson
Photographers: Tina Cornett, William Dickey, Beth Dreiling
Senior Photo Stylist: Buffy Hargett
Photo Stylist: Rose Nguyen
Assistant Photo Stylists: Lisa Powell, Cari South
Photo Production Manager: Larry Hunter
Photo Librarian: Tracy Duncan
Photo Assistant: Catherine Carr
Assistant Production Manager: Jamie Barnhart
Production Coordinators: Christy Coleman, Paula Dennis
Production Assistant: Allison Brooke Wilson

Oxmoor House, Inc.
Editor in Chief: Nancy Fitzpatrick Wyatt
Executive Editor: Susan Carlisle Payne
Copy Chief: Allison Long Lowery

Southern Living® *2006 Annual Recipes*
Editor: Susan Hernandez Ray
Copy Editor: Donna Baldone
Editorial Assistant: Julie Boston
Director of Production: Laura Lockhart
Senior Production Manager: Greg A. Amason
Production Assistant: Faye Porter Bonner

Contributors
Designer: Nancy Johnson
Indexer: Mary Ann Laurens
Editorial Consultant: Jean Wickstrom Liles
Editorial Interns: Jill Baughman, Mary Katherine Pappas,
  Lucas Whittington
Proofreaders: Dolores Hydock, Barzella Papa, Laura K. Womble

contents

favorite columns at a glance

Each month we focus on topics that are important to our readers—from Southern classics to fast dinners to delicious menus.

>> top-rated menus

■ The secret to **Our Best Chicken-fried Steak** is in the breading. One taste of its crunchy coating and you'll see why we list it among our favorites. Easy Creamy Mashed Potatoes are a comforting companion (page 39).

■ Our scrumptious **Dinner for Two** with Beef Fillets With Cognac-Onion Sauce and Baby Blue Salad was created with Valentine's Day in mind. We reduced these favorite recipes for two with no leftovers (pages 52–53).

■ Serve **Catfish With All the Fixin's** at your next family get-together. This timeless Southern menu includes Classic Fried Catfish, Baked Beans, and Hush Puppies (page 78).

■ Try something inherently Southern for supper—**Our Favorite Vegetable Plate** with Tee's Corn Pudding, Butterbeans and Bacon, and Skillet Cornbread (pages 198–199).

■ Make a meal out of these **Appetizer Favorites,** which include Marinated Cheese and Peppered Pork With Pecan Biscuits (page 240).

■ **Entertain With Ease** during the busy holiday season with one of our most-requested recipes, Shrimp Destin, paired with Asparagus With Curry Sauce (page 295).

>> taste of the south

■ **Cheese Grits** (page 31) A blend of two cheeses gives the perfect balance of creaminess and flavor in this good old-fashioned stick-to-your-ribs Southern dish.

■ **King Cake** (page 51) Similar to coffee cake, this ring-shaped Mardi Gras dessert is as rich in tradition as it is in color and taste.

■ **Cheese Straws** (page 72) Sample each variety of these bite-sized treats. They're great as appetizers, picnic favorites, or simple afternoon pick-me-ups.

■ **Hot Cross Buns** (page 104) Many Southerners serve these nutmeg-and-cinnamon-spiced buns during Lenten season, but you can bake these melt-in-your-mouth treats anytime.

■ **Strawberry Shortcake** (page 121) True shortcake is a big, slightly sweet biscuit. Top these Southern favorites with sugar-kissed berries and sweetened whipped cream.

■ **Margarita** (page 201) This sweet-and-sour sipper, a signature drink of the Southwest, complements a tall glass and a beach chair.

■ **Smoked Mullet** (page 215) A longtime favorite of Gulf Coast Floridians, this rich, dark meat gets its characteristic salty flavor from a quick chill in a salt-water solution before smoking on the grill.

>> quick & easy

■ Mix a few fresh ingredients with some cupboard staples for a delicious New Year's dinner (page 33).

■ Start with ready-to-serve rice pouches for meals that deliver mighty taste in minimum time. (page 49).

■ Slather these speedy sauces over cooked rice, rotisserie chicken, open-faced turkey sandwiches or mashed potatoes for tasty supper options (page 76).

■ Get creative by dressing up ground round and turkey with some unexpected ingredients for your next burger bash (page 101).

■ Try these surprising new twists on tacos for easy weeknight suppers (page 140).

■ Satisfy both fish and shrimp lovers with delicious seafood sandwiches made to order (page 199).

■ Fast and simple, pasta is just right for those nights when you're in a hurry. While the water heats up, you have time to chop, measure, and sauté everything else (page 208).

■ Use either a coating made from cornflake or saltine crackers for crispy pork chops from the oven—the ultimate in comfort food (page 243).

■ Convenience products make these Chicken and Dumplings recipes super simple (page 276).

■ Stack up big flavor in a flash with a satisfying soup and club sandwich (page 294).

>> what's for supper

■ Make a jazzy ground beef base—then serve it on buns for an easy Sloppy Joe supper or baked in a casserole that's big enough to serve your family and a couple of friends (page 79).

■ When you're craving a filling dinner, try our slow-cooker chili lightened for spring weather with ground turkey, bell pepper, and corn. Or a family-pleasing chili and potato tot casserole (page 97).

■ A hot pan, meat or poultry, and simple seasonings are all you need for a quick, stylish dinner. Top it off with Chocolate Soufflés that take just 10 minutes to prepare (page 111).

■ Simmer a beef roast with a few simple ingredients for several hours for an easy weeknight supper (page 133).

■ Pair steak and potatoes on the grill for a streamlined dinner for two (page 193).

■ The University of Georgia created a program where the staff selects, cooks, and serves students' favorite recipes sent in by parents. Sample one of their featured main dishes and desserts (page 218).

■ Easy Lasagna makes it a snap for your family to dine in like they might dine out at a family-style Italian restaurant (page 240).

■ For a fresh twist on Italian, serve up a scrumptious sausage supper. Each recipe in our menu boasts just seven ingredients or less (page 253).

■ When you're in the mood for Tex-Mex, this is the dinner to make (page 296).

>> healthy & light

♥ Staying healthy during cold and flu season can be as simple as fixing nutrient-packed meals (page 36).

♥ Three servings of milk, cheese, or yogurt in your diet each day could lead to a healthier, more-slender you (page 54).

♥ These tasty recipes are loaded with super foods that help prevent disease, aid in weight loss, and maintain a healthy body (page 70).

♥ We jazzed up these already-good dishes with a few simple and healthful ingredients, and tell you how to do the same with your favorite recipes (page 90).

♥ Share a meal with friends and sample a host of miniature main dishes, known as tapas. They'll let you taste a variety of Southern-inspired recipes without overeating (page 118).

♥ Get the kids in the kitchen for a hands-on experience that will enhance their appreciation and basic knowledge of different foods, good nutrition, and simple cooking (page 132).

♥ You won't want to skip dessert with these cool and creamy treats that leave no room for guilt (page 141).

♥ Give your day a great start with a well-rounded breakfast that could also help you consume fewer calories throughout the day (page 194).

♥ Enjoy surprising options from the grill for burgers and potato salad with recipes that are loaded with healthful carbs, fiber, vitamins, and minerals (page 216).

♥ Including whole grains in your diet gives you more energy and helps to control your appetite (page 244).

♥ Lightened holiday party starters let you entertain with great flavor and no guilt (page 252).

♥ One bite of these recipes and you'll agree that sweet potatoes are one of the best-tasting vegetables (page 290).

cook's chat

Our readers chat online about what they think about our recipes and how they use them. Here, they brag about some of their favorites.

≫ appetizers and beverages

White Sangria, page 66—"Very fruity. I cut the recipe with a little extra gingerale because I thought it was a little too sweet."

Blue Cheese Thumbprints, page 72—"These were wonderful and very easy to make. They had just the right kick to them! I made half a recipe which was very easy to do."

Tequila Mojitos, page 125—"Outstanding! These are going to be my new signature summer cocktails . . . cool and refreshing, and not too sweet. I used bottled lime juice, which was fine, and a decent tequila. Double (or triple) the recipe in advance because it barely makes one pitcher and it goes quickly!"

Watermelon-Mint Margaritas, page 111—"I brought these to a pool party and they were a hit—lots of compliments. I tripled the recipe and cut the sugar slightly because my melon was already very sweet; I added a little more tequila. These were not too sweet and people liked the mint taste."

≫ soups and stews

Baked Potato-and-Broccoli Soup, page 28—"This is one of the best creamed soups I have ever made or tasted. It's a family winner! It beats some of the creamed soups you get in the restaurants or deli. It was fast to make—and easy! I had everything on hand in the house and whipped it up quickly. It would be great for special occasions—very impressive. We had a bowl of soup and half a sandwich, which were perfect for lunch. I did alter the recipe; I used one can of chicken stock and one can cream of mushroom soup. I also used a block of cheese that I grated myself. (I prefer to grate my own cheese for all my recipes.) I used the cream soup for a creamier consistency, and I used frozen florets. The month of January *Southern Living* always has great soup recipes!"

Loaded Potato Soup, page 47—"This recipe is wonderful and so easy to make! I don't particularly care for new potatoes, so I use russets in mine. I have halved the recipe because it was just for my husband and me. I have already used this recipe several times; it will become a weekly staple in my home."

≫ entrées

Chicken-fried Steak, page 39—"Absolutely delicious! Definitely will make this again and again. My family loved it! Fairly easy to make; prepared my cracker mix ahead to make it easier. Almost didn't make the gravy, but my husband and I were so glad we did; the dish was excellent!"

Chicken Cobbler Casserole, page 41—"My husband said this is the best chicken casserole he has ever had! Everyone loved it. I added a little thyme, salt, and pepper to the sauce and used a sour dough loaf instead of rolls. The bread crust was wonderful. I served it with a green salad. I will make this over and over again!"

Beef Fillets With Cognac-Onion Sauce, page 52—"This is an absolutely fabulous recipe! We made it for Valentine's Day, and the dinner was better than going out! Easy to make; the only change I made was using red wine instead of the cognac. You will love this!"

Richard's Sloppy Joes, page 79—"Finally a recipe without the proverbial celery and green bell pepper so often included in this type of food item. Thank you; it was great!"

Oven-Fried Bacon-Wrapped Chicken Thighs, page 73—"These were really tasty and so easy to assemble. Once they're in the oven, you then have 50 minutes to an hour to do other tasks around the kitchen or just relax. A good, simple recipe that's great for a weeknight meal. I made them just as the recipe stated and served them with a salad."

Ellie's Lasagna, page 84—"This recipe was excellent! It had a wonderful flavor and was very easy to make. I made it for a group of about 20 plus people, and it got rave reviews. It is also great without the meat—just cheese lasagna!"

Crab Cakes With Lemon Rémoulade, page 113—"Best recipe for crab cakes ever! Lemon Rémoulade was the absolute perfect accompaniment. I have made this recipe for my family several times, and has since become one of our favorites. Served the crab cakes over spring mix as suggested, with a side of fresh green beans and grape tomatoes tossed with thyme. Thanks for an outstanding recipe."

BBQ Shrimp, page 144—"This recipe was delicious! The whole family loved it, and it couldn't have been easier to prepare! Definitely a keeper!"

Slow-cooker Beef Brisket, page 158—"This is one of the best briskets I've ever tasted! It was very simple to make. We had several friends over the night we made it, and everyone thought it was delicious!"

Linguine With Clam Sauce, page 200—"This was a huge hit and absolutely delicious. On a whim, I made this easy dinner one night for my husband and me. We 'ummed and ahhhhed' all the way through the meal. (I halved the recipe for us.) It's company-easy and company-worthy for a rustic, delicious meal."

❯❯ sandwiches

Black Bean-and-Brown Rice Pitas, page 103—"A friend made these for us as a light, end-of-summer dinner, and they were enjoyed by all! Be sure to use sour cream and salsa as toppings."

Barbecue Pork Sandwiches, page 127—"An easy recipe when preparing for guests. Prepare it in the morning and you're done! I've made this recipe twice now, and it was a hit both times. I used the boneless pork loin, as they were on sale, and the sandwiches couldn't have been better. The first time, I served the pork sandwiches with coleslaw, and the second time, my guests provided potluck salads and desserts. Very easy entertaining!"

Tomato-Egg Sandwiches, page 136—"This recipe is simple to make ahead of time. What a great spread to have on hand for a sandwich bar! I didn't have horseradish sauce so I mixed straight horseradish with mayo—about half of each. Turned out delicious—not too hot but a hint of it. Yummy! I got lots of compliments, too."

Mango-Chicken Wraps, page 148—"Very good. I made this last night and was pleasantly surprised at how the flavors worked together so well, including the lettuce in the wrap, which added a nice crunch to the dish. I did not grill the chicken, but cooked it in a frying pan, and it worked wonderfully. I will definitely make this again for a nice light summer meal."

❯❯ salads

Chicken-and-Artichoke Salad, page 40—"This was good chilled, but excellent served hot! I used Texas Garlic Toast and no cheese. My family loves it—new favorite chicken salad!"

Baby Blue Salad, page 52—"This salad is out of this world. My guests are still talking about it. I have served this for elegant Christmas dinners and a bridal shower luncheon, and it's always a big hit. It's so easy to prepare and quick to put together at the last minute. I served chicken salad for the bridal shower with this and prime rib for an elegant dinner. It fits in anywhere."

Lemon-Basil Shrimp Salad, page 95—"This is a wonderful dish to serve to family or guests. It's a shrimp cocktail and salad in one! I served it with garlic crudites and goat cheese rounds. It was a big hit. I will certainly make this again!"

Honey-Chicken Salad, page 131—"Fabulous! Served it at a wedding luncheon and had rave reviews! Thanks for a great recipe! When I made it at home, I did not have the dried cranberries but used the dried apples, cranberries and cherries mix along with some jicama, which adds a wonderful crunch."

Texas Pecan-and-Avocado Salad, page 149—"This was so beautiful that I almost didn't want to serve it—but it was delicious! A real winner when served to company."

Grilled Sweet Potato Salad With Basil Vinaigrette, page 216—"Delicious! I doubled the dressing. I left the sweet potatoes on the grill too long and they formed a black crust . . . which I scraped off. They were still delicious. I took this dish to our family Labor Day celebration, and everyone loved it."

>> sides

Marinated Tomatoes, page 38—"I made this recipe for my family and friends on New Year's Day, and they all loved it. The flavors were great; I had some left over and put them on my green salad the next day, and it tasted great."

Asparagus With Dill Sauce, page 44—"I served this at a dinner party. Guests raved about the perfect crunch of the asparagus and the lightness of the sauce. I also added other fresh veggies."

Cheesy Tomato Casserole, page 65—"This dish is now a staple in my repertoire, after preparing it three times already. Everyone who has tasted it has raved. I do use garlic and butter croutons rather than crackers. I also added fresh bacon pieces (three strips) for more flavor. I've served it at casual parties and as a side with beef. It's very versatile."

White Cheddar-and-Squash Casserole, page 113—"I had family members who do not like squash taking seconds. It's appropriate for everyday or special occasions. I have served turkey and pork tenderloin with this dish."

Pan-fried Okra, Onion, and Tomatoes, page 155—"Being from the north, okra is not a vegetable we have access to. My Southern sister made this, and I must say, it was fabulous. I'm trying to figure out if frozen okra will work, or any other vegetable. This is one of those keepers that may require a trip down South to make."

Tee's Corn Pudding, page 198—"Summer leaves us with a lot of fresh corn. This recipe was extremely delicious. The texture was very light and fluffy. I will freeze some corn and use it again on Thanksgiving. I did increase the sugar to ½ cup since I like things sweeter. I mixed the flour and sugar thoroughly with the corn before adding any wet ingredients."

>> breads

Honey-Oatmeal Wheat Bread, page 70—"I really enjoyed making and eating this bread. Usually, wheat bread is dense. This recipe had a great texture and a wonderful taste. I certainly would make it again."

Brown Sugar-Banana Muffins, page 94—"Wonderful! I didn't have baking soda or powder, so I substituted Bisquick reduced-fat pancake mix for the flour/baking soda/powder. The muffins turned out delicious. My husband ate four!"

Sausage Bread, page 119—"I made this using canned croissant dough since the store was out of French bread dough. We used sage sausage instead of hot sausage. Everyone loved it, from the six-year-old to the teen to the adults!"

Cinnamon-Raisin Rolls, page 212—"Very good! I did not have any raisins, but the rolls were just as good! Very easy and such a comfort food to have with coffee in the mornings! I'm adding this to my brunch recipes and will make them at the next brunch I prepare."

>> desserts

Uptown Banana Pudding Cheesecake, page, 67—"Loved making it—easy—great for any occasion that you have to take a dessert. It's very rich so small slices are the norm—goes a long way. Best cheesecake I've tasted, and everyone raves when they eat it."

So-Easy Chocolate Soufflés, page 112—"This was truly so easy and delicious! Don't skip the last step of moving your thumb around the edge. I had forgotten the first time and noticed (the second time) when I did move my thumb around the edge, the soufflé rose much higher. One guest loved whipped topping, so I served it on the side for dipping with a slice of strawberry garnish."

Sour Cream Pound Cake, page 134—"This is the yummiest sour cream pound cake recipe . . . so rich with butter! It gets better after it sits for a day. My husband thinks it's the best . . . plain or with fruit. A real *Southern Living* classic."

Key Lime Pie, page 141—"I have made this almost weekly since I got my July issue. It's delicious and hard to believe it's 'light.' In my oven, I have to bake it slightly more than 12 minutes to set the filling. I have also substituted egg whites for the egg substitute with equal success."

Cream-Filled Chocolate Chip Wafers, page 149—"I couldn't find the wafers so I substituted chocolate graham crackers. All the family loved this."

Toffee-Almond Blondies, page 197—"Delicious! Very easy, quick, and rich. The guys at our preseason tailgate party devoured them."

january

Eating Together

Check out this Kentucky family's nutritious, hearty recipes and cold-weather activities.

Sherry and David Bryant of Bowling Green, Kentucky, stay busy raising five children ages 2 to 14. We gave them ideas for making their favorite recipes more healthful and for finding new ways to experience quality family time.

Baked Potato-and-Broccoli Soup
family favorite
PREP: 20 MIN., COOK: 20 MIN.
Sherry's original potato-cheese soup recipe used butter, cream cheese, and cream of mushroom soup. We lightened hers by using lower fat ingredients and adding broccoli and onions for fiber, while still maintaining the rich flavor with freshly shredded cheese and bacon pieces.

¼ cup all-purpose flour
2 (14¼-oz.) cans low-sodium
  fat-free chicken broth, divided
3 cups peeled, cubed potato
  (about 1¼ lb.)
2 cups broccoli florets, chopped
1 small onion, chopped
1¼ cups 2% reduced-fat milk
1 (8-oz.) block 2% reduced-fat sharp
  Cheddar cheese, shredded
7 tsp. shredded 2% reduced-fat sharp
  Cheddar cheese
7 tsp. fully cooked bacon pieces
7 tsp. chopped green onions

1. Whisk together flour and ⅓ cup chicken broth until smooth.
2. Combine remaining chicken broth and next 3 ingredients in a Dutch oven. Bring to a boil; cover, reduce heat, and simmer 8 minutes or until potatoes are tender. Gradually stir in flour mixture. Cook, stirring often, 5 minutes.
3. Stir in milk and 8 oz. shredded cheese. Cook over medium-low heat, stirring mixture constantly, until cheese melts. Top each serving of soup with 1 tsp. cheese, 1 tsp. bacon pieces, and 1 tsp. chopped green onions. **Makes** 7 servings.

Note: We recommend freshly shredded cheese (versus the preshredded variety) for additional creaminess and even melting.

Per (1-cup) serving: Calories 223 (32% from fat); Fat 7.9g (sat 4.5g, mono 0.5g, poly 0.1g); Protein 17.3g; Carb 20.3g; Fiber 2.6g; Chol 31mg; Iron 1mg; Sodium 667mg; Calc 395mg

Hearty Lasagna With Italian Meat Sauce
family favorite
PREP: 15 MIN.; BAKE: 1 HR., 5 MIN.; STAND: 15 MIN.

1 (15-oz.) container part-skim ricotta
  cheese
½ cup (2 oz.) shredded Italian three-
  cheese blend *
2 egg whites
½ tsp. pepper
6 cups Italian Meat Sauce
Vegetable cooking spray
1 (9-oz.) package dried precooked
  lasagna noodles
1½ cups (6 oz.) shredded part-skim
  mozzarella cheese, divided

1. Stir together first 4 ingredients.
2. Spread 1½ cups Italian Meat Sauce in a 13- x 9-inch baking dish coated with cooking spray. Arrange 4 noodles over meat sauce; top with half of ricotta mixture, 1½ cups Italian Meat Sauce, and ¾ cup shredded mozzarella. Arrange 4 noodles over cheese; top with remaining ricotta cheese mixture and 1½ cups Italian Meat Sauce. Arrange 4 noodles over sauce; top with remaining 1½ cups Italian Meat Sauce. Sprinkle evenly with remaining ¾ cup mozzarella cheese.
3. Bake, covered, at 350° for 50 minutes to 1 hour. Uncover and bake 5 more minutes. Remove from oven; let stand 15 minutes. **Makes** 12 servings.

* Substitute ½ cup freshly shredded Parmesan cheese, if desired.

Per serving: Calories 328 (32% from fat); Fat 11.7g (sat 5.3g, mono 3.4g, poly 0.4g); Protein 23.5g; Carb 30.9g; Fiber 2.6g; Chol 38mg; Iron 1.6mg; Sodium 515mg; Calc 250mg

Italian Meat Sauce:
freezeable
PREP: 15 MIN.; COOK: 1 HR., 45 MIN.
This hearty sauce makes 14 cups, but only 6 cups are needed for the lasagna. Freeze the extra sauce in zip-top plastic freezer bags, and save it to use later for another meal.

3 lb. extra-lean ground beef
2 large onions, chopped
2 medium-size green bell peppers,
  chopped
1½ tsp. minced garlic
2 (26-oz.) jars vegetable pasta sauce
2 (14½-oz.) cans chopped diced
  tomatoes with basil, garlic, and
  oregano
3 (8-oz.) cans no-salt-added tomato
  sauce
2 tsp. dried Italian seasoning
1½ tsp. pepper

1. Cook first 4 ingredients, in batches, in a large Dutch oven over medium-high heat, stirring until meat crumbles and is no longer pink. Drain well, and return to pan. Stir in pasta sauce and remaining ingredients.
2. Bring to a boil, and reduce heat to medium-low; cover and simmer, stirring occasionally, 45 minutes. Uncover and simmer, stirring occasionally, 45 minutes or until sauce is thickened. **Makes** 14 cups.

Note: For testing purposes only, we used Classico Traditional Favorites Garden Vegetable Primavera Pasta Sauce.

Per (½-cup) serving: Calories 151 (34% from fat); Fat 5.7g (sat 1.8g, mono 1.9g, poly 0.2g); Protein 11.6g; Carb 13g; Fiber 1.9g; Chol 18mg; Iron 1.4mg; Sodium 359mg; Calc 29mg

Garlic-and-Herb-Stuffed Chicken Breasts

family favorite

PREP: 15 MIN., COOK: 10 MIN., BAKE: 20 MIN.
This simple stuffed chicken is a favorite when Sherry and David entertain. Although this recipe serves only four, it can easily be doubled for a larger crowd.

4 (6-oz.) skinned and boned chicken breasts
1 (8-oz.) container light buttery-garlic-and-herb spreadable cheese
2 large egg whites
¼ cup nonfat buttermilk
½ cup Italian-seasoned breadcrumbs
½ cup whole wheat cracker crumbs
¼ tsp. salt
¼ tsp. pepper
2 tsp. olive oil

1. Place chicken between 2 sheets of heavy-duty plastic wrap, and flatten to a ¼-inch thickness using a meat mallet or rolling pin.
2. Spread cheese evenly over 1 side of each chicken breast. Fold short ends of each chicken breast over center, covering cheese, and secure with wooden picks.
3. Whisk together egg whites and buttermilk in a small bowl. Combine breadcrumbs and next 3 ingredients in a shallow dish. Dip chicken in egg white mixture, and dredge in breadcrumb mixture.
4. Cook chicken breasts in hot oil in a large nonstick skillet 4 to 5 minutes on each side or until chicken breasts are browned. Place chicken on a wire rack, and place wire rack in a jelly-roll pan.
5. Bake at 400° for 20 minutes or until a meat thermometer inserted into the thickest portion of chicken breast registers 170°. **Makes** 4 servings.

Note: For testing purposes only, we used Alouette Light Garlic & Herbs Spreadable Cheese, and Neva Betta Whole Wheat Crackers.

Per serving: Calories 392 (32% from fat); Fat 14g (sat 6.2g, mono 2.7g, poly 1.3g); Protein 47.8g; Carb 17.4g; Fiber 1.3g; Chol 129mg; Iron 1.8mg; Sodium 660mg; Calc 93mg

Pralines-and-Cream Cheesecake

family favorite • make ahead

PREP: 15 MIN., BAKE: 25 MIN., STAND: 10 MIN., CHILL: 3 HRS.
We shaved off 163 calories and 16 fat grams from each serving of Sherry's original cheesecake recipe.

2 (8-oz.) packages ⅓-less-fat cream cheese, softened
½ cup sugar
½ tsp. vanilla extract
2 egg whites
1 large egg
½ cup toffee bits
1 (6-oz.) reduced-fat graham cracker crust
8 Tbsp. reduced-fat whipped topping
8 tsp. caramel syrup
8 tsp. toffee bits

1. Beat first 3 ingredients at medium speed with an electric mixer until blended. Add egg whites, 1 at a time, beating just until blended. Add egg, and beat mixture just until blended. Stir in ½ cup toffee bits. Pour into graham cracker crust.
2. Bake at 325° for 25 minutes or until edges of cheesecake are set and center is almost set. Turn off oven; let cheesecake stand in oven 10 minutes. Remove from oven, and cool completely on a wire rack. Cover and chill at least 3 hours. Serve each slice with 1 Tbsp. whipped topping, 1 tsp. caramel syrup, and 1 tsp. toffee bits. **Makes** 8 servings.

Note: For testing purposes only, we used Heath Bits O'Brickle Almond Toffee Bits.

Per serving: Calories 401 (49% from fat); Fat 21.8g (sat 10.8g, mono 0.2g, poly 0.1g); Protein 8.9g; Carb 42.8g; Fiber 0g; Chol 72mg; Iron 0.5mg; Sodium 459mg; Calc 45mg

Superfast Suppers

You don't have to sacrifice good-for-you meals when you need dinner ready in 30 minutes or less. Get a jump start by using convenience items.

Mediterranean Chicken Couscous

PREP: 15 MIN., COOK: 5 MIN., STAND: 5 MIN.

1¼ cups low-sodium fat-free chicken broth
1 (5.6-oz.) package toasted pine nut couscous mix
3 cups chopped cooked chicken (about 1 rotisserie chicken)
¼ cup chopped fresh basil
1 (4-oz.) package crumbled feta cheese
1 pt. grape tomatoes, halved
1½ Tbsp. fresh lemon juice
1 tsp. grated lemon rind
¼ tsp. pepper
Garnish: fresh basil leaves

1. Heat broth and seasoning packet from couscous in the microwave at HIGH for 3 to 5 minutes or until broth begins to boil. Place couscous in a large bowl, and stir in broth mixture. Cover and let stand 5 minutes.
2. Fluff couscous with a fork; stir in chicken and next 6 ingredients. Serve warm or cold. Garnish, if desired. **Makes** 8 servings.

Tips: You'll need to buy a ⅔-oz. package of fresh basil and 1 rotisserie chicken to get the right amount of basil and chicken for this recipe. Substitute 4 tsp. of dried basil if you can't find fresh.

No pots and pans are required for this easy, no-mess recipe. Simply use a glass measuring cup to heat the broth in the microwave, place dry couscous in the serving bowl, and then add the broth. Once the remaining ingredients are stirred in, the dish is ready to serve.

RAMI PERRY
BIRMINGHAM, ALABAMA

Per 1-cup serving: Calories 212 (29% from fat); Fat 6.8g (sat 3.1g, mono 1.9g, poly 1.1g); Protein 21.3g; Carb 16.9g; Fiber 1.4g; Chol 58mg; Iron 1.2mg; Sodium 455mg; Calc 89mg

Warm Prosciutto-Stuffed Focaccia

PREP: 10 MIN., BAKE: 15 MIN.
It's easy to stack and bake this trendy sandwich. See photos at right. (Pictured on page 162)

1 (9-oz.) round loaf focaccia bread
3 oz. thinly sliced prosciutto ✱
4 oz. thinly sliced Muenster cheese
1 (6-oz.) package fresh baby spinach
¼ cup bottled roasted red bell peppers, drained
2 Tbsp. light balsamic vinaigrette

1. Cut bread in half horizontally, using a serrated knife. Top bottom bread half with prosciutto and next 3 ingredients. Drizzle with balsamic vinaigrette; cover with top bread half. Wrap in aluminum foil; place on a baking sheet.
2. Bake at 350° for 15 minutes or until warm. Cut focaccia into six wedges. Serve immediately. **Makes** 6 servings.

✱Substitute 6 oz. of ham for prosciutto for approximately the same amount of calories, if desired.

NATALIE GAVIN
NASHVILLE, TENNESSEE

Per serving: Calories 233 (35% from fat); Fat 9.4g (sat 4.4g, mono 2.5g, poly 0.5g); Protein 13.5g; Carb 24.9g; Fiber 1.4g; Chol 30mg; Iron 2.4mg; Sodium 648mg; Calc 133mg

If You Can Boil Water, You Can Make Couscous

Light and fluffy couscous is a quick alternative to rice, pasta, or potatoes that cooks in just 5 minutes. Made from semolina, the same ingredient as in pasta, couscous provides a good source of complex carbohydrates and B vitamins. Find it on the rice aisle of most grocery stores, and enjoy it by itself or with meat and vegetables. To add more fiber and whole grains to your diet, look for whole wheat couscous in specialty food stores.

1. Bring broth to a boil. Stir hot broth into dry couscous.

2. Cover couscous with a plate, and let stand 5 minutes.

3. Uncover couscous and fluff with a fork.

4. Stir in chicken, basil, feta, tomatoes, lemon, and pepper.

5. Toss ingredients, and serve warm or cold.

Warm Prosciutto-Stuffed Focaccia Step-by-Step

1. Slice bread horizontally using a serrated knife.

2. Layer with prosciutto and cheese.

3. Top with fresh baby spinach.

4. Add roasted red bell peppers.

5. Drizzle with balsamic vinaigrette.

6. Cover with top bread half and wrap in foil. Bake at 350° for 15 minutes or until warm.

taste of the south
Cheese Grits

The food in our "Taste of the South" column often generates intense discussions at our tasting table, and cheese grits proved no exception. We all agreed that this straightforward dish embodies the very definition of good, old-fashioned, stick-to-your-ribs Southern food. The rest was open to a little friendly debate.

We tested a number of recipes, which included everything from garlic to bacon and just about every kind of cheese you can imagine. In the end, it was the unadorned but extraordinarily delicious Creamy Cheese Grits that won, hands down. The reason? The cheese. Specifically, sharp Cheddar and Monterey Jack. We found that the combination of tangy sharp Cheddar and mild Monterey Jack creates the perfect balance of creaminess and flavor. Here's why: The sharper the cheese, the less moisture it has. This is a good thing when eaten out of hand, but it's not so good when the cheese is heated. When sharp and extra-sharp Cheddar are melted, they can taste greasy and grainy. Enter Monterey Jack, whose high moisture content makes it just right for melting. When you try the recipe, you'll know why they're the perfect match.

For a more dressed-up, savory recipe, don't miss Baked Cheese Grits. We took the basic ingredients from Creamy Cheese Grits, replaced the water with chicken broth, and kicked up the flavor with the addition of ground red pepper and Worcestershire sauce.

Creamy Cheese Grits
PREP: 10 MIN., COOK: 15 MIN.
(Pictured on page 8)

5 cups water
1 tsp. salt
1¼ cups uncooked quick-cooking grits **∗**
½ (8-oz.) block sharp Cheddar cheese, shredded (about 1 cup)
½ (8-oz.) block Monterey Jack cheese, shredded (about 1 cup)
½ cup half-and-half
1 Tbsp. butter
¼ tsp. pepper

1. Bring 5 cups water and salt to a boil in a medium saucepan over medium-high heat. Gradually whisk in grits, and bring to a boil. Reduce heat to medium-low, and simmer, stirring occasionally, 10 minutes or until thickened. Stir in Cheddar cheese and remaining ingredients until cheese is melted and mixture is blended. Serve immediately. **Makes** 6 to 8 servings.

Note: For testing purposes only, we used White Lily Quick Grits.

∗ Substitute stone-ground grits, if desired. Increase liquid to 6 cups, and increase cook time to 50 minutes.

Baked Cheese Grits
PREP: 15 MIN., COOK: 15 MIN., BAKE: 45 MIN.

5 cups chicken broth
1¼ cups uncooked quick-cooking grits **∗**
½ (8-oz.) block extra-sharp Cheddar cheese, shredded (about 1 cup)
½ (8-oz.) block Monterey Jack cheese, shredded (about 1 cup)
¼ cup whipping cream
1 tsp. hot sauce
¼ tsp. ground black pepper
⅛ to ¼ tsp. ground red pepper
1 tsp. Worcestershire sauce (optional)
3 large eggs, lightly beaten

1. Bring chicken broth to a boil in a medium saucepan over medium-high heat. Gradually whisk in grits; bring to a boil. Reduce heat to medium-low, and simmer, stirring occasionally, 10 minutes or until thickened. Stir in Cheddar cheese, next 5 ingredients, and, if desired, Worcestershire sauce, stirring until cheese melts. Remove from heat, and stir in eggs.
2. Pour grits into a lightly greased 2-qt. or 11- x 8-inch baking dish. Bake, uncovered, at 350° for 40 to 45 minutes or until golden and set. **Makes** 6 to 8 servings.

Note: For testing purposes only, we used White Lily Quick Grits.

∗ Substitute stone-ground grits, if desired. Increase liquid to 6 cups, and increase cook time to 50 minutes.

Cakes to Flip Over

Try two new spins on a classic Southern dessert.

This version of pineapple upside-down cake takes the dessert to new heights. Bake two single cakes; then layer and frost with whipped cream. No cast-iron skillet is required; these fruit-on-the-bottom layers bake in regular cake pans. Crushed pineapple, instead of slices, makes it easy to slice and serve.

Pineapple Upside-Down Layer Cake
PREP: 20 MIN., BAKE: 40 MIN., COOL: 10 MIN.

¾ cup butter, softened and divided
1 cup firmly packed brown sugar
2 (8-oz.) cans crushed pineapple, drained
½ cup chopped toasted pecans
¼ cup shortening
1½ cups granulated sugar
2 large eggs
2¼ cups all-purpose flour
2¼ tsp. baking powder
¼ tsp. salt
1⅛ cups milk
1½ tsp. vanilla extract
Whipped Cream Frosting

1. Melt ½ cup butter; pour evenly into 2 (9-inch) round cakepans. Sprinkle brown sugar evenly over butter. Top sugar in each pan evenly with pineapple and pecans. Set pans aside.
2. Beat remaining ¼ cup butter and shortening at medium speed with an electric mixer until fluffy. Gradually add granulated sugar, beating well. Add eggs, 1 at a time, beating until blended after each addition.
3. Combine flour, baking powder, and salt; add to shortening mixture alternately with milk, beginning and ending with flour mixture. Beat at low speed until blended after each addition. Stir in vanilla. Spoon batter over pineapple mixture in prepared pans.
4. Bake at 350° for 40 minutes or until a wooden pick inserted in center comes out clean. Cool in pans on wire racks 10 minutes; invert onto wire racks to cool completely.
5. Place 1 cake layer, pineapple side up, on a serving plate. Spread top with ½ cup Whipped Cream Frosting. Place remaining layer, pineapple side up, on top. Spread top and sides of cake with remaining Whipped Cream Frosting. **Makes** 8 to 10 servings.

Whipped Cream Frosting:
fast fixin's
PREP: 10 MIN.

2 cups whipping cream
3 Tbsp. brown sugar
½ tsp. vanilla extract

1. Beat whipping cream at medium-high speed with an electric mixer until foamy; gradually add brown sugar and vanilla, beating until soft peaks form. **Makes** 4½ cups.

MARY BETH PEDERSON
MORTON, ILLINOIS

Upside-Down Pear Cake
PREP: 30 MIN., BAKE: 50 MIN., COOL: 15 MIN.
If you don't have a springform pan, you'll need a 10-inch cake pan for this one. (Bake time will be 40 minutes in the 10-inch pan.)

¾ cup butter, softened and divided
⅓ cup firmly packed brown sugar
2 cups sliced fresh pears
4 maraschino cherries
5 pecan halves
1 cup granulated sugar
2 large eggs
½ cup sour cream
2 cups self-rising flour
½ cup milk
1 tsp. ground cinnamon
1 tsp. vanilla extract

1. Grease bottom and sides of a 9-inch springform pan or a 10-inch cakepan with 3 Tbsp. butter. Sprinkle evenly with brown sugar. Arrange pear slices in a pinwheel pattern on brown sugar. Place maraschino cherries and pecan halves in center of pinwheel.
2. Beat remaining ½ cup plus 1 Tbsp. butter at medium speed with an electric mixer until fluffy; gradually add granulated sugar, beating well. Add eggs, 1 at a time, beating until blended after each addition. Add sour cream, beating until smooth. Add flour and next 3 ingredients, beating until batter is smooth. Spoon batter evenly over arranged pear slices.
3. Bake at 350° for 45 to 50 minutes or until a wooden pick inserted in center comes out clean. Cool in pan 15 minutes. Remove side of pan; invert onto a serving plate, and remove bottom of pan. **Makes** 8 to 10 servings.

CAROL S. NOBLE
BURGAW, NORTH CAROLINA

Always Ready for Supper

Stir a few fresh ingredients into cupboard staples for sensational eats.

New Year's Dinner

Serves 6

Cooktop Cassoulet

New Year's Lucky Peas over rice

Texas Cornbread Sticks

Opening a can of beans or peas is all you need to get a meal under way on your busiest evenings.

Cooktop Cassoulet

PREP: 15 MIN., COOK: 50 MIN.

This recipe takes a little longer to prepare than others featured in this column, but the resulting flavors will taste like a traditional, slowly cooked oven version.

1 lb. smoked sausage, cut into ½-inch rounds
4 skinned and boned chicken breasts, diced
1 large onion, chopped
1 green bell pepper, chopped
1 garlic clove, minced
1 (14.5-oz.) can diced tomatoes, undrained
1 bay leaf
1 tsp. dried thyme
¼ tsp. salt
¼ tsp. pepper
2 (16-oz.) cans great Northern beans, undrained
¼ cup chicken broth

1. Brown sausage in a large skillet over medium-high heat 10 minutes, stirring often. Remove with a slotted spoon, and drain on paper towels; set aside.
2. Sauté chicken in hot sausage drippings in skillet 8 to 10 minutes or until done; remove with slotted spoon, and drain on paper towels.
3. Sauté onion, bell pepper, and garlic in hot drippings in skillet 5 to 6 minutes or until tender. Stir in chicken, sausage, tomatoes, and next 4 ingredients. Bring to a boil, stirring occasionally; cover, reduce heat, and simmer 10 minutes. Stir in beans and broth. Cook, covered, 10 more minutes. Remove and discard bay leaf. Serve immediately. **Makes** 8 servings.

LINDA NIX
ARLINGTON, TEXAS

New Year's Lucky Peas

PREP: 10 MIN., COOK: 30 MIN.
Serve these peas over rice.

1 medium onion, chopped
2 Tbsp. vegetable oil
1 cup chopped cooked ham
1 garlic clove, minced
2 (15-oz.) cans black-eyed peas, rinsed and drained
1 (14-oz.) can chicken broth
1 tsp. rubbed sage
½ tsp. dried thyme
½ tsp. pepper
Toppings: chopped tomato, sliced green onions, pepper sauce

1. Sauté chopped onion in hot oil in a medium saucepan over medium-high heat 3 minutes. Stir in ham and garlic, and sauté 3 minutes. Stir in peas and next 4 ingredients. Bring to a boil; reduce heat, and simmer, stirring occasionally, 20 minutes. Serve with desired toppings. **Makes** 6 servings.

JUDY BYARS
PITTSBORO, MISSISSIPPI

Texas Cornbread Sticks

fast fixin's

PREP: 10 MIN., BAKE: 18 MIN.

1 cup yellow cornmeal
½ cup all-purpose flour
1 tsp. salt
¼ tsp. baking soda
¼ tsp. ground red pepper
1¼ cups buttermilk
¼ cup butter, melted
1 large egg
1 Tbsp. vegetable oil

1. Combine first 5 ingredients; make a well in center. Stir together buttermilk, butter, and egg. Add to flour mixture, stirring just until moistened.
2. Heat cast-iron cornstick pans in a 450° oven 5 minutes or until hot. Remove from oven, and brush lightly with oil. Spoon batter into hot pans. Bake at 450° for 18 minutes or until golden brown. Remove from pans immediately; cool slightly on wire racks. **Makes** 16 sticks.

BETTY MCCRAY
KELLER, TEXAS

Cooking Up Family Fun

The Davis brothers make great food and a lifetime of memories in their grandparents' kitchen.

Family Fun Feast

Serves 8

Lemony Baked Fish Sticks with
Quick-and-Easy Tartar Sauce

Parsleyed New Potatoes

Microwave Corn on the Cob

Cream Puffs With Chocolate Sauce

The hottest Friday night action in Bryan, Texas, may be the Davis family's boys'-night-out gathering. It's a once-a-month happening dreamed up by Elizabeth and Cletus Davis. "My aliases are Bets and Bebe," Elizabeth jokes. Her husband earned his nickname, "Cowboy," back in the day when he was one.

The couple hit on this idea to teach their grandsons a lifetime skill—cooking—as a novel and practical way to spend time together. The boys come over a week ahead to pick recipes, plan the menu, and make a shopping list. They rotate the chief chef position; this child gets to invite a buddy to come as guest chef. "When a grandson learns to read, he joins the group," Bets explains, "and when he marries, he leaves it."

Goof-off time is a-ok here. "When we built our house, we included a lure to coax the boys over," Bets says with a wink. "We have a room outfitted with computers, games, a TV, and three sets of bunk beds, so all of them can sleep over." Spend a mere hour with this family, and you'll realize it's not the bunk room that brings them to Bets and Cowboy's house time after time. It's love.

Lemony Baked Fish Sticks
family favorite
PREP: 20 MIN., BAKE: 20 MIN.
The Davises often use Hey Kids! You're Cooking Now! *by Dianne Pratt (Harvest Hill Press, 1-888-288-8900, 1998) when selecting recipes for their cooking sessions. We adapted this recipe and Quick-and-Easy Tartar Sauce from this book.*

Vegetable cooking spray
1 Tbsp. canola oil
2 lb. cod, flounder, or other white fish
    fillets
½ tsp. salt
2 large eggs
2 egg whites
½ cup 2% reduced-fat milk
Lemony Breading Mix

1. Coat a jelly-roll pan with cooking spray. Coat bottom of pan evenly with canola oil. Set aside.
2. Rinse fish fillets in running water; pat dry on paper towels. Sprinkle salt evenly on each side of fillets. Cut fish into 1- x 2-inch strips; set aside.
3. Beat eggs, egg whites, and milk in a pieplate or shallow dish with a fork until well blended.
4. Place Lemony Breading Mix in a large zip-top plastic bag. Dip fish strips into egg mixture; add a few at a time to breading mix in bag. Shake to coat. Place breaded fish in prepared jelly-roll pan; repeat with remaining fish strips. Bake at 400° for 15 to 20 minutes or until breaded fillets are golden brown. Serve immediately. **Makes** 8 servings.

Lemony Breading Mix:
fast fixin's
PREP: 10 MIN.

8 bread slices
½ cup grated Parmesan cheese
2 tsp. grated lemon rind
½ tsp. pepper

1. Place bread in a food processor, and pulse to form fine crumbs.
2. Combine breadcrumbs, Parmesan cheese, grated lemon rind, and pepper. **Makes** 3½ cups.

Quick-and-Easy Tartar Sauce

family favorite • fast fixin's

PREP: 5 MIN.

Have the kids grate a lemon for zest for the Lemony Breading Mix; then cut it in half, and squeeze to get the juice for this recipe.

1 cup light mayonnaise
¼ cup sweet pickle relish
2 Tbsp. fresh lemon juice

1. Stir together all ingredients in a small bowl until blended. Cover and chill until ready to serve. **Makes** about 1¼ cups.

Parsleyed New Potatoes

family favorite

PREP: 10 MIN., COOK: 25 MIN.

We used a vegetable peeler to remove a band of peeling around the center of the potato to introduce the children to a handy kitchen gadget. It's pretty and less difficult than trying to peel the entire potato with a knife. Add 1 minced garlic clove or use Old Bay or Cajun seasoning instead of salt and pepper to boost the flavor.

3 lb. small new potatoes
⅓ cup butter
¼ cup chopped fresh flat-leaf parsley
1 tsp. salt
¼ tsp. pepper

1. Bring potatoes and water to cover to a boil in a Dutch oven over medium heat, and cook 20 minutes or until tender. Drain and return to Dutch oven.
2. Microwave butter in a microwave-safe glass bowl at HIGH 45 seconds or until melted. Stir in parsley, salt, and pepper. Pour over potatoes, gently tossing to coat. Serve immediately. **Makes** 8 servings.

Microwave Corn on the Cob

family favorite • fast fixin's

PREP: 10 MIN., COOK: 12 MIN., STAND: 2 MIN.

8 ears fresh corn with husks
Butter
Salt
Pepper

1. Remove husks from corn, and wrap corn individually in plastic wrap. Place corn on a microwave-safe plate, and microwave at HIGH 12 minutes, turning once. Let stand in microwave 2 minutes. Unwrap and, if desired, cut or break corn in half. Serve with butter, salt, and pepper. **Makes** 8 servings.

Cream Puffs With Chocolate Sauce

family favorite

PREP: 10 MIN., COOK: 5 MIN., BAKE: 20 MIN.

You'll be amazed at how easy it is to make your own cream puffs (also known as choux [shoo] pastry). **Tips:** *Once the water-and-butter mixture comes to a full, rolling boil, it's time to pull it off the heat. Drop dough onto a baking sheet using a coffee scoop (most measure ⅛ cup). You can also fill the puffs with pudding. This recipe was adapted from* Children's Quick & Easy Cookbook *by Angela Wilkes (DK Publishing, Inc., www.dk.com, 1997).*

1 tsp. butter
½ tsp. water
¾ cup all-purpose flour
1½ tsp. granulated sugar
¾ cup water
⅓ cup butter, cut into pieces
3 large eggs, beaten
¾ cup whipping cream
2 Tbsp. powdered sugar
Chocolate Sauce

1. Grease a large baking sheet with 1 tsp. butter; sprinkle evenly with ½ tsp. water. Set aside.
2. Stir together flour and sugar.
3. Bring ¾ cup water and ⅓ cup butter to a boil, stirring constantly, in a saucepan over medium-high heat; remove from heat, and quickly stir in flour mixture. Beat mixture with a wooden spoon until mixture is smooth and leaves the sides of pan, forming a ball of dough. Gradually add beaten eggs to dough, beating well until mixture is smooth and glossy. Drop dough by rounded ⅛-cupfuls (about 14 mounds) evenly onto the prepared baking sheet.
4. Bake at 400° for 20 minutes or until puffy and golden brown. Pierce 1 side of each cream puff with a knife to allow steam to escape; let cool on baking sheet on a wire rack.
5. Beat whipping cream at medium speed with an electric mixer until foamy; gradually add powdered sugar, beating until soft peaks form. Cut each cream puff in half horizontally. Fill bottom halves evenly with whipped cream mixture; top with top halves. Drizzle with Chocolate Sauce, and serve immediately. **Makes** 14 cream puffs.

Chocolate Sauce:

fast fixin's

PREP: 5 MIN., COOK: 3 MIN.

1 cup semisweet chocolate morsels
¼ cup whipping cream
2 Tbsp. butter

1. Stir together all ingredients in a small saucepan over low heat, and cook, stirring constantly, until chocolate and butter melt and sauce is warm. **Makes** 1 cup.

Power Foods Fight the Flu

These recipes will set you on the path to good health.

Staying healthy during cold and flu season can be as simple as fixing nutrient-packed meals. Test Kitchens Professional Alyssa Porubcan researched nature's most healthful foods, and then created these fresh and flavorful recipes that protect your body against illness. Best of all, they taste amazing and are easy to prepare. For a dose of vitamin C, try our Fresh Fruit With Lemon-Mint Sauce. Or dig into Beef-and-Butternut Squash Chili for a satisfying meal with a surprising kick that's sure to ward off the sniffles.

Cold and Flu Fighters

Stock up on these immunity boosters to help protect your body against illness and aid in healing.

■ **Beta-carotene:** butternut squash, pumpkin, sweet potatoes, spinach, broccoli
■ **B Vitamins (folate and B12):** spinach, legumes, peanuts, whole grains, leafy green vegetables, eggs, milk
■ **Vitamin C:** oranges, grapefruits, strawberries, green peppers, cabbage
■ **Vitamin E:** peanuts, sunflower seeds, eggs, spinach, whole grains, vegetable oils, poultry
■ **Zinc:** fish, poultry, beef, pork, eggs, cheese, milk, peanut butter, whole grains

Beef-and-Butternut Squash Chili

PREP: 20 MIN., COOK: 50 MIN.
We've loaded this chili with beef and beans for zinc and B vitamins, tomatoes and green peppers for vitamin C, and butternut squash for beta-carotene.

1 lb. extra-lean ground beef
1 green bell pepper, chopped
1 medium onion, chopped
2 garlic cloves, minced
2 (14.5-oz.) cans Mexican-style stewed tomatoes, chopped
1 (16-oz.) can chili beans
½ small butternut squash, peeled and cubed (about 1½ cups)
1 cup low-sodium beef broth
1½ tsp. ground cumin
1½ tsp. chili powder
1 cup frozen corn kernels

1. Cook first 4 ingredients in a Dutch oven over medium-high heat until meat crumbles and is no longer pink. Drain well, and return to Dutch oven.
2. Stir in tomatoes and next 5 ingredients; bring to a boil over medium-high heat. Cover, reduce heat to medium-low, and simmer, stirring occasionally, 15 minutes. Stir in corn, and cook, uncovered, 15 minutes or until squash is tender and chili is thickened. **Makes** 8 servings.

Per (1-cup) serving: Calories 234 (22% from fat); Fat 6g (sat 2.3g, mono 2.3g, poly 0.4g); Protein 17g; Carb 30g; Fiber 6.8g; Chol 21mg; Iron 2.9mg; Sodium 642mg; Calc 65mg

Basil Chicken Parmigiana
family favorite
PREP: 25 MIN., COOK: 4 MIN. PER BATCH, BAKE: 20 MIN.
Open a bag of prewashed mixed salad greens, and top with sliced grape or cherry tomatoes, red onion slices, and a drizzle of light balsamic vinaigrette for a zesty accompaniment.

8 oz. uncooked whole wheat rotini
4 (6-oz.) skinned and boned chicken breasts
⅔ cup Italian-seasoned breadcrumbs
½ cup grated Parmesan cheese, divided
½ cup egg substitute
1 Tbsp. olive oil
1 (26-oz.) jar low-fat pasta sauce
¼ cup sliced fresh basil
1 cup (4 oz.) shredded low-fat mozzarella cheese
2 Tbsp. minced fresh flat-leaf parsley

1. Prepare pasta according to package directions, omitting salt and oil. Drain pasta, and keep warm.
2. Cut each chicken breast into 2 pieces. Place each chicken piece between 2 sheets of heavy-duty plastic wrap; flatten to ¼-inch thickness using a meat mallet or rolling pin.
3. Combine ⅔ cup breadcrumbs and ¼ cup Parmesan cheese. Dip chicken in egg substitute, and dredge in breadcrumb mixture.
4. Brown chicken, in batches, in hot olive oil in a large nonstick skillet over medium-high heat, 1 to 2 minutes on each side; remove chicken from skillet.
5. Stir together pasta sauce and basil; spoon half of sauce into an 11- x 7-inch baking dish. Arrange chicken in an even layer over sauce; pour remaining sauce over chicken. Sprinkle evenly with mozzarella cheese and remaining ¼ cup Parmesan cheese.
6. Bake at 350° for 20 minutes or until mozzarella cheese is lightly browned and sauce is bubbly around edges. Remove from oven, and sprinkle with 2 Tbsp. parsley. Serve chicken over hot cooked pasta. **Makes** 8 servings.

Per serving (1 chicken breast half and ½ cup pasta): Calories 337 (21% from fat); Fat 8g (sat 2.9g, mono 2.2g, poly 0.8g); Protein 33.8g; Carb 33.2g; Fiber 4g; Chol 61mg; Iron 2.8mg; Sodium 732mg; Calc 364mg

Antioxidants and Your Heart

Recent studies suggest that taking oral antioxidant supplements have no significant effect on heart health. However, eating a diet rich in antioxidant-packed foods such as fruits, vegetables, and whole grains, which also contain fiber and nutrients, has been found to help reduce the risk of cardiovascular disease.

Fresh Fruit With Lemon-Mint Sauce

make ahead

PREP: 20 MIN., CHILL: 2 HRS.

Oranges, grapefruits, and lemons are packed with vitamin C, the antioxidant that helps boost the immune system, fight infection, and protect the body against influenza. Serve this refreshing dish after a meal for a light dessert, enjoy it as a snack, or try it for breakfast.

(Pictured on page 162)

3 large oranges, peeled and sectioned
2 large red grapefruits, peeled and sectioned
2 cups seedless red grapes, halved
2 Tbsp. chopped fresh mint
1 (6-oz.) container low-fat vanilla yogurt
1 tsp. grated lemon rind
2 Tbsp. fresh lemon juice
1 tsp. honey
Garnish: fresh mint sprigs

1. Place first 4 ingredients in a medium bowl, gently tossing to combine. Cover and chill 2 hours.
2. Stir together yogurt and next 3 ingredients just before serving, and serve with fruit mixture. Garnish, if desired. **Makes** 5 servings.

Per (1-cup) serving: Calories 173 (0% from fat); Fat 0.8g (sat 0.4g, mono 0.2g, poly 0.1g); Protein 4g; Carb 42g; Fiber 4.9g; Chol 2mg; Iron 0.5mg; Sodium 24mg; Calc 133mg

Kitchen Express Fresh Fruit With Lemon-Mint Sauce: Substitute 2 (24-oz.) jars refrigerated orange-and-grapefruit salad mix, drained, for the oranges and grapefruits.

Note: For testing purposes only, we used Del Monte SunFresh Citrus Salad in Extra Light Syrup in the Kitchen Express version.

Toasted Barley-Vegetable Salad

PREP: 25 MIN., COOK: 20 MIN.,
STAND: 5 MIN., CHILL: 3 HRS.

Don't let the long ingredient list deter you from preparing this recipe; many of the ingredients may already be in your pantry or refrigerator. Plus, the salad can be made and chilled up to three days ahead.

1 cup uncooked quick-cooking barley
2 tsp. olive oil
2 cups low-sodium fat-free chicken broth
1 (16-oz.) can chickpeas, rinsed and drained
2 medium tomatoes, seeded and chopped
1 medium cucumber, peeled, seeded, and chopped
1 large garlic clove, minced
¾ cup chopped fresh parsley
½ cup chopped fresh mint
½ cup diced celery
⅓ cup finely chopped red onion
1 tsp. grated lemon rind
3 Tbsp. fresh lemon juice
½ tsp. salt
½ tsp. freshly ground pepper
1 (4-oz.) package crumbled feta cheese with basil and tomatoes

1. Sauté barley in hot oil in a medium saucepan over medium-high heat 4 minutes or until lightly browned; stir in broth. Bring to a boil; cover, reduce heat, and simmer 10 to 12 minutes or until barley is just tender. Remove from heat, and let stand 5 minutes. Cover and chill 1 hour.
2. Stir together chilled barley, chickpeas, and next 11 ingredients in a large bowl. Cover and chill at least 2 hours. Add cheese just before serving, and toss gently. **Makes** 6 servings.

Per (1¼-cup) serving: Calories 250 (26% from fat); Fat 7.7g (sat 3.5g, mono 1.4g, poly 0.8g); Protein 11g; Carb 37g; Fiber 6.6g; Chol 14mg; Iron 2.2mg; Sodium 735mg; Calc 110mg

Test Kitchen *Notebook*

If you're looking for a quick—and delicious—dose of vitamin C, try this refreshing spritzer made with a variety of fruit juices.

Quick Cranberry-Orange Spritzer

PREP: 5 MIN.

To make the spritzer ahead, combine the first three ingredients in a pitcher and chill. Before serving, stir in soft drink.

1 cup cranberry juice cocktail, ✱ chilled
⅓ cup frozen orange juice concentrate, thawed
⅓ cup pineapple juice, chilled
1 cup diet lemon-lime soft drink, chilled

1. Combine first 3 ingredients in a small pitcher. Stir in soft drink. Serve immediately. **Makes** 4 servings.

✱ Substitute mango-flavored pomegranate juice, if desired.

Per (⅔-cup) serving: Calories 86 (0% from fat); Fat 0.1g (sat 0g, mono 0g, poly 0g); Protein 0.6g; Carb 21g; Fiber 0.3g; Chol 0mg; Iron 0.2mg; Sodium 2.2mg; Calc 13mg

Holley Johnson

ASSISTANT FOODS EDITOR

Cooking With Paula Deen

The moment Senior Writer Andria Scott Hurst met Paula Deen, Paula's bubbly personality and open arms made her feel like they've been friends for years. This author, restaurateur, and Food Network regular led Andria straight to the heart of her home—the kitchen.

Her most recent cookbook, *Paula Deen & Friends: Living It Up, Southern Style* (Simon & Schuster, 2005), is a collection of down-home entertaining menus and dishes that will please any palate. You'll make winter tomatoes taste fabulous and turn ordinary cornbread mix into a wonderful side dish just right for company. "Here's the book I always wish I had, with the parties laid out for me," says Paula.

So come on, y'all, and join her for a taste of genuine Southern hospitality. And as Paula always says, "Best dishes."

Marinated Tomatoes
make ahead
PREP: 10 MIN., CHILL: 4 HRS., STAND: 30 MIN.
Once you've enjoyed all of the tomatoes, transform the leftover marinade into a quick and fresh vinaigrette by adding ¼ tsp. Dijon mustard.

¾ cup vegetable oil
½ cup red wine vinegar
3 Tbsp. chopped fresh parsley
1 Tbsp. sugar
1½ tsp. garlic salt
1½ tsp. seasoned salt
¾ tsp. dried oregano
½ tsp. pepper
10 plum tomatoes (about 2½ lb.)

1. Combine first 8 ingredients in a large zip-top plastic freezer bag.
2. Core and cut each tomato into 4 wedges; add to marinade in plastic bag. Seal and shake to coat tomato wedges. Chill 4 hours; let stand 30 minutes at room temperature before serving. Serve with a slotted spoon. **Makes** 6 to 8 servings.

Vidalia Onion Cornbread
PREP: 10 MIN., COOK: 7 MIN., BAKE: 30 MIN.
Turn an ordinary package of cornbread mix into a deliciously moist homemade dish that's reminiscent of spoonbread.

¼ cup butter or margarine
1 large Vidalia or other sweet onion, chopped
1 (7.5-oz.) package cornbread mix
1 cup (4 oz.) shredded sharp Cheddar cheese, divided
1 cup sour cream
⅓ cup milk
1 large egg, beaten
¼ tsp. salt
¼ tsp. dried dill (optional)
Vegetable cooking spray

1. Melt butter in a medium saucepan over medium-high heat. Add onion, and sauté 5 minutes or until tender. (Do not brown onion.) Remove pan from heat. Stir in cornbread mix, ½ cup cheese, next 4 ingredients, and, if desired, dill.
2. Coat an 8-inch square pan with cooking spray; pour mixture into pan. Bake at 450° for 25 minutes. Sprinkle evenly with remaining ½ cup cheese, and bake 5 more minutes or until a wooden pick inserted into center comes out clean. Cool slightly before cutting into squares. **Makes** 8 servings.

Test Kitchen *Notebook*

Paula shared with us her baked, budget-friendly chicken quarters recipe that's just right for company.

Rosemary Chicken Quarters
PREP: 10 MIN., CHILL: 2 HRS., BAKE: 1 HR.
Rosemary is a summer herb that's easily enjoyed year-round. We give a range of the amount of rosemary to use in case you are not familiar with its strong flavor.

½ cup butter or margarine, softened
1 to 2 Tbs. finely chopped fresh rosemary
4 bone-in, skin-on chicken quarters (about 3½ lb.)
½ tsp. salt
¼ tsp. pepper

1. Stir together butter and chopped rosemary.
2. Loosen skin from leg and thigh of each quarter, without totally detaching skin; rub 2 tablespoons butter mixture evenly under skin of each chicken quarter. Replace skin.
3. Place chicken in an aluminum foil-lined roasting pan; sprinkle chicken evenly with salt and pepper. Cover and chill 2 hours.
4. Bake, uncovered, at 400° for 1 hour or until done. **Makes** 4 servings.

Andria Scott Hurst
SENIOR WRITER

Savannah Bow Ties
PREP: 20 MIN., BAKE: 15 MIN.

½ cup almond paste
1 large egg, separated
¼ cup firmly packed light brown sugar
2 tsp. milk
½ (17.3-oz.) package frozen puff pastry, thawed
2 Tbsp. granulated sugar
Chocolate Dipping Sauce (optional)

1. Beat ½ cup almond paste, egg yolk, brown sugar, and milk at medium speed with an electric mixer until well combined. (Mixture will be very stiff.) Set aside.
2. Unfold pastry, and roll out on a lightly floured surface into a 14-inch square; cut in half.

3. Press almond mixture gently and evenly over 1 rectangle. Place the remaining rectangle on top of filling.
4. Cut pastry crosswise into 14 (1-inch-wide) strips; cut each strip in half to make 28 pieces.
5. Twist each piece twice. Place the twists about 2 inches apart on lightly greased baking sheets. Lightly beat egg white, and brush evenly on each twist. Sprinkle evenly with granulated sugar.
6. Bake at 400° for 12 to 15 minutes or until golden. Transfer to wire rack to cool. Serve with Chocolate Dipping Sauce, if desired. **Makes** 28 cookies.

Chocolate Dipping Sauce:
make ahead
PREP: 10 MIN., COOK: 25 MIN.

6 (1.55-oz.) milk chocolate bars, chopped
¾ cup sugar
2 Tbsp. cornstarch
¼ tsp. salt
2 cups whipping cream
1 egg yolk, beaten
½ tsp. vanilla extract

1. Combine first 4 ingredients in a medium saucepan. Stir in cream. Cook over low heat, stirring constantly, just until chocolate is melted.
2. Whisk ½ cup warm chocolate mixture into egg yolk in a small bowl; add to remaining warm chocolate mixture. Increase heat to medium-low, and cook 20 minutes, whisking constantly, just until sauce comes to a boil.
3. Remove from heat; stir in vanilla. Pour into a serving bowl. **Makes** about 3 cups.

Note: Store leftover sauce in refrigerator and serve as pudding.

Our Best Chicken-fried Steak

Down-Home Supper
Serves 4

Chicken-fried Steak

Creamy Mashed Potatoes

greens

store-bought pound cake

Veteran Test Kitchens Specialist and native Texan Vanessa McNeil Rocchio introduced her family's chicken-fried steak to *Southern Living* readers in 2001. Because of its crunchy coating, tender inside, and peppery gravy, we gave it our highest rating.

The secret to Vanessa's chicken-fried steak is in the breading. "Saltine crackers make a great crust," she says. To achieve maximum flavor, Vanessa suggests firmly pushing the cracker crumbs into the cube steak to fill the crevices and to keep the steak from shrinking as it cooks. One taste of this amazing dish, and you'll see why we named it one of our best-ever recipes.

Chicken-fried Steak
family favorite
PREP: 10 MIN., FRY: 7 MIN., COOK: 12 MIN.
(Pictured on page 4)

2¼ tsp. salt, divided
1¾ tsp. black pepper, divided
4 (4-oz.) cube steaks
38 saltine crackers (1 sleeve), crushed
1¼ cups all-purpose flour, divided
½ tsp. ground red pepper
½ tsp. baking powder
4¾ cups milk, divided
2 large eggs
3½ cups peanut oil
Garnish: chopped fresh parsley

1. Sprinkle ¼ tsp. salt and ¼ tsp. black pepper evenly over steaks. Combine cracker crumbs, 1 cup flour, 1 tsp. salt, ½ tsp. black pepper, red pepper, and baking powder. Whisk together ¾ cup milk and eggs. Dredge steaks in cracker mixture; dip in milk mixture, and dredge again in cracker mixture.
2. Pour oil into a 12-inch skillet; heat to 360°. (Do not use a nonstick skillet.) Fry steaks 3 to 4 minutes. Turn and fry 2 to 3 minutes or until golden brown. Remove steaks to a wire rack in a jelly-roll pan. Keep steaks warm in a 225° oven. Carefully drain hot oil, reserving cooked bits and 1 Tbsp. drippings in skillet.
3. Whisk together remaining 4 cups milk, ¼ cup flour, remaining 1 tsp. salt, and remaining 1 tsp. black pepper. Add milk mixture to reserved drippings in skillet; cook, whisking constantly, over medium-high heat 10 to 12 minutes or until thickened. Serve gravy with steaks. Garnish, if desired. **Makes** 4 servings.

Creamy Mashed Potatoes
family favorite
PREP: 5 MIN., COOK: 10 MIN., STAND: 5 MIN.
(Pictured on page 4)

3 Tbsp. butter
1 large garlic clove, minced
1 (22-oz.) bag frozen mashed potatoes
2⅓ cups milk
½ tsp. salt
¼ tsp. pepper

1. Melt butter in a medium saucepan over medium-low heat; add garlic, and sauté until tender. Remove from saucepan, and set aside.
2. Prepare mashed potatoes in a large saucepan according to package directions, using 2⅓ cups milk and stirring with a wire whisk.
3. Stir in garlic mixture, salt, and pepper. Let potatoes stand 5 minutes before serving. **Makes** 4 servings.

5-Ingredient Comfort Foods

These hot and hearty recipes can be ready
to cook in 15 minutes or less.

Pull up a chair, and settle in at the kitchen table. Familiar foods are the ones we love best, and these new twists on family favorites are as easy to prepare as they are to eat. We limited each recipe to 5 ingredients or less (not including pepper, salt, water, and oil). Any choice is a good one—all are satisfying and delicious.

Crunchy Pan-fried Chicken

family favorite • fast fixin's
PREP: 10 MIN., COOK: 10 MIN.
This crispy coating is also terrific on skinned and boned chicken thighs or pork chops.

½ cup self-rising cornmeal mix
½ cup seasoned fine, dry breadcrumbs
½ tsp. pepper
4 skinned and boned chicken breasts
1 large egg, beaten
¼ cup vegetable oil

1. Combine first 3 ingredients in a shallow dish. Dip chicken in egg, and dredge in cornmeal mixture.
2. Cook chicken in hot oil in a large skillet over medium-high heat 3 to 5 minutes on each side or until done. **Makes** 4 servings.

Beginner's Roast

family favorite • make ahead
PREP: 5 MIN.; BAKE: 3 HRS., 30 MIN.
The secret to this juicy, fall-apart tender roast is in the baking. Before placing the lid on the Dutch oven, cover it with a double layer of aluminum foil. An eye-of-round roast has far less fat than a chuck roast, but when tightly covered and slowly cooked with moist heat, is every bit as delicious.

This easy recipe is also a terrific make-ahead dish. After baking, cool roast completely, and remove from Dutch oven, reserving gravy. Cut roast into ¼-inch-thick slices, and arrange in a 13- x 9-inch baking dish. Pour gravy over sliced roast; cover and refrigerate up to 3 days. Reheat in a 325° oven for 30 minutes or until thoroughly heated.

1 (3- to 4-lb.) eye-of-round roast
1 large sweet onion, sliced
1 (10¾-oz.) can cream of mushroom
    soup
½ cup water
1 (1.12-oz.) package brown gravy mix
1 garlic clove, minced

1. Place roast in a lightly greased Dutch oven, and top with sliced onion. Stir together soup and next 3 ingredients; pour over roast.
2. Bake, tightly covered, at 325° for 3 hours and 30 minutes or until tender. **Makes** 6 to 8 servings.

Note: For testing purposes only, we used Knorr Classic Brown Gravy Mix.

HAL RIDDLE — *wait*

KARRIE FAYARD
MOBILE, ALABAMA

Slow-Cooker BBQ Pork

family favorite • fast fixin's
PREP: 5 MIN., COOK: 8 HRS.

This super-simple recipe delivers big flavor. If you don't have a slow cooker, follow the easy directions for oven baking in Beginner's Roast at left. Serve on buns with slaw or over hot toasted cornbread.

Reduce the fat but not the flavor in this juicy cut of pork by preparing a day ahead. Cool the barbecue, and refrigerate overnight. Remove and discard any solidified fat before reheating.

1 (3- to 4-lb.) shoulder pork roast
1 (18-oz.) bottle barbecue sauce
1 (12-oz.) can cola soft drink

1. Place pork roast in a 6-qt. slow cooker; pour barbecue sauce and cola over roast.
2. Cover and cook on HIGH 8 hours or until meat is tender and shreds easily. **Makes** 6 servings.

Note: For testing purposes only, we used Kraft Original Barbecue Sauce.

HAL RIDDLE
TRUSSVILLE, ALABAMA
A TASTE OF TRUSSVILLE

Chicken-and-Artichoke Salad

family favorite • fast fixin's
PREP: 10 MIN.
To serve hot, spread salad on slices of frozen Texas toast, sprinkle with shredded Colby-Jack cheese, and bake at 425° for 10 minutes or until golden brown.

4 cups chopped cooked chicken breasts
1 (14-oz.) can artichoke hearts, drained
    and chopped
½ cup chopped toasted pecans
½ cup mayonnaise
1 tsp. celery salt
½ tsp. pepper

1. Stir together all ingredients; cover and chill until ready to serve. **Makes** 4 servings.

LISA BRIGHT
TRUSSVILLE, ALABAMA

Ranch Noodles

family favorite • fast fixin's

PREP: 5 MIN., COOK: 10 MIN.

Just drop the pasta in a pot of boiling water, and heat the add-ins for a fast meal.

1 (8-oz.) package egg noodles
¼ cup butter
½ cup sour cream
½ cup Ranch dressing
½ cup grated Parmesan cheese

1. Cook egg noodles according to package directions; drain and return to pot. Stir in butter and remaining ingredients. Serve immediately. **Makes** 4 to 6 servings.

Note: Substitute 1 (8-oz.) package of thin spaghetti for the egg noodles, and add chopped cooked ham and steamed broccoli, if desired. Sautéing the ham in a lightly greased skillet over medium-high heat gives it a crisp and smoky baconlike flavor.
KATHY PRICKETT
CARTHAGE, NORTH CAROLINA

Rocky Top Brownies

family favorite

PREP: 10 MIN., BAKE: 25 MIN.

Former Executive Editor Susan Dosier came up with this fun recipe. Substitute an equal amount of your favorite chocolate-covered candy for the peanut butter cups, if desired.

1 (19-oz.) package brownie mix
½ cup butter, melted
3 large eggs
1 (13-oz.) package miniature chocolate-covered peanut butter cups, coarsely chopped

1. Stir together first 3 ingredients until blended. Spoon batter into a greased and floured 13- x 9-inch pan.
2. Bake at 350° for 23 minutes or until center is set. Remove from oven, and sprinkle brownies evenly with chopped candy. Return to oven, and bake 2 minutes. Remove from oven, and cool completely on a wire rack. Cut brownies into squares. **Makes** 32 brownies.

TennTucky Blackberry Cobbler

family favorite

PREP: 5 MIN., BAKE: 1 HR.

Scatter a handful of frozen berries over a buttery batter, and this melt-in-your-mouth cobbler will be ready for the oven.

1¼ cups sugar
1 cup self-rising flour
1 cup milk
½ cup butter, melted
2 cups frozen blackberries

1. Whisk together 1 cup sugar, flour, and milk just until blended; whisk in melted butter. Pour batter into a lightly greased 12- x 8-inch or 11- x 8-inch baking dish; sprinkle blackberries and remaining ¼ cup sugar evenly over batter.
2. Bake cobbler at 350° for 1 hour or until golden brown and bubbly. **Makes** 6 servings.
JENNIFER G. BRINDLEY
ADAIRVILLE, KENTUCKY

Mashed Potatoes

family favorite

PREP: 15 MIN., COOK: 35 MIN.

4 lb. Yukon gold potatoes, peeled and quartered
1¾ tsp. salt, divided
¾ cup milk
½ cup butter, softened
½ tsp. pepper

1. Bring potatoes, 1 tsp. salt, and water to cover to a boil in a Dutch oven; cover, reduce heat, and simmer 30 minutes or until tender. Drain.
2. Mash potatoes with remaining ¾ tsp. salt, milk, butter, and pepper until smooth. **Makes** 8 servings.

Five Plus Five

This dish combines the robust flavors and cheesy bread topping of French onion soup with chicken pot pie. It has more than five ingredients, but it's so quick and easy to make you'll hardly notice. Substitute an equal amount of buttermilk for wine, if desired. Serve with a green salad tossed with fresh citrus, sliced avocados, toasted pecans, and bottled raspberry vinaigrette.

Chicken Cobbler Casserole

family favorite

PREP: 10 MIN., COOK: 25 MIN., BAKE: 15 MIN. *(Pictured on page 161)*

6 Tbsp. melted butter, divided
4 cups cubed sourdough rolls
⅓ cup grated Parmesan cheese
2 Tbsp. chopped fresh parsley
2 medium-size sweet onions, sliced
1 (8-oz.) package sliced fresh mushrooms
1 cup white wine
1 (10¾-oz.) can cream of mushroom soup
½ cup drained and chopped jarred roasted red bell peppers
2½ cups shredded cooked chicken

1. Toss 4 Tbsp. melted butter with next 3 ingredients; set aside.
2. Sauté onions in remaining 2 Tbsp. butter in a large skillet over medium-high heat 15 minutes or until golden brown. Add mushrooms, and sauté 5 minutes.
3. Stir in wine and next 3 ingredients; cook, stirring constantly, 5 minutes or until bubbly. Spoon mixture into a lightly greased 9-inch square or 11- x 7-inch baking dish; top evenly with bread mixture.
4. Bake at 400° for 15 minutes or until casserole is golden brown. **Makes** 4 servings.

from our kitchen

Fresh From the Freezer

When cold winter days leave you longing for the farm-stand flavor of fresh vegetables, head for the freezer. Packaged at their seasonal best, frozen vegetables are a bargain this time of year. With no trimming or cleaning (and no costly waste), you can put a taste of summer on the table every night of the week. Here are a few tips and tricks we've learned.

■ Before simmering frozen greens in chicken broth, sauté chopped cooked ham in a Dutch oven until lightly browned for a lean, smoky flavor. Just add the broth directly to the Dutch oven, stirring to loosen the brown bits from the bottom of the pan.

■ Combine the taste and texture of different types of frozen peas, such as butter peas, lady peas, and field peas with snaps. Cook according to package directions in chicken or vegetable broth rather than water.

■ Coarsely chop partially thawed, sliced yellow squash, and use in place of fresh for a quick start on a casserole. Because most frozen vegetables are already blanched, you don't have to precook them before adding them to a casserole.

■ Pulse frozen white shoepeg corn in a food processor 8 to 10 times or until coarsely chopped, and use in place of grated fresh corn when making creamed corn.

Ripe for the Picking

■ Long and slender, frozen whole green beans can easily stand in for fresh ones—even when company's coming. Quickly pan-fried with flavorful lemon-butter and toasted almonds or simmered for hours with bacon drippings and broth, they're equally delicious.

■ Time-saving seasoning blends, featuring frozen diced onion, bell peppers, and celery, add easy and unexpected flavor to pots of field peas and greens as well as soups, stews, and casseroles. If you hate to chop, these frozen blends come to the rescue.

■ Perfect for sautés and stir-fries, frozen blends of colorful red, yellow, and green bell pepper strips are especially appealing when the price of fresh goes sky-high. (Fresh bell peppers can lose up to half their weight when seeded and cored.) Like many other vegetables, these are individually quick-frozen—just pour out as needed, and return the remainder to the freezer.

■ Frozen cut okra delivers fresh flavor year-round. It's terrific in gumbo or coated with cornmeal while still frozen, and fried.

Flash in the Pan

Pan-frying frozen vegetables, such as sugar snap peas, is a great way to retain the bright color and texture. Thaw 1 (16-oz.) package frozen vegetables just long enough to separate into pieces; sauté in 1 Tbsp. hot oil in a large skillet over medium heat 4 to 6 minutes or until crisp-tender. (The type and size of vegetables can shorten or lengthen the cooking time.) Season to taste with salt and pepper, and serve them immediately.

Don't be afraid to combine fresh seasonal produce with frozen. We paired the natural sweetness of fresh grape tomatoes with frozen sugar snap peas. Just cut the tomatoes in half, and toss in the skillet during the last 2 or 3 minutes the sugar snap peas are cooking.

OUR RECIPES—A NEW LOOK

If our ingredient lists look like they've lost weight, well, they have. Beginning this year, we started abbreviating some of the measurements. The list to the right reflects those new abbreviations. We hope you like the change and will continue to suggest ways we can make our recipes more reader-friendly.

■ teaspoon—tsp.
■ tablespoon—Tbsp.
■ ounce—oz.
■ pound—lb.
■ quart—qt.
■ pint—pt.
■ gallon—gal.

february

Living in the Kitchen

We searched the South for kitchens with one thing in common: the color red. Delicious family recipes are an added bonus.

Use Bold Color With Confidence

Susan and Eddie DeGarmo of Brentwood, Tennessee, designed their new kitchen to be a hardworking space. The DeGarmos also used a standout palette of red, black, and white to kick up the style of their kitchen, created with big parties in mind. Every Sunday, three generations of the DeGarmo family gather to cook and eat. Several prep cooks can work around their island and use it as a buffet.

Tennessee Caviar
make ahead
PREP: 10 MIN., CHILL: 2 HRS.
Instead of fish eggs, this Southern version of caviar features down-home veggies. Make it a day ahead for the best flavor.

1 (15.8-oz.) can black-eyed peas
1 (11-oz.) can yellow corn with red and
   green bell peppers
3 plum tomatoes, seeded and chopped
1 small sweet onion, chopped
1 cup hot picante sauce
¼ cup chopped fresh cilantro
2 garlic cloves, minced
2 Tbsp. fresh lime juice
Tortilla chips

1. Rinse and drain peas and corn.
2. Stir together peas, corn, tomatoes, and next 5 ingredients in a serving bowl; cover and chill at least 2 hours. Serve with tortilla chips. **Makes** 4 cups.

Bruschetta-Goat Cheese Cups
fast fixin's
PREP: 15 MIN., BAKE: 5 MIN.
Bruschetta topping can be found in the refrigerated section or with pasta sauces.

1 (1.4-oz.) package crispy pastry shells
1 (4-oz.) goat cheese log, crumbled
⅓ cup refrigerated sweet pepper,
   vegetable, and olive bruschetta
   topping or tapenade
Garnish: fresh thyme leaves

1. Place shells in a shallow pan. Divide goat cheese evenly between shells, pressing gently to fill bottom of each. Spoon 1 tsp. bruschetta topping into each shell.
2. Bake at 350° for 4 to 5 minutes or until thoroughly heated. Garnish, if desired. **Makes** 24 cups (about 6 servings).

Pesto-Goat Cheese Cups: Substitute ¼ cup prepared basil pesto for ⅓ cup bruschetta topping. Proceed as directed, omitting thyme leaves. Top with finely chopped tomato and toasted pine nuts after baking.

Note: We used Siljans Croustades Crispy Shells and Gia Russa Sweet Pepper, Vegetable & Olive Bruschetta Topping.

Asparagus With Dill Sauce
make ahead
PREP: 15 MIN., CHILL: 1 HR., COOK: 4 MIN.
Make the sauce up to 2 days ahead, and prepare the asparagus the morning you plan to serve it. Older kids can help prep the asparagus for this appetizer spread.

½ cup mayonnaise
½ cup sour cream
1 Tbsp. fresh lemon juice
1 tsp. grated lemon rind
1 tsp. onion powder
½ tsp. dried dillweed
⅛ tsp. salt
2 lb. fresh asparagus
Garnish: lemon rind strips

1. Stir together first 7 ingredients in a small bowl; cover and chill at least 1 hour.
2. Snap off tough ends of asparagus; arrange asparagus in a steamer basket over boiling salted water. Cover and steam 4 minutes or until crisp-tender. Plunge asparagus into ice water to stop the cooking process; drain.
3. Arrange asparagus on a serving platter. Serve with Dill Sauce. Garnish, if desired. **Makes** 10 to 12 servings.

Ultimate Family Kitchen

Busy lifestyles often leave little time for a huge kitchen redo. Frannie and Al Kimsey of Madison, Georgia, have their hands full with four children and full-time jobs so they used the power of paint and fabric to make over the room. They created a kid-friendly space that maxes out style and comfort to make baking together a real treat.

Try some of Frannie's recipes with your family; kids can measure and mix the ingredients. Cooking together creates great memories. Soon your little ones may ask for more chances to help.

Morning Glory Muffins
family favorite

PREP: 20 MIN., BAKE: 23 MIN., COOL: 5 MIN.
Combine a muffin mix and a few fresh ingredients for a delicious breakfast treat.

¼ cup milk
¼ cup vegetable oil
2 large eggs
1 (15.2-oz.) package cinnamon streusel
    muffin mix
½ tsp. ground cinnamon
1 (8-oz.) can crushed pineapple in juice
¾ cup grated peeled Granny Smith
    apple (about 1 small apple)
¾ cup shredded carrots
¾ cup chopped toasted pecans
½ cup raisins
Vegetable cooking spray
1 cup powdered sugar (optional)
½ tsp. grated lemon rind (optional)
1 to 2 Tbsp. fresh lemon juice (optional)

1. Whisk together first 3 ingredients until blended.
2. Remove and reserve streusel packet from muffin mix package. Stir together contents of muffin mix packet and cinnamon in a large bowl. Make a well in center of mixture. Add egg mixture, pineapple, and next 4 ingredients, stirring just until moistened.
3. Place baking cups in muffin pans. Spray with cooking spray. Spoon batter into cups, filling two-thirds full. Sprinkle evenly with reserved streusel packet.
4. Bake at 425° for 18 to 23 minutes or until golden. Cool in pans on wire racks 5 minutes. Remove from pans, and cool on wire racks.
5. Stir together powdered sugar, lemon rind, and lemon juice until smooth, and drizzle over muffins, if desired. **Makes** about 1½ dozen.

Note: For testing purposes only, we used Betty Crocker Cinnabon Cinnamon Streusel Premium Muffin Mix.

Candy-Print Cookies
family favorite

PREP: 20 MIN., CHILL: 30 MIN.,
BAKE: 11 MIN. PER BATCH
Use your favorite candy pieces to top these easy sugar cookies. You can even use jelly in the center for old-fashioned thumbprint cookies.

1 cup butter, softened
⅔ cup sugar
2 egg yolks
½ tsp. vanilla extract
2¼ cups all-purpose flour
¼ tsp. salt
Toppings: candy-coated peanut butter
    pieces, white and milk chocolate
    kisses, halved miniature chocolate-
    coated caramel-peanut nougat bars

1. Beat butter at medium speed with an electric mixer until creamy; add sugar, beating well. Add egg yolks, 1 at a time, beating well after each addition; add vanilla, beating until blended.
2. Combine flour and salt; gradually add to butter mixture, beating at low speed just until blended. Cover and chill 30 minutes.
3. Shape dough into 1-inch balls; place dough 2 inches apart on ungreased baking sheets. Press thumb into each ball to make an indentation.
4. Bake at 350° for 9 to 11 minutes or until set. (Tops of cookies will not be brown.) Remove from oven, and immediately press desired topping in center of each cookie. Remove cookies to wire racks to cool. **Makes** 3½ dozen.

Dream-Come-True Cooking Space

Kris and John Maclay put a lot of thought into the kitchen of their new house in Houston, Texas. They spent a lot of time discussing with an architect how the family would use the kitchen. That allowed them to create a space in an efficient layout to accommodate the family's needs and desires. A fantastic design, paired with an easy weeknight recipe (plus dessert), makes life run a little smoother for the Maclay crew.

Buttery Pound Cake

PREP: 15 MIN.; BAKE: 1 HR., 20 MIN.;
COOL: 15 MIN.
For a special dessert, serve toasted slices of this cake with vanilla ice cream, chocolate fudge sauce, and sliced fresh strawberries.

1 lb. butter, softened
3 cups sugar
6 large eggs
1 tsp. vanilla extract
½ tsp. almond extract
4 cups all-purpose flour
⅓ cup milk
Toppings: chocolate sauce, sliced
    strawberries

1. Beat butter and sugar at medium speed with an electric mixer until light and fluffy. Add eggs, 1 at a time, beating just until the yellow disappears after each addition. Add extracts, beating just until blended. Gradually add flour, beating at low speed until combined. Add milk, beating until smooth. Pour batter into a greased and floured 12-cup Bundt pan.
2. Bake at 325° for 1 hour and 20 minutes or until a long wooden pick inserted in center of cake comes out clean. Cool in pan on a wire rack 15 minutes. Remove from pan; cool completely on wire rack. Serve with desired toppings. **Makes** 10 to 12 servings.

Red-Hot Style Secrets

■ Give furniture that you already own a makeover with a coat of paint. Kris Maclay painted her chairs a distressed red hue.
■ Consider adding electrical outlets to a pantry to eliminate the clutter that small appliances add.
■ Spend money on items that will have the most impact.

Simple Shrimp Creole
PREP: 15 MIN., COOK: 30 MIN.

The children love Kris's mild shrimp Creole. Add more Cajun seasoning and red pepper if you like it spicier. Serve rice, salad, and hot sauce on the side.

1 medium onion, chopped
½ cup chopped green bell pepper
½ cup chopped celery
1 tsp. minced garlic
3 Tbsp. olive oil
3 Tbsp. all-purpose flour
1 (28-oz.) can crushed tomatoes
½ cup chicken broth
1 tsp. Cajun seasoning
½ tsp. salt
¼ tsp. ground red pepper
2 bay leaves
1 lb. peeled, medium-size fresh shrimp
3 cups hot cooked rice

1. Sauté first 4 ingredients in hot oil in a large skillet over medium heat 5 minutes or until onion is tender; gradually stir in flour until smooth. Stir in tomatoes and next 5 ingredients.
2. Cover, reduce heat to low, and cook, stirring occasionally, 20 minutes. Stir in shrimp, and cook 5 more minutes or until shrimp turn pink. Remove and discard bay leaves. Serve over hot cooked rice. **Makes** 4 servings.

Chicken Creole: Prepare recipe as directed, substituting 1 lb. skinned and boned chicken breast, cut into bite-size pieces, for shrimp. Cook chicken an additional 5 minutes or until done. Proceed as directed. Prep: 15 min., Cook: 35 min.

Slow-Cooker Suppers

Turn it on, and prop up your feet. These easy recipes are practically hands-free.

Save time and energy in the kitchen by trying these simple and satisfying slow-cooker dishes. You'll love the versatility and minimal effort. Each dish is straightforward: There's no browning meat before putting it in the slow cooker, high and low temperatures are provided when applicable, and a 6-qt. oval slow cooker is always used. Plus, prepping ingredients is as easy as opening a bag of frozen lima beans, chopping an apple, or adding a can of chicken broth

Beef With Red Wine Sauce
PREP: 15 MIN., COOK: 6 HRS.

3 lb. boneless beef chuck roast, cut into 1-inch pieces
1 medium onion, sliced
1 lb. fresh mushrooms, halved
1 (1.61-oz.) package brown gravy mix
1 (10½-oz.) can beef broth
1 cup red wine
2 Tbsp. tomato paste
1 bay leaf
Hot cooked egg noodles or rice
Garnish: chopped fresh parsley

1. Place first 3 ingredients in a 6-qt. slow cooker.
2. Whisk together gravy mix and next 3 ingredients; pour evenly over beef and vegetables. Add bay leaf.
3. Cover and cook on HIGH 6 hours. Remove and discard bay leaf. Serve over noodles. Garnish, if desired. **Makes** 6 servings.

Braised Chicken Thighs With Carrots and Potatoes
PREP: 20 MIN., COOK: 8 HRS.

Substitute an extra ¼ cup chicken broth in place of the wine, if you prefer.

1 medium onion, halved lengthwise and sliced
4 medium-size new potatoes (about 1 lb.), cut into ¼-inch-thick slices
2 cups baby carrots
1¼ tsp. salt, divided
½ tsp. pepper, divided
¼ cup chicken broth
¼ cup white wine
1 tsp. minced garlic
½ tsp. dried thyme
1 tsp. paprika
6 bone-in, skinned chicken thighs (about 1½ to 1¾ lb.)
Garnish: lemon slices

1. Place onion in a lightly greased 6-qt. slow cooker; top with potatoes and carrots. Combine ¾ tsp. salt, ¼ tsp. pepper, broth, and next 3 ingredients. Pour broth mixture over vegetables. Combine paprika, remaining ½ tsp. salt, and remaining ¼ tsp. pepper; rub evenly over chicken thighs, and arrange over vegetables.
2. Cover and cook on LOW 8 hours or until chicken and vegetables are tender. Garnish, if desired. **Makes** 6 servings.

Easy Brunswick Stew
make ahead
PREP: 15 MIN., COOK: 12 HRS.
Cooking on LOW heat for a long time makes the meat extremely tender, so it shreds easily; HIGH heat yields a less tender product. (Pictured on page 163)

3 lb. boneless pork shoulder roast (Boston butt)
3 medium-size new potatoes, peeled and chopped
1 large onion, chopped
1 (28-oz.) can crushed tomatoes
1 (18-oz.) bottle barbecue sauce
1 (14-oz.) can chicken broth
1 (9-oz.) package frozen baby lima beans, thawed
1 (9-oz.) package frozen corn, thawed
6 Tbsp. brown sugar
1 tsp. salt

1. Trim roast, and cut into 2-inch pieces. Stir together all ingredients in a 6-qt. slow cooker.
2. Cover and cook on LOW 10 to 12 hours or until potatoes are fork-tender. Remove pork with a slotted spoon, and shred. Return shredded pork to slow cooker, and stir well. Ladle stew into bowls. **Makes** 8 servings.

Loaded Potato Soup
family favorite • make ahead
PREP: 15 MIN.; COOK: 5 HRS., 20 MIN.

4 lb. new potatoes, peeled and cut into ¼-inch-thick slices
1 small onion, chopped
2 (14-oz.) cans chicken broth
2 tsp. salt
½ tsp. pepper
1 pt. half-and-half
Toppings: shredded Cheddar cheese, crumbled bacon, green onion slices

1. Layer sliced potatoes in a lightly greased 6-qt. slow cooker; top with chopped onion.
2. Stir together chicken broth, salt, and pepper; pour over potatoes and onion. (Broth will not completely cover potatoes and onion.) Cover and cook on HIGH 3 to 5 hours or until potatoes are tender. Mash mixture with a potato masher; stir in half-and-half. Cover and cook on HIGH 20 more minutes or until mixture is thoroughly heated. Ladle into bowls, and serve with desired toppings. **Makes** 8 servings.

Apple-Pecan Crisp
family favorite • make ahead
PREP: 15 MIN., COOK: 3 HRS.
Be sure to check the apples at 2 hours because overcooking can make them mushy.

5 large Granny Smith apples, peeled and cut into ¼-inch-thick slices
2 Tbsp. lemon juice
¾ cup all-purpose flour
¾ cup firmly packed dark brown sugar
1 tsp. ground cinnamon
⅛ tsp. salt
½ cup cold butter
¾ cup chopped toasted pecans
Vanilla ice cream

1. Place apples in a lightly greased 6-qt. slow cooker; drizzle with lemon juice, and toss to coat.
2. Combine flour and next 3 ingredients in a medium bowl. Cut butter into flour mixture with a pastry blender or 2 forks until mixture resembles coarse meal; sprinkle over apples.
3. Cover and cook on HIGH 3 hours or until apples are tender. Sprinkle with pecans. Serve warm with ice cream. **Makes** 6 servings.

Spicy White Cheese Dip
freezeable • make ahead
PREP: 8 MIN., COOK: 3 HRS.
To prevent the bottom of the cheese dip from burning, we recommend cooking on the LOW setting and holding on the WARM setting when serving.

1 small onion, diced
2 garlic cloves, minced
2 (10-oz.) cans diced tomatoes and green chiles
¾ cup milk
½ tsp. ground cumin
½ tsp. fresh coarsely ground black pepper
2 lb. processed white American deli cheese slices, torn
Assorted tortilla and corn chips

1. Place first 7 ingredients in a 6-qt. oval slow cooker. Cover and cook on LOW 3 hours, stirring gently every hour. Stir before serving. Serve with assorted tortilla and corn chips. **Makes** about 8 cups.

To Make Ahead and Freeze: Spoon into quart-size freezer containers, and freeze up to 1 month. Thaw overnight in the refrigerator. Microwave at HIGH, stirring every 60 seconds until thoroughly heated.

Chocolate Paradise

If you love chocolate, you'll want to indulge in these prizewinners from past competitions of the Chocolate Lovers' Festival at the Inn of the Ozarks in Eureka Springs, Arkansas. Part of the fun of the festival is a chocolate cooking and baking contest.

Double Chocolate Cheesecake

PREP: 20 MIN.; BAKE: 1 HR., 5 MIN.; STAND: 30 MIN.; CHILL: 9 HRS.

The sweetness of this cheesecake checks in at just the right level to let the chocolate flavor stand out. This recipe took first place in the cake category at the 2005 festival. (Pictured on page 2)

1½ cups cream-filled chocolate sandwich cookie crumbs (about 18 cookies)
1 (12-oz.) package semisweet chocolate morsels
3 (8-oz.) packages cream cheese, softened
1 (14-oz.) can sweetened condensed milk
2 tsp. vanilla extract
4 large eggs
Ganache Topping

1. Press cookie crumbs into bottom and halfway up sides of a 9-inch springform pan; set aside.
2. Microwave chocolate morsels in a microwave-safe bowl at HIGH 1½ minutes or until melted, stirring at 30-second intervals.
3. Beat cream cheese at medium speed with an electric mixer 2 minutes or until smooth. Add sweetened condensed milk and vanilla, beating at low speed just until combined. Add eggs, 1 at a time, beating at low speed just until combined after each addition. Add melted chocolate, beating just until combined. Pour cheesecake batter into prepared crust.
4. Bake at 300° for 1 hour and 5 minutes or just until center is set. Turn oven off. Let cheesecake stand in oven 30 minutes with oven door closed. Remove cheesecake from oven; run a knife along outer edge of cheesecake, and cool in pan on a wire rack until room temperature. Cover and chill 8 hours.
5. Remove sides of springform pan, and place cake on a serving plate. Slowly pour and spread warm Ganache Topping over top of cheesecake, letting it run down sides of cheesecake. Chill 1 hour before serving. **Makes** 8 to 10 servings.

Ganache Topping:

PREP: 10 MIN., COOK: 3 MIN., COOL: 30 MIN.

Ganache is a mixture of chocolate and whipping cream that's heated, cooled to lukewarm, and then poured over a cake like a glaze.

¾ cup whipping cream
1 (6-oz.) package semisweet chocolate morsels (1 cup)
1 (6-oz.) package milk chocolate morsels (1 cup)

1. Bring cream to a boil in a saucepan over medium heat; quickly remove from heat, and stir in semisweet and milk chocolate morsels until melted and smooth. Let mixture cool (about 30 minutes) until slightly warm before pouring and spreading over cheesecake. **Makes** 1½ cups.

LISA MCKINNEY
BERRYVILLE, ARKANSAS

Oatmeal-Chocolate Chip Cookies

family favorite

PREP: 20 MIN., BAKE: 10 MIN. PER BATCH

A crisp outside, soft middle, hint of chocolate, and combo of nuts make this one remarkable cookie. It took first prize in the chocolate chip cookie category in a previous festival and remains a favorite treat in many Eureka Springs kitchens.

1¼ cups butter, softened
½ cup granulated sugar
¾ cup firmly packed light brown sugar
1 large egg
1 Tbsp. vanilla extract
1½ cups all-purpose flour
1 tsp. baking powder
½ tsp. salt
3 cups uncooked quick-cooking oats
1 cup semisweet chocolate morsels
½ cup chopped walnuts, toasted
½ cup chopped pecans, toasted

1. Beat butter at medium speed with an electric mixer until creamy; gradually add sugars, beating well. Add egg and vanilla, beating until combined.
2. Combine flour, baking powder, and salt; gradually add to butter mixture, beating until blended. Stir in oats and remaining ingredients. Drop by rounded tablespoonfuls onto ungreased baking sheets.
3. Bake at 375° for 10 minutes or until lightly browned. Cool cookies on baking sheets 1 minute; remove to wire racks to cool completely. **Makes** 4 dozen.

MAGGIE MCCARTHY
DALLAS, TEXAS

Test Kitchen *Notebook*

The Chocolate Lovers' Festival is a tongue-tingling excuse to visit this charming mountain town, filled with bed-and-breakfasts and very nice people. Visitors to the event sample chocolate goodies of all sorts. You won't get to eat the items in the chocolate contest, but you can walk through and admire all the perfectly decorated cakes, cookies, and chocolate sculptures. The festival benefits The Clear Spring School; visit **www.eurekachocfest.org** for details.

Shirley Harrington
ASSOCIATE FOODS EDITOR

Turn Rice Into Something Special

Make a meal that delivers mighty taste in minimum time.

You can chop minutes off meal preparation by using ready-to-serve rice pouches. The fluffy grains are fully cooked and all set to heat in the microwave. Take this Southern staple to the next level by adding chicken or sausage.

Chicken-and-Rice
family favorite
PREP: 10 MIN., COOK: 22 MIN.

1½ lb. skinned and boned chicken
  breasts
2 (8.8-oz.) pouches ready-to-serve
  long-grain rice
4 bacon slices, diced
½ cup chopped onion
½ cup frozen green peas, thawed *
1 (4-oz.) can sliced mushrooms, drained
¾ tsp. salt
¼ tsp. pepper
Garnish: fresh parsley sprigs

1. Cut chicken into ¼-inch slices, and set aside.
2. Heat rice according to package directions; set aside.
3. Sauté bacon in a large skillet over medium-high heat 8 minutes or until crisp; remove bacon with a slotted spoon, reserving 1 Tbsp. drippings in skillet.
4. Sauté onion in hot drippings in skillet 3 minutes or until tender. Stir in chicken, and sauté 8 minutes or until chicken is done. Stir in rice, bacon, peas, and next 3 ingredients; cook, stirring occasionally, 3 minutes or until thoroughly heated. Garnish, if desired. **Makes** 4 servings.

Note: For testing purposes only, we used Uncle Ben's Original Long Grain Ready Rice.

*Substitute 4 oz. (about 1 heaping cup) snow peas for green peas, if desired. Microwave snow peas and ¼ cup water in a microwave-safe bowl 2 minutes before adding to chicken mixture. Proceed with recipe as directed.

CAROL NOBLE
BURGAW, NORTH CAROLINA

Skillet Rice and Sausage
fast fixin's
PREP: 5 MIN., COOK: 11 MIN.

2 (8.8-oz.) pouches ready-to-serve
  yellow rice
1 (14-oz.) package beef smoked
  sausage
1 (14.5-oz.) can diced
  tomatoes
1 Tbsp. chopped fresh parsley
¼ cup water

1. Heat rice according to package directions; set aside.
2. Cut sausage into ½-inch-thick slices. Cook in a large nonstick skillet over medium-high heat 4 minutes on each side or until browned. Drain on paper towels. Wipe skillet clean, and return sausage to skillet.
3. Stir in rice, diced tomatoes, parsley, and ¼ cup water. Cook 3 minutes or until thoroughly heated. **Makes** 6 to 8 servings.

Note: For testing purposes only, we used Zatarain's New Orleans Style Ready-to-Serve Yellow Rice.

LYNN COCKRELL
AIKEN, SOUTH CAROLINA

Black Bean-and-Rice Salad
make ahead
PREP: 10 MIN., STAND: 10 MIN.,
CHILL: 30 MIN.

This tasty make-ahead dish is great for a potluck. Stir it together in 20 minutes; cover and chill for 30 minutes, and you're out the door. You can also stir in 2 cups chopped cooked chicken or pork for a main dish.

2 (8.8-oz.) pouches ready-to-serve
  Spanish rice
2 (15.5-oz.) cans black beans, rinsed and
  drained
1 (10-oz.) can diced tomatoes and
  green chiles, drained
1 medium-size green bell pepper, diced
½ cup diced red onion
¼ cup red wine vinegar
1 Tbsp. vegetable oil
½ tsp. salt
½ tsp. ground cumin
¼ tsp. garlic powder
¼ tsp. pepper

1. Heat rice according to package directions. Pour into a large bowl, and let stand 10 minutes to cool.
2. Stir in black beans and remaining ingredients until well combined. Cover and chill rice mixture at least 30 minutes before serving. **Makes** 10 servings.

Note: For testing purposes only, we used Uncle Ben's Spanish Style Ready Rice.

GENEVA YARBER
GOLDSBY, OKLAHOMA

Sweet & Simple

Four great-tasting desserts get a speedy start from one rich and buttery lemon pie filling.

Pass-Along Pies

Best-loved recipes are often those we inherit from family and friends. Passed along on bits and pieces of tattered paper and dog-eared recipe cards, they are treasures.

This recipe for Lemon Chess Pie Filling came to us from our Editor's late mother, Louise Floyd of Potters Station, Alabama. It's one of our favorites, and it's the inspiration for all of these top-rated treats.

Each recipe can be made ahead and frozen for up to one month. Just bake according to directions, and then cool completely before placing in large zip-top plastic freezer bags.

Deep-dish frozen ready-to-bake piecrusts in disposable aluminum pans can be substituted for refrigerated piecrusts in these recipes. When using frozen piecrusts in disposable aluminum pans, bake on a preheated baking sheet.

Lemon Chess Pie Filling
PREP: 10 MIN.

2 cups sugar
4 large eggs
¼ cup butter, melted
¼ cup milk
1 Tbsp. grated lemon rind
¼ cup fresh lemon juice
1 Tbsp. all-purpose flour
1 Tbsp. cornmeal
¼ tsp. salt

1. Whisk together all ingredients. Use filling immediately. **Makes** about 3 cups.

The bright citrus flavor of a fresh lemon pie is as welcome as sunshine on a winter day. The pie is easy enough to make anytime. You can stir up a single pie for supper, or bake an ovenful of tiny Lemon Chess Tassies to share. If you're lucky enough to have leftovers, you'll find they're every bit as good the second time around.

Lemon Cheesecake Pies
freezeable • make ahead
PREP: 30 MIN., BAKE: 42 MIN.
(Pictured on page 2)

1 (15-oz.) package refrigerated piecrusts
2 (8-oz.) packages cream cheese, softened
½ cup sugar
1 large egg
Lemon Chess Pie Filling
Garnishes: whipped topping, crushed lemon candies

1. Fit each refrigerated piecrust into a 9-inch pieplate according to package directions; fold edges under, and crimp. Line pastry with aluminum foil, and fill with pie weights or dried beans.
2. Bake at 425° for 5 minutes. Remove weights and foil. Bake 2 more minutes or until light golden brown. Cool crusts completely on wire racks.
3. Beat cream cheese, sugar, and egg at low speed with an electric mixer until smooth. Spread cream cheese mixture evenly over crusts. Spoon Lemon Chess Pie Filling evenly over cream cheese mixture in crusts.
4. Bake at 350° for 35 minutes or until set, shielding edges to prevent excess browning, if needed. Cool completely on wire racks. Garnish, if desired. **Makes** 16 servings.

Lemon Chess Tassies
freezeable • make ahead
PREP: 30 MIN., CHILL: 1 HR., BAKE: 25 MIN., COOL: 10 MIN.

1 cup butter, softened
1 (8-oz.) package cream cheese, softened
2½ cups all-purpose flour
Lemon Chess Pie Filling

1. Beat butter and cream cheese at medium speed with an electric mixer until creamy. Gradually add flour to butter mixture, beating at low speed. Shape mixture into 48 balls; cover and chill 1 hour. Place 1 dough ball into each lightly greased muffin cup in miniature muffin pans, shaping each into a shell. Spoon Lemon Chess Pie Filling evenly into tart shells.
2. Bake at 350° for 25 minutes or until filling is set. Cool in pans on wire racks 10 minutes. Remove from pans; cool completely on wire racks. **Makes** 4 dozen.

Lemon-Coconut Bars
freezeable • make ahead
PREP: 10 MIN., BAKE: 1 HR.

2 cups all-purpose flour
1 cup powdered sugar, divided
1 cup butter, softened
½ cup chopped slivered almonds, toasted
Lemon Chess Pie Filling
1 cup sweetened flaked coconut

1. Combine flour and ½ cup powdered sugar. Cut butter into flour mixture with a pastry blender until crumbly; stir in almonds. Firmly press mixture into a lightly greased 13- x 9-inch pan.
2. Bake at 350° for 20 to 25 minutes or until light golden brown.
3. Stir together Lemon Chess Pie Filling and coconut; pour over baked crust.
4. Bake at 350° for 30 to 35 minutes or until set. Cool in pan on a wire rack. Sprinkle evenly with remaining ½ cup powdered sugar, and cut into bars. **Makes** 32 bars.

Lemon Chess Pie

freezeable • make ahead
PREP: 10 MIN., BAKE: 57 MIN.

½ (15-oz.) package refrigerated
    piecrusts
Lemon Chess Pie Filling

1. Fit piecrust into a 9-inch pieplate according to package directions; fold edges under, and crimp. Line pastry with aluminum foil, and fill with pie weights or dried beans.
2. Bake at 425° for 5 minutes. Remove weights and foil. Bake 2 more minutes or until light golden brown. Cool crust completely on a wire rack.
3. Pour Lemon Chess Pie Filling into piecrust. Bake at 350° for 50 minutes or until pie is firm, shielding edges to prevent excess browning, if needed. Cool completely on a wire rack. **Makes** 8 servings.

taste of the south

A Salute to King Cake

Watching her first Mardi Gras parade in the French Quarter from atop her cousin's shoulders is a memory Associate Foods Editor Kate Nicholson loves to conjure up. Right there with that parade, she also recalls her first bite of king cake. Similar to coffee cake, this ring-shaped confection is as rich in tradition and history as it is in color and taste. Trademark decorations—sugars in the royal colors of purple (justice), green (faith), and gold (power)—honor the three kings who visited the Christ child on Epiphany, the 12th day after Christmas. Also known as King's Day, it marks the start of merrymaking that continues until the grand finale on Fat Tuesday, the day before Ash Wednesday.

Hopefully the streets of New Orleans and other cities along the Southern coast will again be filled with the magic of Mardi Gras. So no matter where you live, toast our friends on the Gulf Coast with your favorite beverage and a piece of king cake.

Traditional King Cake

PREP: 30 MIN.; COOK: 10 MIN.; STAND: 5 MIN.;
RISE: 1 HR., 30 MIN.; BAKE: 16 MIN.
This recipe uses bread flour, which makes for a light, airy cake. You still get tasty results with all-purpose flour—the cake will just be more dense. (Pictured on page 7.)

1 (16-oz.) container sour cream
⅓ cup sugar
¼ cup butter
1 tsp. salt
2 (¼-oz.) envelopes active dry yeast
½ cup warm water (100° to 110°)
1 Tbsp. sugar
2 large eggs, lightly beaten
6 to 6½ cups bread flour ✱
⅓ cup butter, softened
½ cup sugar
1½ tsp. ground cinnamon
Creamy Glaze
Purple-, green-, and gold-tinted
    sparkling sugar sprinkles

1. Cook first 4 ingredients in a medium saucepan over low heat, stirring often, until butter melts. Set aside, and cool mixture to 100° to 110°.
2. Stir together yeast, ½ cup warm water, and 1 Tbsp. sugar in a 1-cup glass measuring cup; let mixture stand 5 minutes.
3. Beat sour cream mixture, yeast mixture, eggs, and 2 cups flour at medium speed with a heavy-duty stand mixer until smooth. Reduce speed to low, and gradually add enough remaining flour (4 to 4½ cups) until a soft dough forms.
4. Turn dough out onto a lightly floured surface; knead until smooth and elastic (about 10 minutes). Place in a well-greased bowl, turning to grease top.
5. Cover and let rise in a warm place (85°), free from drafts, 1 hour or until dough is doubled in bulk.
6. Punch down dough, and divide in half. Roll each portion into a 22- x 12-inch rectangle. Spread ⅓ cup softened butter evenly on each rectangle, leaving a 1-inch border. Stir together ½ cup sugar and cinnamon, and sprinkle evenly over butter on each rectangle.
7. Roll up each dough rectangle, jelly-roll fashion, starting at 1 long side. Place 1 dough roll, seam side down, on a lightly greased baking sheet. Bring ends of roll together to form an oval ring, moistening and pinching edges together to seal. Repeat with second dough roll.
8. Cover and let rise in a warm place, free from drafts, 20 to 30 minutes or until doubled in bulk.
9. Bake at 375° for 14 to 16 minutes or until golden. Slightly cool cakes on pans on wire racks (about 10 minutes). Drizzle Creamy Glaze evenly over warm cakes; sprinkle with colored sugars, alternating colors and forming bands. Let cool completely. **Makes** 2 cakes (about 18 servings each).

✱Substitute 6 to 6½ cups all-purpose flour, if desired.

Creamy Glaze:
PREP: 5 MIN.

3 cups powdered sugar
3 Tbsp. butter, melted
2 Tbsp. fresh lemon juice
¼ tsp. vanilla extract
2 to 4 Tbsp. milk

1. Stir together first 4 ingredients. Stir in 2 Tbsp. milk, adding more milk, 1 tsp. at a time, until spreading consistency. **Makes** 1½ cups.

Cream Cheese-Filled King Cake: Prepare each 22- x 12-inch dough rectangle as directed. Omit ⅓ cup softened butter and 1½ tsp. ground cinnamon. Increase ½ cup sugar to ¾ cup sugar. Beat ¾ cup sugar; 2 (8-oz.) packages cream cheese, softened; 1 large egg; and 2 tsp. vanilla extract at medium speed with an electric mixer until smooth. Spread cream cheese mixture evenly on each dough rectangle, leaving 1-inch borders. Proceed with recipe as directed.

Flour Power

Always spoon (not scoop) your flour into the dry measuring cup; then level with a knife. Scooping the flour with a dry measuring cup can add more flour, compromising the results of your recipe.

Dinner for Two

Celebrate with this special Valentine's Day menu.

Readers often request recipes for two. In celebration of our 40th anniversary, we selected two all-time popular dishes, reduced their serving size, and created a truly memorable menu.

Baby Blue Salad is our staff's favorite salad ever. Period. Also don't miss Beef Fillets With Cognac-Onion Sauce; its rich combination of flavors will have you savoring every bite. Served with potatoes and dessert, the meal is designed with Valentine's Day in mind, but you can enjoy it any time of the year.

Test Kitchen Notebook

The Baby Blue Salad is the tasty creation of Birmingham-area chef Franklin Biggs. In revisiting the recipe for this story, Test Kitchens Director Lyda Jones remarked, "The Sweet-and-Spicy Pecans make a cup, but you'll need more than that because you eat half of them before you ever make the salad." If you're easily tempted, you'd better go ahead and double the recipe.

Don't miss the Beef Fillets With Cognac-Onion Sauce, which, according to Associate Foods Editor Mary Allen Perry, was the go-to entrée whenever the Test Kitchens hosted guests back in the late nineties. This recipe must have been way ahead of its time because it feels as contemporary as ever, and its rich combination of flavors hasn't missed a beat.

Scott Jones
EXECUTIVE EDITOR

Beef Fillets With Cognac-Onion Sauce

PREP: 30 MIN., COOK: 36 MIN.,
BAKE: 20 MIN., STAND: 10 MIN.

2 (6- to 8-oz.) beef fillets
½ tsp. salt
¼ tsp. pepper
1 Tbsp. canola oil
1 Tbsp. butter or margarine
1 small yellow onion, sliced and
    separated into rings
1 small red onion, sliced and
    separated into rings
1 bunch green onions, chopped
6 shallots, chopped
2 garlic cloves, minced
¼ cup cognac *
¼ cup beef broth
Salt and pepper to taste

1. Sprinkle beef with ½ tsp. salt and ¼ tsp. pepper. Brown fillets in hot oil in an oven-proof or cast-iron skillet over medium-high heat 3 minutes on each side. Remove fillets, reserving drippings in skillet.
2. Melt butter in drippings over medium-high heat. Add yellow and red onion rings, and sauté 5 minutes. Add green onions, shallots, and garlic, and sauté 10 to 15 minutes or until lightly browned. Stir in cognac and broth; cook over medium-high heat, stirring constantly, until liquid evaporates (about 5 minutes). Place fillets on top of onion mixture in skillet. Cover with aluminum foil.
3. Bake at 400° for 15 to 20 minutes or until a meat thermometer inserted into thickest portion of meat registers 135° (medium rare).
4. Remove fillets from skillet, reserving onion mixture in skillet; cover fillets loosely, and let stand at room temperature 10 minutes.
5. Cook onion mixture over medium heat, stirring constantly, 5 minutes or until liquid evaporates. Add salt and pepper to taste. Serve with fillets. **Makes** 2 servings.

***** Substitute ¼ cup red wine or beef broth for cognac, if desired.

BEVERLE GRIECO
HOUSTON, TEXAS

Baby Blue Salad
fast fixin's
PREP: 10 MIN.
For ease, make the Sweet-and-Spicy Pecans and Balsamic Vinaigrette ahead. (Pictured on page 3)

1 (5-oz.) bag mixed spring salad greens
2 oz. crumbled blue cheese
1 orange, peeled and sectioned
½ pt. fresh strawberries, quartered
½ cup Sweet-and-Spicy Pecans
Balsamic Vinaigrette

1. Toss together first 5 ingredients in a large bowl. Drizzle with ½ cup Balsamic Vinaigrette, gently tossing to coat. Serve with remaining vinaigrette. **Makes** 2 servings.

Sweet-and-Spicy Pecans:
PREP: 5 MIN., SOAK: 10 MIN., BAKE: 10 MIN.
Extras of these pecans make a great snack—but they won't last long.

¼ cup sugar
1 cup warm water
1 cup pecan halves
2 Tbsp. sugar
1 Tbsp. chili powder
⅛ tsp. ground red pepper

1. Stir together ¼ cup sugar and warm water until sugar dissolves. Add pecans; soak 10 minutes. Drain; discard liquid.
2. Combine 2 Tbsp. sugar, chili powder, and red pepper. Add pecans; toss to coat. Place pecans in a single layer on a lightly greased baking sheet.
3. Bake at 350° for 10 minutes or until golden brown, stirring once. **Makes** 1 cup.

Balsamic Vinaigrette:
PREP: 5 MIN.
Store leftover vinaigrette in the refrigerator for up to 2 weeks.

½ cup balsamic vinegar
3 Tbsp. Dijon mustard
3 Tbsp. honey
2 garlic cloves, minced
2 small shallots, minced
¼ tsp. salt
¼ tsp. pepper
1 cup olive oil

1. Whisk together first 7 ingredients until blended. Gradually whisk in olive oil, blending well. **Makes** 2 cups.

FRANKLIN BIGGS
HOMEWOOD GOURMET
BIRMINGHAM, ALABAMA

Pick of the Season

These quick-to-fix side dishes are so delicious you'll want to scoop up every bite. Honey and horseradish add a sweet kick to glazed carrots. Beans and Greens, loaded with smoked sausage and sautéed onions, is a great match for a hot skillet of cornbread—especially on a cold night.

Savory Sweet Potato Hash
PREP: 15 MIN., COOK: 20 MIN.
Equally good with chicken or pork, Savory Sweet Potato Hash combines the tart taste of a green apple with smoky bits of crumbled bacon and toasted pecans.

4 bacon slices, diced
1 Tbsp. olive oil
½ medium onion, diced
3 medium-size sweet potatoes, chopped
1 large Granny Smith apple, peeled and chopped
½ cup chicken broth
¼ tsp. dried thyme
¼ tsp. ground allspice
½ cup chopped toasted pecans
1 Tbsp. chopped fresh parsley

1. Sauté bacon in hot oil in a large non-stick skillet over medium-high heat 3 minutes or until brown. Add onion, and sauté 2 minutes. Stir in sweet potatoes, and sauté 5 minutes. Stir in apple and next 3 ingredients, and cook, stirring often, 8 to 10 minutes or until potatoes and apple are tender.
2. Spoon mixture into a serving dish, and sprinkle evenly with pecans and parsley. **Makes** 4 to 6 servings.

ALFRED LESTER
WILMINGTON, NORTH CAROLINA

Carrots With Horseradish Glaze
fast fixin's
PREP: 5 MIN., COOK: 20 MIN.

1 (16-oz.) package baby carrots
1¼ tsp. salt, divided
3 Tbsp. butter
⅓ cup honey
2 Tbsp. prepared horseradish

1. Cook carrots and 1 tsp. salt in boiling water to cover in a large saucepan 15 minutes or until tender; drain.
2. Melt 3 Tbsp. butter in saucepan over medium-high heat; stir in honey, horseradish, and remaining ¼ tsp. salt. Add carrots, and cook, stirring gently, 5 minutes. **Makes** 4 servings.

ELIZABETH T. CLARKE
BURLINGTON, NORTH CAROLINA

Beans and Greens
PREP: 10 MIN., COOK: 30 MIN.

1 lb. smoked sausage
1 large onion, diced
2 (16-oz.) cans great Northern beans, undrained
2 (16-oz.) packages frozen chopped turnip greens with diced turnips
1 tsp. dried crushed red pepper
1 tsp. salt
½ tsp. seasoned pepper

1. Cut sausage into ¼-inch-thick slices; sauté in a Dutch oven over medium-high heat 5 minutes or until brown. Add onion, and sauté 3 minutes. Stir in beans and remaining ingredients; bring to a boil. Reduce heat, cover, and simmer, stirring occasionally, 15 to 20 minutes or until greens are tender. **Makes** 6 to 8 servings.

BARBARA A. CHERNICK
PENSACOLA, FLORIDA

Baked Winter Squash
PREP: 10 MIN., BAKE: 45 MIN.
This cooking method works well for all types of winter squash. Adding water to the baking dish prevents the bottom of the squash from burning. Substitute sorghum or maple syrup for the honey, if desired.

2 small butternut squash (about 1 lb. each)
¼ cup butter
4 tsp. honey
¼ tsp. salt
¼ tsp. pepper

1. Cut squash in half lengthwise; remove and discard seeds. Place squash, skin side down, in a 13- x 9-inch baking dish. Place 1 Tbsp. butter and 1 tsp. honey in the cavity of each squash half; sprinkle squash evenly with salt and pepper. Add water to baking dish to a depth of ¼ inch.
2. Bake, covered, at 400° for 30 minutes; uncover and bake 15 more minutes or until squash is tender. **Makes** 4 servings.

ADELYNE SMITH
DUNNVILLE, KENTUCKY

Add a Dose of Dairy

Three servings of milk, cheese, or yogurt in your diet each day could lead to a healthier, more-slender you.

By having a glass of milk, a carton of yogurt, or a handful of cubed cheese, you can improve your health and trim your waistline. The unique nutrient package of calcium, protein, phosphorous, and magnesium helps build strong bones, aids in weight loss, lowers blood pressure, and improves the overall quality of your diet. For more information about the healthful benefits of dairy and ideas on incorporating these products into your diet, visit www.nationaldairycouncil.org.

Mocha Frappé
PREP: 10 MIN., FREEZE: 2 HRS.
To make strong brewed coffee, use 3 Tbsp. coffee grounds to 1 cup water.

1 cup strong brewed coffee
2 Tbsp. sugar
1 Tbsp. 2% reduced-fat milk
1¼ cups 2% reduced-fat milk
2 Tbsp. chocolate syrup
3 Tbsp. fat-free frozen whipped topping, thawed
1 tsp. chocolate shavings

1. Stir together coffee, sugar, and 1 Tbsp. milk in a small glass measuring cup. Pour into ice cube trays and freeze at least 2 hours or until firm.
2. Process coffee ice cubes, 1¼ cups milk, and chocolate syrup in a blender until smooth. Dollop evenly with whipped topping, and sprinkle with chocolate shavings. Serve immediately. **Makes** 3 servings.

Per (1-cup) serving: Calories 133 (17% from fat); Fat 2.5g (sat 1.5g, mono 0.6g, poly 0.1g); Protein 4.1g; Carb 23.7g; Fiber 0.1g; Chol 8mg; Iron 0.2mg; Sodium 66mg; Calc 131mg

Key Lime Frozen Yogurt
PREP: 5 MIN., FREEZE: 30 MIN.
Serve with fresh raspberries or blackberries, pressed between graham crackers or ginger-snaps, or on its own for a tangy treat.

1 (32-oz.) container whole milk French vanilla yogurt
1 (14-oz.) can fat-free sweetened condensed milk
½ cup Key lime juice

1. Whisk together all ingredients in a large bowl until well blended. Pour mixture into the freezer container of a 1½-qt. electric ice-cream maker, and freeze according to manufacturer's instructions. (Instructions and times will vary.) Cover and freeze until desired firmness. **Makes** 12 servings.

Note: For testing purposes only, we used Stonyfield Farm Organic Whole Milk French Vanilla Yogurt and Nellie & Joe's Famous Key West Lime Juice.

JOYCE MCGLAUN
ABILENE, TEXAS

Per (½-cup) serving: Calories 178 (14% from fat); Fat 2.7g (sat 1.7g, mono 0g, poly 0g); Protein 5.6g; Carb 32.8g; Fiber 1g; Chol 12mg; Iron 0mg; Sodium 75mg; Calc 211mg

Test Kitchen Notebook

Which Milk is for You?

■ **Conventional cow's milk:** This is a naturally nutrient-dense food source that contains protein, calcium, potassium, magnesium, and vitamins A and D. Studies have found a positive link between cow's milk and weight loss, heart health, and bone density.
■ **Organic cow's milk:** According to the USDA, there are no safety or nutrition differences between organic milk and conventional milk products. The main differences are in the handling and processing procedures. Organic milk is produced without the use of antibiotics, hormones, or pesticides and has the same benefits as conventional cow's milk.
■ **Soy milk:** This is produced from whole soy beans and contains very little natural calcium. It's usually fortified to have the same amount of calcium as cow's milk, but research has found that the body does not absorb fortified calcium as efficiently; therefore, cow's milk is a better choice. Soy milk also does not carry the weight-loss benefits offered by cow's milk. It's simply a dairy-free alternative for those who are lactose-intolerant, vegans, allergic to cow's milk, or who just want to add soy to their diet. Increasing dietary soy helps to lower cholesterol and the risk of heart disease.

Holley Johnson
ASSOCIATE FOODS EDITOR

One-Serving Equivalent
Milk: 8 oz. (1 cup)
Yogurt: 8 oz. (1 cup)
Cheese: 1½ oz.

Buttermilk-Blue Cheese Dressing

make ahead

PREP: 10 MIN., CHILL: 4 HRS.

Drizzle this dressing over an iceberg lettuce wedge, and top with blue cheese crumbles for an impressive-looking and tasty salad.

½ cup reduced-fat mayonnaise
½ cup light sour cream
¼ cup fat-free buttermilk
1 Tbsp. fresh lemon juice
½ tsp. Dijon mustard
¼ tsp. Worcestershire sauce
¼ tsp. salt
¼ tsp. freshly ground pepper
⅛ tsp. garlic powder
2 oz. crumbled blue cheese (½ cup)

1. Stir together first 9 ingredients until blended. Stir in blue cheese. Cover and chill at least 4 hours. **Makes** 1½ cups.

Per (2-Tbsp.) serving: Calories 47 (61% from fat); Fat 3.4g (sat 1.7g, mono 0.4g, poly 0g); Protein 1.6g; Carb 3.3g; Fiber 0g; Chol 7mg; Iron 0mg; Sodium 221mg; Calc 45mg

Grilled Pimiento Cheese Sandwiches

fast fixin's • make ahead

PREP: 20 MIN., COOK: 6 MIN.

This recipe makes 4 cups of pimiento cheese but uses only 1⅓ cups in the recipe. Cover leftover pimiento cheese, and store in the refrigerator for up to 1 week.

1 (4-oz.) jar diced pimiento, drained
½ cup reduced-fat mayonnaise
½ cup light sour cream
1 tsp. finely grated onion
1 tsp. Worcestershire sauce
¼ tsp. ground red pepper
1 (8-oz.) block 2% reduced-fat sharp Cheddar cheese, finely shredded
1 (8-oz.) block light white Cheddar cheese, finely shredded
8 (¾-oz.) light white or wheat bread slices
2 medium tomatoes, sliced
2 Tbsp. light butter, melted
Vegetable cooking spray

1. Stir together first 6 ingredients in a large bowl until blended, and stir in cheeses.

2. Heat an electric griddle to 350° or a nonstick skillet over medium-high heat. Spread ⅓ cup cheese mixture on each of 4 bread slices. Top evenly with tomato slices and remaining 4 bread slices. Brush 1 side of sandwiches evenly with 1 Tbsp. melted butter.

3. Spray hot griddle or skillet with cooking spray. Place sandwiches, buttered sides down, on griddle or in skillet. Brush tops evenly with remaining melted butter. Cook 2 to 3 minutes on each side or until golden. Serve immediately. **Makes** 4 sandwiches.

Note: For testing purposes only, we used Kraft 2% Milk Sharp Cheddar Cheese and Cabot 50% Light Vermont Cheddar Cheese.

CHRISTINA POWELL
ATLANTA, GEORGIA

Per (1-sandwich) serving: Calories 241 (40% from fat); Fat 12.4g (sat 7.1g, mono 0g, poly 0.1g); Protein 17.3g; Carb 24.9g; Fiber 5.6g; Chol 30mg; Iron 3mg; Sodium 551mg; Calc 329mg
Per (⅓-cup pimiento cheese) serving: Calories 125 (58% from fat); Fat 8.1g (sat 4.9g, mono 0g, poly 0g); Protein 11.2g; Carb 4.5g; Fiber 0.2g; Chol 24mg; Iron 0.2mg; Sodium 332mg; Calc 271mg

---

Simple Ways to Sneak in Dairy

Adopting a low-fat diet that's rich in dairy products, fruits, and vegetables will help reduce blood pressure and lower the risk of coronary heart disease.

■ Top multigrain waffles with fruit-flavored yogurt and berries.
■ Prepare oatmeal with milk instead of water.
■ Add a sprinkle of chopped fresh chives and a dollop of plain yogurt to a baked potato in place of sour cream.
■ Melt low-fat Cheddar cheese over steamed vegetables instead of butter.
■ Dress up a salad with crumbled feta cheese and toasted nuts.
■ Toss shredded cheese and fresh-cut veggies into scrambled eggs or omelets.

Start With Frozen Pasta

We've paired two things everyone enjoys—casseroles and pasta. The secret ingredient in each of these recipes is frozen pasta, which is sold at your local grocery store in a variety of shapes and stuffings. The flavors are great, and the pastas conveniently go from the freezer into the baking dish without any thawing or precooking.

Tex-Mex Ravioli Casserole

family favorite

PREP: 20 MIN., BAKE: 50 MIN., STAND: 5 MIN.

For an extra pop of flavor, top individual servings with a dollop of sour cream and a sprinkle of chopped pickled jalapeños.

1 (16-oz.) jar mild salsa
1 (10¾-oz.) can tomato puree
½ tsp. ground cumin
1 (28-oz.) bag frozen cheese ravioli, unthawed
2 (19-oz.) cans black beans, rinsed and drained
½ cup chopped fresh cilantro
1 bunch green onions, thinly sliced
2 cups (8 oz.) shredded sharp Cheddar cheese
1 cup (4 oz.) shredded Monterey Jack cheese

1. Combine first 3 ingredients. Pour ½ cup sauce mixture in a lightly greased 2-qt. oval or 11- x 7-inch baking dish. Top evenly with frozen cheese ravioli. Layer with black beans, chopped cilantro, green onions, and remaining sauce mixture; top evenly with shredded Cheddar and Monterey Jack cheeses.

2. Bake, covered with aluminum foil, at 350° for 45 minutes or until bubbly. Remove foil, and bake 5 more minutes. Let stand 5 minutes. **Makes** 6 servings.

LOUEVA HATFIELD
FLATONIA, TEXAS

Vegetable Manicotti
vegetarian

PREP: 25 MIN., COOK: 21 MIN.,
BAKE: 50 MIN., STAND: 10 MIN.

2 garlic cloves, minced
3 Tbsp. olive oil
1 medium eggplant, peeled and
  cubed
2 medium zucchini, cut in half
  lengthwise and thinly sliced
1 small onion, cut in half and thinly
  sliced (about ½ cup)
1 (8-oz.) package sliced fresh
  mushrooms
½ tsp. salt
½ tsp. dried Italian seasoning
¼ tsp. pepper
2 (14.5-oz.) cans diced tomatoes with
  oregano and basil, undrained
1 (15-oz.) package frozen cheese-
  stuffed manicotti, unthawed
½ cup freshly grated Parmesan cheese
1 (16-oz.) package shredded mozzarella
  cheese, divided

1. Sauté minced garlic in hot olive oil in a large skillet over medium heat 1 minute.
2. Stir in eggplant and next 3 ingredients; cook, stirring occasionally, 15 to 20 minutes or until vegetables are tender and liquid evaporates. Stir in salt, Italian seasoning, and pepper; add diced tomatoes, and remove mixture from heat.
3. Spoon half of vegetable mixture in a lightly greased 13- x 9-inch baking dish. Layer evenly with stuffed frozen manicotti, grated Parmesan cheese, and half of mozzarella cheese; top with remaining half of vegetable mixture.
4. Bake, uncovered, at 375° for 40 minutes. Sprinkle evenly with remaining half of mozzarella cheese, and bake 10 more minutes or until cheese is melted and bubbly. Let stand 10 minutes before serving. **Makes** 6 servings.

BRENDA REYNOLDS
PIEDMONT, ALABAMA

Salmon Made Easy

Follow our tips for perfectly cooked fish.

Supper Tonight

Serves 4

Blackened Salmon With Hash Browns and Green Onions

green salad with peppercorn-Ranch dressing

cherry vanilla ice cream drizzled with hot fudge and sprinkled with toasted slivered almonds

You can buy frozen salmon and cook it with great results, which makes it a convenient, healthful choice for supper. Purchase individually wrapped fillets bagged in 2-lb. packages from a wholesale club, as we did for testing this recipe. To thaw, place wrapped fillets in the fridge while you're at work, or submerge them in cold water for 30 minutes when you get home. For great tips, see "Cooking Salmon" below. Try it, and you'll see how delicious it is.

Cooking Salmon

It's easy to tell when salmon is done. The portion that is closest to the heat will change color first—from bright orange and shiny to pale and dull. When the dull color moves halfway up the fillet, turn the fish over. (A broad, flat spatula helps.) Watch for the same thing as the other side cooks. As soon as the two cooked areas meet, remove the fish from the heat. (Insert a fork or paring knife into the thickest portion—you should see a hint of bright orange in the center.) The salmon will continue to cook when removed from the heat and should be perfectly done and moist when everyone grabs a plate for dinner.

Blackened Salmon With Hash Browns and Green Onions

PREP: 15 MIN., COOK: 26 MIN.

All fillets are not equal in thickness, so cooking times will vary. Plan on about 10 minutes total cooking time for 1-inch-thick pieces and 15 minutes for 1½ inches thick, and so on. Place the largest piece on the heat first.

3 bunches green onions
6 cups frozen shredded hash browns
1 Tbsp. chopped fresh dill or 1 tsp. dried dillweed
½ to ¾ tsp. salt
4 Tbsp. olive oil, divided
2 tsp. blackened seasoning
4 (6- to 8-oz.) salmon fillets
Garnish: fresh dill sprigs

1. Remove and discard root ends and 1 inch of top green portions of green onions, and set green onions aside.
2. Toss together hash browns, dill, and salt in a large bowl.
3. Heat 2 Tbsp. oil in a large nonstick skillet over medium heat. Add hash brown mixture in an even layer, and cook 5 minutes or until lightly browned. (Do not stir.) Place a lightly greased baking sheet, greased side down, onto skillet; invert hash browns onto baking sheet. Place skillet back on heat. Slide hash browns back into skillet, cooked side up, and cook 5 more minutes or until golden brown.
4. Press hash browns down with a spatula to flatten. Remove from skillet onto same lightly greased baking sheet, and keep warm in oven at 300°. Sprinkle blackened seasoning evenly over fillets.
5. Cook salmon in 1 Tbsp. hot oil in same nonstick skillet over medium heat 4 to 6 minutes on each side or just until fish begins to flake with a fork. Remove from pan onto serving plates.
6. Sauté green onions in 1 Tbsp. hot oil in same nonstick skillet over medium heat 4 minutes or until tender. Remove from pan; serve with salmon and hash browns. **Makes** 4 servings.

Note: For testing purposes only, we used Old Bay Blackened Seasoning. Use a skillet with flared sides so the cooked hash browns slide out of the pan easily.

BILL ROYAL
BIRMINGHAM, ALABAMA

Sunny Fruit Salads

Just because it's winter, you don't have to eliminate fresh fruits from your table.

Citrus Salad With Banana-Poppy Seed Dressing

PREP: 25 MIN., CHILL: 30 MIN.

You'll make a delicious dressing thick enough to cling to all the salad ingredients when you blend a ripe banana with plain yogurt.

1 (6-oz.) container plain fat-free yogurt
1 ripe banana, mashed
¼ cup sugar
1 Tbsp. poppy seeds
1 Tbsp. fresh lemon juice
1 tsp. dry mustard
¼ tsp. salt
1 head iceberg lettuce, shredded
2 oranges, peeled and sectioned
2 red grapefruit, peeled and sectioned

1. Stir together first 7 ingredients in a small bowl. Cover and chill 30 minutes.
2. Place lettuce on a serving platter; arrange orange and grapefruit sections around shredded lettuce. Drizzle evenly with chilled dressing. **Makes** 6 servings.

DONNA SPINDLER
PORT CHARLOTTE, FLORIDA

Suffolk Waldorf Salad

PREP: 10 MIN., CHILL: 30 MIN.

We've updated this classic with dried cherries and spinach in place of raisins and lettuce. Apples are key, but make sure you use a crisp snacking variety such as the heart-shaped Gala apple with its yellow-orange skin and red stripes.

⅓ cup light mayonnaise
2 Tbsp. peanut butter
1 tsp. lemon juice
2 large Gala apples, chopped
1 celery rib, chopped
¼ cup dried cherries, chopped
1 cup spinach leaves
¼ cup pecans, chopped

1. Whisk together first 3 ingredients in a large bowl. Stir in apples, celery, and cherries; toss to coat. Cover and chill 30 minutes. Arrange spinach leaves on a serving platter; top with chilled apple mixture, and sprinkle evenly with pecans. **Makes** 6 servings.

AMY PARMAR
VIRGINIA BEACH, VIRGINIA

Test Kitchen Notebook

And here's another fruit-filled recipe sent to us from Suzan L. Wiener of Spring Hill, Florida. Tuna Fruity Salad pairs fruit and albacore tuna with celery and red grapes to give an old standby a new taste.

Tuna Fruity Salad

PREP: 10 MIN.

Serve with crunchy breadsticks or toasted raisin bread.

2 (12-oz.) cans albacore tuna packed in water, drained
1 (8-oz.) can pineapple chunks in juice, drained
¾ cup chopped celery
¾ cup red seedless grapes, halved
¼ cup creamy poppy seed salad dressing
½ cup chopped pecans or almonds, toasted
6 Bibb lettuce leaves

1. Stir together first 5 ingredients and ¼ cup nuts. Cover and chill until ready to serve. Serve over lettuce leaves; sprinkle with remaining ¼ cup nuts. **Makes** 6 servings.

from our kitchen

Diced and sautéed in butter or oil until tender, vegetables such as bell pepper, carrot, onion, celery, and garlic add flavor to soups and stews. Store the cooked mixture in an airtight container in the refrigerator for up to three days or in the freezer for up to two months. You can make a quick heat-and-serve soup by combining broth with vegetables and leftover chicken or beef. It's a smart way to use up extras that might otherwise get tossed.

Quick Starts

A good broth or long-simmered stock adds richness to soups and stews that water alone cannot provide. If you don't have time for homemade, there are some terrific shortcuts on the market that deliver big flavor—from quick-dissolving granules and foil-wrapped bouillon cubes to canned broths and concentrated soup stocks. Just follow the package directions. Most of these products contain high levels of sodium, so hold off adding any extra salt unless it's needed.

Packets of dried soup mix also amp up the flavor, as do leftover cooking liquids from meats and vegetables. If you're going meatless, opt for Knorr Vegetarian Vegetable Bouillon cubes rather than canned vegetable broth. Smoky ham-flavored bouillon cubes pair well with dried beans and greens.

Tips and Tidbits

Don't be tempted to skip the browning step when adding meats to soups and stews. As the meat browns, bits and pieces cling to the bottom of the skillet or pan and develop a mellow, sweet flavor as they caramelize.

After browning, add a small amount of broth or wine to the pan; then stir and scrape the surface of the pan with a wooden spoon to loosen any caramelized portions. These bits impart a lot of flavor to any soup or stew. Here are a few secrets for successful browning.

- Use paper towels to pat the meat dry before browning. Moisture, as well as a pan that isn't hot enough, will cause the meat to stick.
- Use a heavy stainless steel or well-seasoned cast-iron skillet set over medium-high heat. The meat should sizzle as soon as it hits the pan.
- Don't try to brown frozen meat, which cools the pan, causing the meat to release juices and steam rather than form a crisp, caramelized crust.

- Use a small amount of oil or a combination of butter and oil to prevent the butter from burning. You'll need to use a little more oil if the meat is floured.
- Brown the meat in batches, if necessary. Meats brown quickly if the pan isn't too crowded for the juices to evaporate.

march

Gather 'Round the Grill

See what these women are cooking up; then start a grilling club of your own.

Outdoor Gathering

Serves 6 to 8

Bacon-Wrapped Mushrooms
With Honey-Barbecue Sauce

Spicy Flank Steak

Herbed Salad With
Grilled Balsamic Vegetables

Corn-Arugula-Tomato Medley

grilled bread

Sour Cream Pound Cake

Grilling isn't only for guys. Just ask these Valdosta, Georgia, women, who have made an art of entertaining around the grill. They started their "Girls on the Grill, Too" supper club more than five years ago, and now there are nearly 20 members. "We all love to entertain," says Rhonda Thagard, host of this month's gathering. "We try to make every event special with different themes, unique recipes, and fun decorations."

This group is ultra-organized, with a 12-month calendar of recipe assignments and scrapbooks of each event. "It's an outlet for most of us, who are either busy raising kids, volunteering in the community, or building careers," says second-grade teacher Kristy Johnson.

Just wait until you taste what these grill-savvy girlfriends fired up for us. Here are a few of their favorites, including Herbed Salad With Grilled Balsamic Vegetables, just in time for spring.

Bacon-Wrapped Mushrooms With Honey-Barbecue Sauce
fast fixin's
PREP: 15 MIN., COOK: 4 MIN., GRILL: 10 MIN.

24 small fresh mushrooms
12 bacon slices
1 cup Honey-Barbecue Sauce

1. Wash mushrooms thoroughly. Cut bacon slices in half crosswise, and microwave, in 2 batches, at HIGH 1½ to 2 minutes or until bacon is partially cooked. Pat dry with paper towels. Wrap each mushroom with a bacon slice, and secure with wooden picks. Dip wrapped mushrooms in Honey-Barbecue Sauce.
2. Grill mushrooms (using a grill basket, if necessary), covered with grill lid, over medium-high heat (350° to 400°) 4 to 5 minutes on each side or until bacon is crisp and thoroughly cooked. **Makes** 8 appetizer servings.

Honey-Barbecue Sauce:
make ahead
PREP: 10 MIN., COOK: 25 MIN.
Cover and store leftover sauce in the refrigerator up to 1 week.

2 cups ketchup
1 cup dry white wine
⅓ cup honey
1 small onion, diced
2 garlic cloves, minced
1 Tbsp. dried parsley flakes
2 Tbsp. white vinegar
2 Tbsp. lemon juice
1 Tbsp. Worcestershire sauce
1 tsp. hot sauce
¼ tsp. salt

1. Bring all ingredients to a boil in a large saucepan; reduce heat, and simmer, stirring often, 15 to 20 minutes or until slightly thickened. **Makes** about 2¾ cups.
LAURA P. HANSEN
VALDOSTA, GEORGIA

Spicy Flank Steak
PREP: 5 MIN., STAND: 20 MIN., GRILL: 14 MIN.
For a more pungent spice rub, add 1 tsp. ground coriander.

1 (1½- to 2-lb.) flank steak
2 tsp. vegetable oil
2 tsp. ground cumin
2 tsp. chili powder
1 tsp. kosher salt
¾ tsp. black pepper
½ tsp. dried crushed red pepper
¼ tsp. ground cinnamon

1. Rub both sides of steak evenly with vegetable oil.
2. Stir together ground cumin and next 5 ingredients. Rub cumin mixture evenly over both sides of steak. Let stand 10 minutes.
3. Grill, covered with grill lid, over medium-high heat (350° to 400°) 5 to 7 minutes on each side or to desired degree of doneness. Remove from grill. Cover steak loosely with aluminum foil, and let stand 10 minutes. Cut across the grain into thin slices. **Makes** 4 to 6 servings.
JILL BRIGHT
HAHIRA, GEORGIA

Herbed Salad With Grilled Balsamic Vegetables

fast fixin's • make ahead

PREP: 15 MIN.

To prepare ahead, rinse the greens, and spin them dry. Wrap them in damp paper towels. Store them in zip-top plastic bags in the refrigerator. (Pictured on page 3)

8 cups mixed baby greens
3 tomatoes, sliced
Grilled Balsamic Vegetables
½ cup pitted ripe black olives
½ cup olive oil
3 Tbsp. balsamic vinegar
3 Tbsp. chopped fresh basil
2 Tbsp. chopped fresh chives or green onions
1 Tbsp. chopped fresh marjoram (optional)
½ cup crumbled feta or goat cheese
⅓ cup refrigerated shredded Romano or Parmesan cheese

1. Place mixed greens on a large serving platter. Arrange tomato slices in center of platter over greens. Arrange Grilled Balsamic Vegetables and black olives around edge of platter over greens.

2. Whisk together olive oil and vinegar; drizzle over tomatoes and grilled vegetables. Sprinkle tomatoes evenly with basil, chives, and, if desired, marjoram. Top evenly with cheeses. **Makes** 6 to 8 servings.

Grilled Balsamic Vegetables:

PREP: 15 MIN., GRILL: 18 MIN.

4 medium-size fresh beets
2 large red bell peppers
2 small zucchini
1 small eggplant
1 large red onion
¼ cup extra-virgin olive oil
1½ Tbsp. balsamic vinegar
½ tsp. salt
½ tsp. freshly ground black pepper

1. Trim stems from beets to 1 inch; cut into quarters. Cut bell peppers into 1-inch-wide strips. Cut off ends of zucchini and eggplant; cut each lengthwise into 4 slices. Cut eggplant slices lengthwise into 1½-inch strips. Cut onion into ¾-inch-thick rounds.

2. Whisk together olive oil and vinegar in a large bowl. Add vegetables, and sprinkle evenly with salt and pepper; toss to coat.

3. Grill vegetables, covered with grill lid, over medium-high heat (350° to 400°). Grill beets 6 minutes on each side (we grilled on 3 sides) or until tender; grill onion, zucchini, eggplant, and bell peppers 4 to 6 minutes on each side or until crisp-tender. Cool beets slightly, and, if desired, peel. **Makes** 6 to 8 servings.

LISA HARP
QUITMAN, GEORGIA

Corn-Arugula-Tomato Medley

fast fixin's

PREP: 15 MIN., GRILL: 15 MIN.

Vegetable cooking spray for grilling
6 large ears fresh corn, husks removed
3 cups lightly packed baby arugula
2 cups cherry or grape tomatoes
5 bacon slices, cooked and crumbled
¼ cup chopped fresh cilantro
¼ cup fresh lime juice
2 garlic cloves, minced
Salt and freshly ground pepper to taste

1. Coat cold grill cooking grate with cooking spray; place on grill over medium-high heat (350° to 400°). Coat corn with cooking spray. Place corn on cooking grate, and grill, covered with grill lid, turning occasionally, 12 to 15 minutes or until lightly browned and done. Remove corn from grill, and cool slightly.

2. Hold each grilled cob upright on a cutting board, and carefully cut downward, cutting kernels from cob. Discard cobs.

3. Combine corn kernels, arugula, and next 5 ingredients, tossing to coat. Season to taste with salt and pepper. Serve immediately. **Makes** 6 to 8 servings.

CARYN ALVARADO
VALDOSTA, GEORGIA

Light Your Coals With Ease

You can use a gas or charcoal grill to make these recipes. If the thought of grilling over charcoal sends you running indoors, fear no more. Lighting the coals is easier than you think. Consider purchasing a charcoal chimney, available at any home-improvement store for about $20. It eliminates the need for lighter fluid or treated charcoal, which can affect the flavor of your food. Just follow these simple steps, and you'll have hot coals in no time.

1. Pack the bottom of the charcoal chimney with newspaper, and fill the canister with untreated charcoal.

2. Place the chimney upright on the grill food grate. Light the newspaper through the chimney holes at the bottom.

3. Let the coals smolder in the canister until they turn completely ashy in color. Remove the food grate, and carefully pour the hot coals onto the bottom of the grill. Replace the food grate, and start grilling.

Sour Cream Pound Cake
family favorite

PREP: 15 MIN.; BAKE: 1 HR., 30 MIN.;
STAND: 30 MIN.

To make sweetened whipped cream, beat 1 cup whipping cream with 2 Tbsp. powdered sugar until stiff peaks form.

1 (8-oz.) container sour cream
½ tsp. baking soda
3¼ cups sugar, divided
1 cup shortening or butter
6 large eggs
3 cups all-purpose flour
⅛ tsp. salt
1 tsp. vanilla extract
2 pt. fresh strawberries, sliced
Sweetened whipped cream

1. Stir together sour cream and ½ tsp. baking soda; set mixture aside.
2. Beat 3 cups sugar and 1 cup shortening at medium speed with an electric mixer until fluffy. Add eggs, 1 at a time, beating just until blended after each addition.
3. Stir together 3 cups flour and salt. Add to egg mixture alternately with sour cream mixture, beginning and ending with flour mixture. Beat at low speed just until blended after each addition. Stir in 1 tsp. vanilla. Pour batter into a greased and floured 10-inch tube pan.
4. Bake at 325° for 1 hour and 30 minutes or until a long wooden pick inserted in center comes out clean. Cool in pan on a wire rack 10 minutes. Remove from pan, and cool completely on wire rack.
5. Toss together sliced fresh strawberries and remaining ¼ cup sugar; let stand 30 minutes. Serve pound cake with sliced strawberries and sweetened whipped cream. **Makes** 12 to 16 servings.

JENNIFER ALLEN
VALDOSTA, GEORGIA

Grilled Pound Cake: Bake and cool pound cake as directed. Brush 2 Tbsp. melted butter evenly over both sides of 6 (1½-inch-thick) cake slices. Grill, covered with grill lid, over medium-high heat (350° to 400°) 1 to 2 minutes on each side or until lightly toasted. Serve pound cake with sliced fresh strawberries and sweetened whipped cream.

Test Kitchen *Notebook*

After you've finished grilling your meal, and while you've got the grill hot, throw on some bread for a crispy and delicious way to round out your menu. We liked this one sent to us by Lisa Harp of Quitman, Georgia.

Grilled Peppered Bread
PREP: 5 MIN., GRILL: 4 MIN.

12 (½-inch-thick) French bread
  slices
Olive oil
1 tsp. freshly ground black pepper

1. Brush both sides of bread slices with olive oil; sprinkle both sides evenly with pepper. Grill bread, uncovered, over medium-high heat (350° to 400°) 1 to 2 minutes on each side or until lightly toasted and browned. **Makes** 6 to 8 servings.

Shannon Sliter Satterwhite

FOODS EDITOR

Creative Kabobs

Think of a skewer as a blank slate on which to mix and match ingredients. We tried new flavor combinations, such as shrimp and okra, with delicious results.

Skewered Fruit With Rum Drizzle

PREP: 25 MIN., SOAK: 30 MIN.,
BROIL: 10 MIN. PER BATCH

Serve these dessert kabobs with vanilla ice cream and a sprinkle of toasted coconut.

16 (12-inch) wooden or metal skewers
4 bananas, cut into ½-inch slices
¼ cup lemon juice
1 pineapple, peeled and cut into 1-inch
  pieces
8 star fruit, cut into ½-inch pieces *
½ cup sugar
1 tsp. ground cinnamon
¼ cup dark rum

1. Soak wooden skewers 30 minutes to prevent burning.
2. Toss banana slices with lemon juice. Thread banana slices, pineapple, and star fruit onto skewers, alternating fruit. Place on an aluminum foil-lined broiling rack. Cover and chill up to 8 hours, if desired.
3. Combine sugar and cinnamon; sprinkle evenly over fruit.
4. Broil in 2 batches 4 inches from heat 5 minutes on each side or until lightly browned. Drizzle with rum. **Makes** 16 servings.

*Substitute 4 papayas, peeled and cut into ½-inch pieces, for star fruit, if desired.

Creole Shrimp Kabobs With Tomato Rice

PREP: 20 MIN., SOAK: 30 MIN., CHILL: 20 MIN., GRILL: 16 MIN.

8 (12-inch) wooden or metal skewers
24 unpeeled, jumbo fresh shrimp
1 (10-oz.) package frozen whole okra, thawed
18 cherry tomatoes (about 1 pt.)
1 Tbsp. Creole seasoning
2 Tbsp. olive oil
1 tsp. garlic powder
¼ tsp. ground black pepper
⅛ tsp. ground red pepper
Tomato Rice

1. Soak wooden skewers 30 minutes to prevent burning.
2. Peel shrimp, leaving tails on, if desired; devein shrimp, if desired. Thread shrimp, okra, and tomatoes alternately onto skewers. Place on a baking sheet.
3. Whisk together Creole seasoning and next 4 ingredients. Brush mixture on kabobs, and chill 20 minutes.
4. Grill, covered with grill lid, over medium-high heat (350° to 400°) 7 to 8 minutes on each side or until done. Serve immediately with Tomato Rice. **Makes** 4 servings.

Tomato Rice:

PREP: 5 MIN., COOK: 25 MIN.

1 cup uncooked long-grain rice
2 tsp. olive oil
1 Tbsp. tomato paste
2 cups water

1. Sauté rice in hot oil in a saucepan over medium-high heat 2 to 3 minutes. Stir in tomato paste, and sauté 2 minutes; add 2 cups water. Bring to a boil; cover, reduce heat, and cook 20 minutes. **Makes** 4 servings.

Salad on the Side

Asparagus and lettuces are at their peak now, and this recipe offers a great way to showcase them. We used Bibb lettuce, but any tender kind works equally well. Best of all would be those from your own garden or window box. Splash the salad with Basil Vinaigrette, or add some fresh herbs to a subtly flavored bottled dressing.

Asparagus-and-Goat Cheese Salad

fast fixin's

PREP: 12 MIN., COOK: 3 MIN.

Enjoy this as an elegant side or a light entrée.

1 lb. fresh asparagus
1 large head Bibb lettuce, torn
3 plum tomatoes, diced
⅛ tsp. salt
1 (3-oz.) package goat cheese, crumbled
¼ cup pine nuts, toasted
Basil Vinaigrette

1. Snap off and discard tough ends of asparagus.
2. Cook in boiling salted water to cover 3 minutes or until crisp-tender; drain. Plunge into ice water to stop the cooking process; drain.
3. Arrange lettuce on a serving platter. Sprinkle tomatoes with salt. Top lettuce with asparagus, goat cheese, tomatoes, and pine nuts. Drizzle with Basil Vinaigrette before serving. **Makes** 4 servings.

Basil Vinaigrette:

fast fixin's

PREP: 5 MIN.

2 Tbsp. chopped fresh basil
2 Tbsp. balsamic vinegar
1 tsp. sugar
½ tsp. salt
½ tsp. freshly ground pepper
½ cup olive oil

1. Whisk together first 5 ingredients. Gradually whisk in oil, blending well. **Makes** ⅔ cup.

Comfort Food at Its Best

These recipes will make your family say, "Pass the plate, please."

Don't miss this tempting collection of recipes gathered from some of the South's most famous family-style eateries. We adapted timeless favorites from The Dinner Bell in McComb, Mississippi; The Jarrett House in Dillsboro, North Carolina; and Miss Mary Bobo's Boarding House in Lynchburg, Tennessee. All are made with familiar ingredients, many of which are probably already in your pantry.

John's Creole Red Beans and Boarding House Meat Loaf are sure crowd-pleasers and the leftovers are freezer friendly. We suggest making Cheesy Tomato Casserole and Chicken-and-Cornbread Casserole the day before you plan to serve them because they don't freeze well. Cheesy Tomato Casserole begins with canned whole tomatoes and has a prep time of only 15 minutes before you put it in the oven, so it's a snap to pull together for dinner.

Jack Daniel's Whiskey Butter
fast fixin's • make ahead
PREP: 10 MIN.
Spread this rich, flavorful butter over warm biscuits and combine with bacon or sausage. It also makes a quick sauce for grilled or broiled beef, pork, or chicken.

½ cup butter, softened
1 to 2 Tbsp. Jack Daniel's whiskey
1 Tbsp. white wine vinegar
1 Tbsp. Worcestershire sauce
1 tsp. dry mustard
¼ tsp. salt
⅛ tsp. ground red pepper

1. Whisk together all ingredients until well blended. Cover and chill until ready to serve. **Makes** about ¾ cup.
MISS MARY BOBO'S BOARDING HOUSE
LYNCHBURG, TENNESSEE

Boarding House Meat Loaf
freezeable
PREP: 10 MIN.; BAKE: 1 HR., 10 MIN.

½ green bell pepper, chopped
½ small onion, chopped
1½ lb. lean ground beef
2 large eggs, beaten
¾ cup uncooked regular oats
¼ cup ketchup
1½ tsp. salt
Meat Loaf Sauce

1. Microwave green bell pepper and onion in a microwave-safe bowl at HIGH 2 minutes.
2. Combine onion mixture, ground beef, and next 4 ingredients. Shape into a loaf. Place in a lightly greased 9- x 5-inch loaf pan.
3. Bake at 350° for 45 minutes. Remove from oven, and pour off pan juices. Spread half of Meat Loaf Sauce evenly over meat loaf; bake 25 more minutes. Remove from pan, and serve with remaining Meat Loaf Sauce. **Makes** 6 servings.

Meat Loaf Sauce:
fast fixin's
PREP: 10 MIN., COOK: 10 MIN.

2 Tbsp. butter
½ small onion, chopped
½ green bell pepper, chopped
¾ cup ketchup *
1 Tbsp. cider vinegar

1. Melt butter in a large skillet over medium-high heat; add onion and bell pepper, and sauté 5 minutes or until vegetables are tender. Stir in ketchup and vinegar, and simmer, stirring constantly, until sauce thickens. **Makes** about 1 cup.

*For a spicier sauce, substitute ¾ cup chili sauce for ketchup, if desired.
MISS MARY BOBO'S BOARDING HOUSE
LYNCHBURG, TENNESSEE

Chicken-and-Cornbread Casserole
make ahead
PREP: 20 MIN., COOK: 7 MIN., BAKE: 40 MIN.
Pick up a deli-roasted chicken if you don't have 3½ cups of chopped chicken on hand. It yields just enough meat for this recipe. The delicious recipe is sure to put a smile on every face.

2 celery ribs, chopped
½ medium onion, chopped
1 Tbsp. vegetable oil
3 cups packed crumbled cornbread
1 Tbsp. poultry seasoning
3½ cups chopped cooked chicken
1¼ cups low-sodium chicken broth
1 cup sour cream
1 large egg, lightly beaten
1 (4.5-oz.) jar sliced mushrooms, drained
¼ tsp. dried crushed red pepper
¼ tsp. salt
2 Tbsp. butter, melted
1 cup (4 oz.) shredded sharp Cheddar cheese
Garnish: chopped fresh parsley

1. Sauté celery and onion in hot oil in a medium skillet over medium-high heat 7 minutes or until vegetables are tender; set aside.

2. Combine cornbread and poultry seasoning in a large bowl.

3. Layer half of cornbread mixture on bottom of a lightly greased 11- x 7-inch baking dish.

4. Combine onion mixture, chicken, and next 6 ingredients in a bowl. Spoon mixture evenly over cornbread mixture in dish. Top evenly with remaining half of cornbread mixture, and drizzle with butter.

5. Bake, covered, at 350° for 30 minutes or until bubbly. Remove from oven, and top with cheese. Bake, uncovered, 10 more minutes or until cheese is golden. Garnish, if desired. **Makes** 6 servings.

MISS MARY BOBO'S BOARDING HOUSE
LYNCHBURG, TENNESSEE

John's Creole Red Beans

freezeable

PREP: 20 MIN., SOAK: 8 HRS., COOK: 3 HRS.

We tested John's Creole Red Beans with a spicy pork sausage. Substitute your favorite turkey or chicken sausage to lighten this hearty recipe and still get that full-bodied flavor. Diners who gather at The Dinner Bell restaurant sit around lazy Susan-style tables, where they can easily spin the table to put mouthwatering comfort food within their reach.

1 (16-oz.) package dried red kidney beans
1 lb. spicy smoked sausage
1 Tbsp. vegetable oil
3 celery ribs, chopped
1 medium-size green bell pepper, chopped
1 large onion, chopped
3 garlic cloves, minced
1 (14½-oz.) can crushed tomatoes
1 (32-oz.) container chicken broth
3½ cups water
2 bay leaves
1 tsp. sugar
½ tsp. salt
½ tsp. pepper
Hot cooked rice
Garnish: chopped green onions

1. Rinse and sort beans according to package directions. Place beans in a Dutch oven; cover with water 2 inches above beans, and let soak 8 hours. Drain beans, and rinse thoroughly; drain and set aside.

2. Cut smoked sausage into ¼-inch-thick slices.

3. Sauté sausage in hot oil in Dutch oven over medium heat 5 to 7 minutes or until sausage is golden brown. Remove sausage with a slotted spoon, and drain on paper towels, reserving drippings in Dutch oven. (Store sausage in refrigerator until you're ready to stir into bean mixture.) Add celery and next 3 ingredients to hot drippings, and sauté 5 minutes or until vegetables are tender. Add tomatoes, and simmer, stirring occasionally, 7 minutes.

4. Stir in beans, broth, and next 5 ingredients; increase heat to medium-high, and bring to a boil. Boil 10 minutes; reduce heat, and simmer, uncovered, stirring occasionally, 1½ to 2 hours or until beans are tender. Stir in sausage, and simmer 30 more minutes. Remove and discard bay leaves. Serve beans over hot cooked rice. Garnish, if desired. **Makes** 8 servings.

Note: For quick soaking, place kidney beans in a Dutch oven; cover with water 2 inches above beans, and bring to a boil. Boil 1 minute; cover, remove from heat, and let stand 1 hour. Drain as directed, and proceed with recipe. For testing purposes only, we used Conecuh Original Smoked Sausage, which is spicy.

THE DINNER BELL RESTAURANT
MCCOMB, MISSISSIPPI

Cheesy Tomato Casserole

make ahead

PREP: 15 MIN., BAKE: 30 MIN.

If you've never had this baked tomato dish, try it. The tangy tomatoes are sweetened by the buttery cracker crumbs and cheese. Serve it as a side to your favorite pork, chicken, or beef main dish.

1 (35-oz.) can whole tomatoes, drained and chopped
½ cup round buttery cracker crumbs (about 15 crackers)
½ cup (2 oz.) shredded sharp Cheddar cheese
1 Tbsp. butter, melted
½ small onion, finely chopped
1 large egg, well beaten
½ tsp. salt
¼ tsp. paprika

1. Stir together all ingredients. Spoon mixture into a lightly greased 8-inch square baking dish.

2. Bake at 325° for 30 minutes or until golden. **Makes** 4 to 6 servings.

THE JARRETT HOUSE
DILLSBORO, NORTH CAROLINA

Take a Sip of Spring

Frozen juices add tangy sweetness to these quick refreshers.

Chances are you have fruit juices and concentrates in your freezer. If not, grab some on your next grocery run, and stir up these cooling quenchers. We used everything from lemonade to fresh-tasting frozen citrus juice in these recipes, and all are prepared in minutes with eight ingredients or less. Got leftovers? Save unused juices and concentrates to flavor your iced tea, blend a tropical smoothie, or perk up a marinade.

Lemon-Mint Ice

PREP: 10 MIN., COOK: 15 MIN., STAND: 1 HR., FREEZE: 8 HRS.

Make a cool, icy treat with little effort by pouring the lemon-mint mixture into plastic frozen pop molds. Freeze any leftover mixture, or drizzle over fresh cut fruit for a refreshing snack.

2 cups firmly packed fresh mint leaves
1 qt. water
¾ cup sugar
¾ cup thawed lemonade concentrate*
¼ cup fresh raspberries (optional)

1. Bring fresh mint leaves and 1 qt. water to a boil over medium-high heat in a medium saucepan. Boil 7 to 8 minutes or until leaves darken; stir in ¾ cup sugar. Cook, stirring constantly, 2 minutes or until sugar dissolves; remove from heat. Stir in ¾ cup lemonade concentrate, and let mixture stand 30 minutes.
2. Pour lemon-mint mixture through a wire-mesh strainer into a large zip-top freezer bag; discard mint leaves. Seal and freeze 8 hours or until mixture is firm. Remove lemonade mixture from freezer, and let stand, turning bag occasionally, 30 minutes or until slushy. Serve with fresh raspberries, if desired. **Makes** about 4 cups.

Basil-Lemon Ice: Substitute 2 cups firmly packed fresh basil leaves for fresh mint leaves, and proceed with recipe as directed.

*Substitute limeade concentrate for lemonade concentrate, if desired.

SYBIL ANDRUS
ANGLETON, TEXAS

White Sangría

fast fixin's

PREP: 20 MIN. *(Pictured on page 167)*

1 (750-milliliter) bottle dry white wine
1 cup thawed orange juice concentrate
⅓ cup thawed lemonade concentrate
⅓ cup thawed limeade concentrate
1 navel orange, sliced
1 lemon, sliced
1 lime, sliced
3 cups club soda, chilled

1. Stir together first 4 ingredients. Stir in half of fruit slices. Cover and chill until ready to serve. Stir in club soda just before serving. Serve over ice with remaining fruit slices. **Makes** about 2 qt.

BETTY SIMS
DECATUR, ALABAMA

Cool Lavender Lemonade

PREP: 5 MIN., COOK: 5 MIN., STAND: 2 HRS.

The intensity of lavender and mint flavors can be easily adjusted by adding more or less herbs or by steeping for longer or shorter periods of time. (Pictured on page 167)

7 cups water
1 cup sugar
1½ cups frozen lemon juice from concentrate, thawed
4 mint sprigs
3 lavender sprigs*
Garnishes: lemon slices, lavender and mint sprigs

1. Bring 7 cups water to a boil over medium-high heat. Stir in 1 cup sugar, and cook, stirring constantly, 1 to 2 minutes or until sugar dissolves; remove from heat. Stir in lemon juice, mint sprigs, and lavender sprigs; let stand at least 2 hours.
2. Pour lemonade mixture through a wire-mesh strainer into a large pitcher, discarding herbs. Serve over ice. Garnish, if desired. **Makes** about 2 qt.

*Substitute 2 Tbsp. dried lavender flowers, if desired.

JOHN FLEER
MARYVILLE, TENNESSEE

Test Kitchen Notebook

Cool off with this refreshing ice cream drink from Bebe May of Pensacola, Florida.

Orange-Pineapple Frosty

PREP: 5 MIN.

1 pt. vanilla ice cream
1 cup orange juice
1 cup pineapple juice
¾ cup thawed limeade concentrate

1. Process all ingredients in a blender until smooth, stopping to scrape down sides. **Makes** about 5 cups.

Shannon Sliter Satterwhite

FOODS EDITOR

Banana Pudding With Pizzazz

One bite will change the way you think about this cherished dessert.

RHONDA HARMS
CLEARWATER, FLORIDA

D on't miss these spectacular recipes. Pound Cake Banana Pudding and Uptown Banana Pudding Cheesecake not only both received our highest rating, they were also absolute revelations—one using pound cake in place of vanilla wafers, the other combining elements of banana pudding in a rich cheesecake. You can make pudding from scratch, even if you're a new cook. The key is to keep the heat on medium-low while cooking the egg yolk, sugar, and milk mixture. So, grab a whisk and saucepan, and give it a try. The extra effort yields a thick, luscious dessert that's light-years ahead of its instant mix brethren in both flavor and appearance. Guaranteed.

Uptown Banana Pudding Cheesecake

make ahead

PREP: 15 MIN., BAKE: 1 HR., COOK: 1 MIN., CHILL: 8 HRS.

1½ cups finely crushed vanilla wafers
¼ cup chopped walnuts, toasted
¼ cup butter, melted
2 large ripe bananas, diced
1 Tbsp. lemon juice
2 Tbsp. light brown sugar
3 (8-oz.) packages cream cheese, softened
1 cup granulated sugar
3 large eggs
1 Tbsp. coffee liqueur
2 tsp. vanilla extract
Meringue

1. Combine first 3 ingredients in a bowl. Press evenly into bottom of a lightly greased 9-inch springform pan.
2. Bake at 350° for 10 minutes. Cool on a wire rack.
3. Combine diced bananas and 1 Tbsp. lemon juice in a small saucepan. Stir in 2 Tbsp. brown sugar. Place pan over medium-high heat, and cook, stirring constantly, about 1 minute or just until sugar melts. Set aside.
4. Beat cream cheese at medium speed with an electric mixer 3 minutes or until smooth. Gradually add 1 cup granulated sugar; beat until blended. Add eggs, 1 at a time, beating until blended after each addition. Beat in coffee liqueur and vanilla. Pour into prepared vanilla wafer crust. Spoon tablespoonfuls of banana mixture evenly over top, and swirl gently into cream cheese mixture.
5. Bake at 350° for 35 to 40 minutes or until center is almost set.
6. Drop spoonfuls of Meringue gently and evenly over hot filling.
7. Bake at 400° for 10 minutes or until Meringue is golden brown. Remove from oven, and gently run a knife around edge of cheesecake in springform pan to loosen. Cool cheesecake completely on a wire rack. Cover loosely, and chill 8 hours. Release and remove sides of pan. **Makes** 10 to 12 servings.

Meringue:

fast fixin's

PREP: 5 MIN.

3 egg whites
¼ tsp. salt
6 Tbsp. sugar

1. Beat egg whites and salt at high speed with an electric mixer until foamy. Add sugar, 1 Tbsp. at a time, beating until soft peaks form and sugar dissolves (about 1 to 2 minutes). **Makes** about 2 cups.

Blastin' Banana-Blueberry Pudding

PREP: 10 MIN., COOK: 20 MIN., STAND: 10 MIN., CHILL: 4 HRS.

For a less sweet banana pudding, omit the powdered sugar from the whipped cream.

4 cups milk
4 egg yolks
1½ cups granulated sugar
⅓ cup all-purpose flour
2 Tbsp. butter
1 Tbsp. vanilla extract
1 (12-oz.) box vanilla wafers
4 large ripe bananas, sliced
2 cups frozen blueberries
1½ cups whipping cream
3 Tbsp. powdered sugar

1. Whisk together first 4 ingredients in a large saucepan over medium-low heat. Cook, whisking constantly, 20 minutes or until thickened. Remove from heat; stir in butter and vanilla until butter melts. Let stand 10 minutes.
2. Arrange half of vanilla wafers in a 13- x 9-inch baking dish; top with half of banana slices and half of blueberries. Spoon half of pudding mixture evenly over fruit. Repeat layers. Cover and chill 4 hours.
3. Beat whipping cream at high speed with an electric mixer until foamy; gradually add powdered sugar, beating until soft peaks form. Spread evenly over chilled pudding. Serve immediately. **Makes** 10 to 12 servings.

SHARON LAPPOHN
LEISURE CITY, FLORIDA

Rum Banana Pudding

make ahead

PREP: 10 MIN., COOK: 8 MIN., STAND: 5 MIN.,
BAKE: 10 MIN.

*A touch of rum turns this dish into an
adult-friendly banana pudding. Serve cold,
if desired, by allowing to cool 15 minutes
after baking, and then chilling 4 hours.*

1½ cups milk
⅔ cup sugar
2 egg yolks
3 Tbsp. cornstarch
3 Tbsp. light rum
1 tsp. vanilla extract
6 medium bananas, sliced
30 vanilla wafers
1 cup chopped toasted pecans
2 egg whites
⅛ tsp. cream of tartar
2 Tbsp. sugar

1. Whisk together first 5 ingredients in
a large saucepan over medium-low
heat; cook, whisking constantly, 6 to 8
minutes or until thickened. Remove
from heat, and stir in vanilla. Let stand
5 minutes. Gently stir bananas into
pudding mixture.
2. Arrange 15 vanilla wafers in a single
layer on bottom of a 1½-qt. baking
dish; sprinkle ½ cup pecans evenly on
vanilla wafers. Pour half of pudding
mixture on top of pecans in dish.
Repeat layers with remaining vanilla
wafers, pudding, and ending with
pecans.
3. Beat egg whites and ⅛ tsp. cream of
tartar at high speed with an electric
mixer until foamy. Add 2 Tbsp. sugar,
1 Tbsp. at a time, beating until soft
peaks form and sugar dissolves (about
1 to 2 minutes). Spread meringue evenly over top of banana mixture, sealing
edges.
4. Bake at 400° for 8 to 10 minutes or
until golden brown. **Makes** 10 to 12
servings.
JEAN MARIE CINOTTO
COLLEYVILLE, TEXAS

Pound Cake Banana Pudding

family favorite • make ahead

PREP: 20 MIN., COOK: 15 MIN., CHILL: 6 HRS.,
BAKE: 15 MIN.

*This recipe is inspired by the one served at
the famous Mrs. Wilkes' Dining Room in
Savannah, Georgia. Look for pound cake in
the frozen dessert case of the supermarket.*
(Pictured on page 5)

4 cups half-and-half
4 egg yolks
1½ cups sugar
¼ cup cornstarch
¼ tsp. salt
3 Tbsp. butter
2 tsp. vanilla extract
1 (1-lb.) pound cake, cubed
4 large ripe bananas, sliced
Meringue

1. Whisk together first 5 ingredients in
a saucepan over medium-low heat;
cook, whisking constantly, 13 to 15
minutes or until thickened. Remove
from heat; stir in butter and vanilla
until butter melts. Layer half of pound
cake cubes, half of bananas, and half of
pudding mixture in a 3-qt. round baking dish. Repeat layers. Cover pudding,
and chill 6 hours.
2. Spread Meringue over pudding.
3. Bake at 375° for 15 minutes or until
golden brown. **Makes** 10 to 12 servings.

Note: For testing purposes only, we
used Sara Lee Family Size All Butter
Pound Cake.

Meringue:

fast fixin's

PREP: 10 MIN.

¼ cup sugar
⅛ tsp. salt
4 egg whites
¼ tsp. vanilla extract

1. Combine sugar and salt.
2. Beat egg whites and vanilla at high
speed with an electric mixer until
foamy. Add sugar mixture, 1 Tbsp. at a
time, and beat 2 to 3 minutes or until
stiff peaks form and sugar dissolves.
Makes about 3½ cups.

Oh-So-Easy Eggs

Fix a frittata (frih-TAH-tuh) for a
twist on breakfast *or* supper. The
zucchini-onion version featured here is
filled with wholesome vegetables,
Parmesan cheese, and fresh basil. The
heartier Sausage-and-Cheese Frittata is
flavored with Cheddar cheese and spicy
meat. The eggs and other ingredients
are layered in a skillet and start cooking
on the cooktop; then they finish in the
oven. Best of all, there's no flipping or
folding. These will be the easiest
"omelets" you've ever made.

Sausage-and-Cheese Frittata

family favorite

PREP: 15 MIN., BAKE: 20 MIN.

10 large eggs
½ cup milk
½ tsp. salt
½ tsp. pepper
2 Tbsp. butter
1 (12-oz.) package reduced-fat ground
   pork sausage, cooked and crumbled
1 cup (4 oz.) shredded Cheddar cheese

1. Whisk together first 4 ingredients at
least 1 minute or until well blended.
2. Melt butter in a 12-inch ovenproof
skillet over medium heat; remove skillet from heat, and pour half of egg mixture into skillet. Sprinkle evenly with
cooked sausage and cheese. Top with
remaining egg mixture.
3. Bake at 350° for 15 to 20 minutes or
until set. **Makes** 8 servings.
MARY PAPPAS
RICHMOND, VIRGINIA

Here's a lighter version of the Sausage-and-Cheese Frittata that we think you'll find just as tasty as the hearty original.

Lightened Sausage-and-Cheese Frittata: Substitute 1 (15-oz.) carton cheese-and-chive egg substitute for 10 eggs and ½ cup low-fat milk for ½ cup milk. Omit salt, and whisk together egg substitute, low-fat milk, and pepper until well blended. Omit butter. Heat a 12-inch nonstick ovenproof skillet over medium-high heat until hot; remove from heat, and spray with vegetable cooking spray. Pour half of egg substitute mixture into skillet. Sprinkle evenly with cooked sausage; reduce shredded Cheddar cheese to ¾ cup (3 oz.), and sprinkle over sausage. Top with remaining egg substitute mixture. Bake as directed. **Makes** 8 servings.

Charla Draper
ASSOCIATE FOODS EDITOR

Zucchini-Onion Frittata

family favorite

PREP: 15 MIN., COOK: 15 MIN.,
BAKE: 15 MIN., BROIL: 2 MIN.

Combine the eggs and vegetables in a skillet, and finish it in the oven.

3 Tbsp. butter
2 Tbsp. vegetable oil
2 medium zucchini, thinly sliced
1 medium onion, cut in half and sliced
½ cup grated Parmesan cheese, divided
8 large eggs
¼ cup milk
1 tsp. salt
½ tsp. pepper
¼ cup chopped fresh basil
Garnish: chopped seeded plum tomatoes

1. Melt butter with oil in a 12-inch ovenproof skillet over medium-high heat; add zucchini and onion, and sauté 12 to 14 minutes or until onion is tender. Remove from heat, and stir in ¼ cup grated Parmesan cheese.
2. Whisk together eggs and next 3 ingredients at least 1 minute or until well blended. Pour over vegetable mixture.
3. Bake at 350° for 13 to 15 minutes or until set; increase oven temperature to broil, and broil 5½ inches from heat

1 to 2 minutes or until edges are lightly browned. Sprinkle evenly with remaining ¼ cup grated Parmesan cheese and basil. Garnish, if desired. **Makes** 6 to 8 servings.

SUE-SUE HARTSTERN
LOUISVILLE, KENTUCKY

Lightened Zucchini-Onion Frittata: Reduce butter to 1 Tbsp., and omit oil. Sauté zucchini and onion as directed; remove from heat. Reduce grated Parmesan cheese to ¼ cup, stirring 2 Tbsp. into vegetable mixture. Substitute 1 (15-oz.) carton garden vegetable egg substitute for 8 eggs and ¼ cup low-fat milk for ¼ cup milk, and whisk together with salt and pepper. Pour over vegetable mixture. Bake as directed; do not broil. Sprinkle evenly with remaining 2 Tbsp. grated Parmesan cheese and basil. Garnish, if desired.

Pasta in a Snap

This seasonal gem gets a jump start from refrigerated cheese-filled pasta and prepared basil pesto. Round out your meal with a loaf of your favorite bread.

Spring Tortellini With Pesto

fast fixin's

PREP: 10 MIN., COOK: 10 MIN.

Skim off and reserve the oil from the top of the packaged pesto; it will still contain enough oil to coat the pasta without becoming greasy. The skimmed oil is an ideal dip for bread.

1 lb. fresh asparagus
2 (9-oz.) packages refrigerated cheese-filled tortellini
1 (7-oz.) container basil pesto
½ tsp. grated lemon rind
¼ tsp. salt
¼ cup pine nuts, toasted

1. Snap off and discard tough ends of asparagus. Cut asparagus into 2-inch pieces.
2. Prepare cheese-filled tortellini according to package directions. Add asparagus pieces to pasta water during last 2 minutes of cooking; drain.
3. Pour off any excess oil from top of pesto container. Toss together tortellini mixture, pesto, lemon rind, and salt. Sprinkle with pine nuts, and serve immediately. **Makes** 4 to 6 servings.

Note: For testing purposes only, we used Buitoni Pesto with Basil.

LISA JACKSON
BLOOMFIELD HILLS, MICHIGAN

Super Foods, Super Flavor

Power up your plate and your taste buds with these nutrient-packed options.

Honey-Oatmeal Wheat Bread
freezeable

PREP: 25 MIN.; STAND: 15 MIN.;
RISE: 1 HR., 45 MIN.; BAKE: 35 MIN.

This recipe makes two loaves, so freeze one after cooling to help it stay fresh longer. Slice first, if desired; then wrap the loaf in plastic wrap and aluminum foil, and place in a zip-top plastic freezer bag. Keep frozen up to 1 month. (Pictured on page 165)

2 cups warm water (100° to 110°)
3 Tbsp. molasses
1 (1/4-oz.) envelope active dry yeast
3 cups all-purpose flour, divided
2 1/2 cups whole wheat flour
1 cup uncooked regular oats
1 Tbsp. salt
1/4 cup honey
3 Tbsp. olive oil
6 Tbsp. all-purpose flour
Vegetable cooking spray

1. Combine first 3 ingredients in a 2-cup glass measuring cup; let yeast mixture stand 5 minutes.
2. Combine 2 cups all-purpose flour, whole wheat flour, oats, and salt.
3. Beat yeast mixture, 1 cup all-purpose flour, honey, and olive oil at medium speed with a heavy-duty stand mixer until well blended. Gradually add whole wheat flour mixture, beating at low speed until a soft dough forms.
4. Turn out dough onto a well-floured surface, and knead 9 minutes, adding additional all-purpose flour (up to 6 Tbsp.) as needed. (Dough will be slightly sticky.) Place dough in a large bowl sprayed with cooking spray, turning to grease top of dough.
5. Cover bowl with plastic wrap, and let rise in a warm place (85°), free from drafts, 1 hour or until doubled in bulk.
6. Punch down dough, and divide in half. Roll each portion into a 13- x 8-inch rectangle on a lightly floured surface. Roll up each dough rectangle, jelly-roll fashion, starting at 1 short side; pinch ends to seal. Place loaves, seam sides down, into 2 (8 1/2- x 4 1/2-inch) loaf pans sprayed with cooking spray.
7. Cover loosely with plastic wrap, and let rise in a warm place (85°), free from drafts, 45 minutes or until almost doubled in bulk. Remove and discard plastic wrap.
8. Bake at 350° for 30 to 35 minutes or until loaves sound hollow when tapped and are golden. Cool in pans on wire racks 10 minutes. Remove loaves from pans, and cool on wire racks. **Makes** 2 loaves (12 slices per loaf).

Note: If you don't have a heavy-duty stand mixer, you can mix dough by hand with a wooden spoon.

Cook's Tip: To measure flour, spoon into a dry measuring cup, and then level the top with a knife. Never scoop the measuring cup into the flour—you'll get too much flour, resulting in a dense, thick bread.

LORAELEI TEMONEY
NEW BRAUNFELS, TEXAS

Per (1-slice) serving: Calories 150 (14% from fat); Fat 2.4g (sat 0.3g, mono 1.4g, poly 0.4g); Protein 4g; Carb 29.2g; Fiber 2.4g; Chol 0mg; Iron 1.6mg; Sodium 297mg; Calc 14mg

Our Top 5 Super Foods

■ **Berries:** Packed with antioxidants and vitamins A, C, E, and folic acid, berries reduce the risk of cancer and protect the body from the stresses of aging by boosting the immune system. They also help prevent bladder infections and reduce the risk for Alzheimer's.
■ **Legumes:** Loaded with protein, complex carbohydrates, soluble and insoluble fiber, and iron, beans are a one-stop source for essential nutrients. Beans also contain certain phytochemicals that can offer cancer-inhibiting abilities.
■ **Nuts:** High in "good" monounsaturated fat, nuts such as almonds, walnuts, and pistachios help prevent heart disease and control blood pressure. Because of their high fiber content, they help reduce the chance of colon cancer and improve glucose and insulin stability. Nuts are higher in calories than other super foods, so they should be eaten in moderation (about 1 to 2 oz. per day).
■ **Oats:** Fiber-rich oats lower the risk for a number of diseases, including diabetes, hypertension, cancer, and heart disease. Whole grain products such as whole wheat bread, brown rice, and multigrain pasta also offer these same benefits.
■ **Spinach:** Fresh, frozen, or canned spinach contains a significant amount of vitamin A and the carotenoid lutein to help reduce the risk of cataracts and vision loss. Additionally, vitamins C and K, folic acid, and fiber help lower the incidence of heart disease and stroke, prevent osteoporosis, and build strong bones. Other leafy greens with these beneficial effects include kale, arugula, bok choy, and romaine lettuce.

Black Bean Cakes With Chipotle Cream

freezeable • make ahead

PREP: 15 MIN., COOK: 25 MIN., CHILL: 1 HR.

For a quick dinner option, freeze black bean cakes up to 3 weeks in advance; then prepare Chipotle Cream just before serving.

1 red bell pepper, diced
½ cup sliced green onions
½ cup frozen corn kernels, thawed
4 garlic cloves, minced
6 tsp. olive oil, divided
2 (15-oz.) cans black beans, rinsed and drained
1½ tsp. ground cumin
½ tsp. dried crushed red pepper
¼ tsp. salt
¼ tsp. pepper
¾ cup fine, dry breadcrumbs, divided
3 Tbsp. chopped fresh cilantro
2 Tbsp. light mayonnaise
1 large egg, beaten
Chipotle Cream

1. Sauté first 4 ingredients in 2 tsp. hot oil in a large nonstick skillet over medium-high heat 5 minutes or until tender. Remove from heat; cool slightly.
2. Mash 1½ cups black beans in a large bowl. Stir in remaining black beans, red bell pepper mixture, cumin, and next 3 ingredients. Add ½ cup breadcrumbs, cilantro, mayonnaise, and egg, stirring until well blended.
3. Shape black bean mixture into 8 (½-inch-thick) patties. Place on a wax paper-lined baking sheet. Cover and chill 1 hour. Lightly dredge chilled patties in remaining ¼ cup breadcrumbs.
4. Cook 4 patties in 2 tsp. hot oil in a large nonstick skillet over medium heat 5 minutes on each side or until brown. Remove from skillet; keep warm. Repeat procedure with remaining 4 patties and 2 tsp. oil. Serve with Chipotle Cream. **Makes** 8 servings.

Per serving (1 cake and 1 Tbsp. cream): Calories 169 (33% from fat); Fat 6.7g (sat 1.9g, mono 2.5g, poly 0.7g); Protein 6.9g; Carb 23.4g; Fiber 5.1g; Chol 28mg; Iron 2.1mg; Sodium 440mg; Calc 58mg

Chipotle Cream:

fast fixin's

PREP: 5 MIN.

½ cup light sour cream
2 tsp. fresh lime juice
1 tsp. minced canned chipotle peppers in adobo sauce

1. Stir together all ingredients in a small bowl. **Makes** about ½ cup.

ANNE CLOSE
CHICAGO, ILLINOIS

Per (1-Tbsp.) serving: Calories 21 (56% from fat); Fat 1.3g (sat 1g, mono 0g, poly 0g); Protein 1g; Carb 1.2g; Fiber 0.1g; Chol 0mg; Iron 0mg; Sodium 19mg; Calc 0mg

Spinach, Blue Cheese, Pecan, and Cranberry Wraps

fast fixin's • make ahead

PREP: 15 MIN.

Make these sandwiches up to 4 hours in advance, and store them, wrapped individually in plastic wrap, in the refrigerator.

1 (8-oz.) container light spreadable cream cheese
2 Tbsp. nonfat buttermilk
¼ tsp. garlic powder
¼ tsp. onion powder
1 (4-oz.) package crumbled blue cheese
½ cup chopped toasted pecans
½ cup sweetened dried cranberries
8 (8-inch) 98% fat-free flour tortillas
1 Granny Smith apple, thinly sliced
4 cups baby spinach leaves

1. Stir together first 4 ingredients until blended; stir in blue cheese, pecans, and cranberries. Spread about ⅓ cup cream cheese mixture evenly over each tortilla. Layer evenly with apple slices and spinach. Roll up, and secure with wooden picks. **Makes** 8 servings.

ANNA GINSBERG
AUSTIN, TEXAS

Per (1-wrap) serving: Calories 321 (40% from fat); Fat 14.5g (sat 6.2g, mono 4.2g, poly 1.8g); Protein 10.1g; Carb 37.1g; Fiber 4.1g; Chol 24mg; Iron 2.1mg; Sodium 694mg; Calc 171mg

Blueberry-Almond Cobbler

PREP: 15 MIN., BAKE: 50 MIN.

For a tangy treat, serve with low-fat lemon frozen yogurt.

1 cup reduced-fat all-purpose baking mix
½ cup uncooked regular oats
¼ cup firmly packed brown sugar
¼ cup chopped toasted almonds
½ tsp. ground cinnamon
¼ tsp. ground nutmeg
½ cup chilled light butter, cut up
¼ cup granulated sugar
2 Tbsp. all-purpose flour
5 cups frozen blueberries
2 Tbsp. lemon juice

1. Combine first 6 ingredients in a large bowl; cut in butter with a pastry blender until mixture is crumbly and begins to stick together.
2. Combine granulated sugar and flour. Toss together granulated sugar mixture, blueberries, and lemon juice in a medium bowl. Transfer blueberry mixture to a lightly greased 2-qt. baking dish. Sprinkle oat mixture evenly over blueberry mixture.
3. Bake at 350° for 50 minutes or until bubbly and golden. **Makes** 8 servings.

Note: For testing purposes only, we used Bisquick Heart Smart All-Purpose Baking Mix.

Per (1-cup) serving: Calories 248 (33% from fat); Fat 9.7g (sat 4.4g, mono 1.9g, poly 0.5g); Protein 4.4g; Carb 40.2g; Fiber 3.7g; Chol 20mg; Iron 1.4mg; Sodium 247mg; Calc 34mg

Round Out Your Plate

Here are some more stellar, nutrient-dense choices: sweet potatoes, salmon, dark chocolate, whole grain flour, olive oil, tomatoes, low-fat dairy products, dark leafy greens, and soy.

Cheese Straws

Sample each variety of these bite-size treats.

Cheese straws are like deviled eggs—every Southern cook wants to make great ones. Here we've pulled together a couple of our all-time favorites, which can be served as appetizers, picnic snacks, or simple afternoon pick-me-ups. We've updated this classic by incorporating different types of cheese, ground spices, and nuts. These recipes pair well with soups or salads, whether you prefer wafers cut into round or square slices or you choose to put the dough through a cookie press to make the traditional straws. They can also go solo with a glass of Champagne or beer. No matter the shape, that's an idea worth toasting.

Blue Cheese Thumbprints
make ahead
PREP: 15 MIN., CHILL: 2 HRS.,
BAKE: 15 MIN. PER BATCH

2 (4-oz.) packages crumbled blue
  cheese
½ cup butter, softened
1⅓ cups all-purpose flour
3 Tbsp. poppy seeds
¼ tsp. ground red pepper
⅓ cup cherry preserves

1. Beat blue cheese and butter at medium speed with an electric mixer until fluffy. Add flour, poppy seeds, and red pepper, beating just until combined. Roll dough into ¾-inch balls; cover and chill 2 hours.
2. Arrange balls on ungreased baking sheets, and press thumb into each ball of dough, leaving an indentation.
3. Bake at 350° for 15 minutes or until golden. Transfer to wire racks to cool completely. Place about ¼ tsp. preserves in each indentation. **Makes** about 5 dozen.

Blue Cheese Crisps: Combine ingredients for dough as directed. Shape dough into 2 (9-inch-long) logs. Wrap each log in plastic wrap, and chill 2 hours. Cut each log into ¼-inch-thick slices, and place on ungreased baking sheets. Bake at 350° for 10 to 12 minutes or until golden brown. Transfer to wire racks to cool completely. Omit cherry preserves. Store crisps in an airtight container up to 1 week.

SHIRLEY DRAPER
CHARLOTTESVILLE, VIRGINIA

Cheddar Cheese Straws
make ahead
PREP: 30 MIN., BAKE: 12 MIN. PER BATCH
If you don't have a heavy-duty stand mixer, you can use a handheld mixer. Just divide the ingredients in half, and work with two batches.

1½ cups butter, softened
1 (1-lb.) block sharp Cheddar cheese,
  shredded
1½ tsp. salt
1 to 2 tsp. ground red pepper
½ tsp. paprika
4 cups all-purpose flour

1. Beat first 5 ingredients at medium speed with a heavy-duty stand mixer until blended. Gradually add flour, beating just until combined.
2. Use a cookie press with a star-shaped disk to shape mixture into long ribbons, following manufacturer's instructions, on parchment paper-lined baking sheets. Cut ribbons into 2-inch pieces.
3. Bake at 350° for 12 minutes or until lightly browned. Remove to wire racks to cool. **Makes** about 10 dozen.

Test Kitchen Notebook

Follow these simple instructions to prepare Cheddar Cheese Straws. You can find cookie presses online or in retail stores where quality kitchen equipment is sold.
1. Load the dough into the canister of a cookie press until it's about three-fourths full, being careful not to overfill. (Don't chill the dough—it may be too stiff to go through the press.) Attach the desired disk (star, bar, etc.).
2. Line a baking sheet with parchment paper. Hold the press at a 45° angle to the baking sheet. Starting at one end of baking sheet, turn the handle clockwise to push out dough, slowly pulling the press back toward you and continuing to turn the handle. Make rows until the baking sheet is full. (Tip: Parchment paper is available at large supermarkets on the same aisle as plastic wrap and aluminum foil.) With a knife, cut dough crosswise at 2-inch intervals to make individual cheese straws. (You don't need to separate them.) Trim ragged edges, if desired.

Cheese Wafers: Combine ingredients as directed; chill dough 2 hours. Shape dough into 4 (8-inch-long) logs; wrap each in plastic wrap, and chill 8 hours. Cut each log into ¼-inch-thick slices; place on parchment paper-lined baking sheets. Bake at 350° for 13 to 15 minutes or until lightly browned. Remove to wire racks to cool. Store in an airtight container 1 week.

ANN PORTER
JEFFERSON CITY, TENNESSEE

Our Best Cheese Straw Tips

- Shred your own cheese; it's stickier and blends better than preshredded cheese.
- Refrigerate unbaked dough between batches to keep wafers from spreading too thin when baked.
- Store baked cheese straws in an airtight container for 1 week. Store unbaked dough in the fridge for 1 week or in the freezer for 1 month.
- Bake stored cheese straws in the oven at 350° for 3 to 4 minutes to make them crispy again.
- Bake on parchment paper to yield the best results; one sheet can be used multiple times.

Dressed-up Chicken

These dishes are low maintenance yet company-worthy

Here's how to serve a special meal on a budget: Gussy up some chicken. Any of these recipes will do nicely for entertaining. Add an apricot glaze to a deli chicken for an entrée you can serve even if you get home late. Champagne Chicken and Mushrooms takes more time, so plan it for a weekend. Serve it with rice, noodles, or bread to sop up the delicious sauce.

Deli Chicken With Apricot Glaze
family favorite
PREP: 5 MIN., COOK: 11 MIN., BAKE: 15 MIN.

1 Tbsp. olive oil
3 shallots, thinly sliced
½ cup apricot preserves
1 Tbsp. lemon juice
½ tsp. hot sauce
¼ tsp. Creole seasoning
1 (2½-lb.) whole deli chicken

1. Heat oil in a small saucepan over medium-high heat; add shallots, and sauté 3 to 5 minutes or until tender. Stir in preserves and next 3 ingredients. Reduce heat to low, and cook 5 to 6 minutes or until thoroughly heated. Brush glaze over chicken. Place chicken on a lightly greased rack in an aluminum foil-lined roasting pan.
2. Bake at 350° for 15 minutes. **Makes** 4 servings.

Oven-Fried Bacon-Wrapped Chicken Thighs
family favorite
PREP: 20 MIN., BAKE: 1 HR.
You can buy the thighs already boned at the supermarket. This recipe is adapted from Appalachian Home Cooking: History, Culture, and Recipes by Mark F. Sohn (University Press of Kentucky, 2005).

8 bacon slices
8 skinned and boned chicken thighs
1 cup cornmeal *
1 Tbsp. salt
1 tsp. paprika
1 tsp. black pepper

1. Arrange bacon slices on paper towels on a microwave-safe plate in microwave oven. Top with paper towel. Microwave at HIGH 30 seconds to 1 minute or just until bacon is limp and heated through. (Do not fully cook bacon.)
2. Wrap each chicken thigh with a piece of bacon; secure with a wooden pick, if desired.
3. Combine cornmeal and next 3 ingredients in a small bowl. Dredge chicken in cornmeal mixture. Arrange on a wire rack coated with cooking spray in a lightly greased broiler or roasting pan.
4. Bake at 350° for 50 minutes to 1 hour or until chicken is done. **Makes** 8 servings.

*Substitute cornmeal mix for cornmeal, if desired.

Champagne Chicken and Mushrooms

PREP: 30 MIN., STAND: 15 MIN.,
COOK: 50 MIN.

Champagne adds delicate flavor, but you could substitute white wine. Ask your butcher to bone the chicken breasts, which offer the best results, or use skinned and boned breasts.

½ cup all-purpose flour
1 tsp. salt
½ tsp. pepper
6 skin-on, boned chicken breasts
2 Tbsp. unsalted butter
2 Tbsp. olive oil
½ cup minced shallots (about
   3 medium)
2 (3.5-oz.) packages shiitake mushrooms, stems removed and sliced
3 garlic cloves, minced
2 cups Champagne or sparkling wine
2 tsp. chopped fresh thyme
½ cup whipping cream
Salt and pepper to taste

1. Stir together first 3 ingredients in a shallow bowl. Dredge chicken in flour mixture; place on a wire rack. Let stand 15 minutes. Dredge chicken in flour mixture again; return to rack.
2. Melt butter with olive oil in a large skillet over medium heat. Cook chicken, in batches, 5 minutes on each side or until golden brown. Remove chicken to a plate.
3. Add shallots to skillet; cook, stirring often, 2 minutes or until golden brown. Add mushrooms and garlic, and cook, stirring often, 10 minutes or until mushrooms are tender. Stir in Champagne and thyme; bring to a boil, stirring to loosen browned particles from bottom of skillet. Reduce heat, and return chicken to skillet. Cover and simmer 10 minutes or until done.
4. Transfer chicken to a serving platter. Stir cream into mushroom mixture. Cook 5 to 6 minutes or until thickened. Add salt and pepper to taste. Serve sauce immediately over chicken. **Makes** 6 servings.   WES HOLLOWELL
   BIRMINGHAM, ALABAMA

News About New Potatoes

You're sure to fall in love with this "youngster" of the potato world.

What makes a potato "new?" Simply put, it's any kind that's harvested before it's fully matured. This makes for a smaller size; sweet, tender white flesh; and signature skins that are thin and waxy in texture. Because of the thin skin, it's okay to have a few bald spots. They're petite enough to cook whole and are ideal for salads because they retain their shape after cooking. Just remember to buy potatoes that are uniform in size so they cook evenly. You can store them in a dark, dry place for several weeks.

Southwest Twice-Baked New Potatoes

family favorite

PREP: 25 MIN.; BAKE: 1 HR., 5 MIN.

A small melon baller is perfect for scooping out the potato pulp.

2 lb. medium-size new potatoes
1 Tbsp. canola oil
½ cup shredded Cheddar cheese
2 Tbsp. sour cream
1 Tbsp. melted butter
2 Tbsp. buttermilk
½ tsp. pepper
½ tsp. salt
1 (4.5-oz.) can diced green chiles, drained
Garnish: paprika

1. Cut a thin slice from the bottom of each potato to form a flat base; brush potatoes evenly with oil, and place on a baking sheet.
2. Bake at 350° for 45 minutes or until tender. Remove from oven, and let cool slightly.

3. Cut a thin slice from the top of each potato. Carefully scoop out potato pulp into a bowl, leaving shells intact. Add shredded Cheddar cheese and next 5 ingredients to potato pulp in bowl, and beat at medium speed with an electric mixer until smooth and creamy. Stir in green chiles. Spoon mixture evenly into each potato shell, and place on baking sheet.
4. Bake potatoes at 350° for 20 minutes or just until lightly browned. Garnish, if desired. **Makes** 6 servings.

   ELAINE SWEET
   DALLAS, TEXAS

Lemon-and-Herb Roasted New Potatoes

PREP: 15 MIN., BAKE: 25 MIN.

¾ cup loosely packed fresh parsley
   leaves
2 tsp. coarsely chopped fresh rosemary
2 garlic cloves
½ tsp. grated lemon rind
1 Tbsp. fresh lemon juice
4 Tbsp. olive oil, divided
1 tsp. salt, divided
2 lb. new potatoes, halved
½ tsp. pepper

1. Process first 5 ingredients, 2 Tbsp. oil, and ½ tsp. salt in a food processor or blender until smooth, stopping to scrape down sides. Set aside.
2. Toss together halved potatoes, ½ tsp. pepper, remaining 2 Tbsp. oil, and remaining ½ tsp. salt in a large bowl; spread potato mixture in a single layer

in an aluminum foil-lined 15- x 10-inch jelly-roll pan.

3. Bake at 425° for 25 minutes or until potatoes are golden brown and tender, stirring after 10 minutes. Toss potatoes with lemon-and-herb mixture until evenly coated. **Makes** 6 to 8 servings.

New Potato Salad With Feta Cheese
make ahead
PREP: 10 MIN., COOK: 30 MIN., CHILL: 2 HRS.
At 6 servings, this salad is an ample main dish. As a side dish, it will serve 8 to 10.

3 lb. small new potatoes
⅔ cup olive oil
½ cup fresh lemon juice
1 tsp. Dijon mustard
1 tsp. salt
¾ tsp. pepper
1 bunch green onions, sliced
1 (4-oz.) package crumbled
    garlic-and-herb feta cheese
¼ cup chopped fresh parsley
Mixed salad greens (optional)

1. Bring potatoes and water to cover to a boil, and cook 25 minutes or just until tender; drain well. Cool slightly, and cut into wedges.
2. Whisk together oil and next 4 ingredients in a large bowl; add potatoes, green onions, and feta cheese, tossing to coat. Cover and chill at least 2 hours or up to 8 hours. Sprinkle with parsley before serving. Serve over mixed salad greens, if desired. **Makes** 6 servings.

KAY GLENOS
BIRMINGHAM, ALABAMA

Sharing With Neighbors

Greet new friends with move-in day munchies.

You'll be sold on these easy ideas to welcome families into your neighborhood. You make one recipe and then fill in the basket with simple foods purchased from the grocery store. Each recipe also provides a few practical ideas to help personalize the welcome package. Deliver, say "hi," and offer your new neighbors a tasty break from unpacking boxes.

White Cheddar Cheese Ring
make ahead
PREP: 20 MIN., CHILL: 2 HRS.
Deliver this basket with bottles of cold sparkling water and a list of your favorite places and shops in the community. Use real bacon pieces; they add a great smoky flavor to this cheesy, sweet, and salty snack.

1 (10-oz.) block white Cheddar cheese,
    shredded
6 Tbsp. mayonnaise
6 Tbsp. fully cooked bacon pieces
¼ cup minced green onions (about
    4 onions)
½ cup seedless raspberry preserves
Scoop-size corn chips or crackers

1. Stir together first 4 ingredients until well blended. Shape mixture into a ring with a 2-inch center on a serving platter. Cover with plastic wrap, and chill at least 2 hours.
2. Fill center of ring with preserves just before serving. Serve with corn chips or crackers. **Makes** 8 servings.

Note: For testing purposes only, we used Cracker Barrel Natural Extra Sharp-White Cheddar Cheese.

CAROL N. CROWE
SUMMERDALE, ALABAMA

Honey-Pecan Shortbread
make ahead
PREP: 20 MIN.; BAKE: 1 HR., 5 MIN.
Deliver these delicate cookies along with fresh strawberries (washed and ready to eat) and bright-colored napkins. Add a bottle of sparkling cider and clear plastic glasses for a truly festive welcome.

1 cup butter, softened
⅓ cup honey
2 Tbsp. brown sugar
1 tsp. vanilla extract
2½ cups all-purpose flour
¾ cup pecan pieces, toasted and
    chopped

1. Beat butter at medium speed with an electric mixer until fluffy; add honey, brown sugar, and vanilla, and beat until blended, stopping to scrape down sides. Gradually add flour, beating at low speed until blended. Stir in pecans.
2. Press dough evenly into bottom of an ungreased 9-inch square pan.
3. Bake at 300° for 55 to 65 minutes or until golden (begin checking for doneness at 50 minutes just in case your oven runs hot). Let cool in pan on a wire rack. Cut into bars. Store in an airtight container. **Makes** about 24 bars.

Note: This shortbread can also be baked in an ungreased 10-inch cast-iron skillet, if desired.

JACKIE CASEY
MOUNTAIN VIEW, ARKANSAS

Creamy Basil-Pesto Dip

make ahead

PREP: 15 MIN., COOK: 5 MIN., CHILL: 1 HR.

For families with children, tuck in a list of babysitters and phone numbers (check with them first to make sure they want to be included) and a recreation center bulletin. Add a jug of sweet tea and plastic cups to make this gift over-the-top great.

2 Tbsp. pine nuts
2 cups loosely packed fresh basil leaves
½ cup grated Parmesan cheese
½ cup sour cream
1 garlic clove, chopped
1 Tbsp. fresh lemon juice
1 tsp. sugar
¼ tsp. salt
½ cup olive oil
Fried chicken strips or hot wings, cherry
    tomatoes, crispy breadsticks
Garnish: fresh basil sprig

1. Heat pine nuts in a small nonstick skillet over medium-low heat, stirring often, 3 to 5 minutes or until toasted.
2. Process pine nuts and next 7 ingredients in a food processor until smooth, stopping to scrape down sides. With processor running, pour oil through food chute in a slow, steady stream. Transfer to serving bowl.
3. Cover and chill at least 1 hour. Serve with fried chicken strips or hot wings, cherry tomatoes, and crispy breadsticks. Garnish, if desired. **Makes** about 1⅓ cups.

Note: If using purchased basil, 4 (1-oz.) packages will equal 2 cups loosely packed fresh basil leaves.

DEVON DELANEY
PRINCETON, NEW JERSEY

Simple, Satisfying Sauces

Here are speedy fixes to slather over cooked rice, rotisserie chicken, open-face turkey sandwiches, or mashed potatoes.

You might be thinking these sauces sure sound a lot like gravy. But here's the difference: Gravies require pan drippings, while sauces do not. Gravy is a sauce, but not all sauces are gravy.

However that technicality isn't really important. Getting flavorful food on the table is. And these recipes do just that.

Onion Sauce

fast fixin's

PREP: 10 MIN., COOK: 10 MIN.

Don't let the name fool you. The flavor of this sauce is subtle—not oniony at all.

3 Tbsp. butter
⅓ cup finely chopped sweet onion
¼ cup all-purpose flour
1 (14-oz.) can chicken broth
2 tsp. soy sauce
¼ tsp. freshly ground pepper
Garnish: chopped fresh chives

Steps to Successful Sauces

Follow these guidelines for perfect Onion Sauce, Mushroom-Onion Sauce, and Beef-Onion Sauce.

Step 1: Sauté onion in melted butter until lightly browned.
Step 2: Whisk in flour, whisking constantly, until the flour is fully combined with the butter.
Step 3: Keep whisking, and cook until flour is lightly browned.
Step 4: Gradually add chicken or beef broth, straight from the can, whisking the entire time until smooth. If lumps start to form, remove pan from heat to stop cooking the flour, and whisk until smooth. Return to heat, if necessary, and whisk in remaining ingredients. Cook, whisking constantly, until mixture is thickened and bubbly.

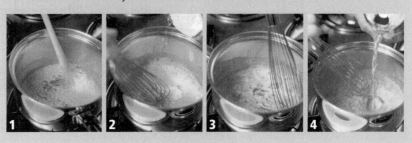

1. Melt butter in a medium saucepan over medium heat; add onion, and sauté 5 to 7 minutes or until lightly browned. Whisk in flour. Cook, whisking constantly, until lightly browned (about 1 minute). Gradually whisk in broth and next 2 ingredients. Cook, whisking constantly, until thickened and bubbly. Garnish, if desired. **Makes** about 1½ cups.
HOWARD WIENER
SPRING HILL, FLORIDA

Mushroom-Onion Sauce: Melt 1 Tbsp. butter in a large nonstick skillet over medium-high heat. Add 1 (8-oz.) package sliced fresh mushrooms, and sauté 10 minutes or until browned. Remove from heat. Prepare Onion Sauce as directed; stir in mushrooms, and cook, stirring constantly, until thoroughly heated. **Makes** about 2½ cups. Prep: 10 min., Cook: 20 min.

Beef-Onion Sauce: Prepare Onion Sauce as directed, substituting 1 (14-oz.) can beef broth for chicken broth. **Makes** about 1½ cups. Prep: 10 min., Cook: 10 min.

Simple Mushroom Sauce
PREP: 10 MIN., COOK: 25 MIN.

½ cup butter, divided
2 (8-oz.) containers sliced fresh
    mushrooms
3 Tbsp. chopped fresh chives *
3 Tbsp. all-purpose flour
1 tsp. dry mustard
2 cups milk
2 tsp. hot sauce
¾ tsp. salt
¾ tsp. freshly ground pepper

1. Melt ¼ cup butter in a large skillet over medium-high heat; add mushrooms, and sauté 12 to 14 minutes or until liquid evaporates. Add chives, and sauté 2 minutes. Remove from heat.
2. Melt remaining ¼ cup butter in a large saucepan over medium heat; whisk in flour until smooth. Cook, whisking constantly, 1 minute; whisk in dry mustard. Gradually whisk in milk and next 3 ingredients; cook,

whisking constantly, until mixture is thickened and bubbly. Stir in mushroom mixture, and cook until thoroughly heated. **Makes** about 4 cups.

* Substitute 3 Tbsp. chopped green onions, if desired.
BETTY H. CLEVELAND
JEFFERSON CITY, TENNESSEE

Chop This Way

Cooking like the pros is easy. All you have to do is learn the basics and practice them. Just check out our photo and simple definitions to make sure your food looks and tastes like ours does in the Test Kitchens.

At times, getting the right cut can be critical to the success of your recipe. You want to make sure your guests get the perfect hint of garlic or jalapeño in a salad dressing or salsa. Cut them too big, and watch out! Have you ever taken a bite of casserole and bitten into an unexpected hunk of onion that didn't quite get cooked? It's not pleasant. This quick guide should help you avoid such situations and turn those little bits into perfect bites.

Mango-Avocado Salsa
make ahead
PREP: 15 MIN., CHILL: 1 HR.
You'll need 2 avocados and 2 mangoes for this deliciously fresh salsa. If you prefer it spicier, leave the seeds in the jalapeño before mincing.

2 cups diced fresh mango
1 cup chopped avocado
3 Tbsp. fresh lime juice
2 Tbsp. minced fresh chives
2 Tbsp. finely chopped fresh cilantro
1 jalapeño pepper, seeded and minced
Pinch of salt

1. Combine all ingredients in a medium bowl; cover and chill 1 hour before serving. **Makes** about 3 cups.

Smart Cuts
Here's what we mean when we use the following terms.
- **Chopped:** Make rough-cut pieces the size of a dime.
- **Diced:** These are cubed pieces, smaller than chopped and all the same size. An even cut promotes even cooking.
- **Finely chopped:** Make rough cuts. Pieces don't have to be the same size, but they should all be smaller than a pea.
- **Minced:** Create very small pieces; cut until you can't cut them anymore.

Catfish With All the Fixin's

Celebrate any occasion with this timeless Southern menu.

Catfish Fry

Serves 6 to 8

Classic Fried Catfish

Baked Beans

Hush Puppies

coleslaw from your
favorite barbecue restaurant

Pound Cake Banana Pudding
(page 68)

Growing up on the Tennessee River, Test Kitchens Director Lyda Jones learned that every Friday night meant one thing: a catfish fry at the cabin. Carrying on the tradition, she prepares these recipes at her family's get-togethers.

Classic Fried Catfish

PREP: 15 MIN., FRY: 6 MIN. PER BATCH
For an extra-crispy crust, use stone-ground yellow cornmeal, if available. (Pictured on page 166)

1 cup yellow cornmeal
⅓ cup all-purpose flour
1¼ tsp. ground red pepper
½ tsp. garlic powder
2½ tsp. salt
12 catfish fillets (about 3¾ lb.)
Vegetable oil

1. Combine first 4 ingredients and 2 tsp. salt in a large shallow dish. Sprinkle catfish fillets evenly with remaining ½ tsp. salt, and dredge in cornmeal mixture, coating evenly.
2. Pour vegetable oil to a depth of 2 inches into a Dutch oven; heat to 350°. Fry fillets, in batches, 5 to 6 minutes or until golden; drain on paper towels. **Makes** 6 to 8 servings.

Note: For a quick weeknight version, skip the deep fryer. Cook catfish in 2 Tbsp. hot oil, per batch, in a nonstick skillet 5 minutes on each side.

Baked Beans

PREP: 15 MIN., COOK: 11 MIN., BAKE: 45 MIN.
The thick, rich taste of sorghum gives this quick recipe that all-day, slow-cooked flavor.

4 bacon slices
1 small onion, diced
4 (15-oz.) cans pork and beans in
  tomato sauce, drained
⅓ cup firmly packed brown sugar
½ cup ketchup
½ cup sorghum syrup or molasses
1½ tsp. Worcestershire sauce
1 tsp. dry mustard

1. Cook bacon in a large skillet over medium-high heat 4 minutes; drain, reserving 1 tsp. drippings in skillet.
2. Sauté onion in hot bacon drippings 7 minutes or until tender. Stir together onions, pork and beans, and next 5 ingredients in a lightly greased 11- x 7-inch baking dish. Top bean mixture with bacon.
3. Bake at 350° for 45 minutes or until bubbly. **Makes** 6 to 8 servings.

Hush Puppies

PREP: 10 MIN., STAND: 10 MIN.,
FRY: 6 MIN. PER BATCH
This recipe was adapted from a favorite of The Catfish Institute in Mississippi. Substituting beer for milk makes these lighter and tangier.

1 cup self-rising white cornmeal mix
½ cup self-rising flour
½ cup diced onion
1 Tbsp. sugar
1 large egg, lightly beaten
½ cup milk or beer
Vegetable oil

1. Combine first 4 ingredients in a large bowl. Add egg and milk to dry ingredients, stirring just until moistened. Let stand 10 minutes.
2. Pour oil to a depth of 2 inches into a Dutch oven; heat to 375°. Drop batter by rounded tablespoonfuls into hot oil, and fry in batches 2 to 3 minutes on each side or until golden brown. Drain on a wire rack over paper towels; serve immediately. **Makes** 1½ dozen (about 6 servings).

Note: Keep fried hush puppies warm in a 200° oven while frying catfish. For testing purposes only, we used White Lily Self-Rising White Cornmeal Mix.

Jalapeño Hush Puppies: Add 1 seeded, diced jalapeño to batter. Proceed with recipe as directed.

Double-Duty Sloppy Joes

In 30 minutes, you can whip up these warm, tasty sandwiches. Plus, you'll have time to make a homemade honey-mustard salad dressing. If you have another 30 minutes, you can put together and bake the Shepherd's Pie variation, leisurely make the dressing, and even mix up the pan-cookie dough. (Bake dessert while you eat.)

Change It Up

Take the Sloppy Joe ground beef base, and make it into a casserole that's big enough to serve your family and a couple of friends.

Sloppy Joe Shepherd's Pie:
- Prepare Richard's Sloppy Joes, omitting hamburger buns; spoon into a lightly greased 13- x 9-inch baking dish.
- Prepare 1 (22-oz.) package frozen mashed potatoes according to package directions. Stir in 1 cup (4 oz.) shredded Cheddar cheese, ⅓ cup sliced green onions, ½ tsp. salt, and ¼ tsp. pepper. Spread evenly over meat mixture in baking dish, spreading potatoes to edge of dish.
- Bake at 350° for 25 minutes; sprinkle 1 cup (4 oz.) shredded Cheddar cheese on top of potatoes. Bake 5 more minutes or until cheese is melted. Let stand 5 minutes before serving. **Makes** 8 to 10 servings. Prep: 10 min., Bake: 30 min., Stand: 5 min.

Sloppy Joe Supper

Serves 6 to 8

Richard's Sloppy Joes

mixed salad greeens with Honey-Mustard Vinaigrette

PB & Chocolate Pan Cookie

Richard's Sloppy Joes
family favorite • fast fixin's
PREP: 10 MIN., COOK: 20 MIN.

Our adult taste-testers described this dish as mildly hot. If your family prefers less kick, adjust the amount of pickled jalapeños (and liquid from the jar) to suit their tastes.

1½ lb. lean ground beef
1 (14½-oz.) can diced tomatoes
1¼ cups ketchup
½ cup bottled barbecue sauce
1 Tbsp. Worcestershire sauce
2 Tbsp. chopped pickled jalapeños (optional)
1 Tbsp. liquid from pickled jalapeños (optional)
8 hamburger buns, toasted

1. Cook ground beef in a large skillet over medium-high heat, stirring until beef crumbles and is no longer pink; drain well. Return cooked beef to skillet.
2. Stir in tomatoes, next 3 ingredients, and, if desired, jalapeños and liquid. Reduce heat to low, and simmer 15 minutes or until thickened. Serve mixture on toasted buns. **Makes** 6 to 8 servings.

Note: For testing purposes only, we used KC Masterpiece Original Barbecue Sauce. RICHARD COLEMAN
ORANGE PARK, FLORIDA

Honey-Mustard Vinaigrette

1. Whisk together ¼ cup olive oil, 2 Tbsp. red wine vinegar, 1 Tbsp. Dijon mustard, 1 Tbsp. honey, ½ tsp. salt, ¼ tsp. pepper, and, if desired, ⅛ tsp. nutmeg. Cover and chill up to 4 days. Serve over mixed salad greens with your favorite toppings. **Makes** ½ cup. Prep: 10 min. URSULA HENNESSY
SPRINGFIELD, VIRGINIA

PB & Chocolate Pan Cookie
family favorite
PREP: 10 MIN., BAKE: 20 MIN., STAND: 5 MIN.
Leave the mixer in the cabinet—you can mix this dough with a spoon.

¾ cup chunky peanut butter
2 large eggs
1 tsp. vanilla extract
1 cup firmly packed light brown sugar
2 cups all-purpose baking mix
1 (12-oz.) package dark chocolate morsels, divided

1. Stir together peanut butter, eggs, and vanilla in a large bowl.
2. Stir in brown sugar until combined. Add baking mix and ¾ cup dark chocolate morsels, stirring just until moistened. Spread mixture in a lightly greased 15- x 10-inch jelly-roll pan.
3. Bake at 325° for 20 minutes or until golden brown. Remove from oven, and sprinkle evenly with remaining 1¼ cups dark chocolate morsels; let stand 5 minutes or until chocolate melts. Spread melted chocolate evenly over top. Cut into triangles, bars, or squares. **Makes** about 24 pieces.

Note: For testing purposes only, we used Bisquick All-Purpose Baking Mix and Hershey's Special Dark Chips.

from our kitchen

Warm days find us craving the cool comforts of a crisp, green salad. Served as a side dish or a main course for a super-quick supper, salads are versatile enough to enjoy every day.

To keep lettuce fresh all week, wash and dry thoroughly before refrigerating. Loosely wrap the leaves in paper towels, and place in a large zip-top plastic bag; seal and store in the vegetable crisper. If the towels become damp during the week, replace with dry ones.

Transporting salads for meals on the go isn't a problem when they're tucked into pita pockets. Sliced turkey, sliced pears, crumbled blue cheese, and toasted pecans turn a package of gourmet greens and a handful of alfalfa sprouts into a take-along treat. Opt for wrapping these hearty sandwiches in wax paper rather than plastic wrap to prevent the bread from absorbing excess moisture.

Tips and Tidbits

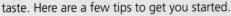

Best Dressed

Flavored oils and vinegars offer endless possibilities for creating your own salad dressing. The ratio for a classic vinaigrette is three parts oil to one part vinegar or fresh lemon juice, but the proportions can be adjusted according to taste. Here are a few tips to get you started.

■ Substitute fruit preserves or jam for a portion of the oil. Fresh herbs and aromatics, such as minced shallots or garlic, and fresh ginger are also great options.

■ Whisking in a little mustard will emulsify the mixture and will help prevent the oil and vinegar from separating. Just remember to always add the oil after all the other ingredients have been mixed together.

■ Nut oils can vary in strength and richness. You may want to combine them with a little olive oil when preparing a vinaigrette. To ensure freshness, look for a production date on the label, and refrigerate after opening.

■ White balsamic vinegar has the same sweet taste as the traditional brown balsamic vinegar, but it can be added to foods without discoloring them.

■ A terrific way to flavor and tenderize less expensive cuts of meat, vinaigrettes also make a memorable marinade.

Hot Toppers

Creative toppings can transform a simple salad into something special. Bake a pan of breaded chicken pieces, or roast those extra vegetables lying around in the crisper. Strips of leftover egg roll and won ton wrappers fry up in seconds, and they pair perfectly with the new Asian-flavored salad dressings.

For a tasty twist on traditional croutons, cut leftover cornbread or biscuits into ¾-inch cubes. Drizzle with a little olive oil or melted butter, and sprinkle with grated Parmesan cheese. Spread evenly on a baking sheet, and bake at 375° for 15 to 20 minutes or until golden brown, turning once.

Quick-cooking and low in fat, turkey tenderloins are always a favorite and are a great addition to a salad. They're every bit as easy to prepare as pork tenderloin. Just season as desired, and grill, covered with grill lid, over medium-high heat (350° to 400°) for 25 to 30 minutes or until a meat thermometer inserted into the thickest portion registers 170°. Remove from heat, and let stand 10 minutes. Cut into ¼-inch-thick slices.

april

Top-Rated Pasta

These recipes are our best of the best, so you can't go wrong. Start the water boiling!

Whether you're planning a quick and casual get-together with friends or packing the freezer for busy weeknight suppers, these pasta dishes keep everyone coming back for more. Perfect for any season, they have it all: ease, versatility, and fresh flavors the whole family will love.

Baked Macaroni and Cheese
family favorite
PREP: 15 MIN., COOK: 10 MIN., BAKE: 1 HR., STAND: 10 MIN.

1 (8-oz.) package large elbow macaroni
16 saltine crackers, finely crushed
1 tsp. seasoned pepper
1 tsp. salt
1 (10-oz.) block extra-sharp Cheddar cheese, shredded
1 (10-oz.) block sharp Cheddar cheese, shredded
6 large eggs, lightly beaten
4 cups milk

1. Cook macaroni according to package directions; drain.
2. Layer one-third each of pasta, crackers, pepper, salt, and cheeses into a lightly greased 13- x 9-inch baking dish. Repeat layers twice.
3. Whisk together eggs and milk; pour over pasta mixture.
4. Bake at 350° for 55 to 60 minutes or until golden and set. Let stand 10 minutes before serving. **Makes** 8 to 10 servings.

Note: For testing purposes only, we used Kraft Cracker Barrel cheeses.

Late-Night Pasta Chez Frank
chef recipe • fast fixin's
PREP: 10 MIN., COOK: 10 MIN.
(Pictured on page 169)

1 (8-oz.) package vermicelli
6 garlic cloves, pressed
2 Tbsp. olive oil
4 jalapeño peppers, seeded and minced
8 plum tomatoes, chopped
½ tsp. salt
½ cup chopped fresh basil
Freshly grated Parmesan cheese

1. Cook vermicelli according to package directions; drain and keep warm.
2. Sauté garlic in hot oil in a large skillet over medium heat 1 to 2 minutes or until golden. Add peppers, and cook, stirring constantly, 1 minute.
3. Add tomatoes and salt; cook 3 minutes or until thoroughly heated. Stir in chopped basil. Serve immediately over pasta, and sprinkle with Parmesan cheese. **Makes** 4 servings.   FRANK STITT
HIGHLANDS BAR & GRILL
BIRMINGHAM, ALABAMA

Three-Cheese Baked Pasta
make ahead
PREP: 10 MIN., COOK: 10 MIN., BAKE: 30 MIN.
Serve alongside grilled chicken, beef, or pork or as a meatless main dish. Prepare up to 1 day ahead; cover and refrigerate. Let stand at room temperature 30 minutes, and bake as directed. (Pictured on page 168)

1 (16-oz.) package ziti pasta
2 (10-oz.) containers refrigerated Alfredo sauce
1 (8-oz.) container sour cream
1 (15-oz.) container ricotta cheese
2 large eggs, lightly beaten
¼ cup grated Parmesan cheese
¼ cup chopped fresh parsley
1½ cups mozzarella cheese

1. Cook ziti according to package directions; drain and return to pot.
2. Stir together Alfredo sauce and sour cream; toss with ziti until evenly coated. Spoon half of ziti mixture into a lightly greased 13- x 9-inch baking dish.
3. Stir together ricotta cheese and next 3 ingredients; spread evenly over pasta mixture. Spoon remaining pasta mixture evenly over ricotta cheese layer; sprinkle with mozzarella cheese.
4. Bake at 350° for 30 minutes or until bubbly. **Makes** 8 to 10 servings.

Note: Ziti pasta is shaped in long, thin tubes; penne or rigatoni pasta can be substituted. For testing purposes only, we used refrigerated Buitoni Alfredo Sauce.   AMY FAGGART
CONCORD, NORTH CAROLINA

Cook's Notes

■ Be careful not to overcook pasta. When preparing pasta for a casserole, keep in mind that it will continue to cook in the oven.
■ Save those extra bits and pieces of cheese to shred and toss with pasta. Shredded cheese, as well as pasta, absorbs liquid from the sauce, so add at the last minute to prevent the dish from drying out.
■ Fry leftover cooked pasta (without sauce) in a small amount of oil in a non-stick skillet. Like hash brown potatoes, the noodles will become crisp and golden brown on the outside and soft and tender on the inside.
■ Pantry ingredients, such as canned artichokes, roasted red bell peppers, sun-dried tomatoes, and olives, are great for spur-of-the-moment pasta creations.
■ Fire up the flavor of commercial marinara sauce with hot and spicy salsa or a dash of dried crushed red pepper flakes. Just before serving, toss in a handful of finely chopped fresh vegetables for texture, or whisk in a little light cream cheese or sour cream for richness.

Chicken Tetrazzini

freezeable • make ahead

PREP: 10 MIN., COOK: 10 MIN., BAKE: 35 MIN.

Freeze unbaked casserole up to 1 month, if desired. Thaw overnight in refrigerator. Let stand 30 minutes at room temperature, and bake as directed. (Pictured on page 169)

1 (16-oz.) package vermicelli
½ cup chicken broth
4 cups chopped cooked chicken breasts
1 (10¾-oz.) can cream of mushroom soup
1 (10¾-oz.) can cream of chicken soup
1 (10¾-oz.) can cream of celery soup
1 (8-oz.) container sour cream
1 (6-oz.) jar sliced mushrooms, drained
½ cup (2 oz.) shredded Parmesan cheese
½ tsp. salt
1 tsp. pepper
2 cups (8 oz.) shredded Cheddar cheese

1. Cook vermicelli according to package directions; drain. Return to pot, and toss with chicken broth.
2. Stir together chicken and next 8 ingredients; add vermicelli, and toss well. Spoon mixture into 2 lightly greased 11- x 7-inch baking dishes. Sprinkle evenly with cheese.
3. Bake, covered, at 350° for 30 minutes; uncover and bake 5 more minutes or until cheese is melted and bubbly. **Makes** 12 servings.

MARTA'S BAKERY
BIRMINGHAM, ALABAMA

Test Kitchen *Notebook*

Don't be afraid to combine dried herbs with fresh. To preserve the delicate flavor of fresh herbs, always add them at the end of cooking, or sprinkle over the finished dish.

Mary Allen Perry
ASSOCIATE FOODS EDITOR

Second Helpings

Cooked pasta can be stored in the refrigerator for up to 3 days or frozen for up to 1 month. Prepare pasta according to package directions, cooking for the minimum amount of time; drain and rinse under cold running water.

Toss pasta with a splash of olive oil, or lightly coat with vegetable cooking spray to prevent the strands from sticking together. Place in a zip-top plastic freezer bag, and refrigerate or freeze.

When ready to serve, remove the cold or frozen pasta from the bag, and drop into a large pot of rapidly boiling water, stirring just until hot (about 1 to 3 minutes). Drain and use as desired.

Tortellini Alfredo With Prosciutto and Artichoke Hearts

PREP: 10 MIN., COOK: 35 MIN.

2 (9-oz.) packages refrigerated cheese-filled tortellini
1 cup whipping cream
½ cup (2 oz.) freshly grated Parmesan cheese
3 strips prosciutto, chopped
3 marinated artichoke hearts, sliced

1. Cook tortellini according to package directions; drain and set aside.
2. Heat cream in a large skillet over low heat. Gradually sprinkle in cheese, stirring constantly, until blended. Simmer, stirring occasionally, 15 to 20 minutes.
3. Add tortellini, prosciutto, and artichoke hearts; simmer, stirring occasionally, 5 to 10 minutes or until sauce is slightly reduced. Serve immediately. **Makes** 4 to 6 servings.

DEBBIE ABBOTT
ROCKWELL, TEXAS

Noodle-and-Spinach Casserole

freezeable • make ahead

PREP: 15 MIN., COOK: 10 MIN., BAKE: 30 MIN.

To make ahead, bake as directed, cover, and freeze. Let thaw overnight in refrigerator. Bake, covered, at 350° for 30 minutes. Uncover and bake 10 more minutes.

1 (8-oz.) package wide egg noodles
1½ lb. ground beef
2 garlic cloves, minced
½ tsp. salt
½ tsp. pepper
1 (26-oz.) jar spaghetti sauce
1 tsp. dried Italian seasoning
1 (10-oz.) package frozen chopped spinach, thawed and drained
2 cups (8 oz.) shredded Monterey Jack cheese
1½ cups sour cream
1 large egg, lightly beaten
1 tsp. garlic salt
1½ cups (6 oz.) shredded Parmesan cheese

1. Cook noodles according to package directions; drain and set aside.
2. Cook beef and next 3 ingredients in a large nonstick skillet over medium heat, stirring until beef crumbles and is no longer pink. Drain and return to skillet. Stir in spaghetti sauce and Italian seasoning.
3. Combine spinach and next 4 ingredients. Fold in noodles; spoon mixture into a lightly greased 13- x 9-inch baking dish. Sprinkle with half of Parmesan cheese. Top evenly with beef mixture and remaining Parmesan cheese.
4. Bake at 350° for 30 minutes or until bubbly and golden. **Makes** 8 to 10 servings.

SUSANNE PETTIT
MEMPHIS, TENNESSEE

Ellie's Lasagna

family favorite
PREP: 15 MIN., COOK: 15 MIN.,
BAKE: 40 MIN., STAND: 10 MIN.

This super-simple recipe gets rave reviews from our readers. Some add mushrooms or a dash or two of dried Italian seasoning, while others substitute ground turkey or chicken for the ground beef.

12 lasagna noodles
1 (15-oz.) container ricotta cheese
1 tsp. pressed garlic
1 lb. ground beef
2 (26-oz.) jars spaghetti sauce
4 cups (16 oz.) shredded Italian
　　three-cheese blend

1. Cook lasagna noodles according to package directions; drain noodles, and set aside.
2. Stir together ricotta cheese and garlic; set aside.
3. Cook 1 lb. ground beef in a large skillet, stirring until meat crumbles and is no longer pink; drain. Stir in spaghetti sauce.
4. Layer a lightly greased 13- x 9-inch baking dish with one-third each of noodles, ricotta mixture, shredded cheese blend, and meat sauce. Repeat layers twice.
5. Bake at 375° for 35 to 40 minutes. Let lasagna stand 5 to 10 minutes before serving. **Makes** 6 servings.

Note: For testing purposes only, we used Classico di Napoli Tomato & Basil pasta sauce.

BETTY RUFFLE
ELLICOTT CITY, MARYLAND

Broiling Makes It Fast

Try these flavorful recipes when company's coming and you don't know what to cook.

When you need a fast main dish, broiling can solve your dinner dilemma. Broiled Herb Chicken With Lemon-Butter Sauce is seasoned with oregano, lemon pepper, and paprika. The sauce adds a splash of citrus. If you fancy fish, try Green Chile Broiled Catfish. The fillets are brushed with a ketchup-based sauce of chopped green chiles, cumin, lime, and hot sauce. For entertaining, consider making Broiled Steaks With Mushrooms. Garlic-rubbed steaks broiled to perfection are hard to beat. The finishing touch to the steaks is mushrooms sautéed in butter. Round out your meal with a side of rice or pasta (to help soak up the delectable sauce) and a green salad. Dinner is ready.

Broiling 101

This quick-cooking method will help you put together a full-flavored meal using freezer staples such as chicken, fish, or steak. Use a broiler pan, or place the meat on a rack in a baking pan so the fat can drip off. Just watch the meat carefully because it can brown quickly. Pay attention to the distance between the oven rack and your broiler. We measured ours at 7 and 8 inches. If your rack is closer to the broiler, the cook time will likely shorten.

Green Chile Broiled Catfish

PREP: 15 MIN., BROIL: 18 MIN.

When broiling, keep in mind that ovens can vary. In our ovens, the distance between the heat element and the oven rack measured 7 and 8 inches. The thickness of the fish can make a difference as well. A good test for doneness with fish is to cook it until the fish flakes easily with a fork. If you're not sure how powerful your broiler is, start checking for doneness halfway through the cooking time.

6 (4- to 6-oz.) catfish or tilapia fillets
1 tsp. salt
¼ tsp. freshly ground pepper
1 (4-oz.) can chopped green chiles
2 Tbsp. ketchup
1 Tbsp. extra-virgin olive oil
1 tsp. grated lime rind
1 Tbsp. fresh lime juice
¼ tsp. ground cumin
⅛ to ¼ tsp. hot sauce

1. Sprinkle fillets evenly with salt and pepper. Arrange fillets on a lightly greased wire rack in an aluminum foil-lined broiler pan.
2. Stir together green chiles, ketchup, and next 5 ingredients. Spoon half of mixture evenly over fillets, reserving remaining half.
3. Broil 7 to 8 inches from heat 18 minutes or until fish flakes with a fork. (Do not overcook.) Serve fish with reserved green chile mixture. **Makes** 6 servings.

Broiled Herb Chicken With Lemon-Butter Sauce
family favorite
PREP: 10 MIN., BROIL: 25 MIN.

Broiler-fryers are usually 2½ to 4 lb.; larger chickens, known as roasters, usually weigh 4 to 7 lb.

1 tsp. salt
1 tsp. dried oregano
½ tsp. garlic powder
½ tsp. lemon pepper
½ tsp. paprika
¼ tsp. ground red pepper
1 (3- to 3½-lb.) broiler-fryer, cut into pieces
Lemon-Butter Sauce

1. Combine first 6 ingredients.
2. Arrange chicken pieces, skin side down, on a lightly greased rack in an aluminum foil-lined roasting pan. Sprinkle evenly with 2 tsp. salt mixture.
3. Broil 7 to 8 inches from heat 12 to 15 minutes or until chicken is golden brown. Turn chicken pieces, and sprinkle evenly with remaining salt mixture. Broil 8 to 10 more minutes or until a meat thermometer inserted into thickest portion of white meat registers 170° and dark meat registers 180°. Serve chicken pieces with Lemon-Butter Sauce. **Makes** 4 to 6 servings.

Lemon-Butter Sauce:
fast fixin's
PREP: 5 MIN.

3 Tbsp. butter, melted
2 tsp. grated lemon rind
2 tsp. fresh lemon juice
1 tsp. chopped fresh parsley

1. Stir together first 3 ingredients until blended. Stir in chopped parsley. **Makes** about ⅓ cup.

JEAN LUMLEY
PFAFFTOWN, NORTH CAROLINA

Broiled Steaks With Mushrooms
family favorite
PREP: 15 MIN., BROIL: 14 MIN., COOK: 3 MIN.

4 (1-inch-thick) boneless chuck-eye steaks
1⅛ tsp. salt, divided
½ tsp. freshly ground pepper
½ tsp. garlic powder
¼ cup butter
2 cups sliced fresh mushrooms
Chopped fresh parsley

1. Sprinkle steaks evenly with 1 tsp. salt, pepper, and garlic powder. Place steaks on a lightly greased rack in an aluminum foil-lined broiler pan.
2. Broil steaks 7 to 8 inches from heat 6 to 7 minutes on each side or to desired doneness. Remove steaks from oven.
3. Melt ¼ cup butter in a small saucepan over medium-high heat; add mushrooms. Sauté mushrooms 3 minutes or until lightly browned; add remaining ⅛ tsp. salt. Arrange steaks on a serving platter, and top evenly with sautéed mushrooms. Sprinkle with chopped fresh parsley. **Makes** 4 servings.

CHARLOTTE BRYANT
GREENSBURG, KENTUCKY

Blend the Easy Way

Creamy soups, pureed vegetables, and fruit smoothies are easier to make than ever with a handheld, or immersion, blender. Place the appliance—also called a stick blender—right into the pot, and puree until the food mixture is smooth. With this handy gadget, there's no more processing soup in batches in a blender or food processor and then returning the pureed mixture to the pot to reheat. Cleanup is a breeze; the blade end can be detached and placed in the dishwasher.

Creamy Tomato Soup With Crispy Croutons
PREP: 10 MIN., COOK: 30 MIN., COOL: 10 MIN.

1 small onion, diced
2 Tbsp. olive oil
3 garlic cloves, minced
2 (28-oz.) cans chopped tomatoes
1 (14-oz.) can chicken broth
1 (5-oz.) package Brie without rind, cut into pieces *
1 tsp. salt
½ tsp. freshly ground pepper
Chopped fresh basil (optional)
Crispy Croutons

1. Sauté diced onion in 2 Tbsp. hot oil in a Dutch oven over medium-low heat 8 minutes or until tender; add minced garlic, and sauté 1 minute. Increase heat to medium-high; stir in chopped tomatoes and chicken broth, and bring to a boil. Simmer, stirring often, 10 minutes. Remove pan from heat. Allow tomato mixture to cool 10 minutes; stir in Brie pieces until melted.
2. Process soup with immersion blender until smooth.
3. Cook soup over medium-low heat until thoroughly heated. Stir in salt, pepper, and, if desired, chopped fresh basil. Serve with Crispy Croutons. **Makes** 6 to 8 servings.

Note: For testing purposes only, we used Alouette Crème de Brie.

*Substitute 2 (3-oz.) packages cream cheese for Brie, if desired.

SUSAN MARTIN
BIRMINGHAM, ALABAMA

Crispy Croutons: Thinly slice 1 French bread baguette. Brush cut sides with olive oil; place on a baking sheet. Sprinkle with ¼ tsp. salt and ¼ tsp. pepper. Bake at 350° for 8 to 10 minutes or until golden. Prep: 5 min., Bake: 10 min.

The Start of Something Good

It's impossible to resist the rich and nutty taste of browned butter. It pairs well with everything from savory pan-fried cutlets to sweet frosted cupcakes. Toss it with green beans, garlic, and grated lemon rind, or add it to your favorite dessert recipe. Almost anytime you use butter, you can use browned butter instead.

Browned Butter Frosting
PREP: 5 MIN., COOK: 8 MIN., CHILL: 1 HR.

1 cup butter
1 (16-oz.) package powdered sugar
¼ cup milk
1 tsp. vanilla extract

1. Cook butter in a small heavy saucepan over medium heat, stirring constantly, 6 to 8 minutes or until butter begins to turn golden brown. Remove pan from heat immediately, and pour butter into a small bowl. Cover and chill 1 hour or until butter is cool and begins to solidify.
2. Beat butter at medium speed with an electric mixer until creamy; gradually add powdered sugar alternately with milk, beginning and ending with powdered sugar. Beat mixture at low speed until well blended after each addition. Stir in vanilla. **Makes** about 3½ cups.

Cupcakes With Browned Butter Frosting: Prepare 1 (16-oz.) package pound cake mix according to package directions. Place 24 paper baking cups in muffin pans; spoon batter evenly into paper cups, filling two-thirds full. Bake at 350° for 20 minutes or until a wooden pick inserted in center of cupcake comes out clean. Remove from pans, and let cool completely on wire racks. Spread cupcakes evenly with Browned Butter Frosting; garnish with fresh mint leaves and edible violas, if desired. **Makes** 24 cupcakes. Prep: 15 min., Bake: 20 min.

Browned Butter-Pecan Shortbread
PREP: 30 MIN., COOK: 8 MIN., CHILL: 5 HRS., BAKE: 10 MIN. PER BATCH

1½ cups butter
¾ cup firmly packed brown sugar
¾ cup powdered sugar
3 cups all-purpose flour
1½ cups chopped pecans, toasted

1. Cook butter in a small heavy saucepan over medium heat, stirring constantly, 6 to 8 minutes or until butter begins to turn golden brown. Remove pan from heat immediately, and pour butter into a small bowl. Cover and chill 1 hour or until butter is cool and begins to solidify.
2. Beat butter at medium speed with an electric mixer until creamy. Gradually add brown sugar and powdered sugar, beating until smooth. Gradually add flour to butter mixture, beating at low speed just until blended. Stir in pecans.
3. Shape dough into 4 (8-inch) logs. Wrap logs tightly in plastic wrap, and chill 4 hours or until firm.
4. Cut logs into ¼-inch-thick rounds; place on lightly greased baking sheets.
5. Bake at 350° for 8 to 10 minutes or until lightly browned. Transfer shortbread to wire racks to cool. **Makes** about 10½ dozen.

Panning for Gold

Browning butter is a simple technique. It's so easy, you'll make it often. Just cook butter in a small heavy saucepan over medium heat, stirring constantly, 6 to 8 minutes or until the butter begins to turn golden brown.

After a few minutes, the butter will begin to foam, which is caused by heating the milk solids (the white liquid that appears when butter is melted). It's the milk solids in butter that actually brown as the foam drops to the bottom of the pan. (You'll always need to use real butter rather than margarine because margarine doesn't contain milk solids.)

Once the butter begins to brown, it will go from golden to black very quickly, so remove the pan from the heat immediately. And be sure to use a light-colored saucepan so you can accurately judge the color of the butter as it browns.

Our Grand Prize Winner— Lightened

After winning the *Southern Living* Cook-Off 2005, registered dietitian Sharon Collison returned to us with the lightened version of her $100,000 cheesecake. She did a full-fat version for our contest and won. Ironically, the skinnier version (with half the fat and calories) received the same outstanding rating in our Test Kitchens.

Lightened Chocolate-Coffee Cheesecake With Mocha Sauce

PREP: 20 MIN.; BAKE: 1 HR., 10 MIN.;
STAND: 30 MIN.; COOL: 1 HR.; CHILL: 4 HRS.
(Pictured on page 174)

2 cups crushed chocolate graham
    crackers (about 18 crackers)
⅓ cup light butter,
    melted
Vegetable cooking spray
4 (8-oz.) packages ⅓-less-fat cream
    cheese, softened
1 cup sugar
¼ cup coffee liqueur
1 tsp. vanilla extract
1 tsp. instant coffee granules
4 large eggs
4 (1-oz.) bittersweet baking chocolate
    squares
Mocha Sauce

1. Stir together crushed graham crackers and melted butter; press mixture into bottom and up sides of a 9-inch spring-form pan coated with cooking spray.
2. Bake at 350° for 10 minutes. Cool on a wire rack. Reduce oven temperature to 325°.
3. Beat cream cheese and sugar at medium speed with an electric mixer until blended. Add liqueur, vanilla, and coffee granules, beating at low speed until well blended. Add eggs, 1 at a time, beating just until yellow disappears after each addition.
4. Remove and reserve 1 cup cream cheese mixture. Pour remaining batter into prepared crust.
5. Microwave chocolate in a medium-size, microwave-safe bowl 1 minute or until melted, stirring after 30 seconds. Stir reserved 1 cup cream cheese mixture into melted chocolate, blending well. (Mixture will be thick.) Spoon mixture in lines on top of batter in pan; gently swirl with a knife.
6. Bake at 325° for 1 hour or until almost set. Turn oven off. Let cheesecake stand in oven, with door closed, 30 minutes. Remove cheesecake from oven, and gently run a knife around outer edge of cheesecake to loosen from sides of pan. (Do not remove sides of pan.) Cool 1 hour on a wire rack. Cover and chill at least 4 hours.

7. Remove sides of springform pan. Serve with Mocha Sauce. **Makes** 10 servings.

Note: For testing purposes only, we used Kahlúa for coffee liqueur.

Mocha Sauce:
fast fixin's
PREP: 10 MIN., COOK: 3 MIN.

1 cup semisweet chocolate morsels
¼ cup half-and-half
2 tsp. light butter
3 Tbsp. strong-brewed coffee

1. Cook first 3 ingredients in a small heavy saucepan over low heat, stirring often, 2 to 3 minutes or until smooth. Remove from heat, and stir in coffee. Serve warm. **Makes** ¾ cup.

SHARON COLLISON
NEWARK, DELAWARE

Per serving (1 slice cheesecake and about 1 Tbsp. mocha sauce): Calories 464 (46% from fat); Fat 24.8g (sat 13.7g, mono 2.9g, poly 0.4g); Protein 14.9g; Carb 48.5g; Fiber 2g; Chol 131mg; Iron 1.2mg; Sodium 411mg; Calc 88mg

Per serving (about 1 Tbsp. mocha sauce): Calories 92 (54% from fat); Fat 6g (sat 3.7g, mono 1.9g, poly 0.2g); Protein 1g; Carb 10.8g; Fiber 1g; Chol 4mg; Iron 0.5mg; Sodium 10mg; Calc 13mg

A Special Dessert

A great dessert doesn't have to take hours to prepare. You can make Brandy-Caramel Ice-cream Puffs in 40 minutes, and most of that is hands-off baking time. While the pastry shells are baking, stir together the sauce. Then all that's left is to scoop the ice cream, and drizzle the sauce. Have someone else pour the coffee or Champagne for a lavish ending to your meal.

Brandy-Caramel Ice-cream Puffs

PREP: 10 MIN., BAKE: 30 MIN.

1 (10-oz.) package ready-to-bake
    frozen puff pastry shells
Vanilla ice cream (about 1 qt.)
Brandy-Caramel Sauce
Garnishes: whole strawberries, fresh
    mint sprigs

1. Bake puff pastry shells according to package directions. Remove tops according to package directions after baking. Top each shell evenly with ice cream, and drizzle with warm Brandy-Caramel Sauce. Garnish, if desired. **Makes** 6 servings.

Note: For testing purposes only, we used Pepperidge Farm Puff Pastry Shells.

Brandy-Caramel Sauce:
fast fixin's • make ahead
PREP: 5 MIN., COOK: 10 MIN.
This sauce is super easy—no worrying about scorching the sugar as with traditional caramel sauces. It's also terrific without the brandy.

1 cup whipping cream
1½ cups firmly packed brown sugar
1 Tbsp. brandy
¼ cup butter
1 tsp. vanilla extract

1. Bring whipping cream to a simmer in a large saucepan over medium heat, stirring occasionally. Add sugar, and cook, stirring occasionally, 5 minutes or until smooth. Remove from heat, and stir in brandy, butter, and vanilla. **Makes** 2 cups.

To make ahead: Cool and store sauce in an airtight container in the refrigerator for up to 2 weeks. To reheat, microwave sauce in a glass bowl at HIGH for 1 to 1½ minutes or until warm, stirring once.

Serve a Holiday Ham

Prepare this popular choice for your Easter meal.

Ham is a perennial favorite that's easy to prepare. It's also a crowd-pleasing choice of meat with minimal fat and great flavor. So if you're hamstrung on what to cook this holiday, try one of our simple recipes. Both are irresistible and will be the hot dish on the menu.

Classic Cola-Glazed Ham
family favorite
PREP: 10 MIN.; BAKE: 2 HRS., 30 MIN.; STAND: 15 MIN.

1 (6- to 7-lb.) fully cooked, bone-in ham
30 to 32 whole cloves
1 (16-oz.) package dark brown sugar
1 cup spicy brown mustard
1 cup cola soft drink
½ cup bourbon or apple juice

1. Remove skin from ham, and trim fat to ¼-inch thickness. Make ¼-inch-deep cuts in a diamond pattern, and insert cloves at 1-inch intervals. Place ham in an aluminum foil-lined 13- x 9-inch pan.
2. Stir together brown sugar and next 3 ingredients until smooth. Pour mixture evenly over ham.
3. Bake at 350° on lower oven rack 2 hours and 30 minutes, basting with pan juices every 20 minutes. Remove ham, and let stand 15 minutes before serving. **Makes** 12 to 14 servings.

Citrus-Glazed Ham
family favorite
PREP: 10 MIN.; BAKE: 2 HRS., 30 MIN.; STAND: 15 MIN.
This ham takes only a few steps to make. Dress it up with salad greens, sliced oranges and apples, and ribbons of orange rind.

1 (6- to 7-lb.) fully cooked, bone-in ham
30 to 32 whole cloves
1 (10-oz.) bottle orange juice-flavored soft drink
1¼ cups orange marmalade
½ cup firmly packed light brown sugar
¼ cup Dijon mustard
Garnishes: apple slices, orange slices, orange rind, salad greens

1. Remove skin from ham; trim fat to ¼-inch thickness. Make ¼-inch-deep cuts in a diamond pattern; insert cloves at 1-inch intervals. Place ham in an aluminum foil-lined 13- x 9-inch pan.
2. Stir together soft drink and next 3 ingredients until smooth. Pour mixture evenly over ham.
3. Bake at 350° on lower oven rack 2 hours and 30 minutes, basting with pan juices every 20 minutes. Remove ham; let stand 15 minutes before serving. Garnish, if desired. **Makes** 12 to 14 servings.

Note: For testing purposes only, we used Orangina Sparkling Citrus Beverage.

Ham 101

Ham comes from the leg of the hog. You can buy it cooked, uncooked, dry cured, or wet cured.
■ **Cooked ham** can be served directly from the refrigerator. If you'd like to serve it hot, heat in a 350° oven to an internal temperature of 140°. At 140°, the ham will be thoroughly warmed and moist.
■ **Uncooked ham** should be heated to an internal temperature of 160° in a 350° oven. Depending on the size, plan to cook it 18 to 25 minutes per pound.
■ **Dry-cured ham** is rubbed with salt, sugar, and other seasonings, and then stored until the salt penetrates the meat.
■ **Wet-cured ham** is seasoned with a brine solution, which keeps the meat moist and produces a more tender texture.

25 Ideas for Strawberries

Bite into a fresh, juicy strawberry. Here are five simple recipes to get you started, as well as 20 ideas for indulging in these berries all season long.

Billie's Favorite Strawberry Milk Shake

PREP: 5 MIN.

For a thinner shake, add up to ¼ cup more milk.

1 (16-oz.) container fresh strawberries, hulled
1 qt. vanilla ice cream
½ cup milk

1. Process all ingredients in a blender until desired consistency, stopping to scrape down sides. Serve immediately. **Makes** 4 servings.

Note: For testing purposes only, we used Häagen-Dazs Vanilla ice cream.

BILLIE CAINE
HELENA, ALABAMA

Strawberry-Mint Milk Shake: Add 2 Tbsp. chopped fresh mint. Proceed as directed.

Strawberry Lemonade

PREP: 10 MIN.

Make a strawberry lemonade slush by freezing lemonade in ice cube trays and then processing frozen cubes in a blender.

1 (12-oz.) can lemonade concentrate, thawed *****
1 (16-oz.) container fresh strawberries, hulled
¼ cup powdered sugar
Ice cubes

1. Prepare lemonade according to package directions.
2. Process strawberries and powdered sugar in a food processor until smooth, stopping to scrape down sides; stir into lemonade. Serve over ice. Store in refrigerator up to 3 days. **Makes** 8 cups.

* Substitute 1 (12-oz.) can limeade concentrate, if desired.

LIZA OSBUN PINARD
SAN DIEGO, CALIFORNIA

Strawberry Soup

fast fixin's

PREP: 8 MIN.

Add a dollop of sour cream to this dessert soup, and garnish with fresh mint sprigs or lemon rind for a pretty presentation.

1 (16-oz.) container fresh strawberries, hulled
1 cup light sour cream
½ cup milk
¼ cup sugar
1 Tbsp. fresh lemon juice

1. Process all ingredients in a blender until smooth, stopping to scrape down sides. **Makes** 4 cups.

HELEN MAURER
CLERMONT, GEORGIA

Strawberry-Spinach Salad

fast fixin's

PREP: 10 MIN.

For a tasty twist, replace the almonds, blue cheese, and red wine vinaigrette with pecans, goat cheese, and balsamic vinaigrette.

¼ red onion, thinly sliced
2 (6-oz.) bags baby spinach
1 (16-oz.) container strawberries, quartered
1 (4-oz.) package crumbled blue cheese
½ cup sliced almonds, toasted
Bottled red wine vinaigrette
Salt and freshly ground pepper to taste

1. Toss together first 5 ingredients in a large bowl. Drizzle with red wine vinaigrette; sprinkle with salt and pepper to taste. **Makes** 6 servings.

BRIDGET DRENNEN
ATLANTA, GEORGIA

No-Cook Ways to Enjoy Strawberries

After rinsing the fruit under cool water and patting them dry, try some of these fun ways to savor them.
- By themselves.
- Accompany berries with good-quality dark chocolate or warm chocolate sauce.
- Accompany with Champagne.
- Layer sliced strawberries in parfait glasses with nonfat vanilla yogurt and granola.
- Spread lemon curd on pound cake slices; top with sweetened strawberries and whipped cream.
- Toss sliced strawberries with lemon juice and fresh mint. Serve over vanilla ice cream.
- Sandwich peanut butter and strawberry and banana slices between two vanilla wafers.
- Dip in lemon yogurt.
- Spread cream cheese frosting on ladyfingers, and top with sliced strawberries.
- Toss sliced strawberries with sugar, and serve over pound cake with chocolate syrup.
- Drizzle cubed pound cake with orange liqueur; layer in glasses with vanilla pudding and sliced strawberries. Top with sweetened whipped cream.
- Enjoy a peanut butter sandwich filled with sliced strawberries.
- Stir together 2 cups sour cream and ½ cup brown sugar; dip strawberries.
- Dip in powdered sugar.
- Slice over cereal.
- Slice over oatmeal.
- Drizzle sliced strawberries with balsamic vinegar and sugar; sprinkle with freshly ground black pepper.
- Drizzle with lime juice, and sprinkle with sugar and salt.
- Dip in orange liqueur and powdered sugar.
- Spread orange marmalade on toasted English muffins, and top with sliced strawberries.

Add a Burst of Flavor

Take your recipes from good to great by adding a few simple and healthful ingredients. The majority of these products can be found in your pantry or refrigerator, are big on taste, and add very little fat and calories to your dish. See our box of favored flavors for other ideas.

Bacon-Wrapped Beef Fillets
family favorite
PREP: 15 MIN., STAND: 40 MIN.,
GRILL: 20 MIN.
Use salt-free seasoning to add big flavor without additional sodium.

1 Tbsp. salt-free Greek seasoning
¼ tsp. garlic powder
¼ cup steak sauce
¼ cup orange juice
4 (4-oz.) 1½-inch-thick beef tenderloin
   steaks
4 turkey bacon slices

1. Combine first 4 ingredients in a shallow dish or large zip-top freezer bag; add steaks, turning to coat. Cover or seal, and let stand 30 minutes. Remove steaks from marinade, and discard marinade. Set steaks aside.
2. Microwave turkey bacon at HIGH 30 seconds.
3. Wrap 1 slice of bacon around each steak, and secure with wooden picks.

4. Grill, covered with grill lid, over medium-high heat (350° to 400°) 8 to 10 minutes on each side or to desired degree of doneness. Remove steaks from grill, and let stand, loosely covered with aluminum foil, 10 minutes before serving. **Makes** 4 servings.

Note: For testing purposes only, we used A.1. Sauce.

Per serving: Calories 219 (44% from fat); Fat 10.4g (sat 3.7g, mono 3g, poly 0.3g); Protein 27.2g; Carb 2.4g; Fiber 0g; Chol 89mg; Iron 1.8mg; Sodium 374mg; Calc 28mg

Orange-Ginger Grilled Chicken Thighs
family favorite
PREP: 13 MIN., CHILL: 1 HR., GRILL: 8 MIN.

⅓ cup orange juice
3 Tbsp. rice wine vinegar
3 Tbsp. lite soy sauce
1 Tbsp. minced garlic
1 Tbsp. minced fresh ginger
1 Tbsp. sesame oil
8 (4-oz.) skinned and boned chicken
   thighs
Garnishes: fresh cilantro sprigs, orange
   slices

1. Combine first 6 ingredients in a shallow dish or large zip-top freezer bag; add chicken. Cover or seal, and chill at least 1 hour, turning chicken occasionally.
2. Remove chicken thighs from marinade, and discard marinade.
3. Grill, covered with grill lid, over medium-high heat (350° to 400°) 4 minutes on each side or until done. Garnish, if desired. **Makes** 8 servings.

Per serving: Calories 146 (31% from fat); Fat 5.1g (sat 1.2g, mono 1.6g, poly 1.3g); Protein 22.5g; Carb 0.8g; Fiber 0g; Chol 94mg; Iron 1.2mg; Sodium 161mg; Calc 12mg

Mediterranean Salmon
PREP: 20 MIN., BAKE: 20 MIN.
If your sun-dried tomatoes are packed in oil, be sure to drain and pat dry with a paper towel before using.

4 (6-oz.) salmon fillets
¾ tsp. lemon pepper
¾ tsp. dried dillweed
¼ tsp. salt
½ cup coarsely chopped sun-dried
   tomatoes
1 (2.25-oz.) can sliced ripe black olives,
   drained
2 oz. reduced-fat crumbled feta cheese
   with basil and tomatoes
¼ cup pine nuts, toasted

1. Place each salmon fillet on a 16- x 12-inch piece of heavy-duty aluminum foil. Sprinkle fillets evenly with lemon pepper, dill, and salt. Top fillets evenly with tomatoes and next 3 ingredients. Fold long sides of foil over fillets; roll up short sides of foil to seal. Place foil packets, seam sides up, on a baking sheet.
2. Bake at 400° for 18 to 20 minutes or until fish flakes with a fork. **Makes** 4 servings.
CHARLOTTE HINSON
BOSSIER, LOUISIANA

Per serving: Calories 334 (47% from fat); Fat 17.4g (sat 3.3g, mono 5.5g, poly 6g); Protein 38.4g; Carb 5.9g; Fiber 1.7g; Chol 98mg; Iron 2.8 mg; Sodium 770mg; Calc 84mg

Balsamic-Roasted New Potatoes
PREP: 10 MIN., BAKE: 45 MIN.

2 tsp. olive oil
2 tsp. minced garlic
1 tsp. chopped fresh thyme ✳
½ tsp. kosher salt
¼ tsp. pepper
2 lb. small new potatoes,
   quartered
3 Tbsp. balsamic vinegar, divided
Vegetable cooking spray

1. Stir together first 5 ingredients in a large bowl or large zip-top plastic bag; add potatoes. Drizzle with 2 Tbsp. balsamic vinegar, and stir or shake well to coat. Arrange potatoes in an aluminum foil-lined jelly-roll pan coated with cooking spray.

Go Beyond Bland

Jazz up your favorite recipes with these suggestions.
■ **Dressings and marinades:** Add red or white wine, balsamic vinegar, sesame oil, minced garlic.
■ **Salads and sandwiches:** Top with sun-dried tomatoes, strong cheeses (blue or Parmesan), capers.
■ **Fish and poultry:** Season with Dijon mustard, citrus juice and rind, ground spices, fresh herbs.

2. Bake, uncovered, at 450° for 45 minutes or until potatoes are tender, stirring once. Drizzle with remaining 1 Tbsp. vinegar, and toss well. Serve immediately. **Makes** 6 servings.

✱ Substitute ¼ tsp. dried thyme for fresh, if desired.

Per serving: Calories 132 (13% from fat); Fat 1.9g (sat 0.2g, mono 1.1g, poly 0.2g); Protein 2.9g; Carb 25.5g; Fiber 2.6g; Chol 0mg; Iron 1.2mg; Sodium 168mg; Calc 16mg

Rosemary Green Beans
family favorite
PREP: 20 MIN., COOK: 15 MIN.

1 lb. fresh green beans, trimmed
½ tsp. salt, divided
2 green onions, sliced (about ¼ cup)
2 tsp. chopped fresh rosemary
1 tsp. olive oil
¼ cup chopped pecans, toasted
2 tsp. grated lemon rind
Garnish: fresh rosemary sprigs

1. Sprinkle green beans evenly with ¼ tsp. salt, and place in a steamer basket over boiling water; cover and steam 10 minutes or until crisp-tender. Plunge green beans into ice water to stop the cooking process, and drain.
2. Sauté green onions and rosemary in hot oil in a nonstick skillet over medium-high heat 2 to 3 minutes or until softened. Add green beans, pecans, lemon rind, and remaining ¼ tsp. salt, stirring until thoroughly heated. Garnish, if desired, and serve immediately. **Makes** 6 servings.

MARY PAPPAS
RICHMOND, VIRGINIA

Per serving: Calories 68 (54% from fat); Fat 4.5g (sat 0.5g, mono 2.6g, poly 1.3g); Protein 1.9g; Carb 6.9g; Fiber 3g; Chol 0mg; Iron 0.7mg; Sodium 195mg; Calc 40mg

Sweet Onion Sides

Try this mild yet flavorful vegetable for a change of pace at your table. You may be most familiar with the Vidalia of Georgia, but Texas grows its share of sweet onions too. They are coming into the market in full force right now, so keep an eye out. You'll find them loose or in small, marked bags in the produce section. Go ahead, and give them a try.

Sweet Onion Bake
PREP: 15 MIN., COOK: 25 MIN., BAKE: 20 MIN.
Serve this instead of macaroni and cheese with your favorite entrée.

6 Tbsp. butter, divided
3 medium-size sweet onions, chopped (about 2 cups)
1 (8-oz.) block Swiss cheese, shredded
¾ cup finely crushed saltine crackers, divided (about 20 crackers)
2 large eggs
1 cup half-and-half
1 tsp. salt
⅛ tsp. freshly ground pepper

1. Melt 4 Tbsp. butter in a large skillet over medium heat; add onions, and sauté 20 minutes or until golden brown. Place half of cooked onions in a lightly greased 8-inch square baking dish. Sprinkle evenly with half of cheese and ¼ cup cracker crumbs. Top with remaining onions and cheese.
2. Whisk together eggs and next 3 ingredients in a medium bowl; pour over onion mixture.
3. Melt remaining 2 Tbsp. butter in skillet over medium heat; add remaining ½ cup cracker crumbs, and cook, stirring often, until crumbs are lightly browned. Sprinkle crumbs evenly over mixture in dish.
4. Bake at 350° for 20 minutes or until lightly browned and set. **Makes** 4 to 6 servings.

RENEE RAND-CESMIROSKY
SAN ANTONIO, TEXAS

Minted Onion Relish
make ahead
PREP: 10 MIN., COOK: 20 MIN.,
COOL: 30 MIN., CHILL: 2 HRS.
This is great with grilled chicken or pork. It's also good on a relish tray for hamburgers and hot dogs.

2 cups white vinegar
1 cup loosely packed fresh mint sprigs
¼ cup sugar
½ tsp. salt
2 large sweet onions, thinly sliced and separated into rings
1 (4-oz.) jar diced pimiento, drained
2 Tbsp. chopped fresh mint

1. Cook first 4 ingredients in a Dutch oven over low heat, stirring occasionally, until sugar dissolves. Increase heat to medium, and cook 10 minutes. Pour mixture through a wire-mesh strainer into a bowl, discarding mint sprigs. Return vinegar mixture to Dutch oven, and bring to a boil. Add onion rings; bring to a boil, and boil 1 minute. Remove onion mixture from heat, and stir in diced pimiento. Cool 30 minutes.
2. Stir 2 Tbsp. chopped mint into onion mixture; cover and chill at least 2 hours. **Makes** 3 cups.

EDNA CHADSEY
CORPUS CHRISTI, TEXAS

Begin With Breakfast

Make your morning meal a priority, and enjoy these hearty, nutritious dishes.

Morning Menu

Serves 8

Oatmeal Pancakes With Cider Sauce
Brown Sugared Turkey Bacon
Parmesan-Portobello Grits

Increase your chances of living a healthier, happier life by eating a well-balanced breakfast daily. Short on time? Try a smoothie or low-fat muffin. Either way, you'll feel satisfied and full of energy.

Breakfast on-the-Go

Crunched for time in the morning? Just grab a nutritious option on your way out.
■ Top whole wheat waffles with a tablespoon of peanut butter.
■ Toss fruit and yogurt in the blender to whip up a quick smoothie.
■ Mix together dried fruit, toasted seeds, and nuts for a protein-packed pick-me-up.
■ Prepare low-fat muffins ahead, freeze, and pop in the microwave before leaving.

Oatmeal Pancakes With Cider Sauce

freezeable • make ahead
PREP: 10 MIN., COOK: 4 MIN. PER BATCH
The pancake and sauce recipes can easily be halved for a smaller crowd, or you can prepare the entire pancake recipe, and freeze leftovers for a quick, hearty breakfast on another day.

1 cup uncooked regular oats
1 cup whole wheat flour
¼ cup instant nonfat dry milk powder
¼ cup wheat germ
1 Tbsp. brown sugar
1 tsp. baking soda
¼ tsp. salt
2 cups nonfat buttermilk
2 large eggs
¼ cup light butter, melted
Vegetable cooking spray
Cider Sauce

1. Pulse oats in food processor 5 or 6 times until ground.
2. Combine ground oats, wheat flour, and next 5 ingredients in a large bowl. Whisk together buttermilk, eggs, and butter; stir into oat mixture.
3. Pour ¼ cup batter for each pancake onto a hot griddle coated with cooking spray. Cook pancakes until tops are covered with bubbles and edges look cooked; turn and cook other side. Serve with Cider Sauce. **Makes** 10 servings.

Per serving (2 pancakes and ¼ cup sauce): Calories 209 (27% from fat); Fat 6.7g (sat 3.7g, mono 0.6g, poly 0.4g); Protein 8.4g; Carb 32.2g; Fiber 2.5g; Chol 59mg; Iron 1.4mg; Sodium 321mg; Calc 118mg

Cider Sauce:
fast fixin's
PREP: 5 MIN., COOK: 5 MIN.

2 cups apple cider
3 Tbsp. light brown sugar
2 Tbsp. cornstarch
2 Tbsp. lemon juice
¼ tsp. ground nutmeg
¼ tsp. ground cinnamon
¼ cup light butter

1. Whisk together first 6 ingredients in a medium saucepan. Bring to a boil over medium heat, whisking constantly; boil, whisking constantly, 1 minute. Remove from heat, and add butter, whisking until melted. Serve immediately. **Makes** 2½ cups.

LAURA PATTERSON
DECATUR, ALABAMA

Per (¼-cup) serving: Calories 66 (31% from fat); Fat 2.4g (sat 1.6g, mono 0g, poly 0g); Protein 0.6g; Carb 11.4g; Fiber 0.1g; Chol 8mg; Iron 0.1mg; Sodium 29mg; Calc 3mg

Brown Sugared Turkey Bacon

family favorite • fast fixin's
PREP: 5 MIN., COOK: 18 MIN.
Sweet and salty with a hint of pepper, this crispy bacon is sure to please everyone at your breakfast table.

1 (12-oz.) package turkey bacon
Vegetable cooking spray
⅓ cup firmly packed light brown sugar
1 to 1½ tsp. coarsely ground pepper

1. Arrange bacon in a single layer in an aluminum foil-lined broiler pan coated with cooking spray. Sprinkle evenly with brown sugar and pepper.
2. Bake at 425° for 14 to 18 minutes or until done. Serve immediately. **Makes** 12 servings.

Note: For testing purposes only, we used Butterball Turkey Bacon.

Per (1-oz.) serving: Calories 94 (55% from fat); Fat 5.8g (sat 1.5g, mono 2.1g, poly 1.3g); Protein 4.3g; Carb 6.5g; Fiber 0.1g; Chol 26mg; Iron 0.6mg; Sodium 346mg; Calc 17mg

Parmesan-Portobello Grits

PREP: 10 MIN., COOK: 25 MIN.

These savory grits also pair well as a dinner side with pork chops or steaks.

1 Tbsp. light butter
1 small sweet onion, finely chopped
2 portobello mushroom caps, cleaned and finely chopped
2 garlic cloves, minced
2 tsp. chopped fresh thyme
½ tsp. salt
¼ tsp. ground red pepper
1 (32-oz.) container low-sodium fat-free chicken broth
½ cup water
1 cup uncooked quick-cooking grits
½ cup (2 oz.) freshly shredded Parmesan cheese

1. Melt butter in a large nonstick skillet over medium-high heat; add onion. Cook, stirring occasionally, 8 minutes or until golden. Stir in mushrooms and next 4 ingredients; cook 5 minutes or until mushrooms are tender. Remove skillet from heat.
2. Bring broth and ½ cup water to a boil in a medium saucepan; gradually stir in grits. Cover, reduce heat, and simmer, stirring occasionally, 5 minutes or until grits are thickened. Stir in portobello mixture and Parmesan cheese. Serve immediately. **Makes** 8 servings.

EILEEN WATSON
WINTER PARK, FLORIDA

Per (½-cup) serving: Calories 114 (19% from fat); Fat 2.4g (sat 1.4g, mono 0.5g, poly 0.2g); Protein 5g; Carb 18g; Fiber 0.8g; Chol 6mg; Iron 1mg; Sodium 491mg; Calc 69mg

Healthy Benefits

■ Studies show that eating breakfast improves your overall nutrition and ability to concentrate and maintain your weight.
■ Aim to incorporate starch, fiber, and fat into your breakfast to maintain satiety throughout the morning.

Try Quiche Tonight

When you need a meal that's family-friendly yet special enough for entertaining, try quiche. Our ham-and-bacon version blends a popular duo into one delicious dish and will be a popular addition to your recipe book. But you can also mix-and-match ingredients to find your favorite pairing for this versatile meal.

Ham-and-Bacon Quiche

family favorite

PREP: 20 MIN.; BAKE: 1 HR., 5 MIN.;
COOK: 10 MIN.; STAND: 10 MIN.

1 (15-oz.) package refrigerated piecrusts
1 egg white, lightly beaten
6 bacon slices
½ cup chopped onion
1 cup sliced fresh mushrooms
1½ cups half-and-half
1 cup chopped cooked ham
6 eggs, lightly beaten
½ tsp. seasoned salt
½ tsp. black pepper
2 cups (8 oz.) shredded Swiss cheese
2 Tbsp. all-purpose flour

1. Fit 1 piecrust into a 9-inch deep-dish pieplate according to package directions; trim dough around edges of pieplate.
2. Place remaining piecrust on a lightly floured surface; cut desired shapes with a decorative 1-inch cookie cutter. Brush edge of piecrust in pieplate with beaten egg white; gently press dough cutouts onto edge of piecrust. Pierce bottom and sides with a fork.
3. Line piecrust with parchment paper or aluminum foil; fill piecrust with pie weights or dried beans.
4. Bake at 400° for 10 minutes. Remove weights and parchment paper; bake 5 more minutes, and set aside. Reduce oven temperature to 350°.
5. Cook bacon in a large skillet over medium-high heat until crisp. Remove bacon, and drain on paper towels,

reserving 2 tsp. drippings in pan. Crumble bacon, and set aside.
6. Sauté chopped onion and mushrooms in hot drippings 3 to 4 minutes or until tender.
7. Stir together bacon, onion mixture, half-and-half, and next 4 ingredients in a large bowl. Combine cheese and flour; add to bacon mixture, stirring until blended. Pour mixture into crust.
8. Bake at 350° for 45 to 50 minutes or until a wooden pick inserted in center comes out clean. (Shield edges with aluminum foil to prevent excess browning, if necessary.) Let stand 10 minutes before serving. **Makes** 6 to 8 servings.

KAREN WILCHER
MITCHELLVILLE, MARYLAND

Dress It Up

Use one refrigerated piecrust for the bottom of the quiche, and make it pretty with the second one. On a lightly floured surface, cut desired shapes from the piecrust using a decorative 1-inch cookie cutter. (Dress up any piecrust with this technique.) Brush edge of piecrust in pieplate with beaten egg white. Gently press cutouts onto edge of piecrust.

Enjoy Muffins Anytime

Muffins are so easy to make that you can serve them piping hot from the oven to round out any meal. Freeze a batch for up to a month to enjoy when there's no time to make breakfast. Wrap a frozen muffin in a paper towel, and microwave it for 15 seconds (or until heated through) for bakery-fresh flavor.

Brown Sugar-Banana Muffins

freezeable

PREP: 15 MIN., BAKE: 25 MIN., COOL: 10 MIN.

Bananas get softer and sweeter as they ripen. Make sure yours are ripe enough (almost black) for these luscious treats. We use a mixer here to achieve a more cakelike, even texture.

½ cup butter, softened
1 cup firmly packed brown sugar
2 large eggs
1 cup mashed ripe banana (about 2 large)
¼ cup buttermilk
1 tsp. vanilla extract
2¼ cups all-purpose flour
¾ tsp. baking soda
½ tsp. baking powder
½ tsp. salt
½ cup toasted pecans, chopped

1. Beat butter at medium speed with an electric mixer until creamy. Gradually add brown sugar, beating until light and fluffy. Add eggs, 1 at a time, beating just until blended after each addition.
2. Stir together mashed banana, buttermilk, and vanilla. Stir together flour and next 3 ingredients; add to butter mixture alternately with banana mixture, beginning and ending with flour mixture. Beat at low speed just until blended after each addition. (Do not overbeat.) Spoon batter into 12 lightly greased muffin cups, filling two-thirds full. Sprinkle evenly with pecans.
3. Bake at 350° for 20 to 25 minutes or until a wooden pick inserted in center comes out clean. Remove from pans immediately, and cool 10 minutes on wire racks. **Makes** 1 dozen.

Tip: If you don't have buttermilk, stir ¾ tsp. lemon juice or vinegar into ¼ cup milk.

Freezer-Friendly Peanut Butter-Chocolate Chip Muffins:

Stir together 2 cups all-purpose baking mix, 1 cup milk, ½ cup sugar, and 2 large eggs in a large mixing bowl, stirring just until dry ingredients are moistened. Stir in ½ cup chunky peanut butter and ½ tsp. vanilla extract just until blended; stir in 1 cup semisweet chocolate morsels. Spoon batter into lightly greased paper-lined muffin cups, filling two-thirds full. Bake at 350° for 24 minutes or until lightly browned. Remove from pans; serve warm. **Makes** 16 to 18 muffins. Prep: 10 min., Bake: 24 min.

Note: For testing purposes only, we used Bisquick Original All-Purpose Baking Mix.

MARLENE J. MURPHY
WINTER SPRINGS, FLORIDA

Pizza Muffins

family favorite

PREP: 15 MIN., COOK: 3 MIN., BAKE: 20 MIN., STAND: 3 MIN.

Tomato juice lends these zesty muffins a tawny color. Serve them with a cup of soup or a salad for a satisfying lunch.

¼ cup finely chopped onion
1 garlic clove, minced
6 Tbsp. olive oil, divided
2 cups all-purpose flour
1 cup (4 oz.) shredded mozzarella cheese
¼ cup diced turkey pepperoni
2¾ tsp. baking powder
1 tsp. dried oregano
¾ tsp. salt
1 cup tomato juice
1 large egg
½ cup freshly grated Parmesan cheese

1. Sauté onion and garlic in 2 Tbsp. hot oil in a large skillet over medium-high heat 2 to 3 minutes or until tender. Set aside.
2. Combine flour and next 5 ingredients in a large bowl; make a well in center of mixture.
3. Stir together onion mixture, tomato juice, egg, and remaining 4 Tbsp. oil, blending well; add to flour mixture, stirring just until dry ingredients are moistened. Spoon mixture into lightly greased muffin cups, filling two-thirds full. Sprinkle evenly with grated Parmesan cheese.
4. Bake at 400° for 20 minutes or until lightly browned. Let stand 3 minutes before removing from pans. **Makes** 1 dozen.

AGNES MIXON
OCALA, FLORIDA

Test Kitchen Notebook

Muffins are one of the ultimate morning comfort foods—perfect with a glass of milk or cup of coffee. Their single-serving size charms children and offers adults built-in portion control. Muffins are equally at home as midafternoon snacks or, in the case of nonsweet versions, on the dinner table. Bake them in cupcake liners for a festive touch, and pass them in a cloth-lined basket, as you would any other bread.

Donna Florio
SENIOR WRITER

A Fresh Twist on Spring

Enjoy our spin on a classic spring lunch, and rediscover the pleasures of sharing a light repast on a glorious afternoon.

Lemon-Basil Shrimp Salad
make ahead
PREP: 20 MIN., CHILL: 8 HRS.

Don't skip the fresh lemon rind and juice in the marinade—it makes this recipe special. These shrimp also make a terrific appetizer. The shrimp and dressing, as well as the Parmesan Baskets, can all be made a day ahead. (Pictured on page 164)

3 lb. unpeeled, cooked large shrimp
1 large red onion, sliced
1 red bell pepper, sliced
1 yellow bell pepper, sliced
Lemon-Basil Marinade
½ cup chopped fresh basil
16 cups salad greens
8 Parmesan Baskets (optional)
Fresh Lemon Vinaigrette

1. Peel shrimp, and devein, if desired. Place shrimp and next 4 ingredients in a large zip-top plastic freezer bag. Seal and chill 8 hours or up to 24 hours, turning bag occasionally. Stir in basil 1 hour before serving. Drain and discard marinade just before serving.
2. Divide greens evenly between Parmesan Baskets or serving bowls; arrange drained shrimp mixture evenly over lettuce. Serve with Fresh Lemon Vinaigrette. **Makes** 8 servings.

Lemon-Basil Marinade:
fast fixin's • make ahead
PREP: 10 MIN.

1 cup vegetable oil
1 cup red wine vinegar
2 Tbsp. grated lemon rind
¼ cup fresh lemon juice
3 Tbsp. sugar
2 Tbsp. hot sauce
2 Tbsp. Dijon mustard
2 garlic cloves, pressed
½ tsp. salt

1. Whisk together all ingredients. **Makes** about 2½ cups.

Note: To prepare marinade ahead, store in an airtight container in the refrigerator up to 1 week. Bring to room temperature, and whisk before using.

Fresh Lemon Vinaigrette:
fast fixin's • make ahead
PREP: 5 MIN.

¼ cup fresh lemon juice
1 tsp. Dijon mustard
1 large garlic clove, pressed
¼ tsp. salt
¼ tsp. freshly ground black pepper
½ cup vegetable oil

1. Whisk together first 5 ingredients. Gradually add oil in a slow, steady stream, whisking until blended. **Makes** about ¾ cup.

Note: To prepare ahead, store in an airtight container in the refrigerator up to 1 week. Bring to room temperature, and whisk before serving.

How to Make a Parmesan Basket

You can bake these a day ahead, and store them in individual zip-top plastic bags. You'll need to move quickly to shape them when they come out of the oven, so make them one at a time.
1. Wrap the outside of an inverted 6-inch terra-cotta pot in aluminum foil. Coat foil with vegetable cooking spray.
2. Place a 12-inch square of parchment paper on a baking sheet. Spread ½ cup shredded Parmesan cheese onto the parchment paper, patting it into an 8½-inch circle. (**Note:** Don't use grated cheese in this recipe—only shredded will work.) Bake at 375° for 5 to 7 minutes or until pale gold in color. Remove from oven, and let cool 10 seconds.
3. Carefully lift off the parchment paper from the baking sheet.
4. Working quickly, invert the Parmesan circle over the prepared pot.
5. Carefully remove the parchment from the Parmesan circle. (Reserve the parchment to use again.) Gently press the cheese over inverted pot into desired bowl shape. (**Tip:** If the cheese circle is too hot, it will slide down the pot, causing small tears. If this happens, gently press the cheese together to seal any large gaps.) Cool basket completely (about 5 minutes), and remove from pot. Repeat to create as many baskets as you need.

Celebrate the Baby to Come

Dianne Simmons of Madison, Georgia, is an expert when it comes to entertaining. A professional food stylist for 20 years, Dianne expresses her passion for food and art through casual gatherings.

She invited us to a baby shower that she helped put together for expectant parents Tracy and Randy Hoexter. To make things easy on everyone, each of the six cohosts was assigned a job, from tending bar to greeting guests. Dianne didn't have time to experiment with new recipes, so she relied on faithful standbys perfect for any occasion.

She shares these words of wisdom: "Always be a part of your party—and have as much fun as your guests do."

Dianne's Entertaining Secrets

- Monitor your guest list. Don't invite more people than you can comfortably seat. As a rule of thumb, a third of your guests won't be able to attend.
- Simplify the menu. Build a collection of all-time favorites that are easy to prepare and include make-ahead options.
- Minimize last-minute tasks. For example, choose garnishes that can be made the day before.

Raspberry Lemonade
fast fixin's
PREP: 10 MIN.
Slice lemons and limes with a serrated knife the day before. Wrap in damp paper towels, and store in a zip-top plastic bag in the refrigerator.

2 cups sugar
3 cups fresh lemon juice (about 9 lemons)
4 cups cold water
5 cups ice cubes
1 pt. frozen raspberries in syrup, thawed
3 lemons, sliced
2 limes, sliced

1. Combine sugar and juice in a large serving container, stirring until sugar dissolves. Stir in 4 cups cold water and ice cubes; add raspberries, lemon slices, and lime slices. **Makes** 10 cups.

Chicken Salad Croissants
make ahead
PREP: 15 MIN., CHILL: 30 MIN.
Tarragon adds a fresh flair to this Southern favorite. If desired, prepare the chicken salad two days ahead, and then assemble the sandwiches the morning of the party.

1 cup mayonnaise
1 cup sour cream
1 tsp. salt
1 tsp. pepper
¼ to ½ tsp. fresh tarragon
3 cups chopped cooked chicken
1 cup seedless green or red grapes
¾ cup pecans, toasted and coarsely chopped
20 croissants
Red leaf lettuce
Fresh tarragon sprigs

1. Stir together first 5 ingredients in a large bowl. Add chicken, grapes, and chopped pecans, tossing to coat. Cover and chill at least 30 minutes.
2. Cut a slit horizontally on 1 side of each croissant; fill evenly with lettuce and chicken salad. Skewer sandwiches with fresh tarragon sprigs to hold together. **Makes** 20 sandwiches.

Fresh Corn Salad
make ahead
PREP: 15 MIN., COOK: 4 MIN., CHILL: 2 HRS.
This recipe doubles easily for a crowd.

5 large ears white corn
¼ cup sugar
¼ cup cider vinegar
¼ cup olive oil
½ tsp. salt
½ tsp. pepper
1 medium-size red onion, diced
1 medium-size red bell pepper, diced
¼ cup coarsely chopped fresh parsley

1. Cook corn in boiling salted water in a large stockpot 3 to 4 minutes; drain. Plunge corn into ice water to stop the cooking process; drain. Cut kernels from cobs.
2. Whisk together ¼ cup sugar and next 4 ingredients in a large bowl; add corn, onion, bell pepper, and parsley, tossing to coat. Cover and chill at least 2 hours. **Makes** 6 cups.

Chocolate Fondue
fast fixin's • make ahead
PREP: 10 MIN.
Make ahead, and store in an airtight container in the refrigerator. Reheat in the microwave at LOW at 15-second intervals until thoroughly heated, stirring often.

2 (10-oz.) bittersweet or semisweet chocolate bars, coarsely chopped
3 cups whipping cream
Fresh fruit, angel food cake

1. Combine chocolate bars and whipping cream in a large microwave-safe glass bowl. Microwave at LOW until chocolate is melted and mixture is blended, stirring every 30 seconds. Keep warm in a chafing dish. Serve fondue with assorted fresh fruit or angel food cake. **Makes** 4 cups.

what's for supper?
Freshened-Up Favorites

Busy-Day Dinner #1

Serves 4

Slow-cooker Turkey Chili
orange wedges and green grapes
focaccia or cornbread crackers

Busy-Day Dinner # 2

Serves 8

Chili-Cheese-Potato Tot Casserole
mixed green salad with peppercorn-Ranch dressing (Add chopped avocado for a Southwestern touch.)
hot dinner rolls with honey butter

Try these recipes when you're craving a filling dinner. Ground turkey, bell pepper, and corn lighten up chili for the spring weather. Diced tomatoes and reduced-fat cheese, exchanged for the traditional cream soup base, do the same for a potato tot casserole. Round out the meal with a mixed green salad or fruit and hot dinner rolls. And save room for the cobbler—it's really good.

Slow-cooker Turkey Chili
PREP: 15 MIN., COOK: 8 HRS.
Choose the cooking time that best fits your schedule and slow cooker. (Newer slow cookers tend to cook faster than older models.)

1¼ lb. lean ground turkey
1 large onion, chopped
1 garlic clove, minced
1½ cups frozen corn kernels
1 red bell pepper, chopped
1 green bell pepper, chopped
1 (28-oz.) can crushed tomatoes
1 (15-oz.) can black beans, rinsed and drained
1 (8-oz.) can tomato sauce
1 (1.25-oz.) package chili seasoning mix
½ tsp. salt
Toppings: shredded Colby and Monterey Jack cheese blend, finely chopped red onion

1. Cook first 3 ingredients in a large skillet over medium-high heat, stirring until turkey crumbles and is no longer pink; drain. Spoon mixture into a 5½-qt. slow cooker; stir in corn and next 7 ingredients until well blended.
2. Cook on HIGH 4 to 5 hours or at LOW 6 to 8 hours. Serve with desired toppings. **Makes** 4 to 6 servings.

CARY HOLLADAY
MEMPHIS, TENNESSEE

Chili-Cheese-Potato Tot Casserole
PREP: 10 MIN., COOK: 10 MIN., BAKE: 1 HR.
The chili starter contains beans, chili powder, cumin, garlic, onion, and oregano, packing lots of flavor and keeping the ingredients list short.

2 lb. lean ground beef
1 onion, chopped
2 (15½-oz.) cans chili starter
1 (14½-oz.) can petite diced tomatoes
1 (11-oz.) can whole kernel corn with red and green peppers, rinsed and drained
1 (8-oz.) package reduced-fat shredded Colby and Monterey Jack cheese blend
1 (32-oz.) package frozen potato tots
¼ cup pickled sliced jalapeño peppers or 2 fresh jalapeño peppers, sliced

1. Cook ground beef and onion in a large skillet over medium-high heat, stirring until beef crumbles and is no longer pink. Drain well, and return to skillet. Stir in chili starter, tomatoes, and corn.
2. Pour mixture into a lightly greased 13- x 9-inch baking dish. Sprinkle evenly with cheese; top evenly with potato tots.
3. Bake at 350° for 1 hour or until tots are golden. Top with jalapeño slices. **Makes** 8 servings.

Note: For testing purposes only, we used Bush's Chili Magic Chili Starter Traditional Recipe and Ore-Ida Tater Tots. To kick up the flavor, substitute 1 (14½-oz.) can petite diced tomatoes with jalapeños for the petite diced tomatoes.

CYNTHIA GIVAN
FORT WORTH, TEXAS

Three Ingredients= a Sweet Treat

This cobbler is destined to become the most requested recipe at your house, as it was at our table.
Lemon Cream-Topped Blackberry Cobbler: Stir together ½ cup lemon curd and ½ cup sour cream. Cover and chill 1 hour. Bake 2 (8-oz.) packages frozen individual blackberry cobblers according to package directions. Top warm cobblers with lemon curd mixture. **Makes** 4 servings. Prep: 5 min., Chill: 1 hr., Bake: 15 min.

Note: For testing purposes only, we used Sara Lee Blackberry Cobbler Anytime (in the freezer section) and Dickinson's Lemon Curd (with jams and jellies). Store leftover curd in the fridge 5 to 7 days.

Sensational Appetizers

Host a laid-back party with no-fuss recipes and fun serving ideas.

Springtime is the perfect time to take your dining room outside. In fact, the cool night breezes, along with the twinkle of candles, delicious food, and great friends, will make you want to stay outside forever. And with neighbors stopping by to catch up on the latest, a menu of appetizers, most of which can be made ahead, becomes delectable porch fare.

Pickled Okra-Ham Rolls
make ahead
PREP: 15 MIN., CHILL: 4 HRS.

1 (16-oz.) jar pickled okra
1 (8-oz.) container whipped cream cheese with chives
½ lb. thinly sliced Virginia ham

1. Drain pickled okra, and pat dry with paper towels.
2. Spread about 3 Tbsp. whipped cream cheese on 1 side of each ham slice, leaving a ¼-inch border on all sides. Trim off ends of pickled okra. Place 2 okra, end to end, across 1 short side of each ham slice; roll up, jelly-roll fashion. Cover and chill ham rolls at least 4 hours or up to 24 hours. Slice each ham roll into 1-inch pieces before serving. **Makes** 18 appetizer servings (about 36 rolls).

FOOD FOR THOUGHT
THE JUNIOR LEAGUE OF BIRMINGHAM, ALABAMA

Catfish Poppers With Spicy Dipping Sauce
PREP: 10 MIN., FRY: 6 MIN. PER BATCH

½ tsp. salt
½ tsp. Cajun seasoning
⅔ cup all-purpose flour
1 large egg
¼ cup milk
1¾ lb. catfish fillets, cut into 1½-inch pieces
1½ cups Japanese breadcrumbs (panko)
Vegetable oil
Spicy Dipping Sauce

1. Combine first 3 ingredients; whisk together egg and milk. Dredge catfish pieces in flour mixture, and dip in egg mixture. Dredge in breadcrumbs.
2. Pour oil to a depth of ½ inch in a large skillet; heat to 375°. Fry catfish pieces, in batches, 2 to 3 minutes on each side or until golden brown. Drain on paper towels. Serve with Spicy Dipping Sauce. **Makes** 15 appetizer servings (about 45 poppers).

Spicy Dipping Sauce:
make ahead
PREP: 5 MIN.

¾ cup mayonnaise
¼ cup spicy cocktail sauce
2 tsp. fresh lemon juice
¼ tsp. ground red pepper
Old Bay seasoning (optional)

1. Stir together first 4 ingredients. Cover and chill until ready to serve. Sprinkle with Old Bay seasoning, if desired. **Makes** 1 cup.

Cindy's Cheese Wafers
make ahead
PREP: 15 MIN., CHILL: 8 HRS.,
BAKE: 16 MIN. PER BATCH

1 (10-oz.) block sharp Cheddar cheese, finely grated
½ cup butter, softened
1 tsp. ground red pepper
1 tsp. Worcestershire sauce
½ tsp. onion salt
1¾ cups all-purpose flour
Pecan halves

1. Beat cheese and butter in a large mixing bowl at medium speed with an electric mixer until blended. Add red pepper, Worcestershire sauce, and onion salt, beating just until blended. Gradually add flour, beating until mixture is blended and smooth.

2. Shape dough into 2 (10-inch-long) logs. Wrap each log in plastic wrap; chill at least 8 hours or up to 24 hours.

3. Cut logs into ¼-inch-thick slices, and place on lightly greased baking sheets. Gently press 1 pecan half into center of each slice.

4. Bake at 350° for 14 to 16 minutes or until lightly browned. Remove to wire racks, and let cool completely. **Makes** about 6½ dozen.

Olive Cheese Bites: Omit pecan halves. Drain 1 (7½-oz.) jar pimiento-stuffed olives on paper towels. Prepare cheese wafer dough as directed. Pinch off a 1-inch piece of dough. Wrap dough around 1 olive; roll in hands to form a ball, covering entire olive with dough, and place on a lightly greased baking sheet. Repeat procedure with remaining dough and olives. Bake at 350° for 15 minutes or until lightly browned. **Makes** about 4 dozen. Prep: 15 min., Bake: 15 min. per batch.

CINDY BLEDSOE CROSBY
PLANO, TEXAS

Tomato Chutney Cheesecake
make ahead
PREP: 15 MIN., CHILL: 8 HRS.

4 (8-oz.) packages cream cheese, softened and divided
2 cups shredded Cheddar cheese
½ tsp. ground red pepper
4 or 5 green onions, finely chopped
⅔ cup red tomato chutney
1 to 2 Tbsp. milk
Assorted raw vegetables
Cornbread crackers
Garnishes: chopped fresh chives or green onions, cherry tomato halves

1. Beat 3 packages cream cheese, Cheddar cheese, and red pepper at medium speed with an electric mixer until blended and smooth. Stir in green onions.

2. Spread half of cream cheese mixture into an 8-inch round cakepan lined with plastic wrap; spread top with tomato chutney, leaving a ½-inch border of cream cheese around outside edge. Spread remaining cream cheese mixture over chutney and cream cheese border. Cover and chill at least 8 hours or up to 24 hours.

3. Invert cheesecake onto a serving platter; remove plastic wrap. Stir together 1 Tbsp. milk and remaining 1 package cream cheese, stirring until spreading consistency and adding additional milk, if needed. Frost top and sides of cheesecake. Serve with vegetables and crackers. Garnish, if desired. **Makes** 18 to 20 appetizer servings.

MELANIE BACON
SHREVEPORT, LOUISIANA

Chocolate Chess Tartlets
make ahead
PREP: 20 MIN., BAKE: 25 MIN.

1½ cups sugar
3 Tbsp. unsweetened cocoa
1½ Tbsp. cornmeal
1 Tbsp. all-purpose flour
2 tsp. white vinegar
½ cup butter, melted
Dash of salt
3 large eggs, lightly beaten
5 (2.1-oz.) packages frozen mini phyllo pastry shells, thawed
Garnish: thawed frozen whipped topping

1. Stir together first 7 ingredients until blended. Add eggs, stirring well. Spoon about 1 heaping tsp. chocolate mixture into each pastry shell, and place on 2 large ungreased baking sheets.

2. Bake at 350° for 25 minutes or just until set. Remove to wire racks, and let cool completely. Garnish, if desired. **Makes** about 6 dozen.

Note: For testing purposes only, we used Athens Mini Fillo Shells. Store tartlets in an airtight container up to 3 days.

MARY CARMAN
BIRMINGHAM, ALABAMA

Streusel-Topped Lemon Shortbread Bars
family favorite
PREP: 15 MIN.; BAKE: 1 HR., 8 MIN.

2 cups all-purpose flour
3 Tbsp. sugar
½ tsp. salt
1 cup cold butter, cut into ½-inch pieces and divided
2 egg yolks
6 large eggs
2½ cups sugar, divided
1¼ cups all-purpose flour, divided
1 tsp. baking powder
4 tsp. grated lemon rind
½ cup fresh lemon juice
¼ tsp. salt
Powdered sugar

1. Combine first 3 ingredients in a food processor. Add ¾ cup butter pieces to food processor; pulse 12 to 15 times or until mixture resembles coarse meal. Chill remaining ¼ cup butter pieces. Add egg yolks; process just until mixture forms clumps. (Clumps will be moist.) Press mixture onto bottom of a lightly greased 13- x 9-inch pan.

2. Bake at 350° for 16 to 18 minutes or just until golden brown around edges. Remove pan from oven, and reduce temperature to 325°.

3. Whisk together eggs and 2 cups sugar in a large bowl until blended. Combine ½ cup flour and baking powder; whisk into egg mixture until blended. Whisk in 4 tsp. grated lemon rind and ½ cup fresh lemon juice. Immediately pour lemon mixture over hot crust in pan.

4. Bake at 325° for 20 to 25 minutes or until filling is set. Remove from oven.

5. Combine ¼ tsp. salt, remaining ½ cup sugar, and remaining ¾ cup flour. Cut in reserved ¼ cup butter pieces with a pastry blender or fork until crumbly. Sprinkle topping over hot lemon mixture, and bake 25 more minutes or just until lightly golden. Let cool completely on a wire rack. Cut into 32 (1½- x 2-inch) bars, and sprinkle evenly with powdered sugar. **Makes** 32 bars.

PEGGY SHARPE
MICHIGAN CITY, MISSISSIPPI

Fire Up the Grill Tonight

Here's a flavorful menu that your family will love.

Enjoy Southwestern flair with these recipes. They're perfect for a weeknight supper or casual entertaining (especially when you round them out with a ready-to-serve rice pouch). For a truly laid-back approach, serve the menu family style, and pile everything into warm tortillas for hearty burritos.

Test Kitchen *Notebook*

Prepare the Guacamole Sauce, cut the vegetables, and whisk together the marinade for the Easy Grilled Vegetables the night before. (The marinade starts with a bottled salad dressing.) When you're ready to cook, marinate the vegetables while you season the flank steak and prepare the grill. Grilling doesn't get much simpler than that. *Scott Jones*

EXECUTIVE EDITOR

Grilled Flank Steak With Guacamole Sauce
family favorite
PREP: 10 MIN., GRILL: 20 MIN., STAND: 5 MIN.
Find dried chipotle powder on the spice aisle of your supermarket. If you serve the flank steak without the Guacamole Sauce, reduce the chipotle powder to 1 tsp. to moderate the heat.

1 (2-lb.) flank steak, trimmed
2 tsp. dried chipotle powder
½ tsp. salt
2 tsp. minced fresh garlic
16 (8-inch) flour tortillas (optional)
Guacamole Sauce

1. Sprinkle steak evenly with chipotle powder and salt; rub with garlic.
2. Grill steak, covered with grill lid, over medium-high heat (350° to 400°) 8 to 10 minutes on each side or to desired degree of doneness. Cover loosely with aluminum foil, and let stand 5 minutes.
3. Cut steak diagonally across the grain into thin strips. Serve with tortillas, if desired, and Guacamole Sauce. **Makes** 8 servings.

Note: For testing purposes only, we used McCormick Gourmet Collection Chipotle Chile Pepper for dried chipotle powder.

Guacamole Sauce:
make ahead
PREP: 15 MIN.
Prepare this sauce up to 1 day ahead. Cover tightly with plastic wrap, and store in the refrigerator. Let stand at room temperature at least 30 minutes before serving.

2 small ripe avocados, peeled and cut
    into quarters
1 small jalapeño pepper, seeded and
    minced
1 green onion, sliced
½ cup fat-free sour cream
½ tsp. grated lime rind
¼ cup fresh lime juice
½ tsp. salt
½ tsp. sugar
¼ tsp. minced fresh garlic
Garnish: chopped green onions

1. Process first 9 ingredients in a blender or food processor 30 seconds or until smooth. Garnish, if desired. **Makes** about 1½ cups.

Easy Grilled Vegetables
PREP: 30 MIN., CHILL: 30 MIN., GRILL: 14 MIN.
If you don't have a grill wok or metal basket, feel free to place the tomatoes on skewers. (Remember to soak wooden skewers in water for at least 30 minutes before using on the grill.)

2 green bell peppers
2 yellow squash
2 zucchini
10 large fresh mushrooms
¾ cup balsamic vinaigrette
1 Tbsp. lemon pepper
¼ tsp. salt
12 cherry tomatoes

1. Cut bell peppers in half, and remove seeds. Slice squash and zucchini into ¼-inch-thick rounds. Place peppers, squash, zucchini, and mushrooms in a large shallow dish or large zip-top plastic bag.

2. Whisk together vinaigrette, lemon pepper, and salt until blended. Pour over vegetables. Cover and chill at least 30 minutes. Remove vegetables from marinade, reserving marinade.

3. Grill vegetables, covered with grill lid, over medium-high heat (350° to 400°), basting with reserved marinade. Grill peppers 7 minutes on each side or until tender; grill squash and zucchini 3 minutes on each side or until tender. Grill mushrooms 5 minutes or until tender. Grill tomatoes in a grill wok or metal basket 2 to 3 minutes or until skins begin to split. **Makes** 8 servings.

ALEXANDRA JANNUZZI
DANIEL ISLAND, SOUTH CAROLINA

quick & easy
Better Burgers

Get creative by dressing up ground round and turkey with unexpected ingredients for your next get-together. We guarantee your family and friends will rave about the results.

Make Your Burgers Better Than Ever

Black Olive Pesto and Best-Ever Cajun Seasoning are great in burgers and on chicken or fish.

Herb-Blend Turkey Burgers
fast fixin's
PREP: 10 MIN., GRILL: 12 MIN.

1 lb. lean ground turkey
¼ cup chopped fresh basil
2 tsp. grated lemon rind
¾ tsp. minced garlic
⅛ tsp. salt
4 kaiser rolls, split
Tomato slices
Shredded spinach leaves

1. Combine first 5 ingredients in a large bowl until blended. (Do not overwork meat mixture.) Shape mixture into 4 (5-inch) patties.
2. Grill, covered with grill lid, over medium-high heat (350° to 400°) 5 to 6 minutes on each side or until done.
3. Scoop out soft centers from bottom half of rolls, leaving ¼-inch-thick shells. Place burgers in shells; top evenly with tomato slices and spinach, and cover with roll tops. **Makes** 4 servings.

NORA HENSHAW
OKEMAH, OKLAHOMA

Best-Ever Cajun Seasoning
fast fixin's • make ahead
PREP: 5 MIN.
Make Cajun-Spiced Burgers by combining 3 Tbsp. seasoning with 1½ lb. ground chuck. Top them with flavorful Cajun Mayonnaise; make this by mixing ½ cup light mayonnaise with 2 tsp. seasoning.

2 Tbsp. paprika
1 Tbsp. salt
1 Tbsp. black pepper
2 tsp. garlic powder
2 tsp. onion powder
2 tsp. ground red pepper
1 tsp. dried oregano
1 tsp. dried thyme

1. Combine all ingredients. Store in an airtight container up to 6 weeks. **Makes** about ⅓ cup.

DONIA KIRCHMAN
GAINESVILLE, FLORIDA

Pesto-Topped Burgers
fast fixin's
PREP 10 MIN., GRILL: 12 MIN.

1½ lb. ground round
1 Tbsp. grill seasoning mix
4 toasted hamburger buns
Black Olive Pesto
Toppings: romaine lettuce, tomato slices

1. Combine ground round and seasoning; shape into 4 (4-inch) patties.
2. Grill, covered with grill lid, over medium-high heat (350° to 400°) 5 to 6 minutes on each side or until no longer pink in center. Serve on buns with Black Olive Pesto and desired toppings. **Makes** 4 servings.

Note: For testing purposes only, we used McCormick Grill Mates Hamburger Seasoning.

Olive Burgers: Add ¼ cup Black Olive Pesto to ground round. Grill, covered with grill lid, over medium-high heat (350° to 400°) 5 to 6 minutes on each side or until no longer pink in center. Serve on buns with desired toppings.

Black Olive Pesto
fast fixin's
PREP: 10 MIN.
Stir Black Olive Pesto into pasta or serve as an appetizer with pita chips.

1 (6-oz.) jar pitted kalamata olives, drained
1 garlic clove
1 Tbsp. olive oil
1 tsp. dried basil
2 tsp. Dijon mustard
¼ tsp. pepper

1. Process all ingredients in a food processor until a coarse paste forms, stopping to scrape down sides. **Makes** ¾ cup.

GLORIA C. MALARO
BRANFORD, CONNECTICUT

Tacos With a Twist

Try this updated version with a seafood filling and Southwest flavor.

Just about every culture has a handheld food for easy eating. Tacos are an easy grab-and-go meal from Mexico. We've filled the ones here with fish, reeling in the coastal trend of using seafood in place of the traditional beef, pork, or chicken.

Cook's Notes

While we love the fried fish flavor, we also tried baking and grilling the flounder fillets. Both are great options. Here's how to do it.

■ **Baked Flounder Fillets:** Omit oil from Spicy Fish Tacos recipe. Assemble as directed. Spray cornmeal-coated fish with vegetable cooking spray. Bake at 350° on a lightly greased rack on a baking sheet 12 minutes or until fish flakes with a fork.

■ **Grilled Flounder Fillets:** Omit oil and cornmeal from Spicy Fish Tacos recipe. Assemble as directed. Reduce salt to 1 tsp. Sprinkle fish evenly with chili powder, salt, cumin, and red pepper. Lightly grease a large piece of heavy-duty aluminum foil; line cooking grate with foil. Place fish on lightly greased side of foil; grill, covered with grill lid, over high heat (400° to 500°) 8 minutes or until fish flakes with a fork, turning once.

Spicy Fish Tacos With Mango Salsa and Guacamole

PREP: 20 MIN., FRY: 3 MIN. PER BATCH

These flavorful tacos are made with flounder seasoned with chili powder, cumin, and red pepper. It's equally delicious whether the fish is fried, baked, or grilled.

6 (6-oz.) flounder fillets
1 lime
2 Tbsp. chili powder
2 tsp. salt
2 tsp. ground cumin
½ tsp. ground red pepper
1½ cups yellow cornmeal
Vegetable oil
4 to 6 flour or corn tortillas
Mango Salsa
Guacamole
Toppings: shredded iceberg lettuce, chopped tomato
Garnishes: lime wedges, fresh cilantro sprigs

1. Place fish in a shallow dish. Squeeze juice of 1 lime over fillets.
2. Combine chili powder and next 3 ingredients. Sprinkle 1½ Tbsp. seasoning mixture evenly over fish, coating both sides of fillets. Reserve remaining seasoning mixture.
3. Combine cornmeal and reserved seasoning mixture in a shallow dish. Dredge fish fillets in cornmeal mixture, shaking off excess.
4. Pour oil to a depth of 1½ inches in a Dutch oven; heat to 350°. Fry fillets, in batches, 2 to 3 minutes or until golden brown. Drain fillets on wire racks over paper towels.
5. Break each fillet into chunks, using a fork. Place fish in warmed tortillas, and serve with Mango Salsa, Guacamole, and desired toppings. Garnish, if desired. **Makes** 4 to 6 servings.

Mango Salsa:
fast fixin's • make ahead
PREP: 15 MIN.

1 mango, chopped
1 jalapeño pepper, seeded and finely chopped
1 garlic clove, minced
1 Tbsp. fresh lime juice
1 Tbsp. finely chopped red onion
1 Tbsp. chopped fresh cilantro
¼ tsp. salt

1. Stir together all ingredients. Cover and chill until ready to serve. **Makes** 1 cup.

Guacamole:
fast fixin's • make ahead
PREP: 15 MIN.

2 ripe avocados
1 jalapeño pepper, seeded and finely chopped
1 garlic clove, minced
¼ cup sour cream
1 Tbsp. lime juice
½ Tbsp. finely chopped red onion
½ tsp. salt

1. Cut avocados in half, and discard pits. Scoop pulp into a medium bowl, and mash into chunks with a fork. Stir in chopped jalapeño and remaining ingredients, stirring well. Cover and chill avocado mixture until ready to serve. **Makes** 1⅓ cups.

Eat Outside

With a few items from the grocery store, you'll be ready for a refreshing outdoor lunch. Black Bean-and-Brown Rice Pitas, a deliciously healthful choice, uses canned and frozen vegetables for a speedy filling that can easily be made ahead.

Outdoor Lunch

Serves 6

Black Bean-and-Brown Rice Pitas

Couscous and Garbanzo Salad

Caramel Dip with apple slices

lemonade and iced tea

Black Bean-and-Brown Rice Pitas

PREP. 15 MIN., COOK: 40 MIN.
You can substitute leftover brown or white rice in these hearty sandwiches.

⅔ cup water
⅓ cup uncooked brown rice
1 (15-oz.) can black beans, rinsed and drained
1 (4-oz.) can diced green chiles
¾ cup frozen corn kernels, thawed
3 green onions, chopped
1 tsp. salt
¼ tsp. pepper
½ cup Fresh Salsa
3 pita bread rounds, halved
Romaine lettuce leaves
Plain nonfat yogurt or sour cream
Fresh Salsa

1. Bring ⅔ cup water to a boil in a small saucepan; stir in rice. Cover, reduce heat, and simmer 35 to 40 minutes or until water is absorbed and rice is tender. Cool.
2. Combine rice, black beans, green chiles, and next 5 ingredients in a large bowl; gently toss. Cover and chill, if desired.
3. Line each pita half with lettuce. Spoon rice mixture evenly into each half. Top with plain yogurt and additional Fresh Salsa. **Makes** 6 servings.

Fresh Salsa:
make ahead
PREP: 10 MIN., CHILL: 1 HR.

2 medium tomatoes, chopped
1 Tbsp. fresh lime juice
½ small red onion, diced
2 garlic cloves, minced
1 (4-oz.) can diced green chiles
2 Tbsp. chopped fresh cilantro
½ tsp. salt
¼ tsp. dried crushed red pepper

1. Combine all ingredients in a large bowl. Cover and chill at least 1 hour. **Makes** 2 cups.

Caramel Dip
fast fixin's • make ahead
PREP: 5 MIN., COOK: 5 MIN.
Store this dip in an airtight container in the refrigerator. Simply reheat in the microwave for 1 minute or until hot, stirring at 20-second intervals.

½ cup butter
1 (8-oz.) container sour cream
1 (16-oz.) package light brown sugar
2 cups coarsely chopped pecans, toasted (optional)
Apple, pear, or other fruit slices

1. Cook first 3 ingredients over low heat in a 3-qt. saucepan, stirring constantly, 5 minutes or until mixture is smooth.
2. Stir in pecans, if desired. Serve with fruit slices. **Makes** about 2 cups.

MICHELE BAKER
RICHARDSON, TEXAS

Test Kitchen Notebook

If salad is your fancy, you'll enjoy this refreshing recipe.

Couscous and Garbanzo Salad
PREP: 25 MIN., COOK: 5 MIN., STAND: 10 MIN.

1 (14½-oz.) can chicken broth
1 cup uncooked couscous
1 (15-oz.) can garbanzo beans, rinsed and drained
4 green onion tops, sliced
3 carrots, shredded
1 red bell pepper, seeded and diced
½ cup pitted kalamata olives, coarsely chopped
Mint Vinaigrette
Shredded lettuce or cabbage
1 (4-oz.) package crumbled feta cheese (optional)

1. Bring chicken broth to a boil in a saucepan; add couscous, cover, and remove pan from heat. Let stand 10 minutes.
2. Toss together couscous, beans, and next 4 ingredients in a large bowl. Drizzle with Mint Vinaigrette, gently tossing to coat. Cover and chill until ready to serve. Serve over shredded lettuce, and, if desired, sprinkle with feta just before serving. **Makes** 6 to 8 servings.

Mint Vinaigrette:
PREP: 5 MIN.

⅔ cup fresh mint, chopped
3 Tbsp. white wine vinegar
2 garlic cloves
1 tsp. Dijon mustard
¼ tsp. sugar
¼ tsp. salt
⅛ tsp. pepper
½ cup olive oil

1. Process first 7 ingredients in a food processor until minced, stopping to scrape down sides. With food processor running, add olive oil in a slow, steady stream until blended. **Makes** ¾ cup.

Shannon Sliter Satterwhite
FOODS EDITOR

Hot Cross Buns

Bake these beautiful buns—they're truly a treat. Make it a family project, or call a friend. You'll need a heavy-duty stand mixer to make these yeast rolls. If necessary, borrow one from a neighbor, and pay her back with rolls.

The recipes vary, so we baked buns until we found the right combination of spices, spice levels, dried fruit, and icing that pleased everyone at our tasting table. Have no worries about the yeast—our method avoids the step of dissolving it in a warm liquid. All the tips here ensure your success.

Hot Cross Buns

PREP: 50 MIN., COOK: 5 MIN., COOL: 20 MIN., RISE: 2 HRS., BAKE: 15 MIN.
(Pictured on page 7)

4½ to 5 cups all-purpose flour, divided
⅔ cup sugar
1 (¼-oz.) envelope rapid-rise yeast
1 tsp. salt
¾ tsp. ground nutmeg
½ tsp. ground cinnamon
1 cup milk
¼ cup water
⅓ cup unsalted butter, cut up
2 large eggs
Vegetable cooking spray
⅔ cup currants
⅓ cup golden raisins
1 Tbsp. all-purpose flour
1 egg white, lightly beaten
Hint of Lemon Icing

1. Combine 2½ cups flour, sugar, and next 4 ingredients in mixing bowl of a heavy-duty stand mixer, stirring well. Set aside.

2. Combine milk, ¼ cup water, and butter pieces in a saucepan; cook over medium heat, stirring constantly, just until butter melts. Cool 5 minutes (to 130°).

3. Pour milk mixture into flour mixture, and beat at low speed with dough hook attachment 2 minutes or until dry ingredients are moistened. Increase speed to medium; add eggs, 1 at a time, beating just until yellow disappears after each addition. Beat 3 more minutes. Reduce speed to low, and gradually beat in enough remaining flour (up to 2½ cups) to make a soft dough (dough will be sticky). Beat at medium speed with dough hook attachment 5 minutes.

Steps for Success for Hot Cross Buns

1. Use a heavy-duty stand mixer to mix and knead. The dough will be too sticky to be kneaded by hand. The dry yeast goes directly into the flour. Lightly spoon flour into a dry measuring cup; then level it with a straight-edge spatula or knife. **Don't scoop the flour directly out of the container.** Too much flour will compromise your results. A rainy, humid day will require the full 5 cups of flour; a dry, cool day will take less. Definitely start with the minimum amount.

2. It's okay to let dough rise in a glass, metal, or pottery bowl. Spray the top of the dough with vegetable cooking spray to prevent the dough from drying out and crusting, which could inhibit rising.

3. Your oven is the ideal warm, draft-free place for the dough. Heat the oven, and then turn it off. Allow oven to cool to 85° or below. Put dough in oven, along with a cup of hot water to add moisture and keep the dough soft. Leave on the oven light, and close the door.

4. You'll have to work those arms to knead in the raisins and currants. But you can goof off during the rising times.

5. It's tempting to pinch off dough to shape rolls, but don't. Pinching will stretch the dough, resulting in tough rolls. Instead, use a bench scraper or sharp knife to cut dough in half; then cut each in half again, and so on until you have 20 pieces. Let rolls rise one more time, and bake.

6. Let baked rolls cool 15 minutes before icing them—otherwise the icing will melt, rather than hold the shape of a cross.

4. Scrape dough into a large bowl coated with cooking spray, and lightly spray the top of the dough.

5. Cover and let rise in a warm place (85°), free from drafts, 1 hour. (Dough will almost double in bulk.)

6. Punch dough down, and turn out onto a floured surface. Combine ⅔ cup currants, ⅓ cup raisins, and 1 Tbsp. flour, stirring to coat. Knead about one-fourth of fruit mixture at a time into dough until all fruit mixture is evenly dispersed.

7. Divide dough into 20 equal portions; shape each portion into a 2-inch ball. Evenly space dough balls on a parchment paper-lined 15- x 10-inch jelly-roll pan; cover and let rise in a warm place (85°), free from drafts, 1 hour or until doubled in bulk. Gently brush tops with beaten egg white.

8. Bake at 375° for 15 minutes or until buns are a deep golden brown and sound hollow when tapped. Cool buns 15 minutes in pan on a wire rack.

9. Spoon icing into a zip-top plastic freezer bag; snip a ¼-inch piece from 1 corner of bag, and pipe an "X" on top of warm buns, forming a cross. Serve remaining icing with buns, if desired. **Makes** 20 buns.

Hint of Lemon Icing:
fast fixin's
PREP: 5 MIN.

2 cups powdered sugar
1 Tbsp. butter, melted
3 Tbsp. milk
½ tsp. grated lemon rind
¼ tsp. vanilla extract

1. Whisk together all ingredients until smooth. **Makes** ½ cup.

Make the World's Easiest Candy

Now's the time to enjoy Rock Candy again. It's probably been years (dating back to your first school science experiment) since you last thought of it, but making Rock Candy is as simple as boiling water and sugar. It's also something the entire family can enjoy. The hardest part is waiting for the crystals to form—about two weeks. (But it sure is fun to watch.)

In addition to eating them out of hand, dip the sugar-coated strands into hot beverages such as coffee, tea, and cider for ideal sweeteners (especially when the candy is made with your favorite flavoring). We recommend cinnamon oil as well as extracts such as mint, strawberry, and orange.

Tip: To promote the formation of sugar crystals, avoid touching or adjusting the string once you've poured the syrup mixture into jars. Typical of most candy-making, this recipe involves very hot liquid, so it requires adult supervision.

Rock Candy
PREP: 15 MIN., COOK: 20 MIN., STAND: 14 DAYS
Crystals will form on the surface of the liquid. This is not a problem. Simply break them up, and scoop them out to enjoy.

4 (12-oz.) glass canning jars
4 (7-inch) pieces clean kitchen string
4 wooden skewers or pencils
4½ cups sugar
2 cups water
10 drops red liquid food coloring *
⅛ tsp. cinnamon oil *
2 tsp. vanilla extract

1. Arrange jars in a large Dutch oven, and fill with enough water to cover jars by 1 inch. Bring to a boil over medium-high heat; boil 2 minutes (this is to sterilize). Carefully remove jars with kitchen tongs to a wire rack; cool completely, and dry.

2. Tie strings around centers of wooden skewers or pencils. Place 1 string in each jar, resting skewer or pencil across rim of jar, and making sure strings do not touch bottoms of jars. Set aside.

3. Bring sugar and 2 cups water to a boil in a large saucepan over medium-high heat, stirring occasionally; boil, stirring occasionally, 5 minutes. Remove from heat. Stir in food coloring, cinnamon oil, and vanilla. Let stand 5 minutes.

4. Pour about 1 cup syrup mixture carefully around skewer into each jar. Loosely cover with aluminum foil (including skewer); pierce aluminum foil several times with a skewer or knife. Let stand 10 to 14 days or until crystals form on strings. (Occasionally break up hard sugar layer on surface using a wooden skewer.) Remove strings from jars, and suspend strings between jars until crystals are dry (about 1 hour). Remove strings from skewers or pencils. **Makes** 4 candies.

*Substitute 10 drops of your favorite shade of food coloring for red food coloring, and 2 tsp. of your favorite flavored extract, such as mint, strawberry, or orange, for cinnamon oil.

CHARLIE CUNDIFF
LOS ANGELES, CALIFORNIA

Watch the crystals grow. The examples on the strings are after 3 days, 1 week, and 2 weeks.

from our kitchen

Eggs are the ultimate fast food. Versatile and inexpensive, they can be enjoyed anytime of day in dozens of different ways. The secret to great eggs is in the timing. Whether boiled, scrambled, or baked in a casserole, it's important not to overcook them.

For perfect scrambled eggs every time, melt a little butter in a nonstick skillet over medium heat, and add lightly beaten eggs. Cook eggs, without stirring, until eggs begin to set on the bottom. Draw a spatula across the bottom of the skillet to form large curds. Continue cooking until eggs are thickened but still moist (do not stir constantly). Remove eggs from heat, and serve immediately.

Ready-Made Meringues

Weather affects the texture of meringues, so when the hot, humid days of summer settle in, you might want to opt for a box of store-bought ones rather than making your own. These crisp little cookies come in a variety of flavors and sizes and make a quick start for some fun desserts.

Partially dip whole meringue cookies into melted chocolate, and sprinkle with finely chopped toasted pecans; or coarsely crush the cookies, and layer with sliced strawberries and whipped cream. Use meringues to garnish a cheesecake or pie, or create a border for a layer cake.

Tips and Tidbits

Special Deliveries

Make-ahead breakfast casseroles are great for entertaining and are all the more festive when baked in colorful ramekins. These individual portions of bread pudding can be prepared and baked immediately or refrigerated overnight and baked the next morning.

Most bread-and-egg-based casseroles can be baked in individual servings. Prepare the recipe as directed; divide evenly between lightly greased ramekins, filling about three-fourths full.

Cinnamon-Raisin Bread Puddings:

Tear 1 (16-oz.) loaf of sliced cinnamon-raisin bread into 1-inch pieces; place in a large bowl. Whisk together 1 (14-oz.) can sweetened condensed milk, ¾ cup hot water, 4 large eggs, and 2 tsp. vanilla; pour over bread pieces, tossing gently to coat. Divide bread mixture evenly between 6 (10-oz.) lightly greased ramekins or custard cups. Bake at 350° for 25 to 30 minutes or until a knife inserted in center comes out clean. Stir together 1 cup powdered sugar and 2 Tbsp. milk or maple syrup; drizzle evenly over bread puddings. Serve warm. **Makes** 6 servings. Prep: 10 min., Bake: 30 min.

may

Front-Yard Fiesta

Grab your sombreros, and bring on the flavor—it's time to party.

Party Menu

Serves 12

Beer 'Garitas (triple the recipe)

Smoky Hot Sauce, Tomatillo Sauce

tortilla chips

Smoked Lemon-Chipotle Chickens

Wheat Berry Tabbouleh

green salad with Avocado-Ranch Dressing

Lemon Chill With Raspberry Sauce

Welcome, amigos, to a fabulous Cinco de Mayo party. Julie and Kevin Nisbet know how to entertain with fun style—from a sombrero-decorating contest to the luscious Lemon Chill With Raspberry Sauce finale. Their Irmo, South Carolina, home invites spring and early summer entertaining.

These busy parents rely on friends to pull off a mucho grande get-together. "We never deny anyone the fun of hanging lanterns in trees, setting tables, and lugging ice from car to cooler," says Julie, flashing a smile of appreciation.

Just before sunset, the guests head to the Nisbet home to enjoy a unique menu. Olé!

Beer 'Garitas
fast fixin's
PREP: 5 MIN.

For a bolder flavor, use a dark beer. Serve in 16-oz. mason jars for fun.

1 cup frozen limeade concentrate, thawed
1 cup tequila
½ cup orange liqueur
Crushed ice
½ to 1 cup cold beer

1. Stir together first 3 ingredients until well blended. Fill 4 medium glasses with crushed ice. Pour limeade mixture evenly into glasses. Add beer to taste. **Makes** 4 servings.

Note: For testing purposes only, we used Minute Maid Frozen Concentrate for Limeade, José Cuervo Especial tequila, and Triple Sec for orange liqueur.

Smoky Hot Sauce
make ahead
PREP: 10 MIN., COOK: 35 MIN., CHILL: 8 HRS.

If you prefer a milder sauce, remove the chipotle pepper before pureeing the tomato mixture.

1 large onion, chopped
1 Tbsp. olive oil
4 tsp. minced garlic
5 medium tomatoes, coarsely chopped (about 1½ lb.)
¾ cup water
1 chicken bouillon cube
1 canned chipotle pepper in adobo sauce
2 Tbsp. adobo sauce from can
1 Tbsp. balsamic vinegar
1 tsp. hot sauce
¼ tsp. salt
Tortilla chips

1. Sauté onion in hot olive oil in a large saucepan over medium-high heat 5 minutes or until softened; add garlic, and sauté 1 minute. Stir in tomatoes and next 7 ingredients. Bring to a boil; reduce heat, and simmer, stirring occasionally, 25 minutes. Remove from heat, and cool slightly.
2. Remove chipotle pepper, if desired. Process tomato mixture in a food processor or blender until smooth. Cover and chill at least 8 hours. Serve at room temperature with tortilla chips. **Makes** about 3 cups.

Tomatillo Sauce
make ahead
PREP: 10 MIN., COOK: 20 MIN., CHILL: 8 HRS.

Buy tomatillos, or Mexican green tomatoes, that are firm with tight-fitting, papery green skins.

1¼ lb. small tomatillos (about 30)
1 medium onion, chopped
1 Tbsp. olive oil
4 tsp. minced garlic
1 cup water
1 jalapeño pepper, minced
½ cup chopped fresh cilantro
1 Tbsp. fresh lime juice
1 tsp. salt
Tortilla chips

1. Remove husks from tomatillos; wash thoroughly.
2. Sauté onion in hot olive oil in a large saucepan over medium-high heat 5 minutes or until softened. Add garlic, and sauté 1 minute. Stir in tomatillos, 1 cup water, and jalapeño; bring to a boil. Reduce heat to medium; cover and simmer, stirring occasionally, 10 to 12 minutes or until tomatillos are softened. Remove from heat; cool slightly.
3. Process tomatillo mixture, cilantro, lime juice, and salt in a food processor or blender until smooth. Cover and chill at least 8 hours. Serve at room temperature with tortilla chips. **Makes** about 3½ cups.

Smoked Lemon-Chipotle Chickens

PREP: 45 MIN., SOAK: 30 MIN.,
SMOKE: 4 HRS., STAND: 10 MIN.
On a chilly day, the chicken will take longer to cook—up to 45 minutes more. Don't skip the step of tying the chicken with string; the more compact the chicken, the better the smoking results will be, according to Kevin.

1 small sweet onion, quartered
8 large garlic cloves, peeled
¾ cup fresh lemon juice
¼ cup olive oil
3 Tbsp. white vinegar
3 chicken bouillon cubes
3 canned chipotle peppers in adobo sauce
2 Tbsp. adobo sauce from can
2 tsp. salt, divided
3 (4½-lb.) whole chickens
Kitchen string
2½ cups hickory or oak wood chips

1. Process first 8 ingredients and ¾ tsp. salt in a food processor or blender until smooth, stopping to scrape down sides. Set mixture aside.
2. Remove excess skin from necks and cavities of chickens, if desired. Starting at large cavities, loosen skin from breasts and legs by inserting fingers and gently pushing between skin and meat. (Do not completely detach skin.)
3. Place chickens in a large roasting pan. Using a bulb baster, squeeze lemon-chipotle mixture evenly into chicken cavities and under skin on breasts and legs.
4. Sprinkle chickens evenly with remaining 1¼ tsp. salt. Tuck wings under, if desired. Position the center of a 3-foot piece of kitchen string under back of 1 chicken near tail. Wrap string around legs and around body of chicken. Tie securely at neck. Repeat with remaining chickens.
5. Soak wood chips in water for at least 30 minutes. Set aside.
6. Prepare smoker according to manufacturer's directions. Bring internal temperature to 225° to 250°, and maintain temperature for 15 to 20 minutes. Place chickens on upper cooking grate; cover with smoker lid.
7. Cook chickens, maintaining the temperature inside the smoker between 225° and 250°, for 1 hour and 30 minutes. Drain reserved wood chips, and place on coals. Cover with smoker lid; smoke chickens 2 hours to 2 hours and 30 minutes more or until a meat thermometer inserted into thighs registers 175°. Remove chickens from smoker; cover loosely with aluminum foil, and let stand 10 minutes or until thermometer registers 180° before slicing. **Makes** 12 servings.

Wheat Berry Tabbouleh
make ahead

PREP: 20 MIN., SOAK: 24 HRS., COOK: 1 HR.
Find hard red or white wheat berries at health food stores, specialty grocery stores, and some supercenters. You can visit **www.bobsredmill.com** *to locate a store near you or to order the berries online. This fabulous side dish is great cold, warm, or at room temperature.*

3 cups hard wheat berries*
12 cups water
2 medium tomatoes, seeded and chopped
1 cup pine nuts, toasted
⅔ cup chopped dried apricots
⅔ cup chopped dried mango
⅔ cup sweetened dried cranberries
⅔ cup golden raisins
⅔ cup chopped fresh cilantro
⅓ cup diced celery
⅓ cup fresh lime juice
1 Tbsp. olive oil
1 tsp. salt
1 tsp. freshly ground pepper
Garnish: fresh parsley sprigs

1. Soak wheat berries in 12 cups water in a large Dutch oven 24 hours.
2. Bring wheat berries and soaking water to a boil over medium-high heat. Reduce heat, cover, and simmer 45 to 50 minutes or until tender. Drain wheat berries, and cool.
3. Stir together wheat berries, tomatoes, and next 11 ingredients until well blended. Serve immediately, or cover and chill up to 2 days. Garnish, if desired. **Makes** 12 servings.

*Substitute 3 cups quick-cooking barley for wheat berries, if desired. Sauté barley in 2 Tbsp. hot olive oil in a Dutch oven over medium-high heat 5 to 6 minutes or until barley is lightly browned. Stir in 6 cups water. Bring to a boil over medium-high heat; reduce heat, cover, and simmer 10 to 12 minutes or until tender. Remove from heat, and let stand 5 minutes. Drain barley, and cool. Stir together barley, tomatoes, and next 7 ingredients. Stir in lime juice and next 3 ingredients just before serving. Garnish, if desired.

Avocado-Ranch Dressing

make ahead

PREP: 10 MIN., CHILL: 1 HR.

Toss with a salad of romaine lettuce, grape tomatoes, and toasted sunflower seeds.

2 ripe avocados
1 cup Ranch dressing
½ cup milk
½ cup sour cream
¼ cup fresh lime juice
2 tsp. hot sauce
½ tsp. pepper
¼ tsp. garlic powder

1. Cut avocados in half; scoop pulp into a food processor or blender.
2. Add 1 cup Ranch dressing and remaining ingredients to food processor. Process until avocado mixture is smooth, stopping to scrape down sides. Cover and chill at least 1 hour or up to 3 days. **Makes** about 2⅔ cups.

Lemon Chill With Raspberry Sauce

freezeable • make ahead

PREP: 20 MIN., FREEZE: 1 HR., STAND: 15 MIN.

For a fancier presentation, freeze in lemon cups (see tip box at right).

2 (10-oz.) packages frozen raspberries
   in syrup, thawed
2 cups whipping cream
1 (12-oz.) can frozen lemonade
   concentrate, thawed
½ cup sweetened condensed milk
3 Tbsp. fresh lemon juice
Garnish: fresh mint sprigs

1. Process raspberries in a blender or food processor until smooth, stopping to scrape down sides. Press mixture through a wire-mesh strainer into a bowl, using the back of a spoon to squeeze out juice. Discard pulp and seeds. Cover sauce, and chill until ready to serve.
2. Place 12 foil baking cups in muffin pans; discard paper liners in cups.
3. Beat whipping cream at medium-high speed with an electric mixer until soft peaks form. Reduce speed to

medium-low; gradually add lemonade concentrate, sweetened condensed milk, and lemon juice, beating until blended. Increase speed to medium-high, and beat until stiff peaks form. Spoon into 12 foil baking cups in muffin pans by heaping one-third cupfuls. Freeze at least 1 hour or until whipped cream mixture is firm.
4. Place on serving plates, and let stand at room temperature 10 to 15 minutes or until slightly softened. Serve with raspberry sauce. Garnish, if desired. **Makes** 12 servings.

Note: For testing purposes only, we used Minute Maid Frozen Concentrate for Lemonade. To make ahead, freeze as directed for 1 hour; cover whipped cream mixture in pans or lemon cups with plastic wrap. Wrap pans or lemon cups securely with heavy-duty aluminum foil. Freeze pans up to 4 days and lemon cups up to 1 day.

How to Make a Lemon Cup

Cut stem end off each lemon (top one-third of lemon). Save tops to garnish plates, if desired. Cut a small slice off bottoms of lemons to allow them to stand upright. Run a grapefruit knife around lemon between the peel and pulp, loosening pulp. Scoop out pulp with a spoon. Remove excess juice from inside shells by scraping against the sides with a spoon.

Cook Smart; Eat Well

Pick a day when there's some breathing room to cook, and end up with two nights' worth of suppers. To start, we put together a Sunday menu and cooked two pork loin roasts. We served one and then saved the other for a second night's one-dish meal.

Two Speedy Suppers

Serves 6

Zesty Pork Loin With
Apricot-Pan Sauce

Potato-and-Carrot Amandine

mixed salad greens

—and—

Pork-and-Soba Noodle Bowl

orange slices

fortune cookies

Double-Duty Marinade

fast fixin's

PREP: 10 MIN.

Be sure to whisk the marinade well and divide it quickly, so that the oil evenly distributes into each portion. You will use half the mixture to marinate the pork and the other half as a sauce for the Pork-and-Soba Noodle Bowl. Discard any leftover marinade after marinating the meat.

1 cup lite soy sauce
6 Tbsp. fresh lime juice (about 4 limes)
½ cup olive oil
¼ cup water
¼ cup honey
2 garlic cloves, pressed
4 tsp. minced fresh ginger
½ tsp. dried crushed red pepper

1. Whisk together all ingredients. **Makes** about 2½ cups.

Zesty Pork Loin With Apricot-Pan Sauce

family favorite

PREP: 10 MIN., CHILL: 6 HRS., BAKE: 1 HR., STAND: 10 MIN.

2 (2-lb.) boneless pork loin roasts
1¼ cups Double-Duty Marinade
½ tsp. pepper
⅓ cup apricot preserves

1. Place pork roasts in a large zip-top plastic freezer bag, and add 1¼ cups Double-Duty Marinade, turning to coat. Seal and chill 6 hours or up to 24 hours.
2. Remove pork from marinade, discarding marinade. Sprinkle pork evenly with pepper. Place on a lightly greased rack in an aluminum foil-lined roasting pan.
3. Bake at 400° for 50 minutes to 1 hour or until a meat thermometer inserted into thickest portion registers 155°. Remove pan from oven, and cover with foil; let stand 10 minutes or until thermometer registers 160°. Remove roasts from pan, reserving drippings in pan; cut 1 roast into slices. Cover sliced roast, and keep warm. Cover and chill remaining whole roast.
4. Combine ¼ cup pan drippings with ⅓ cup apricot preserves in a small microwave-safe bowl. Microwave at HIGH 1 minute or until melted, stirring once. Serve with sliced pork. **Makes** 6 servings.

Speedy Tuesday Supper

Use the second cooked pork roast and reserved marinade within 2 days to make Pork-and-Soba Noodle Bowl. You've got your protein, carbs, and veggies covered, so simply serve with orange slices and fortune cookies.

Pork-and-Soba Noodle Bowl

PREP: 15 MIN., COOK: 20 MIN.

Mollie Bell of Cedar Park, Texas, sent us her meatless version of this recipe. We added the pork to make it heartier.

12 oz. soba (buckwheat) noodles *
2 tsp. salt
1 (12-oz.) package fresh stir-fry vegetables
1 cooked Zesty Pork Loin, cut into strips
1¼ cups Double-Duty Marinade
1 Tbsp. sesame oil
Toppings: chopped peanuts, chopped fresh cilantro, thinly sliced red onion

1. Cook noodles with 2 tsp. salt in a large Dutch oven according to package directions. Stir vegetables into noodles during the last 3 minutes of cooking time; drain.
2. Cook pork strips, marinade, and oil in Dutch oven over medium-high heat 5 minutes or until thoroughly heated. Stir in noodle mixture, tossing to coat. Serve immediately with desired toppings. **Makes** 6 to 8 servings.

Note: For testing purposes only, we used Eat Smart Vegetable Stir-Fry.

***** Substitute 1 (10-oz.) package Chinese noodles or 1 (13.75-oz.) package whole wheat thin spaghetti, if desired.

MOLLIE BELL
CEDAR PARK, TEXAS

Potato-and-Carrot Amandine

family favorite

PREP: 15 MIN., BAKE: 50 MIN.

Amandine, often misspelled as "almondine," is a French word meaning "garnished with almonds." We also tested this recipe using presliced refrigerated potatoes, but they did not brown, so we recommend buying fresh whole potatoes.

8 small red potatoes, quartered (about 1¼ lb.)
1 (16-oz.) package baby carrots
3 Tbsp. olive oil
1 tsp. salt
½ tsp. pepper
¼ cup slivered almonds, toasted
2 Tbsp. chopped fresh parsley
1 Tbsp. lemon juice (optional)

1. Place potatoes and carrots in a single layer on a 15- x 10-inch jelly-roll pan. Drizzle with 3 Tbsp. olive oil, tossing to coat; sprinkle evenly with salt and pepper.
2. Bake at 400° for 45 to 50 minutes or until vegetables are tender and lightly browned, stirring once. Transfer vegetables to a serving bowl; stir in almonds, parsley, and, if desired, lemon juice. Toss to coat. **Makes** 6 servings.

---

what's for supper?

Fast and Fun Food

Stop here for a quick, stylish meal. We took a lesson from Peg Lee. She's raised a family, now cooks for one, and manages the Cooking School for Central Market, a top-notch grocery store in Houston (**www.centralmarket.com**). Her sellout sauté class on what she calls "the fastest way to cook" features a dish called piccata. "A hot pan, poultry or meat, simple seasonings, lemon juice, and parsley, and voilà—a scrumptious dinner," she says. Make Peg's 10-minute-prep soufflés after supper, and you'll have a creative meal tonight.

Turkey Piccata
fast fixin's

PREP: 15 MIN., COOK: 15 MIN.

Pull out your largest nonstick skillet for this recipe. (An electric one would be great.) Don't crowd the pan, and add each turkey cutlet slowly so temperature will stay hot.

1 lb. boneless turkey breast cutlets ✱
½ cup all-purpose flour
1 tsp. salt
1 tsp. white pepper
3 Tbsp. butter, divided
2 Tbsp. olive oil
½ cup dry white wine
⅓ cup fresh lemon juice
1 Tbsp. drained capers
6 lemon slices, halved
1 Tbsp. chopped fresh flat-leaf parsley

1. Place turkey between 2 sheets of heavy-duty plastic wrap, and flatten to ¼-inch thickness, using a rolling pin or the flat side of a meat mallet.
2. Combine flour, salt, and pepper in a shallow dish. Dredge turkey cutlets in flour mixture.
3. Melt 1 Tbsp. butter in 1 Tbsp. olive oil in a large nonstick skillet over medium-high heat. Add half of turkey, and cook 2 to 3 minutes on each side or until golden brown. Remove turkey from skillet, and place on a wire rack in a jelly-roll pan in a 200° oven to keep warm. Repeat with remaining turkey, 1 Tbsp. butter, and 1 Tbsp. oil as needed.
4. Stir wine and next 3 ingredients into skillet; cook over medium-high heat 2 minutes or until sauce is slightly thickened. Remove from heat; stir in remaining 1 Tbsp. butter. Place turkey on a serving platter; pour sauce over turkey, and sprinkle evenly with parsley. **Makes** 4 to 6 servings.

✱ Substitute 1 lb. boneless, skinless chicken thighs or thin-cut boneless pork chops, if desired.

So-Easy Chocolate Soufflés
fast fixin's

PREP: 10 MIN., BAKE: 20 MIN.

Before baking, run your thumb around edges of ramekins or measuring cups (see step 3) to help the soufflés rise higher.

2 tsp. butter
2 Tbsp. sugar
1 (4-oz.) semisweet chocolate baking bar
⅓ cup seedless strawberry jam
1½ tsp. vanilla extract
4 egg whites

1. Grease bottom and sides of 4 (6-oz.) ramekins or 4 (1-cup) stainless steel dry measuring cups evenly with butter. Lightly coat bottom and sides with sugar, shaking out excess. Place cups on a baking sheet; set aside.
2. Microwave chocolate and jam in a small microwave-safe bowl at MEDI-UM (50% power) 1½ minutes, stirring at 30-second intervals until melted. Stir in vanilla.
3. Beat egg whites at high speed with an electric mixer until soft peaks form. Stir about one-third of egg whites into chocolate mixture. Fold chocolate mixture into remaining egg whites. Spoon evenly into ramekins. Run tip of thumb around edges of each ramekin, wiping clean and creating a shallow indentation around outside edge of egg mixture.
4. Bake at 350° for 18 to 20 minutes or until soufflés rise and begin to brown on top. **Makes** 4 servings.

Note: For testing purposes only, we used Ghirardelli Semi-Sweet Chocolate Baking Bar.

After-Supper Treat

Turn off the TV, and instead watch Peg's So-Easy Chocolate Soufflés rise in the oven. Bake them in ramekins or 1-cup stainless steel dry measuring cups. (**Tip:** Don't use measuring cups with a nonstick coating, and don't use plastic.)

Try Our Best Crab Cakes

Special Occasion Menu

Serves 4

Crab Cakes With Lemon Rémoulade

mixed baby greens

green beans with grape tomatoes

So-Easy Chocolate Soufflés
(recipe at left)

Test Kitchen Specialist Rebecca Kracke Gordon and her husband chose their favorite recipes from the last 40 years of *Southern Living* for their anniversary dinner.

Make-Ahead Timeline

The Day Before:
1. Shape crab cakes.
2. Blanch green beans in boiling water for about 8 minutes; shock in ice water to stop the cooking process. Cover and chill.
3. Prepare Lemon Rémoulade.

The Day of:
1. Sauté crab cakes as directed.
2. To reheat green beans, toss with halved grape tomatoes and melted butter in a warm skillet; season with fresh thyme, salt, and pepper.
3. Toss mixed baby greens in olive oil, salt, and pepper.
4. Stir together the soufflé ingredients just before eating, bake them while you're eating, and enjoy them warm from the oven.

Crab Cakes With Lemon Rémoulade

PREP: 20 MIN., COOK: 30 MIN., CHILL: 1 HR.

Just before serving, toss mixed baby greens with olive oil, salt, and pepper to taste, as many restaurants do. Place crab cakes on top.

3 Tbsp. butter, divided
1 large red bell pepper, finely chopped
½ medium onion, finely chopped
1 cup saltine cracker crumbs (finely crushed)
½ cup mayonnaise
1 large egg, lightly beaten
2 tsp. Old Bay seasoning
2 tsp. Worcestershire sauce
¾ tsp. dry mustard
¼ tsp. hot sauce
1 lb. fresh lump crabmeat, drained and picked
1 Tbsp. vegetable oil
Lemon Rémoulade
Garnishes: mixed baby greens, lemon wedges, parsley sprigs

1. Melt 2 Tbsp. butter in a large non-stick skillet over medium heat; add bell pepper and onion, and sauté 10 minutes or until tender. Remove from heat; stir in cracker crumbs and next 6 ingredients. Gently stir in crabmeat. Shape mixture into 8 patties; cover and chill at least 1 hour or up to 24 hours.
2. Melt ½ Tbsp. butter with ½ Tbsp. oil in a large skillet over medium-high heat. Cook 4 crab cakes 4 to 5 minutes on each side or until golden. Drain on paper towels. Repeat procedure. Serve with Lemon Rémoulade; garnish, if desired. **Makes** 4 servings.

Lemon Rémoulade:

PREP: 10 MIN., CHILL: 30 MIN.

2 cups mayonnaise
¼ cup Creole mustard
2 garlic cloves, pressed
2 Tbsp. chopped fresh parsley
1 Tbsp. fresh lemon juice
2 tsp. paprika
¾ tsp. ground red pepper

1. Whisk together all ingredients until blended. Cover and chill 30 minutes or up to 3 days. **Makes** about 2¼ cups.

Fresh Vegetable Sides

Take advantage of spring and summer, and enjoy these veggies at their peak.

White Cheddar-and-Squash Casserole

make ahead

PREP: 20 MIN., COOK: 30 MIN., BAKE: 20 MIN., STAND: 10 MIN.

4 Tbsp. butter, divided
1 medium onion, chopped
3 lb. yellow squash, sliced
2 tsp. salt, divided
¾ tsp. pepper
2 Tbsp. all-purpose flour
1½ cups milk
1 (10-oz.) block white Cheddar cheese, shredded
2 Tbsp. Italian-seasoned breadcrumbs
Garnish: chopped fresh parsley

1. Melt 2 Tbsp. butter in a large skillet over medium-high heat; add onion, and sauté 5 minutes or until tender. Add squash, 1½ tsp. salt, and pepper; cover and cook, stirring occasionally, 15 minutes or until squash is tender. Remove from heat; drain well.
2. Melt remaining 2 Tbsp. butter in a saucepan over medium-high heat; whisk in flour until smooth. Whisk in milk. Bring to a boil; reduce heat, and simmer 2 minutes. Remove from heat; whisk in cheese and remaining ½ tsp. salt. Gently stir together squash and cheese mixture in a large bowl. Pour into a lightly greased 11- x 7-inch baking dish. Sprinkle breadcrumbs evenly over top.
3. Bake at 400° for 20 minutes or until bubbly. Let stand 10 minutes before serving. Garnish, if desired. **Makes** 6 to 8 servings.

Note: To make ahead, prepare recipe as directed; do not top casserole with breadcrumbs. Cover and chill overnight. Remove from refrigerator; let stand 45 minutes. Uncover and top with breadcrumbs; bake as directed.

Orange-Mint Peas

PREP: 5 MIN., COOK: 10 MIN.

Even though fresh is always better, frozen peas work well in this recipe. You don't even have to change the cooking times.

2 Tbsp. butter
3 cups fresh early green peas *
1 Tbsp. grated orange rind
2 Tbsp. fresh orange juice
1 Tbsp. chopped fresh mint
½ tsp. salt
¼ tsp. pepper
Garnish: orange rind curls

1. Melt butter in a medium saucepan over medium heat; add peas, rind, and juice. Cook, stirring occasionally, 8 to 10 minutes or until thoroughly heated. Stir in fresh mint, salt, and pepper. Garnish, if desired. **Makes** 4 servings.

* Substitute 3 cups frozen early green peas, if desired.
BETH GEWANT
BIRMINGHAM, ALABAMA

Hot Boiled Cabbage

PREP: 10 MIN., COOK: 30 MIN.

1 large cabbage (about 2½ lb.), cut into bite-size pieces
2 green tomatoes, chopped
1 large green bell pepper, chopped
1 cup water
⅓ cup hot pickled banana peppers, chopped
1 Tbsp. vegetable oil
1 tsp. salt
½ tsp. pepper

1. Bring all ingredients to a boil in a large nonstick skillet over medium-high heat. Cover, reduce heat, and simmer, stirring occasionally, 25 minutes or until cabbage is tender. **Makes** 6 servings.

ELMER BURGESS
KNOXVILLE, TENNESSEE

Springtime Entertaining

Stacked sandwiches frosted with fluffy, seasoned cream cheese add flavor to any celebration.

With warm weather calling you, Frosted Party Sandwiches are a timeless choice to kick off spring get-togethers. We mixed-and-matched several of our favorite salad recipes for a fun and festive variety.

Serve the sandwiches for brunch with fresh fruit, an egg casserole, and purchased sweet rolls. For lunch, simply add a crisp salad and picnic-style side dishes. Whatever the occasion, you'll be set to entertain with ease.

Step-by-Step: Ice Tray

We tried baby carrots for this project, but some were too short and slid into the water. The carrots create small cavities in the ice to hold your choice of flowers.

Materials:
Whole carrots
Paring knife
Vegetable cooking spray
13- x 9-inch pan
Water
Self-sealing plastic wrap
Heavy-duty tape
Flowers

Step 1: Cut carrots into 4-inch pieces; spray with vegetable cooking spray.
Step 2: Fill pan with water. Cover top of pan with self-sealing plastic wrap. Place 2 strips of tape about ½ inch apart on the plastic wrap ½ inch from inside edge on each short side of pan. Using the paring knife, evenly cut Xs, smaller than the diameter of the carrots, in between strips of tape on each side. Fit carrots into Xs; secure with tape, if necessary.
Step 3: Place pan on level rack in freezer, and freeze at least 24 hours. Remove plastic wrap, carrots, and, if necessary, tape. Run tap water over ice block to remove from pan. The frozen carrots will be soft and easy to dig out of the ice with a small spoon, if necessary. Place your choice of flowers in ice cavities.

Frosted Party Sandwiches
make ahead
PREP: 30 MIN., CHILL: 1 HR.
Make these sandwiches the night before your celebration. An electric knife works really well to cut the sandwiches, but a serrated knife will also do the trick.

1 cup Chicken Salad
12 whole wheat bread slices, crusts removed
1 cup Egg Salad
1 cup purchased pimiento cheese
1 (8-oz.) tub chive-and-onion cream cheese
1 (8-oz.) package cream cheese, softened
2 tsp. milk
Garnishes: celery leaves, paprika, shredded Cheddar cheese

1. Spread ⅓ cup Chicken Salad evenly on 1 side of 3 bread slices. Stack Chicken Salad-topped slices; top with 1 bread slice. Repeat procedure with 4 more bread slices and Egg Salad. Repeat procedure with remaining bread slices and pimiento cheese. (You will have 3 stacked sandwiches.)
2. Beat cream cheeses and milk at medium speed with an electric mixer until smooth. Spread over top and sides of each stack. Cover and chill at least 1 hour or up to 24 hours. Garnish chicken salad sandwich with celery leaves; egg salad sandwich with paprika; and pimiento cheese sandwich with Cheddar cheese, if desired. **Makes** 10 to 12 servings.
JANE WHEELER
PONTE VEDRA BEACH, FLORIDA

Chicken Salad:

PREP: 15 MIN., COOK: 35 MIN.,
STAND: 15 MIN., CHILL: 4 HRS.

1½ lb. skinned and boned chicken
  breasts
2 (14-oz.) cans chicken broth
¾ cup finely chopped celery
½ cup finely chopped green bell pepper
¼ cup finely chopped red onion
1 cup mayonnaise
¾ tsp. salt
¼ tsp. ground black pepper
¼ tsp. ground red pepper

1. Place chicken breasts in a large skillet; add broth. Cover and bring to a boil over medium-high heat. Reduce heat to medium-low, and simmer, covered, 30 minutes or until done. Remove chicken from skillet, and let stand 15 minutes or until cool to touch. Pulse chicken in food processor until finely chopped, stopping to scrape down sides.
2. Combine chicken, celery, bell pepper, and onion in a large bowl. Stir mayonnaise and next 3 ingredients into chicken mixture. Cover and chill at least 4 hours. Store any remaining chicken salad in an airtight container up to 1 week in refrigerator. **Makes** 4 cups.

TERRI MATHEWS
LEEDS, ALABAMA

Egg Salad:

fast fixin's • make ahead
PREP: 10 MIN.

4 large hard-cooked eggs, chopped
¼ cup mayonnaise
1 Tbsp. mustard
⅛ tsp. salt
⅛ tsp. pepper

1. Stir together all ingredients. Cover and chill until ready to serve. Store any remaining egg salad in an airtight container up to 1 week in refrigerator. **Makes** 1¼ cups.

JANE WHEELER
PONTE VEDRA BEACH, FLORIDA

Help Yourself to Tacos

Easy Taco Bar

Serves 8

Slow-cooker Beef Tacos
favorite toppings
Mexican Slaw
Black Beans and Yellow Rice

Meals are easier—and tastier—with this menu. Plus, you can freeze the filling for other meals.

Slow-cooker Beef Tacos

freezeable • make ahead
PREP: 20 MIN.; COOK: 6 HRS., 10 MIN.
We brown the beef before slow-cooking to add color and enhance flavor.

2 lb. boneless beef chuck roast, cut into
  1-inch cubes
1 tsp. salt
1 Tbsp. vegetable oil
1 Tbsp. chili powder
1 (6-oz.) can tomato paste
2 cups beef broth
1 small white onion
1 (8-oz.) can tomato sauce
½ medium-size green bell pepper
1 tsp. ground cumin
½ tsp. pepper
Flour or corn tortillas, warmed
Toppings: shredded Cheddar or
  Monterey Jack cheese, sour cream

1. Sprinkle beef with salt. Cook in batches in hot oil in a Dutch oven over medium-high heat 5 to 7 minutes or until browned on all sides. Remove beef, reserving drippings in Dutch oven. Add 1 Tbsp. chili powder to Dutch oven; cook, stirring constantly, 1 minute. Stir in tomato paste, and cook, stirring constantly, 2 minutes. Add 2 cups beef broth, and stir, scraping bits from bottom of Dutch oven.

Return beef to Dutch oven, and stir.
2. Place beef mixture in a 4½-quart slow cooker. Add onion and next 4 ingredients. Cook on HIGH 4 hours or on LOW 6 hours or until beef is tender. Serve with warm tortillas and desired toppings. **Makes** 8 servings.

Mexican Slaw

make ahead
PREP: 15 MIN., CHILL: 4 HRS.

⅓ cup olive oil
2 Tbsp. orange juice
2 Tbsp. lime juice
1 garlic clove, minced
½ tsp. ground cumin
½ tsp. salt
½ tsp. pepper
1 (10-oz.) package finely shredded
  cabbage
½ lb. jicama, shredded (2 cups)
1 large carrot, shredded (about ½ cup)
1 jalapeño pepper, seeded and diced
¼ cup chopped fresh cilantro

1. Whisk together first 7 ingredients in a large bowl. Add shredded cabbage and remaining ingredients, and toss to coat. Cover and chill slaw mixture at least 4 hours. **Makes** 8 servings.

SHANNON RALEY
VESTAVIA HILLS, ALABAMA

Black Beans and Yellow Rice

PREP: 10 MIN., COOK: 25 MIN.

1 (10-oz.) package yellow rice mix
2 (15-oz.) cans black beans, rinsed and
  drained
1 (14½-oz.) can Mexican-style stewed
  tomatoes
1 (4.5-oz.) can chopped green chiles
1 cup (4 oz.) shredded Monterey Jack
  cheese with peppers

1. Prepare rice mix according to package directions.
2. Heat beans, tomatoes, and chiles in a large skillet over medium heat. Add rice and cheese, stirring until cheese melts. **Makes** 8 servings.

DEBORAH DIETZLER ANDERSON
ATHENS, GEORGIA

Simple, Stylish Salads

Toss one of these salads to add great taste and good health to any meal, or make them extra-special with a great presentation.

Orange-Avocado Salad
fast fixin's
PREP: 20 MIN.
Create unique "croutons" by cutting a French baguette into roughly 3-inch portions. Hollow out each portion, leaving a ¼-inch-thick shell. Place the shells upright on 4 serving plates, and fill with salad. Arrange additional salad around the shells.

2 medium avocados, sliced
2 navel oranges, peeled and sectioned
1 (5-oz.) bag mixed baby greens
3 slices prosciutto, cut into thin strips
¼ cup thinly sliced red onion
⅓ cup chopped walnuts, toasted
Honey-Balsamic Vinaigrette

1. Arrange avocado slices and orange sections on mixed greens on a large serving platter. Sprinkle evenly with prosciutto, red onion, and walnuts. Drizzle with desired amount of Honey-Balsamic Vinaigrette. **Makes** 4 servings.

Honey-Balsamic Vinaigrette:
PREP: 5 MIN.
You can use regular balsamic vinegar if you don't have white, but it will change the color of the vinaigrette.

½ cup olive oil
¼ cup white balsamic vinegar
1 Tbsp. honey
½ tsp. salt
¼ tsp. pepper

1. Whisk together all ingredients in a small bowl. **Makes** ¾ cup.

Iceberg Stack
PREP: 20 MIN.

1 small head iceberg lettuce
3 radishes, grated
1 cucumber, peeled, seeded, and thinly sliced
½ pt. grape tomatoes, halved
½ (4-oz.) container alfalfa sprouts
4 bacon slices, cooked and crumbled
Creamy Blue Cheese Dressing

1. Cut lettuce into 4 (1-inch-thick) slices, reserving ends for another use. Place 1 slice on each of 4 salad plates. Sprinkle radishes evenly over lettuce. Layer cucumber, tomatoes, alfalfa sprouts, and bacon evenly over radishes. Drizzle with Creamy Blue Cheese Dressing. **Makes** 4 servings.

Creamy Blue Cheese Dressing:
PREP: 5 MIN.

1 (8-oz.) container whipped garlic-and-herb cream cheese
⅓ cup buttermilk
¼ cup sliced green onion tops
½ tsp. grated lemon rind
1 tsp. fresh lemon juice
¼ tsp. salt
1 (4-oz.) container crumbled blue cheese

1. Process first 6 ingredients in a blender until smooth. Stir in crumbled blue cheese. Cover and chill dressing until ready to serve. **Makes** about 1½ cups.

Fix-and-Freeze Lasagna

Great for families or company, lasagna is one popular dish with its layers of zesty sauces and gooey cheeses. Our readers shared their favorite recipes, showing how easy it is to mix-and-match ingredients to personalize this casserole. Better still, you can fix and freeze any of them (see the box on the opposite page for make-ahead instructions).

Classic Lasagna
freezeable • make ahead
PREP: 20 MIN.; COOK: 50 MIN.; STAND: 25 MIN.; BAKE: 1 HR., 10 MIN.
Homemade sauce is time-consuming but worth the extra effort. Make it on a weekend, and freeze it to enjoy later with lasagna or your favorite pasta.

2 medium onions, chopped
2 Tbsp. olive oil, divided
4 garlic cloves, minced
1 lb. lean ground beef
1 (14.5-oz.) can basil, garlic, and oregano diced tomatoes
2 (6-oz.) cans tomato paste
1 (8-oz.) can basil, garlic, and oregano tomato sauce
1 bay leaf
1 tsp. dried Italian seasoning
1¼ tsp. salt, divided
¾ tsp. pepper, divided
12 lasagna noodles, uncooked
8 cups boiling water
1 (16-oz.) container ricotta cheese
2 large eggs, lightly beaten
¼ cup grated Parmesan cheese
2 (6-oz.) packages part-skim mozzarella cheese slices
Garnish: chopped fresh parsley

1. Sauté onion in 1 Tbsp. hot oil in a large skillet over medium-high heat 5 minutes or until tender. Add garlic; sauté 1 minute. Add beef; cook, stirring occasionally, 10 minutes or until beef crumbles and is no longer pink. Drain beef mixture, and return to skillet. Stir in diced tomatoes, next 4 ingredients, 1 tsp. salt, and ½ tsp. pepper; bring to a boil. Reduce heat; cover, and simmer, stirring occasionally, 30 minutes. Remove and discard bay leaf; set meat sauce aside.
2. Place lasagna noodles in a 13- x- 9-inch pan. Carefully pour 8 cups boiling water and remaining 1 Tbsp. olive oil over noodles. Let stand 15 minutes.
3. Stir together ricotta cheese, eggs, Parmesan cheese, remaining ¼ tsp. salt, and remaining ¼ tsp. pepper until blended.
4. Spoon half of the meat sauce mixture into a lightly greased 13- x 9-inch baking dish. Shake excess water from noodles, and arrange 6 noodles over meat sauce; top with half of ricotta

mixture and 1 package mozzarella cheese slices. Repeat layers once.

5. Bake, covered, at 350° for 55 minutes. Uncover and bake 10 to 15 more minutes or until bubbly. Let lasagna stand 10 minutes before serving. Garnish, if desired. **Makes** 8 to 10 servings.

COLETTE GIRARD
BALTIMORE, MARYLAND

Eggplant Parmesan Lasagna

freezeable • make ahead
PREP: 50 MIN., COOK: 1 HR., BAKE: 40 MIN., STAND: 20 MIN.

2 (26-oz.) jars tomato, garlic, and onion
    pasta sauce
¼ cup chopped fresh basil
½ tsp. dried crushed red pepper
½ cup whipping cream
1 cup grated Parmesan cheese
1 large eggplant (about 1½ lb.)
½ tsp. salt
¼ tsp. black pepper
3 large eggs, lightly beaten
3 Tbsp. water
1 cup all-purpose flour
6 Tbsp. olive oil
6 lasagna noodles, cooked and
    drained *
1 (15-oz.) container part-skim ricotta
    cheese
2 cups (8 oz.) shredded mozzarella
    cheese

1. Cook first 3 ingredients in a 3½-quart saucepan over medium-low heat 30 minutes. Remove from heat; stir in cream and Parmesan cheese. Set aside.
2. Peel eggplant, and cut crosswise into ¼-inch-thick slices. Sprinkle slices evenly with salt and black pepper. Stir together eggs and 3 Tbsp. water. Dredge eggplant in flour; dip into egg mixture, and dredge again in flour, shaking to remove excess.
3. Cook eggplant, in batches, in 1½ Tbsp. hot oil in a large nonstick skillet over medium-high heat 4 minutes on each side or until golden brown and slightly softened. Drain on paper towels. Repeat with remaining oil and eggplant, wiping skillet clean after each batch, if necessary.

4. Layer 3 lasagna noodles lengthwise in a lightly greased 13- x 9-inch baking dish. Top with one-third tomato sauce mixture and half of eggplant. Dollop half of ricotta cheese evenly on eggplant in dish; top with half of mozzarella. Repeat layers with remaining noodles, one-third sauce mixture, remaining eggplant, and remaining ricotta. Top with remaining one-third sauce mixture and mozzarella cheese.
5. Bake at 350° for 35 to 40 minutes or until golden brown. Let stand 20 minutes before serving. **Makes** 8 to 10 servings.

Note: For testing purposes only, we used Bertolli Vidalia Onion With Roasted Garlic pasta sauce.

*Substitute 6 no-cook lasagna noodles, if desired. Prepare recipe as directed, reserving last half of mozzarella for top. Bake, covered, at 350° for 45 minutes. Sprinkle top with reserved cheese; bake, uncovered, for 20 more minutes or until golden brown. DEB REYNOLDS
PEORIA, ILLINOIS

Turkey-Mushroom Lasagna

freezeable • make ahead
PREP: 15 MIN.; COOK: 10 MIN.; BAKE: 1 HR., 10 MIN.; STAND: 10 MIN.

1 lb. ground Italian-style turkey
    sausage, casings removed
1 (26-oz.) jar tomato-and-basil pasta
    sauce
1 (8-oz.) can mushroom slices, drained
1 (32-oz.) container low-fat ricotta
    cheese
1 large egg, lightly beaten
2 Tbsp. dried parsley flakes
1 Tbsp. grated Parmesan cheese
¼ tsp. salt
10 lasagna noodles, uncooked
4 cups (16 oz.) shredded mozzarella
    cheese

1. Cook sausage in a lightly greased nonstick skillet over medium-high heat, stirring occasionally, 8 to 10 minutes or

until turkey is no longer pink. Drain turkey, and return to skillet. Stir in pasta sauce and mushrooms; set aside.
2. Stir together ricotta cheese and next 4 ingredients in a large bowl until blended.
3. Arrange 5 uncooked lasagna noodles in a single layer in a lightly greased 13- x 9-inch baking dish; layer evenly with half of the turkey mixture, half of the ricotta cheese mixture, and 2 cups shredded mozzarella cheese. Repeat layers once.
4. Bake, covered, at 375° for 55 minutes; uncover and bake 10 to 15 more minutes or until lasagna is bubbly. Let stand 10 minutes before serving. **Makes** 8 to 10 servings.

Note: For testing purposes only, we used Barilla Tomato & Basil Sauce.

NANCY HILL
NORMAL, ILLINOIS

To Make Ahead

Line a 13- x 9-inch baking dish with heavy-duty nonstick aluminum foil, allowing several inches of foil to extend over sides. Prepare recipe as directed in foil-lined dish. Freeze unbaked lasagna until firm. Remove from baking dish by holding edges of foil; fold foil over lasagna. Wrap in additional foil, making sure it's tightly sealed to keep out the air. Freeze up to 1 month.

The day before serving, remove lasagna from the freezer. Remove foil, and place lasagna in a lightly greased 13- x 9-inch baking dish. Cover and thaw overnight in the refrigerator. Bake as directed. (Note: Lasagna can also be baked frozen. Plan to double the baking times.)

Host a Tasting Party

Southern Tapas Night

Serves 6

Polenta Rounds With
Black-eyed Pea Topping

Grits-Stuffed Greens

Smoky Hot-Buffalo Chicken Pizzas

Ice-cream Crêpes

Share a meal with friends and sample all of these miniature main dishes. Small-plate entrées, also known as tapas, are popular in restaurants right now. You can taste a variety of recipes at one time without overeating. Try our uniquely Southern choices such as Grits-Stuffed Greens and Polenta Rounds With Black-eyed Pea Topping. Ice-cream Crêpes topped with hot fudge are the perfect low-fat finale. Every recipe gives you the nutritional value for each small serving. These little nibbles were made for sharing, so pass the plate.

Polenta Rounds With Black-eyed Pea Topping

fast fixin's

PREP: 15 MIN., COOK: 11 MIN.

Find prepared polenta in the produce section of the supermarket.

½ (16-oz.) tube refrigerated sun-dried
    tomato polenta, cut into 6 even
    slices
Vegetable cooking spray
1 (15-oz.) can black-eyed peas, rinsed
    and drained
½ cup finely chopped onion
¼ cup water
¼ tsp. ground red pepper
¼ tsp. salt
½ cup diced tomatoes
4 Tbsp. chopped fresh cilantro
¼ cup light sour cream

1. Cook polenta rounds in a large non-stick skillet coated with cooking spray over medium-high heat 4 minutes on each side or until lightly browned. Remove from heat, and keep warm.
2. Wipe pan with paper towel, spray with cooking spray, and cook peas and next 4 ingredients over medium heat 3 minutes or until water evaporates. Remove from heat; stir in tomatoes and 3 Tbsp. cilantro. Spoon warm black-eyed pea mixture over polenta rounds, and top evenly with sour cream. Sprinkle with remaining 1 Tbsp. cilantro. **Makes** 6 appetizer servings.

Note: For testing purposes only, we used Melissa's Organic Sun-Dried Tomato Polenta.
SUE WINDHAM
BROOKHAVEN, MISSISSIPPI

Per serving: Calories 92 (11% from fat); Fat 1.1g (sat 0.6g, mono 0g, poly 0.2g); Protein 4g; Carb 17g; Fiber 3g; Chol 3mg; Iron 1.6mg; Sodium 347mg; Calc 16mg

Grits-Stuffed Greens

make ahead

PREP: 20 MIN., COOK: 35 MIN., STAND: 5 MIN.

Egg rolls have gone Southern! Assemble these up to a day ahead, and refrigerate. Just steam them for an extra 5 minutes when ready to serve.

6 large fresh collard green leaves
1 cup 2% reduced-fat milk
1 cup low-sodium fat-free chicken
    broth
½ cup uncooked quick-cooking grits
¾ cup (3 oz.) shredded 2% sharp
    Cheddar cheese
1 Tbsp. butter
½ tsp. garlic salt
¼ tsp. pepper
Pepper sauce

1. Rinse collard greens. Trim and discard thick stems from bottom of collard green leaves (about 2 inches); place greens in a steamer basket over boiling water. Cover and steam 10 to 12 minutes or until greens are tender. Cool completely.
2. Bring milk and broth to a boil in a medium saucepan over medium-high heat. Gradually stir in grits. Cover, reduce heat to low, and simmer, stirring occasionally, 5 minutes or until grits are thickened. Remove from heat; stir in cheese and next 3 ingredients, stirring until cheese is melted. Let stand 5 minutes.
3. Place 1 collard leaf on a flat surface, and spread out sides. Spoon ⅓ cup grits toward bottom center of leaf. Fold 1 side of leaf over filling. Fold opposite side of leaf over filling. Beginning at 1 short side, roll up leaf tightly, jelly-roll fashion. Repeat with remaining collard leaves and grits.
4. Place bundles in a single layer in a steamer basket; steam, covered, 10 to 15 minutes or until thoroughly heated. Serve with pepper sauce. **Makes** 6 appetizer servings.

Note: For testing purposes only, we used Louisiana Hot Peppers in Vinegar for pepper sauce.
RENEÉ POTEET
AUSTIN, TEXAS

Per serving: Calories 133 (39% from fat); Fat 5.9g (sat 3.7g, mono 0.8g, poly 0.2g); Protein 6.3g; Carb 12.5g; Fiber 0.3g; Chol 18mg; Iron 0.6mg; Sodium 312mg; Calc 156mg

20-Minute Pizzas

Don't be intimidated by these homemade pizzas. The convenience of deli chicken and store-bought crusts makes this recipe a cinch. Hot sauce, blue cheese dressing, and Colby-Monterey Jack cheese add the enticing flavor.

Smoky-Hot Buffalo Chicken Pizzas

PREP: 10 MIN., BAKE: 10 MIN.

2 cups diced deli-roasted chicken breast
3 Tbsp. chipotle hot sauce
1 tsp. butter, melted
8 Tbsp. low-fat blue cheese dressing, divided
2 (7-inch) prebaked pizza crusts
½ cup (2 oz.) shredded 2% Colby-Monterey Jack cheese blend
2 green onions, thinly sliced (optional)

1. Stir together chicken, hot sauce, and butter in a microwave-safe bowl. Microwave at HIGH 45 seconds or until heated.
2. Spread 3 Tbsp. blue cheese dressing evenly over each pizza crust, leaving a 1-inch border around edges. Top evenly with chicken mixture. Sprinkle with cheese.
3. Bake directly on oven rack at 450° for 8 to 10 minutes or until crusts are golden and cheese is melted. Drizzle remaining 2 Tbsp. dressing evenly over pizzas; sprinkle with green onions, if desired. Cut each pizza into 3 wedges. **Makes** 6 appetizer servings.

Note: For testing purposes only, we used Mama Mary's Gourmet Pizza Crusts. For a softer crust, bake pizza on a pizza pan or baking sheet.

Per serving: Calories 278 (29% from fat); Fat 8.9g (sat 2.7g, mono 0.7g, poly 0.4g); Protein 20.9g; Carb 27.1g; Fiber 2.6g; Chol 48mg; Iron 0.8mg; Sodium 395mg; Calc 80mg

Ice-cream Crêpes

fast fixin's

PREP: 10 MIN.

This recipe makes 3 crêpes to be shared by 6 people. Scoop ice cream into ⅓ cupfuls, and freeze on a baking sheet until ready to assemble.

3 Tbsp. light hot fudge topping
3 (7-inch) prepared French crêpes
1 cup low-fat chocolate ice cream
½ cup raspberries
1 Tbsp. powdered sugar

1. Warm fudge topping according to package directions; set aside.
2. Microwave French crêpes at HIGH 10 seconds.
3. Spoon ⅓ cup chocolate ice cream in center of 1 crêpe, and wrap sides of crêpe around ice cream. Place seam side down on a serving dish. Repeat procedure with remaining ice cream and crêpes. Drizzle 1 Tbsp. warm fudge topping over each crêpe, and top evenly with raspberries; sprinkle evenly with powdered sugar. Serve immediately. **Makes** 6 appetizer servings.

Note: For testing purposes only, we used Smucker's Toppings Light Hot Fudge and Frieda's French Style Crêpes.

Per serving: Calories 80 (11% from fat); Fat 1g (sat 0.3g, mono 0g, poly 0g); Protein 1.8g; Carb 16.8g; Fiber 1.2g; Chol 4mg; Iron 0.4mg; Sodium 67mg; Calc 39mg

Bake It Quick

The hardest part of making these breads is waiting until they're cool enough to eat. You won't even need a mixer. Pop open a can of refrigerated French bread dough, and get a fast start on a hot and crusty loaf of Sausage Bread. Stir up a batch of Biscuit Breadsticks, or bake a pan of Hush Puppy Muffins. All these breads are ready for the oven in 15 minutes or less.

Sausage Bread

PREP: 10 MIN., COOK: 5 MIN., BAKE: 30 MIN., STAND: 10 MIN.

1 (1-lb.) package hot ground pork sausage
1 (11-oz.) can refrigerated French bread dough
1½ cups shredded pizza cheese blend

1. Cook sausage in a large nonstick skillet over medium-high heat, stirring until sausage crumbles and is no longer pink. Remove from pan; drain well, pressing between paper towels.
2. Unroll dough into a rectangular shape on a lightly greased baking sheet; sprinkle evenly with sausage and cheese. Beginning with 1 long side, roll up, jelly-roll fashion. Turn seam side down on baking sheet, and pinch ends to secure filling inside. Cut 3 (¼-inch-deep) slits across top of dough with a sharp paring knife.
3. Bake at 350° for 30 minutes or until browned. Remove from oven; let stand 10 minutes before slicing. **Makes** 6 servings.

Note: For testing purposes only, we used Pillsbury Crusty French Loaf.

DONNA TEAL
PLANO, TEXAS

Biscuit Breadsticks

PREP: 10 MIN., BAKE: 14 MIN.

Pair these cheesy breadsticks with a warm bowl of marinara sauce for dipping.

1½ cups all-purpose flour
2 tsp. sugar
2 tsp. baking powder
1 tsp. salt
¾ cup milk
3 Tbsp. butter, melted
1 cup shredded mozzarella cheese

1. Stir together first 4 ingredients. Gradually add milk, stirring to form a soft dough.
2. Turn dough out on a lightly floured surface, and knead lightly 5 or 6 times. Pat or roll dough into an 8- x 4-inch rectangle. Cut lengthwise into 8 (½-inch-wide) strips. Arrange strips on a lightly greased baking sheet; brush evenly with melted butter.
3. Bake at 450° for 10 to 12 minutes or until golden brown. Remove from oven, and sprinkle breadsticks evenly with mozzarella cheese. Return to oven, and bake 1 to 2 minutes or until cheese is melted. **Makes** 8 servings.

DANA M. HEBERT
WELSH, LOUISIANA

Hush Puppy Muffins

PREP: 10 MIN., BAKE: 10 MIN.

⅔ cup cornmeal
⅓ cup all-purpose flour
1 tsp. baking powder
½ tsp. salt
½ small onion, minced
⅓ cup fat-free milk
1 large egg, beaten
1 Tbsp. vegetable oil
⅛ tsp. pepper

1. Combine first 4 ingredients in a medium bowl. Add onion and remaining ingredients, stirring just until blended. Spoon batter evenly into lightly greased muffin cups in miniature muffin pans, filling three-fourths full.
2. Bake at 450° for 10 minutes or until muffins are golden brown. **Makes** 1½ dozen.

POLLY BLOODWORTH
ATKINSON, NORTH CAROLINA

Breakfast Anytime

Enjoy one of these comforting selections morning, noon, or night. The time is always right for breakfast.

From weeknight dinners to easy, relaxed weekend entertaining, the morning meal is always a hit. Here's a new way to enjoy an egg casserole. We even have a time-saving Kitchen Express version for when you're especially busy. Expand your lineup of favorites with these recipes.

Brunch for a Bunch

Serves 10 to 12

Blueberry-Honey Breakfast Shake (make 5 times) and orange juice

Southwest Brunch Casserole

fruit salad

biscuits

Blueberry-Honey Breakfast Shake

fast fixin's

PREP: 5 MIN.

½ cup fresh or frozen blueberries
½ cup low-fat vanilla yogurt
½ cup low-fat milk
2 Tbsp. honey
5 ice cubes

1. Process all ingredients in a blender until smooth. Serve immediately. **Makes** 2 servings.

NORA HENSHAW
OKEMAH, OKLAHOMA

Southwest Brunch Casserole

family favorite

PREP: 25 MIN., COOK: 15 MIN., BAKE: 30 MIN.

Start the Chile-Cheese Sauce first, and then begin the casserole. We don't recommend egg substitute for this recipe.

1 (16 oz.) package mild ground pork sausage
¼ cup chopped onion
12 large eggs, lightly beaten
Chile-Cheese Sauce
2 cups self-rising flour
⅓ cup vegetable oil
⅓ cup evaporated milk
1 large egg, lightly beaten
½ tsp. chili powder
1½ cups (6 oz.) shredded sharp Cheddar cheese or Monterey Jack cheese with peppers
2 Tbsp. chopped fresh cilantro or parsley

1. Cook sausage and onion in a large nonstick skillet over medium-high heat, stirring until sausage crumbles and is no longer pink. Reduce heat to medium; add eggs, and cook, without stirring, until eggs begin to set on bottom. Gently stir to slightly break up eggs. Cook, stirring occasionally, until eggs are thickened but still moist. (Do not overstir as this will form small, dry pieces.) Remove from heat; stir in Chile-Cheese Sauce. Spoon into a lightly greased 13- x 9-inch baking dish; set aside.
2. Stir together flour and next 4 ingredients until a dough forms. Turn

dough out onto a lightly floured surface; knead 3 or 4 times.

3. Roll dough into a 12-inch square; sprinkle evenly with shredded cheese and cilantro. Roll up, jelly-roll fashion, and cut into 12 (1-inch-thick) slices. Place dough slices over egg mixture, spacing evenly.

4. Bake at 400° for 25 to 30 minutes or until golden. **Makes** 10 to 12 servings.

Kitchen Express: Prepare sausage, egg, and Chile-Cheese Sauce mixture as directed; spoon into a lightly greased 13- x 9-inch baking dish. Top evenly with 12 frozen Southern-style biscuits. Bake at 400° for 25 to 30 minutes or until golden. **Note:** For testing purposes only, we used Pillsbury Southern Style Oven Baked Biscuits, located in the freezer section of the supermarket.

Chile-Cheese Sauce:
PREP: 10 MIN., COOK: 10 MIN.

2 Tbsp. butter or margarine
2½ Tbsp. all-purpose flour
2 cups milk
1 cup (4 oz.) shredded Cheddar cheese
1 (4.5-oz.) can chopped green chiles
½ tsp. salt
¼ tsp. pepper

1. Melt butter in a heavy saucepan over medium-low heat; add flour, whisking until smooth. Cook, whisking constantly, 1 minute. Increase heat to medium, and gradually add milk; cook, whisking constantly, until slightly thickened. Remove from heat; add cheese and remaining ingredients, stirring until cheese melts. Keep warm. **Makes** about 3 cups.

Strawberry Shortcake

True shortcake is basically a big, sweet biscuit. You can bake the biscuits ahead and freeze them, wrapped in foil and stored in a zip-top freezer bag. Defrost them the morning of the day you plan to serve them. Cut and sugar the berries in the morning as well, and store them in the fridge until you're ready for them. Whip the cream up to two hours before serving. (If you prefer your shortcake warm, reheat the biscuits in a 350° oven for 5 to 7 minutes.)

Classic Strawberry Shortcake
PREP: 20 MIN., STAND: 2 HRS., BAKE: 15 MIN., CHILL: 2 HRS.
If the berries are very sweet, decrease the sugar to suit your taste. Drop the dough easily by using a lightly greased ⅓-cup dry measure. (Pictured on page 5)

2 (16-oz.) containers fresh strawberries, quartered
¾ cup sugar, divided
¼ tsp. almond extract (optional)
1 cup whipping cream
2 Tbsp. sugar
2¾ cups all-purpose flour
4 tsp. baking powder
¾ cup cold butter, cut up
2 large eggs, lightly beaten
1 (8-oz.) container sour cream
1 tsp. vanilla extract
Garnish: fresh mint sprigs

1. Combine strawberries, ½ cup sugar, and, if desired, almond extract. Cover berry mixture, and let stand 2 hours.
2. Beat whipping cream at medium speed with an electric mixer until foamy; gradually add 2 Tbsp. sugar, beating until soft peaks form. Cover and chill up to 2 hours.
3. Combine flour, remaining ¼ cup sugar, and baking powder in a large bowl; cut butter into mixture with a pastry blender or 2 forks until crumbly.

4. Whisk together eggs, sour cream, and vanilla until blended; add to flour mixture, stirring just until dry ingredients are moistened. Drop dough by lightly greased ⅓ cupfuls onto a lightly greased baking sheet. (Coat cup with vegetable cooking spray after each drop.)
5. Bake at 450° for 12 to 15 minutes or until golden.
6. Split each shortcake in half horizontally. Spoon about ½ cup berry mixture onto each shortcake bottom; top each with a rounded Tbsp. chilled whipped cream, and cover with tops. Serve with remaining whipped cream. Garnish, if desired. **Makes** 8 servings.

Strawberry Jam Shortcakes: Prepare recipe as directed. Before topping shortcake bottoms with strawberry mixture, stir together ¼ cup strawberry jam and 2 Tbsp. chopped fresh mint. Spread cut sides of bottom shortcake halves evenly with jam mixture. Proceed with recipe as directed.

Cut cold butter into the flour mixture with a pastry blender. When the butter melts, it creates steam that makes the pastry light and flaky. Tip: If you don't have a pastry blender, use 2 forks.

The mixture is the right consistency when the flour and butter form clumps the size of small peas.

from our kitchen

Winning Tips and Tidbits

Increase your chances of becoming a cook-off finalist this year with this advice from our judges and Test Kitchens professionals.

■ Follow the rules and guidelines. We receive many wonderful recipes that would have been finalists, but they were disqualified because they didn't meet the category requirements. For example, if you enter a recipe in the new Super-Quick Family Favorites category, make sure the hands-on prep time is less than 20 minutes. It might be a terrific recipe, but if it takes 45 minutes to assemble the ingredients, we won't be able to consider it as a finalist. With a fast prep time of just 15 minutes, last year's Kids Love It! Finalist Crispy Ginger-and-Garlic Asian Turkey Lettuce Wraps (pictured left) was a big hit with our staff and judges.

■ Recipes are selected based on taste, appearance, and appeal to our readers. Dishes don't need to be complicated. We're just as likely to choose a quick-and-easy recipe with a unique combination of flavors as a recipe with a long list of hard-to-find ingredients and complex procedures. The end result needs to justify not only the cost of the ingredients, but also the amount of time spent preparing the recipe.

■ Have a friend or relative prepare your recipe before you send it in to make sure it reads correctly. Give the exact measurement for each ingredient. Be sure the instructions for using each ingredient are included in the body of the recipe. Be specific about pan sizes, procedures, and cook times.

■ If you have a recipe that fits the specifications for more than one category, go ahead and enter it twice. For example, a great-tasting cake or pie might be suitable for both Your Best Recipe and Southern Desserts. A Super-Quick Family Favorite might also be Healthy and Good for You.

Finishing Touches

Visual appeal can often be the deciding factor when we're judging two equally delicious recipes, so add a note to your entry that describes creative garnishes and serving ideas. For example, Brand Winner Balsamic Steaks With Blue Cheese-Pecan Confetti (below) is everyday-easy to prepare, yet the addition of fresh thyme makes it special enough for entertaining. And be sure to share any personal tips and secrets that make your recipe special. Do you always add a handful of hickory chips to the fire before grilling? Is frequent basting the key to your perfectly roasted chicken? Do you partially bake the crust on your pecan pie before pouring in the filling or use only Granny Smith apples in that cobbler everyone can't get enough of? Let us know!

june

Make-Ahead Backyard Party

Try 'em all, or sample a few of these recipes. Either way, you can enjoy the picnic as much as your guests.

Glorious Texas Hill Country Menu

Serves 8

Cold Marinated Shrimp and Avocados

Roast Pork Loin With Peach Glaze served with Chunky Peach Chutney

Green Bean-and-New Potato Salad

Marinated Cherry Tomatoes

Tequila Mojitos

bakery-bought decorated cookies

You have to be really quick to catch up with Rebecca Rather. This always-on-the-go Texan might be on a nationwide tour teaching cooking classes, running a marathon, preparing the menu for a charity dinner, or serving up mighty fine food at her Rather Sweet Bakery & Cafe in Fredericksburg.

Here, Rebecca offers some new recipes, developed just for *Southern Living* readers. She's packed a picnic, and we're off in a blue pickup truck to a friend's home for fly-fishing, canoeing, and fun and games. This relaxing day by the Pedernales River is topped off with wonderful food.

Cold Marinated Shrimp and Avocados
make ahead
PREP: 20 MIN., CHILL: 1 HR.

If making this ahead, get all the ingredients (except the avocados) ready to combine; place in individual zip-top plastic bags, and store in the refrigerator. Once you arrive at your destination, peel and chop the avocados; gently stir together up to 2 hours before serving, and chill.

1 lb. large cooked, peeled shrimp
2 medium avocados, chopped
1 cup fresh corn kernels
¼ cup chopped fresh cilantro
2 Tbsp. chopped red onion
Lime Vinaigrette
Garnishes: fresh cilantro leaves, red onion slices

1. Combine first 5 ingredients. Gently stir in Lime Vinaigrette to coat. Cover and chill at least 1 hour. Garnish, if desired. **Makes** 8 appetizer servings.

Lime Vinaigrette:
fast fixin's
PREP: 5 MIN.

½ cup fresh lime juice
¼ cup honey
1 garlic clove, pressed
½ tsp. salt
¼ tsp. pepper
⅓ cup olive oil

1. Whisk together first 5 ingredients. Gradually whisk in olive oil until blended. **Makes** about ¾ cup.

Roast Pork Loin With Peach Glaze
make ahead
PREP: 15 MIN., BAKE: 53 MIN., STAND: 15 MIN.
Make this recipe the day before; then cover and chill. Unwrap, cut into slices, and wrap for travel. Transfer to a platter just before serving. This recipe easily doubles for a crowd and can be served with rolls to make sandwiches.

1 (4-lb.) boneless pork loin roast, trimmed
1 Tbsp. olive oil
1 tsp. salt
½ tsp. pepper
½ cup peach preserves
Chunky Peach Chutney (optional)
Garnishes: sliced fresh peaches, fresh rosemary sprigs

1. Rub pork loin roast on all sides with 1 Tbsp. olive oil, and sprinkle evenly with 1 tsp. salt and ½ tsp. pepper.
2. Place roast on a rack in an aluminum foil-lined broiler pan.
3. Bake at 450° for 45 minutes. Brush roast evenly with ½ cup peach preserves. Bake roast 8 more minutes or until a meat thermometer inserted into thickest portion registers 155°. Remove from oven, and let stand 15 minutes or until thermometer reaches 160° before slicing.

4. Serve roast with Chunky Peach Chutney, if desired, and garnish, if desired. **Makes** 8 servings.

Chunky Peach Chutney
make ahead
PREP: 25 MIN.; COOK: 1 HR., 20 MIN.
This ingredients list looks long, but after chopping and measuring everything, it all goes into a Dutch oven to simmer. Because the yield is 7 cups, you might consider giving jars of this tasty chutney to guests as they head home. Store up to 1 week in the refrigerator.

2 medium-size sweet onions, chopped
2 Tbsp. finely chopped fresh ginger
2 garlic cloves, minced
2 Tbsp. olive oil
4 lb. peaches, cut into chunks (do not peel)
2 Granny Smith apples, chopped
2 cups white wine vinegar
1 cup pitted dried cherries
1 cup granulated sugar
1 cup firmly packed light brown sugar
½ cup dried sweetened cranberries
¼ cup fresh lime juice (about 2 limes)
2 Tbsp. brandy＊
1 tsp. salt
¾ cup chopped toasted pecans

1. Sauté first 3 ingredients in hot oil in a Dutch oven over medium-high heat 3 to 5 minutes. Stir in peaches and next 9 ingredients, and cook, stirring occasionally, until sugar dissolves. Bring to a boil, reduce heat, and simmer, stirring occasionally, 1 hour or until thickened. (Do not cook until fruit is mushy.) Stir in pecans. **Makes** 7 cups.

＊Substitute apple cider or juice for brandy, if desired.

Green Bean-and-New Potato Salad
make ahead
PREP: 10 MIN., COOK: 36 MIN.
This can be prepared the night before and stored in the refrigerator.

2 lb. new red potatoes, quartered
1 tsp. salt
2 qt. water
2 Tbsp. salt
2 lb. thin fresh green beans, trimmed
Rosemary Vinaigrette

1. Bring new potatoes, 1 tsp. salt, and water to cover to a boil in a Dutch oven; cook 18 to 20 minutes or until potatoes are tender. Drain and let cool.
2. Bring 2 qt. water and 2 Tbsp. salt to a boil in a Dutch oven; add beans. Cook 6 minutes or until crisp-tender; drain. Plunge beans into ice water to stop the cooking process; drain.
3. Combine green beans and potatoes in a large bowl. Pour Rosemary Vinaigrette over green bean mixture, tossing to coat. Cover and chill until ready to serve. **Makes** 8 servings.

Rosemary Vinaigrette:
fast fixin's
PREP: 5 MIN.
Store dressing in an airtight container in the refrigerator up to 2 days.

½ cup white balsamic vinegar
¼ cup honey
2 garlic cloves
2 Tbsp. chopped fresh rosemary leaves
¼ medium-size red onion
1 Tbsp. Dijon mustard
½ tsp. salt
Freshly ground pepper to taste
½ cup extra-virgin olive oil

1. Process first 8 ingredients in a blender or food processor 15 to 20 seconds, stopping to scrape down sides. With blender or processor running, gradually add olive oil in a slow, steady stream; process until smooth. **Makes** 1⅓ cups.

Marinated Cherry Tomatoes
PREP: 10 MIN., CHILL: 3 HRS.

2 pt. grape tomatoes
½ cup vodka
1 tsp. salt
1 (8-oz.) log goat cheese
Garnishes: fresh cilantro leaves, grape tomato halves

1. Pierce stem ends of tomatoes once with a wooden pick.
2. Combine tomatoes, vodka, and salt in a 4-cup liquid measuring cup or bowl; cover and chill at least 3 hours. Shape goat cheese into a disk, and serve with marinated tomatoes. Garnish, if desired. **Makes** 8 servings.

Tequila Mojitos
make ahead
PREP: 10 MIN., COOK: 8 MIN., STAND: 2 HRS.
The simple syrup needed for this beverage can be made up to 1 week ahead and stored in the refrigerator.

1 cup water
¾ cup sugar
1 cup fresh mint sprigs
2 cups lemon-lime soft drink, chilled
1 cup fresh lime juice
½ cup tequila
Garnishes: fresh mint sprigs, lime slices

1. Bring 1 cup water and sugar to a boil in a medium saucepan. Boil, stirring often, until sugar dissolves. Remove from heat; add mint sprigs, and let stand 2 hours or until mixture is completely cool.
2. Pour mixture through a wire-mesh strainer into a pitcher, discarding mint. Stir in lemon-lime soft drink, lime juice, and tequila. Serve over ice. Garnish, if desired. **Makes** 5 cups.

Get Together With Friends

Each year, these neighbors share their love of beautiful landscapes and great food.

Every summer these Richmond friends, also known as Garden G8 (Gate), host an all-day progressive garden party at their homes, where they enjoy healthful meals and share gardening ideas, favorite recipes, and lots of laughter.

Veggie Frittata
vegetarian
PREP: 20 MIN., COOK: 13 MIN.,
BAKE: 15 MIN., STAND: 3 MIN.

1 medium-size yellow onion, chopped
½ (8-oz.) container sliced fresh
　 mushrooms
1 Tbsp. olive oil
1 (6-oz.) bag fresh baby spinach *
4 large eggs
6 egg whites
½ (8-oz.) block 2% reduced-fat sharp
　 Cheddar cheese, shredded (about
　 1 cup)
¼ cup freshly grated Parmesan
　 cheese
2 Tbsp. fat-free milk
½ tsp. pepper
¼ tsp. salt
¼ tsp. ground nutmeg
Garnishes: black pepper, chopped fresh
　 parsley

1. Sauté onion and mushrooms in hot oil in an ovenproof nonstick 10-inch skillet over medium-high heat 10 minutes or until tender. Stir in spinach, and sauté 3 minutes or until water evaporates and spinach wilts. Remove from heat, and set aside.

2. Whisk together 4 large eggs, 6 egg whites, Cheddar cheese, and next 5 ingredients.
3. Pour egg mixture into skillet with onion mixture, stirring to combine.
4. Bake at 350° for 12 to 15 minutes or just until set. Let stand 3 minutes. Cut into wedges. Garnish, if desired. **Makes** 8 servings.

*Substitute 1 (10-oz.) package chopped frozen spinach, thawed and well drained, for fresh, if desired.

BETH ROYAL
RICHMOND, VIRGINIA

Per serving: Calories 139 (54% from fat); Fat 8.5g (sat 3.7g, mono 2.2g, poly 0.5g); Protein 12.5g; Carb 3.9g; Fiber 0.9g; Chol 119mg; Iron 1.3mg; Sodium 231mg; Calc 202mg

Banana-Nut Bread
family favorite
PREP: 20 MIN., BAKE: 1 HR., COOL: 10 MIN.
This sweet bread has less oil than most traditional recipes, but you won't even notice.

1½ cups whole wheat flour
1 tsp. baking soda
1 tsp. baking powder
1 tsp. ground cinnamon
4 medium-size ripe bananas, mashed
½ cup sugar
1 large egg, lightly beaten
2 Tbsp. canola oil
2 tsp. vanilla extract
½ cup chopped walnuts, toasted
Vegetable cooking spray
Light whipped cream cheese spread
　 (optional)

1. Stir together first 4 ingredients in a large bowl; make a well in center of mixture.
2. Stir together bananas and next 4 ingredients; add to flour mixture, stirring just until dry ingredients are moistened. Gently fold in walnuts.
3. Pour batter into a 9- x 5-inch loaf pan coated with cooking spray.
4. Bake at 350° for 55 minutes to 1 hour or until a wooden pick inserted in center comes out clean. Cool in pan on a wire rack 10 minutes; remove from pan, and cool completely on wire rack. Serve with light whipped cream cheese spread, if desired. **Makes** 10 servings.

LISA DAVIS
RICHMOND, VIRGINIA

Per serving (not including cream cheese): Calories 217 (28% from fat); Fat 7.2g (sat 0.6g, mono 2.7g, poly 3.4g); Protein 5g; Carb 35.9g; Fiber 4.2g; Chol 21mg; Iron 1.3mg; Sodium 183mg; Calc 42mg

---

All-day Garden Hop
Serves 8

Breakfast:
- Veggie Frittata
- sliced tomatoes
- Banana-Nut Bread
- juice or coffee

Lunch:
- Barbecue Pork Sandwiches
- mixed veggie-potato chips
- soft drinks

**Afternoon
Hors d'Oeuvres:**
- wine and cheese

Dinner:
- Shrimp Penne
- green tossed salad
- Peach-and-Blueberry Parfaits

Healthy Benefits

■ Hosting a garden hop, such as this one, keeps guests active and on the move, a fun way to burn calories.
■ Planting a garden—big or small—can be relaxing and therapeutic.
■ Spinach and other dark green leafy vegetables contain lutein and zeaxanthin, which help your eyes eradicate some harmful pollutants.

Barbecue Pork Sandwiches

fast fixin's

PREP: 20 MIN., COOK: 9 HRS.

2 Tbsp. barbecue seasoning, divided
1½ tsp. salt, divided
1 (5-lb.) bone-in pork loin center rib roast
1 (15-oz.) can no-salt-added diced tomatoes
⅓ cup cider vinegar
¼ cup no-salt-added tomato paste
1 Tbsp. Worcestershire sauce
¼ cup firmly packed brown sugar
2 Tbsp. spicy brown mustard
1 tsp. black pepper
2 tsp. dried crushed red pepper
12 multigrain buns
Dill pickles (optional)

1. Combine 1 Tbsp. barbecue seasoning and 1 tsp. salt; rub evenly over pork roast.
2. Stir together tomatoes, next 7 ingredients, remaining 1 Tbsp. barbecue seasoning, and remaining ½ tsp. salt in a 6.5-qt. slow cooker. Add roast; cover and cook on LOW 9 hours or until meat shreds easily.
3. Remove roast; remove and discard bone. Shred meat using the tines of 2 forks. Return to slow cooker, and stir together with sauce; spoon over multigrain buns. Serve with pickles, if desired. **Makes** 12 servings.

Note: For testing purposes only, we used Chef Paul Prudhomme's Magic Barbecue Seasoning.

MARY ALEXANDER
RICHMOND, VIRGINIA

Per serving (including ⅔ cup barbecue mixture and 1 bun): Calories 461 (28% from fat); Fat 14g (sat 5.9g, mono 5.3g, poly 2.1g); Protein 39.9g; Carb 40.4g; Fiber 3.2g; Chol 81mg; Iron 2.7mg; Sodium 712mg; Calc 105mg

Shrimp Penne

PREP: 30 MIN., COOK: 35 MIN.

12 oz. uncooked multigrain penne pasta
1½ lb. uncooked large, fresh shrimp
1 yellow bell pepper, cut into thin strips
1 red bell pepper, cut into thin strips
2 Tbsp. olive oil
2 garlic cloves, chopped
1 pt. grape tomatoes, halved
1 cup dry white wine
½ tsp. salt
½ tsp. freshly ground black pepper
¼ tsp. dried crushed red pepper
¼ cup chopped fresh basil
Freshly grated Parmesan cheese (optional)

1. Cook pasta according to package directions; drain and set aside.
2. Peel shrimp, and, if desired, devein.
3. Sauté bell peppers in hot oil in a large skillet over medium-high heat 10 minutes or until tender. Add garlic; sauté 1 minute. Add tomatoes; sauté 3 minutes. Add wine and next 3 ingredients; cook 10 minutes, stirring occasionally. Add shrimp and basil, and cook, stirring occasionally, 3 minutes or just until shrimp turn pink. Stir in pasta; cook until thoroughly heated. Sprinkle with Parmesan cheese, if desired. **Makes** 12 (1-cup) servings.

Note: For testing purposes only, we used Barilla Plus Penne Pasta.

LISA DAVIS
RICHMOND, VIRGINIA

Per serving: Calories 194 (17% from fat); Fat 3.6g (sat 0.5g, mono 1.8g, poly 0.5g); Protein 13g; Carb 24g; Fiber 3.3g; Chol 84mg; Iron 2.4mg; Sodium 202mg; Calc 34mg

Peach-and-Blueberry Parfaits

make ahead

PREP: 30 MIN., COOK: 15 MIN., CHILL: 2 HRS.

This refreshing summer dessert is served in mason jars or tall glasses for a decorative touch.

2 cups 1% low-fat milk
1 large egg
⅓ cup sugar
1 Tbsp. cornstarch
1 tsp. vanilla extract
3 lb. fresh peaches, peeled and chopped (about 7 cups)
1 pt. fresh blueberries
½ (14-oz.) angel food cake, cubed (about 6 cups)
Garnish: fresh mint sprigs

1. Whisk together first 4 ingredients in a small nonaluminum saucepan over medium-low heat, and cook, stirring constantly, 15 minutes or until slightly thickened. (Mixture should lightly coat the back of a spoon.) Remove from heat; stir in vanilla.
2. Pour mixture into a small mixing bowl, and place plastic wrap directly over surface of custard to prevent film from forming; chill 2 hours or until ready to serve.
3. Layer fruit and cake in 8 mason jars or tall glasses. Drizzle each with ¼ cup vanilla sauce. Garnish, if desired. **Makes** 8 servings.

MARY ALEXANDER
RICHMOND, VIRGINIA

Per serving: Calories 215 (8% from fat); Fat 2g (sat 0.7g, mono 0.6g, poly 0.4g); Protein 5.9g; Carb 46g; Fiber 3.5g; Chol 29mg; Iron 0.8mg; Sodium 226mg; Calc 124mg

Test Kitchen Notebook

Besides the fun, there's also a little friendly competition. As the couples venture from home to home, they tour each other's artful landscapes and judge the work. The rule is: You must incorporate a new element into your garden each year—and deductions are given for dead leaves.

Shannon Sliter Satterwhite

FOODS EDITOR

Good-for-You Grilling

Get ready to cook outdoors with these wholesome recipes and simple techniques.

Grilling is one of the easiest—and most flavorful—ways to cook. Just a light marinade or seasoning will do, and the grill takes care of the rest. Test Kitchens Specialist Vanessa McNeil Rocchio developed these light recipes that you can serve at any outdoor gathering.

Refreshing Beverage

Treat your guests to iced herb tea. It makes a great accompaniment with a meal straight from the grill. For a fun garnish, serve the tea with rock candy stirrers. (We found them at a local candy store. See page 105 for our Rock Candy recipe.)

Lemon-Grilled Salmon

PREP: 15 MIN., SOAK: 8 HRS., GRILL: 20 MIN.

2 (15- x 6-inch) cedar grilling planks
3 Tbsp. chopped fresh dill
3 Tbsp. chopped fresh parsley
2 tsp. grated lemon rind
3 Tbsp. fresh lemon juice
1 Tbsp. olive oil
1 garlic clove, pressed
½ tsp. salt
¼ tsp. pepper
4 (6-oz.) salmon fillets

1. Weigh down cedar planks with a heavier object in a large container. Add water to cover, and soak at least 8 hours.
2. Combine dill and next 5 ingredients; set aside.
3. Sprinkle salt and pepper evenly on salmon.
4. Remove cedar planks from water, and place planks on cooking grate on grill.
5. Grill soaked planks, covered with grill lid, over medium-high heat (350° to 400°) 2 minutes or until the planks begin to lightly smoke. Place 2 fillets on each cedar plank, and grill, covered, with grill lid, 15 to 18 minutes or until fish flakes with a fork. Remove fish from planks to individual serving plates using a spatula. (Carefully remove planks from grill using tongs.) Spoon herb mixture over fish, and serve immediately. **Makes** 4 servings.

Per serving: Calories 310 (47% from fat); Fat 15.7g (sat 2.4g, mono 6.6g, poly 5.3g); Protein 38.7g; Carb 1.4g; Fiber 0.3g; Chol 107mg; Iron 1.8mg; Sodium 378mg; Calc 31mg

Pork Kabobs

PREP: 10 MIN., CHILL: 1 HR., SOAK: 30 MIN., GRILL: 9 MIN.

¼ cup fresh lime juice
2 Tbsp. olive oil
1 tsp. red or yellow curry powder
¼ tsp. dried crushed red pepper
1 (3-lb.) pork loin, trimmed and cut into 1-inch pieces
18 (8-inch) wooden or metal skewers

1. Whisk together first 4 ingredients. Place pork in a shallow dish or large zip-top plastic freezer bag; pour lime juice mixture over pork. Cover or seal, and chill 1 hour, turning occasionally.
2. Soak wooden skewers in water 30 minutes to prevent burning.
3. Remove pork from marinade, discarding marinade. Thread 5 pork pieces evenly onto each skewer, leaving a little space between pieces.
4. Grill pork, covered with grill lid, over medium-high heat (350° to 400°) 7 to 9 minutes or until done, turning once. **Makes** about 6 servings.

Per serving: Calories 342 (41% from fat); Fat 15.1g (sat 5g, mono 7.4g, poly 1.2g); Protein 47.8g; Carb 0.8g; Fiber 0.2g; Chol 130mg; Iron 1.5mg; Sodium 95mg; Calc 52mg

A Simple Way to Grill Fish

Grilling fish on cedar planks is so easy. Not only does the wood add smoky flavor to the fish, but the planks also prevent it from flaking and falling through the food grate. Soak the planks in water at least 8 hours beforehand to prevent burning. Keep a spray bottle of water handy for any flare-ups. Look for the planks in the grilling section of your grocery store, home-improvement center, or specialty kitchen or garden shop.

Grilled Peppered Bread
fast fixin's
PREP: 5 MIN., GRILL: 4 MIN.

12 (½-inch-thick) French bread slices
2 Tbsp. olive oil
1 tsp. freshly ground black
    pepper

1. Brush both sides of bread slices evenly with olive oil; sprinkle both sides evenly with pepper.
2. Grill bread, uncovered, over medium-high heat (350° to 400°) 1 to 2 minutes on each side or until lightly toasted and browned. **Makes** 6 servings.

LISA HARP
QUITMAN, GEORGIA

Per serving (2 slices): Calories 171 (28% from fat); Fat 5.5g (sat 0.6g, mono 3.3g, poly 0.5g); Protein 5.1g; Carb 26g; Fiber 1.1g; Chol 0mg; Iron 1.5mg; Sodium 290mg; Calc 81mg

Strawberry Napoleons
fast fixin's
PREP 10 MIN., GRILL: 4 MIN.

2 (5.3-oz.) containers plain fat-free
    yogurt
3 Tbsp. honey
1 (16-oz.) container fresh strawberries,
    sliced
2 Tbsp. sugar
4 frozen phyllo sheets, thawed
Vegetable cooking spray
1 tsp. sugar
Garnishes: mint sprigs, whole
    strawberries

1. Stir together yogurt and honey; cover and chill yogurt sauce until ready to serve.
2. Combine strawberries and 2 Tbsp. sugar; cover and chill until ready to serve.
3. Place 1 phyllo sheet on a flat work surface. Coat with cooking spray, and sprinkle evenly with ¼ tsp. sugar. Top with 1 phyllo sheet; coat again with cooking spray, and sprinkle with ¼ tsp. sugar. Cut phyllo stack into thirds lengthwise; cut each in half, creating 6 even rectangular stacks. Repeat procedure with remaining phyllo sheets, cooking spray, and ½ tsp. sugar.
4. Grill phyllo stacks, without grill lid, over medium-low heat (300° to 350°)

1 to 2 minutes on each side or until lightly browned.
5. Place 1 grilled phyllo stack on each of 6 serving plates; top evenly with half of strawberry slices. Drizzle evenly with half of yogurt sauce. Top each with 1 grilled phyllo stack. Top with remaining strawberry slices and yogurt sauce. Garnish, if desired. Serve immediately. **Makes** 6 servings.

Per serving: Calories 156 (7% from fat); Fat 1.2g (sat 0.2g, mono 0.4g, poly 0.3g); Protein 5.3g; Carb 33.1g; Fiber 2.2g; Chol 1mg; Iron 0.9mg; Sodium 118mg; Calc 117mg

Healthy Benefits

- Omega-3 fatty acids in salmon help prevent blood clots that can cause heart attacks.
- Red fruits such as strawberries, cherries, pomegranates, raspberries, and watermelon help improve memory function, lower the risk of certain cancers, and help maintain urinary tract health.

healthy living
Celebrate the Season

Gather your family or a few good friends, and take a Saturday morning stroll around the local farmers market. In this community environment, you can savor summer's bounty of freshly picked fruits and vegetables in an array of colors and flavors. In addition to peak produce, many markets offer flowers by the bunch, handmade crafts, and live local entertainment. We've showcased the abundant produce in the recipes here. They're easy to make, and knowing you selected fresh ingredients from a local vendor will make them taste even better.

Roasted Plums With Sour Cream
PREP: 10 MIN., BAKE: 30 MIN.
Dark purple plums hold up better for baking than the lighter ones.

4 large purple plums, cut in half and
    pitted
⅓ cup water
½ tsp. vanilla extract
¼ cup firmly packed brown sugar
¼ cup low-fat sour cream
2 Tbsp. brown sugar

1. Place plum halves, cut sides down, in an 8-inch square baking dish. Stir together ⅓ cup water and vanilla; pour over fruit. Sprinkle ¼ cup brown sugar evenly over fruit.
2. Bake plums at 450° for 25 to 30 minutes or until skins just start to blister. Divide fruit and syrup evenly among 4 bowls. Top each with 1 Tbsp. low-fat sour cream and ½ Tbsp. brown sugar. **Makes** 4 servings.

KATHY EAKIN
BIRMINGHAM, ALABAMA

Per serving: Calories 137 (6% from fat); Fat 1g (sat 0.8g, mono 0g, poly 0g); Protein 1g; Carb 32.7g; Fiber 1g; Chol 5mg; Iron 0.6mg; Sodium 23mg; Calc 18mg

Asian Cucumber Salad
make ahead
PREP: 15 MIN., CHILL: 1 HR.

¾ cup seasoned rice vinegar
¼ cup water
1 Tbsp. sugar
1 Tbsp. minced garlic
1 Tbsp. lite soy sauce
1 tsp. sesame oil
½ tsp. freshly ground pepper
2 large cucumbers, peeled and sliced
2 Tbsp. sesame seeds, toasted

1. Stir together first 7 ingredients in a large bowl. Add cucumbers, tossing to coat. Cover and chill 1 hour. Add sesame seeds, and toss; serve immediately. **Makes** 6 servings.

NORA HENSHAW
OKEMAH, OKLAHOMA

Per 1-cup serving: Calories 52 (44% from fat); Fat 2.4g (sat 0.3g, mono 0.8g, poly 0.9g); Protein 1.3g; Carb 5.8g; Fiber 1g; Chol 0mg; Iron 0.4mg; Sodium 97mg; Calc 18mg

Sugar Snap Peas With Ginger

fast fixin's

PREP: 10 MIN., COOK: 6 MIN.

1 lb. fresh sugar snap peas
2 tsp. olive oil
2 garlic cloves, chopped
2 tsp. grated fresh ginger
1 tsp. chopped walnuts, toasted *
¾ tsp. salt

1. Cook peas in hot oil in a nonstick skillet over medium-high heat, stirring occasionally, 3 to 5 minutes or until crisp-tender. Stir in garlic and remaining ingredients; cook 1 minute. Serve immediately. **Makes** 5 servings.

*Substitute1 tsp. toasted sesame seeds, if desired.

Per ½-cup serving: Calories 62 (30% from fat); Fat 2.1g (sat 0.3g, mono 1.4g, poly 0.4g); Protein 2.5g; Carb 8.7g; Fiber 3.5g; Chol 0mg; Iron 0.9mg; Sodium 354mg; Calc 72mg

Blueberry-Lime Granita

freezeable • make ahead

PREP: 15 MIN., FREEZE: 8 HRS., STAND: 5 MIN.

2 cups blueberries
½ cup sugar *
½ tsp. grated lime rind
2 tsp. fresh lime juice
3 cups diet lemon-lime soft drink, chilled
Garnish: lime rind twists

1. Process blueberries in a food processor or blender until smooth, stopping to scrape down sides. Add sugar, lime rind, and lime juice; process until well blended. Pour into an 11- x 7-inch dish. Stir in soft drink. Cover and freeze 8 hours. Remove from freezer; let stand 5 minutes.
2. Chop mixture into large chunks, and place in food processor in batches; pulse 5 or 6 times or until mixture is smooth. Serve immediately, or freeze until ready to serve. Garnish, if desired. **Makes** 7 servings.

*Substitute ½ cup of no-calorie sweetener (such as Splenda), if desired.

Per 1-cup serving with sugar: Calories 80 (0% from fat); Fat 0.1g (sat 0g, mono 0g, poly 0g); Protein 0.3g; Carb 20.4g; Fiber 1g; Chol 0mg; Iron 0.1mg; Sodium 0mg; Calc 3mg

Per 1-cup serving with no-calorie sweetener: Calories 25 (0% from fat); Fat 0.1g (sat 0g, mono 0g, poly 0g); Protein 0.3g; Carb 6.2g; Fiber 1g; Chol 0mg; Iron 0.1mg; Sodium 0mg; Calc 3mg

Easy Meals With Pasta and Veggies

Pasta is one of the most versatile ingredients. Combine it with fresh veggies, and it's even better. It's a fast-cooking, affordable addition to menus for parties, picnics, or simple meals.

Vegetable-Bacon Noodle Toss mixes squash, tomatoes, and parsley with bacon and balsamic vinaigrette for a hearty, wholesome main dish. Broccoli-Pasta Alfredo is a meat-free, creamy mixture of broccoli, shallots, basil, and Parmesan cheese. Serve either of these with a salad and a toasted, herb-flavored Italian bread—and pronto, you're ready to dine.

Broccoli-Pasta Alfredo

vegetarian

PREP: 15 MIN., COOK: 25 MIN.

½ (16-oz.) package uncooked farfalle or bow-tie pasta
2 cups broccoli florets
2 Tbsp. butter
¼ cup finely chopped shallots *
1 cup half-and-half
1 cup refrigerated grated Parmesan cheese
¼ cup loosely packed fresh basil, chopped
½ tsp. freshly ground black pepper
¼ tsp. dried crushed red pepper

1. Cook pasta according to package directions, adding broccoli during last 3 minutes of cooking time; drain and keep warm.
2. Melt butter in a large saucepan over medium-high heat. Add shallots, and sauté 3 minutes or until lightly browned. Stir in half-and-half. Cook, stirring constantly, 3 minutes or until thoroughly heated. Stir in Parmesan cheese and next 3 ingredients until smooth. Stir in pasta and broccoli. Serve immediately. **Makes** 4 servings.

*Substitute ¼ cup finely chopped onion, if desired.

Vegetable-Bacon Noodle Toss

PREP: 20 MIN., COOK: 20 MIN.

For a vegetarian version of this dish, omit the bacon, and sauté the chopped onion in 2 tsp. olive oil.

½ (16-oz.) package uncooked wide egg noodles
4 bacon slices
½ small onion, chopped
2 yellow squash, cut in half lengthwise and sliced
1 zucchini, cut in half lengthwise and sliced
2 medium tomatoes, seeded and chopped
½ cup light balsamic vinaigrette
2 Tbsp. chopped fresh flat-leaf parsley
½ tsp. salt
½ tsp. freshly ground pepper
Garnish: flat-leaf parsley sprig

1. Prepare egg noodles according to package directions; drain noodles, and keep warm.
2. Cook bacon in a large nonstick skillet over medium-high heat until crisp; remove bacon, and drain on paper towels, reserving 2 tsp. drippings in a small bowl. Discard remaining drippings. Wipe skillet clean with a paper towel. Crumble bacon.
3. Sauté chopped onion in hot reserved drippings over medium-high heat 5 minutes or until tender. Add squash, zucchini, and tomatoes; sauté 6 minutes or until squash and zucchini are crisp-tender. Add egg noodles, bacon, vinaigrette, and next 3 ingredients, stirring until well blended. Cook, stirring constantly, until thoroughly heated. Serve immediately. Garnish, if desired. **Makes** 4 to 6 servings.

Note: For testing purposes only, we used Newman's Own Light Balsamic Vinaigrette.

Fast and Fresh Party Salads

Entertaining is easier than ever with this carefree menu of cool and refreshing salads. Steamed shrimp and rotisserie chicken from the supermarket make quick starts for our main-dish salads.

Summer Sampler

Serves 4 to 6

Honey-Chicken Salad

Shrimp Salad

tomato-and-cucumber salad with Sugar-and-Vinegar Dressing

cornbread madeleines

iced tea

Sour Cream Pound Cake with fresh peaches (see recipe on page 134)

Honey-Chicken Salad

PREP: 20 MIN.

The mayonnaise-honey mixture is reminiscent of poppy seed dressing. For a less sweet dressing, reduce the amount of honey. (Pictured on page 172)

4 cups chopped cooked chicken
3 celery ribs, diced (about 1½ cups)
1 cup sweetened dried cranberries
½ cup chopped pecans, toasted
1½ cups mayonnaise
⅓ cup honey
¼ tsp. salt
¼ tsp. pepper
Garnish: chopped toasted pecans

1. Combine first 4 ingredients.
2. Whisk together mayonnaise and next 3 ingredients. Add to chicken mixture, stirring gently until combined. Garnish, if desired. **Makes** 4 to 6 servings.

TERESA MOSHER
BRADENTON, FLORIDA

Shrimp Salad

fast fixin's • make ahead
PREP: 15 MIN. *(Pictured on page 172)*

Stir together 4 cups chopped cooked shrimp, ¾ cup mayonnaise, 4 thinly sliced green onions, 2 diced celery ribs, 2 tsp. grated lemon rind, ½ tsp. ground red pepper, and salt and black pepper to taste. **Makes** 4 to 6 servings.

Sugar-and-Vinegar Dressing

PREP: 5 MIN.

Top salad greens with sliced vine-ripened tomatoes, cucumbers, and red onion. Drizzle with dressing just before serving.(Pictured on page 172)

⅓ cup raspberry or red wine vinegar
¼ cup sugar
2 tsp. Dijon mustard
1 garlic clove
½ tsp. salt
½ tsp. freshly ground pepper
½ cup vegetable oil
2 Tbsp. chopped fresh basil

1. Process first 6 ingredients in a blender or food processor until smooth. With blender or processor running, add oil in a slow, steady stream; process until smooth. Stir in basil. **Makes** about ¾ cup.

Make It Special

■ Bake your favorite cornbread mix in shell-shaped madeleine pans. Lightly grease pans, and fill each mold two-thirds full. Bake at 425° for 6 to 8 minutes or until cornbread is golden brown. *(Pictured on page 173)*
■ Serve scoops of Honey-Chicken Salad in individual pastry shells. Use refrigerated piecrusts to make your own, or take a super-shortcut, and simply bake a package of frozen tart shells.

Cook Smart With Kids

Gather everyone in the kitchen, and prepare a meal the whole family will love. It's a great opportunity to teach your children safe ways to handle food as well as how to whisk, stir, measure, and chop ingredients. This hands-on experience will enhance their appreciation and basic knowledge of different foods, good nutrition, and simple cooking skills. Plus, it's a fun way to spend time together and to encourage a lifetime of healthful eating.

Fun and Safe Kitchen Skills

Here are our recommendations for age-appropriate tasks.
- **Age 3:** wash fruits and vegetables, and stir ingredients in large, deep bowls
- **Age 4:** open packages, squeeze citrus, measure and spoon out cookies, and tear lettuce
- **Ages 5-6:** measure ingredients, set the table, and cut soft foods with a fork or table knife
- **Ages 7-8:** help plan the meal, find ingredients in the pantry or spice rack, knead dough, and crack eggs
- **Ages 9-12:** open cans, use small appliances, follow a recipe, and prepare a meal with few ingredients
- **Ages 13-16:** prepare recipes with multiple ingredients

Turkey-and-Ham Rollups

fast fixin's • make ahead
PREP: 10 MIN.

1 (8-oz.) container garlic-and-herb whipped cream cheese spread
½ cup chopped roasted red bell peppers
6 (8-inch) 98% fat-free flour tortillas
3 cups firmly packed baby spinach leaves
12 oz. sliced lean deli ham
12 oz. sliced deli turkey breast

1. Stir together cream cheese and peppers until smooth. Spread about ¼ cup cream cheese mixture evenly over 6 tortillas. Place ½ cup spinach on each tortilla. Top evenly with ham and turkey slices. Roll up, jelly-roll fashion, and cut in half. Secure each half with a wooden pick. **Makes** 12 servings.

Note: For testing purposes only, we used Philadelphia Garlic 'N Herb Whipped Cream Cheese Spread.

ANNA GINSBERG
AUSTIN, TEXAS

Per serving: Calories 184 (38% from fat); Fat 7.8g (sat 3.9g, mono 1.8g, poly 0.6g); Protein 14.2g; Carb 14.5g; Fiber 1.3g; Chol 56mg; Iron 1.7mg; Sodium 865mg; Calc 27mg

Oven-Fried Parmesan Chicken Strips

freezeable
PREP: 15 MIN., BAKE: 30 MIN.

2 Tbsp. butter
⅓ cup reduced-fat baking mix
⅓ cup grated Parmesan cheese
1½ tsp. Old Bay seasoning
⅛ tsp. black pepper
2 lb. chicken breast strips

1. Melt butter in a 15- x 10-inch jelly-roll pan in a 425° oven.
2. Place baking mix and next 3 ingredients in a large zip-top plastic bag; shake well to combine. Add chicken, several pieces at a time, shaking well to coat. Arrange chicken in melted butter in hot pan.
3. Bake at 425° for 30 minutes or until chicken is done, turning once. Serve immediately. **Makes** 5 servings.

Note: To freeze, place uncooked, coated chicken strips on a baking sheet in the freezer. Once frozen, place strips in a zip-top plastic freezer bag, and freeze until ready to prepare. Bake frozen strips on a hot buttered jelly-roll pan (according to previous directions) at 425° for 35 minutes, turning after 25 minutes. For testing purposes only, we used Bisquick Heart Smart mix.

TERESA PATTEN
CHATTANOOGA, TENNESSEE

Per serving (3 strips): Calories 294 (28% from fat); Fat 8.7g (sat 4.5g, mono 2.1g, poly 0.9g); Protein 44.7g; Carb 6g; Fiber 0g; Chol 123mg; Iron 1.8mg; Sodium 516mg; Calc 87mg

Mini Sweet-and-Sour Sloppy Joes

family favorite
PREP: 15 MIN., COOK: 50 MIN.
Because these are child-size portions, adults may choose to eat two of these tasty little sandwiches.

1½ lb. extra-lean ground beef
Vegetable cooking spray
1 cup finely chopped onion
½ cup finely chopped green bell pepper
3 (8-oz.) cans basil, garlic, and oregano tomato sauce
¼ cup cider vinegar
1 Tbsp. brown sugar
2 tsp. Worcestershire sauce
1 tsp. chili powder
¼ tsp. salt
1 (13.9-oz.) package dinner rolls, toasted

1. Cook ground beef in a large non-stick skillet coated with cooking spray over medium-high heat 10 minutes or until beef crumbles and is no longer pink. Remove meat from skillet, and drain well.
2. Sauté onion and bell pepper in skillet 5 minutes or until tender. Return meat to skillet; stir in tomato sauce and next 5 ingredients. Bring mixture to a boil; cover, reduce heat, and simmer, stirring occasionally, 30 minutes. Spoon mixture evenly into toasted dinner rolls, and serve immediately. **Makes** 12 sandwiches.

Note: For testing purposes only, we used Pepperidge Farm Soft Dinner Rolls Country Style. They're about the size of a baseball.

MARIAN TETOR
HOLLAND, PENNSYLVANIA

Per serving (1 sandwich): Calories 216 (28% from fat); Fat 6.7g (sat 2g, mono 2.2g, poly 1.2g); Protein 15.8g; Carb 23.6g; Fiber 1.8g; Chol 21mg; Iron 2.8mg; Sodium 506mg; Calc 31mg

Breakfast Pizza Cups
family favorite
PREP: 20 MIN., COOK: 10 MIN., BAKE: 20 MIN.

½ lb. lean ground turkey sausage
2 (13.8-oz.) cans refrigerated pizza crust
  dough
½ cup frozen hash browns, thawed
½ cup (2 oz.) shredded 2% reduced-fat
  sharp Cheddar cheese
1¼ cups egg substitute
½ cup fat-free milk
⅛ tsp. pepper
2 Tbsp. grated Parmesan cheese
1½ cups pizza sauce

1. Cook sausage in a large skillet over medium-high heat 10 minutes or until sausage crumbles and is no longer pink. Drain well on paper towels, and set aside.
2. Roll or pat 1 can pizza dough into a 15- x 10-inch rectangle on a lightly floured surface; cut into 6 (5-inch) squares. Press squares into lightly greased muffin cups, skipping every other muffin cup. Repeat procedure with remaining can of pizza dough.
3. Spoon sausage evenly into crusts; sprinkle evenly with hash browns and Cheddar cheese.
4. Stir together egg substitute, milk, and pepper; pour evenly into pizza cups, and sprinkle with grated Parmesan cheese.
5. Bake at 375° for 18 to 20 minutes or until golden. Serve with pizza sauce. **Makes** 12 servings.

PATSY BELL HOBSON
LIBERTY, MISSOURI

Per serving (1 pizza cup and 2 Tbsp. pizza sauce): Calories 238 (20% from fat); Fat 5.4g (sat 2g, mono 0.8g, poly 0.7g); Protein 12.8g; Carb 34.6g; Fiber 0.6g; Chol 20mg; Iron 2.5mg; Sodium 763mg; Calc 64mg

what's for supper?
A Family Favorite

Weekday Supper
Serves 6

Easy Shredded Beef Over Rice
Seasoned Green Beans
Texas toast or hot dinner rolls
Warm Cookie Sundaes

Easy Shredded Beef Over Rice
make ahead
PREP: 20 MIN., COOK: 4 HRS.
This dish is known as ropa vieja [ROH-pah VYAY-hoh], Spanish for "old clothes." Fajita seasoning gives it a tasty twist.

1 (4-lb.) boneless top chuck
  roast
2 tsp. fajita seasoning
2 Tbsp. vegetable oil
2 (14½-oz.) cans Mexican-style stewed
  tomatoes
2 cups water
4 cups hot cooked rice
2 Tbsp. chopped fresh parsley

1. Rub both sides of roast evenly with fajita seasoning.
2. Cook roast in hot oil in a large Dutch oven over medium-high heat 5 minutes or until browned on all sides.
3. Combine stewed tomatoes and 2 cups water; pour over roast in Dutch oven. Cover, reduce heat to low, and cook 4 hours or until roast is tender. Remove roast, and shred using 2 forks.
4. Skim fat from tomato liquid in Dutch oven, and discard. Stir shredded beef into tomato liquid.
5. Combine rice and parsley. Serve beef mixture over rice. **Makes** 6 to 8 servings.

Seasoned Green Beans
fast fixin's
PREP: 15 MIN., COOK: 10 MIN.
Cook beans longer in boiling water if you prefer more tender vegetables.

6 cups water
1 Tbsp. Greek seasoning
1½ lb. thin fresh green beans,
  trimmed
1 Tbsp. butter
½ tsp. Greek seasoning

1. Bring 6 cups water and 1 Tbsp. Greek seasoning to a boil in a Dutch oven over high heat; add green beans. Cook 6 minutes or until beans are crisp-tender; remove beans, draining well. Wipe Dutch oven dry with paper towels.
2. Melt butter in Dutch oven over medium heat. Add green beans and ½ tsp. Greek seasoning, tossing to coat; cook, stirring constantly, 2 minutes or until thoroughly heated. **Makes** 6 to 8 servings.

Warm Cookie Sundaes
family favorite
PREP: 5 MIN., BAKE: 30 MIN., COOL: 5 MIN.
We liked the cookie cups soft, but for a more crisp cookie, increase the bake time. Experiment with other cookie-and-ice cream combos.

6 packaged ready-to-bake peanut
  butter cookie dough rounds with
  mini peanut butter cups
Vanilla ice cream
Toppings: hot fudge sauce, whipped
  cream, chopped peanuts

1. Place each cookie dough round into a lightly greased 8-oz. ramekin or individual soufflé dish.
2. Bake at 350° for 25 to 30 minutes or until cookies are lightly browned. Let cool 5 minutes. Scoop vanilla ice cream into each ramekin, and top sundaes with desired toppings. Serve immediately. **Makes** 6 servings.

Note: For testing purposes only, we used half of an 18-oz. package of Pillsbury Ready to Bake Peanut Butter Cup Cookies.

The Sweet Taste of Peaches

Pass out the plates for this fresh-picked fruit and pound cake.

Whatever the season, pound cake rates as a perennial favorite in the South. Warm from the oven or tossed on the grill—it's always irresistible.

Leavened with a dash of baking soda, the fine-crumb texture and delicate lemon-almond flavor of Sour Cream Pound Cake pairs perfectly with summer fruits. We especially love it with fresh peaches, but feel free to substitute nectarines or berries if you'd like.

For a real treat, sprinkle sliced fruit with sugar to taste, and cook over low heat, stirring gently, 3 to 4 minutes or until warm. Spoon over warm pound cake, and top with your favorite ice cream. It's so good, everyone will want seconds.

Sour Cream Pound Cake

freezeable • make ahead

PREP: 20 MIN.; BAKE: 1 HR., 30 MIN.; STAND: 10 MIN.

Bake this delicious cake, and store at room temperature up to 3 days; or place it in a large zip-top freezer bag, and store in the freezer up to 2 months. (Pictured on page 170)

1½ cups butter, softened
3 cups sugar
6 large eggs
3 cups all-purpose flour
½ tsp. salt
¼ tsp. baking soda
1 (8-oz.) container sour cream
1 tsp. lemon extract
¼ tsp. almond extract

1. Beat butter at medium speed with an electric mixer until creamy. Gradually add sugar, beating at medium speed until light and fluffy. Add eggs, 1 at a time, beating just until the yolk disappears.
2. Sift together flour, salt, and soda. Add to butter mixture alternately with sour cream, beginning and ending with flour mixture. Beat batter at low speed just until blended after each addition. Stir in extracts. Pour into a greased and floured 12-cup tube pan.
3. Bake at 325° for 1 hour and 20 minutes to 1 hour and 30 minutes or until a long wooden pick inserted in center of cake comes out clean. Cool in pan on a wire rack 10 minutes. Remove cake from pan, and cool completely on wire rack. **Makes** 10 to 12 servings.

ANITA GUIDRY
CHURCH POINT, LOUISIANA

Whipped Cream

fast fixin's

PREP: 5 MIN.

Try replacing the tsp. of vanilla extract with a Tbsp. of your favorite liqueur. Almond-flavored liqueur is a perfect match for peaches, while orange liqueur pairs especially well with berries. (Pictured on page 170)

1 cup whipping cream
2 Tbsp. powdered sugar
1 tsp. vanilla extract

1. Beat whipping cream at low speed with an electric mixer until foamy; increase speed to medium-high, and gradually add powdered sugar, beating until soft peaks form. Stir in vanilla. **Makes** about 2 cups.

Simple Syrup

fast fixin's • make ahead

PREP: 5 MIN., COOK: 5 MIN.

1 cup water
1 cup sugar
6 strawberries, sliced (optional)

1. Bring water, sugar, and, if desired, strawberries to a boil in a saucepan, stirring until sugar dissolves; boil 1 minute. Remove from heat. If necessary, pour syrup through a wire-mesh strainer into a bowl, discarding fruit; cool. **Makes** about 1½ cups.

A Spoonful of Sugar

Tossing fresh fruit with sugar enhances the fruit's sweetness and flavor. The sugar draws the natural juices from the fruit, creating a heavenly syrup when the fruit is allowed to stand 30 minutes to an hour.

Basic syrups, easily made by boiling equal amounts of sugar and water, offer delicious alternatives to sprinkling fruit with sugar. Store syrups in the refrigerator for up to 3 weeks. (Leftovers are great in iced tea.)

To be festive, we tossed in some strawberries when making our syrup. They don't add flavor but do tint the syrup a pretty pink color.

july

Tomato Time

These juicy gems are at their peak now, and our scrumptious recipes are ripe and ready to go.

So take advantage of the too-short tomato season, and try these recipes while you can

Broiled Tomatoes With Feta Cheese
fast fixin's
PREP: 5 MIN., BROIL: 3 MIN.

6 plum tomatoes
Salt and pepper to taste
½ tsp. dried Italian seasoning
⅔ cup crumbled feta cheese
¼ cup Italian dressing

1. Cut tomatoes in half lengthwise, and place, cut sides up, on a baking sheet. Sprinkle evenly with salt and pepper to taste, Italian seasoning, and feta cheese. Drizzle evenly with ¼ cup Italian dressing.
2. Broil 3 inches from heat 2 to 3 minutes or just until cheese starts to brown. **Makes** 6 servings.
PAM FLOYD
TRUSSVILLE, ALABAMA

Tomato-Egg Sandwiches
fast fixin's • make ahead
PREP: 20 MIN.
This recipe is a snap to make ahead. The day before serving, combine the first 4 ingredients; cover and chill. Boil eggs, peel, and slice; cover and chill. Slice the tomatoes and toast the bread just before assembling the sandwiches. It's not necessary to cut the toasted bread slices with a cutter, but it looks really nice.

1 (8-oz.) package cream cheese, softened
1 (9-oz.) jar horseradish sauce
1 small onion, grated (about ¼ cup)
1 (1-oz.) package Ranch dressing mix
12 white sandwich bread slices, toasted
12 whole wheat sandwich bread slices, toasted
24 tomato slices (about 6 medium-size ripe tomatoes)
48 hard-cooked egg slices (about 8 large eggs)
Chopped fresh dill
Freshly ground pepper

1. Beat first 4 ingredients at medium speed with an electric mixer until blended; set aside.
2. Cut 24 rounds from toasted bread using a 3-inch cutter. (Select a cutter close to the size of the tomato slices.) Reserve bread trimmings for another use, if desired.
3. Spread 1 side of each round evenly with cream cheese mixture; top with 1 tomato slice and 2 egg slices. Sprinkle evenly with dill and pepper. **Makes** 12 appetizer servings.
CAROL SWILLEY
BRANDON, MISSISSIPPI

Italian Tomato Salad
make ahead
PREP: 15 MIN., CHILL: 30 MIN.

6 medium-size ripe tomatoes, diced (about 2½ lb.)
⅓ cup cider vinegar or balsamic vinegar
1 Tbsp. chopped fresh basil
2 Tbsp. olive oil
3 tsp. salt
1½ tsp. chopped fresh oregano
1 tsp. fresh ground pepper
1 garlic clove, minced
Mixed salad greens

1. Stir together first 8 ingredients in a medium bowl. Cover and chill at least 30 minutes. Serve over or toss with salad greens. **Makes** 6 to 8 servings.
CAROL S. NOBLE
BURGAW, NORTH CAROLINA

How to Pick a Tasty Tomato

According to Linda Sapp of Tomato Growers Supply Company in Fort Myers, Florida, "You can't judge a book by its cover. Looks can be deceiving." She offers these tips on selecting good tomatoes.
- A ripe tomato has deep, uniform color. If there is too much green, you know it was picked green and shipped.
- You want it to feel firm and full, but not too soft.
- A freshly picked tomato will smell like a tomato. Aromatics in tomatoes go away quickly.
- Look for tomatoes that are plump and heavy for their size.
- Avoid soft spots, blemishes, deep cracks, or leathery dark patches.
- Know your suppliers, and ask questions. Did they grow this tomato, or was it purchased from a produce broker?
- The longer a tomato is allowed to ripen on the vine, the more flavorful it is.

Fresh Tomato Slices With Basil Mayonnaise

fast fixin's

PREP: 5 MIN.

3 Tbsp. fresh lemon juice
¼ cup egg substitute
¼ cup chopped fresh basil
2 tsp. coarse-grained mustard
½ to ¾ tsp. salt
½ tsp. pepper
⅔ cup vegetable oil
2 large ripe tomatoes, sliced

1. Process first 6 ingredients in a food processor or blender until smooth, stopping to scrape down sides. With processor running, pour vegetable oil through food chute in a slow, steady stream; process until smooth and thickened. Spoon over sliced tomatoes. **Makes** 8 servings.

Kitchen Express: Stir together ½ cup mayonnaise, ¼ cup chopped fresh basil, 2 tsp. coarse-grained mustard, and salt and pepper to taste. Cover and chill up to 1 week. Serve mayonnaise mixture over tomatoes.

Terrific Tips

■ For faster ripening results, place tomatoes in a brown paper bag.
■ Tomatoes will ripen more quickly when stored next to bananas.
■ 1 lb. tomatoes will yield about 2½ cups chopped, 3 cups wedged, or 3 cups sliced.
■ Never store a fresh tomato in the refrigerator, which reduces the quality of its flavor and texture. Leave at room temperature on the kitchen counter.
■ You should refrigerate tomatoes once they have been cooked, sliced, chopped, or made into a salsa.
■ Tomatoes are available year-round, but they are at their peak July through August.

Amazing Avocados

G rocery store bins are filled with avocados this time of year, so now's your chance to enjoy their tropical flavor. To effortlessly pit an avocado, Test Kitchens Specialist Vanessa McNeil Rocchio suggests slicing all the way around the pit and through both ends of the avocado with a large knife. Then twist the halves in opposite directions, and pull them apart. If the avocado flesh is firm, tap the pit sharply with the knife, and twist the blade to lift out the pit. For those with a softer flesh, gently squeeze the outside of the avocado, and remove the pit with your fingers.

Corn-and-Avocado Salsa

PREP: 25 MIN., COOK: 8 MIN., CHILL: 30 MIN.
Serve with tortilla chips. To add flavor without more heat, increase the fajita seasoning by ½ Tbsp.

4 cups fresh or frozen corn kernels
1 Tbsp. fajita seasoning
½ tsp. pepper
2 Tbsp. vegetable oil
1 red bell pepper, chopped
½ jalapeño pepper, seeded and chopped
½ cup chopped green onions
¼ cup fresh chopped cilantro
¼ cup fresh lime juice
2 Tbsp. orange juice
¾ tsp. salt
2 ripe avocados, diced

1. Sauté first 3 ingredients in hot oil in a large skillet over medium-high heat 6 to 8 minutes or until corn is slightly golden. Remove from heat; let cool.
2. Stir together corn mixture, bell pepper, and next 6 ingredients. Cover and chill at least 30 minutes. Stir in avocado just before serving. **Makes** 4½ cups.

Note: For testing purposes only, we used Badia Fajita Seasoning.

MICHAEL RUSSO
LAFAYETTE, LOUISIANA

Cook's Notes

■ Two varieties are widely available: **Hass** (from California and Mexico) and **Florida** (also sold as **Fuerte**). Smaller Hass avocados have bumpy, dark green skin and a vibrant, buttery flesh. Its skin turns almost black as it ripens. Florida avocados are larger with almost smooth, emerald-green skin and a firm, mild flesh.
■ Hass avocados contain about 30% more fat than Florida ones, but both are filled with monounsaturated fat, which boosts HDL (good cholesterol) levels. The creamy flesh of the higher fat Hass is ideal for mashing or pureeing for guacamole or salad dressing; Florida's mild, firm flesh is perfect for dicing and slicing for sandwiches and salsa.

Melted Avocado Club

PREP: 20 MIN., COOK: 12 MIN.

2 ripe avocados, mashed
1 Tbsp. fresh lime juice
1 Tbsp. mayonnaise
1 Tbsp. yellow mustard
⅛ tsp. ground red pepper
8 whole wheat bread slices
½ lb. thinly sliced deli ham
½ lb. thinly sliced deli roast beef
4 tomato slices
8 bacon slices, cooked
¼ lb. provolone cheese slices
3 Tbsp. butter, softened and divided

1. Stir together first 5 ingredients. Spread avocado mixture evenly on 1 side of each of 4 bread slices. Top each evenly with ham, next 4 ingredients, and remaining bread slices. Spread butter on both sides of each sandwich.
2. Cook sandwiches in a nonstick skillet or on a griddle over medium heat 6 minutes on each side or until golden. **Makes** 4 sandwiches.

CLAIRE CARDWELL
MADISON, GEORGIA

Bring Home Fresh Flavor

Stroll, shop, and savor. Let our great recipes, inspired by a trip to Atlanta's Dekalb Farmers Market, guide you the next time you visit your favorite local spot for produce.

Wear comfy shoes, plan to stay awhile, and bring your wallet when you visit Your Dekalb Farmers Market in Decatur, Georgia. Whatever your taste in food, when you experience this culinary mecca, you're going to want to shop.

The 140,000-square-foot superstore just outside of Atlanta offers virtually every foodstuff you can imagine—as well as plenty you've never heard of—all at reasonable prices. It attracts the city's large ethnic population looking for hard-to-find items, as well as folks shopping for okra to fry, corn to grill, or freshly roasted coffee to brew.

The great prices reflect owner Robert Blazer's commitment to making top-notch foods available to people of limited means. "Our goal is to make [fresh food] as affordable as we can," he says. "What I've always wanted the market to be is a service to the community."

Robert and his wife, Barbara, and a staff of 450 people of some 30 different nationalities serve the 7,000 daily customers. Though most of the staff speak English, their nametags list the other languages they speak, useful to customers with a limited grasp of English.

No language is needed, though, to select from top-quality fruits and vegetables. The produce comes in daily, both from local farmers and from 50 different countries. Looking for melons? You'll likely find a dozen kinds. If you favor exotic ingredients, there is galangal, lemon grass, horseradish root, and even durian. The in-house bakery produces 75 kinds of breads, bagels, cookies, pies, and muffins. At the seafood counter, customers line up for octopus and live crabs, as well as dozens of different fish and shellfish. Meats and dairy products round out the perishable items, complemented by wines, fresh flowers, jams, pastas, and sauces.

Enjoy these recipes inspired by the international flavors of this marvelous market.

Spicy Curried Fried Chicken

PREP: 15 MIN.; CHILL: 3 HRS.; STAND: 30 MIN.; FRY: 1 HR., 5 MIN.

The wings cook more quickly than larger pieces, so we recommend that you cook them first. While we normally fry at 375°, this recipe requires a lower temperature to keep the chicken from overbrowning.

1 (3½-lb.) cut-up whole chicken
Spicy Yogurt Marinade
1½ cups all-purpose baking mix
⅓ cup sesame seeds
1½ tsp. garam masala
1 tsp. coarsely ground pepper
Canola oil
Minted Mango Dipping Sauce

1. Place chicken in a 13- x 9-inch dish; pour Spicy Yogurt Marinade over chicken, turning to coat. Cover and chill at least 3 hours or overnight, turning occasionally.

2. Remove chicken from marinade, and place on a wire rack on an aluminum foil-lined baking sheet; let stand 10 minutes.

3. Stir together baking mix and next 3 ingredients in a large bowl; toss chicken in mixture until coated, shaking off excess. Repeat coating process. Return chicken to rack; let stand 15 minutes.

4. Pour oil to a depth of 1 inch in a large heavy skillet; heat to 350°. (Temperature will reduce as chicken is added. For best results, keep temperature between 300° and 325°.) Fry wings 6 minutes; turn and cook 6 more minutes. Remove wings to a rack on an aluminum foil-lined baking sheet. Keep warm in a 200° oven. Fry remaining chicken, 2 pieces at a time, skin sides down, 6 minutes; turn and cook 6 more minutes. Turn pieces; cover and cook 6 minutes or until done, turning during the last 3 minutes for even browning, if necessary. (Chicken pieces will be very dark.) Remove to wire rack; let stand 5 minutes. Serve with Minted Mango Dipping Sauce. **Makes** 4 servings.

Spicy Curried Fried Shrimp: Substitute 2 lb. peeled and deveined jumbo shrimp for chicken; proceed as directed. Fry shrimp, in batches, at 350° for 3 minutes or until golden; drain on paper towels.

Spicy Yogurt Marinade:

fast fixin's • make ahead
PREP: 10 MIN.
You can make this marinade up to 1 day ahead and store it in the fridge.

2 cups plain yogurt
6 Tbsp. chopped fresh cilantro
4 tsp. red curry powder
1 Tbsp. grated lemon rind
2 garlic cloves, minced
1½ tsp. ground ginger
1 tsp. salt

1. Stir together all ingredients in a medium bowl. **Makes** about 2 cups.

Minted Mango Dipping Sauce:
fast fixin's
PREP: 5 MIN.
Stir together 1 (9-oz.) jar mango chutney (about ¾ cup), 3 Tbsp. fresh lime juice, and 1 Tbsp. chopped fresh mint. **Makes** about 1 cup.

CAMILLA SAULSBURY
BLOOMINGTON, INDIANA

Roasted Vegetable Sandwiches
vegetarian
PREP: 20 MIN., BAKE: 12 MIN.

¼ cup butter, softened
1 garlic clove, pressed
¼ tsp. dried Italian seasoning
4 French hamburger buns, split
4 tsp. mayonnaise
3 cups Roasted Summer Vegetables
4 provolone cheese slices

1. Stir together first 3 ingredients.
2. Spread butter mixture evenly on cut sides of top bun halves; spread mayonnaise evenly on cut sides of bottom bun halves. Place ¾ cup Roasted Summer Vegetables evenly on each bottom bun half; top each with 1 provolone cheese slice and remaining bun halves. Wrap each sandwich lightly in aluminum foil, and place on a baking sheet.
3. Bake at 400° for 10 to 12 minutes or until cheese melts. **Makes** 4 sandwiches.

Note: For testing purposes only, we used Publix Deli French Hamburger Buns.

Roasted Summer Vegetables:
PREP: 30 MIN., STAND: 20 MIN., BAKE: 20 MIN.
Enjoy these vegetables as a flavorful side dish, or use them in salads, sandwiches, or with deli-roasted chicken.

1 medium eggplant
1 tsp. salt, divided
2 medium zucchini (about 1 lb.)
3 yellow squash (about 1¼ lb.)
1 red bell pepper
1 medium-size sweet onion, halved
3 Tbsp. olive oil
½ tsp. pepper
3 Tbsp. chopped fresh basil
1 Tbsp. chopped fresh parsley

1. Cut eggplant into ¼-inch-thick slices, and place in a single layer on paper towels. Sprinkle with ½ tsp. salt, and let stand 20 minutes.
2. Cut zucchini and yellow squash into ¼-inch-thick slices. Cut bell pepper into ½-inch strips. Cut onion halves into ½-inch slices.
3. Toss together vegetables, olive oil, remaining ½ tsp. salt, and pepper; place in 3 lightly greased broiler pans or jelly-roll pans.
4. Bake at 450° for 20 minutes or until vegetables are tender, stirring once. Remove from oven, and sprinkle evenly with basil and parsley. **Makes** 6 to 8 servings.

Green Beans With Bacon and Shallots
PREP: 25 MIN., COOK: 30 MIN.

2½ lb. fresh green beans, trimmed
8 bacon slices, chopped
1 Tbsp. butter
⅔ cup finely chopped shallots (about 4 large)
½ tsp. salt
¼ tsp. pepper

1. Cook beans in boiling salted water 9 minutes or until crisp-tender; drain. Plunge into ice water to stop the cooking process; drain.
2. Cook chopped bacon in a large skillet until crisp; remove bacon, and drain on paper towels, reserving 1 Tbsp. drippings in skillet. Add 1 Tbsp. butter to hot drippings in skillet over medium heat; add chopped shallots, and sauté 4 minutes or until tender. Add beans; sauté 6 minutes or until thoroughly heated. Sprinkle evenly with salt, pepper, and bacon. **Makes** 10 servings.

MARLENE MCDONALD
SANFORD, NORTH CAROLINA

Add Fresh Flavor to Sweet Tea

Pour a tall glass of tea on a sultry summer day—but make it a jazzed-up version of the Southern standard by using one of these variations. Peach nectar and fresh mint are the stars in Governor's Mansion Summer Peach Tea Punch. The delicious recipe makes a gallon, so you're guaranteed to have plenty for family and friends. Refreshing, citrus-kissed Fruited Mint Tea blends orange and lemon juices. No matter how you flavor it, cold tea is hard to beat on a hot day.

Fruited Mint Tea
fast fixin's • make ahead
PREP: 5 MIN., COOK: 5 MIN., STEEP: 10 MIN.
Add a fresh twist to this summertime favorite with fruit juice and mint tea leaves.

3 cups water
4 regular-size tea bags
12 fresh mint sprigs
1 cup sugar
1 cup orange juice
¼ cup lemon juice
5 cups cold water

1. Bring 3 cups water to a boil in a medium saucepan; add tea bags. Boil 1 minute; remove from heat. Add mint; cover and steep 10 minutes.
2. Remove and discard tea bags and mint. Add 1 cup sugar, stirring until dissolved.
3. Pour into a 1-gal. heatproof container; add orange juice, lemon juice, and 5 cups cold water. Chill or serve over ice. **Makes** about 2½ qt.

MAURICE MALLOW
BRADY, TEXAS

Governor's Mansion Summer Peach Tea Punch

make ahead

PREP: 5 MIN., COOK: 5 MIN., STEEP: 10 MIN., CHILL: 8 HRS.

Fruit juice nectars are blends of fruit puree, water, and cane sugar. You can find them in a variety of flavors in the fruit juice aisle of the supermarket. (Pictured on page 171)

4 cups water
3 family-size tea bags
2 cups loosely packed fresh mint leaves
1 (33.8-oz.) bottle peach nectar
1 (6-oz.) can frozen lemonade
    concentrate, thawed
½ cup Simple Sugar Syrup
1 (1-liter) bottle ginger ale, chilled
1 (1-liter) bottle club soda, chilled
Garnish: fresh mint sprigs

1. Bring 4 cups water to a boil in a medium saucepan; add tea bags and 2 cups mint leaves. Boil 1 minute; remove from heat. Cover and steep 10 minutes.
2. Remove and discard tea bags and mint. Pour into a 1-gal. container; add peach nectar, lemonade concentrate, and Simple Sugar Syrup. Cover and chill 8 hours or overnight.
3. Pour chilled tea mixture into a punch bowl. Stir in ginger ale and club soda just before serving. Garnish, if desired. **Makes** about 1 gal.

Simple Sugar Syrup:

fast fixin's

PREP: 5 MIN., COOK: 8 MIN.

2 cups sugar
1 cup water

1. Bring 2 cups sugar and 1 cup water to a boil in a medium saucepan over medium-high heat. Boil, stirring occasionally, 4 minutes or until sugar is dissolved and mixture is clear. Cool to room temperature. **Makes** 2½ cups.

AUSTIN ENTERTAINS
JUNIOR LEAGUE OF AUSTIN, TEXAS

quick & easy

New Ways With Tacos

This popular Mexican dish is a no-recipe-required, budget-stretching, familiar meal. We've tweaked the taco concept with surprising new suppers. Once you try these recipes, you'll know them by heart in no time.

Taco Pizzas

family favorite

PREP: 20 MIN., COOK: 10 MIN.,
BAKE: 10 MIN. PER PIZZA, STAND: 5 MIN.
PER PIZZA

This recipe makes 2 (12-inch) pizzas. If your family won't eat both pizzas on the same night, save half the ingredients for the second pizza at another meal.

1 lb. ground pork ∗
1 (1.25-oz.) package 40%-less-sodium
    taco seasoning mix
⅔ cup water
¼ cup chopped fresh cilantro
1 (11-oz.) can Mexican-style corn, rinsed
    and drained
1 (10-oz.) can mild diced tomatoes and
    green chiles
1½ cups (6 oz.) shredded Colby-
    Monterey Jack cheese blend
1 (24-oz.) package prebaked pizza
    crusts
1 (16-oz.) can fat-free refried beans
Toppings: sliced green onions, shredded
    lettuce, sour cream

1. Cook ground pork in a large skillet over medium-high heat 5 minutes, stirring until meat crumbles and is no longer pink; drain well on paper towels. Wipe skillet with a paper towel. Return pork to skillet; stir in taco seasoning mix and ⅔ cup water; cook according to package directions on seasoning mix. Remove mixture from heat, and stir in chopped cilantro and next 3 ingredients.
2. Place pizza crusts on baking sheets. Spread half of refried beans evenly over each crust, leaving a ¼-inch border around edges. Top beans evenly with pork mixture.
3. Bake, 1 pizza at a time, at 400° for 8 to 10 minutes or until thoroughly heated and cheese melts. Remove from oven; let stand 5 minutes. Serve with desired toppings. **Makes** 6 servings.

Note: For testing purposes only, we used Old El Paso 40% Less Sodium Taco Seasoning Mix and Mama Mary's Gourmet Pizza Crusts.

∗Substitute 1 lb. ground chuck for ground pork, if desired.

TINA KILLEN
CLARKSVILLE, TENNESSEE

Mini Taco Cups

PREP: 20 MIN., BAKE: 25 MIN.

Serve Mini Taco Cups as an appetizer for a party or gathering. Treat your family to these tasty bites by serving the meat mixture in regular-size taco shells for supper tonight.

½ lb. mild pork sausage
½ lb. ground chuck
1 (8-oz.) jar taco sauce
½ cup (2 oz.) shredded Monterey Jack
    cheese
1 (4.5-oz.) can chopped green chiles
1 (16-oz.) package won ton wrappers
Toppings: sour cream, shredded cheese,
    salsa, chopped lettuce

1. Crumble sausage and ground beef into a microwave-safe container. Microwave at HIGH 1 minute, and stir.

Microwave at HIGH 4 to 4½ minutes, stirring every 60 seconds, or until meat is done and no longer pink. Drain well on paper towels. Stir together sausage mixture, taco sauce, ½ cup shredded cheese, and green chiles. Set aside.

2. Press won ton wrappers into 24 lightly greased mini muffin cups. Reserve remaining wrappers for another use.

3. Bake at 350° for 8 minutes or until wrappers start to brown. Remove muffin pans to wire racks. Fill baked won ton cups evenly with sausage mixture. Return pans to oven, and bake 15 more minutes or until thoroughly heated and cheese melts. Serve with desired toppings. **Makes** 24 cups.

Note: For testing purposes only, we used an 1,100-watt microwave oven and Old El Paso Taco Sauce.

TERESA METZGER
LOUISVILLE, KENTUCKY

healthy & light

Dessert Without the Guilt

Don't skip dessert! These cool, creamy treats are low fat and low calorie and taste so great that you'll never notice the difference. Each has 7 or fewer ingredients, and one doesn't even require cooking. Tangy Key Lime Pie is just right for those concerned with heart health. For a calcium boost, sample the Caramel Custard. If you're watching your sugar intake, try the Chocolate Parfaits. All are sure to please.

Caramel Custard
make ahead
PREP: 5 MIN., COOK: 5 MIN., STAND: 5 MIN.,
BAKE: 1 HR., CHILL: 3 HRS.
The hot water bath helps insulate the custard from the direct heat of the oven and provides a more gentle environment for even baking.

½ cup sugar
2 egg yolks
1 large egg
1 (14-oz.) can fat-free sweetened
    condensed milk
1 (12-oz.) can evaporated fat-free milk
3 oz. ⅓-less-fat cream cheese, softened
1 Tbsp. vanilla extract

1. Cook sugar in an 8-inch round cakepan (with 2-inch sides) over medium heat, shaking pan occasionally, 5 minutes or until sugar melts and turns light golden brown. Remove pan from heat, and let stand 5 minutes. (Sugar will harden.)

2. Process egg yolks and next 5 ingredients in a blender until smooth. Pour mixture over caramelized sugar in pan. Cover mixture with aluminum foil.

3. Place cakepan in a broiler pan. Add hot water (150°) to pan to a depth of ⅔ inch.

4. Bake at 350° for 1 hour or until a knife inserted in center of custard comes out clean. Remove cakepan from water bath; cool completely on a wire rack. Cover and chill at least 3 hours.

5. Run a knife around edge of pan to loosen; invert onto a serving plate. **Makes** 10 servings.

Tip: The 8-oz. blocks of ⅓-less-fat cream cheese have marks on the packaging noting 1 oz. measurements. By using these marks, it's easy to measure the 3 oz. of cream cheese that you need for this recipe.

Per (1-slice) serving: Calories 220 (13% from fat); Fat 3.3g (sat 1.7g, mono 0.6g, poly 0.2g); Protein 7.7g; Carb 38.9g; Fiber 0g; Chol 75mg; Iron 0.3mg; Sodium 127mg; Calc 214mg

Banana-Caramel Custard: Prepare the custard recipe as directed, adding 1 medium-size ripe banana to egg yolk mixture in blender.

Per (1-slice) serving: Calories 231 (13% from fat); Fat 3.3g (sat 1.7g, mono 0.6g, poly 0.2g); Protein 7.8g; Carb 41.8g; Fiber 0.4g; Chol 75mg; Iron 0.3mg; Sodium 127mg; Calc 214mg

Key Lime Pie
make ahead
PREP: 10 MIN., BAKE: 12 MIN.
Place the unbaked pie on a baking sheet for easy removal from the oven. (Pictured on page 175)

1 (14-oz.) can fat-free sweetened
    condensed milk
¾ cup egg substitute
2 tsp. grated lime rind (about 2 limes)
½ cup fresh lime juice
1 (6-oz.) reduced-fat ready-made
    graham cracker crust
1 (8-oz.) container fat-free whipped
    topping, thawed
Garnishes: lime wedges, lime curls

1. Process first 4 ingredients in a blender until smooth. Pour mixture into piecrust.

2. Bake at 350° for 10 to 12 minutes or until golden. Let pie cool completely, and top with whipped topping. Garnish, if desired. **Makes** 8 servings.

BARBARA PETIT
COLUMBIA, SOUTH CAROLINA

Per (1-slice) serving: Calories 290 (12% from fat); Fat 3.7g (sat 0.5g, mono 0g, poly 0g); Protein 7.4g; Carb 55.1g; Fiber 0.1g; Chol 3mg; Iron 0.4mg; Sodium 185mg; Calc 143mg

Easy Blending

You can achieve creamy desserts by using your electric blender to combine the ingredients. Whipping everything together results in a smoother consistency and a silkier feel in your mouth. Quickly clean the appliance by processing warm tap water and a small amount of liquid detergent in the blender for a few seconds. Then rinse and dry.

Chocolate Parfaits
make ahead

PREP: 20 MIN., CHILL: 1 HR.

We tried using both sugar-free instant and regular pudding mixes. To our surprise, we preferred the flavor of the sugar-free. (Pictured on page 175)

1 (1.4-oz.) package fat-free, sugar-free chocolate instant pudding mix
2 cups 1% low-fat milk
½ cup light sour cream
1 (8-oz.) container fat-free frozen whipped topping, thawed and divided
¾ cup chocolate graham cracker crumbs (4 cracker sheets)
1 Tbsp. freshly grated chocolate

1. Whisk together first 3 ingredients in a bowl until blended and smooth. Fold in 1½ cups whipped topping.
2. Spoon 1 Tbsp. crumbs into each of 6 (4-oz.) glasses, and top with ⅓ cup pudding mixture. Repeat layers with remaining crumbs and pudding mixture. Top each parfait evenly with remaining whipped topping and grated chocolate. Cover and chill at least 1 hour. **Makes** 6 servings.

MARGARET GROVES
NORTHPORT, ALABAMA

Per serving: Calories 196 (22% from fat); Fat 4.6g (sat 2.3g, mono 1.3g, poly 0.3g); Protein 4.9g; Carb 31.8g; Fiber 0.2g; Chol 10mg; Iron 0.7mg; Sodium 306mg; Calc 101mg

Weeknight Chicken

Looking for some ideas to jazz up chicken breasts? Let these recipes provide inspiration. Grilled Chicken Burritos serve up a taste of the Southwest with ease by using convenient canned ingredients. Sesame-Pecan Crusted Chicken, with a mix of sweet and spicy flavors, offers Asian flair.

Both of these recipes can be made in about an hour, and you can shortcut the burritos even more by substituting shredded cooked chicken for the grilled breasts. Either way, the results are terrific.

Test Kitchen *Notebook*

Packaged saffron rice adds color and flavor to this one-dish meal sent to us by Tracey Ferrell of Nashville, Tennessee.

Lowcountry Chicken and Saffron Rice

PREP: 15 MIN., COOK: 40 MIN.

¼ cup diced sweet onion
1 celery rib, diced
¼ cup diced green bell pepper
2 tablespoons vegetable oil
1 garlic clove, minced
3 skinned and boned chicken breasts, cut into ½-inch pieces
3 cups low-sodium chicken broth
1 (14½-ounce) can diced tomatoes, undrained
¼ teaspoon dried thyme
2 (5-ounce) packages saffron rice mix

1. Sauté onion, celery, and bell pepper in 1 tablespoon oil in Dutch oven over medium-high heat 4 to 5 minutes or until onion is tender. Add garlic, and sauté 1 minute. Remove vegetables and set aside. Heat remaining 1 tablespoon oil in Dutch oven, add chicken, and cook until lightly browned.
2. Add broth, tomatoes, thyme, and vegetables; bring to a boil. Add rice mix. Reduce heat to low. Cover and cook 20 to 25 minutes or until rice is done. **Makes** 4 servings.

Donna Florio
SENIOR WRITER

Sesame-Pecan Crusted Chicken
family favorite

PREP: 15 MIN., CHILL: 10 MIN., COOK: 15 MIN.

Serve this dish with steamed rice and green beans for a simply satisfying meal.

2 lb. skinned and boned chicken breasts
⅓ cup reduced-sodium teriyaki sauce
1 cup pecans, finely ground
2 Tbsp. all-purpose flour
1 Tbsp. sesame seeds
¾ tsp. garlic powder
½ tsp. Chinese five-spice powder
2 Tbsp. vegetable oil
½ cup reduced-sodium teriyaki sauce
¼ cup water
1 Tbsp. cornstarch
¼ cup crushed pineapple
2 tsp. chopped green onions
Garnish: sliced green onions

1. Combine chicken breasts and ⅓ cup teriyaki sauce in a large zip-top plastic freezer bag; seal and chill 10 minutes.
2. Stir together pecans and next 4 ingredients in a shallow dish. Dredge chicken in pecan mixture.
3. Cook chicken in hot oil in a large skillet over medium heat 6 minutes on each side or until golden. Remove to a serving platter, and keep warm. Reserve drippings in skillet.
4. Stir together ½ cup teriyaki sauce, ¼ cup water, and cornstarch until smooth; add crushed pineapple and green onions. Stir mixture into drippings in skillet, stirring to loosen browned particles. Cook mixture over low heat, stirring constantly, 1 to 2 minutes or until thickened. Serve sauce over chicken. Garnish, if desired. **Makes** 6 servings.

GINNIE PRATER
ANNISTON, ALABAMA

Grilled Chicken Burritos
family favorite

PREP: 10 MIN., GRILL: 20 MIN., BAKE: 30 MIN., STAND: 10 MIN.

Use the meat from a deli-roasted chicken in these burritos if you're in a hurry.

3 skinned and boned chicken breasts
½ tsp. salt
¼ tsp. pepper
Vegetable cooking spray
2 (10-oz.) cans tomatoes with green chiles, divided
1 (19.75-oz.) can black beans, rinsed, drained, and divided
2 cups (8 oz.) shredded Monterey Jack cheese, divided
8 (8-inch) flour tortillas
1 (10-oz.) can green enchilada sauce
2 avocados, sliced
1 (8-oz.) container sour cream

1. Sprinkle chicken breasts with salt and pepper.
2. Coat food rack with cooking spray; place on grill over medium-high heat (350° to 400°). Place chicken on rack, and grill 10 minutes on each side or until done.
3. Shred chicken, and place in a large bowl. Stir in 1 can tomatoes with green chiles, half of black beans, and 1 cup of cheese.
4. Spoon chicken mixture evenly down center of each tortilla; roll up tortillas, and place, seam sides down, in a 13- x 9-inch baking dish. Top with enchilada sauce and remaining tomatoes with green chiles, black beans, and cheese.
5. Bake at 350° for 30 minutes. Remove from oven, and let stand 10 minutes. Top each serving with avocado slices and sour cream. **Makes** 4 servings.

CHRISTINA VALENTA
HOUSTON, TEXAS

Secrets to Perfect Pork Tenderloin

Your calls and e-mails confirm that pork tenderloin is more popular than ever. This lean cut is easy to cook, a great value, and right at home on the grill or in the oven. We've discovered it's important to remove the thick outer membrane called silver skin. This sinewy layer shrinks during cooking, causing the tenderloin to curl and cook unevenly. When the silver skin is removed, recipes taste and look much better. With a little practice and a sharp knife, you can master this in a snap.

Mustard-Glazed Pork Tenderloin
family favorite

PREP: 20 MIN., CHILL: 2 HRS., GRILL: 24 MIN., STAND: 10 MIN.

1 (8-oz.) jar Dijon mustard (1 cup)
⅓ cup orange juice
2 Tbsp. Creole seasoning
1½ lb. pork tenderloins
Garnish: fresh thyme sprigs

1. Stir together first 3 ingredients.
2. Place pork in a shallow dish or a zip-top plastic freezer bag; pour mustard mixture over pork. Cover or seal, and chill 2 hours, turning occasionally.
3. Remove pork from marinade, discarding marinade.
4. Grill, covered with grill lid, over medium-high heat (350° to 400°) 10 to 12 minutes on each side or until a meat thermometer inserted into thickest portion registers 155°. Remove from grill; let stand until thermometer registers 160°. Let stand 5 more minutes before slicing. Garnish, if desired. **Makes** 8 servings.

JUSTIN SAYER
ORLANDO, FLORIDA

Removing the Silver Skin

1. Place meat on a cutting board. Use your sharpest knife to trim away the layer of silver skin, being careful not to remove edible meat.

2. Pull the end of the silver skin tight above the meat, and gently cut the layer away, making sure to keep the blade of the knife angled slightly upward and just underneath the skin.

3. A trimmed pork tenderloin should be free of any visible fat and silver skin.

Summer Living®

*Celebrate the season with our creative menu ideas and tips
for outdoor entertaining.*

Casual at the Beach

Start these scrumptious dishes at home,
and finish them when you arrive.

Here's how to enjoy great food and still have time to lounge by the ocean: Prep some of the food at home, and carry it to the beach with you. Make our flavored mayonnaises, shrimp barbecue sauce, and dressing ahead, put them in containers with snug lids, chill, and pack them in a cooler. The process couldn't be simpler.

When you get to the coast, visit your favorite seafood market for fresh shrimp and fish fillets to use in these recipes.

Basil Mayonnaise
fast fixin's • make ahead
PREP. 10 MIN.

1 cup light mayonnaise
1 tsp. grated lemon rind
1 Tbsp. fresh lemon juice
1 cup loosely packed fresh basil leaves

1. Process all ingredients in a food processor or blender until smooth, stopping to scrape down sides. Store in an airtight container in the refrigerator up to 1 week. **Makes** 1½ cups.

Garlic-Chili Mayonnaise: Omit lemon rind and basil. Substitute fresh lime juice for lemon juice. Stir together mayonnaise, juice, and 2 Tbsp. Asian garlic-chili sauce. **Makes** about 1 cup.

Fish Sandwiches
PREP: 15 MIN.
Use steamed, poached, or baked fish in this sandwich. Any firm white fish, such as tilapia or grouper, works well. (Pictured on page 176)

2 lb. firm white fish, cooked
¼ tsp. grated lemon rind
¼ cup fresh lemon juice
2 Tbsp. olive oil
¼ tsp. salt
¼ tsp. pepper
½ cup Basil Mayonnaise (recipe at left)
4 French bread rolls, split
4 romaine lettuce leaves
¼ cup thinly sliced red onion

1. Flake fish in a medium bowl. Add ¼ tsp. lemon rind, ¼ cup lemon juice, 2 Tbsp. olive oil, ¼ tsp. salt, and ¼ tsp. pepper, tossing gently to coat.
2. Spread Basil Mayonnaise evenly on cut sides of rolls. Place lettuce and fish on bottom halves of rolls; top with onion, and cover with roll tops. **Makes** 4 servings.

BBQ Shrimp
PREP: 5 MIN., BAKE: 35 MIN.
To make cleanup easier, bake in a disposable foil pan. If you transport the lemon wedges in the marinade, it's okay to bake them with the shrimp. (Pictured on page 177)

4 lb. unpeeled, large fresh
    shrimp
2 lemons, cut into wedges
2 bay leaves
1 cup butter, melted
1 cup ketchup
½ cup Worcestershire sauce
4 garlic cloves, chopped
3 Tbsp. Old Bay seasoning
1 tsp. dried rosemary
1 tsp. dried thyme
French bread

1. Place shrimp in a 13- x- 9-inch pan; top with lemon wedges and bay leaves.
2. Stir together butter and next 6 ingredients. Pour over shrimp.
3. Bake, uncovered, at 400° for 35 minutes or until shrimp are pink, stirring every 10 minutes. Discard bay leaves. Serve with bread and lemon wedges. **Makes** 6 to 8 servings.

Basil Shrimp Salad
fast fixin's
PREP: 20 MIN.

4 to 6 large tomatoes
2 lb. peeled cooked shrimp
½ cup finely chopped celery
¼ cup sliced green onions
¼ cup Basil Mayonnaise (recipe on opposite page)

1. Cut a ¼-inch slice from tops of tomatoes; scoop out and discard pulp, leaving shells intact. Drain tomato shells upside down on paper towels.
2. Stir together shrimp and next 3 ingredients. Spoon evenly into tomato shells. **Makes** 4 to 6 servings.

Asian Beef Salad
PREP: 15 MIN., CHILL: 1 HR., GRILL: 14 MIN., STAND: 5 MIN.
No grill available? Cook the beef in a grill skillet on the cooktop. Napa cabbage may be called Chinese cabbage in some grocery stores.

¼ cup teriyaki sauce
2 Tbsp. olive oil
2 (1-lb.) flank steaks
1 (1¾-lb.) napa cabbage, chopped
1 large head romaine lettuce, chopped
2 large tomatoes, cut into wedges
2 cucumbers, thinly sliced
½ small red onion, thinly sliced
½ cup loosely packed fresh cilantro
Soy-Sesame Dressing

1. Combine teriyaki sauce and oil in a shallow dish or large zip-top plastic freezer bag; add steaks, turning to coat. Cover or seal, and chill 1 hour, turning steaks occasionally.
2. Remove steaks from marinade, discarding marinade.
3. Grill steaks, covered with grill lid, over medium-high heat (350° to 400°) 5 to 7 minutes on each side or to desired degree of doneness. Let stand 5 minutes; cut diagonally across the grain into thin slices.

4. Toss steak slices, cabbage, and next 5 ingredients together; drizzle with desired amount of Soy-Sesame Dressing, tossing gently to coat. **Makes** 8 servings.

Soy-Sesame Dressing:
fast fixin's • make ahead
PREP: 5 MIN.
Sesame oil lends a nutty flavor. Use the higher amount of Asian garlic-chili sauce for a spicier dressing. Store dressing in the refrigerator up to 1 week.

¼ cup fresh lime juice
1 Tbsp. light brown sugar
3 Tbsp. olive oil
3 Tbsp. sesame oil
2 Tbsp. lite soy sauce
1 to 2 tsp. Asian garlic-chili sauce

1. Whisk together all ingredients. **Makes** ¾ cup.

Thai Iced Coffee
make ahead
PREP: 10 MIN., STAND: 12 HRS.

½ lb. dark roast ground coffee
8 cups cold water
½ tsp. vanilla extract
1 (14-oz.) can sweetened condensed milk

1. Stir together ground coffee and 8 cups cold water in a pitcher until well combined; let stand at room temperature 12 hours.
2. Pour coffee mixture through a large, fine wire-mesh strainer into a Dutch oven or other large container, discarding grounds. Clean strainer; place a coffee filter or double layer of cheesecloth in strainer, and pour coffee mixture through lined strainer into a pitcher. Add vanilla extract. (Cover and store in refrigerator up to 1 week, if desired.)
3. Stir together coffee mixture and sweetened condensed milk. Serve over ice. **Makes** about 7 cups.

Pack It Right

Taking food you've prepared at home to the beach is a great idea—as long as you keep it properly chilled on the journey. Food needs to be kept colder than 40° to prevent bacteria from growing. Here are some tips for maintaining the proper temperature.
■ Pack food snugly in a well-insulated cooler with a secure lid. This should be your last chore before leaving the house. Do not open the cooler until you're ready to unpack it. Keep cold drinks and snacks for the trip in a separate cooler.
■ If possible, store the cooler in an air-conditioned area of the car rather than the trunk.
■ Make sure all the food is cold when it goes into the cooler. If any of the items you're transporting can be frozen, put them in the cooler that way. They'll help keep the other food cold.
■ Ice is terrific for keeping things really cold, but as it melts, it can seep into containers. Ice packs (also called gel packs or Blue Ice) are good alternatives.

Island Family Reunion

Share this family's favorite recipes from their annual beach gathering.

It's easy to eat well in the Lowcountry. Fresh, local seafood and regional specialties inspire a lot of the dishes at the Drennen family reunion.

Sullivan's Island, South Carolina, has been Betty Drennen's summer vacation spot for generations—a place that inspired some of her fondest childhood memories. "My family has been coming here since the 1930s," she says. To continue this cherished tradition, Betty and her husband, Jerry, take their adult children and all the grandkids every year to the South Carolina coast. "We laugh, play, and eat very well," she adds.

Of course, you don't have to go to the coast to enjoy these family favorites, but it's important to choose fresh seafood. Read on for our Test Kitchens tips, and share these flavorful recipes at your summer gathering.

Shrimp Sullivan's Island
make ahead
PREP: 45 MIN., COOK: 10 MIN., CHILL: 12 HRS.

10 qt. water
2 lemons, cut in half
5 lb. unpeeled, medium-size fresh shrimp
3 medium-size sweet onions, thinly sliced
3 (13.75-oz.) cans quartered artichoke hearts, drained
2 cups olive oil
1¾ cups cider vinegar
1 (3.5-oz.) jar capers, undrained
¼ cup Worcestershire sauce
1 tsp. salt
½ to 1 tsp. hot sauce
Garnish: chopped fresh parsley

1. Bring 10 qt. water to a boil in a 12-qt. stockpot over medium-high heat; squeeze lemon halves over water, and add squeezed halves to water in stockpot. Add shrimp, and cook 3 minutes or just until shrimp turn pink. Drain and rinse with cold water to stop the cooking process.
2. Peel shrimp; devein, if desired.
3. Layer shrimp, onions, and artichoke hearts in 2 (13- x 9-inch) baking dishes.
4. Stir together olive oil and next 5 ingredients; pour evenly over shrimp mixture. Cover and chill at least 12 hours or up to 48 hours, stirring occasionally. Garnish, if desired, and serve with a slotted spoon. **Makes** 18 appetizer servings.
BETTY DRENNEN
BIRMINGHAM, ALABAMA

Bacon-Wrapped Scallops
PREP: 30 MIN., CHILL: 30 MIN., GRILL: 8 MIN.

3 Tbsp. fresh lime juice
2 Tbsp. chopped fresh cilantro
2 garlic cloves, minced
¼ tsp. salt
¼ tsp. pepper
Dash hot sauce
½ cup olive oil
4 lb. sea scallops, rinsed and drained (about 48)
24 bacon slices (about 1 lb.), cut in half
Wooden picks
¼ tsp. salt
¼ tsp. pepper
Vegetable cooking spray

1. Combine first 6 ingredients in a small bowl; whisk in olive oil in a slow, steady stream. Place scallops in a zip-top plastic freezer bag; add lime juice mixture. Cover or seal, and chill 30 minutes, turning once. Drain scallops, discarding marinade.
2. Microwave bacon, covered with paper towels, in 4 batches, at HIGH 3 to 4 minutes or until slightly brown. Wrap 1 bacon piece around each scallop; secure with a wooden pick. Sprinkle with ¼ tsp. salt and ¼ tsp. pepper.
3. Coat a cold cooking grate with cooking spray, and place grate on grill over medium-high heat (350° to 400°). Place scallops on grate, and grill, covered with grill lid, 3 to 4 minutes on each side or until bacon is crisp and scallops are done. **Makes** 12 appetizer servings.
GREG HAYNES
FAIRHOPE, ALABAMA

West Indies Salad
PREP: 15 MIN., CHILL: 8 HRS.

1 lb. lump crabmeat, picked
1 medium-size sweet onion, diced
½ cup vegetable oil
⅓ cup cider vinegar
½ cup ice cubes
¾ tsp. salt
½ tsp. pepper
Assorted crackers
Garnish: fresh chopped parsley

1. Toss together first 7 ingredients gently. Cover and chill at least 8 hours or up to 48 hours. Serve with assorted crackers, and garnish, if desired. **Makes** 3½ cups.

ZEB HARGETT
BIRMINGHAM, ALABAMA

Greek Snapper on the Grill
fast fixin's
PREP: 15 MIN., GRILL: 15 MIN.

12 (8-oz.) snapper or grouper fillets
¼ cup olive oil
1 Tbsp. Greek seasoning
24 (¼-inch-thick) lemon slices
Dot's Tartar Sauce

1. Rub fish fillets with oil; sprinkle evenly with Greek seasoning. Top each fillet with 2 lemon slices.
2. Place a large piece of lightly greased heavy-duty aluminum foil over grill cooking grate. Arrange fish on foil.
3. Grill fillets, covered with grill lid, over medium-high heat (350° to 400°) 15 minutes or until fish flakes with a fork. Serve with Dot's Tartar Sauce. **Makes** 12 servings.

Note: For testing purposes only, we used Cavender's All-Purpose Greek Seasoning

PRISCILLA CARROLL
OZARK, ALABAMA

Dot's Tartar Sauce
fast fixin's • make ahead
PREP: 10 MIN.

1 cup mayonnaise
2 Tbsp. dill pickle relish
2 Tbsp. drained capers
2 Tbsp. chopped fresh chives
1 Tbsp. chopped fresh tarragon
1 Tbsp. Dijon mustard
2 tsp. fresh lemon juice
¼ tsp. black pepper
Garnish: fresh chopped chives

1. Stir together first 8 ingredients until blended. Cover and chill until ready to

serve. Garnish, if desired. **Makes** 1½ cups.

Note: For testing purposes only, we used Wickles Relish.

DOT ASHBY
BIRMINGHAM, ALABAMA

Red Rice
PREP: 10 MIN., COOK: 50 MIN.
Tomato paste tends to scorch easily, so be sure to stir as directed.

1½ cups uncooked long-grain rice
8 bacon slices
1 large sweet onion, chopped
4 garlic cloves, pressed
2½ cups chicken broth
1½ (6-oz.) cans tomato paste
½ tsp. salt
¼ tsp. pepper
3 Tbsp. chopped fresh parsley
Garnish: chopped fresh parsley

1. Rinse rice with cold running water 3 minutes or until water is no longer cloudy. Drain and set aside.
2. Cook bacon slices in a 3½-qt. saucepan over medium heat 10 minutes or until crisp. Drain bacon and set aside, reserving 2 Tbsp. bacon drippings in pan.
3. Sauté onion in hot drippings in saucepan over medium-high heat 8 minutes or until onion is tender; add garlic, and sauté 1 minute.
4. Stir in rinsed rice, chicken broth, and next 3 ingredients; bring to a boil. Cover, reduce heat to low, and simmer

30 minutes, stirring mixture every 7 to 10 minutes.
5. Remove from heat; fluff with a fork. Stir in crumbled bacon and 3 Tbsp. parsley; garnish, if desired. **Makes** 10 to 12 servings.

BETTY DRENNEN
BIRMINGHAM, ALABAMA

Sweet-and-Sour Slaw
PREP: 20 MIN.

2 (3-oz.) packages Ramen noodles
¼ cup butter
½ cup sliced almonds
¼ cup olive oil
2 Tbsp. sugar
2 Tbsp. white vinegar
1½ tsp. soy sauce
¼ tsp. salt
1 large cabbage, finely shredded
  (about 8 cups)

1. Remove seasoning packets from noodle packages, and reserve for another use. Break up uncooked noodles.
2. Melt butter in a large skillet over medium-high heat; add noodle pieces and almonds. Cook, stirring constantly, 5 minutes or until toasted. Remove from heat.
3. Whisk together olive oil and next 4 ingredients in a large bowl. Add cabbage, tossing to coat. Sprinkle with toasted noodles and almonds before serving. **Makes** about 12 servings.

PRISCILLA CARROLL
OZARK, ALABAMA

Pick Fresh Seafood

Before joining the *Southern Living* Foods staff, Test Kitchens Director Lyda Burnette spent time on the coast as a restaurant chef preparing seafood delicacies. Here are some of her suggestions for buying fresh ingredients.
■ If you're visiting the coast, ask around for a reputable seafood market. Most local markets offer fresh selections and lower prices.
■ Avoid fish that smells fishy. Fresh fish should not have an odor. Look for scallops with a sweet smell; a sulfurous odor indicates a spoiled scallop.
■ Choose shrimp that are slightly firm in texture, avoiding those that are soft and limp. Shelled shrimp should be moist and translucent. If purchasing unshelled shrimp, make sure the shells are tightly attached. Avoid dark spots, which might mean the shrimp are past their peak.

Lakeside Picnic

This active Austin family works up an appetite for a Southwestern lunch by the water.

Whether you're landlocked or living on the lake, this easy Southwestern menu is great for picnics, weeknight meals, or any summer occasion.

Steve and Cindy Present of Austin, Texas, have mastered casual outdoor entertaining. They're always inviting friends to their Lake Austin home for good food and fun activities.

Layered Bean Dip

fast fixin's • make ahead
PREP: 10 MIN.
Look for fresh salsa and guacamole at your supermarket deli for this make-ahead dip. Substitute mild refried beans if you prefer.

1 (15.6-oz.) can spicy refried beans
¼ cup sour cream
1 (8-oz.) package refrigerated
   guacamole
1 cup refrigerated salsa
1 cup (4 oz.) shredded Monterey Jack
   cheese
Toppings: chopped green onions, grape
   tomato halves, sour cream
Tortilla chips

1. Stir together beans and sour cream. Spoon evenly into an 8-inch-square serving dish. Spread guacamole over bean mixture; top evenly with salsa, and sprinkle with cheese. Cover and chill until ready to serve. Add desired toppings, and serve with tortilla chips. **Makes** 8 servings.

Note: For testing purposes only, we used Pace Traditional Refried Beans.

Papaya Gazpacho

make ahead
PREP: 15 MIN., CHILL: 4 HRS.
Serve this gazpacho in nonbreakable plastic stemware for a refreshing soup sipper. Coat the rims in salt by dipping them first in lime juice.

3 cups tomato juice
3 cups pineapple juice
1 cup chopped fresh papaya or mango
1 cup finely chopped avocado (about
   1½ avocados)
⅔ cup chopped yellow bell pepper
⅔ cup chopped yellow tomatoes
3 Tbsp. fresh lime juice (2 limes)
4 tsp. chopped fresh mint
1 tsp. sea salt
½ tsp. pepper
Lime juice (optional)
Sea salt (optional)
Hot sauce (optional)

1. Pulse first 10 ingredients in blender until smooth, stopping to scrape down sides. Cover and chill at least 4 hours.
2. Dip rims of margarita glasses in lime juice, and dip rims in sea salt to coat, if desired. Serve chilled soup in prepared glasses; serve with hot sauce, if desired. **Makes** 8 cups.

Mango-Chicken Wraps

PREP: 15 MIN., CHILL: 1 HR., GRILL: 8 MIN.

⅔ cup vegetable broth
¼ cup chopped cilantro
1 green onion, chopped
1 garlic clove
1 Tbsp. fresh lime juice (1 lime)
1 Tbsp. white wine vinegar
½ tsp. sea salt
2 fresh mangoes, peeled, chopped,
   and divided
½ tsp. chopped and seeded serrano
   chile pepper (optional)
1½ lb. chicken breast strips
¼ tsp. salt
Romaine lettuce leaves
10 (8-inch) flour tortillas
Wooden picks (optional)

1. Process first 7 ingredients, 1 chopped mango, and, if desired, chile pepper in food processor until smooth, stopping to scrape down sides. Pour half of mixture into a shallow dish or zip-top plastic freezer bag; add chicken. Cover or seal, and chill at least 1 hour. Cover, chill, and reserve other half of cilantro mixture.
2. Remove chicken from marinade, discarding marinade. Sprinkle chicken evenly with ¼ tsp. salt.
3. Grill chicken, covered with grill lid, over medium-high heat (350° to 400°) 4 minutes on each side or until done.
4. Shred chicken into bite-size pieces. Stir together chicken, remaining chopped mango, and reserved cilantro mixture.
5. Place lettuce leaves on each tortilla, and top each evenly with chicken mixture. Roll up tortillas, and secure with wooden picks, if desired. **Makes** 10 wraps.

Texas Pecan-and-Avocado Salad
fast fixin's
PREP: 15 MIN. *(Pictured on page 173)*

1 head Bibb lettuce
2 avocados, thinly sliced
1 red bell pepper, thinly sliced
1 yellow bell pepper, thinly sliced
½ cup chopped toasted pecans
Tangy Dijon Dressing

1. Arrange lettuce leaves on a serving platter. Top evenly with avocados and bell pepper slices; sprinkle with pecans. Drizzle with desired amount of dressing. **Makes** 8 servings.

Tangy Dijon Dressing:
fast fixin's
PREP: 5 MIN.

⅓ cup olive oil
2 Tbsp. lemon juice
2 Tbsp. water
1 Tbsp. sugar
2 tsp. Dijon mustard
⅛ tsp. salt
⅛ tsp. pepper

1. Whisk together all ingredients. Store in an airtight container in the refrigerator up to 1 week. **Makes** about ⅔ cup.

Cilantro Potato Salad
make ahead
PREP: 20 MIN., COOK: 15 MIN., CHILL: 4 HRS.
Canned green chiles add extra zest to this picnic favorite.

3 lb. red potatoes
2 tsp. salt, divided
1 cup mayonnaise
1 (4.5-oz.) can chopped green chiles
⅓ cup chopped fresh cilantro
3 green onions, chopped
2 Tbsp. fresh lime juice (about 2 limes)
1 garlic clove, minced
½ tsp. pepper
4 slices maple bacon, cooked and crumbled
Garnish: chopped fresh cilantro

1. Cook potatoes and 1 tsp. salt in boiling water to cover in a large Dutch oven 15 minutes or until fork tender. Drain and cool. Cut potatoes into quarters.
2. Stir together mayonnaise, next 6 ingredients, and remaining 1 tsp. salt in a large bowl; add potatoes, and toss to coat. Cover and chill at least 4 hours. Stir in bacon just before serving; garnish, if desired. **Makes** 8 servings.

Cream-Filled Chocolate Chip Wafers
make ahead
PREP: 20 MIN., CHILL: 2 HRS.

1 (8-oz.) package ⅓-less-fat cream cheese, softened
⅓ cup butter, softened
¼ tsp. vanilla extract
¾ cup powdered sugar
2 Tbsp. brown sugar
¾ cup semisweet chocolate mini-morsels
¾ cup finely chopped pecans, toasted
2 (9-oz.) boxes chocolate wafers

1. Beat first 3 ingredients at medium speed with an electric mixer until creamy. Gradually add sugars, beating until blended. Stir in chocolate morsels and pecans.
2. Spread about 1 Tbsp. cream cheese mixture evenly on 1 side of a chocolate wafer; top with another wafer. Repeat procedure with remaining wafers and cream cheese mixture. Cover cookies, and chill 2 hours. Store in refrigerator. **Makes** about 3½ dozen.

Note: For testing purposes only, we used Nabisco Famous Chocolate Wafers for chocolate wafers.

Icy Treats

Conquer the sweltering heat and entertain the youngsters with thirst-quenching, refreshing snow cones. As an alternative to packaged drink mixes, you can choose healthful options such as orange juice, a sports drink, or pomegranate juice. They'll all leave sweet mustaches on lips and huge smiles on faces.

Super-Sour Snow Cone Syrup
PREP: 10 MIN., COOK: 5 MIN., STAND: 20 MIN.

2 cups sugar
1¼ cups water
2 (0.23-oz.) envelopes unsweetened pink lemonade drink mix
1 (0.13-oz.) envelope unsweetened cherry drink mix
Crushed or shaved ice

1. Bring sugar and 1¼ cups water to a boil in a medium saucepan. Remove from heat, and stir in drink mixes. Cover and chill until ready to serve. Let stand at room temperature about 20 minutes. Spoon 1 to 2 Tbsp. syrup over 1 cup crushed or shaved ice for each serving. **Makes** 2½ cups.

Note: For testing purposes only, we used Kool-Aid Pink Lemonade and Kool-Aid Cherry drink mixes.

Snow Cone Syrup

PREP: 10 MIN., COOK: 5 MIN., STAND: 20 MIN.
You can substitute your favorite flavor drink mix.

2 cups sugar
1¼ cups water
1 (0.23-oz.) envelope unsweetened lemonade drink mix
Crushed or shaved ice

1. Bring sugar and 1¼ cups water to a boil in a medium saucepan. Remove from heat, and stir in drink mix. Cover and chill until ready to serve. Let stand at room temperature about 20 minutes. Spoon 1 to 2 Tbsp. syrup over 1 cup crushed or shaved ice for each serving. **Makes** 2½ cups.

Note: For testing purposes only, we used Kool-Aid Pink Lemonade drink mix.

Cool Off in Style

Discover the secret to the best-ever homemade snow cones, a Snow Cone Maker. This inexpensive, easy-to-use gadget from Rival shaves ice cubes straight from your freezer. Associate Foods Editor Vicki Poellnitz first used this appliance at her 12-year-old's birthday party, where it was a big hit. At least 15 of the preteens stood in line, because each one wanted to make his or her own icy treat. By the way, parents can also use it for their own frozen drinks.

Look for snow cone makers at large discount stores or online. Prices range from $20 to $40 for most home models.

New Twist on Watermelon

Don't miss these fun, no-fuss ideas the entire family can enjoy.

Watermelon season is in full swing, so now's the time to feast on these ruby-hued gems. Most of the time we enjoy this tasty melon in chunks or slices straight out of hand. Some folks add a sprinkling of salt to coax out a tad bit more of the fruit's tropical sweetness.

Once you've cut into your just-right find, use these creative recipes for that leftover hunk or two. We've even included an edible Watermelon Cup, which is sure to get rave reviews at your next gathering.

Watermelon Cups

These colorful cups look like a million bucks and can be made up to 4 hours ahead. Use them for everything from chicken or tuna salad to fresh fruit.

1. Cut a 2-inch-thick slice from a seedless watermelon. (We recommend using a large chef's knife.)

2. Using a 3-inch round cutter, press through the watermelon slice, forming a cylinder.

3. Scoop out the center of each cylinder, leaving a ½-inch-thick border, to form a cup, reserving the watermelon centers for another use. (**Tip:** A grapefruit spoon works great here.) Place cups on paper towels, and chill until ready to use.

Test Kitchen Secret: We use a melon baller to get perfectly round honeydew and cantaloupe balls (which, when combined with fresh blackberries and sprigs of fresh mint, make a simple yet beautiful presentation.) Most melon ballers are designed with a single handle and different-size scoops at each end.

Watermelon Salsa

fast fixin's • make ahead

PREP: 20 MIN.

This recipe doubles as a healthful and refreshing topping for grilled, baked, or broiled fish, shrimp, or chicken.

1½ tsp. grated lime rind
¼ cup fresh lime juice (about 3 limes)
1 Tbsp. sugar
¾ tsp. ground black pepper
3 cups seeded and finely chopped watermelon
1 cucumber, peeled, seeded, and diced
2 jalapeño peppers, seeded and minced
¼ cup chopped red onion
¼ cup chopped fresh basil
½ tsp. salt
Tortilla chips

1. Whisk together first 4 ingredients in a large bowl. Add watermelon and next 4 ingredients, gently tossing to coat. Chill until ready to serve. Stir in salt just before serving. Serve with tortilla chips. **Makes** about 3 cups.

WALKER OGLESBY
VESTAVIA HILLS, ALABAMA

Layered Fruit Salad

Check out our easy instructions to create layers of color using summer's bounty. We used a 2-qt. round glass bowl with straight sides, but you can use a different size, adjusting the amount of fruit as needed.

■ Cut 2 (1½-inch-thick) crosswise slices from center of a seedless watermelon. Place 1 slice on a cutting board. Using a paring knife, cut around the rind, and remove from slice, forming a watermelon disc. Repeat procedure with remaining slice.

■ Cut 1 or 2 honeydew melons and 1 cantaloupe in half lengthwise; peel and seed halves. Cut halves, crosswise, into ¼-inch-thick slices.

■ Place 1 watermelon disc on bottom of glass bowl. Layer half of honeydew melon slices in a circular pattern, slightly overlapping, on top of disc. Repeat procedure with remaining watermelon disc and honeydew slices.

■ Layer cantaloupe slices in a circular pattern, slightly overlapping, on top of honeydew slices.

■ Garnish, if desired, with fresh peach slices, raspberries, blackberries, strawberry halves, and mint leaves. If desired, place bowl on a cake stand.

Frozen Watermelon Dippers

PREP: 10 MIN., FREEZE: 4 HRS., STAND: 10 MIN.

Cantaloupe and pineapple can easily be used with the watermelon for a colorful variation.

15 (1-inch) seeded watermelon cubes
15 (4-inch) wooden skewers
Toppings: chocolate chips, vanilla yogurt, strawberry yogurt, candy sprinkles, sweetened toasted coconut, crystallized ginger, honey, chopped macadamia nuts, kosher salt, ground cumin

1. Place 1 watermelon cube on each of 15 skewers, and freeze 4 hours or until firm.
2. Remove from freezer, and let stand 10 minutes before serving.
3. Dip cubes in desired toppings. **Makes** 15 skewers.

Watermelon-Mint Margaritas

PREP: 10 MIN., FREEZE: 4 HRS.

Use leftover watermelon to make this slushy summer drink. (Pictured on page 6)

4 cups seeded and chopped watermelon
Fresh lime juice
Sugar
½ cup tequila ✱
¼ cup sugar
1 Tbsp. grated lime rind
¼ cup fresh lime juice (about 3 limes)
2 Tbsp. chopped fresh mint leaves
Garnish: fresh mint sprig

1. Place watermelon in a single layer on a baking sheet. Freeze 4 hours or until firm.
2. Coat rims of cocktail glasses with lime juice; dip in sugar.
3. Process frozen watermelon, tequila, and next 4 ingredients in a blender until slushy. Pour into glasses. Garnish, if desired. **Makes** 5 cups.

✱ Substitute ½ cup orange or apple juice for tequila, if desired.

Test Kitchen *Notebook*

To find the perfect watermelon, look for melons with smooth, blemish- and wrinkle-free skin. When you turn the melon over, look for a creamy yellow spot. This tells you it's been on the ground and allowed to ripen in the sun. Finally, because watermelons are about 92% water, they should be heavy for their size.

Scott Jones
EXECUTIVE EDITOR

Host a Block Party

Welcome all your neighbors to a great get-together. We'll tell you how.

Street Party

Serves 4

Pimiento Cheese-Stuffed Burgers
Marinated Green Beans
Egg-and-Olive Potato Salad
ice cream sandwiches

It's so much fun to play in the road. Close off the street in your neighborhood, and start your own festive celebration. With a little teamwork and tempting recipes, a block party will create fond memories. Here's a menu that everyone will love.

Pimiento Cheese-Stuffed Burgers

family favorite

PREP: 15 MIN., CHILL: 30 MIN., GRILL: 16 MIN.

Purchase pimiento cheese from your favorite deli, or make your own. This recipe is easy to increase for a crowd. Just prepare one recipe at a time to ensure the seasonings are correct.

2 lb. ground chuck
1 tsp. freshly ground black pepper
1⅓ cups prepared pimiento cheese, divided
1 tsp. salt
Hamburger buns
Toppings: tomato slices, red onion slices, lettuce leaves, mustard, mayonnaise, ketchup

1. Combine ground beef and pepper in a large bowl until blended. (Do not overwork meat mixture.) Shape mixture into 8 (4-inch) patties; spoon 1½ Tbsp. pimiento cheese in center of each of 4 patties. Top with remaining 4 patties; pressing edges to seal. Cover and chill at least 30 minutes. Sprinkle evenly with salt.
2. Grill, covered with grill lid, over medium-high heat (350° to 400°) for 7 to 8 minutes on each side or until beef is no longer pink. Serve on buns with desired toppings and remaining pimiento cheese. **Makes** 4 servings.

LIZ PITTMAN
HOMEWOOD, ALABAMA

Marinated Green Beans

make ahead

PREP: 20 MIN., COOK: 5 MIN., CHILL: 4 HRS.

1½ lb. fresh green beans, trimmed
¾ cup white vinegar
¼ cup sugar
2 Tbsp. vegetable oil
1 garlic clove, minced
¾ tsp. salt
½ tsp. pepper
1 small red onion, thinly sliced

1. Cook beans in boiling water to cover 4 to 5 minutes or until crisp-tender; drain. Plunge into ice water to stop the cooking process; drain.
2. Whisk together vinegar and next 5 ingredients in a large bowl; add beans and onion, tossing to coat. Cover and chill 4 hours. Serve with a slotted spoon. **Makes** 4 to 6 servings.

HILDA MORRISON
CHILDERSBURG, ALABAMA

Egg-and-Olive Potato Salad

make ahead

PREP: 20 MIN., COOK: 18 MIN.,
COOL: 10 MIN., CHILL: 2 HRS.

3½ lb. potatoes (about 4 large)
1 tsp. salt
5 hard-cooked eggs, grated
1 (7-oz.) jar pimiento-stuffed olives, drained and chopped
1 large celery rib, diced
½ small sweet onion, grated
1½ cups mayonnaise
½ tsp. pepper
Paprika (optional)

1. Peel potatoes, and cut into 1-inch cubes. Cook potatoes and salt in boiling water to cover in a Dutch oven 15 to 18 minutes or just until tender. Drain potatoes, and let cool 10 minutes.
2. Stir together eggs and next 5 ingredients. Add potatoes; toss gently to coat. Cover; chill 2 hours. Sprinkle with paprika, if desired. **Makes** 8 servings.

LARRY D. HEDGE
FORT WORTH, TEXAS

Block Party Basics

■ Telephone several families to help. Set up a meeting to pick a date and make plans.
■ Contact your local police department about barricading the street. You might have to submit a special-event form and pay a small fee. Regulations will vary.
■ Decide on a tentative menu, and figure out how you will divide the cost.
■ Create invitations; be sure to include food and beverage assignments. Use the first letter of each family's last name to assign items (A-E brings side dishes, F-H desserts, etc.). Include requests for extra grills and coolers.
■ Decide who will be in charge of what tasks. It helps to ask for more helpers than you really need. Something always comes up, and a few people will back out.
■ Set up food stations around the street for easy access. Use sturdy tables for serving.
■ Practice food safety by keeping perishable foods in coolers or in trays of crushed ice.
■ Consider ages of adults and children when planning activities such as playing in the sprinkler, drawing with sidewalk chalk, and playing T-ball or musical chairs.

Fun Dough

Kids will enjoy sculpting this dough. Use any color of food coloring paste to create a rainbow of gifts.

PREP: 20 MIN.

½ to ¾ cup warm water, divided
1 tsp. white vinegar
2 cups all-purpose flour
1 cup salt
Food coloring paste

1. Stir together ½ cup warm water and 1 tsp. vinegar.
2. Combine flour and salt in a large bowl. Slowly stir in water mixture with a wooden spoon until a stiff dough forms, adding up to ¼ cup more water, if necessary. Knead until smooth and workable. Divide dough into portions, and add desired amount of food coloring paste. Shape dough portions into blocks. Store in refrigerator in a zip-top plastic bag. **Makes** about 2½ cups nonedible dough.
TIFFANY WILLIS
TERRELL, TEXAS

Easy Pasta Meals

These recipes prove quick-to-cook entrées can be flavorful too. Try Layered Antipasto Salad for a new twist on the usual seven-layer salad. Pour on the flavor with bottled dressing, and this make-ahead dish is ready to chill. Regardless of which one you try, none of these recipes has a prep time of more than 15 minutes. Serve toasted Italian bread with any of these choices to round out your menu.

Layered Antipasto Salad
make ahead
PREP: 10 MIN., COOK:12 MIN., CHILL: 2 HRS.
This recipe uses mostaccioli, which is tube-shaped pasta that can be ridged or smooth and is usually about 2 inches long. Penne is a good alternative.

3 cups (9-oz.) uncooked mostaccioli or penne pasta
2½ cups broccoli florets
1 Tbsp. chopped fresh parsley
2 cups chopped tomato
½ lb. deli roast beef slices, cut into strips
½ small red onion, sliced
1 cup Caesar dressing
6 provolone cheese slices, cut into strips

1. Cook pasta according to package directions, adding broccoli during the last 2 minutes of cooking time; drain. Rinse and cool. Toss with parsley.
2. Place half of pasta mixture in a 4-qt. glass bowl; top with half each of tomatoes, beef, and onions. Repeat layers once. Pour dressing evenly over salad. Cover and chill at least 2 hours or overnight. Top with cheese before serving. **Makes** 6 servings.

Note: For testing purposes only, we used Ken's Caesar Dressing.

Fresh Tomato-Mushroom-Basil Pasta

PREP: 15 MIN., COOK: 35 MIN.
Use a sturdy pasta such as bow tie or rotini.

1 (16-oz.) package bow tie pasta
1 small onion, chopped (about ½ cup)
2 garlic cloves, minced
2 Tbsp. olive oil
2 cups seeded and chopped plum
  tomatoes
1 (8-oz.) package sliced fresh
  mushrooms
¾ tsp. salt
¼ to ½ tsp. dried crushed red pepper
½ cup whipping cream
3 oz. ⅓-less-fat cream cheese
3 Tbsp. chopped fresh basil
3 Tbsp. grated Romano cheese

1. Cook pasta according to package directions. Drain and set aside.
2. Sauté onion and garlic in hot oil in a large skillet over medium-high heat 5 minutes or until onion is tender. Stir in tomatoes and next 3 ingredients; cook, stirring occasionally, 10 minutes.
3. Stir in whipping cream, cream cheese, and basil. Cook, stirring constantly, until cream cheese melts and sauce is smooth. Serve over cooked pasta; sprinkle with Romano cheese. **Makes** 6 to 8 servings.

Chicken Spaghetti Supreme

PREP: 15 MIN., BAKE: 45 MIN.,
STAND: 10 MIN., COOK: 10 MIN.

4 skinned and boned chicken breasts
2 bunches green onions, chopped
1 (8-oz.) package sliced fresh
  mushrooms
1 pt. grape tomatoes, halved
1 cup Italian dressing
1 (8-oz.) package spaghetti
½ cup freshly grated Parmesan cheese

1. Place chicken breasts in a single layer in a lightly greased 13- x 9-inch baking dish. Top evenly with onions, mushrooms, and tomatoes. Pour dressing evenly over chicken and vegetables.

2. Bake, covered, at 375° for 45 minutes. Remove chicken and vegetables from oven; let stand 10 minutes. Shred chicken using 2 forks.
3. Cook pasta according to package directions, and drain. Combine shredded chicken mixture and spaghetti, tossing well. Top evenly with ½ cup Parmesan cheese. **Makes** 6 servings.

Note: For testing purposes only, we used Kraft Zesty Italian Dressing.

KATHY MOSS
SILOAN SPRINGS, ARKANSAS

Barbecue With a View

Summer Picnic

Serves 6

Smoky Ribs

Pan-fried Okra, Onion, and Tomatoes

Chili-Lime Grilled Corn

Grilled Parmesan-Garlic Bread

Caramel–Cashew Ice Cream

Now, this is not just your ordinary picnic. This picnic on the lake just isn't complete for father-and-son pilots Wally and Michael Kirkpatrick without a ride in one of their seaplanes and some slow-cooked barbecue. They share this fun each year with 100 people at Wally's Seaplane Splash In party on Alabama's Lake Guntersville.

Seaplane pilots from around the Southeast, airplane enthusiasts, friends, and family join together for wonderful eats and exciting aerial action. Throughout the meal, the vintage planes will "splash in" as their pilots perform tricks for onlookers gathered onshore and in boats for the spectacle.

But make no mistake—the star of this waterside cookout is the food, especially the smoked ribs. The recipes are so good, you won't need a lakeside setting to enjoy them; your own patio will do just fine.

So rev up the smoker, call a few friends over, and have a splashy good time.

Smoky Ribs

PREP: 30 MIN.; STAND: 30 MIN.;
SOAK: 30 MIN.; SMOKE: 4 HRS., 30 MIN.
The Kirkpatricks use a secret rub and a commercial smoker for their Smoky Ribs, but you can make your own version with a home smoker and purchased Cajun seasoning.

3 slabs baby back pork ribs
  (about 6 lb.)
¼ cup Cajun seasoning
Hickory wood chunks
Bottled barbecue sauce

1. Rinse and pat ribs dry. Remove thin membrane from back of ribs by slicing into it with a knife and then pulling. (This makes for more tender ribs and allows smoke and rub to penetrate meat better.)
2. Sprinkle meat evenly with Cajun seasoning, and massage into meat. Let stand at room temperature 30 minutes.
3. Soak wood chunks in water for at least 30 minutes.
4. Prepare smoker according to manufacturer's directions. Bring internal temperature to 225° to 250°; maintain temperature for 15 to 20 minutes.
5. Drain wood chunks, and place on coals. Place rib slabs in a rib rack on upper cooking grate; cover with smoker lid.
6. Smoke ribs, maintaining temperature in smoker between 225° and 250°, for 3½ to 4 hours. Remove ribs from grill, and wrap in heavy-duty aluminum foil; return ribs to smoker. Cover with smoker lid, and smoke 30

more minutes. Serve with barbecue sauce. **Make** 6 servings.

Note: For testing purposes only, we used Luzianne Cajun Seasoning.

Pan-fried Okra, Onion, and Tomatoes
PREP: 15 MIN., FRY: 6 MIN. PER BATCH
(Pictured on page 8)

2 lb. fresh okra
½ cup vegetable oil
1 medium-size red onion, thinly sliced
2 large tomatoes, seeded and thinly sliced
2 Tbsp. lime juice
1½ tsp. salt
1½ tsp. pepper
1 tsp. chicken bouillon granules

1. Cut okra in half lengthwise.
2. Pour ¼ cup oil into a large skillet over medium-high heat. Cook okra in hot oil, in batches, 6 minutes or until browned, turning occasionally. Remove from skillet, and drain well on paper towels. Repeat with remaining okra, adding remaining ¼ cup oil as needed. Cool.
3. Stir together onion and next 5 ingredients in a large bowl; Add okra, tossing to coat. Serve at room temperature. **Makes** 8 servings.

ROMEY JOHNSON
WOODBRIDGE, VIRGINIA

Chili-Lime Grilled Corn
PREP: 15 MIN., STAND: 1 HR., GRILL: 25 MIN.
Soak corn husks in a cooler of water before grilling to prevent the husks from burning. After grilling, drain water, and put corn back into cooler for up to 20 minutes to keep warm until ready to serve.

8 ears fresh corn with husks
½ cup butter, softened
1 tsp. grated lime rind
1 tsp. fresh lime juice
Chili powder

1. Remove heavy outer husks from corn; pull back inner husks. Remove and discard silks. Pull husks over corn. Cover corn with water; let stand 1 hour.
2. Stir together ½ cup softened butter, 1 tsp. grated lime rind, and 1 tsp. lime juice.
3. Drain corn, and pat dry.
4. Grill corn, without grill lid, over medium heat (300° to 350°) 25 minutes or until tender, turning often. Remove corn from grill. Carefully pull back husks, and tie with a leftover husk or kitchen string. Spread with desired amount of butter mixture. Sprinkle corn evenly with desired amount of chili powder. **Makes** 8 servings.

Note: Stir ½ tsp. chili powder into the butter mixture, if desired.

SABINE HEFFELFINGER
MADISON, ALABAMA

Grilled Parmesan-Garlic Bread
fast fixin's
PREP: 5 MIN., COOK: 2 MIN., GRILL: 10 MIN.
For a softer bread crust, wrap bread in aluminum foil when grilling.

¼ cup butter
4 garlic cloves, crushed
1 (12-oz.) French bread loaf, split horizontally
½ cup freshly grated Parmesan cheese
2 Tbsp. chopped fresh parsley

1. Melt butter in a small saucepan over medium heat; add garlic, and cook 2 minutes. Remove and discard garlic. Brush cut sides of bread evenly with butter mixture, and sprinkle cut sides evenly with Parmesan cheese and parsley. Place cut sides together.
2. Grill, covered with grill lid, over medium heat (300° to 350°) 5 minutes on each side or to desired degree of doneness. **Makes** 6 servings.

Note: To prepare bread in the oven, wrap loaf in aluminum foil, place on a baking sheet, and bake at 350° for 15 minutes or until hot.

MICHAEL KIRKPATRICK
MADISON, ALABAMA

Caramel-Cashew Ice Cream
make ahead
PREP: 10 MIN., FREEZE: 8 HRS.
Only 4 ingredients are needed to prepare this simple, creamy ice cream.

2 cups whipping cream
1 (14-oz.) can sweetened condensed milk
½ cup butterscotch-caramel topping
1 cup salted cashews, chopped
Toppings: butterscotch-caramel topping, chopped cashews

1. Beat whipping cream at high speed with an electric mixer until stiff peaks form.
2. Stir together sweetened condensed milk and ½ cup butterscotch-caramel topping in a large bowl. Fold in whipped cream and 1 cup cashews. Place in an airtight container; freeze 6 to 8 hours or until firm. Serve with desired toppings. **Makes** about 1 qt.

from our kitchen

Peaches Year-round

Savoring the sun-kissed flavor of juicy peaches all year long is easy—simply freeze them at their peak. Freeze sliced, peeled peaches with or without a sugar syrup, depending on how you plan to serve them. Either way, add lemon juice or commercial powdered fruit preservative such as Fruit-Fresh to protect color and texture. Look for fruit preservatives in the produce or canning sections of your supermarket.

For jams and jellies or cooked dishes, such as pies and cobblers, freeze peaches without sugar, and thaw only partially prior to use. Thaw in the refrigerator about 6 hours or until peach slices can be separated but are still semi-frozen; use immediately.

As sugar syrup further helps retain color and texture, peaches frozen with syrup are the better bet for serving uncooked, such as over pound cake or ice cream. Thaw syrup-packed peaches in the refrigerator 8 to 10 hours, and plan to use thawed peaches within 1 day.

Unsweetened peaches: Gently toss 4 cups sliced, peeled peaches with 1 Tbsp. powdered fruit preservative or a mixture of 1 tsp. lemon juice and 1 Tbsp. water. Pack into a 1-qt. zip-top plastic freezer bag, leaving 1 inch of headspace. Squeeze out excess air, and seal; freeze. Use within 3 to 6 months.

Syrup-packed peaches: Stir together 2½ cups sugar, 1 Tbsp. lemon juice or 4 tsp. powdered fruit preservative, and 1 qt. water until sugar dissolves. Pour ½ cup sugar syrup into a 1-qt. zip-top plastic freezer bag. Add 4 cups sliced, peeled peaches and additional syrup to cover peaches (about 1 cup), leaving 1 inch of headspace. Squeeze out excess air, and seal; freeze. Use within 8 months.

Flavored Seasoning Butter

Prepared in minutes and kept on hand in the freezer, this herb- and citrus-scented butter gives last-minute meals a burst of fresh flavor. Try it atop grilled fish and meats or melted into hot cooked pasta or rice; it's especially delicious stirred into steamed or grilled veggies. Give it your signature by substituting your favorite herb or by adding a touch of lime or orange zest or a small amount of minced garlic. (Note: Use less of stronger herbs such as rosemary, sage, or tarragon.)

Lemon-Herb Seasoning Butter: Stir together ½ cup softened butter, 3 Tbsp. chopped fresh chives, 2 Tbsp. chopped fresh parsley, and 2 tsp. grated lemon rind until well blended. Cover and refrigerate to use within a few days. For longer storage, form into a log or press into ice cube trays, and wrap tightly with plastic wrap; freeze up to 1 month.

Puttin' Up Peas

It's the perfect time to freeze fresh Southern field peas. Whether you lean towards delicate lady creams or heartier black-eyed or crowder peas, head down to your local farmers market to pick up your favorite types. You can even include some snap beans to add a different texture and color to your frozen mix. When choosing peas in the shell, look for pods that are flexible and well-filled with tender seeds.

To prepare for freezing, wash shelled peas, and cook in boiling water (1 gal. per lb. of peas) for 2 minutes. (Cook snap beans 3 minutes.) Drain and immediately plunge into ice water; let stand 2 minutes. Drain well. Transfer peas to airtight containers, leaving ½-inch headspace, or pack into zip-top plastic freezer bags, squeezing out excess air. Freeze up to 6 months. Use frozen field peas as you would fresh; do not thaw them before using.

august

Jump-Start Supper

You'll love these great-tasting, stress-free weeknight meals.

Midweek Beef Brisket Menu

Serves 6

Slow-cooker Beef Brisket

flour tortillas

Tomato-and-Corn Chip Salad

Honeydew-Orange Toss

lemonade

Get cooking. All it takes is some simple preplanning and a little advance prep work. For instance, cook the Zesty Pork Roast With Vegetables, which takes less than an hour. Slice the cooled, cooked roast, wrap in aluminum foil, and refrigerate for dinner one to two days later.

Five Tips for Next-Day Dishes

Use these ideas to turn leftovers into a quick supper.
1. Toss shredded Slow-cooker Beef Brisket with iceberg lettuce and chopped tomatoes. Serve with sweet-spicy tomato-flavored salad dressing and tortilla chips.
2. Top Honeydew-Orange Toss with vanilla yogurt, and stir in chopped nuts for a healthful breakfast or snack.
3. Spoon shredded beef brisket over long-grain rice to make beef hash.
4. Cut Zesty Pork Roast slices into strips or cubes, and heat with cooked stir-fry vegetables. Serve with soy sauce, if desired.
5. Cut Zesty Pork Roast slices into strips; toss with lettuce, drained mandarin oranges, and slivered toasted almonds or chow mein noodles. Serve with oil-and-vinegar or sesame-flavored salad dressing.

Slow-cooker Beef Brisket

make ahead

PREP: 15 MIN., COOK: 8 HRS.

South-of-the-border flavors add zest to this dish. Be sure to select a brisket that's uniform in thickness to make shredding the meat easier.

2 medium onions, thinly sliced
2 celery ribs, thinly sliced
2 garlic cloves, pressed
1 (2- to 3-lb.) beef brisket
2 tsp. salt
1½ tsp. ground chipotle powder
1 cup coarsely chopped fresh cilantro
Flour tortillas
Toppings: shredded Mexican cheese blend, sour cream, salsa, chopped fresh cilantro
Lime wedges

1. Place first 3 ingredients in a 6-qt. slow cooker.

2. Trim fat from brisket; cut brisket into 3-inch pieces. Rub brisket pieces evenly with 2 tsp. salt and 1½ tsp. chipotle powder, and place on top of vegetables in slow cooker. Top with 1 cup cilantro.
3. Cover and cook on HIGH 6 to 8 hours or until brisket pieces shred easily with a fork.
4. Remove brisket from slow cooker, and cool slightly. Using 2 forks, shred meat into bite-size pieces. Serve in flour tortillas with desired toppings and lime wedges. **Makes** 6 servings.

WANDA JENSEN
EL PASO, TEXAS

Tomato-and-Corn Chip Salad

fast fixin's

PREP: 15 MIN.

Try a time-saving, ready-to-use bottled Italian salad dressing instead of the homemade vinaigrette on days when time is really short.

1 head iceberg lettuce, torn into bite-size pieces
3 small tomatoes, chopped
1 (15-oz.) can dark red kidney beans, rinsed and drained
½ (8-oz.) package shredded Cheddar cheese
1 cup coarsely crushed corn chips
Italian Vinaigrette

1. Layer first 5 ingredients in a large bowl. Serve with Italian Vinaigrette. **Makes** 6 servings.

Italian Vinaigrette:

make ahead

PREP: 5 MIN., CHILL: 30 MIN.

½ cup cider vinegar
½ cup vegetable oil
1 (0.7-oz.) package Italian dressing mix

1. Whisk together all ingredients. Cover; chill 30 minutes. **Makes** 1 cup.

Note: For testing purposes only, we used Good Seasons Italian Salad Dressing & Recipe Mix.

VICTORIA SAMPSON
HENDERSONVILLE, NORTH CAROLINA

Honeydew-Orange Toss

make ahead

PREP: 20 MIN.

We used honeydew melon, but this recipe is just as refreshing with cantaloupe, Crenshaw, or watermelon.

⅓ cup fresh lemon juice (about 3 lemons)
¼ cup powdered sugar
2 Tbsp. fresh lime juice (1 lime)
½ honeydew melon, peeled and cut into 1-inch cubes (about 4 cups)
2 cups navel orange sections (2 oranges)*

1. Whisk together first 3 ingredients in a large bowl. Add honeydew melon and orange sections, and gently toss. **Makes** 6 cups.

*Substitute 1 (11-oz.) can mandarin oranges, drained, if desired.

CAROL S. NOBLE
BURGAW, NORTH CAROLINA

Weeknight Pork Roast Supper

Serves 6

Zesty Pork Roast
With Vegetables

Herbed Rice

ice cream

iced tea

Zesty Pork Roast With Vegetables

PREP: 10 MIN., BAKE: 50 MIN., STAND: 10 MIN.

2 tsp. Creole seasoning
2 tsp. ground cumin
2 tsp. garlic powder
2 medium-size yellow squash, cut lengthwise into ¼-inch-thick slices
2 medium zucchini, cut lengthwise into ¼-inch-thick slices
2 Tbsp. olive oil, divided
1 (3- to 4-lb.) boneless pork loin roast

1. Combine first 3 ingredients in a small bowl.
2. Toss squash and zucchini slices with 1 Tbsp. olive oil in a large bowl; sprinkle vegetables with 1 tsp. Creole mixture. Arrange seasoned vegetables on an aluminum foil-lined baking sheet, and set aside.
3. Stir remaining 1 Tbsp. olive oil into remaining Creole mixture. Rub mixture evenly on boneless pork loin roast.
4. Place roast on a lightly greased rack in a roasting pan. Place pan on middle rack in oven.
5. Bake at 425° for 30 minutes.
6. Place vegetables in oven on lowest rack, and bake, with roast, 15 to 20 more minutes or until a meat thermometer inserted into thickest portion of pork registers 155°. Remove roast and vegetables from oven. Let roast stand 10 minutes before slicing or until meat thermometer registers 160°. **Makes** 6 servings.

Zesty Grilled Pork Chops: Toss vegetables with 1 Tbsp. oil, and sprinkle with 1 tsp. Creole mixture as directed. Do not place on baking sheet. Substitute 6 (1¼-inch-thick) bone-in pork chops for pork loin roast. Stir remaining oil into remaining Creole mixture. Rub evenly on pork chops. Grill vegetables and pork chops over high heat (400° to 500°) 3 minutes on each side or until pork is done. **Makes** 6 servings. Prep: 10 min., Grill: 6 min.

MILLIE FETZER
JACKSONVILLE, FLORIDA

Slice squash and zucchini lengthwise with your sharpest knife.

Herbed Rice

fast fixin's • family favorite

PREP: 10 MIN., COOK: 15 MIN.

Try fresh herbs from your local farmers market or supermarket. If fresh herbs are not available, you can substitute dried herbs. The general rule of thumb for using dried herbs in place of fresh is 1 part dried herbs to 3 or 4 parts fresh herbs.

2 Tbsp. butter
2 green onions, finely chopped
2½ cups water
½ tsp. garlic powder
½ tsp. salt
3 cups uncooked quick-cooking brown rice
2 Tbsp. finely chopped fresh parsley
1 tsp. chopped fresh or ¼ tsp. dried thyme
1 tsp. chopped fresh or ¼ tsp. dried sage
½ tsp. grated lemon rind (optional)

1. Melt butter in a medium saucepan over medium-high heat. Add green onions to pan, and sauté 1 minute. Add 2½ cups water, garlic powder, and salt; bring to a boil. Add brown rice; reduce heat to medium, and cook, uncovered, stirring occasionally, 10 minutes or until water is absorbed. Stir in parsley, thyme, sage, and, if desired, lemon rind. **Makes** 6 servings.

Note: Long-grain rice can be substituted for quick-cooking brown rice. Reduce water to 2 cups, and reduce rice to 1 cup. Bring to a boil over medium-high heat. Reduce heat to low; cover and cook 20 minutes or until water is absorbed. Proceed as directed.

SUZAN L. WIENER
SPRING HILL, FLORIDA

Cool Desserts

For the price of a double-scoop, wow an entire crowd.

This dessert duo never looked so good. Pair everyone's favorite combination, cake and ice cream, as a rolled frozen treat.

Chocolate Angel Food Cakes

PREP: 20 MIN., BAKE: 20 MIN.,
COOL: 10 MIN., CHILL: 30 MIN.
If you don't have 2 jelly-roll pans, use 2 (15- x 10¼-inch) disposable foil pans.

1 (16-oz.) package angel food cake mix
¼ cup unsweetened cocoa
⅔ cup powdered sugar

1. Line 2 (15- x 10-inch) jelly-roll pans with parchment or wax paper. Prepare angel food cake mix batter according to package directions, adding unsweetened cocoa. Pour batter into prepared pans.
2. Bake at 325° for 15 to 20 minutes or until a wooden pick inserted in center comes out clean. Cool in pans on wire racks 10 minutes. (If baking cakes in 1 oven, bake on middle 2 racks for 10 minutes; then switch places, and continue baking for 5 to 10 minutes.)
3. Sift ⅔ cup powdered sugar over 2 (24- x 18-inch) pieces heavy-duty aluminum foil.
4. Loosen edges of cakes from pans. Invert each slightly warm cake onto a prepared foil piece. Carefully remove parchment paper, and discard. Place a cloth towel on top of each cake. Starting at 1 long side, roll up foil, cake, and towel together.

5. Chill rolled cakes 30 minutes or until completely cool. Unroll cakes, and remove towels. (Keep each cake on foil piece.) **Makes** 2 (15- x 10-inch) cakes.

Hot Fudge Sundae Cake Rolls

PREP: 20 MIN., FREEZE: 8 HRS.

1 recipe Chocolate Angel Food Cakes
½ gal. vanilla ice cream, softened
1 (10-oz.) jar maraschino cherries, drained and chopped
1 (16-oz.) container frozen whipped topping, thawed
Garnishes: grated chocolate, maraschino cherries
Hot Fudge Sauce

1. Bake, roll, and chill cakes as directed. Remove towels.
2. Spread half of ice cream over top of 1 prepared cake on foil piece, leaving a 1-inch border; sprinkle with half of chopped cherries, and roll up, jelly-roll fashion, ending seam side down. Wrap cake roll with foil piece, sealing at both ends. Place in freezer. Repeat procedure with remaining ice cream, cherries, and prepared cake on foil piece.
3. Freeze cake rolls at least 8 hours or until firm. Unwrap; frost each evenly with whipped topping. Serve immediately, or freeze cake roll 1 hour or until whipped topping is firm; rewrap with foil, and freeze until ready to serve. Garnish, if desired, and serve with Hot Fudge Sauce. **Makes** 2 cake rolls (10 to 12 servings each).

Hot Fudge Sauce:

PREP: 5 MIN., COOK: 10 MIN.

Stir together 5 (1-oz.) semisweet chocolate baking squares and ½ cup butter in a heavy saucepan over medium-low heat, whisking constantly until melted. Whisk in 1 cup evaporated milk until blended. Gradually whisk in 1 (16-oz.) package powdered sugar; stir constantly until blended and smooth, and simmer 1 minute. Serve warm. Store sauce in an airtight container in the refrigerator up to 2 weeks. **Makes** 3½ cups.

SHIRLEY CARTER
WALLS, MISSISSIPPI

Key Lime Pie Ice-cream Cake Rolls
Omit cocoa from Chocolate Angel Food Cakes recipe; bake and roll as directed. Stir 1 cup coarsely crumbled graham crackers (4 sheets), 5 Tbsp. Key lime juice, and 1 tsp. grated lime rind into ½ gal. softened vanilla ice cream. Spread ice-cream mixture over cakes as directed; roll and freeze as directed (see recipe for Hot Fudge Sundae Cake Rolls). Frost with 1 (16-oz.) container frozen whipped topping, thawed; sprinkle with grated lime rind. Serve with Raspberry Sauce. **Makes** 2 cake rolls (10 to 12 servings each).

Raspberry Sauce:

PREP: 10 MIN.

Process 1 (12-oz.) package frozen raspberries, thawed, in a blender until smooth, stopping to scrape down sides. Pour through a fine wire-mesh strainer into a bowl, pressing mixture with the back of a spoon. Discard seeds. Stir in 3 Tbsp. powdered sugar. Store sauce in an airtight container in the refrigerator up to 2 weeks. **Makes** about 1 cup.

Fast and Delicious

For a quick dessert, cut a store-bought angel food cake in 3 or 4 horizontal slices. Spread ice cream between slices, frost all over with whipped topping, and freeze.

Chicken Cobbler Casserole, page 41

Fresh Fruit With Lemon-Mint Sauce, page 37

Warm Prosciutto–Stuffed Focaccia, page 30

Easy Brunswick Stew, page 47

Lemon–Basil Shrimp Salad, page 95

Honey–Oatmeal Wheat Bread, page 70

Classic Fried Catfish, page 78

Cool Lavender Lemonade (front) and
White Sangría, page 66

Three-Cheese Baked Pasta, page 82

Chicken Tetrazzini, page 83

Late-Night Pasta
Chez Frank, page 82

Sour Cream Pound Cake with fresh peaches and Whipped Cream, page 134

Governor's Mansion Summer
Peach Tea Punch, page 140

Honey–Chicken Salad; Shrimp Salad; and tomato-and-cucumber salad with Sugar-and-Vinegar Dressing, page 131

Texas Pecan-and-Avocado Salad, page 149

hot and crispy cornbread madeleines, page 131

Lightened Chocolate-Coffee Cheesecake With
Mocha Sauce, page 87

Key Lime Pie, page 141

Chocolate Parfaits, page 142

175

Fish Sandwiches, page 144

BBQ Shrimp, page 144

Butterbeans and Bacon, sliced tomatoes, fried okra, Tee's Corn Pudding, and Skillet Cornbread, pages 198 and 199

Brick-Grilled Cornish Hens, mixed salad greens, and Squash Casserole, page 204

John's Bananas Foster, page 206

Bananas Foster Upside-down Coffee Cake,
page 206

Chocolate Chip Cheesecake Bars, page 226

Pasta Salad Niçoise, page 230

Linguine Alfredo, page 229

Antipasto Platter, page 229

Maryland Crab Cakes With Creamy Caper-Dill Sauce and Roasted Sweet Potato Salad, page 237

Chesapeake Chowder, page 236

Sun-dried Tomato Cheese Spread, page 236

Quick Mocha Latte, page 268

Sausage-Cheese Muffins, page 274

Breakfast Pizza and Cheesy Baked Grits,
page 289

Apricot-Ginger Salmon, page 257; Sautéed Beans and Peppers, page 258; and Citrus Sweet Potatoes, page 257

Easy Apple Tart With Ol' South Custard, page 258

Champagne Salad With Pear-Goat Cheese Tarts, page 256

Chocolate-and-Almond Macaroons, page 262

Roasted Pecan Fudge, page 263

Fruit-Filled Cookies, page 262; Oatmeal Carmelitas, page 263; and Snowflake Cookies, page 262

Caramel Cream Cake, page 285

Grill a Meal Tonight

Sometimes two is the perfect number for supper. To get just the right recipes for you, we turned to Debby Maugans of Birmingham. She's a mom, author, and expert in downsizing recipes. Feeding more than a duo? No problem, Debby's recipes easily double.

Dinner for Two

Serves 2

Grilled Steak and Potatoes
With Red Onion Relish

buttered, steamed green beans

Outrageous Peanut Butter Cookies

iced tea

Grilled Steak and Potatoes With Red Onion Relish

family favorite

PREP: 10 MIN., COOK: 15 MIN.,
GRILL: 22 MIN., STAND: 10 MIN.

3 small red potatoes (about ¾ lb.)
1½ Tbsp. olive oil
2 garlic cloves, pressed
½ tsp. salt
½ tsp. freshly ground pepper
1 (12-oz.) flank steak
Red Onion Relish

1. Bring potatoes and water to cover to a boil in a medium saucepan. Cook 10 to 15 minutes or just until tender. Drain, cool, and cut into ½-inch-thick slices.
2. Stir together olive oil and garlic. Brush half of mixture over both sides of potato slices. Sprinkle potatoes evenly with ¼ tsp. salt and ¼ tsp. pepper, and set aside. Brush both sides of steak with remaining half of olive oil mixture; sprinkle evenly with remaining ¼ tsp. salt and ¼ tsp. pepper.
3. Grill steak, covered with grill lid, over medium-high heat (350° to 400°) 6 to 7 minutes on each side or to desired degree of doneness. Cover loosely with aluminum foil, and let stand 10 minutes.
4. Grill potato slices, covered with grill lid, over medium-high heat 3 to 4 minutes on each side or until browned.
5. Cut steak diagonally across the grain into thin strips. Serve with potatoes and Red Onion Relish. **Makes** 2 servings.

Red Onion Relish:
fast fixin's • make ahead
PREP: 10 MIN., GRILL: 8 MIN.

1 small red onion
½ Tbsp. olive oil
⅓ cup crumbled feta cheese
¼ cup chopped pitted oil-cured olives (about 10 olives)
2 tsp. drained capers
2 tsp. balsamic vinegar
¼ tsp. freshly ground pepper

1. Cut onion into ¾- to 1-inch-thick slices. Brush both sides of onion slices evenly with olive oil.
2. Grill onion slices, covered with grill lid, over medium-high heat (350° to 400°) 3 to 4 minutes on each side or until grill marks appear and onion is tender. Transfer to cutting board, and let cool slightly. Coarsely chop onion slices.
3. Toss together onion, feta, and remaining ingredients. **Makes** about 1½ cups.

Outrageous Peanut Butter Cookies

fast fixin's • make ahead
PREP: 10 MIN., BAKE: 20 MIN.

This recipe is adapted from Debby's cookbook, Small-Batch Baking *(Workman Publishing, 2004).*

¼ cup all-purpose flour
⅛ tsp. baking soda
¼ cup firmly packed dark brown sugar
2 Tbsp. butter, softened
2 tsp. well-beaten egg *
¼ tsp. vanilla extract
⅓ cup extra-chunky peanut butter
1½ Tbsp. uncooked regular oats
½ (1.8-oz.) chocolate-coated caramel-peanut butter-peanut candy bar, chopped
1 Tbsp. granulated sugar

1. Combine flour and baking soda.
2. Beat brown sugar and next 3 ingredients at low speed with an electric mixer 1 minute or until blended. Add peanut butter, and beat 20 seconds or until blended. Add flour mixture, and beat 30 seconds or until well blended. Stir in oats and chopped candy bar.
3. Drop dough by heaping tablespoonfuls 2 inches apart on an aluminum foil- or parchment paper-lined baking sheet. Dip bottom of a drinking glass in granulated sugar, and flatten mound of dough. Repeat process with remaining sugar and mounds of dough.
4. Bake at 325° for 15 to 20 minutes or until lightly browned. Cool on baking sheet 2 minutes; remove cookies to wire rack to cool completely. **Makes** 8 cookies.

*Substitute 2 tsp. egg substitute, if desired.

Note: For testing purposes only, we used Reese's NutRageous candy bar.

Test Kitchen Notebook

To get dinner on the table fast, make the relish first; then put the steak on. Grill the potatoes directly on the grate while the steak stands for 10 minutes. Standing time for the meat helps lock in the juices that keep slices moist and flavorful. Serve the Red Onion Relish warm or at room temperature. Top a green salad with any leftover relish and sliced steak; drizzle with a simple oil-and-vinegar salad dressing.

Shirley Harrington
ASSOCIATE FOODS EDITOR

Get a Good Start

Recent research finds that a well-rounded breakfast helps you consume fewer calories throughout the day. These recipes are so fuss-free that you can whip them up anytime.

Grillades and Grits

PREP: 15 MIN., COOK: 35 MIN.

3 Tbsp. all-purpose flour
1 tsp. Creole seasoning, divided
1 lb. lean breakfast pork cutlets, trimmed
2 tsp. olive oil, divided
1 cup finely diced onion
1 cup finely diced celery
½ cup finely diced green bell pepper
1 (14.5-oz.) can no-salt-added diced tomatoes
1 (14-oz.) can low-sodium fat-free chicken broth
Creamy Grits

1. Combine flour and ½ tsp. Creole seasoning in a shallow dish. Dredge pork in flour mixture.
2. Cook pork, in 2 batches, in ½ tsp. hot oil per batch in a large skillet over medium-high heat 2 minutes on each side or until done. Remove from skillet, and keep warm.
3. Add remaining 1 tsp. oil to skillet. Sauté diced onion, celery, and bell pepper in hot oil 3 to 5 minutes or until vegetables are tender. Stir in remaining ½ tsp. Creole seasoning. Stir in diced tomatoes and chicken broth, and cook 2 minutes, stirring to loosen particles from bottom of skillet. Simmer 15 to 18 minutes or until liquid reduces to about 2 Tbsp. Serve tomato mixture over Creamy Grits and pork. **Makes** 4 servings.

Per serving (includes ½ cup Creamy Grits): Calories 371 (25% from fat); Fat 10.3g (sat 3.1g, mono 5.2g, poly 1.1g); Protein 33.8g; Carb 36.1g; Fiber 3.4g; Chol 66mg; Iron 2.7mg; Sodium 350mg; Calc 149mg

Creamy Grits:

fast fixin's

PREP: 5 MIN., COOK: 20 MIN.

1 (14-oz.) can low-sodium fat-free chicken broth
1 cup fat-free milk
½ cup quick-cooking grits

1. Bring broth and milk to a boil in a medium saucepan over medium-high heat; reduce heat to low, and whisk in ½ cup grits. Cook, whisking occasionally, 15 to 20 minutes or until creamy and thickened. **Makes** 2 cups.

Per (½-cup) serving: Calories 109 (7% from fat); Fat 0.9g (sat 0.2g, mono 0.3g, poly 0.2g); Protein 5.8g; Carb 20g; Fiber 0.3g; Chol 1.2mg; Iron 1mg; Sodium 56mg; Calc 81mg

Oatmeal Scones

make ahead • freezeable

PREP: 10 MIN., BAKE: 21 MIN.

¾ cup uncooked quick-cooking oats
⅓ cup sugar
1¾ cups all-purpose flour
2 tsp. baking powder
½ tsp. baking soda
¼ tsp. salt
2 Tbsp. cold butter, cut up
⅔ cup fat-free buttermilk
1 large egg
Vegetable cooking spray
3 Tbsp. sugar
½ tsp. ground cinnamon
1½ Tbsp. fat-free buttermilk
2 Tbsp. chopped pecans, toasted

1. Bake oats in a 15- x 10-inch jelly-roll pan at 400° for 6 minutes or until lightly browned. Cool.
2. Combine uncooked oats and next 5 ingredients.
3. Cut butter into oats mixture with a pastry blender or fork until crumbly. Stir together ⅔ cup buttermilk and

egg. Add to oats mixture, stirring just until dry ingredients are moistened and dough forms.
4. Turn dough out onto a jelly-roll pan coated with cooking spray. Shape dough into a 7½-inch circle.
5. Combine 3 Tbsp. sugar and ½ tsp. cinnamon. Brush dough with 1½ Tbsp. buttermilk. Sprinkle with sugar mixture and pecans.
6. Bake at 400° for 15 minutes or until a wooden pick inserted in center comes out clean. Cut into 8 wedges; serve immediately. **Makes** 8 servings.

FLORINE BRUNS
FREDERICKSBURG, TEXAS

Per serving: Calories 232 (21% from fat); Fat 5.6g (sat 1.9g, mono 2.3g, poly 0.9g); Protein 5.7g; Carb 40.5g; Fiber 1.7g; Chol 34mg; Iron 1.9mg; Sodium 327mg; Calc 110mg

Black Walnut French Toast

fast fixin's

PREP: 10 MIN., COOK: 12 MIN.

2 Tbsp. chopped black walnuts ∗
1 Tbsp. light butter
1 large ripe banana, sliced
¼ cup honey
2 large eggs, lightly beaten
¼ cup fat-free milk
½ tsp. ground cinnamon
⅛ tsp. ground nutmeg
8 (0.8-oz.) white bread slices
Vegetable cooking spray
¼ cup reduced-calorie maple syrup

1. Place a small skillet over medium-high heat until hot; add 2 Tbsp. chopped black walnuts, and cook, stirring constantly, 5 minutes or until toasted. Remove from skillet.
2. Melt 1 Tbsp. light butter in small skillet over medium heat; add banana slices, and cook 3 minutes or until thoroughly heated. Stir in toasted black walnuts and ¼ cup honey, and remove from heat.
3. Whisk together eggs and next 3 ingredients in a shallow dish or pieplate. Lightly press bread slices, 1 at a time, into egg mixture, coating both sides of bread. Cook bread, in batches, on a nonstick griddle coated with cooking spray over medium heat 1 to 2 minutes on each side or until done.

Repeat procedure, if necessary. Transfer to a serving plate. Serve with banana mixture and syrup. **Makes** 4 servings.

* Substitute chopped pecans or traditional walnuts, if desired.

DEBORAH MARKS
SUMTER, SOUTH CAROLINA

Per serving (2 slices French toast, about 2 Tbsp. banana mixture, and 1 Tbsp. syrup): Calories 315 (21% from fat); Fat 7.9g (sat 1.8g, mono 1.5g, poly 1.8g); Protein 10.3g; Carb 54.9g; Fiber 1.3g; Chol 110mg; Iron 1.6mg; Sodium 371mg; Calc 84mg

Black Walnuts

These have a stronger, nuttier flavor than their better known counterpart, the traditional, or English, walnut. Their distinctive taste lends punch to confections, baked goods, and more. Black walnuts are an essential source of omega-3 fats, which help lower cholesterol, aid in brain function, and promote anti-inflammatory benefits for arthritis, asthma, and eczema. Because black walnuts have a high fat content, they tend to go rancid if not stored properly. Store them in an airtight container in the fridge for a year, or freeze for two.

Test Kitchen Notebook

To make scones ahead, simply cool after baking and wrap individually in plastic wrap. Store individual scones in a large zip-top freezer bag for up to one month.

When toasting nuts, such as in Black Walnut French Toast, once you begin to smell the nutty aroma, remove from heat to avoid burning.

Holley Johnson
ASSOCIATE FOODS EDITOR

Chicken Salad Sampler

Most Southerners have a favorite chicken salad in their recipe collection. If you're an enthusiast, then you'll love this scrumptious sampler. Here, we offer new flavors and creative combinations, including creamy mixtures with fruits and vegetables. These recipes are so good, you'll want to add them to your collection of favorites.

Chicken Salad With Grapes and Pecans
make ahead
PREP: 20 MIN., CHILL: 1 HR.

"This recipe was inspired by a favorite dish served at the former Sweetbriar restaurant in Gadsden, Alabama," says reader Linda Banning. Serve it with assorted crackers and grapes for a filling lunch or a delicious brunch contribution. To dress up individual servings, line a petite footed glass with lettuce leaves and fill it with the salad.

½ cup light or regular mayonnaise
½ cup light or regular sour cream
1 Tbsp. fresh lemon juice
1 tsp. salt
½ tsp. pepper
2 lb. skinned and boned chicken breasts, cooked and chopped
3 cups red and white seedless grapes, halved
1 cup chopped pecans, toasted
Lettuce leaves (optional)

1. Stir together first 5 ingredients in a large bowl. Add chopped chicken and grapes, tossing gently to coat. Cover and chill at least 1 hour. Stir in toasted pecans just before serving. Serve in stemware lined with lettuce leaves, if desired. **Makes** 4 servings.

LINDA BANNING
DECATUR, ALABAMA

Creamy Dill Chicken Salad Pitas
make ahead
PREP: 20 MIN., CHILL: 2 HRS.

3 cups chopped cooked chicken (about 6 breasts)
3 green onions, chopped
2 celery ribs, chopped
1 cup plain nonfat yogurt
¼ cup dill pickle relish
1 tsp. dried dillweed
½ tsp. salt
½ tsp. pepper
1 Tbsp. poppy seeds (optional)
3 pita bread rounds
Lettuce leaves
Tomato slices

1. Stir together first 8 ingredients and, if desired, poppy seeds. Cover and chill 2 hours.
2. Heat pitas according to package directions. Cut pitas in half, and line with lettuce leaves and tomato slices. Spoon ½ cup chicken mixture into each pita half. **Makes** 6 servings.

Chicken BLT Salad
fast fixin's
PREP: 15 MIN.

Packaged chopped cooked chicken, leftover grilled chicken, or a deli-roasted chicken are all options for this salad.

½ cup garlic-and-herb-flavored cheese spread
3 cups chopped cooked chicken (about 6 breasts)
½ cup grape tomatoes, halved
⅓ cup chopped green onion tops
2 bacon slices, cooked and crumbled
Salt and freshly ground pepper to taste
Assorted mixed greens (optional)

1. Microwave cheese in a small bowl at HIGH 20 seconds. Stir in next 4 ingredients, tossing well. Add salt and pepper to taste. Serve on assorted greens, if desired. **Makes** 4 servings.

Note: For testing purposes only, we used Alouette Garlic & Herbs Spreadable Cheese.

PATTY ROBERTS
MANCHESTER, TENNESSEE

Invite the Neighbors

Ice the drinks and fire up the grill—no kitchen required for "ears and beers."

Before summer's end, invite your neighbors over for a quirky little party called "Ears and Beers." This late-afternoon gathering gets people cooking and talking together as they shuck and grill fresh corn, and then meet up at a seasonings table to doctor their hot ears. You'll probably shake in your flip-flops, hoping this off-the-wall idea works. Associate Foods Editor Shirley Harrington knows it does—she tried it. As neighbors arrive, toting their favorite beverages, the laughter starts and everything falls into place. Near the end, whip out a sweet treat of Toffee-Almond Blondies.

Grilled Corn on the Cob

PREP: 15 MIN., GRILL: 20 MIN.

10 ears fresh corn with husks
Olive oil (about ¼ cup)
1¼ tsp. salt

1. Remove heavy outer husks from corn; pull back (but do not remove) inner husks. Remove and discard silks; rinse corn, and dry with paper towels. Tie inner husks together with string, leaving ears exposed.
2. Brush corn cobs lightly with oil; sprinkle evenly with salt. Position corn so that tied husks hang over edge of grill to avoid burning husks.
3. Grill corn, covered with grill lid, over medium-high heat (350° to 400°) 20 minutes, turning every 5 minutes, or until done. (Some kernels will begin to char and pop.) Serve immediately. **Makes** 10 servings.

Spicy Wasabi Spread

make ahead

PREP: 5 MIN., CHILL: 30 MIN.

Here's a unique, tangy-hot spread. Toast sesame seeds in a skillet over medium heat, stirring constantly, until lightly browned.

⅓ cup sour cream
⅓ cup mayonnaise
1 Tbsp. prepared wasabi
½ tsp. grated lemon rind
¼ tsp. dried ground ginger
¼ cup toasted sesame seeds

1. Whisk together first 5 ingredients in a small bowl until smooth. Cover and chill at least 30 minutes. Brush sour cream mixture on hot grilled corn, and sprinkle evenly with sesame seeds. **Makes** about ⅔ cup.

Smoky Chipotle-Lime Butter

fast fixin's • make ahead

PREP: 5 MIN.

Try our fun Tex-Mex twist on your grilled corn.

½ cup butter
1½ Tbsp. chipotle hot sauce
2 tsp. fresh lime juice
⅔ cup crushed tortilla chips

1. Let butter stand until room temperature. (Butter should be very soft.)
2. Stir together butter, hot sauce, and lime juice in a small bowl. Brush on hot grilled corn; sprinkle with crushed tortilla chips. **Makes** about ½ cup.

Creamy Lemon-Dill Spread

make ahead

PREP: 10 MIN., CHILL: 30 MIN.

This spread is also great on tomato or smoked turkey sandwiches, grilled fish, and as a dip for raw vegetables.

⅓ cup sour cream
⅓ cup mayonnaise
1 small shallot, minced
2 tsp. chopped fresh dill
1 tsp. grated lemon rind
1 tsp. fresh lemon juice

1. Stir together all ingredients in a small bowl; cover and chill at least 30 minutes. Brush on hot grilled corn. **Makes** about ⅔ cup.

Seasoning the Ears

Set up a station of special butters, spreads, and sprinkle-on toppings for Grilled Corn on the Cob. Each spread can be made the day before, covered, and refrigerated. Take Roasted Garlic-Red Pepper and Smoky Chipotle-Lime Butters out of the fridge, and place on the table as guests arrive. As the first round of corn comes off the grill, they'll be spreadable. Keep the mayonnaise-and-sour cream-based spreads—Creamy Lemon-Dill Spread, Spicy Wasabi Spread, and Cheesy Onion Spread—food-safe by placing decorative bowls in larger bowls of ice or replacing with a new batch every 30 minutes. We bought inexpensive pastry brushes at a dollar store to use as spreaders. Place sprinkle-on toppings next to their respective spreads. For example, crushed tortilla chips go alongside Smoky Chipotle-Lime Butter. Each recipe seasons 10 ears.

Simple Appetizers

Spice up a gathering with one or both of these easy offerings.

Cheesy Onion Spread

make ahead
PREP: 10 MIN., CHILL: 30 MIN.
With crispy crumbled bacon on top, this one will remind you of a loaded baked potato.

⅓ cup sour cream
⅓ cup mayonnaise
2 tsp. finely chopped green onion
½ cup (2 oz.) finely shredded Colby-Jack cheese blend
⅔ cup finely chopped, cooked bacon

1. Stir together first 4 ingredients in a small bowl; cover and chill at least 30 minutes. Brush on hot grilled corn, and sprinkle evenly with bacon. **Makes** about ⅔ cup.

Roasted Garlic-Red Pepper Butter

make ahead
PREP: 15 MIN., BAKE: 1 HR.

½ cup butter
1 garlic bulb
½ tsp. olive oil
2 Tbsp. finely chopped jarred roasted red bell peppers
1 Tbsp. chopped fresh basil
⅔ cup grated Parmesan cheese

1. Let butter stand until room temperature. (Butter should be very soft.)
2. Cut off pointed end of garlic; place garlic on a piece of aluminum foil, and drizzle with oil. Fold foil to seal.

3. Bake at 400° for 1 hour; cool. Squeeze pulp from garlic cloves. Combine 1½ tsp. pulp and butter in a medium bowl, reserving remaining garlic for another use. Stir in peppers and basil. Brush butter mixture on hot grilled corn, and sprinkle evenly with Parmesan cheese. **Makes** about ⅔ cup.

Toffee-Almond Blondies

PREP: 10 MIN., BAKE: 30 MIN.

½ cup butter, softened
1 large egg
1 (17.5-oz.) package chocolate chip cookie mix
1 tsp. vanilla extract
1 (8-oz.) package toffee bits
¾ cup chopped toasted slivered almonds

1. Stir together butter and egg in a large bowl. (Mixture will not fully blend together.) Stir in cookie mix and vanilla until a soft dough forms. Stir in toffee bits and almonds until well blended. Press mixture into a lightly greased 13- x 9-inch pan.
2. Bake at 350° for 25 to 30 minutes or until golden and a wooden pick inserted in center comes out clean. Cool in pan on a wire rack, and cut into bars. **Makes** 2 dozen bars.

Note: For testing purposes only, we used Betty Crocker Chocolate Chip Cookie Mix and Heath Bits O' Brickle Toffee Bits.

Special Deviled Eggs

PREP: 15 MIN.
To hard-cook eggs, place in a pot and cover with cold water. Boil for 1 minute; remove from heat. Cover and let stand 15 minutes.

1 dozen hard-cooked eggs, peeled
5 bacon slices, cooked and crumbled
½ cup finely shredded Swiss cheese
¼ cup plus 1 Tbsp. mayonnaise
2½ Tbsp. cider vinegar
2 tsp. sugar
2 tsp. honey mustard
1½ tsp. freshly ground pepper
¼ tsp. salt
Finely chopped green onions or chives (optional)

1. Cut eggs in half lengthwise; carefully remove yolks, and place in a bowl. Set egg whites aside.
2. Mash yolks until smooth. Add bacon and next 7 ingredients; stir until blended.
3. Spoon yolk mixture evenly into egg whites. Sprinkle with green onions, if desired. **Makes** 24 appetizers.

KELSEY CORBIN
SHAWNEE MISSION, KANSAS

Italian Brie

PREP: 5 MIN.
Serve with black olives and French baguette slices or crackers.

1 (8-oz.) round Brie
1 (3.5-oz.) jar prepared pesto
½ cup sun-dried tomatoes in oil, drained and chopped

1. Trim and discard rind from top of Brie. Place Brie on a serving plate; spread top with pesto, and sprinkle with tomatoes. **Makes** 8 appetizer servings.

NATALIE ASMAN
BIRMINGHAM, ALABAMA

Our Favorite Vegetable Plate

Home-Cooked Flavor

Serves 6

Tee's Corn Pudding

fried okra

Butterbeans and Bacon

sliced tomatoes

Skillet Cornbread

sweet tea

Try something new for supper—scrumptious corn pudding and butterbeans. Add some extras, including your favorite fried okra. Pick up some at the deli or in the freezer section. Complete your plate with fresh, peeled tomato slices (late-season tomatoes tend to have tougher skins) and a warm wedge of cornbread.

Tee's Corn Pudding
family favorite

PREP: 15 MIN., BAKE: 30 MIN., STAND: 5 MIN.
If you'd like to add Southwestern flair to this recipe, try our flavor variation. (Pictured on page 178)

¼ cup sugar
3 Tbsp. all-purpose flour
2 tsp. baking powder
1½ tsp. salt
6 large eggs
2 cups whipping cream
½ cup butter, melted
6 cups fresh corn kernels (about 12 ears) *****

1. Combine first 4 ingredients.
2. Whisk together eggs, whipping cream, and butter in a large bowl. Gradually add sugar mixture, whisking until smooth; stir in corn. Pour mixture into 8 lightly greased 8-oz. ramekins or individual soufflé dishes, and place on a baking sheet.
3. Bake at 350° for 30 minutes or until pudding is set and deep golden. Let stand 5 minutes. **Makes** 8 servings.

*Substitute 6 cups frozen whole kernel corn or canned shoepeg corn, drained, if desired.

Note: You can substitute 1 (13- x 9-inch) baking dish for ramekins. Bake at 350° for 40 to 45 minutes or until set. Let stand 5 minutes. For testing purposes only, we used Silver Queen corn.

Southwestern Corn Pudding: Stir in 1 (4.5-oz.) can chopped green chiles and ¼ tsp. ground cumin.

Butterbeans and Bacon
chef recipe

PREP: 20 MIN.; COOK: 1 HR., 30 MIN.
Cooked beans freeze beautifully, so you can make a double batch to enjoy later. When the season's over, just use plum tomatoes and frozen butterbeans.(Pictured on page 178)

3 thick-cut bacon slices, chopped
1 cup diced onion (1 medium onion)
3 garlic cloves, minced
1 bay leaf
¾ cup chopped green bell pepper
2 small tomatoes, seeded and chopped (optional)
1 (32-oz.) container chicken broth
4 cups fresh or thawed frozen butterbeans
½ tsp. salt
1 tsp. pepper
1 tsp. Worcestershire sauce
½ tsp. hot sauce

1. Cook bacon in a skillet over medium heat, stirring often, 8 minutes or until crisp. Remove bacon, and drain on paper towels, reserving drippings in skillet. Add onion, garlic, and bay leaf; cook, stirring often, 3 minutes or until onion is tender.
2. Add bell pepper; cook, stirring often, 3 minutes. Add tomatoes, if desired, and cook, stirring often, 3 minutes.
3. Add broth and butterbeans; bring to a boil. Cover, reduce heat, and simmer, stirring occasionally, 30 minutes.
4. Uncover and simmer 30 minutes, stirring often. Stir in salt and next 3 ingredients. Cook, stirring often, 5 minutes. Remove and discard bay leaf. Sprinkle with cooked bacon. **Makes** 6 servings.

CHEF JOHNNY EARLES
CRIOLLA'S
GRAYTON BEACH, FLORIDA

Skillet Cornbread
family favorite
PREP: 15 MIN., BAKE: 15 MIN.
This recipe was adapted from Hoppin' John's Lowcountry Cooking *(Houghton Mifflin, 2000) by John Martin Taylor. (Pictured on page 178)*

2 to 3 tsp. bacon drippings or vegetable oil
2 cups buttermilk
1 large egg
1¾ cups white cornmeal
1 tsp. baking powder
1 tsp. baking soda
1 tsp. salt
Butter

1. Coat bottom and sides of a 10-inch cast-iron skillet with bacon drippings; heat in a 450° oven for 10 minutes. (Skillet may smoke a bit.)
2. Whisk together buttermilk and egg. Add cornmeal, stirring well.
3. Stir in baking powder, baking soda, and salt. Pour batter into hot skillet.
4. Bake at 450° for 15 minutes. Serve with butter. **Makes** 6 servings.

quick & easy
Seafood for Dinner

Sandwich Supper
Serves 4

Cumin-Dusted Catfish Sandwiches or Cumin-Dusted Shrimp Sandwiches

Sweet Potato Fries

coleslaw

You'll be able to satisfy both fish and shrimp lovers without feeling like a short-order cook. These recipes work with fresh or frozen selections.

The Cumin-Dusted Catfish and Shrimp Sandwiches are easy to prepare on a weeknight. You'll recognize the aromatic, nutty-flavored cumin from Southwestern dishes. Cook both on the same night by using half shrimp and half fish.

Cumin-Dusted Catfish Sandwiches
fast fixin's
PREP: 10 MIN., GRILL: 8 MIN.
Thin fillets of mild, firm-textured fish, such as cod, tilapia, perch, or orange roughy, can be substituted. If the grilled fillets hang over the sides of the bun, break them in half to stack on the bun. You can also serve remaining halves on the side.

1 cup mayonnaise
3 Tbsp. orange juice
1 to 2 tsp. minced canned chipotle chiles in adobo sauce
1½ tsp. salt, divided
¼ cup self-rising cornmeal
2 tsp. ground cumin
4 (6-oz.) catfish fillets
Vegetable cooking spray
4 whole wheat buns, split and toasted
Tomato slices, shredded lettuce

1. Stir together first 3 ingredients and ½ tsp. salt. Set aside.
2. Combine cornmeal, cumin, and remaining 1 tsp. salt. Rinse fish, and dredge in cornmeal mixture. Spray fish evenly with cooking spray.
3. Grill fish, covered with grill lid, over medium-high heat (350° to 400°) 3 to 4 minutes on each side or just until fish begins to flake with a fork.
4. Serve on buns with mayonnaise mixture, tomato slices, and shredded lettuce. **Makes** 4 servings.

MARY LOU COOK
WELCHES, OREGON

Sweet Potato Fries
fast fixin's
PREP: 10 MIN., STAND: 5 MIN., GRILL: 4 MIN.
This easy side dish is ready to serve in just under 20 minutes.

1½ lb. sweet potatoes (about 3 medium size)
Vegetable cooking spray
½ tsp. seasoned salt

1. Pierce sweet potatoes several times with tines of a fork. Place on a microwave-safe plate; cover with damp paper towels. Microwave at HIGH 6 to 8 minutes or until tender. Let stand 5 minutes. Peel and cut in half lengthwise. Cut into (½- x 3-inch) strips. Coat evenly with cooking spray, and sprinkle evenly with salt.
2. Coat cold grill cooking grate with cooking spray; place on grill over medium-high heat (350° to 400°). Place potato strips on grate.
3. Grill potatoes, covered with grill lid, 1 to 2 minutes on each side or until grill marks appear on fries. **Makes** 4 servings.

Note: For testing purposes only, we used an 1,100-watt microwave oven.

A Sure-to-Please Option

Not in the mood for a sandwich? Pair these shrimp with a mixed green salad and spicy dressing.

Cumin-Dusted Shrimp Sandwiches
If using wooden skewers, soak in water for 30 minutes before grilling.

Stir together 1 cup mayonnaise, 3 Tbsp. orange juice, and 1 to 2 tsp. minced canned chipotle peppers in adobo sauce, and set aside. Combine ¼ cup cornmeal, 2 tsp. cumin, and 1 tsp. salt. Peel and, if desired, devein 1 lb. fresh shrimp; rinse shrimp. Toss shrimp in cornmeal mixture. Thread shrimp onto skewers; spray evenly with cooking spray. Grill, covered with grill lid, over medium-high heat (350° to 400°) 2 to 3 minutes on each side or until shrimp turn pink. Serve shrimp on whole wheat buns with mayonnaise mixture, tomato slices, and shredded lettuce. **Makes** 4 servings. Prep: 10 min., Grill: 6 min.

He Cooks Pasta

Join these newlyweds as they re-create their Italian culinary experience.

Sample one of these fresh and flavorful pasta dishes that Wes Hollowell created after honeymooning in Italy with his wife, Leesa. "I had always thought of Italian food as just noodles and tomato sauce," says Wes, "but in Italy, we tried a lot of recipes that used fresh herbs and olive oil or chicken stock as a base." Adds Leesa, "Everytime we would go to a restaurant, Wes commented on how he could re-create the recipe at home." Though Wes says it took some trial and error to perfect his dishes, we think he got it just right. See what you think.

Linguine With Clam Sauce
PREP: 20 MIN., COOK: 25 MIN.

1 (12-oz.) package linguine
2 (6½-oz.) cans chopped clams
1 Tbsp. butter
¼ cup olive oil
1 (8-oz.) package sliced fresh
    mushrooms
3 garlic cloves, minced
⅓ cup dry white wine
2 Tbsp. chopped fresh basil
2 Tbsp. chopped fresh parsley
2 tsp. crushed Italian seasoning*
¼ tsp. freshly ground black
    pepper
⅛ tsp. crushed dried red pepper
Garnish: freshly grated Parmesan
    cheese

1. Cook pasta in a Dutch oven according to package directions. Drain and return to Dutch oven; set aside.
2. Drain clams, reserving juice.
3. Melt butter with oil in a large skillet over medium heat; add mushrooms and garlic, and sauté 5 minutes or until

mushrooms are tender. Add clams, white wine, basil, and next 4 ingredients; cook, stirring often, 5 minutes.
4. Stir reserved clam juice into pasta in Dutch oven; cook over medium heat 5 minutes. Remove from heat; add mushroom mixture, tossing to coat. Garnish, if desired. **Makes** 6 servings.

*Substitute 1 tsp. dried Italian seasoning, if desired.

Note: For testing purposes only, we used Dean Jacob's Grinder Fresh Italiano All Natural Seasoning.

Chicken Bow Tie Pasta
family favorite
PREP: 20 MIN., COOK: 25 MIN.
If you prefer to use frozen broccoli florets, simply thaw under cool running water, pat dry, and proceed with directions.

1 (16-oz.) package bow tie pasta
3 skinned and boned chicken breasts
¾ tsp. salt
¼ tsp. pepper
⅓ cup olive oil
1 (8.5-oz.) jar sun-dried tomatoes in oil,
    drained
¾ cup chicken broth
½ cup white wine
¼ cup chopped fresh basil
4 garlic cloves, minced
1 tsp. dried Italian seasoning
⅛ tsp. dried crushed red pepper
1 (12-oz.) package fresh broccoli florets

1. Cook pasta according to package directions; drain and keep warm.
2. Cut chicken into 1-inch cubes. Sprinkle evenly with salt and pepper.

Sauté chicken in hot oil in a large skillet over medium-high heat 5 minutes or until done. Remove from skillet; drain on paper towels.
3. Add sun-dried tomatoes and next 6 ingredients to skillet; bring to a boil over medium heat. Stir in broccoli, and cook 5 minutes or until broccoli is tender. Stir in cooked chicken and warm cooked pasta. Serve immediately. **Makes** 6 servings.

Fresh Tomato Penne With Oregano
family favorite
PREP: 20 MIN., COOK: 20 MIN.
We prefer the flavor of fresh oregano instead of dried for this recipe.

1 (16-oz.) package penne pasta
¼ lb. prosciutto, chopped
¼ cup olive oil
3 plum tomatoes, seeded and diced
4 garlic cloves, minced
1 (2-oz.) package pine nuts, lightly
    toasted
¼ cup chopped fresh oregano
½ tsp. dried crushed red pepper
¼ tsp. sugar
¼ tsp. freshly ground black
    pepper
⅛ tsp. salt
Freshly grated Parmesan cheese
    (optional)

1. Cook pasta according to package directions; drain and keep warm.
2. Cook prosciutto in hot oil in a large skillet over medium heat 8 minutes or until crisp. Add tomatoes and next 7 ingredients; cook, stirring often, 5 minutes or until tomatoes are tender. Toss with warm cooked pasta. Serve with Parmesan cheese, if desired. **Makes** 6 servings.

taste of the south

The Legendary Margarita

Summer is definitely here, and it's the perfect season to feature one of Foods Editor Shannon Sliter Satterwhite's favorite concoctions—the margarita, which complements a tall glass and a beach chair.

Though this sweet-and-sour sipper is undeniably a signature of the Southwest, its history is unclear. Perhaps the most documented tale involves bar owner Danny Herrera of Rancho La Gloria in Mexico. He claimed to have developed the libation for a frequent customer, 1930s Hollywood showgirl Marjorie King, who was allergic to every kind of alcohol but tequila.

Whatever the real story is, one thing's for sure—everyone has a different way of mixing this drink. Needless to say, Shannon's search for the quintessential margarita led her to an array of recipes, so she decided to go back to the basics. Just three ingredients—tequila, fresh lime juice, and orange liqueur—are the fundamental flavors that make up this cocktail. The rest is history.

Classic Margarita
fast fixin's
PREP: 10 MIN.

Make any size batch of this recipe and all the variations by simply multiplying the ingredient measurements by the desired number of servings. For larger batches, stir together all ingredients in a pitcher until powdered sugar is dissolved. Chill and serve over ice. For a sweeter drink, use ½ cup powdered sugar instead of ⅓ cup.

Fresh lime wedge (optional)
Margarita salt (optional)
Ice
⅓ cup fresh lime juice ✱
3 Tbsp. orange liqueur
2 Tbsp. tequila
⅓ to ½ cup powdered sugar
Garnish: lime slice

1. Rub rim of a chilled margarita glass with lime wedge, and dip rim in salt to coat, if desired.
2. Fill cocktail shaker half full with ice. Add lime juice, liqueur, tequila, and powdered sugar; cover with lid, and shake until thoroughly chilled. Strain into prepared glass. Garnish, if desired, and serve immediately. **Makes** 1 serving.

✱Substitute ⅓ cup thawed frozen limeade concentrate for fresh lime juice, if desired. Omit powdered sugar, and proceed with recipe as directed.

Note: For testing purposes only, we used Cointreau for orange liqueur and Jose Cuervo Especial for tequila.

Frozen Margarita: Combine lime juice, liqueur, tequila, and powdered sugar in a small pitcher or measuring cup; stir until powdered sugar is dissolved. Pour into a zip-top plastic freezer bag. Seal and freeze 8 hours. Let stand 5 minutes at room temperature before serving. Pour into prepared glass. **Makes** 1 serving.

Frozen Strawberry Margaritas: Process lime juice, liqueur, tequila, powdered sugar, 1 cup fresh or frozen strawberries✱, and 1 cup crushed ice in a blender until slushy. Rub rim of 2 chilled margarita glasses with lime wedge, and dip rim in red decorator sugar to coat, if desired. Serve immediately in prepared glasses. **Makes** 2 servings.

✱Substitute your favorite fruit, such as watermelon, peaches, or berries, if desired.

Margarita Sunrise: Pour lime juice, liqueur, tequila, powdered sugar, and 3 Tbsp. orange juice over ice in a cocktail shaker. Cover with lid; shake until thoroughly chilled. Strain into prepared glass. Add 3 Tbsp. club soda or lemon-lime soft drink for a little fizz, if desired. Top with 2 tsp. grenadine. Serve immediately. **Makes** 1 serving.

Melon Margarita: Substitute melon liqueur for orange liqueur. Proceed with recipe as directed. **Makes** 1 serving.

Note: For testing purposes only, we used Midori for melon liqueur.

The Perfect Margarita Glass

1. Moisten the rim of the glass with a lime wedge. You can also use orange liqueur or other sticky juices that allow the salt to cling.

2. Dip the prepared rims into margarita salt or other coarse salt varieties. Substitute sugar for salt, if desired.

from our kitchen

Freezing Seasonal Berries

Take advantage of the luscious blueberries, raspberries, and blackberries available now. Buy extra, and freeze them for summer-fresh flavor year-round. Frozen berries make great additions to smoothies, pancakes, muffins, pies, and cobblers. The best part is, it's a cinch to freeze berries; here's how.

■ Sort berries, discarding any mushy, underripe, or damaged ones. Gently rinse in cool water. (Do not wash blueberries.) Pat dry with a paper towel.

■ Place berries in a single layer on a jelly-roll pan; freeze until firm.

■ Transfer berries to a labeled and dated zip-top plastic freezer bag, squeezing out excess air. Freeze up to nine months.

■ Add berries to your favorite recipes while still frozen. Briefly rinse frozen blueberries with cool water just before using.

Fresh Peach Salsa

fast fixin's • make ahead
PREP: 20 MIN., COOK: 10 MIN.

This versatile salsa is equally delicious made with fresh nectarines. You'll need a 4- to 5-inch-long piece of ginger (about 1 inch thick) to get 2 Tbsp. grated ginger.

1 large sweet onion, chopped
1 jalapeño pepper, seeded and minced
¼ cup sugar
2 Tbsp. grated fresh ginger
2 Tbsp. olive oil
6 large firm peaches, peeled and chopped
¼ cup fresh lemon juice
¼ tsp. salt
2 Tbsp. chopped fresh cilantro

1. Sauté first 4 ingredients in hot oil in a large skillet over medium heat 5 minutes or until onion is tender. Stir in peaches and remaining ingredients, and cook, stirring gently, 5 minutes. Serve warm or at room temperature. Store leftovers in an airtight container in the refrigerator up to 2 days. **Makes** about 4 cups.

Juicy peaches take a savory spin in this hot and spicy salsa, created by Associate Foods Editor Mary Allen Perry. She serves the chutneylike condiment with grilled pork, chicken, or fish and as a dip for tortilla chips and quesadillas. It even makes a great appetizer—simply pair it with goat cheese or cream cheese and crackers or toasted baguette slices.

Easy Summer Treat

Just the mention of cobbler during berry season is enough to make anyone's mouth water. Here, we've updated the well-known dessert with the crunch of cornmeal and a hint of lemon. Frozen berries may be substituted for fresh; just increase the baking time by about 10 minutes. Serve with a scoop of vanilla ice cream for the ultimate indulgence.

Fresh Berry Cobbler
PREP: 15 MIN., BAKE: 45 MIN.

1 cup sugar, divided
1½ Tbsp. cornstarch
6 cups fresh berries (raspberries, blueberries, blackberries)
1½ tsp. grated lemon rind
1 cup all-purpose flour
¾ cup self-rising yellow cornmeal mix
⅓ cup butter, melted and slightly cooled
1 cup milk

1. Combine ⅓ cup sugar and 1½ Tbsp. cornstarch in a small bowl. Combine berries, cornstarch mixture, and lemon rind in a large bowl until well blended; spoon berry mixture into a lightly greased 2-qt. baking dish.
2. Combine flour, cornmeal mix, and remaining ⅔ cup sugar in a medium bowl. Stir in butter and milk until blended. Gently spread batter evenly over berry mixture.
3. Bake at 350° for 40 to 45 minutes or until a wooden pick inserted in center of topping comes out clean. Serve warm. **Makes** 6 to 8 servings.

september

Here's to Food, Wine, & Friends

For your next gathering, try this group's mouthwatering menu, and take the guesswork out of what to pour.

Festive Fall Menu

Serves 8

Brick-Grilled Cornish Hens

Lump Blue Crab Salad Wraps

Squash Casserole

Bourbon-Chocolate Cake With Praline Frosting

In 1993, Birmingham wine wholesaler Jerome Crawford and local businessman Elias Hendricks, Jr., started a supper club in the city's African American community to celebrate Birmingham's African American chefs. The group was so popular that it formalized into the Palm Wine Society. This menu was developed by Clayton Sherrod, who is one of the city's most respected chefs, for a gathering at his home.

Brick-Grilled Cornish Hens

chef recipe

PREP: 15 MIN., CHILL: 1 HR., GRILL: 40 MIN., STAND: 8 MIN. *(Pictured on page 179)*

8 (1½- to 1¾-lb.) Cornish hens
3 Tbsp. kosher salt
3 Tbsp. freshly ground black pepper
3 Tbsp. minced garlic
3 Tbsp. chopped fresh rosemary
1 Tbsp. dried crushed red pepper
¼ cup lemon juice
¼ cup olive oil
8 aluminum foil-wrapped bricks *
Garnishes: lemon wedges, flat-leaf
    parsley sprigs

1. Cut Cornish hens lengthwise through the backbone using kitchen shears, and flatten.
2. Combine salt and next 4 ingredients; rub evenly over hens. Place hens in 2-qt. zip-top freezer bags or 2 large baking dishes. Whisk together lemon juice and olive oil; drizzle lemon juice mixture over hens. Seal or cover, and chill 1 hour or up to 24 hours. Remove hens from marinade, discarding marinade.
3. Place hens on cooking grate of grill, and top each with an aluminum foil-wrapped brick. Grill, covered with grill lid, over medium heat (300° to 350°) 18 to 20 minutes on each side, replacing bricks on hens after flipping. Turn grill off, and let stand, covered with grill lid, 5 to 8 minutes or until done. (If using a charcoal grill, transfer hens to a 350° oven, and bake 5 to 8 minutes or until done.) Garnish, if desired. **Makes** 8 servings.

* Substitute cast-iron skillets for foil-wrapped bricks, if desired. Place a sheet of foil between each skillet and hen.

Lump Blue Crab Salad Wraps

chef recipe • make ahead

PREP: 20 MIN., CHILL: 8 HRS.

⅔ cup cider vinegar
½ cup vegetable oil
½ cup ice water
½ tsp. salt
⅛ tsp. pepper
1 lb. fresh lump crabmeat, picked and
    drained
1 medium onion, diced
3 bay leaves
1 Tbsp. drained capers
½ tsp. celery seeds
Bibb lettuce leaves

1. Whisk together first 5 ingredients. Add crabmeat and next 4 ingredients to dressing, tossing gently to coat. Cover and chill 8 hours. Drain crabmeat mixture, reserving ¼ cup dressing. Discard bay leaves. Spoon mixture into lettuce leaves, and serve with reserved dressing. **Makes** 8 servings.

Squash Casserole

chef recipe • make ahead

PREP: 15 MIN., COOK: 30 MIN., BAKE: 30 MIN.
(Pictured on page 179)

3 lb. yellow squash, cut into ¼-inch-
    thick slices
1 small onion, chopped
1½ Tbsp. salt
16 saltine crackers, divided
1½ cups (6 oz.) shredded sharp
    Cheddar cheese, divided
½ cup mayonnaise
1 large egg, lightly beaten
2 Tbsp. butter, melted
¼ tsp. pepper
⅛ tsp. salt

1. Cook first 3 ingredients in boiling water to cover in a Dutch oven 25 minutes or until squash is very tender. Drain well, and mash mixture with a fork.
2. Crush 10 crackers, and stir into squash mixture; stir in ½ cup cheese and next 5 ingredients. Spoon mixture into a lightly greased 11- x 7-inch baking dish.
3. Crush remaining 6 crackers, and sprinkle over casserole; sprinkle remaining 1 cup cheese evenly over casserole.

4. Bake, uncovered, at 350° for 30 minutes or until cheese melts and casserole is bubbly. **Makes** 8 servings.

Note: To make ahead, prepare recipe as directed; do not top with crackers or cheese. Cover and chill overnight. Remove from refrigerator; let stand 30 minutes. Uncover and top with crackers and cheese; bake as directed.

Bourbon-Chocolate Cake With Praline Frosting
chef recipe

PREP: 30 MIN., COOK: 5 MIN., BAKE: 28 MIN., COOL: 10 MIN., CHILL: 30 MIN.

1 cup butter
¼ cup unsweetened cocoa
1 cup water
½ cup buttermilk
2 large eggs
1 tsp. baking soda
1 tsp. vanilla extract
2 cups sugar
2 cups all-purpose flour
½ tsp. salt
Chocolate Ganache
Praline Frosting
Bourbon Glaze

1. Grease bottoms of 3 (8-inch) round cake pans; line with wax paper. Grease and flour wax paper and sides of pans; set pans aside.
2. Cook first 3 ingredients in a saucepan over low heat, stirring constantly, 3 to 5 minutes or until butter melts and mixture is smooth; remove from heat, and let cool.
3. Beat buttermilk and next 3 ingredients at medium speed with an electric mixer until smooth. Add butter mixture to buttermilk mixture, beating until blended. Combine sugar, flour, and salt; gradually add to buttermilk mixture, beating until blended. (Batter will be thin.) Pour batter evenly into prepared pans.
4. Bake at 350° for 25 to 28 minutes or until a wooden pick inserted into centers comes out clean. Cool in pans on wire racks 10 minutes. Remove from pans, and cool completely on wire racks. (Cake layers will be thin.)

5. Spread about ½ cup Chocolate Ganache between each cake layer; spread remaining Chocolate Ganache on sides of cake. (Do not frost top of cake.) Chill cake 30 minutes. Pour warm Praline Frosting slowly over top of cake, spreading to edges. (Cover and let stand up to 24 hours, if desired.)
6. Pierce about 25 holes in top of cake using a wooden or metal skewer. Pour warm Bourbon Glaze over cake. **Makes** 12 servings.

Chocolate Ganache:
PREP: 10 MIN., COOL: 35 MIN.

2 cups (12 oz.) semisweet chocolate morsels
⅓ cup whipping cream
¼ cup butter, cut into pieces

1. Microwave chocolate morsels and cream in a glass bowl at MEDIUM (50% power) 2 to 3 minutes or until morsels are melted, stirring after 1½ minutes; whisk until smooth. Gradually add butter, whisking until smooth. Cool about 35 minutes or until spreading consistency, whisking every 10 minutes. **Makes** about 2½ cups.

Praline Frosting:
PREP: 10 MIN., BAKE: 15 MIN., COOK: 2 MIN.

½ cup chopped pecans
2 Tbsp. butter
½ cup firmly packed light brown sugar
3 Tbsp. whipping cream
½ cup powdered sugar
½ tsp. vanilla extract

1. Bake pecans on a baking sheet at 350° for 15 minutes or until golden brown, stirring once.
2. Bring butter, brown sugar, and cream to a boil in a 2-qt. saucepan over medium heat, stirring often; boil, stirring often, 1 minute. Remove from heat, and whisk in powdered sugar and vanilla until smooth. Add toasted pecans; stir gently 3 minutes or until frosting begins to cool and thicken slightly. **Makes** ¾ cup.

Bourbon Glaze:
PREP: 5 MIN., COOK: 2 MIN.

4 Tbsp. butter
¼ cup granulated sugar
¼ cup firmly packed brown sugar
1 tsp. vanilla extract
⅓ cup bourbon

1. Melt 4 Tbsp. butter in a skillet over medium-high heat; stir in granulated sugar, brown sugar, and vanilla. Cook, stirring constantly, 1 minute. Remove skillet from heat, and stir in bourbon. Carefully ignite the fumes just above liquid mixture with a long match or long multipurpose lighter. Let stand until flames disappear. **Makes** about 1 cup.

Celebrating the South

One of the wineries Jerome works with is Garretson Wine Company in Paso Robles, California, owned and operated by Georgia native Mat Garretson. Mat introduced a line of red and white wines in 2003 to pay tribute to the South.

The full-bodied white wine, Camellia Cuvee (in honor of Alabama), served at this supper was outstanding. It's perfect with everything from artichoke-and-spinach dip to grilled pork chops and spicy curry chicken. The splurge-worthy wines retail for about $19.

Everything Bananas Foster

This showstopping dessert is easier than you think and oh so versatile. And by the way, it only takes about 15 minutes.

Butter, brown sugar, rum, and bananas turn dessert into an event. Igniting the sauce of bananas Foster tableside will wow friends and family. Chef Paul Blangé created the festive treat for one of his favorite customers, Richard Foster, at Brennan's Restaurant more than 50 years ago. Some say he was also motivated by enormous shipments of bananas. Whatever inspired Paul, his sweet dish is an enduring hit.

Some versions of the sauce call for both banana liqueur and rum, while others list only rum. When we call for rum, it can be light or dark unless specified. We don't recommend spiced rum in these recipes.

You'll like the flavor of bananas Foster in these other presentations too: a warm upside-down cake and a hot gratin. No matter how you serve it, this dessert will turn you into a devoted fan.

John's Bananas Foster
fast fixin's
PREP: 10 MIN., COOK: 6 MIN.
Working quickly, prescoop ice cream into a large bowl, and store in the freezer to make serving easy. If you don't have countertops that accommodate a hot skillet, just move the skillet to an unlit burner on your stovetop before igniting. (Pictured on page 180)

4 medium-size ripe bananas
½ cup butter
1 cup firmly packed brown sugar
¼ cup banana liqueur
½ cup rum
Vanilla ice cream

1. Cut bananas in half crosswise; cut each half in half lengthwise. Melt butter in a large skillet over medium-high heat; add brown sugar, and cook, stirring constantly, 2 minutes.
2. Add bananas to skillet, and remove from heat. Stir in liqueur and rum, and carefully ignite the fumes just above mixture with a long match or long multipurpose lighter. Let flames die down.
3. Return skillet to heat, and cook 3 to 4 minutes or until bananas are soft and curl slightly. Remove from heat. Serve banana mixture immediately over vanilla ice cream. **Makes** 6 to 8 servings.

JOHN ALEX FLOYD, JR.
TRUSSVILLE, ALABAMA

Bananas Foster Upside-down Coffee Cake
family favorite
PREP: 20 MIN., COOK: 3 MIN., BAKE: 50 MIN., COOL: 10 MIN. *(Pictured on page 181)*

½ cup butter, softened and divided
2 Tbsp. rum
1 cup firmly packed light brown sugar
½ cup chopped pecans, toasted
2 medium-size ripe bananas
7 maraschino cherries
¾ cup granulated sugar, divided
2 large eggs, separated
¾ cup milk
½ cup sour cream
1 tsp. vanilla extract
2 cups all-purpose baking mix
¼ tsp. ground cinnamon
Whipped cream (optional)

John's Bananas Foster Step-by-Step

1. Melt ¼ cup butter in a 10-inch cast-iron skillet over low heat; stir in rum. Sprinkle brown sugar evenly over butter mixture. Remove from heat.

2. Sprinkle pecans evenly over brown sugar mixture. Cut bananas in half crosswise; cut each half lengthwise into 3 slices. Arrange banana slices in a spoke pattern over pecans. Cut 6 cherries in half. Place 1 cherry half between each banana slice. Place remaining whole cherry in center of skillet.

3. Beat remaining ¼ cup butter and ½ cup granulated sugar in a large bowl at medium speed with an electric mixer until blended. Add egg yolks, 1 at a time, beating just until blended after each addition. Add milk, sour cream, and vanilla, beating just until blended. Combine baking mix and cinnamon. Add cinnamon mixture to milk mixture, beating just until blended.

4. Beat egg whites in a large bowl with an electric mixer until soft peaks form. Gradually beat in remaining ¼ cup granulated sugar until stiff peaks form. Fold into batter. Spread batter evenly over bananas in skillet.

5. Bake at 350° for 45 to 50 minutes or until a wooden pick inserted in center comes out clean. Cool in skillet on wire rack 10 minutes. Invert onto a serving plate. Serve warm with whipped cream, if desired. **Makes** 8 to 10 servings.

Note: For testing purposes only, we used Bisquick All-Purpose Baking Mix.

LOUIS DELAUNAY
GRAPEVINE, TEXAS

Bananas Foster Gratin
fast fixin's

PREP: 10 MIN., COOK: 4 MIN., BAKE: 10 MIN.

Get all the flavor without the flaming in this version of the famous dessert.

¼ cup firmly packed light brown sugar
3 Tbsp. water
1 Tbsp. dark rum
¼ tsp. ground cinnamon
2 tsp. butter
4 medium-size ripe bananas
1 almond biscotti, crushed (about ⅓ cup)
Vanilla ice cream

1. Stir together first 4 ingredients in a 10-inch skillet over medium heat, and bring to a boil. Reduce heat to medium-low, and simmer, stirring constantly, 2 minutes. Remove from heat, and stir in butter.

2. Slice bananas diagonally. Add to brown sugar mixture in skillet, tossing to coat.

3. Spoon banana mixture evenly into 4 lightly greased (1- to 1½-cup) gratin dishes or a shallow, lightly greased 1-qt. baking dish.

4. Bake at 450° for 10 minutes or until bubbly. Remove from oven, and sprinkle evenly with biscotti crumbs. Serve warm with vanilla ice cream. **Makes** 4 servings.

CAROLINE W. KENNEDY
COVINGTON, GEORGIA

Casual Gathering

It's a staple on most brunch menus. And with an assortment of condiments to make it mild or hot, with alcohol or not, a Bloody Mary bar helps gather neighbors for a little libation. Offer a variety of ingredients (see box on following page), so guests can mix their drinks to suit their tastes. Add this flavorful casserole and your favorite dip to turn the gathering into a laid-back party.

Golden Egg Casserole
family favorite

PREP: 30 MIN., COOK: 10 MIN., BAKE: 30 MIN.

2 Tbsp. butter or margarine
1 cup sliced fresh mushrooms
1 medium-size green bell pepper, chopped
10 large eggs
½ cup all-purpose flour
1 tsp. baking powder
¼ tsp. salt
1 (16-oz.) container small-curd cottage cheese
2 cups (8 oz.) shredded Monterey Jack cheese
½ lb. ground pork sausage, cooked and drained
6 bacon slices, cooked and crumbled
1 (2¼-oz.) can sliced ripe black olives, drained

1. Melt butter in a large skillet over medium-high heat; add mushrooms and bell pepper, and sauté 8 minutes or until tender. Remove from heat; cool slightly.

2. Whisk together eggs and next 3 ingredients in a large bowl until smooth. Stir in mushroom mixture, cottage cheese, and remaining ingredients. Pour into a greased 13- x 9-inch baking dish.

3. Bake at 400° for 15 minutes. Reduce heat to 350°, and bake 15 more minutes or until set and lightly browned. **Makes** 8 to 10 servings.

ELLIE WELLS
LAKELAND, FLORIDA

Basic Bloody Mary
fast fixin's
PREP: 5 MIN.

Lime juice
Seasoned pepper or Old Bay seasoning
1 cup tomato juice, chilled
3 Tbsp. vodka
3 Tbsp. lemon or lime juice
¾ tsp. Worcestershire sauce
4 drops hot sauce
½ tsp. prepared horseradish
¼ tsp. pepper
¼ tsp. celery salt
¼ tsp. salt
Garnishes: lime wedges, pickled green
    beans, pickled peppers

1. Dip rim of a cocktail glass in lime juice; dip in seasoned pepper, coating well.
2. Add 1 cup chilled tomato juice and next 8 ingredients to prepared glass, stirring until blended. Add ice to tomato juice mixture in glass. Garnish, if desired. **Makes** 1 serving.

Stock Up

This generous assortment of ingredients allows guests to create perfectly seasoned cocktails.

vodka
spicy-hot vegetable juice
plain vegetable juice
plain tomato juice
Bloody Mary mix
Worcestershire sauce
pickled tomatoes
pickled onions
pickled okra
pickled peppers
pickled green beans
lemons
limes
prepared horseradish
Old Bay seasoning
seasoned pepper
celery sticks
carrot sticks
olives
hot sauce

---

quick & easy
Ready, Set, Pasta

Fast and simple, pasta is just right for nights when you're really in a hurry. Save time by immediately putting a big pot of water, covered with the lid, on the stove to boil. While the water heats up, you'll have time to chop, measure, and sauté everything else. Cook the pasta, drain, and toss the meal together. Serve with a satisfied smile.

Penne With Vodka
PREP: 20 MIN., COOK: 25 MIN.

1 lb. uncooked penne or ziti pasta
2 Tbsp. butter or margarine
2 Tbsp. olive oil
1 medium onion, diced
3 garlic cloves, minced
½ tsp. dried crushed red pepper
1 cup vodka*
1 (14½-oz.) can crushed tomatoes
1 Tbsp. chopped fresh parsley
1 Tbsp. chopped fresh basil
1 cup whipping cream
½ tsp. salt
¾ cup freshly grated Parmesan cheese
Cracked black pepper to taste

1. Prepare pasta according to package directions. Set aside.
2. Melt butter with oil in a Dutch oven over medium-high heat; add onion and garlic, and sauté 5 minutes. Add red pepper. Remove from heat; stir in vodka. Return to heat, and simmer 5 minutes.
3. Stir in tomatoes, parsley, and basil; simmer 5 minutes.
4. Stir in cream and salt; simmer, stirring occasionally, 5 minutes. Stir in pasta; cook 2 more minutes. Sprinkle with cheese and pepper, and toss. Serve immediately. **Makes** 4 to 6 servings.

∗Substitute chicken broth, if desired.
GRETCHEN OHAR
LOCKPORT, NEW YORK

Pork Lo Mein
fast fixin's
PREP: 15 MIN., COOK: 12 MIN.
If you cook the pork and vegetables in vegetable oil instead of sesame oil, this dish will have a milder flavor and fragrance.

8 oz. uncooked lo mein noodles or thin
    spaghetti
1 Tbsp. sesame oil or vegetable oil
4 boneless pork loin chops (1 lb.), cut
    into ¼-inch strips
1 small onion, sliced
1 cup chopped fresh mushrooms
¾ cup chopped celery (about 2 ribs)
⅓ cup soy sauce
¼ tsp. pepper

1. Prepare noodles according to package directions. Drain well; keep warm.
2. Heat oil in a large skillet or wok over medium-high heat 2 minutes. Add pork, and stir-fry 5 minutes or until done. Remove from skillet.
3. Add onion, mushrooms, and celery to skillet; stir-fry 4 minutes. Stir in soy sauce. Return pork to skillet; stir-fry 1 minute. Stir in cooked pasta and pepper, tossing to coat. Serve immediately. **Makes** 4 servings.

KIMBERLY TUCKER
HUNTERSVILLE, NORTH CAROLINA

Bow Tie Pasta Toss
fast fixin's
PREP: 15 MIN., STAND: 10 MIN.

8 oz. uncooked bow tie pasta
¾ tsp. salt, divided
1 cup grape tomatoes, cut in half
1 (2.25-oz.) can sliced ripe black olives,
    drained
1 Tbsp. finely chopped sweet onion
3 Tbsp. olive oil
3 Tbsp. balsamic vinegar
1 small garlic clove, pressed
1 tsp. chopped fresh oregano
½ (4-oz.) package crumbled feta
    cheese
Garnish: fresh oregano sprigs

1. Prepare pasta according to package directions, adding ½ tsp. salt to water; drain well.
2. Place pasta in a large bowl, and stir in tomatoes, olives, and onion.

3. Whisk together olive oil, next 3 ingredients, and remaining ¼ tsp. salt; add to pasta mixture, tossing to coat. Let stand 10 minutes; stir in feta. Garnish, if desired. **Makes** 2 to 3 main-dish or 4 to 6 side-dish servings.

PHAEDRA SPENCER
BETHLEHEM, GEORGIA

Kitchen Express: Substitute 6 Tbsp. balsamic vinaigrette for olive oil, vinegar, garlic, and oregano. Proceed as directed.

Main-Dish Rice

Quick-cooking bags or pouches of rice just might become your new best friends. They cook in no time and can easily evolve into hearty main dishes with just a few additions. We've included a group of recipes that are sure to please, and with all the choices out there, you'll have main-dish rice options galore.

Skillet Sausage 'n' Rice
fast fixin's
PREP: 10 MIN., COOK: 20 MIN.

1 (16-oz.) package smoked sausage
1 medium-size green bell pepper, chopped
1 small onion, chopped
1 garlic clove, minced
1 cup chicken broth
2 (3.5-oz.) bags quick-cooking brown rice
½ tsp. salt
¼ tsp. pepper
Garnish: chopped fresh parsley

1. Cut sausage into ½-inch slices. Sauté sausage in a large nonstick skillet over medium-high heat 8 to 10 minutes or until lightly browned. Remove sausage slices, and drain on paper towels, reserving 1 Tbsp. drippings in skillet.
2. Add bell pepper, onion, and garlic to skillet, and sauté over medium-high heat 4 minutes or until tender. Add chicken broth, stirring to loosen particles from bottom of skillet, and bring to a boil. Remove rice from cooking bag; add rice, sausage, salt, and pepper to skillet. Reduce heat to medium-low, cover, and cook 5 minutes or until rice is tender. Garnish, if desired. **Makes** 4 to 6 servings.

Speedy Black Beans and Mexican Rice
fast fixin's
PREP: 5 MIN., COOK: 2 MIN.
This hearty dish is the perfect answer for a meatless main-dish choice and doubles perfectly.

1 (8.8-oz.) pouch ready-to-serve Mexican rice
1 (15-oz.) can black beans, rinsed and drained
1 (4.4-oz.) can chopped green chiles
2 Tbsp. chopped fresh cilantro
Toppings: sour cream, salsa, diced tomato, shredded Cheddar cheese

1. Cook rice according to package directions.
2. Combine black beans and green chiles in a microwave-safe bowl. Microwave at HIGH 90 seconds. Stir in rice and cilantro. Serve immediately with desired toppings. **Makes** 2 servings.

Note: For testing purposes only, we used Rice-A-Roni Express Heat & Serve Mexican Rice.

Mexican Beef 'n' Rice: Substitute 1 lb. cooked lean ground beef for black beans. Substitute 1 cup salsa for green chiles. Prepare recipe as directed, omitting toppings. Serve with corn chips or in lettuce leaves, if desired. **Makes** 4 servings.

Dinner in Less Than 10 Minutes

Even on your busiest days, you'll have time to whip up these hearty entrées.

Turkey and Rice With Veggies
fast fixin's
PREP: 5 MIN., COOK: 2 MIN.

1. Cook 1 (8.8-oz.) pouch ready-to-serve garden vegetable rice according to package directions. Stir together cooked rice; 1 lb. lean ground turkey, cooked; and 1 (14.5-oz.) can diced tomatoes with basil, garlic, and oregano, drained. **Makes** 4 servings.

Note: For testing purposes only, we used Uncle Ben's Garden Vegetable Ready Rice With Peas, Carrots, and Corn.

Asian Chicken and Fried Rice
fast fixin's
PREP: 5 MIN., COOK: 2 MIN.

1. Cook 1 (8.8-oz.) pouch ready-to-serve Asian fried rice according to package directions. Stir together cooked rice, 2 cups shredded cooked chicken, 1 Tbsp. chopped fresh basil, and 2 Tbsp. fresh lemon juice. **Makes** 4 servings.

Note: For testing purposes only, we used Rice-A-Roni Express Heat & Serve Asian Fried Rice.

Test Kitchen *Notebook*

Another way to save time is by cooking up a large batch of rice and storing it in an airtight container in the refrigerator up to a week; just reheat it or microwave briefly until heated through.

Kate Nicholson
ASSOCIATE FOODS EDITOR

Weekend Living.

Enjoy an at-home escape any time of day with luscious food and a few hours of leisure.

Breakfast for Two

Brunch on the Double

Serves 2

Sausage-Cheese Breakfast Cups
Mint-Topped Broiled Oranges
Spiced Coffee Cake

Pamper yourself—and a loved one—with an easygoing breakfast. Our menu lets you prep the dishes the night before so you're free to relax in the morning while the meal is baking. Linger over a conversation, or simply settle in with your favorite book or a stack of movies.

Sausage-Cheese Breakfast Cups

PREP: 10 MIN., CHILL: 8 HRS., STAND: 25 MIN., BAKE: 25 MIN.

1 cup cubed white bread (about 2 slices)
¼ cup cooked, crumbled hot ground
   pork sausage
¼ cup shredded Monterey Jack cheese
   with peppers
2 large eggs
¼ cup milk
¼ tsp. salt
¼ tsp. dry mustard
¼ tsp. pepper
⅛ tsp. onion powder

1. Layer cubed bread, cooked sausage, and cheese evenly into 2 greased 8-oz. ramekins or individual soufflé dishes.
2. Whisk together eggs and next 5 ingredients. Pour evenly over cheese in ramekins. Cover and chill 8 hours. Let stand at room temperature 20 minutes before baking.
3. Bake at 350° for 20 to 25 minutes or until set. Let stand 5 minutes before serving. **Makes** 2 servings.

Note: To bake in a muffin pan, layer cubed bread, cooked sausage, and shredded cheese evenly in 4 greased cups in pan. Pour egg mixture evenly over cheese in muffin cups. Cover and chill 8 hours. Let stand at room temperature 20 minutes before baking. Bake at 350° for 15 to 20 minutes or until set. Let stand 5 minutes before serving.

Individual Ham-Swiss Breakfast Cups: Prepare recipe as directed, substituting ¼ cup chopped cooked ham for sausage and ¼ cup shredded Swiss cheese for Monterey Jack cheese with peppers.

Mint-Topped Broiled Oranges
fast fixin's
PREP: 10 MIN., BROIL: 8 MIN.
Cut a very thin slice off the bottom of each orange half to help steady the fruit on the baking sheet.

1 large navel orange
2 tsp. butter, melted
½ tsp. chopped fresh mint
1 Tbsp. orange liqueur
   (optional)

1. Cut orange in half crosswise. Run a sharp knife or grapefruit knife around each section to loosen from membrane. (Do not remove sections.)
2. Stir together butter, chopped mint, and, if desired, orange liqueur. Spoon evenly over cut sides of orange halves. Place orange halves, cut side up, on an aluminum foil-lined baking sheet.
3. Broil 5 inches from heat 5 to 8 minutes or until thoroughly heated. **Makes** 2 servings.

Spiced Coffee Cake
PREP: 25 MIN., BAKE: 40 MIN.

2 cups all-purpose flour
¾ tsp. ground cinnamon
½ tsp. ground nutmeg
½ tsp. baking soda
½ tsp. salt
½ cup butter, softened
¾ cup firmly packed dark brown sugar
⅔ cup granulated sugar
2 large eggs
1 tsp. vanilla extract
1 cup buttermilk
Streusel Topping

1. Combine first 5 ingredients in a small bowl.
2. Beat butter, brown sugar, and granulated sugar at medium speed with an electric mixer until combined. Add eggs, 1 at a time, beating until blended after each addition. Add vanilla, beating until blended. Add flour mixture to butter mixture alternately with buttermilk, beginning and ending with flour mixture. Beat at low speed until blended after each addition. Pour batter into

a lightly greased 9-inch square pan; sprinkle evenly with Streusel Topping. **3.** Bake at 350° for 35 to 40 minutes or until a wooden pick inserted in center comes out clean. Serve warm or at room temperature. **Makes** 9 servings.

Streusel Topping:
fast fixin's
PREP: 5 MIN.

½ cup chopped pecans, toasted
⅓ cup firmly packed dark brown sugar
2 Tbsp. all-purpose flour
¼ tsp. ground cinnamon
2 Tbsp. butter, melted

1. Combine first 4 ingredients in a small bowl; stir in melted butter. **Makes** about ¾ cup.

No-Fuss Get-together

Easy Entertaining

Serves 8

Layered Spicy Black Bean Dip with chips

Smoky Ranch Dip with raw veggies

Simple Antipasto Platter

Invite a few friends over for a bite to eat, and feel the stress of the workweek melt away. Keep it simple, and take the party outside; light up the chiminea, and savor the cool, crisp air.

Offer guests easy-to-make Layered Spicy Black Bean Dip or Simple Antipasto Platter, both with prep times of 10

minutes or less. Try one of the chip and vegetable dips that start with a package of Ranch dressing mix and combine diverse ingredients for any taste.

Continue the casual theme by offering an assortment of icy drinks, or cut costs and have everyone bring a six-pack of their favorite beverage to share. To keep the gathering laid-back, divide up the recipes, and purchase wrapped chocolate candies from your local supermarket to nibble on for a sweet ending. Without a lot of fuss, you can unwind and relax into the evening.

Layered Spicy Black Bean Dip
fast fixin's
PREP: 10 MIN.

1 (8-oz.) package cream cheese, softened
1 (16-oz.) jar spicy black bean dip
½ (8-oz.) package shredded Mexican cheese blend
Toppings: sliced green onions, chopped tomatoes, sliced ripe black olives
Assorted tortilla and corn chips

1. Layer cream cheese, dip, and cheese in a 1-qt. serving dish. Add toppings, and serve with chips. **Makes** 8 servings.

Note: For testing purposes only, we used Desert Pepper Trading Company Spicy Black Bean Dip.

MARROW GORDON
BIRMINGHAM, ALABAMA

Smoky Ranch Dip
make ahead
PREP: 5 MIN., CHILL: 30 MIN.

1 (1-oz.) envelope Ranch dressing mix
1½ cups light sour cream
2 tsp. finely chopped chipotle peppers in adobo sauce
1 tsp. adobo sauce from can
Potato chips or assorted raw vegetables

1. Whisk together first 4 ingredients. Cover and chill 30 minutes. Serve with

chips or assorted raw vegetables. **Makes** about 1½ cups.

MATT CAINE
HELENA, ALABAMA

Barbecue Ranch Dip: Omit chipotle peppers and adobo sauce. Stir in 2 Tbsp. barbecue sauce. Serve with roasted red new potatoes.

Lime-Cilantro Ranch Dip: Omit chipotle peppers and adobo sauce. Stir in 1 Tbsp. fresh lime juice and 1 Tbsp. chopped cilantro. Serve with quesadillas, tacos, or chili.

Lemon-Parsley Ranch Dip: Omit chipotle peppers and adobo sauce. Stir in 1 Tbsp. fresh lemon juice and 1 Tbsp. chopped fresh parsley. Serve with steamed asparagus.

Horseradish Ranch Spread: Omit chipotle peppers and adobo sauce. Stir in 2 tsp. prepared horseradish. Spread on dinner rolls, and top with thinly sliced deli roast beef.

Simple Antipasto Platter
fast fixin's
PREP: 10 MIN.

If you can open a jar, you can arrange this platter. Simply roll a log of goat cheese in chopped fresh parsley, and then just arrange the other items around it for an effortless and tasty offering.

1 (5-oz.) log goat cheese
2 Tbsp. chopped fresh parsley
1 (16-oz.) jar pickled okra, drained
1 (10-oz.) jar pitted kalamata olives, rinsed and drained
1 (7-oz.) jar roasted red bell peppers, drained and cut into strips
1 (4-oz.) package sliced salami
Assorted crackers and breadsticks

1. Roll goat cheese log in parsley; place on a serving platter. Arrange okra and next 3 ingredients on platter around goat cheese. Serve with crackers and breadsticks. **Makes** 8 servings.

Shortcut to Amazing Cinnamon Rolls

Turn frozen biscuits into something scrumptious.

Homemade flavor is inside every sweet and buttery bite of these delicious biscuit cinnamon rolls. They're so easy to make, you won't even need a rolling pin. Just start with a package of frozen biscuits.

Apricot-Pecan Cinnamon Rolls

PREP: 10 MIN., STAND: 55 MIN., BAKE: 40 MIN.
To prepare individual rolls such as those shown at right, prepare as directed; place one slice in each of 12 lightly greased 3-inch muffin cups. Bake at 375° for 20 to 25 minutes or until golden brown. Cool slightly, and remove from pan. (Pictured on page 9)

1 (26.4-oz.) package frozen biscuits
1 (6-oz.) package dried apricots
All-purpose flour
¼ cup butter, softened
¾ cup firmly packed brown sugar
1 tsp. ground cinnamon
½ cup chopped pecans, toasted
1 cup powdered sugar
3 Tbsp. milk
½ tsp. vanilla extract

1. Arrange frozen biscuits, with sides touching, in 3 rows of 4 biscuits on a lightly floured surface. Let stand 30 to 45 minutes or until biscuits are thawed but still cool to the touch.
2. Pour boiling water to cover over dried apricots, and let stand 10 minutes; drain well. Chop apricots.
3. Sprinkle thawed biscuits lightly with flour. Press biscuit edges together, and pat to form a 12- x 10-inch rectangle of dough; spread evenly with softened butter. Stir together brown sugar and cinnamon; sprinkle evenly over butter. Sprinkle chopped apricots and pecans evenly over brown sugar mixture.
4. Roll up, starting at 1 long end; cut into 12 (about 1-inch-thick) slices. Place rolls into a lightly greased 10-inch cast-iron skillet, 10-inch round pan, or 9-inch square pan.
5. Bake at 375° for 35 to 40 minutes or until center rolls are golden brown and done; cool slightly.
6. Stir together 1 cup powdered sugar, 3 Tbsp. milk, and ½ tsp. vanilla; drizzle evenly over rolls. **Makes** 1 dozen.

Cinnamon-Raisin Rolls: Prepare Apricot-Pecan Cinnamon Rolls as directed, substituting 1 cup golden raisins for 1 (6-oz.) package dried apricots.

Peaches-and-Cream Cinnamon Rolls: Prepare Apricot-Pecan Cinnamon Rolls as directed, substituting ½ (8-oz.) package softened cream cheese for ¼ cup butter and 1 (6-oz.) package dried peaches for 1 (6-oz.) package dried apricots.

Chocolate-Cherry-Cream Cheese Cinnamon Rolls: Prepare Apricot-Pecan Cinnamon Rolls as directed, substituting ½ (8-oz.) package softened cream cheese for ¼ cup butter, 1 (6-oz.) package dried cherries for 1 (6-oz.) package dried apricots, and 1 cup semisweet chocolate morsels for ½ cup pecans.

Pimiento Cheese Rolls
family favorite
PREP: 15 MIN., STAND: 45 MIN., BAKE: 25 MIN.
We enjoyed the sweet versions of our cinnamon rolls so much that we decided to create a few savory ones as well. You can also bake these in a 10-inch skillet or pan, but we liked them best baked in 3-inch muffin cups. This gave each roll a crispy brown edge that held the fillings in snugly—perfect for breakfast on the go.

1 (26.4-oz.) package frozen biscuits
All-purpose flour
2 cups Pimiento Cheese

1. Arrange frozen biscuits, with sides touching, in 3 rows of 4 biscuits on a lightly floured surface. Let stand 30 to 45 minutes or until biscuits are thawed but cool to the touch.
2. Sprinkle thawed biscuits lightly with flour. Press biscuit edges together, and pat to form a 12- x 10-inch rectangle of dough; spread evenly with Pimiento Cheese.
3. Roll up, starting at 1 long end; cut into 12 (about 1-inch-thick) slices. Place 1 slice into each of 12 lightly greased 3-inch muffin pan cups.
4. Bake at 375° for 20 to 25 minutes or until golden brown. Cool slightly, and remove from pan. **Makes** 1 dozen.

Pimiento Cheese:
fast fixin's
PREP: 10 MIN.

2 cups (8 oz.) shredded sharp Cheddar cheese
¾ cup mayonnaise
1 (2-oz.) jar diced pimiento, drained
1 tsp. minced onion
¼ tsp. ground red pepper

1. Stir together all ingredients until blended. **Makes** 2 cups.

Ham-and-Swiss Rolls: Omit Pimiento Cheese. Stir together ¼ cup each of softened butter, spicy brown mustard, and finely chopped sweet onion. Spread butter mixture evenly over 12- x 10-inch rectangle of thawed dough; sprinkle evenly with 1 cup each of shredded Swiss cheese and chopped

Rise and Shine

Both the sweet and savory variations of these quick-to-fix biscuit rolls are prepared in the same way. Just substitute your favorite fillings for the ones we've shown here.

1 Arrange frozen biscuits, with sides touching, in 3 rows of 4 biscuits on a lightly floured surface. Let stand 30 to 45 minutes or until biscuits are thawed but still cool to the touch.

2 Sprinkle thawed biscuits lightly with flour. Press biscuit edges together, and pat to form a 12- x 10-inch rectangle of dough.

3 Spread rectangle evenly with softened butter or cream cheese, and then sprinkle with desired fillings.

4 Roll up dough carefully, starting at one long end of the rectangle and pressing together any open spaces on the underside of the dough as you roll.

5 Cut into 12 slices. (The rectangle of dough will elongate as it's rolled, yielding 12 slices that are each a little more than 1 inch thick.)

6 Place rolls into a lightly greased 10-inch cast-iron skillet, 10-inch round pan, 9-inch square pan, or 3-inch muffin cups; bake as directed.

cooked ham. Proceed with recipe as directed.

Sausage-and-Cheddar Rolls: Omit Pimiento Cheese. Spread ¼ cup softened butter evenly over 12- x 10-inch rectangle of thawed dough; sprinkle evenly with 1 cup each of shredded Cheddar cheese and cooked, crumbled sausage. Proceed with recipe as directed.

Test Kitchens Tips

■ Thawing activates the leavening agents in frozen biscuits, so be sure to work with the dough as soon as it's soft enough to pat into a rectangle. The biscuits should still be cold when you begin to pat them together. If left to stand too long, the dough will discolor and not rise properly.
■ Soaking dried fruit in boiling water intensifies the natural flavor and makes the fruit moist and tender for baking. This step takes only a few minutes and can be done while the biscuits thaw.
■ Don't worry about small tears or ragged edges when rolling or slicing the dough. Just poke any loose filling back inside, press the dough together, and continue on. The rolls will still bake up beautifully.
■ Warm leftover rolls for a few seconds in the microwave. (Overheating will make them tough and dry.)

One Special Salad

One look at Cornbread Cobb Salad, and you'll want to dive right in. Piled high with chicken, bacon, avocado, lettuce, tomato, and blue cheese-laced croutons, this salad is an enticing meal. Though the croutons and dressing take a little effort, you can prepare them a day ahead and assemble the salad just before serving.

Cornbread Cobb Salad
PREP: 20 MIN., COOK: 15 MIN.

1 (14.5-oz.) can chicken broth
2 skinned and boned chicken breasts
Cilantro-Chile Dressing, divided
1 head romaine lettuce
½ (8-oz.) block Cheddar cheese, shredded
1 (8-oz.) container grape tomatoes, halved
½ cup sliced green onions
2 avocados, sliced
1 (8-oz.) package fully cooked bacon, crumbled
Cornbread Croutons

1. Bring chicken broth to a boil in a medium-size nonstick skillet over medium heat. Reduce heat, and add chicken; cover and simmer 12 minutes or until tender. Remove from heat; cool completely. Cut chicken into ¼-inch strips. Toss with 3 Tbsp. Cilantro-Chile Dressing.
2. Cut or tear lettuce into bite-size pieces. Arrange lettuce pieces on a large serving platter; arrange chicken, cheese, and next 4 ingredients over lettuce. Serve with remaining Cilantro-Chile Dressing and Cornbread Croutons. **Makes** 6 servings.

CAROL ORR
HILLSBORO, OREGON

Cilantro-Chile Dressing:
make ahead
PREP: 15 MIN.

⅓ cup chopped fresh cilantro
⅓ cup rice wine vinegar
1 serrano chile, seeded and coarsely chopped
2 garlic cloves, chopped
2 tsp. sugar
½ tsp. salt
¼ tsp. pepper
1 cup vegetable oil

1. Process first 7 ingredients in a food processor or blender until combined, stopping to scrape down sides. With processor running, pour oil in a slow, steady stream; process until thickened. **Makes** about 1⅓ cups.

Cornbread Croutons:
make ahead
PREP: 10 MIN., BAKE: 23 MIN., COOL: 10 MIN.

1 cup all-purpose flour
1 cup yellow cornmeal
1 Tbsp. sugar
2 tsp. baking powder
¼ tsp. salt
1 large egg
½ cup milk
¼ cup vegetable oil
1 (4-oz.) container crumbled blue cheese
½ cup canned whole kernel corn, drained

1. Combine first 5 ingredients in a medium bowl.
2. Whisk together egg, milk, and oil. Stir egg mixture into flour mixture just until smooth; fold in blue cheese and corn. (Batter will be thick.) Spread mixture in an even layer (about 1 inch thick) in a greased 8-inch square pan.
3. Bake at 400° for 12 to 15 minutes or until golden brown. Cool in pan on a wire rack for 10 minutes. Remove cornbread from pan; place on rack to cool completely.
4. Cut cornbread into 1-inch cubes; place in a single layer on a baking sheet. Bake at 400° for 8 minutes, turning once after 4 minutes. Remove from oven, and let cool. **Makes** about 6 cups.

Kitchen Express Cornbread Croutons:
Stir together 1 (6-oz.) package yellow cornbread mix, 1 large egg, and ⅔ cup milk. Fold in 1 (4-oz.) container crumbled blue cheese and ½ cup canned whole kernel corn, drained. Pour into a greased 8-inch square pan. Bake at 375° for 12 to 15 minutes or until golden brown. Cool in pan on a wire rack 10 minutes; remove from pan, and place on rack to cool completely. Cut cornbread into 1-inch cubes; place cubes in a single layer on a baking sheet. Bake at 400° for 8 minutes, turning once. Remove from oven, and let cool.

Serve Shrimp Tonight

Whether it's weekend entertaining or a weeknight supper, shrimp fills the bill. These recipes call for fresh shrimp; however, uncooked frozen shrimp will work just fine too. Simply thaw them according to package directions.

Garlic Shrimp is on and off the grill in 6 minutes. Serve Big Easy Barbecue Shrimp, our take on a New Orleans original, with plenty of French bread because sopping up the spicy sauce is half the fun.

Garlic Shrimp
PREP: 20 MIN., SOAK: 30 MIN.,
CHILL: 20 MIN., GRILL: 6 MIN.
This recipe comes from NASCAR driver Jimmie Johnson, who likes to wrap the shrimp in a flour tortilla along with guacamole, sour cream, and salsa for a tasty burrito. It's also good served over rice pilaf.

8 (12-inch) wooden or metal skewers
2 lb. unpeeled, large fresh shrimp
½ cup olive oil
8 to 10 garlic cloves, chopped
3 Tbsp. fresh lime juice
2 Tbsp. fresh orange juice
1 Tbsp. chopped fresh rosemary
¼ tsp. ground red pepper
Lime wedges

1. Soak wooden skewers in water for 30 minutes to prevent burning.
2. Peel shrimp, and devein, if desired; set aside.
3. Combine olive oil and next 5 ingredients in a zip-top plastic freezer bag. Remove and reserve 3 Tbsp. marinade for basting.
4. Add shrimp to plastic bag; seal and shake to coat. Chill 20 minutes.
5. Remove shrimp from marinade, discarding marinade. Thread shrimp evenly onto skewers.
6. Grill shrimp, covered with grill lid, over medium-high heat (350° to 400°) 3 minutes on each side or just until shrimp turn pink, basting occasionally with reserved 3 Tbsp. marinade. Serve shrimp with lime wedges. **Makes** 4 servings.

JIMMIE JOHNSON
MOORESVILLE, NORTH CAROLINA

Oven method: Omit wooden skewers; combine shrimp and next 6 ingredients in a 13- x 9-inch baking dish. Bake at 450° for 10 to 12 minutes or just until shrimp turn pink.

Big Easy Barbecue Shrimp

PREP: 10 MIN., COOK: 5 MIN., BAKE: 25 MIN.
Bay leaves are an integral seasoning in Cajun and Creole cooking. However, when left whole, as in this recipe, they should not be eaten.

3 lb. unpeeled, large fresh shrimp
¾ cup butter
¼ cup Worcestershire sauce
¼ cup ketchup
3 bay leaves
2 lemons, sliced
2 Tbsp. Old Bay seasoning
1 Tbsp. dried Italian seasoning
2 Tbsp. Asian garlic-chili pepper sauce
2 tsp. hot sauce
1 (16-oz.) French baguette, sliced

1. Spread shrimp in a shallow, aluminum foil-lined broiler pan or disposable aluminum roasting pan.
2. Stir together butter and next 8 ingredients in a saucepan over low heat until butter melts; pour mixture over shrimp.

3. Bake at 325° for 25 minutes, stirring and turning shrimp after 10 minutes. Remove and discard bay leaves. Serve with French bread. **Makes** 6 servings.

Note: For testing purposes only, we used A Taste Of Thai Garlic Chili Pepper Sauce, which is found on the Asian foods aisle of the supermarket.

ELIZABETH ROSS
DALLAS, TEXAS

taste of the south
Smoked Mullet

Consider the plight of the mullet. Some people regard its rich, dark meat as a delicacy, while others call it "trash fish." There are those who like it fried, and those who prefer it smoked. Then there's the renowned hairdo—short in the front and long in the back, named for the fishermen who sport it.

Despite its image problem, mullet has been a favorite with Gulf Coast Floridians for generations. From the days when the fish were easily harvested, residents turned to smoking as a way to preserve the plentiful fish and quickly realized that it tasted good too.

Home cooks can prepare mullet in smokers, just as you would ribs or brisket. To give the fish that characteristic salty flavor, they require brining (a long soak in heavily salted liquid). Chilling after brining allows the salt to penetrate and seals in moisture. We liked a simple brine of water, salt, brown sugar, and bay leaves, with a good sprinkling of black pepper on the fish.

While some folks smoke the fish on a gas grill with wood chips, we found the flavor and texture weren't nearly as good as when cooked in a smoker. The most popular form for smoking is split fish, which have the heads and innards removed and are split to the backbone. Leave on the skin and scales—they hold the flesh together and seal in moisture.

Smoked Mullet

PREP: 5 MIN., CHILL: 5 HRS., SOAK: 30 MIN., COOK: 2 HRS.
Disposable turkey roasting pans from the supermarket are great for brining the fish. If you can't find mullet in your area, try mackerel, bluefish, amberjack, or even salmon—lower the smoking time for fillets rather than split fish.

5 lb. split mullet
1 gal. water
¾ to 1 cup kosher salt
1 cup firmly packed brown sugar
1 Tbsp. onion powder
5 bay leaves, crushed
Pepper
Hickory wood chips
Garnish: fresh parsley
Saltines (optional)
Hot sauce (optional)
Lemon wedges (optional)

1. Rinse fish.
2. Combine 1 gal. water and next 4 ingredients in a large bowl, stirring until salt dissolves. Add mullet; cover and chill 45 minutes to 2 hours or to desired degree of saltiness. (Cut off a small piece of fish, and fry it to determine degree of saltiness by tasting. Longer soak times yield saltier fish.)
3. Rinse fish, discarding brine mixture; pat fish dry with paper towels. Place fish on wire racks in roasting pans; cover with paper towels, and chill 2 to 3 hours or until dry. Rub 1 tsp. pepper on both sides of each fish.
4. Soak wood chips in water at least 30 minutes.
5. Prepare charcoal fire in smoker; let burn 15 to 20 minutes.
6. Drain chips, and place on coals. Place water pan in smoker; add water to depth of fill line.
7. Place fish on upper and lower food racks; cover with smoker lid. (If smoking fillets, place skin sides down on racks.)
8. Cook 2 hours or just until fish flakes with a fork. Garnish, if desired. Serve with saltines, hot sauce, and lemon wedges, if desired. **Makes** 6 servings.

Take Dinner Outside

Enjoy the beginning of fall with this tasty menu from the grill. Each recipe is loaded with healthful carbs, fiber, vitamins, and minerals. For a change of pace from traditional beef burgers, try grilling meaty portobello mushrooms. Their hearty texture and earthy flavor are satisfying and pack an additional vegetable serving into your day.

Dinner on the Grill

Serves 4

Portobello Mushroom Burgers
With Carrot-Cabbage Slaw

Grilled Sweet Potato Salad
With Basil Vinaigrette

Portobello Mushroom Burgers With Carrot-Cabbage Slaw

PREP: 10 MIN., CHILL: 1 HR., GRILL: 8 MIN.

4 large portobello mushroom caps
¼ cup white balsamic vinegar
1 Tbsp. olive oil
¼ tsp. salt
4 whole wheat hamburger buns
Carrot-Cabbage Slaw

1. Scrape gills from mushroom caps with a spoon, if desired.
2. Combine vinegar, oil, and salt in a shallow dish or large zip-top plastic freezer bag; add mushrooms, turning to coat. Cover or seal, and chill 1 hour, turning occasionally. Remove mushrooms from marinade, discarding marinade.
3. Grill mushrooms, covered with grill lid, over medium-high heat (350° to 400°) 3 to 4 minutes on each side or until tender.
4. Serve mushrooms on buns with slaw. **Makes** 4 servings.

Per serving (including ½ cup slaw): Calories 258 (31% from fat); Fat 9g (sat 1.3g, mono 5.5g, poly 1.7g); Protein 6.5g; Carb 39.6g; Fiber 6.5g; Chol 0mg; Iron 1.9mg; Sodium 535mg; Calc 73mg

Carrot-Cabbage Slaw:
fast fixin's
PREP: 10 MIN.
For light dressings, we prefer to use white vinegars to prevent the vegetables from becoming discolored.

1 cup shredded carrot (about 2 large carrots)
1 cup shredded red cabbage
½ cup shredded jicama (about ½ small jicama)
3 Tbsp. white balsamic vinegar
1 Tbsp. chopped fresh mint
1 Tbsp. olive oil
1 Tbsp. honey
¼ tsp. salt

1. Stir together all ingredients. Cover and chill until ready to serve. **Makes** 4 servings.

Per (½-cup) serving: Calories 77 (40% from fat); Fat 3.5g (sat 0.5g, mono 2.5g, poly 0.4g); Protein 0.7g; Carb 11.3g; Fiber 2g; Chol 0mg; Iron 0.4mg; Sodium 174mg; Calc 20mg

Grilled Sweet Potato Salad With Basil Vinaigrette
fast fixin's
PREP: 10 MIN., GRILL: 12 MIN.
Dress the potatoes while they're still warm to allow them to absorb the vinaigrette flavor.

4 sweet potatoes, peeled and cut into ½-inch slices
Vegetable cooking spray
½ cup diced red bell pepper
¼ cup sliced green onions
¼ cup chopped flat-leaf parsley
Basil Vinaigrette

1. Coat both sides of sweet potato slices with cooking spray.
2. Grill potatoes, covered with grill lid, over medium-high heat (350° to 400°) 6 minutes on each side or until tender. Cool slightly, and cut into 1-inch cubes. Combine potatoes, bell pepper, green onions, and parsley in a large bowl; toss with Basil Vinaigrette. **Makes** 4 servings.

Per (1½-cup) serving (includes vinaigrette): Calories 194 (11% from fat); Fat 2.4g (sat 0.3g, mono 0g, poly 0.1g); Protein 3.4g; Carb 40.3g; Fiber 6.5g; Chol 0mg; Iron 1.5mg; Sodium 220mg; Calc 72mg

Basil Vinaigrette:
fast fixin's
PREP: 5 MIN.

¼ cup bottled light red wine vinegar-and-olive oil dressing
1 Tbsp. chopped basil
2 tsp. balsamic vinegar

1. Whisk together all ingredients. **Makes** about ¼ cup.

Note: For testing purposes only, we used Newman's Own Lighten Up Red Wine Vinegar & Olive Oil dressing.

CAROLINE KENNEDY
COVINGTON, GEORGIA

Per (1-Tbsp.) serving: Calories 28 (74% from fat); Fat 2.2g (sat 0.2g, mono 0g, poly 0g); Protein 0.2g; Carb 1.6g; Fiber 0.2g; Chol 0mg; Iron 0mg; Sodium 115mg; Calc 5mg

Meatloaf Sandwiches

Plan plenty of leftovers so you can enjoy these two satisfying sandwiches.

Leftover meatloaf is a wonderful thing. While it's warm and comforting when snuggled up to mashed potatoes, meatloaf is downright luscious layered on bread with mayonnaise or tomato sauce. Use your favorite recipe for the basic loaf, or try the one offered here. Because you can't just conjure meatloaf out of the air when the urge for a sandwich strikes, double the recipe and freeze one to keep on hand. One of these midnights, you'll be really glad you did.

Simple Meatloaf
freezeable • make ahead
PREP: 10 MIN., BAKE: 1 HR., STAND: 5 MIN.
Ground chuck offers lots of flavor and is less expensive, but we chose lean ground beef because it has less fat.

1½ lb. 85% lean ground beef
¾ cup quick-cooking oats
¾ cup milk
¼ cup chopped onion
1 large egg, lightly beaten
1½ tsp. salt
¼ tsp. pepper
⅓ cup ketchup
2 Tbsp. brown sugar
1 Tbsp. yellow mustard

1. Combine first 7 ingredients in a large bowl just until blended; place in a lightly greased 9- x 5-inch loaf pan.
2. Stir together ketchup, brown sugar, and yellow mustard; pour evenly over meatloaf.
3. Bake at 350° for 1 hour. Remove from oven; let stand 5 minutes, and remove from pan before slicing. **Makes** 6 servings.

Note: Wrap meatloaf in plastic wrap and aluminum foil, and freeze up to 1 month. Thaw in refrigerator overnight.

NORA HENSHAW
OKEMAH, OKLAHOMA

Italian Meatloaf Sandwich
fast fixin's
PREP: 15 MIN., BAKE: 15 MIN.
This great flavor combo also works with leftover roast beef or pot roast.

1 (14-oz.) French bread loaf
8 (1-inch-thick) cold meatloaf slices
1 cup marinara or spaghetti sauce
1 (8-oz.) package shredded Italian cheese blend
¼ tsp. dried Italian seasoning

1. Cut bread into fourths; cut quarters in half horizontally. Place bread quarters, cut sides up, on a baking sheet. Top each bread bottom with 2 meatloaf slices, 2 Tbsp. marinara sauce, and ¼ cup cheese. Top each bread top with 2 Tbsp. marinara sauce and ¼ cup cheese; sprinkle with Italian seasoning.
2. Bake at 375° for 10 to 15 minutes or until cheese melts and meat is thoroughly heated. Top bread bottoms with bread tops, and serve sandwiches immediately. **Makes** 4 sandwiches.

Basil-Tomato Meatloaf Sandwich
PREP: 10 MIN.
You'll love the flavor boost when you stir fresh basil into mayonnaise. Instead of chopping the basil, snip it with scissors or chop it in a mini-processor. Because the meatloaf slices are not very wide, it takes two to cover a slice of bread.

½ cup mayonnaise
1 Tbsp. chopped fresh basil
8 hearty white bread slices
8 (½-inch-thick) cold meatloaf slices
1 cup shredded iceberg lettuce
2 plum tomatoes, sliced
Salt and pepper to taste

1. Stir together ½ cup mayonnaise and 1 Tbsp. chopped fresh basil. Spread 1 Tbsp. mayonnaise mixture on 1 side of each bread slice. Top 4 bread slices, mayonnaise sides up, evenly with meatloaf slices, shredded lettuce, and tomato slices; sprinkle with salt and pepper to taste. Top with remaining bread slices, mayonnaise sides down. **Makes** 4 sandwiches.

Note: For testing purposes only, we used Sara Lee Honey White Bakery Bread.

Test Kitchen Notebook

Ground beef that's very lean—labeled 93% lean and 7% fat—prevents meatloaf from being greasy and reduces shrinkage.

Use soft breadcrumbs or uncooked oats to help stabilize the loaf and keep it moist.

Let meatloaf stand or "rest" when it comes out of the oven. It will keep cooking from the residual heat, but this also allows the juices to soak back into the meatloaf, adding flavor and moisture.

Donna Florio
SENIOR WRITER

Family Favorites

A School-Day Menu

Serves 4 to 6

Baked Curry-Glazed Chicken

Fruity Couscous
*Stir ¼ cup chopped sweetened dried cranberries,
1 tsp. grated orange rind, and 1 Tbsp. olive oil into a
prepared 10-oz. box of couscous.*

Zucchini Toss
*Sauté sliced zucchini and onion in olive oil. Season with
dried thyme and salt to taste.*

Delta Velvet Pudding Dessert

Getting dinner on the table is a challenge for all parents. Multiply that by 7,650 diners, and you'll know the difficulty facing The University of Georgia Food Services staff. So they created a clever program called "Taste of Home." Parents send in recipes, and the staff selects, cooks, and serves about 120 dishes in the dining halls at the annual "Taste of Home" event. Here's a main dish and dessert that made the grade at UGA.

Baked Curry-Glazed Chicken
family favorite
PREP: 10 MIN.; BAKE: 1 HR., 10 MIN.
Beverly Stichtenoth of Katy, Texas, was honored for this recipe, a favorite of her just-graduated son, Todd.

½ cup honey
¼ cup butter, melted
¼ cup yellow mustard
1 tsp. salt
1 tsp. curry powder
1 (3½- to 4-lb.) whole chicken, cut up *

1. Stir together first 5 ingredients in a shallow dish until blended. Dip chicken in honey mixture, 1 piece at a time, thoroughly coating all sides. Arrange chicken, skin side up, in a single layer in a 15- x 10-inch jelly-roll pan; pour remaining honey mixture over chicken.
2. Bake at 375° for 1 hour to 1 hour and 10 minutes or until done. **Makes** 4 to 6 servings.

*Substitute 4 skinned and boned chicken breasts and 4 skinned and boned chicken thighs for cut-up whole chicken. Proceed as directed, decreasing bake time to 40 to 45 minutes.

Fabulous Finale

Keri Hochgertle, a junior at The University of Georgia, is crazy about this luscious dessert. Her mom, Debi, of Lawrenceville, Georgia, picked up the recipe while in college at the University of Southern Mississippi.

Delta Velvet Pudding Dessert
make ahead
PREP: 20 MIN., BAKE: 20 MIN., CHILL: 2 HRS.

½ cup butter, softened
1 cup all-purpose flour
1 cup finely chopped pecans, toasted
1 (8-oz.) package cream cheese, softened
1½ cups powdered sugar
1 (8-oz.) container frozen whipped topping, thawed
1 (3.4-oz.) package French vanilla instant pudding mix
1 (3.4-oz.) package chocolate instant pudding mix
3 cups milk
Toppings: whipped topping, toasted chopped pecans, toffee bits, shaved chocolate

1. Cut butter into flour with a pastry blender or fork until crumbly; stir in pecans. Press mixture into a 13- x 9-inch pan or baking dish.
2. Bake at 350° for 18 to 20 minutes or until lightly browned. Remove pan to wire rack to cool completely.
3. Beat cream cheese and powdered sugar at medium speed with an electric mixer until fluffy. Fold in whipped topping. Spread cream cheese mixture evenly over cooled crust.
4. Beat pudding mixes and milk in a large bowl at medium speed with an electric mixer 2 minutes. Pour evenly over cream cheese mixture in pan. Cover and chill 2 hours or up to 3 days. Serve pudding in individual bowls with desired toppings. **Makes** 10 to 12 servings.

Fill Up the Lunchbox

Break out of the peanut butter-and-jelly rut with goodies that both kids and adults will enjoy.

School's in, but you're fresh out of lunch ideas. Try our kid-friendly recipes to banish the daily lunchbox blues. Add some unexpected variety to the usual midday fare, and everyone in the class will want to trade lunch with your child. Each of these recipes can easily be made ahead.

Back-to-School Lunch

Serves 6

Festive Turkey Rollups
Crunchy-Munchy Mix
S'more Cupcakes
lemonade

Festive Turkey Rollups

make ahead
PREP: 10 MIN., CHILL: 8 HRS.

6 (8-inch) flour tortillas *
½ cup hot pepper jelly with red jalapeño peppers
½ cup red raspberry preserves
¾ cup Ranch vegetable dip
12 thinly sliced turkey breast slices, halved
1 bunch green leaf lettuce
1½ cups (6 oz.) shredded Cheddar cheese **

1. Microwave tortillas at HIGH 10 to 15 seconds, and set aside.

2. Stir together jelly and preserves.
3. Spread 2 Tbsp. Ranch dip on 1 side of each tortilla. Top each tortilla with 4 turkey slice halves, and spread with 2½ Tbsp. jelly mixture. Top tortillas evenly with lettuce and cheese.
4. Roll up tortillas; wrap with plastic wrap. Chill up to 8 hours. **Makes** 6 servings.

*Substitute 6 pita rounds, if desired.
**Substitute shredded Monterey Jack cheese with peppers, if desired.

MAUDE GRIFFITH
STOW, OHIO

Crunchy-Munchy Mix

make ahead
PREP: 5 MIN., BAKE: 30 MIN.
This crunchy snack mix makes a large yield and stores up to a week. It's perfect for multiple lunch boxes, for giving as gifts, or for serious munchies.

1 (16-oz.) jar dry-roasted peanuts
1 (10-oz.) package pretzel pieces *
1 (7-oz.) can potato sticks
1 (6-oz.) can fried onions
1 (6-oz.) package bite-size bagel chips **
⅓ cup butter or margarine, melted ***
1 (1.25-oz.) package taco seasoning

1. Combine first 5 ingredients in a large roasting pan. Drizzle with butter, gently stirring to coat. Stir in taco seasoning.
2. Bake at 250° for 30 minutes, stirring occasionally. Cool on paper towels.

Store in an airtight container. **Makes** 12 cups.

*Substitute 1 (7-oz.) can potato sticks, if desired.
**Substitute 1 (6-oz.) can fried onions, if desired.
***Substitute butter-flavored cooking spray, if desired.

KATHY HUNT
DALLAS, TEXAS

S'more Cupcakes

fast fixin's • make ahead
PREP: 10 MIN., BAKE: 18 MIN.

⅔ cup shortening
1½ cups sugar
3 large eggs
1½ cups all-purpose flour
1½ cups graham cracker crumbs
2 tsp. baking powder
1 tsp. salt
1¼ cups milk
1 tsp. vanilla extract
24 chocolate nuggets
4 cups miniature marshmallows
1 cup chopped pecans (optional)

1. Beat shortening at medium speed with an electric mixer until fluffy. Gradually add sugar, beating well. Add eggs, 1 at a time, beating after each addition.
2. Combine flour and next 3 ingredients; add to egg mixture alternately with milk, beginning and ending with flour mixture. Beat until blended after each addition. Stir in vanilla.
3. Place paper baking cups in muffin pans; spoon ¼ cup batter into each cup.
4. Bake at 350° for 18 minutes or until done. Quickly insert a chocolate nugget into center of each warm cupcake; top each with 4 or 5 marshmallows, gently pressing into melted chocolate. Sprinkle with pecans, if desired. **Makes** 2 dozen.

Note: For testing purposes only, we used Hershey's Nuggets.

TERRYANN MOORE
OAKLYN, NEW JERSEY

Sample These Tasty Pages

This book is the next best thing to having the *Southern Living* Foods staff in your kitchen.

We don't want to toot our own horn too loudly, but we think *The All-New Ultimate Southern Living Cookbook* will become an indispensable tool in your kitchen.

Whether you're a new cook or a skilled gourmet, you'll be impressed by the wide selection of recipes, step-by-step features, and glorious photography. Julie Gunter, the book's editor, especially likes the "Kitchen Basics" chapter. Enjoy a taste of what's inside with these recipes and tips.

You can find this cookbook wherever books are sold, or call 1-800-765-6400, or visit **www.oxmoorhouse.com.**

Lemon-Baked Cauliflower

PREP: 10 MIN., BAKE: 1 HR.
You can prepare this dish a day ahead and then bake it an hour before serving.

⅓ cup finely chopped shallots
¼ cup butter, softened
¼ cup finely chopped fresh
    parsley
2 garlic cloves, minced
1 Tbsp. grated lemon rind
1 tsp. salt
¼ tsp. pepper
⅛ tsp. ground nutmeg
1 large head cauliflower, cored

1. Stir together first 8 ingredients.
2. Place cauliflower on a large sheet of heavy-duty aluminum foil; spread butter mixture over cauliflower. Bring sides of foil to top; seal edges. Place on a baking sheet.

3. Bake at 375° for 1 hour or until cauliflower is tender. **Makes** 6 servings.

Caramelized Onion Macaroni and Cheese
family favorite
PREP: 20 MIN., COOK: 20 MIN., BAKE: 1 HR., STAND: 10 MIN.
Feel free to omit the pecans in this recipe. It will still taste fantastic.

1 (8-oz.) package large elbow macaroni
2 Tbsp. butter
2 large onions, thinly sliced
1 tsp. sugar
1 (16-oz.) block white Cheddar cheese, shredded
1 cup (4 oz.) shredded Parmesan cheese
32 saltine crackers, finely crushed and divided
6 large eggs
4 cups milk
1 tsp. salt
½ tsp. pepper
2 Tbsp. butter, melted
½ cup chopped pecans (optional)

1. Prepare macaroni according to package directions; drain and set aside.
2. Melt 2 Tbsp. butter in a large skillet over medium-high heat. Add sliced onions and 1 tsp. sugar. Cook, stirring often, 15 to 20 minutes or until onions are caramel-colored.
3. Layer half each of macaroni, onions, cheeses, and cracker crumbs in a lightly greased 13- x 9-inch baking dish. Layer with remaining macaroni, onions, and cheeses.

4. Whisk together eggs and next 3 ingredients; pour over macaroni mixture.
5. Stir together remaining cracker crumbs, melted butter, and, if desired, pecans. Sprinkle evenly over macaroni mixture.
6. Bake at 350° for 1 hour or until golden brown and set. Let stand 10 minutes before serving. **Makes** 8 to 10 servings.

Julie's Favorite Tips

■ Pasta needs plenty of room to roam in rapidly boiling salted water (1 Tbsp. salt per 1 lb. pasta). Resist the urge to add oil to pasta water. Oil merely coats the pasta and prevents sauce from sticking to it.
■ Freeze lemon and lime wedges, and use them to dress up cold drinks in lieu of ice.
■ For well-rounded muffins, a lumpy batter is desirable. Stir batter just until dry ingredients are moistened.

the all-new ultimate
Southern Living
COOKBOOK
Over 1,250 of Our Best Recipes

Southern Favorites

Whether you're preparing a week-night supper or entertaining on the weekend, these doable recipes add an extra Southern touch to the table.

Quick Shrimp Creole

PREP: 15 MIN., COOK: 35 MIN.

Try using kitchen shears to chop the tomatoes in the can instead of using a food processor—it's quick and makes one less dish to wash!

2 (3.5-oz.) bags SUCCESS White Rice
2 (14½-oz.) cans stewed tomatoes, undrained
½ green bell pepper, chopped (about ½ cup)
1 small onion, chopped
½ cup chopped celery (about 2 ribs)
1 Tbsp. olive oil
1 garlic clove, minced
2 tsp. hot sauce
1 tsp. Creole seasoning
1 lb. peeled large fresh shrimp

1. Prepare rice according to package directions; keep warm.
2. Pulse tomatoes in a food processor 3 or 4 times or until chopped.
3. Sauté green pepper, onion, and celery in hot oil in a large nonstick skillet 8 minutes or until tender. Add garlic, and sauté 1 minute. Stir in chopped tomatoes, hot sauce, and Creole seasoning.

Bring to a boil; reduce heat, and simmer, uncovered, 20 minutes.
4. Stir in shrimp; cover and simmer 3 minutes or just until shrimp turn pink. Serve over hot cooked rice. **Makes** 6 servings.

Almond Rice Pilaf

PREP: 10 MIN., COOK: 25 MIN., STAND: 5 MIN.

1 Tbsp. butter
1½ cups uncooked MAHATMA Long-Grain White Rice
3 cups chicken broth
¼ cup chopped, toasted almonds
3 Tbsp. chopped fresh parsley
2 tsp. grated lemon rind
½ tsp. salt
½ tsp. freshly ground pepper

1. Melt butter in a large saucepan over medium-high heat. Stir in rice, and cook, stirring constantly, 5 minutes or until golden. Add chicken broth, and bring to a boil. Cover, reduce heat, and simmer 20 minutes or until liquid is absorbed and rice is tender. Remove from heat, and let stand 5 minutes. Fluff rice with a fork.
2. Stir in almonds and remaining ingredients. **Makes** 6 servings.

Cook's Notes:

You can add extra flavor to rice by cooking it in fruit juice, chicken broth, or beef broth instead of water. Just follow the package directions, and fluff it with a fork when it's ready.

Creamy Mashed Sweet Potatoes

make ahead

PREP: 15 MIN.; BAKE: 1 HR., 20 MIN.

3 lb. sweet potatoes
½ cup firmly packed DOMINO Light Brown Sugar, divided
¼ cup half-and-half
¼ tsp. ground nutmeg
¼ tsp. ground ginger
¾ tsp. ground cinnamon, divided
Vegetable cooking spray
½ cup chopped pecans
½ tsp. grated orange rind

1. Bake potatoes at 400° for 1 hour or until tender; peel. Reduce oven temperature to 350°.
2. Beat potatoes, ¼ cup brown sugar, next 3 ingredients, and ¼ tsp. cinnamon in a large bowl at medium speed with an electric mixer until smooth. Spoon mixture into a 13- x 9-inch baking dish coated with cooking spray.
3. Combine chopped pecans, orange rind, remaining ¼ cup brown sugar, and remaining ½ tsp. cinnamon; sprinkle evenly over potato mixture.
4. Bake at 350° for 20 minutes or until thoroughly heated. **Makes** 6 to 8 servings.

Note: Prepare sweet potatoes a day in advance, if desired. Spoon into a 13- x 9-inch baking dish (do not add topping), cover with plastic wrap, and refrigerate. Remove potatoes from refrigerator, and let stand 20 minutes at room temperature. Sprinkle pecan mixture evenly over potatoes, and bake at 350° for 25 to 30 minutes or until thoroughly heated.

Cozy Up to Comfort Food

These recipes are just like the ones Mom used to make—but a whole lot faster.

Herb-Topped Pasta Bake

PREP: 5 MIN., COOK: 12 MIN., BAKE: 15 MIN., STAND: 5 MIN.

For a delicious and healthful alternate topping, process 3 whole wheat bread slices in a food processor until slices are finely ground. Toss together breadcrumbs and 1 Tbsp. butter, melted. Sprinkle breadcrumb mixture over prepared macaroni before baking.

1 (12-oz.) package VELVEETA Shells & Cheese Dinner
½ cup half-and-half
1 cup (4 oz.) shredded Cheddar cheese, divided
¼ tsp. onion powder
4 white bread slices
¼ cup grated Parmesan cheese
¼ cup butter, melted
1 Tbsp. dried parsley

1. Cook shells and cheese dinner according to basic package directions.
2. Stir half-and-half, ½ cup shredded cheese, and onion powder into shell macaroni mixture. Pour pasta mixture into an 8-inch square baking dish.
3. Remove crusts from bread with a serrated knife. Process bread slices in a food processor or blender until finely ground. Toss together breadcrumbs, Parmesan cheese, melted butter, and parsley.
4. Sprinkle shell macaroni with remaining ½ cup cheese and breadcrumb mixture.

5. Bake at 400° for 15 minutes or until pasta mixture is thoroughly heated. Let stand 5 minutes before serving. **Makes** 6 servings.

How-to

Add a tasty crunch to your usual mac and cheese with this easy trick.

Toss together breadcrumbs, grated Parmesan cheese, butter, and parsley.

Sprinkle macaroni with breadcrumb mixture before baking. This crunchy topping is also delicious on other casseroles and vegetable dishes.

Savory Chicken Pot Pie

PREP: 20 MIN., COOK: 20 MIN., STAND: 15 MIN., BAKE: 35 MIN.

1 small sweet potato
12 PILGRIM'S PRIDE Boneless, Skinless Chicken Thighs, cut into bite-size pieces
½ tsp. seasoned salt
⅓ cup chopped onion
1 tsp. vegetable oil
¼ cup butter
⅓ cup all-purpose flour
3 cups chicken broth
1 (10¾-oz.) can condensed cream of mushroom soup
1 (16-oz.) package frozen peas and carrots, thawed
1 Tbsp. fresh lemon juice
½ tsp. freshly ground pepper
½ (15-oz.) package refrigerated piecrusts

1. Pierce sweet potato several times with a fork. Place in microwave oven, and cover with a damp paper towel. Microwave at HIGH 3 minutes or until done. Let stand 5 minutes; peel and dice. Set aside.
2. Sprinkle chicken evenly with seasoned salt. Sauté chicken and onion in hot oil in a Dutch oven over medium-high heat 5 to 8 minutes or until done. Remove chicken and onion.
3. Melt butter in Dutch oven over medium-high heat; whisk in flour, chicken broth, and soup. Reduce heat to medium-low, and cook, stirring occasionally, 3 to 4 minutes or until thickened. Stir in cooked chicken and onion, sweet potato, peas and carrots, lemon juice, and pepper. Cook, stirring often, 5 minutes or until thoroughly heated. Spoon chicken mixture into a lightly greased 13- x 9-inch baking dish.
4. Roll piecrust into 13- x 9-inch rectangle; fit over chicken mixture in baking dish. Cut several slits in top of crust for steam to escape.
5. Bake at 400° for 30 to 35 minutes or until crust is golden brown and filling is thoroughly heated. Let stand 10 minutes before serving. **Makes** 8 servings.

Bacon-Ranch Quesadillas
fast fixin's
PREP: 15 MIN., COOK: 8 MIN.

PAM Original No-Stick Cooking Spray
¼ cup Ranch dressing
4 (8-inch) flour tortillas
1 cup (4 oz.) shredded Mexican four-cheese blend
4 bacon slices, cooked and crumbled
1 plum tomato, seeded and chopped
Ranch dressing
Salsa

1. Spray a large nonstick skillet with cooking spray. Place skillet over medium-high heat until hot.
2. Spread Ranch dressing evenly on 1 side of each tortilla. Place 1 tortilla, dressing side up, in hot skillet; top evenly with half each of cheese, bacon, and tomato. Lightly press a second tortilla, dressing side down, on top of mixture. Coat lightly with cooking spray, and cook 1 to 2 minutes on each side or until golden.
3. Repeat procedure with remaining tortillas, cheese, bacon, and tomato.
4. Cut each quesadilla into wedges. Serve with Ranch dressing and salsa. **Makes** 4 servings.

Turkey Meatloaf
PREP: 15 MIN.; COOK: 5 MIN.;
BAKE: 1 HR., 30 MIN.; STAND: 10 MIN.

1 Tbsp. butter
1 medium onion, finely chopped
2 (1.25-lb.) packages extra-lean ground turkey
1 (10¾-oz.) can CAMPBELL'S Condensed Cream of Mushroom Soup
⅔ cup Italian-seasoned breadcrumbs
1 tsp. Creole seasoning
½ cup bottled chili sauce

1. Melt butter in a nonstick skillet over medium-high heat; add onion, and sauté 5 minutes or until tender. Cool slightly.

2. Stir together cooked onion, ground turkey, and next 3 ingredients in a large bowl until well blended. Shape into an 8- x 5-inch loaf; place on a lightly greased rack in an aluminum foil-lined broiler pan.
3. Pour chili sauce evenly over meatloaf.
4. Bake at 350° for 1 hour and 20 minutes to 1 hour and 30 minutes or until done. Let stand 10 minutes before serving. **Makes** 6 to 8 servings.

Mocha Pudding Cake
PREP: 15 MIN., BAKE: 30 MIN.

1 cup all-purpose flour
1½ tsp. baking powder
¼ tsp. salt
1 cup sugar, divided
6 Tbsp. unsweetened cocoa, divided
½ cup milk
3 Tbsp. vegetable oil
1 tsp. vanilla extract
½ cup NESTLÉ TOLL HOUSE Mini Morsels
1 cup strong brewed coffee
Vanilla ice cream

1. Combine first 3 ingredients, ⅔ cup sugar, and 4 Tbsp. cocoa in a large bowl. Stir together milk, vegetable oil, and vanilla; add to dry ingredients, stirring just until blended. Spread batter evenly into a lightly greased 8-inch square pan.
2. Combine chocolate morsels, remaining ⅓ cup sugar, and remaining 2 Tbsp. cocoa. Sprinkle over batter. Bring coffee to a boil in a saucepan; pour boiling coffee evenly over batter. (Do not stir.)
3. Bake at 350° for 25 to 30 minutes or until cake springs back when lightly pressed in center. Serve warm with ice cream. **Makes** 6 to 8 servings.

Skillet Drop Biscuits
PREP: 5 MIN., BAKE: 30 MIN.
These tender biscuits are great to serve with just about any entrée.

1⅓ cups milk
1 cup HELLMANN'S Real Mayonnaise
4 cups self-rising flour
1 Tbsp. butter

1. Whisk together milk and mayonnaise until smooth. Stir milk mixture into flour just until blended.
2. Butter a 10-inch cast-iron skillet; place in a 425° oven for 3 minutes.
3. Remove skillet from oven; drop batter by rounded ¼ cupfuls into hot skillet, dropping 8 around edge and 4 in center. (Biscuits will touch.)
4. Bake at 425° for 25 to 30 minutes or until lightly browned. **Makes** 1 dozen.

We used a wire whisk to make blending the biscuit ingredients easier. You can also blend the ingredients together with a spoon or rubber spatula.

Use rounded ¼ cupfuls of biscuit dough. This recipe bakes a dozen that can be kept warm and served right from the skillet.

Take the Cake

Large or small, these desserts make sweet memories.

Next time you're asked to make a treat for a bake sale or potluck, turn to these great recipes. They have short prep times, and when made into cupcakes, they are perfect for pint-size hands to hold. We've created new versions with flavors that are hard to resist: peanut butter cupcakes with a surprise filling, dark chocolate cupcakes with orange frosting, mini-pound cakes, and spiced carrot cake with cream cheese frosting. With this array of treats, we predict plenty of folks will be eating dessert first.

Brown Sugar-Buttermilk Pound Cakes

PREP: 15 MIN., BAKE: 55 MIN., STAND: 10 MIN.

1 cup butter, softened
1 cup granulated sugar
1 cup firmly packed dark brown sugar
3 large eggs
1 cup buttermilk
½ tsp. baking soda
3 cups all-purpose flour
⅛ tsp. salt
2 tsp. vanilla extract
PAM For Baking No Stick Cooking Spray

1. Beat butter at medium speed with an electric mixer until creamy. Gradually add sugars, beating until light and fluffy. Add eggs, 1 at a time, beating at low speed just until blended after each addition.
2. Stir together buttermilk and baking soda. Combine flour and salt; add to butter mixture alternately with buttermilk mixture, beginning and ending with flour mixture. Beat at low speed after each addition just until blended. Stir in vanilla.

3. Spray 5 (5¾- x 3¼-inch) disposable foil loaf pans with baking spray. Pour batter evenly into pans (about 1 cup batter in each pan).
4. Bake at 325° for 50 to 55 minutes or until a wooden pick inserted in center comes out clean. Cool cakes in pans on wire racks 10 minutes. Remove from pans, and cool completely on wire racks. **Makes** 5 small cakes.

Double Chocolate-Orange Cupcakes With Orange Buttercream Frosting

PREP: 20 MIN., BAKE: 18 MIN.

1 (12-oz.) package NESTLÉ TOLL HOUSE Semisweet Chocolate Morsels, divided
1 (18.25-oz.) package German chocolate cake mix
4 large eggs
⅓ cup butter, melted
1¼ cups orange juice
1 tsp. vanilla extract
Orange Buttercream Frosting

1. Microwave 1 cup chocolate morsels in a 2-cup glass measuring cup at HIGH 1 minute, stirring after 30 seconds. Stir until smooth. Cool slightly.
2. Beat cake mix and next 3 ingredients at low speed with an electric mixer until moistened. Increase speed to medium, and beat 1 to 2 minutes or until well blended and smooth. Add melted chocolate and vanilla, beating until blended. Spoon batter by ¼ cupfuls into paper baking cups in muffin pans.
3. Bake at 375° for 16 to 18 minutes or until a wooden pick inserted in center comes out clean. Let cool in pans on

wire racks 5 minutes. Remove from pans, and cool completely on wire racks. Spread Orange Buttercream Frosting evenly over cupcakes.
4. Place remaining chocolate morsels in a 1-qt. zip-top plastic freezer bag; seal bag. Microwave at MEDIUM (50% power) 45 seconds to 1 minute, turning bag over after 30 seconds. Squeeze chocolate in bag until smooth. Cut a tiny hole in 1 corner of bag. Pipe melted chocolate over Orange Buttercream Frosting on cupcakes by gently squeezing bag. **Makes** about 2½ dozen cupcakes.

Orange Buttercream Frosting:
fast fixin's
PREP: 10 MIN.

¾ cup butter, softened
2 tsp. grated orange rind
1 (16-oz.) package confectioners sugar
2 to 3 Tbsp. orange juice

1. Beat butter and orange rind at medium speed with an electric mixer until creamy. Gradually add confectioners sugar, beating until well blended.
2. Stir in 2 Tbsp. orange juice, adding additional orange juice, if necessary, for desired consistency. **Makes** about 2½ cups.

Technique

Beating butter and sugar together, called "creaming," incorporates air into the mixture to help baked goods rise.

Peanut Butter Surprise Cupcakes
family favorite

PREP: 20 MIN., BAKE: 20 MIN., STAND: 5 MIN.
You can use a coffee scoop, which equals about 2 Tbsp., to measure batter into paper baking cups.

¾ cup butter, softened
2 cups DOMINO Granulated Sugar
3 large eggs
1 cup creamy peanut butter
2 cups all-purpose flour
1 tsp. baking soda
½ tsp. salt
1 cup buttermilk
1 tsp. vanilla extract
24 milk chocolate kisses
Confectioners sugar

1. Beat butter at medium speed with an electric mixer until creamy. Gradually add granulated sugar, beating until light and fluffy. Add eggs, 1 at a time, beating after each addition. Add peanut butter, beating until smooth.
2. Combine flour, baking soda, and salt; add to peanut butter mixture alternately with buttermilk, beginning and ending with flour mixture. Beat at low speed just until blended after each addition. Stir in vanilla.
3. Spoon 2 Tbsp. batter into each of 24 paper baking cups in muffin pans. Place 1 chocolate kiss on its side in center of batter in each cup. Top evenly with remaining batter (about 2 Tbsp. in each cup), covering chocolate kisses.
4. Bake at 375° for 18 to 20 minutes or until golden brown. Let cool in pans on wire racks 5 minutes. Remove from pans, and cool on wire racks. Dust with confectioners sugar. Serve warm or at room temperature. **Makes** about 2 dozen cupcakes.

Peanut Butter-Jam Surprise Cupcakes:
Prepare batter as directed. Spoon 2 Tbsp. batter into each of 24 paper baking cups in muffin pans. Omit milk chocolate kisses. Dollop 1 rounded tsp. of your favorite flavor jam in center of batter in each cup. Top evenly with remaining batter (about 2 Tbsp. in each cup). Bake and cool as directed.

Technique

Kitchen utensils can double up on the tasks they perform. Use a mesh tea ball filled with confectioners sugar to lightly dust cupcakes or cakes.

Carrot Cake With Toasted Pecan-Cream Cheese Frosting

PREP: 20 MIN., BAKE: 45 MIN.

1 (18.25-oz.) package spice cake mix
1 (10¾-oz.) can CAMPBELL'S Condensed Tomato Soup
1 (8-oz.) can crushed pineapple in juice, undrained
4 large eggs
1½ cups finely shredded carrot
½ cup butter, melted and slightly cooled
1 tsp. ground cinnamon
1 tsp. vanilla extract
Toasted Pecan-Cream Cheese Frosting

1. Beat first 8 ingredients at low speed with an electric mixer until moistened. Increase speed to medium, and beat 1 to 2 minutes or until well blended. Pour batter into a lightly greased 13- x 9-inch pan.
2. Bake at 350° for 40 to 45 minutes or until a wooden pick inserted in center comes out clean and edges of cake pull away from sides of pan. Cool completely in pan on a wire rack.
3. Spread Toasted Pecan-Cream Cheese Frosting evenly over cake. **Makes** 12 servings.

Toasted Pecan-Cream Cheese Frosting:
fast fixin's

PREP: 10 MIN.

1 (8-oz.) package cream cheese, softened
¼ cup butter, softened
1 (16-oz.) package confectioners sugar
1 cup chopped, toasted pecans
1 tsp. vanilla extract
2 to 3 tsp. milk

1. Beat cream cheese and butter at medium speed with an electric mixer until creamy. Gradually add confectioners sugar, beating until light and fluffy. Stir in pecans and vanilla. Stir in 2 tsp. milk, adding additional milk, if necessary, for desired consistency. **Makes** about 3 cups.

Pick-up Snacks

Whether you're entertaining at home or taking something to a party, these fast bites are just the ticket.

Wow your friends with these easy-to-make recipes. If the guys are planning a football marathon, Kick-Off Beef Pretzel Poppers will be ready before the first quarter ends. Skewered Tortellini Bites and Chocolate Chip Cheesecake Bars can be prepared and chilled ahead of time and transported easily. When you're ready to go, just pull them out of the fridge, and you're out the door to tailgate.

Chocolate Chip Cheesecake Bars
make ahead
PREP: 15 MIN., BAKE: 40 MIN., CHILL: 4 HRS.
(Pictured on page 181)

1 cup all-purpose flour
⅓ cup firmly packed light brown sugar
¼ cup butter, softened
3 (8-oz.) packages cream cheese, softened
¾ cup granulated sugar
3 large eggs
⅓ cup sour cream
½ tsp. vanilla extract
1 (12-oz.) package NESTLÉ TOLL HOUSE Mini Morsels, divided

1. Beat first 3 ingredients at medium-low speed with an electric mixer until combined. Increase speed to medium, and beat until well blended and crumbly. Pat mixture into a lightly greased 13- x 9-inch pan.
2. Bake at 350° for 13 to 15 minutes or until lightly browned.
3. Beat cream cheese at medium speed with an electric mixer until creamy. Gradually add granulated sugar, beating until well blended. Add eggs, 1 at a time, beating at low speed just until blended after each addition. Add sour cream, vanilla, and 1 cup chocolate morsels, beating just until blended. Pour over baked crust.
4. Bake at 350° for 25 minutes or until set. Cool completely on a wire rack.
5. Microwave remaining chocolate morsels in a 2-cup glass measuring cup at HIGH 1 minute, stirring after 30 seconds. Stir until smooth. Cool slightly. Drizzle over cheesecake. Cover and chill at least 4 hours; cut into bars. **Makes** 12 bars.

Skewered Tortellini Bites
PREP: 25 MIN., COOK: 15 MIN., CHILL: 4 HRS.

1 (8-oz.) package BARILLA Three Cheese Tortellini
2 small zucchini, cut into ¼-inch-thick slices
1 cup grape or cherry tomatoes, halved
1 (16-oz.) bottle Italian dressing
4-inch wooden skewers
Grated Parmesan cheese (optional)

1. Cook tortellini according to package directions; drain and rinse with cold water.
2. Toss together tortellini, zucchini slices, tomato halves, and Italian dressing in a large bowl. Cover and chill at least 4 hours, stirring occasionally.
3. Thread tortellini alternately with vegetables onto skewers. Sprinkle with Parmesan cheese, if desired. **Makes** 10 to 12 appetizer servings.

Kick-Off Beef Pretzel Poppers
family favorite • fast fixin's
PREP: 15 MIN.

½ (8-oz.) container soft cream cheese
½ cup (2 oz.) finely shredded sharp Cheddar cheese
½ to 1 Tbsp. minced pickled jalapeño pepper slices
Pinch of garlic powder
20 OSCAR MAYER Deli-Fresh Shaved Roast Beef slices
20 (3-inch) honey wheat pretzel sticks

1. Stir together first 4 ingredients in a small bowl until well blended.
2. Spread about 1 tsp. cream cheese mixture on 1 side of each roast beef slice; top each slice with 1 pretzel stick, and roll up. Serve immediately, or chill up to 1 hour. **Makes** 6 to 8 appetizer servings.

Horseradish-Dijon Pretzel Poppers: Omit shredded Cheddar, jalapeño pepper slices, and garlic powder. Stir together cream cheese, 1 Tbsp. finely chopped green onions, ½ tsp. prepared horseradish, and 2 tsp. Dijon mustard. Proceed with recipe as directed.

Technique

To re-create the decorative look on top of Chocolate Chip Cheesecake Bars, pour melted chocolate into a zip-top plastic freezer bag; close bag. Snip a tiny hole in a bottom corner of the bag to pipe melted chocolate onto the cheesecake bars.

Homemade in a Hurry

These family-friendly recipes—from Slaw Reubens to Taco Salad—have prep times of 10 minutes or less.

White Bean Chili

PREP: 10 MIN., COOK: 1 HR.

2 lb. fresh turkey tenderloins
2 Tbsp. olive oil
1 cup finely chopped onion
2 garlic cloves, minced
2 (15.8-oz.) cans great Northern beans, rinsed and drained
1 (10¾-oz.) can CAMPBELL'S Condensed Chicken Broth
1¼ cups water
1 (4.5-oz.) can chopped green chiles
1 bay leaf
1 tsp. ground cumin
⅛ tsp. ground red pepper
Toppings: sour cream, fresh cilantro

1. Cut turkey into bite-size pieces. Cook turkey in hot oil in a large Dutch oven over medium-high heat 6 to 8 minutes or until browned.
2. Add onion and garlic, and cook 5 to 6 minutes or until onion is tender.
3. Stir in beans and next 6 ingredients; bring to a boil. Reduce heat, and simmer, stirring occasionally, 30 to 45 minutes or until thickened. Remove and discard bay leaf; serve chili with desired toppings. **Makes** about 8 cups.

◀ Use kitchen shears to chop cilantro or any leafy herb in a measuring cup or small mixing bowl.

Orange-Pineapple Smoothie

fast fixin's
PREP: 5 MIN.

2 cups frozen pineapple chunks
1 cup orange juice
1 cup vanilla yogurt
¾ cup milk
¼ cup SPLENDA No Calorie Sweetener, granular
Garnish: orange wedges

1. Process first 5 ingredients in a blender until smooth, stopping to scrape down sides. Garnish, if desired; serve immediately. **Makes** about 4¼ cups.

Note: We tested with bagged frozen pineapple from the freezer section, fresh pineapple we froze in the Test Kitchens, and canned pineapple chunks (in juice) that we placed in the freezer (can and all). After opening the frozen can, we let hot water run over the top for about 10 seconds and then used a fork to pull out 2 cups worth of pineapple. (Tip: Canned pineapple can be frozen up to 3 months.)

Taco Salad

fast fixin's
PREP: 10 MIN., COOK: 15 MIN.

1½ lb. lean ground beef
1 (16-oz.) jar TOSTITOS Medium Salsa
1 (16-oz.) can kidney beans, drained
2 Tbsp. taco seasoning mix
2 avocados
½ cup sour cream
2 Tbsp. chopped fresh cilantro
Bite-size tortilla chips
3 cups shredded lettuce (about ½ head)
Toppings: crumbled bacon, chopped tomatoes, finely chopped red onion, shredded cheese

1. Brown beef in a large nonstick skillet over medium-high heat, stirring until it crumbles and is no longer pink. Drain and return to skillet. Stir in salsa, beans, and taco seasoning; bring to a boil. Reduce heat, and simmer, stirring occasionally, 10 minutes.
2. Peel and mash avocados; stir in sour cream and cilantro.
3. Place desired amount of tortilla chips on a serving platter, and top with shredded lettuce and beef mixture. Serve with avocado mixture and desired toppings. **Makes** 6 servings.

Slaw Reubens

fast fixin's
PREP: 10 MIN., COOK: 4 MIN.

2 cups shredded coleslaw mix
5 Tbsp. Thousand Island dressing, divided
1 Tbsp. white vinegar
¼ tsp. freshly ground pepper
1 tsp. spicy brown mustard
4 slices rye or pumpernickel bread
1 (7-oz.) package OSCAR MAYER Shaved Roast Beef
½ Granny Smith apple, cored and thinly sliced
2 (1-oz.) Swiss cheese slices
2 Tbsp. butter, melted

1. Stir together coleslaw mix, 2 Tbsp. Thousand Island dressing, vinegar, and pepper in a medium bowl.
2. Stir together mustard and remaining 3 Tbsp. Thousand Island dressing; spread mixture evenly on 1 side of bread slices. Top 2 bread slices evenly with beef; top each with half of apple slices and 1 cheese slice. Divide slaw mixture evenly over cheese. Top with remaining bread slices, dressing mixture sides down. Brush both sides of sandwiches evenly with melted butter.
3. Cook sandwiches in a large lightly greased nonstick skillet over medium-high heat 2 minutes on each side or until golden. Serve immediately. **Makes** 2 servings.

Plan Quick Meals

Y ou can never have too many creative ideas for building weeknight menus everyone will enjoy.

Grilled Asian Flank Steak

PREP: 10 MIN., CHILL: 4 HRS., GRILL: 14 MIN., STAND: 10 MIN.

¼ cup lite soy sauce
3 Tbsp. lite teriyaki sauce
3 Tbsp. rice wine vinegar
1 Tbsp. Asian garlic-chili sauce
1 Tbsp. minced fresh ginger
2 green onions, chopped
1½ lb. BEEF Flank Steak

1. Combine first 6 ingredients in a large zip-top plastic freezer bag or shallow dish. Add flank steak, and turn to coat. Seal or cover, and chill 4 hours, turning occasionally.
2. Remove steak from marinade, discarding marinade.
3. Grill steak, covered with grill lid, over medium-high heat (350° to 400°) 5 to 7 minutes on each side or to desired degree of doneness. Let stand 10 minutes before slicing. Cut diagonally across the grain into thin strips. **Makes** 4 to 6 servings.

Skillet Chili Mac

family favorite • fast fixin's
PREP: 5 MIN., COOK: 25 MIN.

1 lb. sweet Italian turkey sausage
2 Tbsp. vegetable oil
1½ tsp. chili powder
2 cups low-sodium chicken broth
¼ cup tomato paste
1 (12-oz.) package VELVEETA Shells & Cheese Dinner
1¾ cups chunky tomatillo salsa
Toppings: sour cream, chopped tomato, chopped fresh cilantro

1. Remove and discard casings from sausage; cut into ½-inch slices.
2. Cook sausage in hot oil in a large skillet over medium-high heat, stirring occasionally, 8 to 10 minutes or until lightly browned. Drain well on paper towels, and return to skillet. Add chili powder, stirring to coat sausage. Stir in chicken broth and tomato paste, stirring to loosen particles from bottom of skillet.
3. Stir in shell macaroni; return to boil. Reduce heat to medium-low; cover and simmer, stirring occasionally, 8 to 10 minutes or until shells are tender.
4. Stir in cheese sauce from packet and tomatillo salsa; simmer, uncovered, 5 minutes or until thoroughly heated. Serve immediately with desired toppings. **Makes** 4 servings.

Cheesy Pasta With Bell Peppers

family favorite
PREP: 10 MIN., COOK: 25 MIN.

1 red bell pepper, chopped
½ medium red onion, chopped
2 garlic cloves, minced
1 Tbsp. olive oil
1 lb. ground beef
2 cups chicken broth, divided
1 (12-oz.) package VELVEETA Shells & Cheese Dinner
¼ cup chopped fresh basil
¼ tsp. black pepper

1. Cook first 3 ingredients in hot oil in a large skillet over medium heat, 5 minutes or until vegetables are tender. Add ground beef, and cook 8 to 10 minutes, stirring until beef crumbles and is no longer pink; drain and set aside.
2. Bring 1½ cups chicken broth to a boil in a Dutch oven over medium-high heat; stir in shell macaroni, and return to a boil. Cook, covered, 8 to 10 minutes or until shells are tender, stirring occasionally.
3. Stir in beef mixture, cheese sauce from packet, basil, pepper, and remaining ½ cup chicken broth. Serve immediately. **Makes** 4 servings.

Cherry-Walnut Bars

PREP: 15 MIN., STAND: 10 MIN., BAKE: 25 MIN.

1 (6-oz.) package dried cherries
2 cups all-purpose flour
1 cup SPLENDA Brown Sugar Blend, firmly packed
¾ cup butter, cut into cubes
1 cup sour cream
1 large egg, lightly beaten
¾ tsp. baking soda
1 cup chopped walnuts

1. Pour boiling water to cover over dried cherries, and let stand 10 minutes; drain well, and set aside.
2. Combine flour and brown sugar blend in a large bowl; cut in butter with a pastry blender until crumbly. Press 2½ cups crumb mixture into a lightly greased 13- x 9-inch pan.
3. Stir together sour cream, egg, and baking soda; add to remaining crumb mixture in bowl, stirring just until dry ingredients are moistened. Stir in cherries. Pour sour cream mixture over prepared crust in pan; sprinkle evenly with walnuts.
4. Bake at 350° for 20 to 25 minutes or until a wooden pick inserted in center comes out clean. Let cool completely on a wire rack, and cut into bars. **Makes** 2 dozen.

Technique

"Cut in" is the term for mixing a cold fat, such as butter or shortening, with dry ingredients until the mixture is crumbly. We use a pastry blender, but you can use 2 knives or a fork.

Make It Italian

Try these dishes for a keep-it-casual evening.

A pasta party is easy with these simple recipes. Sample Antipasto Platter, our version of the traditional assortment of meats and vegetables offered before the meal. Then serve Linguine Alfredo prepared with perfectly cooked pasta and tossed with the classic cheese-laced cream sauce. This menu makes entertaining Italian-style fun.

Pasta Party

Serves 6

Antipasto Platter

Linguine Alfredo

Caesar salad

Lemon Tortoni Dessert

Antipasto Platter

make ahead

PREP: 25 MIN., CHILL: 8 HRS. *(Pictured on page 183)*

1 (8-oz.) block mozzarella cheese
1 (9-oz.) package OSCAR MAYER Shaved Virginia-Brand Ham
1 pt. cherry tomatoes, halved
1 (6-oz.) can whole ripe black olives, drained
12 pickled banana peppers
1 small red onion, thinly sliced
½ cup olive oil
¼ cup lemon juice
¼ cup white wine vinegar
4 garlic cloves, minced
1 tsp. dried oregano
½ tsp. salt
¼ tsp. pepper

1. Cut mozzarella cheese into 24 thin sticks. Wrap each stick with 1 ham slice, and place in an 11- x 7-inch dish. Add tomatoes and next 3 ingredients.
2. Whisk together olive oil and next 6 ingredients. Drizzle over mixture in dish. Cover and chill 8 hours or up to 24 hours, turning occasionally. Drain and transfer to a serving dish. **Makes** 6 servings.

Linguine Alfredo

fast fixin's

PREP: 20 MIN., COOK: 8 MIN. *(Pictured on page 183)*

½ (16-oz.) box BARILLA Linguine
⅓ cup butter
2 garlic cloves, pressed
2 cups whipping cream
1 cup chicken broth
¼ cup finely chopped fresh basil
1¼ cups grated Parmesan cheese
Freshly ground pepper to taste
Garnish: fresh basil sprig

1. Cook pasta according to package directions; drain and keep warm.
2. Melt butter in a large skillet over medium heat. Add garlic, and sauté 2 minutes or until lightly browned. Stir in cream, ½ cup broth, and basil. Increase heat to high, and bring to a boil. Remove from heat; add pasta and remaining ½ cup broth. Sprinkle with Parmesan cheese, and toss to coat. Stir in pepper to taste. Garnish, if desired. **Makes** 6 servings.

Lemon Tortoni Dessert

make ahead

PREP: 20 MIN., FREEZE: 4 HRS.

½ (8-oz.) package cream cheese, softened
½ cup DOMINO Confectioners Sugar
2 Tbsp. half-and-half
1 pt. lemon sorbet, softened
3 biscotti, crushed (about ¾ cup) *
¼ cup sliced almonds, toasted

1. Beat cream cheese at medium speed with an electric mixer until creamy. Gradually add confectioners sugar, beating until blended. Gradually add half-and-half, beating until blended. Fold in lemon sorbet and remaining ingredients.
2. Scoop mixture evenly into 8 paper-lined baking cups in muffin pans. Freeze 4 hours or until firm. **Makes** 8 servings.

Note: Dessert can be stored in an airtight container in the freezer up to 1 month.

*Substitute ¾ cup crushed shortbread cookies, if desired.

Cook Pasta Like a Pro

The keys to making delicious pasta dishes are to start with quality ingredients and to cook the pasta properly.
■ Choose a 4- to 6-qt. pot such as a stock pot, Dutch oven, or pasta pot. Pasta should be cooked in plenty of water; use package directions as a guide.
■ Cook the pasta until it is firm but tender. This is often referred to as *al dente,* an Italian term meaning "to the tooth" or firm to the bite. Pasta should not be overcooked, which results in a mushy texture.

Supper Solutions

These crowd-pleasing dishes are ready in a flash.

Even with busy days and after-school activities, it's important for the family to eat dinner together. We've created tempting choices to minimize the time spent cooking and give you more time together at the table. Any of these dishes will give you ample opportunity for dinner-table chats that will likely include accolades for the cook.

Black Bean Enchiladas
PREP: 15 MIN., BAKE: 35 MIN.

2 (15-oz.) cans black beans, rinsed, drained, and divided
1 tsp. chili powder
½ tsp. ground cumin
½ tsp. onion powder
½ tsp. garlic powder
1 (16-oz.) jar medium salsa
½ cup TOSTITOS Monterey Jack Queso Dip
½ cup sour cream
8 (8-inch) flour tortillas

1. Mash 1 can of beans in a bowl; add remaining beans, chili powder, and next 3 ingredients, stirring until blended. Stir together salsa, queso dip, and sour cream in a medium bowl.
2. Spoon about ½ cup black bean mixture down center of each tortilla. Top each with 2 Tbsp. salsa mixture. Roll up tortillas, and place seam sides down in a lightly greased 13- x 9-inch baking dish. Pour remaining salsa mixture evenly over tortillas.
3. Bake, covered, at 350° for 30 to 35 minutes or until thoroughly heated. **Makes** 8 servings.

Creamy Balsamic Sauce
fast fixin's • make ahead
PREP: 10 MIN.
Keep this balsamic sauce on hand to dress up fresh salad greens, grilled vegetables, meat, or seafood.

1 cup balsamic vinaigrette dressing
½ cup HELLMANN'S Real Mayonnaise
3 Tbsp. freshly grated Parmesan cheese
¼ cup chopped fresh basil
¼ tsp. freshly cracked black pepper

1. Whisk together dressing and mayonnaise until blended. Stir in cheese, basil, and pepper. Cover; store in refrigerator up to 1 week. **Makes** 1½ cups.

Festive Grilled Pineapple
PREP: 20 MIN., GRILL: 6 MIN., COOK: 5 MIN.
For extra convenience, you can buy a peeled, cored fresh pineapple; look for them in the produce section of the supermarket.

1 fresh pineapple
PAM Cooking Spray for Grilling
4 Tbsp. butter
¼ cup firmly packed light brown sugar
Vanilla ice cream
½ cup sweetened flaked coconut, toasted
½ cup chopped macadamia nuts, toasted

1. Peel and core pineapple. Cut crosswise into ½-inch slices.
2. Spray cold cooking grate with cooking spray, and place on grill, over medium-high heat (350° to 400°). Place pineapple slices on cooking grate, and grill 2 to 3 minutes on each side or until grill marks appear.
3. Melt 4 Tbsp. butter in a large skillet over medium heat. Stir in brown sugar, and cook until sugar dissolves. Add grilled pineapple, spooning sugar mixture over pineapple, and cook 3 minutes or until mixture is thickened and pineapple is glazed. Top pineapple with ice cream; sprinkle evenly with coconut and macadamia nuts. **Makes** 4 servings.

Parsleyed Noodles
fast fixin's
PREP: 5 MIN., COOK: 15 MIN.
Noodles are easily prepared and make the perfect companion for quick suppers. Try this simple recipe to round out weeknight menus in a jiffy.

1. Cook ½ (12-oz.) package NO YOLKS Noodles according to package directions. Microwave 2 Tbsp. butter in a microwave-safe bowl or 2-cup liquid measuring cup at HIGH 30 seconds or until melted. Stir in 2 Tbsp. chopped fresh parsley, ¼ tsp. salt, and ⅛ tsp. pepper. Stir butter mixture into cooked noodles. **Makes** 3 servings.

Pasta Salad Niçoise
make ahead
PREP: 20 MIN., COOK: 15 MIN., CHILL: 2 HRS.
(Pictured on page 182)

1 (12-oz.) package NO YOLKS Dumplings
½ lb. fresh green beans, trimmed
1 (16-oz.) bottle Italian dressing, divided
1 (12-oz.) can solid white tuna in water, drained and flaked
1 cup grape tomatoes, halved
½ red bell pepper, cut into thin strips
1 (2.25-oz.) can sliced ripe black olives, drained
¼ cup thinly sliced red onion
½ tsp. freshly ground pepper
2 (5-oz.) packages mixed salad greens

1. Cook dumplings according to package directions, adding green beans during last 3 minutes of cooking. Drain and rinse with cold water.

2. Toss noodle mixture with 1½ cups dressing in a large bowl; stir in tuna and next 5 ingredients. Cover and chill at least 2 hours or up to 24 hours.

3. Place salad greens on a large serving platter; top with noodle mixture. Serve with remaining dressing. **Makes** 8 to 10 servings.

Quick Chicken Stir-fry

family favorite

PREP: 20 MIN., STAND: 30 MIN.,
COOK: 10 MIN.

4 PILGRIM'S PRIDE Boneless, Skinless
    Chicken Breasts
1 (14-oz.) can reduced-sodium chicken
    broth
2 Tbsp. lite soy sauce
1 to 2 Tbsp. chili-garlic paste
2 Tbsp. cornstarch
1 Tbsp. brown sugar
1 Tbsp. grated fresh ginger
2 Tbsp. vegetable oil
2 cups packaged matchstick
    carrots
1 red bell pepper, cut into slices
1 green bell pepper, cut into slices
2 green onions, sliced
Hot cooked rice

1. Cut chicken into ¼-inch-thick strips; place in a shallow dish.

2. Whisk together chicken broth and next 5 ingredients in a small bowl. Pour half of broth mixture over chicken, reserving remaining broth mixture. Turn chicken to coat, and let stand 30 minutes.

3. Heat 2 Tbsp. oil in a wok or large skillet over medium-high heat 2 minutes. Remove chicken from marinade, discarding marinade. Add chicken to wok, and stir-fry 3 to 5 minutes or until lightly browned. Add carrots, bell peppers, and green onions, and stir-fry 3 to 4 minutes. Add reserved broth mixture, and cook 1 minute or until thickened. Serve over hot cooked rice. **Makes** 4 to 6 servings.

Guacamole

fast fixin's

PREP: 15 MIN.

3 ripe avocados
1½ Tbsp. lemon juice
1 garlic clove, minced
1 Tbsp. chopped fresh cilantro
¼ tsp. salt
Pinch of pepper
1 medium tomato, chopped (optional)
1 (12-oz.) bag TOSTITOS Bite Size Gold
    Tortilla Chips

1. Scoop avocado pulp into a bowl; mash with a fork or potato masher, leaving some chunks. Stir in lemon juice until blended.

2. Stir in minced garlic; next 3 ingredients; and, if desired, chopped tomato. Serve with tortilla chips. **Makes** 2 cups.

Beef Pocket Sandwiches

family favorite

PREP: 15 MIN., COOK: 15 MIN., BAKE: 30 MIN.

1 lb. 95% Lean Ground BEEF
1 Tbsp. butter
1 green bell pepper, cut into
    strips
1 cup sliced fresh mushrooms
1 (14-oz.) jar pizza sauce
1 (8-oz.) package shredded Italian
    six-cheese blend
2 (13.8-oz.) cans refrigerated pizza crust
    dough
Olive oil
Pizza sauce (optional)

1. Cook ground beef in a large non-stick skillet over medium-high heat, stirring until it crumbles and is no longer pink. Remove from skillet, and drain well. Wipe skillet clean with a paper towel.

2. Melt butter in skillet over medium-high heat. Add bell pepper strips and sliced mushrooms, and sauté 8 minutes or until mushrooms are lightly browned and liquid evaporates. Remove from heat; stir in beef, 1 jar pizza sauce, and cheese.

3. Unroll each can of pizza crust dough on a lightly floured surface; cut each crust into quarters. Press each dough quarter into a 7- x 6-inch rectangle. Spoon about ⅔ cup meat mixture in the center of each rectangle. Fold 1 short side of dough over filling, pressing or crimping edges to seal. Place beef pockets on 2 lightly greased baking sheets, and cut slits in tops to allow steam to escape. Brush lightly with olive oil.

4. Bake, on separate oven racks, at 375° for 25 to 30 minutes or until golden. (Switch places of baking sheets in oven after 15 minutes if necessary for even baking.) Serve with pizza sauce, if desired. **Makes** 8 servings.

Greek Shrimp Pasta Salad

make ahead

PREP: 20 MIN., COOK: 10 MIN., CHILL: 1 HR.

½ (16-oz.) package BARILLA Rotini
    Pasta
¼ cup lemon juice
1 Tbsp. Greek seasoning
3 Tbsp. mayonnaise
½ tsp. minced garlic
¼ tsp. sugar
¼ cup olive oil
½ lb. peeled cooked medium shrimp
1 cup chopped tomatoes (1 large tomato)
¼ cup chopped red onion
1 (2.5-oz.) can sliced ripe black olives,
    drained
2 Tbsp. chopped fresh parsley
Lettuce leaves (optional)

1. Cook pasta according to package directions. Drain well, and set aside.

2. Whisk together lemon juice and next 4 ingredients. Gradually add olive oil in a slow, steady stream, whisking until blended. Cover and chill until ready to use.

3. Combine cooked pasta, shrimp, and next 4 ingredients in a large bowl. Drizzle with vinaigrette, tossing to coat. Cover and chill 1 hour. Serve on a lettuce-lined plate, if desired. **Makes** 4 to 6 servings.

Quick Chicken Piccata

fast fixin's
PREP: 20 MIN., COOK: 10 MIN.

1 lb. PILGRIM'S PRIDE Chicken
   Breasts
½ tsp. salt
½ tsp. pepper
½ cup Italian-seasoned breadcrumbs
2 Tbsp. olive oil
¼ cup chicken broth
3 Tbsp. fresh lemon juice
2 Tbsp. butter
2 Tbsp. chopped fresh parsley
1 (12-oz.) package cooked noodles

1. Cut each chicken breast in half horizontally. Place chicken between 2 sheets of heavy-duty plastic wrap; flatten to ¼-inch thickness, using a rolling pin or the flat side of a meat mallet.
2. Sprinkle chicken evenly with salt and pepper; lightly dredge in breadcrumbs.
3. Cook half of chicken in 1 Tbsp. hot oil in a large nonstick skillet over medium-high heat 2 minutes on each side or until golden brown and done. Remove chicken to a serving platter, and cover with aluminum foil. Repeat procedure with remaining chicken and 1 Tbsp. olive oil.
4. Add broth and lemon juice to skillet, and cook, stirring to loosen particles from bottom of skillet, until sauce is slightly thickened. Remove from heat; add butter and parsley, stirring until butter melts. Pour sauce over chicken, and serve over warm noodles. **Makes** 4 servings.

Italian Pasta Casserole

PREP: 15 MIN., COOK: 30 MIN., BAKE: 30 MIN.

1 (12-oz.) package WACKY MAC Veggie
   Spirals
1 lb. lean ground beef
1 medium onion, chopped
1 medium-size green bell pepper,
   chopped
1 (8-oz.) package sliced mushrooms
2 garlic cloves, minced
1½ tsp. salt, divided
1 (28-oz.) can diced tomatoes, drained
1 (26-oz.) jar tomato sauce
1½ tsp. sugar
½ tsp. pepper
2 Tbsp. chopped fresh basil
1 Tbsp. chopped fresh oregano
1 (8-oz.) package shredded mozzarella
   cheese

1. Cook pasta according to package directions; drain and set aside.
2. Cook beef, next 4 ingredients, and ½ tsp. salt in a Dutch oven over medium-high heat, stirring often, 10 minutes or until meat is browned and vegetables are tender.
3. Stir in tomatoes, next 5 ingredients, and remaining 1 tsp. salt. Bring tomato mixture to a boil; reduce heat, and simmer 15 minutes.
4. Combine tomato mixture and pasta; spoon into a lightly greased 13- x 9-inch baking dish. Sprinkle evenly with cheese.
5. Bake, uncovered, at 400° for 30 minutes or until bubbly and thoroughly heated. **Makes** 8 to 10 servings.

New Orleans Brunch

Tempt your guests with this fabulous meal. We offer classic recipes, such as hearty Grillades Over Yellow Grits Wedges and irresistible Creamy Rice Pudding With Praline Sauce. When you serve up delicious food inspired by the Big Easy, you can bet everyone will have a great time.

Brunch in the Big Easy

Serves 6

Grillades Over Yellow Grits Wedges

Fruit With Orange-Ginger Dressing

Creamy Rice Pudding With
Praline Sauce

Citrus-Mint Sipper

Grillades Over Yellow Grits Wedges

PREP: 20 MIN.; COOK: 1 HR., 25 MIN.

1½ lb. BEEF Top Round Steak
3 Tbsp. all-purpose flour
2 tsp. Creole seasoning
2 Tbsp. vegetable oil
1 (10-oz.) package frozen diced onion,
   red and green bell pepper, and celery blend
1 (14½-oz.) can stewed tomatoes,
   undrained and chopped
1 cup beef broth
2 tsp. minced garlic
Yellow Grits Wedges

1. Trim steak, and cut into 2-inch squares.
2. Combine flour and Creole seasoning in a large zip-top plastic freezer bag. Add steak; seal bag, and shake to evenly coat.
3. Heat 1 Tbsp. oil in a large skillet or Dutch oven over medium-high heat.

Technique

To flatten a chicken breast, place it on a cutting board between 2 sheets of plastic wrap; flatten to ¼-inch thickness, using the flat side of a meat mallet. (A rolling pin can be used instead of a mallet.)

Add half of steak, and cook 2 to 3 minutes on each side or until browned; remove from skillet. Repeat procedure with remaining 1 Tbsp. oil and remaining steak. (Do not remove steak.) Return cooked steak to skillet.

4. Stir in frozen vegetables and next 3 ingredients. Bring to a boil over medium-high heat. Cover, reduce heat, and simmer, stirring occasionally, 1 hour and 15 minutes or until steak is tender. Spoon over Yellow Grits Wedges; serve immediately. **Makes** 6 servings.

Yellow Grits Wedges:

PREP: 10 MIN., COOK: 30 MIN.,
STAND: 10 MIN.

Vegetable cooking spray
2½ cups low-sodium chicken broth
2 cups milk
1½ cups uncooked stone-ground
    yellow grits
½ tsp. salt
Freshly ground pepper to taste

1. Line a 9-inch square pan with aluminum foil; coat with cooking spray.
2. Bring 2½ cups chicken broth and 2 cups milk to a boil in a large saucepan; stir in grits and salt. Reduce heat, and cook, stirring constantly, 17 to 20 minutes or until very thick. Stir in pepper to taste.
3. Spread hot grits evenly into prepared pan; let stand 10 minutes. Cut into 6 rectangles; cut each in half, forming 2 triangles. Serve immediately. **Makes** 6 servings.

How-to

Grillades may sound fancy, but they're easy to make. Here's how.
1. Trim and cut steak into 2-inch squares. Dredge the squares in the flour mixture by tossing flour mixture and meat together in a zip-top freezer bag.
2. Brown the steak on each side in a small amount of oil in a skillet or Dutch oven.

Fruit With Orange-Ginger Dressing

make ahead

PREP: 15 MIN., COOK: 20 MIN., CHILL: 1 HR.

We found that orange sections and chunks of pineapple, honeydew melon, and cantaloupe work well in this light, refreshing fruit dessert.

⅔ cup orange juice
3 Tbsp. minced crystallized ginger
3 Tbsp. honey
½ cup HELLMANN'S Real Mayonnaise
½ cup plain yogurt
5 cups assorted fruit, cut into bite-size
    pieces

1. Combine first 3 ingredients in a small saucepan; bring to a boil over medium heat. Boil, stirring occasionally, 15 minutes or until mixture thickens and reduces by half (about ⅓ cup). If desired, pour mixture through a wire-mesh strainer into a bowl, discarding solids. Cover and chill at least 1 hour.
2. Whisk together mayonnaise and yogurt. Stir in chilled juice mixture.
3. Place fruit in 6 (1-cup) parfait glasses or a medium serving bowl. Pour dressing evenly over fruit. **Makes** 6 servings.

Creamy Rice Pudding With Praline Sauce

PREP: 15 MIN., COOK: 50 MIN.

2 cups milk
1 cup uncooked MAHATMA Extra
    Long-Grain White Rice
½ tsp. salt
2¾ cups half-and-half, divided
4 egg yolks, beaten
½ cup sugar
1½ tsp. vanilla extract
20 caramels
½ cup chopped pecans, toasted

1. Stir together first 3 ingredients and 2 cups half-and-half in a large saucepan. Cover and cook over medium-low heat, stirring often, 35 to 40 minutes or until rice is tender.

2. Whisk together egg yolks, ½ cup half-and-half, and sugar. Gradually stir about one-fourth of hot rice mixture into yolk mixture; stir yolk mixture into remaining hot mixture. Cook over medium-low heat, stirring constantly, until mixture reaches 160° and is thickened and bubbly (about 7 minutes). Remove from heat; stir in vanilla.
3. Stir together caramels and remaining ¼ cup half-and-half in a small saucepan over medium-low heat until smooth. Stir in pecans. Serve over rice pudding. **Makes** 6 to 8 servings.

Citrus-Mint Sipper

make ahead

PREP: 10 MIN., COOK: 5 MIN.,
STAND: 10 MIN., CHILL: 1 HR.

1 cup water
½ cup lightly packed fresh mint leaves,
    coarsely chopped
2 cups chilled lemonade
¼ cup SPLENDA No Calorie Sweetener,
    granular
½ cup fresh lime juice (about 4 limes)
1 (1-qt.) bottle sparkling water, chilled
Ice

1. Bring 1 cup water to a boil in a saucepan. Remove from heat; add mint. Let stand 10 minutes. Pour mixture through a wire-mesh strainer into a pitcher. Cover and chill at least 1 hour. Stir in lemonade, sweetener, juice, and sparkling water before serving. Serve over ice. **Makes** 6 to 8 servings.

Technique

Braising is a cooking method in which you brown the food first and then simmer it gently in a small amount of liquid in a tightly covered skillet or Dutch oven until tender.

from our kitchen

Tools We Love

The Foods staff spends a lot of time in the kitchen, both personally and professionally, so good tools are high on our must-have lists. Well-designed ones save time or, at least, simplify meal preparation. So, when several Test Kitchens Professionals and Foods Editors sing the praises of a particular gadget, we all take notice. Here are a few that most of us have in our collections, along with some suggested uses.

We can't say this often enough: Among our favorite time-savers to come along in recent years are Microplane® graters. Modeled on a woodworker's plane, these handy utensils shred everything from chocolate to soft cheese with ease. Before buying, consider what you'll be grating most.

The version with the smallest cutting holes makes short work of tedious kitchen tasks, such as grating citrus peel, garlic, and ginger. Most important, when you gently pull the grating edge across an orange, lemon, or lime, it scrapes off only the oil-rich rind without getting the bitter pith. Use the larger Microplane tools to grate chocolate for dusting desserts or pasteurized processed cheese for that veggie-plate standard, macaroni and cheese.

For added convenience, hold the Microplane grater over a flexible cutting board. These are downright cheap—you can buy them at a dollar store—and very versatile. Because they fold, you can easily shake the grated or chopped ingredient into a mixing bowl or pot. Place one over your regular cutting board for slicing meat; then put it in the dishwasher when you're done. That way, you can cut vegetables and raw meat for the same meal without fear of cross contamination.

Small Is Beautiful

Tiny measuring cups, such as the ones shown here, portion out from a Tbsp. to ¼ cup of liquid with ease. No more adding a Tbsp. of water at a time to a recipe, counting how many you've added while trying not to spill. One version even has a 1½-Tbsp. mark.

The cups also are easy to grip, perfect for children. The dainty size of these tools makes them fun to use. They'll take you back to the days when the Easy-Bake Oven was your primary kitchen appliance.

Mini-whisks are equally engaging and useful. They're perfect for whipping up one scrambled egg or a small amount of salad dressing, or for frothing milk for an occasional latte. They fit nicely in a kitchen utensil drawer and the dishwasher.

Reinvented Classic

A silicone basting and pastry brush has two advantages: It cleans up beautifully in the dishwasher, and it won't shed bristles into the food as traditional basting brushes are prone to do.

october

Fall Feast From the Chesapeake

This laid-back menu makes any outdoor gathering a breeze.

Outdoor Menu

Serves 6 to 8

Sun-dried Tomato Cheese Spread

Chesapeake Chowder

Maryland Crab Cakes With Creamy Caper-Dill Sauce

Roasted Sweet Potato Salad

caramel apples
(Prepare your favorite recipe or purchase a kit from the produce section of your grocery store. For a festive twist, add sprinkles of ginger or salt before the caramel hardens.)

spiced cider

Even if you don't live near Chesapeake Bay, you can still enjoy the bountiful seafood it has to offer. Ann and Michael McInerney don't live there full-time either, but their waterfront home in Shady Side, Maryland, is a favorite gathering place for special occasions. "We try to visit as often as we can," says Ann, whose family is spread across the South. "There's nothing like the Chesapeake in the fall."

We agree. The Upper South is truly divine this time of year—and so are these regional recipes. Maryland Crab Cakes topped with Creamy Caper-Dill Sauce are some of the best we've tasted. Pair them with Roasted Sweet Potato Salad drizzled with Warm Bacon Dressing for a hearty taste of the season. Not only is this menu easy to prepare, but it's also sure to entice guests.

Sun-dried Tomato Cheese Spread

make ahead

PREP: 10 MIN., BAKE: 45 MIN.
(Pictured on page 185)

1 garlic bulb
1 tsp. olive oil
1 (11-oz.) package goat cheese
1 (8-oz.) package cream cheese, softened
⅓ cup sun-dried tomatoes in oil, drained and chopped
2 Tbsp. chopped fresh chives
¼ tsp. salt
¼ tsp. freshly ground pepper
Assorted crackers, breads, radishes, carrots

1. Cut off pointed end of garlic; place garlic on a piece of aluminum foil, and drizzle with oil. Fold foil to seal. Place on baking sheet.
2. Bake at 425° for 45 minutes or until cloves are tender. Let cool slightly. Squeeze pulp from garlic cloves; mash.
3. Beat garlic, goat cheese, and next 5 ingredients at medium speed with an electric mixer until well blended. Cover and chill until ready to serve. Serve with assorted crackers, breads, and vegetables. **Makes** about 3 cups.

CAROLINE WILLIAMS
LOOKOUT MOUNTAIN, GEORGIA

Chesapeake Chowder

PREP: 25 MIN., COOK: 45 MIN.
(Pictured on page 185)

½ lb. unpeeled, medium-size fresh shrimp
½ lb. fresh crabmeat
1 onion, chopped
3 garlic cloves, minced
2 celery ribs, chopped
1 Tbsp. olive oil
¼ cup all-purpose flour
2½ cups chicken broth
1 cup dry white wine or chicken broth
1 (8-oz.) bottle clam juice
5 red potatoes, peeled and diced
1 Tbsp. Old Bay seasoning
½ cup heavy cream
Garnish: chopped fresh parsley

1. Peel shrimp; devein, if desired. Drain and flake crabmeat, removing any bits of shell. Set seafood aside.
2. Sauté onion, garlic, and celery in hot oil in a Dutch oven over medium-high heat 8 minutes or until tender. Stir in flour, and cook, stirring constantly, 1 minute. Stir in broth and next 4 ingredients. Bring to a boil; cover, reduce heat, and simmer, stirring occasionally, 30 minutes or until potatoes are tender.
3. Stir in shrimp, crabmeat, and heavy cream; cook over low heat 5 minutes or just until shrimp turn pink. Garnish, if desired. **Makes** 8 cups.

ANN MCINERNEY
BETHESDA, MARYLAND

Maryland Crab Cakes With Creamy Caper-Dill Sauce

make ahead

PREP: 30 MIN., COOK: 30 MIN., CHILL: 1 HR.

These golden cakes have a higher ratio of crabmeat to filling than other recipes, yet they still hold up nicely in the skillet.

(Pictured on page 184)

2 lb. fresh lump crabmeat *
½ cup minced green onions
½ cup minced red bell pepper
1 Tbsp. olive oil
½ cup Italian-seasoned breadcrumbs
1 large egg, lightly beaten
½ cup mayonnaise
1 Tbsp. fresh lemon juice
1½ tsp. Old Bay seasoning
½ tsp. pepper
Dash of Worcestershire sauce
2 Tbsp. butter
Lemon wedges
Creamy Caper-Dill Sauce
Garnish: fresh dill sprigs

1. Rinse, drain, and flake crabmeat, being careful not to break up lumps, and remove any bits of shell. Set aside.
2. Sauté green onions and bell pepper in hot oil in a large nonstick skillet 8 minutes or until tender.
3. Stir together green onion mixture, breadcrumbs, egg, and next 5 ingredients. Gently fold in crabmeat. Shape mixture into 14 (2½-inch) cakes (about ⅓ cup for each cake). Place on an aluminum foil-lined baking sheet; cover and chill at least 1 hour or up to 8 hours.
4. Melt butter in a large nonstick skillet over medium heat. Add crab cakes, and cook, in 2 batches, 4 to 5 minutes on each side or until golden. Drain on paper towels. Serve with a squeeze of lemon and Creamy Caper-Dill Sauce. Garnish, if desired. **Makes** 14 cakes.

*Substitute regular crabmeat for lump, if desired.

Creamy Caper-Dill Sauce:

fast fixin's • make ahead

PREP: 10 MIN.

¾ cup mayonnaise
½ cup sour cream
¼ tsp. grated lemon rind
2 Tbsp. fresh lemon juice
1 Tbsp. drained capers
2 tsp. chopped fresh dill
1 tsp. Dijon mustard
¼ tsp. salt
¼ tsp. pepper

1. Stir together all ingredients. Cover and chill up to 3 days. **Makes** 1¼ cups.

ANN MCINERNEY
BETHESDA, MARYLAND

Seafood Savvy

It's easy to buy the right seafood if you know what to look for. Follow these guidelines for picking it fresh.

■ Purchase seafood from a reputable market or grocery store. Observe how it's stored: Seafood is best packed on ice.
■ Choose shrimp that are slightly firm in texture, avoiding those that are soft and limp. Make sure the shells are tightly attached. Watch out for dark spots, which probably mean that the shrimp are past their peak.
■ Buy shrimp one day before you plan to serve it. This will give you time to peel and, if desired, devein the shrimp in advance.
■ Avoid crab and shrimp that smell fishy. Fresh seafood should not have a strong odor.

Roasted Sweet Potato Salad

PREP: 30 MIN., BAKE: 45 MIN.

(Pictured on page 185)

1½ lb. sweet potatoes
2 large onions
2 garlic cloves, crushed
2 Tbsp. olive oil
½ tsp. salt
½ tsp. pepper
1 (6-oz.) bag baby spinach
Warm Bacon Dressing
Garnish: cooked, crumbled bacon

1. Peel sweet potatoes, and cut into 1-inch cubes. Cut onions into quarters, and cut each quarter in half.
2. Toss together sweet potatoes, onions, crushed garlic, and 2 Tbsp. olive oil; place on a lightly greased aluminum foil-lined 15- x 11-inch jelly-roll pan. Sprinkle evenly with salt and pepper.
3. Bake, stirring occasionally, at 400° for 45 minutes or until tender and lightly brown. Serve over spinach, and drizzle with Warm Bacon Dressing. Garnish, if desired. **Makes** 6 to 8 servings.

Warm Bacon Dressing:

PREP: 10 MIN., COOK: 10 MIN.

4 bacon slices
⅓ cup red wine vinegar
3 Tbsp. orange juice
2 Tbsp. honey
¼ tsp. salt
⅛ tsp. pepper

1. Cook bacon slices in a large skillet until crisp. Remove bacon, and drain on paper towels, reserving 1 Tbsp. drippings in skillet. Crumble bacon.
2. Stir vinegar and next 4 ingredients into hot drippings in skillet; cook over medium heat, stirring until thoroughly heated. Stir in bacon. **Makes** ½ cup.

ANN MCINERNEY
BETHESDA, MARYLAND

Test Kitchen *Notebook*

To plan ahead, prepare Sun-dried Tomato Cheese Spread up to three days in advance. Make Maryland Crab Cakes the day before. Shape the mixture as directed, and place the uncooked cakes on an aluminum foil-lined pan. Cover and chill overnight. Peel and, if desired, devein shrimp for Chesapeake Chowder the day before.

Shannon Sliter Satterwhite
FOODS EDITOR

Comfort Food With an Accent

Add a touch of Southwest flavor to your everyday menus with these recipes and tips.

desired degree of doneness. Remove to a serving plate, and keep warm.

5. Add onions, carrots, and chiles to skillet; cook, stirring often, 10 minutes or until onions are brown. Cut steak pieces diagonally across the grain into thin strips. Spoon vegetables over steak; serve immediately. **Makes** 4 to 6 servings.

Note: For testing purposes only, we used Goya Bitter Orange Marinade.

Southwestern Supper

Serves 4 to 6

Pan-Seared Skirt Steak With Poblano Chiles and Onions

Traditional Frijoles

Tres Leches Cake

Horchata

It's so easy to make Mexican food at home," says Melissa Guerra, cookbook author and star of the PBS show *The Texas Provincial Kitchen*. She shared some favorite recipes and tips with us at her family's ranch near McAllen, Texas. Despite a hectic schedule, Melissa cooks daily for her husband, Enrique ("Kiko"), and children Henry, Diego, and Lorenzo.

To fit with her busy lifestyle, Melissa chooses dishes that are doable and delicious. "Mexican food is very simple and real," she says, "and it doesn't require too many canned or processed products. Most of the produce is fresh and cooked up right away." Grilling and stewing—techniques that most Southerners use regularly—are the two basic cooking methods, she explains.

On special occasions, she'll whip up Tres Leches Cake, a fabulous concoction moistened with a mixture of sweetened condensed milk, evaporated milk, and whipping cream. The dessert is a hands-down favorite.

Pan-Seared Skirt Steak With Poblano Chiles and Onions

PREP: 25 MIN., BROIL: 10 MIN., STAND: 15 MIN., CHILL: 20 MIN., COOK: 35 MIN.

This popular dish is similar to fajitas. Purchase bitter orange juice marinade in the Mexican food section of supermarkets.

3 poblano chiles
2 lb. skirt or flank steak
2 cups bitter orange juice marinade or apple cider vinegar
1 tsp. salt
1 tsp. cracked black pepper
1 Tbsp. olive oil
1 medium-size red onion, sliced
1 white onion, sliced
2 carrots, sliced

1. Broil chiles on an aluminum foil-lined baking sheet 5 inches from heat 5 minutes on each side or until chiles look blistered.

2. Place chiles in a zip-top freezer bag; seal and let stand 15 minutes to loosen skins. Peel chiles; remove and discard seeds. Cut chiles into thin slices, and set aside.

3. Cut steak into 4 to 6 pieces, and place the steak in an 11- x 7-inch baking dish. Pour bitter orange juice marinade over steak, and sprinkle evenly with salt and pepper. Cover and chill 20 minutes.

4. Drain steak, discarding marinade. Heat a cast-iron skillet over medium-high heat 3 minutes; add oil. Cook steak pieces, in batches, 5 minutes on each side or until a meat thermometer inserted in steak reads 135° or to

How to Roast Chiles

Roast poblano chiles over an open flame or under the broiler until they're thoroughly charred. Place the chiles in a zip-top plastic or paper bag, and seal or fold down top. (Melissa likes to intensify the steaming process by wrapping the bags of roasted chiles in a kitchen towel.) Let stand 15 minutes; then pull off the charred skin with your fingers. Remove the seeds and stems before including chiles in the recipe. Poblano chiles are mild, so there's no need to wear gloves.

Traditional Frijoles

PREP: 15 MIN., COOK: 3 HRS.

This tasty, inexpensive recipe goes together in a flash but requires long, slow cooking.

8 cups water
1 lb. dried pinto beans, rinsed, drained, and sorted
4 oz. salt pork
1 medium onion, chopped
1 large tomato, chopped
2 garlic cloves, minced
1 bunch fresh cilantro, chopped
½ tsp. pepper
1¼ tsp. salt, divided
1 serrano chile (optional)

1. Bring first 8 ingredients, ¼ tsp. salt, and, if desired, serrano chile to a boil over medium-high heat in a Dutch oven. Cover and cook, stirring occasionally, over medium-low heat 3 hours or until beans are tender. Stir in remaining 1 tsp. salt. Remove and discard salt pork and chile before serving. **Makes** 6 to 8 servings (about 6 cups).

Refritos: Cook 4 cups Traditional Frijoles in 1 Tbsp. hot vegetable oil in a large skillet over medium heat. Reduce heat, and mash beans with a potato masher as they cook, adding water if necessary to keep moist. Simmer, stirring often, 10 minutes. Prep: 5 min., Cook: 10 min. **Makes** 6 to 8 servings.

Tres Leches Cake

PREP: 25 MIN.; BAKE: 25 MIN.;
STAND: 2 HRS., 10 MIN.

Soaked in three different milks, this butter cake is popular in Latin America. This exceptional dessert takes a little extra effort, but it's worth it. The combination of textures—tender cake, fluffy frosting, and a pool of creamy sauce—will delight your family and friends. If you don't have a double boiler to make the frosting, place a metal mixing bowl over a saucepan instead.

7 large eggs, separated
½ cup butter, softened
1 cup sugar
2½ cups all-purpose flour
1 tsp. baking powder
½ tsp. salt
1 cup milk
1 tsp. vanilla extract
1 (14-oz.) can sweetened condensed milk
1 (12-oz.) can evaporated milk
¾ cup whipping cream
Fluffy Frosting
Garnish: grated lemon rind

1. Beat egg yolks, butter, and sugar at medium speed with an electric mixer 2 minutes or until mixture is creamy.
2. Combine flour, baking powder, and salt. Add flour mixture to egg yolk mixture alternately with milk, beginning and ending with flour mixture. Beat at low speed just until blended after each addition. Stir in vanilla.
3. Beat egg whites until stiff, and fold gently into batter. Pour into a greased and floured 13- x 9-inch pan.
4. Bake at 350° for 25 minutes or until a wooden pick inserted in center comes out clean. Let stand 10 minutes.
5. Pierce top of cake several times with a small wooden skewer. Stir together condensed milk, evaporated milk, and cream; gradually pour and spread over warm cake. (Pour about ¼ cup at a time, allowing mixture to soak into cake before pouring more.) Let stand 2 hours; cover and chill overnight, if desired. Spread top of cake with Fluffy Frosting before serving. Garnish, if desired. **Makes** 16 servings.

Fluffy Frosting:

fast fixin's

PREP: 10 MIN., COOK: 14 MIN.

6 egg whites
1 cup sugar
1 cup light corn syrup
1 Tbsp. fresh lemon juice (about ½ lemon)

1. Pour water to a depth of 1½ inches into bottom of a double boiler over medium-high heat; bring to a boil. Reduce heat to a gentle boil. Place egg whites and sugar in top of double boiler. Beat at high speed with an electric mixer 5 to 7 minutes or until stiff peaks form. Gradually pour in corn syrup and lemon juice, beating 7 minutes or until spreading consistency. **Makes** about 7½ cups.

Tricks to Perfect *Tres Leches*

Use tips from Test Kitchens Director Lyda Jones Burnette when making this cake.
■ Let the cake cool in the pan 10 minutes after removing it from the oven.
■ While it's still warm, poke holes in the cake with a wooden pick or skewer (photo 1).
■ Slowly pour the milk mixture over the cake—about ¼ cup at a time—and smooth it in with a spatula or the back of a large spoon (photo 2). You want most of the liquid to be absorbed by the cake, which will make it extremely moist.

Horchata
make ahead
PREP: 10 MIN., COOK: 30 MIN.

This cool, rice-infused drink is a Mexican staple, served at breakfast and as a thirst quencher on hot afternoons. It can be made with milk rather than water.

2 qt. water
½ cup uncooked long-grain white rice
2 Mexican cinnamon sticks ✱
1 cup sugar

1. Bring 2 qt. water, rice, and cinnamon sticks to a boil in a 3½-qt. saucepan over medium heat; cook 25 minutes or until rice is tender. Let cool to room temperature. Remove cinnamon sticks.
2. Puree rice mixture, in batches, in a blender until smooth. Pour mixture into a pitcher; stir in sugar and enough water to equal 2 qt. Cover and chill; serve over ice. **Makes** 2 qt.

✱Substitute regular cinnamon sticks, if desired.

what's for supper?

Lasagna Tonight

Family Meal

Serves 6 to 8

Easy Lasagna

Italian Salad

toasted garlic bread

Spumoni, pistachio, or Neapolitan ice cream with hot fudge sauce

Dine in like you might dine out at a family-style Italian restaurant. Start the lasagna first. While it bakes (about an hour), make the salad, help the kids with homework, or take a few minutes for yourself.

Easy Lasagna
family favorite
PREP: 15 MIN., BAKE: 55 MIN., STAND: 15 MIN.

Scrape the layer of solidified oil from the top of the container of pesto, and discard. Then measure the pesto.

1 lb. mild Italian sausage
1 (15-oz.) container part-skim ricotta cheese
¼ cup refrigerated ready-made pesto
1 large egg, lightly beaten
2 (26-oz.) jars pasta sauce
9 no-boil lasagna noodles
4 cups (16 oz.) shredded Italian three-cheese blend or mozzarella cheese

1. Remove and discard casings from sausage. Cook sausage in a large skillet over medium heat, stirring until meat crumbles and is no longer pink; drain.
2. Stir together ricotta cheese, pesto, and egg.
3. Spread half of 1 jar pasta sauce in a lightly greased 13- x 9-inch baking dish. Layer with 3 lasagna noodles (noodles should not touch each other or sides of dish), half of ricotta mixture, half of sausage, 1 cup three-cheese blend, and remaining half of 1 jar pasta sauce. Repeat layers using 3 lasagna noodles, remaining ricotta mixture, remaining sausage, 1 cup three-cheese blend. Top with remaining 3 noodles and second jar of pasta sauce, covering noodles completely. Sprinkle evenly with remaining 2 cups three-cheese blend.
4. Bake, covered, at 350° for 40 minutes. Uncover and bake 15 more minutes or until cheese is melted and edges are lightly browned and bubbly. Let stand 15 minutes. **Makes** 6 to 8 servings.

Note: For testing purposes only, we used Classico Tomato & Basil spaghetti sauce and Barilla Lasagna Oven-Ready noodles.

VICTORIA AUSTEN MOON
LOUISVILLE, KENTUCKY

Italian Salad
fast fixin's
PREP: 15 MIN.

No need to cook the frozen artichoke hearts—just thaw, and pat dry.

1 head iceberg lettuce (about 1 lb.), torn
1 (9-oz.) package frozen artichoke hearts, thawed ✱
1 (2.25-oz.) can sliced ripe black olives, drained
1 small red bell pepper, chopped
1¼ cups large-cut croutons
½ cup sliced pepperoncini salad peppers
¼ cup chopped red onion
¾ cup refrigerated creamy Asiago-peppercorn or Parmesan-peppercorn dressing
Cracked black pepper (optional)

1. Place lettuce in a 4-qt. bowl. Arrange artichoke hearts and next 5 ingredients over lettuce. Top with dressing; gently toss to combine. Sprinkle with cracked black pepper, if desired. Serve immediately. **Makes** 8 servings.

✱Substitute 1 (14-oz.) can artichoke hearts, drained, if desired.

top-rated menu

Appetizer Favorites

Tempt your friends with a couple of our best-loved party starters. They're tasty, easy to make ahead, and look terrific.

Party Starters

Serves 12 to 24

Peppered Pork With Pecan Biscuits

Marinated Cheese

assorted veggie tray

Peppered Pork With Pecan Biscuits

freezeable • make ahead

PREP: 15 MIN., BAKE: 37 MIN.,
STAND: 15 MIN.

Bake the biscuits in advance, and freeze in a zip-top freezer bag for up to a month.

2 tsp. pepper
1 tsp. salt
1 (2-lb.) package pork tenderloins
1 (¼-oz.) envelope rapid-rise yeast
1 Tbsp. sugar
¾ cup warm water (100° to 110°)
1 (20-oz.) box all-purpose baking mix
½ cup chopped pecans
1 cup buttermilk
¼ cup butter, melted
2 Tbsp. prepared pesto
½ cup all-purpose flour
Coarse-grained Dijon mustard

1. Combine pepper and salt. Rub evenly over pork tenderloins; place on a lightly greased rack in a roasting pan.
2. Bake at 450° for 20 to 25 minutes or until a meat thermometer inserted into thickest portion registers 155°. Let stand 10 minutes before thinly slicing. Reduce oven temperature to 425°.
3. Combine yeast, sugar, and ¾ cup water in a large bowl, and let stand 5 minutes.
4. Add baking mix and next 4 ingredients to yeast mixture, stirring until dry ingredients are moistened. Stir in flour (up to ½ cup) as needed until dough pulls away from sides of bowl. Turn dough out onto a lightly floured surface, and knead gently 2 or 3 times.
5. Pat or roll dough to a 1-inch thickness; cut biscuits with a 1½-inch round cutter. Place biscuits on lightly greased baking sheets.
6. Bake at 425° for 10 to 12 minutes or until lightly browned. Split biscuits; serve sliced pork in biscuits with mustard. **Makes** 5 dozen appetizer sandwiches.

Marinated Cheese

PREP: 10 MIN., CHILL: 8 HRS.

When assembling this recipe, make sure the cream cheese is thoroughly chilled for easier slicing.

1 (0.7-oz.) envelope Italian dressing mix
½ cup vegetable oil
¼ cup white vinegar
2 Tbsp. minced green onions
2 Tbsp. water
1½ tsp. sugar
1 (8-oz.) block Monterey Jack cheese, chilled
1 (8-oz.) block Cheddar cheese, chilled
1 (8-oz.) package cream cheese, chilled
1 (4-oz.) jar chopped pimiento, drained
Assorted crackers

1. Whisk together first 6 ingredients. Set aside.
2. Cut Monterey Jack cheese in half lengthwise. Cut each half crosswise into ¼-inch-thick slices. Repeat with Cheddar cheese and cream cheese.
3. Arrange cheese in 4 rows in a shallow 2-qt. baking dish, alternating Monterey Jack cheese, Cheddar cheese, and cream cheese. Pour marinade over cheese. Cover and chill at least 8 hours.
4. Drain marinade; arrange cheese on a platter in rows. Top with pimiento, and serve with assorted crackers. **Makes** 25 appetizer servings.

Side Solutions

Round out weeknight suppers with great-tasting, budget-stretching dishes that can be pulled together easily.

Great Garlic Bread

PREP: 10 MIN., COOK: 1 MIN., BAKE: 12 MIN.

⅓ cup butter or margarine
4 garlic cloves, minced
1 (16-oz.) French bread loaf, cut into 1-inch slices
2 Tbsp. shredded Parmesan cheese (optional)
1½ Tbsp. chopped fresh or dried rosemary (optional)

1. Melt butter in a small saucepan over medium heat; add minced garlic, and sauté 1 minute or until tender. Remove from heat.
2. Place bread slices on a baking sheet; brush 1 side of each bread slice with butter mixture. Top with Parmesan cheese and rosemary, if desired.
3. Bake at 375° for 10 to 12 minutes or until toasted. **Makes** 8 servings.

Florentine Potato Gratin

PREP: 15 MIN., COOK: 10 MIN., BAKE: 30 MIN.

1 (1-lb., 4-oz.) package refrigerated potato slices
6 cups water
1 Tbsp. salt
1 (10-oz.) package frozen chopped spinach, thawed
¾ tsp. pepper
8 bacon slices, cooked and crumbled
1 (3-oz.) package cream cheese, softened
¾ cup sour cream
1 cup (4 oz.) shredded sharp Cheddar cheese

1. Bring first 3 ingredients to a boil in a large saucepan over medium-high heat; reduce heat, and simmer 8 minutes or until potatoes are tender. Drain and set aside.
2. Drain spinach well, pressing between paper towels.
3. Spread half of potatoes in a lightly greased, 11- x 7-inch baking dish; sprinkle evenly with half of pepper. Spread spinach over potatoes; sprinkle with bacon. Top with remaining potatoes and remaining pepper.
4. Stir together cream cheese and sour cream. Dollop cream cheese mixture evenly over potatoes; sprinkle with shredded cheese.
5. Bake at 400° for 25 to 30 minutes or until golden and bubbly. **Makes** 4 to 6 servings.

Note: For testing purposes only, we used Simply Potatoes Homestyle Slices.
To Lighten: Substitute turkey bacon for bacon, or reduce the amount of regular bacon; use reduced-fat cream cheese and sour cream.

SUSAN RUNKLE
WALTON, KENTUCKY

Glazed Butternut Squash

PREP: 15 MIN., COOK: 30 MIN.

(Pictured on page 11)

3 lb. butternut squash, peeled **✱**
½ cup apple cider **✱**
¼ cup water
2 Tbsp. butter
1 Tbsp. sugar
1 tsp. salt
½ tsp. pepper
¼ cup chopped pecans, toasted
1 Tbsp. chopped fresh or 1 tsp. dried sage

1. Cut squash in half lengthwise; remove and discard seeds. Cut each half into 4 wedges; cut wedges into 2-inch pieces.
2. Stir together squash, ½ cup apple cider, and next 5 ingredients in a 12-inch, deep-sided, nonstick skillet over medium-high heat; bring to a boil. Cover, reduce heat, and simmer, gently stirring occasionally, 25 minutes. Uncover and cook 5 more minutes or until liquid thickens and squash is tender. Gently stir in pecans and sage until well combined. **Makes** 4 servings.

✱Substitute 3 lb. sweet potatoes for butternut squash and ½ cup apple juice for apple cider, if desired.

ESMÉE PAULSEN
WARREN, RHODE ISLAND

Crowd-Pleasing Casseroles

Convenience is the key to these dishes, which are ready for the oven in 30 minutes or less. Frozen veggies team up with pantry items to deliver down-home comfort.

They're also perfect for a potluck. To keep dishes hot when traveling short distances, wrap in heavy-duty aluminum foil, then in several layers of newspaper. Place in a cardboard box, and cover with a thick towel.

Broccoli-Spinach Casserole

PREP: 15 MIN., BAKE: 45 MIN.

2 (10-oz.) packages frozen chopped broccoli, thawed
2 (10-oz.) packages frozen chopped spinach, thawed and drained
2 (10¾-oz.) cans cream of mushroom soup
4 large eggs, lightly beaten
1 large sweet onion, diced
2 cups (8 oz.) shredded sharp Cheddar cheese
1 cup mayonnaise
1 tsp. salt
½ tsp. pepper
½ tsp. garlic powder
36 round buttery crackers, crushed

1. Stir together first 10 ingredients in a large bowl until combined. Spoon mixture into a lightly greased 13- x 9-inch baking dish. Sprinkle with crushed crackers.
2. Bake at 350° for 40 to 45 minutes or until set. **Makes** 12 to 16 servings.

Note: For testing purposes only, we used Ritz crackers.

NORINNE WILSON
WINTER SPRINGS, FLORIDA

Southern-Stuffed Rosemary Chicken

PREP: 25 MIN., BAKE: 20 MIN., COOK: 10 MIN.

2 (6-oz.) packages cornbread stuffing mix
1 large egg, lightly beaten
½ cup finely chopped pecans, toasted
8 skinned and boned chicken breasts
¼ cup olive oil, divided
1 Tbsp. chopped fresh rosemary
1 tsp. salt
½ tsp. pepper
¼ cup grated Parmesan cheese
1 (8-oz.) package sliced fresh mushrooms
4 green onions, sliced
1 (10¾-oz.) can reduced-fat cream of chicken soup
1 cup chicken broth
Garnish: fresh rosemary sprigs

1. Prepare stuffing mix according to package directions, and let cool. Stir in egg and pecans.

2. Butterfly chicken breasts by making a lengthwise cut in 1 side, cutting to but not through the opposite side; unfold. Spoon stuffing mixture down center of one side of each butterflied chicken breast; fold opposite side over stuffing, and place in a lightly greased baking dish. Stir together 3 Tbsp. olive oil and chopped rosemary; brush over chicken. Sprinkle chicken with salt, pepper, and Parmesan cheese.
3. Bake chicken, uncovered, at 400° for 20 minutes or until done.
4. Sauté mushrooms and onions in remaining 1 Tbsp. oil in a large skillet over medium-high heat 5 minutes or until tender; stir in soup and chicken broth. Reduce heat, and simmer, stirring often, 5 minutes or until thoroughly heated. Spoon mushroom mixture evenly over chicken; garnish, if desired. **Makes** 8 servings.

Note: For testing purposes only, we used Stove Top Cornbread Stuffing Mix.

MARY LOU COOK
WELCHES, OREGON

Speckled Butter Beans With Cornbread Crust

PREP: 20 MIN., COOK: 30 MIN., BAKE: 20 MIN.

4 cups chicken broth
2 (16-oz.) bags frozen butter beans
½ tsp. salt
½ tsp. pepper
1 large sweet onion, diced
1 poblano chile, diced
1 Tbsp. olive oil
Cornbread Crust Batter

1. Bring first 4 ingredients to a boil in a large saucepan over medium-high heat. Reduce heat to low; cover and simmer 25 minutes or until beans are tender. Remove from heat.
2. Sauté onion and chile in hot oil in a large skillet over medium-high heat 2 minutes; remove from heat, and stir into beans. Spoon bean mixture into a lightly greased 13- x 9-inch baking dish.
3. Spoon Cornbread Crust Batter over mixture, spreading to edges of dish.
4. Bake at 425° for 20 minutes or until crust is golden brown. **Makes** 6 to 8 servings.

Cornbread Crust Batter:
PREP: 5 MIN.

2 cups cornmeal mix
½ cup buttermilk
½ cup sour cream
2 large eggs, lightly beaten

1. Stir together all ingredients. **Makes** 3 cups.

RHONDA JONES
CALHOUN, GEORGIA

quick & easy
Crispy Chops From the Oven

These oven-fried pork chops have become our new favorite comfort food.

Cornflake-Coated Pork Chops
PREP: 10 MIN., BAKE: 35 MIN.

2 large eggs, lightly beaten
2 Tbsp. milk
5 cups cornflakes cereal, crushed (about 2 cups crushed)
6 boneless pork chops (about ¾ inch thick)
2 tsp. lemon pepper
1 tsp. salt
1 tsp. garlic powder
1 large lemon, halved
Garnish: halved lemon slices

1. Stir together eggs and milk in a shallow dish. Place cornflakes crumbs in a separate shallow dish. Sprinkle pork with lemon pepper, salt, and garlic powder. Dip pork chops in egg mixture, and dredge in cornflakes crumbs. Place on a lightly greased rack on a baking sheet.
2. Bake at 350° for 30 to 35 minutes or until done. Squeeze lemon juice evenly over chops, and garnish, if desired. **Makes** 6 servings.

JESSICA FRYE
WARRIOR, ALABAMA

Crush It Just Right

Make your own coating for oven-baked pork chops. Store any fresh remaining crumbs (ones that had no contact with eggs, milk, or pork) in an airtight container in the freezer up to one month.

Pulse your choice of coating in a food processor or blender to achieve the desired consistency. If you don't have a food processor or blender, use a rolling pin (or even a large drinking glass with a flat bottom) and a zip-top plastic bag to crush the cornflakes cereal or crackers. Be sure to leave a small portion of the plastic bag unsealed to allow air to escape. Our Test Kitchens professionals prefer a medium-coarse texture that includes a variety of crumb sizes.

Make crumbs that are a medium-coarse texture that includes a variety of crumb sizes.

3 ways to make crumbs: food processor, blender, rolling pin

Oven-Fried Pork Chops
family favorite
PREP: 10 MIN., BAKE: 10 MIN.

4 (½-inch-thick) pork chops (about 1½ lb.)
1 tsp. salt
½ tsp. black pepper
⅛ tsp. ground red pepper
1 sleeve saltine crackers, crushed (about 1 cup crushed)
1 large egg, lightly beaten
Vegetable cooking spray

1. Sprinkle pork chops evenly with salt, black pepper, and red pepper. Place cracker crumbs in a shallow dish.
2. Dip chops in egg, and dredge in cracker crumbs. Place on a lightly greased rack on a baking sheet. Spray chops evenly with cooking spray.
3. Bake at 425° for 8 to 10 minutes or until done. **Makes** 4 servings.

SHERRI MITCHELL
HOOVER, ALABAMA

Good-for-You Grains

4. Bake at 350° for 30 minutes or until golden brown. **Makes** 12 servings.

Note: For testing purposes, we used Barilla Plus pasta and Sara Lee Soft & Smooth Whole Grain White Bread.

Per serving: Calories 232 (38% from fat); Fat 9.5g (sat 6g, mono 0.3g, poly 0.2g); Protein 15.6g; Carb 19g; Fiber 2.3g; Chol 30mg; Iron 1.3mg; Sodium 430mg; Calc 364mg

Delight your taste buds with hearty whole grains.

Stock up on Goodness

The 2005 Dietary Guidelines for Americans recommend making half of your daily servings of grain from whole grains. Here's how.
- Substitute brown, wild, or colored rice for white.
- Purchase whole grain versions of staples such as bread, pasta, cereal, and crackers.
- Snack on popcorn (without butter), instead of chips.
- Substitute whole wheat flour for ¼ to ½ of the white flour called for in a recipe.

Chunky Chicken-Barley Soup
PREP: 15 MIN., COOK: 40 MIN.

1 cup chopped onion
1 cup chopped carrot
½ cup chopped celery
2 garlic cloves, minced
2 tsp. olive oil
2 (14½-oz.) cans low-sodium fat-free chicken broth
1¾ cups water
¼ tsp. salt
¼ tsp. dried thyme
¼ tsp. pepper
1 cup chopped cooked chicken
½ cup uncooked quick-cooking barley

1. Sauté first 4 ingredients in hot oil in a large Dutch oven over medium-high heat 5 minutes. Add chicken broth, 1¾ cups water, and next 3 ingredients.

Bring to a boil; reduce heat, and simmer, partially covered, 23 to 25 minutes or until vegetables are tender.
2. Add chicken and barley; cook 8 to 10 minutes or until barley is tender. **Makes** 4 servings.

FRANCES JOHNSON
CROPWELL, ALABAMA

Per (1¼-cup) serving: Calories 208 (17% from fat); Fat 3.9g (sat 0.8g, mono 2.1g, poly 0.7g); Protein 15.4g; Carb 28.4g; Fiber 6g; Chol 30mg; Iron 1.4mg; Sodium 674mg; Calc 46mg

Macaroni-and-Cheese Florentine
PREP: 20 MIN., BAKE: 30 MIN.

1 (8-oz.) package multigrain or whole wheat elbow macaroni
2 cups 2% reduced-fat milk
¼ cup all-purpose flour
½ tsp. pepper
¼ tsp. salt
Dash of ground red pepper
2 (8-oz.) blocks 2% reduced-fat sharp Cheddar cheese, shredded
1 (10-oz.) package frozen spinach, thawed and drained
Butter-flavored cooking spray
½ cup soft whole grain white breadcrumbs (about 1 oz.)

1. Prepare macaroni according to package directions, omitting salt and butter; drain well.
2. Place milk and next 4 ingredients in a quart jar; cover tightly, and shake vigorously 1 minute. Stir together milk mixture, cheese, spinach, and macaroni.
3. Pour macaroni mixture into a 13- x 9-inch baking dish coated with butter-flavored cooking spray. Sprinkle evenly with breadcrumbs; lightly coat breadcrumbs with cooking spray.

Whole Kernel Corn Cornbread
PREP: 15 MIN., BAKE: 35 MIN.
This recipe can be prepared with corn kernels cut straight from the cob, canned corn kernels, or frozen corn kernels that have been defrosted.

1½ tsp. vegetable oil
1 cup whole kernel corn
1 cup 1% low-fat milk
¼ cup honey
2 Tbsp. light butter, melted
2 large eggs
¾ cup all-purpose flour
¼ cup oat bran flour
1 cup cornmeal
4 tsp. baking powder
¾ tsp. salt

1. Coat a 10-inch cast-iron skillet with oil, and place in a 400° oven 10 minutes or until hot.
2. Process corn and milk in a blender or food processor until smooth. Add honey, butter, and eggs; process until blended.
3. Combine flours and next 3 ingredients in a large bowl. Add corn mixture to flour mixture, and stir just until combined. Pour batter into preheated skillet.
4. Bake at 400° for 20 to 25 minutes or until a wooden pick inserted in the center comes out clean. **Makes** 12 servings.

Note: For testing purposes, we used Arrowhead Mills Oat Flour for oat bran flour.

DEBBIE HEALER
FORT WORTH, TEXAS

Per serving: Calories 139 (20% from fat); Fat 3.3g (sat 1.1g, mono 0.6g, poly 0.7g); Protein 4.2g; Carb 25.7g; Fiber 2.4g; Chol 39mg; Iron 1.4mg; Sodium 352mg; Calc 132mg

Healthy Living

Easy ways to have nutritious options—and great flavor—during busy fall days.

Time-Saving Suppers

Each of these favorite recipes packs lots of nutrition in one dish.

A busy fall season begs for quick meals, but don't resort to the drive-through. Try these stress-free, nutritious dinner options; preparation is simple, and cleanup is a snap. Using convenience products such as canned beans, rotisserie chicken, and packaged shredded cheese, these dishes are so easy to fix that even the kids can get involved.

Cheesy Sausage Quiche
family favorite
PREP: 10 MIN., COOK: 16 MIN., BAKE: 30 MIN., STAND: 5 MIN.

1 (8-oz.) package sliced fresh
   mushrooms
½ cup chopped onion (1 small onion)
Vegetable cooking spray
1 (12-oz.) package lean ground pork
   sausage
4 large eggs, lightly beaten *
8 egg whites, lightly beaten *
¼ cup (1 oz.) shredded 2% reduced-fat
   sharp Cheddar cheese
½ cup fat-free milk
¼ tsp. salt
¼ tsp. pepper

1. Sauté mushrooms and onion in a nonstick skillet coated with cooking spray over medium-high heat 8 minutes or until onion is tender. Remove from skillet, and place in a large bowl.

2. Cook sausage in skillet 8 minutes or until sausage crumbles and is no longer pink; drain well on paper towels. Stir together sausage, eggs, and next 4 ingredients with mushroom mixture in bowl. Pour mixture into a 10-inch quiche dish or deep-dish pieplate coated with cooking spray.

3. Bake at 350° for 30 minutes or until set. Let stand 5 minutes before serving. Slice into 8 wedges. **Makes** 8 servings.

* Substitute 1 (1-pt.) carton of egg substitute for the 4 whole eggs and 8 egg whites, if desired.

CAROL S. HENSON
SHARPSBURG, GEORGIA

Per (1 wedge) serving: Calories 183 (56% from fat); Fat 11.2g (sat 4g, mono 1g, poly 0.4g); Protein 16.4g; Carb 3.8g; Fiber 0.4g; Chol 139mg; Iron 1.3mg; Sodium 472mg; Calc 63mg

Healthy Benefits

■ Children of all ages can help in the kitchen. Allowing them to participate in food preparation enhances their knowledge of basic foods, promotes good nutrition, and teaches simple cooking skills.

■ Beans contain phytochemicals and antioxidants, such as magnesium, copper, and selenium, that fight cancer.

Chicken-and-Black Bean Enchiladas
family favorite
PREP: 10 MIN., BAKE: 35 MIN.

3 cups chopped cooked chicken (about 1 rotisserie chicken)
1 (15-oz.) can black beans, rinsed and drained
1 (10-oz.) can diced tomatoes with green chiles
1 (8¾-oz.) can no-salt-added corn, drained
1 (8-oz.) package shredded reduced-fat Mexican four-cheese blend, divided
8 (8-inch) whole wheat flour tortillas
Vegetable cooking spray
2 (10-oz.) cans enchilada sauce
Garnish: cilantro sprig

1. Combine first 4 ingredients and 1½ cups cheese in a large bowl. Spoon chicken mixture evenly down the center of each tortilla, and roll up. Arrange seam side down in a 13- x 9-inch baking dish coated with cooking spray.
2. Pour enchilada sauce evenly over tortillas, and sprinkle evenly with remaining ½ cup cheese.
3. Bake, covered with aluminum foil, at 350° for 20 minutes. Remove foil, and bake 15 more minutes or until bubbly. Garnish, if desired. **Makes** 8 servings.

HOLLIS RUSSELL
VIRGINIA BEACH, VIRGINIA

Per (1 enchilada) serving: Calories 340 (33% from fat); Fat 12.3g (sat 4.3g, mono 1.8g, poly 1g); Protein 29.1g; Carb 28g; Fiber 4.1g; Chol 55mg; Iron 1.9mg; Sodium 897mg; Calc 229mg

Enchilada Step-by-Step

Use a dry measuring cup to scoop mixture onto each tortilla.

Evenly distribute mixture down center of each tortilla.

Roll up, and place seam side down in the baking dish.

Great Flavor, Better Health

Quite possibly the perfect food, nuts not only make a great snack, but they're also chock-full of nutrients. Plus, they add a delicious crunch to almost any recipe.

Nutty Tips

■ Nuts are high in fat (the good kind of fat), so they tend to go rancid easily. Store them in tightly sealed containers or zip-top freezer bags in the refrigerator or freezer up to one year.
■ Toasting enhances the flavor and crunch of nuts. Simply spread them in a large skillet in a single layer over medium-high heat; cook, stirring constantly, until they are golden and aromatic. (Smaller nuts, such as sliced almonds and pine nuts, may take only a minute or so to toast, while larger nuts, such as pecans, may take about 3 to 4 minutes.)

Lemon Roasted Vegetables
PREP: 15 MIN., BAKE: 20 MIN.

2 Tbsp. olive oil
1 Tbsp. fresh lemon juice
1 garlic clove, minced
½ tsp. salt
1 large red bell pepper, cut into 1-inch pieces
1 yellow squash, cut into 1-inch pieces
1 zucchini, cut into 1-inch pieces
1 Tbsp. chopped fresh basil
⅓ cup sliced almonds, toasted

1. Stir together first 4 ingredients in a large bowl; add vegetables, and toss to coat. Place in a single layer in an aluminum foil-lined jelly-roll pan.

2. Bake at 400° for 10 minutes; stir vegetables. Bake 10 more minutes or until tender.

3. Transfer vegetables to a large serving dish; toss with basil, and sprinkle with almonds. **Makes** 4 servings.

SARAH DRURY
NASHVILLE, TENNESSEE

Per serving: Calories 144 (69% from fat); Fat 11.2g (sat 1.3g, mono 7.5g, poly 1.8g); Protein 4.1g; Carb 10.1g; Fiber 3.6g; Chol 0mg; Iron 1.2mg; Sodium 302mg; Calc 50mg

Healthy Benefits

■ Nuts are naturally cholesterol-free as well as good sources of protein and fiber.

■ Research suggests that people who eat nuts tend to exercise more than those who don't.

■ Nuts can make you feel full and suppress hunger. Snack on nuts instead of foods with empty calories, such as potato chips and candy.

Pecan Pancakes
family favorite • make ahead
PREP: 10 MIN., COOK: 6 MIN. PER BATCH
We prefer the hearty thickness of these pancakes. If you like yours thinner, add up to ⅔ cup additional milk to batter.

1 cup all-purpose flour
⅓ cup finely chopped pecans or walnuts, toasted
1 tsp. granulated sugar
1 tsp. light brown sugar
½ tsp. baking powder
½ tsp. ground cinnamon
¼ tsp. baking soda
⅛ tsp. salt
1 cup nonfat buttermilk *
2 Tbsp. vegetable oil
1 large egg

1. Stir together first 8 ingredients until well combined.

2. Whisk together buttermilk, oil, and egg in a bowl; add to flour mixture, stirring just until dry ingredients are moistened.

3. Pour about ¼ cup batter for each pancake onto a hot, lightly greased griddle or large skillet. Cook pancakes 2 to 3 minutes or until tops are covered with bubbles and edges look cooked. Turn and cook other sides. Serve pancakes immediately. **Makes** about 10 pancakes.

Note: Mix up the dry ingredients to keep on hand for an even quicker breakfast meal. Store the mix in an airtight container up to 1 week.

* Substitute ½ cup fat-free milk and 1½ tsp. lemon juice for buttermilk, if desired. Let stand 10 minutes before whisking mixture with egg and oil.

MARIANA VIZZINA
HOOVER, ALABAMA

Per pancake: Calories 117 (48% from fat); Fat 6.3g (sat 0.8g, mono 2.4g, poly 2.8g); Protein 3.2g; Carb 12.6g; Fiber 0.8g; Chol 21.4mg; Iron 0.9mg; Sodium 87mg; Calc 53mg

Thai Noodle Salad
fast fixin's
PREP: 25 MIN.
Find fish sauce in the Asian foods section of the supermarket.

1 (8-oz.) package vermicelli
⅓ cup chopped fresh cilantro
2 garlic cloves, minced
1 jalapeño pepper, seeded and chopped
¼ cup fresh lime juice
1 Tbsp. fish sauce *
1 Tbsp. honey
1½ tsp. sesame oil
¼ tsp. salt
2 carrots, grated
1 cucumber, peeled, seeded, and thinly sliced
1 cup finely shredded cabbage
¼ cup chopped fresh mint
¼ cup chopped dry-roasted peanuts

1. Cook pasta according to package directions. Drain, rinse, and place in a large bowl; set aside.

2. Process cilantro and next 7 ingredients in a food processor until smooth, stopping to scrape down sides.

3. Toss together pasta, cilantro dressing, carrots, and next 3 ingredients. Sprinkle with peanuts, and serve immediately. **Makes** 4 servings.

* Substitute soy sauce for fish sauce, if desired.

HEIDI KINSELLA
WILMINGTON, DELAWARE

Per serving: Calories 329 (19% from fat); Fat 7.2g (sat 1.1g, mono 2.3g, poly 1.5g); Protein 11.5g; Carb 57g; Fiber 4.6g; Chol 0mg; Iron 2.5mg; Sodium 522mg; Calc 53mg

from our kitchen

Creating spectacular cutouts from rolled cookie dough is easier than it looks. Keep these tips in mind when preparing your favorite recipe.

■ For easy rolling, divide the dough into portions, and flatten slightly before chilling.

■ To prevent sticking, lightly dust both the rolling pin and countertop with flour. Too much flour, which incorporates into the dough as it's rolled, will make cookies dry and less tender.

■ Always place the rolling pin in the center of the dough, and roll outward. Decrease pressure as you roll to prevent thinning near the edges.

■ Don't worry if some cookies are a little thinner than others. Rather than reroll (which toughens the dough), place the thinner cookies in the center of the baking sheet and the thicker ones around the edges.

■ Use heavy-duty, shiny aluminum baking sheets with flat edges that allow you to slide cookies off the pan without distorting the shape. Avoid insulated baking sheets that can cause the butter in some doughs to melt and separate before the cookies are set.

■ For crisp-cut edges, place cutouts at least 1 inch apart on the baking sheet, and refrigerate until firm before baking. Never place cookie dough on a warm baking sheet.

■ Create a quick glaze for cookies with ready-to-spread cake frosting. Add food coloring a drop at a time to prepared vanilla frosting until you like the shade. Microwave at HIGH 10 to 15 seconds or until the frosting begins to melt. Stir until smooth, and spread quickly over cookies.

Tips and Tidbits

Make-Ahead Magic

Treat yourself to a batch of fresh-baked cookies anytime. Cookie dough can be stored in the fridge up to three days or frozen up to six months. Here are three make-ahead options.

■ Shape cookie dough into logs, and wrap in parchment paper. To

prevent flattening on one side, place each log inside an empty cardboard tube from gift wrap or paper towels. Place in zip-top freezer bags.

■ Shape dough with a small ice-cream scoop; lightly roll dough between palms to create smooth balls. Place on a baking sheet, freeze until firm, and transfer to a zip-top plastic freezer bag. Allow 2 to 3 minutes extra baking time for frozen dough.

■ Pack dough in an airtight container or zip-top plastic freezer bag. Before baking, thaw frozen dough overnight in the refrigerator.

Top-Rated Cookie Recipes
Fresh-baked cookies are everyone's favorite treat, and they're super easy to make at home. Crisp and buttery, rich and gooey, big or small batches, the cookie recipes we love most can now be part of your e-cookbook collection. Just visit **southernliving.com,** grab a handful of goodies from our "Test Kitchens Recipe Box," and download some fun.

We also share our best cookie-baking secrets. You'll find everything you need to get a jump start on the holiday season, including clever tricks for baking, decorating, and freezing

cookies. If you don't have Internet access at home, ask your local librarian for information on how to go online.

november

Beachside Celebration

No matter where you are, bring some coastal flavor to your Thanksgiving meal.

Some Thanksgiving guests kick off their shoes and opt for bare feet. That's what happens when Ursula Ann and Ed Mazzolini gather family and friends for this holiday celebration. The dazzling blue-green waters of the Gulf of Mexico along with the sound of splashing waves make the ideal backdrop at their Florida home on Blue Mountain Beach in Santa Rosa Beach.

The spectacular ocean view coupled with this menu is an ideal setting for a Thanksgiving-meets-the-tropics dinner. You won't believe how perfectly a fabulous shrimp appetizer and Key Lime Pie pair with traditional turkey and dressing. As for the main attraction, Ursula Ann's Apple-Bourbon Turkey Breast is delightful and surprisingly easy—check out her secret for a no-fail recipe.

Wherever you live, you might just be inspired to create your own beach-style gathering.

Overnight Marinated Shrimp

make ahead

PREP: 20 MIN., COOK: 3 MIN., CHILL: 24 HRS.
Because fresh seafood is always abundant, Ursula Ann often serves peel-and-eat cooked shrimp with cocktail sauce. We shared a marinated shrimp recipe that received our highest rating, and she liked it so much, she served it to great reviews at her family's gathering. (Pictured on page 10)

7½ cups water
3 lbs. unpeeled, large fresh shrimp
2 small red onions, sliced
1 yellow bell pepper, sliced
1 cup vegetable oil
1 cup red wine vinegar
3 Tbsp. sugar
1 Tbsp. grated lemon rind
3 Tbsp. fresh lemon juice
1 Tbsp. white wine Worcestershire sauce
1 Tbsp. hot sauce
1 Tbsp. Dijon mustard
½ tsp. salt
2 garlic cloves, pressed
½ cup chopped fresh basil

1. Bring 7½ cups water to a boil; add shrimp, and cook 2 to 3 minutes or until shrimp turn pink. Drain and rinse with cold water. Peel shrimp, and, if desired, devein.
2. Layer shrimp, onion slices, and bell pepper slices in an airtight container.
3. Whisk together oil and next 9 ingredients; pour over shrimp. Cover and chill 24 hours, stirring occasionally.
4. Stir in ½ cup chopped basil 1 hour before serving. **Makes** 12 to 15 appetizer servings.

Apple-Bourbon Turkey Breast

PREP: 20 MIN.; COOK: 3 MIN.; CHILL: 8 HRS.;
BAKE: 1 HR., 45 MIN.

1 (6-lb.) bone-in turkey breast
Apple-Bourbon Marinade
1 Tbsp. all-purpose flour
1 large oven bag
2 celery ribs
1 medium onion, sliced
2 Tbsp. butter, melted
Garnishes: Key limes, papaya halves
Apple-Bourbon Gravy

1. Rinse turkey breast thoroughly with cold water; pat dry, and set aside.
2. Remove ½ cup Apple-Bourbon Marinade, and reserve for Apple-Bourbon Gravy. Pour remaining 2 cups Apple-Bourbon Marinade into a 2-gal. zip-top plastic freezer bag; add turkey breast. Seal bag, and chill at least 8 hours or up to 24 hours, turning occasionally.
3. Remove turkey breast from bag, discarding marinade.
4. Place flour in oven bag; shake to coat inside of bag. Place bag in a shallow roasting pan; place celery and sliced onion inside bag. Brush turkey breast with melted butter, and place on top of vegetables in bag. Close bag with nylon tie; cut 6 (½-inch) slits in top of bag.
5. Bake at 350° for 1 hour and 45 minutes or until a meat thermometer inserted into thickest portion of turkey breast registers 170°. Remove turkey breast from bag to a serving platter. Pour bag drippings through a wire-mesh strainer into a medium bowl, discarding solids in strainer and reserving drippings (about 2 cups) in bowl for Apple-Bourbon Gravy. Garnish, if desired, and serve with gravy. **Makes** 6 to 8 servings.

Note: If doubling the recipe, simply place both oven bags side by side in the same roasting pan, and bake as directed.

Apple-Bourbon Marinade:
fast fixin's
PREP: 5 MIN.

2 cups apple juice
½ cup bourbon
¼ cup firmly packed brown sugar

1. Stir together all ingredients, stirring until sugar dissolves. **Makes** about 2½ cups.

Apple-Bourbon Gravy:
fast fixin's
PREP: 10 MIN., COOK: 15 MIN.

¼ cup butter
¼ cup all-purpose flour
2 cups reserved drippings
½ cup reserved Apple-Bourbon Marinade
Salt and pepper to taste

1. Melt butter in a saucepan over medium heat; whisk in flour, and cook, whisking constantly, 1 to 2 minutes or until smooth. Gradually add reserved drippings and marinade to pan, and bring to a boil. Reduce heat, and simmer, stirring occasionally, 5 minutes or until thickened. Add salt and pepper to taste. **Makes** about 2½ cups.

Ursula Ann's Secret

To cook the turkey breast, Ursula Ann uses an oven bag. This is a great way to cook a turkey, especially if it's your maiden voyage. The bags are easy to use, make cleanup a snap, and guarantee a juicy bird cooked to perfection.

Cranberry-Key Lime Sauce
fast fixin's • make ahead
PREP: 10 MIN.
While at the beach, Assistant Test Kitchens Director James Schend was inspired to slightly depart from Ursula Ann's original recipe and use Key limes (peel and all) instead of an orange. Now you have two super choices.

1 (12-oz.) bag fresh cranberries ✱
4 Key limes
1 cup sugar
¼ cup fresh mint leaves
2 Tbsp. orange liqueur or fresh orange juice

1. Pulse all ingredients in a food processor 10 to 12 times or until finely chopped, stopping to scrape down sides. Cover and chill until ready to serve. Store in an airtight container in refrigerator up to 2 weeks. **Makes** about 4 cups.

Note: Key limes are smaller, a bit more round, and have a thinner skin than Persian limes.

✱Substitute 1 (12-oz.) bag frozen cranberries, thawed, if desired.

Cranberry-Orange Sauce: Substitute 1 medium unpeeled orange for 4 Key limes. Proceed with recipe as directed. Thin-skinned oranges, such as Valencia or Indian River, work best in this recipe.

Easy Sweet Potato Casserole
PREP: 10 MIN., BAKE: 45 MIN.

3 (40-oz.) cans cut sweet potatoes in syrup, drained
1¼ cups granulated sugar
½ cup butter, softened
½ cup milk
2 large eggs
1¼ tsp. vanilla extract
½ tsp. salt
1¼ cups firmly packed brown sugar
1¼ cups finely chopped pecans
½ cup all-purpose flour
⅓ cup butter, melted

1. Beat first 7 ingredients at medium speed with an electric mixer until smooth. Spoon potato mixture into a lightly greased 13- x 9-inch baking dish. Combine brown sugar and next 3 ingredients. Sprinkle evenly over top of sweet potato mixture.
2. Bake at 350° for 40 to 45 minutes. **Makes** 8 to 10 servings.

JEAN ELLARD
BIRMINGHAM, ALABAMA

Key Lime Pie
PREP: 20 MIN., BAKE: 27 MIN., CHILL: 8 HRS.

1¼ cups graham cracker crumbs
¼ cup sweetened flaked coconut
⅓ cup butter, melted
3 Tbsp. sugar
4 egg yolks
½ cup Key lime juice
1 (14-oz.) can sweetened condensed milk
4 tsp. grated lime rind
1½ cups whipping cream
1½ Tbsp. sugar
½ tsp. vanilla extract
1½ tsp. dark rum (optional)
Garnish: Key lime halves and slices

1. Stir together first 4 ingredients; firmly press on bottom and sides of a 9-inch pieplate.
2. Bake at 350° for 10 to 12 minutes or until lightly browned. Remove to a wire rack, and let cool.
3. Whisk egg yolks just until blended; whisk in lime juice. Add condensed milk, whisking until blended. Stir in lime rind. Pour into prepared crust.
4. Bake at 350° for 12 to 15 minutes or until set. Remove from oven; cool completely on a wire rack. Cover and chill 8 hours.
5. Beat cream until foamy; gradually add 1½ Tbsp. sugar, beating until soft peaks form. Gently stir in vanilla, and, if desired, rum. Spoon whipped cream on top of pie; garnish, if desired. **Makes** 8 to 10 servings.

SHEILA GOODE
SANTA ROSA BEACH, FLORIDA

Ultimate Appetizers

Entertain with full flavor and no guilt when you serve these lightened starters at your next gathering.

Bean-and-Rosemary Bites
fast fixin's
PREP: 10 MIN., BAKE: 7 MIN., COOK: 5 MIN.

1 (8-oz.) French bread loaf
1 garlic clove, minced
½ tsp. fresh rosemary, minced
1 tsp. extra-virgin olive oil
1 (16-oz.) can cannellini or great
   Northern beans, rinsed and drained
¼ tsp. grated lemon rind
¼ tsp. salt
⅛ tsp. dried crushed red pepper

1. Cut bread into 12 (½-inch) slices. Place on a baking sheet. Bake at 375° for 5 to 7 minutes or until toasted.
2. Sauté garlic and rosemary in hot oil in a nonstick skillet over medium-high heat 2 minutes. Stir in beans and next 3 ingredients. Cook until thoroughly heated, stirring frequently and mashing beans partially to desired consistency.
3. Spread about 2½ Tbsp. bean mixture over each bread slice. **Makes** 12 servings.

DORI LANDRY
ALABASTER, ALABAMA

Per serving: Calories 83 (9% from fat); Fat 0.8g (sat 0.1g, mono 0.3g, poly 0.1g); Protein 3.8g; Carb 15.6g; Fiber 1.6g; Chol 0mg; Iron 1.3mg; Sodium 160mg; Calc 50mg

No-Cook Eggnog
PREP: 10 MIN.

1½ cups 2% reduced-fat milk *
¾ cup fat-free half-and-half
¾ cup egg substitute
½ cup sweetened condensed milk
¾ cup egg substitute
2 Tbsp. bourbon
1 tsp. vanilla extract
⅛ tsp. ground nutmeg

1. Whisk together all ingredients in a bowl or pitcher. Cover and chill until ready to serve. **Makes** 6 servings.

Note: For testing purposes, we used Egg Beaters and Silk Vanilla Soymilk.

* Substitute 1½ cups vanilla-flavored soymilk, if desired.

Per (¾-cup) serving: Calories 158 (20% from fat); Fat 3.4g (sat 2.1g, mono 1g, poly 0.1g); Protein 6.7g; Carb 20.2g; Fiber 0g; Chol 13mg; Iron 0.1mg; Sodium 133mg; Calc 168mg

Baked Spinach-and-Artichoke Dip
PREP: 10 MIN., COOK: 7 MIN., BAKE: 15 MIN.

2 (6-oz.) packages fresh baby spinach
1 Tbsp. butter
1 (8-oz.) package ⅓-less-fat cream
   cheese
1 garlic clove, chopped
1 (14-oz.) can artichoke hearts,
   drained and chopped
½ cup light sour cream
½ cup shredded part-skim
   mozzarella cheese, divided
Fresh pita wedges or baked pita chips

1. Microwave spinach in a large, microwave-safe bowl at HIGH 3 minutes or until wilted. Drain spinach well, pressing between paper towels. Chop spinach.
2. Melt butter in a nonstick skillet over medium-high heat. Add cream cheese and garlic; cook 3 to 4 minutes, stirring constantly, until cream cheese melts. Fold in spinach, artichokes, sour cream, and ¼ cup mozzarella cheese; stir until cheese melts.
3. Transfer mixture to a 1-qt. shallow baking dish. Sprinkle with remaining ¼ cup mozzarella cheese.
4. Bake at 350° for 15 minutes or until hot and bubbly. Serve immediately with fresh pita wedges or baked pita chips. **Makes** 11 servings.

Note: Thoroughly wash bagged spinach before using.

FRAN RIFKIN
WOODLAND HILLS, CALIFORNIA

Per (¼-cup) serving (not including pita wedges or baked pita chips): Calories 113 (53% from fat); Fat 7g (sat 4.7g, mono 0.5g, poly 0.1g); Protein 5.5g; Carb 8.5g; Fiber 2.4g; Chol 24mg; Iron 1mg; Sodium 340mg; Calc 71mg

Fabulous Banana Cakes

Stir up a last-minute dessert or a festive holiday gift with one simple, speedy cake batter. Moist and tender, this cake pairs well with a variety of frostings. The inspiration for all these great cakes comes to us from Lillian Watson of Selma, Alabama. Her Double-Delicious Banana Cake is grand enough for any celebration.

Banana Cake Batter
fast fixin's
PREP: 5 MIN.
Ripe bananas, with brown speckles on the yellow peel, add the best flavor. We often toss extra bananas in the freezer to keep on hand, but don't use them in this recipe—after thawing, their syrupy texture prevents the batter from rising properly.

1 (16-oz.) package pound cake mix
3 large bananas, mashed
2 large eggs
⅓ cup milk

1. Beat all ingredients at low speed with an electric mixer 30 seconds. Scrape down sides, and beat at medium speed 3 minutes. Use batter immediately, following directions for desired cake. **Makes** about 6 cups.

Note: For testing purposes only, we used Betty Crocker Pound Cake Mix.

Banana-Pecan Cake Batter: Prepare Banana Cake Batter as directed; stir 1 cup chopped toasted pecans into batter. Use immediately, following directions for desired cake.

Banana-Pecan Pound Cake: Sprinkle ¼ cup chopped toasted pecans evenly on bottom of a greased and floured 10-inch Bundt pan; spoon Banana-Pecan Cake Batter into pan. Bake at 350° for 35 to 40 minutes or until a long wooden pick inserted in center comes out clean. Cool in pan on a wire rack

10 minutes. Remove from pan; cool completely on wire rack. **Makes** 12 servings. Prep: 5 min., Bake: 40 min.

Mini Banana-Pecan Pound Cake Loaves: Spoon Banana-Pecan Cake Batter evenly into 5 (5- x 3-inch) greased and floured loaf pans. Bake at 350° for 30 to 35 minutes or until a wooden pick inserted in center comes out clean. Cool in pans on wire racks 10 minutes. Remove from pans; cool completely on wire racks. **Makes** 5 loaves. Prep: 10 min., Bake: 35 min.

Banana Cupcakes: Place 24 paper baking cups in muffin pans. Spoon Banana Cake Batter evenly into paper cups, filling two-thirds full. Bake at 350° for 20 to 25 minutes or until a wooden pick inserted in center comes out clean. Remove cupcakes from pans; let cool completely on wire racks. **Makes** 24 cupcakes. Top each with Buttercream Frosting. Prep: 10 min., Bake: 25 min.

Double-Delicious Banana Cake
PREP: 20 MIN., BAKE: 22 MIN.

Banana Cake Batter
3 large bananas
1 Tbsp. lemon juice
Buttercream Frosting

1. Spoon Banana Cake Batter evenly into 3 greased and floured 8-inch round cakepans.
2. Bake at 350° for 20 to 22 minutes or until a wooden pick inserted in center comes out clean. Cool in pans on wire racks 10 minutes. Remove from pans; cool completely on wire racks.
3. Cut bananas into ¼-inch-thick slices; toss with lemon juice, and drain on paper towels.
4. Place 1 cake layer on a serving plate; spread top evenly with ½ cup frosting. Arrange half of banana slices in a single layer over the frosting. Spread top of second cake layer evenly with ½ cup frosting; invert frosted side down over first layer, sandwiching banana slices between 2 frosted cake layers. Repeat sandwiching procedure with remaining cake layer. Frost top and sides with remaining frosting. **Makes** 12 servings.

Buttercream Frosting:
fast fixin's
PREP: 10 MIN.
This recipe makes a generous amount of frosting for all the layers of the Double-Delicious Banana Cake. You'll need only half this amount for a sheet cake.

1 cup butter, softened
2 (16-oz.) packages powdered sugar
⅔ cup milk
1 Tbsp. vanilla extract

1. Beat butter at medium speed with an electric mixer until creamy; gradually add powdered sugar alternately with milk, beating at low speed until blended after each addition. Stir in vanilla. **Makes** about 6 cups.

what's for supper?
Cozy Italian Meal

Chilly Day Dinner

Serves 5

Italian Sausage With
Tomato-Pepper Relish

Parmesan Cheese Grits

garlic toast

tossed salad with Italian
dressing

Chocolate-and-Almond Macaroons
(page 262)

This week, detour from the usual spaghetti dinner with our sausage supper. Each recipe has seven ingredients or less and cooks up in no more than an hour.

Italian Sausage With Tomato-Pepper Relish
PREP: 15 MIN., COOK: 1 HR.
You'll find uncooked Italian sausage in the fresh meat or butcher's case in the grocery store. Check the sell-by date stamped on the package. "Sweet" Italian sausage has fresh basil added. "Hot" is made with dried crushed red pepper and is definitely intense. You can try either of these in this recipe. Use fresh sausage within 3 days of purchase, or freeze for up to 30 days.

1 (14.5-oz.) can diced tomatoes with basil, garlic, and oregano
1 (19.76-oz.) package uncooked sweet Italian sausage links
1 cup water
1 large green bell pepper, cut into thin strips
1 large red bell pepper, cut into thin strips
1 medium onion, thinly sliced
2 Tbsp. olive oil
Parmesan Cheese Grits
Garnish: fresh parsley sprigs

1. Drain tomatoes, reserving juice; set tomatoes aside.
2. Brown sausage links in a nonstick skillet over medium heat 4 to 5 minutes on each side. Add reserved tomato juice and 1 cup water; bring to a boil. Cover, reduce heat, and simmer, turning occasionally, 20 to 25 minutes or until thoroughly cooked.
3. Sauté peppers and onion in hot oil in another large nonstick skillet 15 to 20 minutes or until lightly browned. Stir in tomatoes; cook until thoroughly heated. Remove sausage links from skillet, discarding liquid; cut links into bite-size pieces. Serve sausage over Parmesan Cheese Grits; top evenly with pepper mixture. Garnish, if desired. **Makes** 5 servings.

Note: For testing purposes only, we used Johnsonville Sweet Italian Links.

Parmesan Cheese Grits

PREP: 10 MIN., COOK: 15 MIN.

1 (14-oz.) can chicken broth
1½ cups milk
¾ cup uncooked quick-cooking grits
½ tsp. salt
1 cup freshly grated Parmesan cheese
1 tsp. freshly ground pepper

1. Bring chicken broth and 1½ cups milk just to a boil in a large saucepan. Slowly stir in grits and ½ tsp. salt. Cover, reduce heat to medium-low, and cook, stirring occasionally, 6 to 7 minutes or until mixture is thickened. Add Parmesan cheese and pepper, stirring until cheese is melted. **Makes** 5 servings.

Cheddar Cheese Grits: Cook grits as directed, reducing salt to ¼ tsp. and substituting 2 cups (8 oz.) shredded extra-sharp Cheddar cheese for Parmesan cheese.

Try Some Winning Desserts

The culinary talents of Kate Rovner of Plano, Texas, and her daughters Grace, Rachel, and Hope have scored so many ribbons from the State Fair of Texas that it's hard to count them all. Here are a few of their prized champions.

Flourless Peanut Butter-Chocolate Chip Cookies

family favorite

PREP: 10 MIN., BAKE: 12 MIN., COOL: 5 MIN.

1 cup firmly packed
   brown sugar
1 cup chunky peanut butter
1 large egg
1 tsp. baking soda
½ tsp. vanilla extract
1 cup milk chocolate morsels

1. Stir together first 5 ingredients in a medium bowl, using a wooden spoon. Stir in chocolate morsels.
2. Drop cookie dough by rounded tablespoonfuls onto a parchment paper-lined baking sheet.
3. Bake at 350° for 12 minutes or until puffed and golden. (Cookies will be soft in the center.) Cool cookies on baking sheet 5 minutes. Remove to a wire rack. **Makes** 1½ dozen.

Flourless Peanutty-Peanut Butter Cookies: Substitute 1 cup coarsely chopped lightly salted peanuts for milk chocolate morsels. Proceed with recipe as directed.

Cherry-Filled White Chocolate Blondies

freezeable • make ahead

PREP: 15 MIN., COOK: 5 MIN., BAKE: 45 MIN.

½ cup butter
1 (12-oz.) package white chocolate
   morsels, divided
2 large eggs
½ cup sugar
½ tsp. almond extract
1 cup all-purpose flour
½ tsp. salt
½ cup cherry preserves
½ cup sweetened flaked coconut
½ cup sliced almonds

1. Melt butter in a saucepan over low heat, stirring just until melted. Remove pan from heat, and add 1 cup white chocolate morsels. (Do not stir.)
2. Beat eggs at high speed with an electric mixer 2 minutes or until foamy. Gradually add sugar, beating until blended. Stir in white chocolate mixture and almond extract, stirring until blended. Add flour and salt, stirring just until blended. Spread half of batter into a lightly greased and floured 8-inch square pan.
3. Bake at 325° for 20 minutes or until light golden brown.
4. Melt ½ cup cherry preserves in a small saucepan over low heat, stirring often. Spread evenly over partially baked blondies in pan. Stir together coconut,

remaining 1 cup white chocolate morsels, and remaining half of batter; spread over melted cherry preserves, spreading to edges of pan. Sprinkle batter with ½ cup sliced almonds.
5. Bake at 325° for 25 minutes or until lightly browned. Cool completely in pan on a wire rack. Cut into bars. **Makes** 16 bars.

Note: To freeze, tightly wrap baked bars in aluminum foil. Place in a large zip-top freezer bag; seal bag, and freeze up to 2 months. Let thaw at room temperature before cutting.

Raspberry-Filled White Chocolate Blondies: Substitute ½ cup seedless raspberry preserves for cherry preserves. Proceed with recipe as directed.

Apricot-Filled White Chocolate Blondies: Substitute ½ cup apricot preserves for cherry preserves. Proceed with recipe as directed.

Tres Leches Flan

PREP: 20 MIN., COOK: 7 MIN.,
BAKE: 1 HR., CHILL: 8 HRS.

½ cup sugar
1 (8-oz.) package cream cheese,
   softened to room temperature
2 large eggs, at room temperature
2 egg yolks, at room temperature
1 (14-oz.) can sweetened
   condensed milk
1 (12-oz.) can evaporated milk
1½ cups milk
1 tsp. vanilla extract
Hot water (170° to 175°)

1. Cook sugar in a saucepan over medium heat, stirring often, 5 to 7 minutes or until melted and medium-brown in color. Quickly pour into a 9-inch round cake pan with 2-inch sides. Using oven mitts, tilt cakepan to evenly coat bottom and seal edges.
2. Beat cream cheese at medium speed with an electric mixer in a large bowl 1 minute. (Do not overbeat.) Reduce speed to low; add eggs and yolks, and beat until well blended. Add sweetened condensed milk and next 3 ingredients,

beating at low speed 1 minute. (Mixture should not be foamy and may be slightly lumpy.) Pour milk mixture over sugar in pan. Place cakepan in a roasting pan; add hot water halfway up sides of cakepan.

3. Bake at 325° for 1 hour or until edges are set. (The middle will not be set.) Remove from oven; remove cakepan from water, and place on a wire rack. Let cool completely. Cover and chill at least 8 hours. Run a knife around edges to loosen, and invert onto a serving platter. **Makes** 8 servings.

Note: The flan will continue to set as it cools and will set completely when it is chilled.

Set the Table for Two

Memorable Meal

Serves 2

Cornish Hens With Savory-Sweet Stuffing

Tiny Green Beans Amandine

Basil-Thyme Crème Brûlée

An intimate meal to celebrate Thanksgiving can be really lovely, especially when you plan an elegant menu. Think small—after all, two people and a turkey can be an endless proposition. These cornish game hens offer rich flavor and handsome presentation with easy preparation.

Cornish Hens With Savory-Sweet Stuffing
PREP: 20 MIN.; BAKE: 1 HR., 30 MIN.; STAND: 5 MIN.

2 (1½- to 1¾-lb.) Cornish game hens
1½ tsp. salt, divided
½ tsp. pepper, divided
1 Granny Smith or Golden Delicious apple
1 cup butternut squash, peeled, seeded, and cut into ½-inch cubes
1 cup coarsely chopped fennel, white part only
¼ cup dried cranberries
1 medium shallot, coarsely chopped
1 tsp. olive oil

1. Rinse hens with cold water; pat dry.
2. Combine 1 tsp. salt and ¼ tsp. pepper. Sprinkle cavities and outside of hens with salt mixture. Set hens aside.
3. Peel apple, and cut into 1-inch cubes.
4. Combine apple, remaining ½ tsp. salt, remaining ¼ tsp. pepper, squash, and next 4 ingredients in a medium bowl, tossing to coat.
5. Stuff hen cavities with apple mixture; place extra mixture in a lightly greased 11- x 7-inch baking dish. Place hens on top of apple mixture; cover tightly with aluminum foil.
6. Bake at 350° for 45 minutes; remove foil, and bake 45 more minutes or until meat juices run clear and an instant-read thermometer inserted into thigh registers 180° and internal temperature in center of stuffing registers 190°. Remove from oven; let stand 5 minutes before serving. **Makes** 2 servings.

BARBARA D. SPITZER
LODI, CALIFORNIA

Tiny Green Beans Amandine
fast fixin's
PREP: 5 MIN., COOK: 10 MIN.
Haricots verts (ah-ree-koh-VEHR), tiny French green beans, can be found in the produce section of large supermarkets or in gourmet markets.

½ lb. tiny green beans *(haricots verts)*
1 Tbsp. butter
2 Tbsp. sliced almonds
Salt and pepper to taste

1. Cook beans in boiling salted water 5 minutes or until crisp-tender; drain.
2. Melt butter in a medium skillet over medium heat until hot; add almonds, and sauté 2 minutes or until golden.
3. Add beans to skillet; sauté 2 minutes. Sprinkle beans with salt and pepper to taste. Serve immediately. **Makes** 2 servings.

Basil-Thyme Crème Brûlée
PREP: 10 MIN., COOK: 5 MIN., STAND: 35 MIN., BAKE: 35 MIN., CHILL: 3 HRS., BROIL: 3 MIN.
Make the custards a day or two ahead, and broil them just before serving to produce a crackly topping.

1 cup whipping cream
¼ cup sugar
½ vanilla bean, split lengthwise
1½ Tbsp. chopped fresh basil
1 tsp. chopped fresh thyme leaves
3 large egg yolks
2½ tsp. sugar

1. Heat cream and sugar over medium-high heat, stirring constantly, 3 to 4 minutes or until sugar dissolves. Stir in vanilla bean, basil, and thyme. Bring mixture to a simmer, and remove from heat. Let stand 5 minutes.
2. Whisk in egg yolks. Pour mixture through a fine wire-mesh strainer into a bowl, discarding herbs. Pour mixture evenly into 2 (6-oz.) ramekins; place ramekins in an 11- x 7-inch baking dish. Add hot water to dish to a depth of ½ inch.
3. Bake at 275° for 35 minutes or until almost set. Remove from water bath, and let stand 30 minutes; cover and chill at least 3 hours.
4. Sprinkle 1¼ tsp. sugar evenly over each custard. Broil 5 inches from heat 3 minutes or until sugar is browned. Serve immediately. **Makes** 2 servings.

Holiday Dinners®

"Irresistible" describes the recipes on these pages. Whether you need a fast appetizer, a dinner party plan, a casual potluck idea, or a dessert so tempting you'll sneak a sample before your guests arrive—we have it here.

Host an Amazing Dinner

Peek inside this Virginia couple's Twelfth Night celebration—you'll want to plan your own.

An Elegant Evening Menu
Serves 8

Kir Royale

assorted cheeses, crackers, breads, and fruit

Champagne Salad With Pear-Goat Cheese Tarts

Apricot-Ginger Salmon

Citrus Sweet Potatoes

Sautéed Beans and Peppers

Easy Apple Tart With Ol' South Custard

It's January 6, and in this Roanoke, Virginia, home, you'll find four couples laughing, three beaded Christmas trees sparkling, two fabulous people hosting, and one elegant and easy menu being served. "We wait until the holiday hoopla is behind us and host a Twelfth Night celebration," says Mary Ellen Stokes. "My husband, Bill, and I have what we call the '3K rule' for gatherings. Keep it simple, keep it organized, and keep it familiar."

Kir Royale
fast fixin's
PREP: 10 MIN.

10 Tbsp. crème de cassis
2 (750-milliliter) bottles Champagne or sparkling white wine

1. Pour 1 Tbsp. liqueur into each of 10 Champagne flutes; fill with Champagne. **Makes** 10 servings.

Champagne Salad With Pear-Goat Cheese Tarts
fast fixin's • make ahead
PREP: 10 MIN.
Make the vinaigrette and Sugared Walnuts three days ahead. Partially bake tart shells and mix the pear-goat cheese filling before guests arrive. (Pictured on page 189)

2 (5-oz.) bags gourmet mixed salad greens
⅓ cup sweetened dried cranberries
Sugared Walnuts
Pear-Goat Cheese Tarts
Champagne Vinaigrette

1. Combine salad greens and cranberries in a large bowl. Arrange mixture on a serving plate. Sprinkle evenly with Sugared Walnuts. Top with 8 Pear-Goat Cheese Tarts. Serve immediately with Champagne Vinaigrette. **Makes** 8 servings.

Sugared Walnuts:
fast fixin's • make ahead
PREP: 5 MIN., COOK: 10 MIN.

1½ cups walnut halves
¾ cup sugar

1. Stir together walnuts and sugar in a heavy saucepan over medium heat, and cook, stirring constantly, 8 to 10 minutes or until sugar melts and turns golden brown.

2. Spread mixture in a single layer on lightly greased wax paper; cool. Break into pieces; store in an airtight container up to 3 days. **Makes** 1½ cups.

Pear-Goat Cheese Tarts:
PREP: 20 MIN., BAKE: 18 MIN., COOL: 2 MIN.
Leftover tarts are great for breakfast the next morning.

1 (15-oz.) package refrigerated piecrusts
2 (4-oz.) packages goat cheese, crumbled
1 to 2 ripe pears, chopped
2 Tbsp. honey
½ tsp. dried thyme

1. Unroll piecrusts, and cut each in half; cut each half into 3 pieces. Place 1 piece into a lightly greased muffin cup in a muffin pan. Fold and press pastry piece to form a cup shape. Repeat procedure with remaining pastry pieces.

2. Bake at 375° for 8 minutes or until edges of pastries are lightly browned. Remove pan to a wire rack.

3. Stir together goat cheese and next 3 ingredients. Spoon evenly into pastry shells.

Refrigerated piecrusts and bagged salad greens are the secrets to a swift prep time of Champagne Salad With Pear-Goat Cheese Tarts.

4. Bake at 375° for 8 to 10 minutes or until thoroughly heated. Remove to a wire rack, and let cool 2 minutes. **Makes** 12 tarts.

Champagne Vinaigrette:
make ahead
PREP: 10 MIN., CHILL: 30 MIN.

¼ cup extra virgin olive oil
¼ cup Champagne vinegar
2 Tbsp. Dijon mustard
2 tsp. honey
¾ tsp. salt
¼ tsp. freshly ground pepper

1. Whisk together all ingredients. Cover and chill at least 30 minutes or up to 3 days. **Makes** about ¾ cup.

Apricot-Ginger Salmon
fast fixin's
PREP: 10 MIN., COOK: 4 MIN., BAKE: 6 MIN., STAND: 2 MIN.
If you're unsure whether or not your skillet handle is ovenproof, double-wrap it with heavy-duty aluminum foil. Mary Ellen saves time by using 1 cup of The Greenbrier resort's Apricot-Ginger Grilling Sauce (available in 12-oz. bottles by calling 1-800-321-1168). Allow for shipping time before your party, or use our quick interpretation of the original. (Pictured on page 188)

8 (6-oz.) salmon fillets
½ tsp. salt
½ tsp. pepper
Apricot-Ginger Sauce

1. Sprinkle fillets evenly with salt and pepper. Cook skin sides up in a lightly greased, large, ovenproof nonstick skillet over medium-high heat 2 minutes; turn and cook 2 more minutes. Pour Apricot-Ginger Sauce over salmon.

2. Bake at 350° for 4 to 6 minutes or until a sharp knife is warm to the touch when inserted into center of fillet and removed. Remove from oven, and let stand 2 minutes. **Makes** 8 servings.

Apricot-Ginger Sauce:
fast fixin's • make ahead
PREP: 5 MIN.

½ cup vegetable oil
3 Tbsp. raspberry vinegar
2 Tbsp. apricot preserves
2 Tbsp. honey mustard
1 Tbsp. honey
½ tsp. salt
½ tsp. fresh coarsely ground pepper
½ tsp. ground ginger

1. Process all ingredients in a blender or food processor until smooth. Cover and refrigerate up to 1 week. **Makes** 1 cup.

Citrus Sweet Potatoes
fast fixin's • make ahead
PREP: 15 MIN., COOK: 15 MIN.
For a more intense flavor, bake whole sweet potatoes, instead of boiling them, at 350° for 1½ hours or until tender. (Pictured on page 188)

5 to 6 medium-size sweet potatoes (about 3½ lb.)
2 Tbsp. light brown sugar
2 Tbsp. fresh lime juice
2 Tbsp. honey
½ tsp. salt
⅛ tsp. ground nutmeg
⅛ tsp. ground cinnamon

1. Peel potatoes; cut into 1-inch pieces.

2. Bring potatoes and water to cover to a boil in a large saucepan, and cook 12 minutes or until tender.

3. Drain and return potatoes to pan. Add remaining ingredients. Mash with a potato masher or fork until smooth. **Makes** 8 servings.

Note: To make ahead, spoon mashed potato mixture into a large baking dish; cover and keep warm in a 350° oven up to 1 hour.

Sautéed Beans and Peppers

fast fixin's • make ahead

PREP: 10 MIN., COOK: 10 MIN.

Cook green beans the day before the party. Pat dry with paper towels, and store in a zip-top plastic bag. (Pictured on page 1 and page 188)

2 lb. fresh green beans
1 red bell pepper, cut into thin strips
1 yellow bell pepper, cut into thin strips
1 to 2 Tbsp. olive oil
1 Tbsp. chopped fresh basil
½ tsp. salt

1. Cook green beans in boiling salted water to cover in a Dutch oven over medium-high heat 4 to 5 minutes or until crisp-tender. Drain and plunge into ice water to stop the cooking process; drain.
2. Sauté peppers in hot oil in a Dutch oven over medium-high heat 5 minutes or until tender. Add beans, basil, and salt. Cook, stirring constantly, until thoroughly heated. Serve immediately. **Makes** 8 servings.

Easy Apple Tart With Ol' South Custard

PREP: 20 MIN., COOK: 30 MIN., BAKE: 12 MIN., COOL: 15 MIN.

Roll out the puff pastry no more than 10 minutes before apples are done; the pastry needs to stay as cold as possible for maximum puff. (Pictured on page 189)

12 to 14 Rome or Braeburn apples
    (about 7 lb.)
1½ cups sugar
1 (17.3-oz.) package frozen puff pastry
    sheets, thawed
Ol' South Custard

1. Peel and core apples; cut in half lengthwise. Toss together apples and sugar; place in a 12-inch cast-iron or ovenproof skillet.
2. Cook over medium-high heat, stirring often, 20 to 30 minutes or until apples soften and start to caramelize.
3. Unfold and stack pastry sheets on top of each other on a lightly floured surface. Roll to a 12-inch square. Place on top of cooked apples, with pastry cor-

ners overlapping sides of skillet.
4. Bake at 450° for 10 to 12 minutes or until dark golden brown.
5. Cool on a wire rack 10 to 15 minutes. Carefully invert tart onto a serving plate; remove skillet. Cut tart into wedges, and serve with Ol' South Custard. **Makes** 8 servings.

Ol' South Custard:

make ahead

PREP: 10 MIN., COOK: 20 MIN., CHILL: 24 HRS.

"Our wonderful neighbor Mildred Williams made Ol' South Custard to serve over this masterful dessert," explains Bill.

1 qt. milk
4 large eggs
1 cup sugar
2 tsp. vanilla extract
¼ tsp. salt

1. Cook milk in a heavy nonaluminum saucepan over medium heat, stirring often, 10 minutes or just until it begins to steam. (Do not boil.) Remove from heat.
2. Whisk together eggs and next 3 ingredients until blended. Gradually whisk 1 cup hot milk into egg mixture; whisk egg mixture into remaining hot milk, stirring constantly.
3. Cook over medium heat, stirring constantly, 8 to 10 minutes or until a thermometer registers between 170° and 180°. (Do not boil.)
4. Remove from heat, and pour mixture through a fine wire-mesh strainer into a bowl. Place heavy-duty plastic wrap directly on warm custard to prevent a film from forming on top, and chill at least 24 hours or up to 3 days. Mixture will thicken as it cools. **Makes** 5 cups.

For Easy Apple Tart, place sugared apple halves in a 12-inch skillet (photo 1). As the apples cook, they'll reduce in size and soften. Place puff pastry directly on top of apples in skillet (photo 2).

Friends' Gathering

Christmas Luncheon

Serves 6

Pineapple-Nut Cheese With
Cranberry Chutney

Orange-Cranberry-Glazed
Pork Tenderloin

Pecan Wild Rice

Mandarin-Almond Salad

Belgian Wassail

Each year, a group of friends in Kentucky pulls out their finest serving pieces and gathers for a Christmas luncheon. The only rule: "No husbands allowed," says Kay Buskov, who hosted last year's event at her home in Madisonville. Enjoy this collection of recipes that has shown up on the table during many of the the group's gatherings.

Pineapple-Nut Cheese With Cranberry Chutney

PREP: 20 MIN., CHILL: 1 HR.

Be sure to drain the pineapple well before stirring it in. Simply pour the fruit into a wire-mesh strainer, and press the pineapple with the back of a spoon to remove excess juice.

2 (8-oz.) packages cream cheese,
    softened
1 (8½-oz.) can crushed pineapple,
    well drained
¼ cup finely chopped green bell
    pepper
2 Tbsp. finely chopped onion
1 tsp. seasoned salt
1½ cups chopped pecans, toasted
Cranberry Chutney
Assorted crackers

1. Beat cream cheese at medium speed with an electric mixer until smooth. Gradually stir in pineapple, next 3 ingredients, and 1 cup pecans. Transfer to a serving bowl. Sprinkle evenly with remaining ½ cup pecans. Chill 1 hour or until firm. Serve with Cranberry Chutney and crackers. **Makes** 10 to 12 appetizer servings.

Cranberry Chutney:
fast fixin's

PREP: 15 MIN., COOK: 15 MIN.
Store leftover chutney in an airtight container in the refrigerator up to a week. Serve it with fried turkey, roasted pork tenderloin, or grilled pork chops.

1 cup water
¾ cup sugar
3 cups fresh cranberries (12 oz.)
1 pink grapefruit, peeled, seeded, and
    chopped
1 orange, peeled, seeded, and chopped
1 Granny Smith apple, peeled and diced
1 Anjou pear, peeled and diced
1½ cups mixed dried fruit
1 tsp. ground cinnamon
½ tsp. ground nutmeg
¼ tsp. ground cloves
⅛ tsp. salt

1. Bring 1 cup water to a boil over medium heat; add sugar, stirring until dissolved. Reduce heat to medium-low; stir in cranberries and remaining ingredients, and simmer, stirring constantly, 10 minutes. Remove from heat, and let cool. **Makes** about 4½ cups.

Orange-Cranberry-Glazed Pork Tenderloin

PREP: 10 MIN., COOK: 30 MIN.,
BAKE: 25 MIN., STAND: 5 MIN.

1 (16-oz.) can whole-berry cranberry
    sauce
1 tsp. grated orange rind
⅔ cup fresh orange juice
2 tsp. balsamic vinegar
½ tsp. pepper
¼ tsp. ground allspice
⅛ tsp. salt
⅛ tsp. ground cinnamon
⅛ tsp. ground cloves
1½ lb. pork tenderloin, trimmed
1½ Tbsp. olive oil
Garnishes: halved oranges slices, fresh
    thyme sprigs

1. Bring first 9 ingredients to a boil over medium heat. Reduce heat, and simmer, stirring occasionally, 20 minutes. Remove half of mixture, and set aside.
2. Brown pork in hot oil in a large non-stick skillet over medium-high heat 3 minutes on each side or until golden brown. Place pork in a lightly greased, shallow roasting pan.
3. Bake at 425° for 25 minutes or until a meat thermometer inserted into thickest portion registers 155°, basting occasionally with half of cranberry mixture. Remove from oven; cover pork with aluminum foil, and let stand 5 minutes or until thermometer registers 160°. Slice pork, and serve with reserved cranberry mixture. Garnish, if desired. **Makes** 6 servings.

Cook's Notes: Easy Grating

The rind from some citrus fruits adds bold flavor, but it's important not to grate into the bitter white pith. A Microplane grater, available at any super-store, can help. It delicately grates certain foods, lending a finer grate with more volume than what a box grater produces. Use it for zesting fruits or for grating cinnamon sticks, chocolate, nutmeg, fresh ginger, and hard cheeses such as Parmesan.

Pecan Wild Rice

PREP: 20 MIN., COOK: 8 MIN.

1⅓ cups chicken broth
2 tsp. butter
¼ tsp. salt
1 (2.75-oz.) package quick-cooking wild rice
4 green onions, thinly sliced
½ cup golden raisins
⅓ cup chopped pecans, toasted
1 tsp. grated orange rind
⅓ cup fresh orange juice
¼ cup chopped fresh parsley
1 Tbsp. olive oil
¼ tsp. salt
¼ tsp. pepper

1. Bring first 3 ingredients to a boil in a medium saucepan. Add rice; cover, reduce heat, and simmer 5 minutes or until rice is tender. Drain off excess liquid. Fluff with a fork. Add green onions and remaining ingredients; toss gently to combine. **Makes** 4 to 6 servings.

Mandarin-Almond Salad

PREP: 15 MIN., COOK: 10 MIN., COOL: 20 MIN.

½ cup slivered almonds
¼ cup sugar
¼ cup vegetable oil
2 Tbsp. red wine vinegar
1 Tbsp. minced fresh parsley
½ tsp. salt
⅛ tsp. pepper
3 drops hot pepper sauce
1 Tbsp. sugar
1 bunch green leaf lettuce, torn (8 cups)
1 (11-oz.) can mandarin oranges, drained
½ small red onion, thinly sliced

1. Place almonds and ¼ cup sugar in a small saucepan over medium heat. Cook, stirring constantly, 10 minutes or until sugar coats almonds and turns golden. Spread in a single layer on lightly greased wax paper; cool 20 minutes. Break into pieces, and set aside.

2. Combine oil and next 6 ingredients in a jar with a lid. Tightly close lid, and shake well. Chill until ready to serve.
3. Toss together lettuce, oranges, onion, and almonds. Shake dressing, and drizzle over salad just before serving. **Makes** 6 servings.

Belgian Wassail

PREP: 15 MIN., COOK: 30 MIN.
To make clove-studded orange slices, poke small holes around the edges of each slice with a fork or knife, and insert whole cloves.

2 oranges
2 lemons
1 gal. apple cider
1 cup sugar
2 (3-inch) cinnamon sticks
1 tsp. whole allspice
Garnish: clove-studded orange slices

1. Squeeze juice from oranges and lemons into a bowl, reserving rinds.
2. Bring citrus juice, rinds, apple cider, and next 3 ingredients to a boil over medium-high heat. Reduce heat, and simmer 25 minutes. Pour mixture through a wire-mesh strainer into a container, discarding solids. Garnish, if desired. **Makes** about 1 gal.

Note: This may be enjoyed hot or cold. To serve warm, keep the beverage in coffee carafes or a slow cooker.

Make It Special

Hanukkah Celebration

Serves 8

Beef Tenderloin
Steamed Brussels Sprouts
Lemon Chess Pie

This party is all about combining the perfect atmosphere with simple recipes. Madeline and Jerry E. Abramson, the first lady and mayor of Louisville, Kentucky, go all out for their annual Hanukkah celebrations. The table sets the beautiful mood and includes touches that honor Louisville.

Beef Tenderloin

PREP: 10 MIN., BAKE: 50 MIN., STAND: 15 MIN.

1 cup dry sherry
1 cup lite soy sauce
5 green onions, finely chopped
1 (5- to 6-lb.) beef tenderloin, trimmed
2 Tbsp. olive oil
Garnish: rosemary sprigs

1. Stir together first 3 ingredients.
2. Rub tenderloin with olive oil, and place on a wire rack in a roasting pan. Pour sherry mixture into pan.
3. Bake at 450° for 45 to 50 minutes, basting occasionally, or until a meat thermometer inserted into thickest portion registers 140° for medium rare. Bake longer until thermometer registers 160° for medium or 170° for medium well.
4. Cover tenderloin loosely with aluminum foil; let stand 15 minutes before slicing. Garnish, if desired. Serve with pan drippings. **Makes** 12 to 14 servings.

Steamed Brussels Sprouts

fast fixin's

PREP: 10 MIN., COOK: 12 MIN.

Serve these with one of your favorite potato latke recipes.

3 lb. fresh Brussels sprouts
½ tsp. salt
¼ tsp. pepper
½ cup water
2 Tbsp. olive oil
2 tsp. grated lemon rind (about
   1 lemon)
1 Tbsp. fresh lemon juice

1. Remove discolored leaves from sprouts. Cut off stem ends; cut in half lengthwise. Place sprouts in a 2-qt. microwave-safe dish. Sprinkle with salt and pepper; add water.
2. Cover and microwave squares at HIGH for 10 to 12 minutes or until tender; drain.
3. Toss Brussels sprouts with oil, lemon rind, and lemon juice. Serve immediately. **Makes** 8 servings.

Lemon Chess Pie

PREP: 25 MIN.; BAKE: 1 HR., 6 MIN.

To keep kosher, you'll want to wait at least three hours after the main meal before serving this dairy-enriched dessert.

½ (15-oz.) package refrigerated
   piecrusts
2 cups sugar
1 Tbsp. all-purpose flour
1 Tbsp. yellow cornmeal
¼ cup butter, melted
¼ cup milk
¼ cup fresh lemon juice
1 tsp. grated lemon rind
4 large eggs, lightly beaten
Whipped cream (optional)
Garnishes: fresh raspberries,
   lemon slice

1. Fit pastry into a 9-inch pieplate according to package directions; fold edges under, and crimp. Line piecrust with aluminum foil, and fill with pie weights or dried beans.

2. Bake at 425° for 7 minutes. Remove weights and foil, and bake 4 more minutes. Reduce oven temperature to 350°.
3. Whisk together sugar and next 6 ingredients until blended. Add eggs, whisking well. Pour mixture into prepared piecrust.
4. Bake at 350° for 50 to 55 minutes or until golden, shielding edges with aluminum foil to prevent excessive browning, if necessary. Cool completely on a wire rack. Serve with whipped cream, if desired. Garnish, if desired. **Makes** 8 servings.

Nibbles in No Time

Fig-and-Blue Cheese Bruschetta

fast fixin's

Jill Kucera, owner of Catering Works in Raleigh, North Carolina, said this is one of her most requested holiday recipes.

36 (¼-inch-thick) French baguette slices
1 (3-oz.) package cream cheese, softened
½ cup (2 oz.) crumbled blue cheese
½ cup fig preserves or jam

1. Broil baguette slices on a baking sheet 3 inches from heat 1 to 2 minutes on each side or until lightly toasted. Remove baking sheet, and reduce oven temperature to 350°.
2. Stir together cream cheese and blue cheese in a small bowl until well blended. Spread a heaping ½ tsp. cream cheese mixture onto each baguette slice, and top each with a rounded ½ tsp. fig preserves.
3. Bake at 350° on middle rack for 8 to 10 minutes or until thoroughly heated. **Makes** 12 appetizer servings.

Note: For testing purposes only, we used Braswell's Fig Preserves.

Fast Appetizers

Jill's list of staple ingredients includes blocks of natural cheese, ready-to-use salsa, pesto, pimiento cheese spread, Melba toast rounds, assorted crackers, and chilled wine or sparkling fruit juice. Here are a few of her fast ideas.

Quick Cheese Tray: Slice 1 (8-oz.) block sharp Cheddar or Havarti cheese crosswise into ¼-inch-thick slices. Cut 1 (8-oz.) Edam cheese round into quarters. Cut each quarter into 2 pieces, keeping wax intact. Arrange cheese on tray. Serve with Melba toast rounds, crackers, grapes, and pear slices.

Jalapeño Cream Cheese Appetizer: Place 1 (8-oz.) package cream cheese on a serving dish. Spoon ½ cup jalapeño pepper jelly over cream cheese. Garnish with pickled jalapeño pepper rings and a sprig of cilantro. Serve with bite-size corn chips.

Pimiento Cheese Spread With Vegetables: Spoon 2 cups prepared pimiento cheese into a small serving bowl or 4 (4-oz.) ramekins. Serve with celery sticks and baby carrots.

Pronto Salsa Layered Dip: Spread 2 cups prepared salsa mixed with 2 Tbsp. fresh lime juice on bottom of a large, shallow platter. (Drain off excess liquid from salsa to keep mixture thick.) Spread 1½ cups prepared guacamole over salsa, leaving a 1-inch border of salsa around edges. Spoon ¼ cup sour cream into a small zip-top plastic bag. Snip 1 corner of bag; pipe sour cream across top of guacamole in a decorative pattern. Sprinkle with 1 cup (4 oz.) shredded Monterey Jack cheese and ¼ cup chopped cilantro. Serve with tortilla chips.

Cookie Swap

Enjoy the ultimate goodie exchange
with these yummy recipes.

This trio hosts a gem of a cookie swap in their Long Valley neighborhood in the not-so-Southern state of New Jersey. Diane Kent lived in North Carolina and Terry Holman in Florida before moving to this delightful town one hour west of New York City. One day, while talking about Southern holiday traditions with friend Lila Kosciolek, the three got the idea to host their neighborhood's first cookie exchange. This year marks the sixth event. These recipes just might inspire you to host your own.

Fruit-Filled Cookies
family favorite
PREP: 30 MIN., STAND: 10 MIN.,
CHILL: 30 MIN., BAKE: 20 MIN. PER BATCH,
COOL: 5 MIN.
We loved Sherry Salo's yeast cookie dough so much that we made a variation called Snowflake Cookies. (Pictured on page 191)

3 cups all-purpose flour
1 Tbsp. granulated sugar
½ tsp. salt
1 cup butter, cut into pieces
1 (¼-oz.) envelope active dry yeast
½ cup warm milk (100° to 110°)
1 large egg, lightly beaten
½ tsp. vanilla extract
Powdered sugar
1 (12-oz.) can apricot or cherry dessert filling

1. Stir together first 3 ingredients. Cut butter into flour mixture with a pastry blender or 2 forks until crumbly.
2. Whisk together yeast and warm milk. Let stand 10 minutes. (Mixture does not foam.) Stir in egg and vanilla.

Add milk mixture to flour mixture, stirring until dry ingredients are moistened. Divide dough into fourths; wrap each portion in plastic wrap, and chill 30 minutes.
3. Roll each portion of dough to ⅛-inch thickness on a flat surface lightly dusted with powdered sugar. Cut into 3-inch squares. Spoon 1 heaping teaspoonful of apricot or cherry dessert filling in center of each square.
4. Fold 2 opposite corners to center, slightly overlapping. Place on parchment paper-lined baking sheets.
5. Bake at 350° for 18 to 20 minutes or until lightly golden. Cool cookies on baking sheet 5 minutes. Remove to wire racks, and let cool completely. Sprinkle cookies with powdered sugar before serving. **Makes** 3 dozen.

Note: For testing purposes only, we used Solo Filling for Pastries, Cakes, and Desserts.

SHERRY SALO
LONG VALLEY, NEW JERSEY

Snowflake Cookies: *(Pictured on page 189)* Omit dessert filling. Prepare and roll out dough as directed. Cut dough with a 3¾-inch snowflake-shaped cookie cutter. Place on parchment paper-lined baking sheets. Sprinkle with sparkling sugar. Bake at 350° for 10 minutes or until lightly golden. Cool cookies as directed. **Makes** about 5 dozen. Prep: 20 min., Stand: 10 min., Chill: 30 min., Bake: 10 min. per batch., Cool: 5 min.

Mom's Brown Sugar Bars
family favorite
PREP: 10 MIN., BAKE: 15 MIN., STAND: 5 MIN.
Press dough into the jelly-roll pan with lightly floured fingertips.

1 cup butter, softened
1 cup firmly packed light brown sugar
1 large egg
1 tsp. vanilla extract
2 cups all-purpose flour
½ tsp. baking powder
½ tsp. salt
1 (12-oz.) package semisweet chocolate morsels
1½ cups sliced almonds

1. Beat butter and brown sugar at medium speed with an electric mixer until creamy. Add egg and vanilla, beating until blended.
2. Combine flour, baking powder, and salt; gradually add to butter mixture, beating until blended.
3. Press dough into an ungreased 15- x 10-inch jelly-roll pan.
4. Bake at 350° for 12 to 15 minutes or until golden. Place pan on a wire rack. Sprinkle chocolate morsels evenly over warm cookie. Let stand 5 minutes; spread chocolate morsels evenly over top. Sprinkle evenly with almonds. Cool completely in pan on wire rack. Cut into bars. **Makes** about 3 dozen.

DIANE KENT
LONG VALLEY, NEW JERSEY

Chocolate-and-Almond Macaroons
family favorite
PREP: 15 MIN., BAKE: 17 MIN. PER BATCH
For easy cleanup, put wax paper under the wire rack to catch excess chocolate as you drizzle it on the cookies. (Pictured on page 190)

¾ cup sweetened condensed milk
1 (14-oz.) package sweetened flaked coconut
¼ to ½ tsp. almond extract
⅛ tsp. salt
24 whole unblanched almonds
½ cup dark chocolate morsels

1. Stir together first 4 ingredients. Drop dough by lightly greased tablespoonfuls onto parchment paper-lined baking sheets. Press an almond into top of each cookie.

2. Bake at 350° for 15 to 17 minutes or until golden. Remove to wire racks to cool.

3. Microwave ½ cup chocolate morsels in a microwave-safe bowl at HIGH 1 minute and 15 seconds or until melted and smooth, stirring at 30-second intervals and at end. Transfer to a 1-qt. zip-top plastic freezer bag; cut a tiny hole in 1 corner of bag. Pipe melted chocolate over cooled cookies by gently squeezing bag. **Makes** 2 dozen.

FRAN DEANGELO
LONG VALLEY, NEW JERSEY

Oatmeal Carmelitas
family favorite

PREP: 25 MIN., BAKE: 30 MIN.

Line the pan with nonstick aluminum foil, if desired. Once cookie is baked and cooled, lift the foil and cookie out of the pan. Place on a cutting board, and carefully peel away foil from sides of cookie. Cut into bars. (Pictured on page 191)

2 cups all-purpose flour
2 cups uncooked quick-cooking oats
1½ cups firmly packed light brown sugar
1 tsp. baking soda
¼ tsp. salt
1 cup butter, melted
1 (12-oz.) package semisweet chocolate morsels
½ cup chopped pecans or walnuts, toasted (optional)
1 (14-oz.) package caramels
⅓ cup half-and-half

1. Stir together first 5 ingredients in a large bowl. Add butter, stirring until mixture is crumbly. Reserve half of mixture (about 2¾ cups). Press remaining half of mixture into bottom of a lightly greased 13- x 9-inch pan. Sprinkle evenly with chocolate morsels, and, if desired, pecans.

2. Microwave caramels and half-and-half in a microwave-safe bowl at MEDIUM (50% power) 3 minutes. Stir and microwave at MEDIUM 1 to 3 more minutes or until mixture is smooth. Let stand 1 minute. Pour evenly over chocolate morsels. Sprinkle evenly with reserved crumb mixture.

3. Bake at 350° for 30 minutes or until light golden brown. Cool in pan on a wire rack. Cut into bars. **Makes** 24 to 30 bars.

DIANE GALLAGHER
LONG VALLEY, NEW JERSEY

Heavenly Fudge

Folks on Cynthia Moss's Christmas list are always thrilled to receive her fabulous homemade fudge. It garnered such rave reviews that Cynthia and her husband, George, started a business. Simply Heaven Fudge has developed a strong following in the Birmingham area. The Mosses sell it in specialty stores, including Frankie's Market Café in Helena and V. Richards in Lakeview, as well as at local festivals. In the spirit of the season, they shared recipes for two of their best-sellers. We think you'll agree that the results are divine.

Simply Heaven Fudge
fast fixin's

PREP: 10 MIN., COOK: 12 MIN.

Soft-ball stage (234°) is a candy-making term. Drop a small amount of boiling mixture (in this recipe, the sugar, milk, and butter combination) into a glass cup of cold water. When it forms a soft ball that flattens as you remove it from the water, you've reached the soft-ball stage.

1⅔ cups sugar
⅔ cup evaporated milk
2 Tbsp. butter
2 cups miniature marshmallows
1½ cups semisweet chocolate morsels
2 tsp. vanilla extract

1. Bring first 3 ingredients to a boil in a large heavy saucepan over medium heat; boil, stirring constantly, until a candy thermometer registers 234° (about 7 minutes).

2. Remove from heat; stir in marshmallows and chocolate morsels until smooth. Stir in 2 tsp. vanilla.

3. Pour into a buttered 8-inch square pan; cool completely. Cut into 1-inch squares. **Makes** about 64 pieces.

Roasted Pecan Fudge: *(Pictured on page 190)* Preheat oven to 450°. Soak 2½ cups pecan halves in water to cover 20 minutes; drain well. Sprinkle 2 Tbsp. salt evenly over the bottom of a 15- x 10-inch jelly-roll pan. Arrange pecans in a single layer in pan; sprinkle evenly with 2 more Tbsp. salt. Place pecans in hot oven, and turn off oven. Let stand in oven 1 hour and 30 minutes. Toss pecans in a strainer to remove excess salt. Coarsely chop pecans, and cool. Prepare Simply Heaven Fudge as directed, stirring in chopped pecans with vanilla. **Makes** about 64 pieces. Prep: 15 min.; Soak: 20 min.; Stand: 1 hr., 30 min.

Christmas Eve, Texas Style

Join us in El Paso as Copy Assistant Tara Ivey and her family gather for a Lone Star potluck.

Mexican Soup Supper

Serves 8 to 10

Chile con Queso

Guacamole *Granada*

Chicken Sopa

Spinach Salad With Poppy Seed Dressing

Chocolate Sheet Cake

Frozen Sangria

Chile con Queso

PREP: 15 MIN.; COOK: 1 HR., 30 MIN.
Diced green chiles may be substituted for roasted green chiles.

¼ cup butter or margarine
1 small onion, finely chopped
1 (4-oz.) jar diced pimiento, undrained
2 (4-oz.) cans roasted diced green
  chiles
1 cup cottage cheese
2 (16-oz.) loaves pasteurized prepared
  cheese product, cubed
1 (5-oz.) can evaporated milk
Assorted tortilla and corn chips
Toppings: grape tomato halves, pickled
  jalapeño slices

1. Melt butter in a large skillet over medium heat; add onion, and sauté until tender. Stir in diced pimiento and roasted green chiles, and sauté 1 minute. Set aside.
2. Process 1 cup cottage cheese in blender until creamy.
3. Place onion mixture, cottage cheese, and cubed cheese in a 4-qt. slow cooker; stir in evaporated milk. Cover and cook on LOW 1 hour and 20 minutes, stirring gently every 20 minutes. Stir before serving. Serve with assorted tortilla and corn chips and desired toppings. **Makes** about 8 cups.

KATHY HOLDMAN
TORNILLO, TEXAS

Guacamole *Granada*

fast fixin's
PREP: 20 MIN.
Granada *is the Spanish word for pomegranate. Score the skin of the pomegranate by making four to six shallow lengthwise cuts on the surface. Tara's mom, Kathy, got the idea for this recipe from her sister, Laurie Jones.*

4 large ripe avocados, halved
1 Tbsp. fresh lime juice
½ tsp. garlic salt
6 green onions, chopped
1 (4-oz.) can roasted diced green chiles,
  rinsed and drained (optional)
1 large pomegranate, divided
Garnish: pomegranate seeds
Tortilla chips

1. Scoop avocado pulp into a medium bowl, and mash into small chunks. Stir in lime juice, garlic salt, onions, and, if desired, green chiles. Set mixture aside.
2. Cut off crown of pomegranate. Using a small paring knife, score the outer layer of skin into sections.
3. Working with pomegranate fully submerged in a large bowl of water, break apart sections along scored lines. Roll out seeds with your fingers. (The seeds will sink to the bottom, while the white membrane will float to the top.) Remove and discard membrane with a slotted spoon. Pour seed mixture through a fine wire-mesh strainer. Reserve 3 Tbsp. seeds for garnish, if desired. Stir remaining seeds into avocado mixture. Sprinkle evenly with reserved seeds to garnish, if desired. Serve with tortilla chips. **Makes** 8 to 10 servings.

KATHY IVEY
TORNILLO, TEXAS

Chicken Sopa

freezeable • make ahead
REP: 15 MIN., COOK: 6 MIN., BAKE: 1 HR.
Sopa *(SOH-pah) is Spanish for soup. This recipe comes from Copy Assistant Tara Ivey's aunt Adrienne Ivey Schultz. Ironically, a version of the Chicken Sopa recipe was published in the May 1956 issue of* Progressive Farmer *featuring Tara's great-grandparents K.B. and Marie Ivey.*

1 medium onion, chopped
1 (10¾-oz.) can cream of mushroom
  soup
1 (10¾-oz.) can cream of chicken soup
1 (14-oz.) can chicken broth
2 (4-oz.) cans roasted diced green chiles
¼ tsp. garlic powder
4 cups chopped cooked chicken
12 corn tortillas
1 (8-oz.) block sharp Cheddar cheese,
  shredded and divided

1. Sauté onion in a lightly greased skillet over medium-high heat 5 to 6 minutes or until tender. Stir in next 6 ingredients. Remove from heat. Tear tortillas into bite-size pieces, and stir into soup mixture. Stir in half of shredded cheese.

2. Spread chicken mixture into 6 (2½-cup) buttered oven-safe bowls or ramekins, and top evenly with remaining cheese.

3. Bake, covered, at 325° for 45 minutes or until bubbly. Uncover and bake 15 more minutes or until golden brown. **Makes** 8 to 10 servings.

Note: Chicken Sopa may be baked in a buttered 13- x 9-inch baking dish as directed. To make ahead, assemble, cover tightly, and freeze up to 1 month. Thaw in refrigerator overnight, let stand at room temperature 30 minutes, and bake as directed.

ADRIENNE IVEY SCHULTZ
EL PASO, TEXAS

Spinach Salad With Poppy Seed Dressing
PREP: 15 MIN.

1 (10-oz.) package baby spinach, thoroughly washed
1 pt. cherry tomatoes, halved
2 oranges, peeled, sectioned, and cut into bite-size pieces
½ cup chopped pecans, toasted
½ cup jicama, peeled and cut into small pieces
⅓ cup Poppy Seed Dressing

1. Combine first 5 ingredients in a large bowl; toss with ⅓ cup Poppy Seed Dressing just before serving. **Makes** 8 to 10 servings.

Poppy Seed Dressing:
PREP: 10 MIN.
Also serve this dressing on mixed fruit salad.

½ cup safflower oil
⅓ cup honey
5 Tbsp. red raspberry vinegar
2 Tbsp. poppy seeds
1 Tbsp. minced onion
1 Tbsp. mustard
¼ tsp. salt
⅛ tsp. white pepper

1. Whisk together all ingredients. Store in an airtight container in the refrigerator up to 1 week. **Makes** about 1 cup.

KATHY IVEY
TORNILLO, TEXAS

Chocolate Sheet Cake
family favorite
PREP: 20 MIN., COOK: 5 MIN.,
BAKE: 35 MIN.
Make the icing five minutes before taking the cake out of the oven.

2 cups sugar
2 cups all-purpose flour
1 tsp. baking soda
1 tsp. ground cinnamon
⅛ tsp. salt
½ cup butter or margarine
½ cup shortening
¼ cup unsweetened cocoa
1 cup water
½ cup buttermilk
2 large eggs, lightly beaten
1 tsp. vanilla extract
Chocolate Icing
Vanilla ice cream (optional)

1. Sift together first 5 ingredients in a large bowl.
2. Stir together butter and next 3 ingredients in a medium saucepan over medium-low heat, stirring constantly, 5 minutes or just until butter and shortening melt. Remove from heat, and pour over sugar mixture, stirring until dissolved. Cool slightly.
3. Stir in buttermilk, eggs, and vanilla. Pour into a greased and lightly floured 15- x 10-inch jelly-roll pan.
4. Bake at 350° for 30 to 35 minutes. (Cake will have a fudge-like texture.) Spread Chocolate Icing over hot cake. Serve with vanilla ice cream, if desired. **Makes** 10 to 12 servings.

Chocolate Icing:
fast fixin's
PREP: 5 MIN., COOK: 5 MIN.

½ cup butter or margarine
¼ cup unsweetened cocoa
6 Tbsp. milk
1 (16-oz.) package powdered sugar
1 tsp. vanilla extract
1 cup chopped pecans, toasted

1. Combine butter, cocoa, and milk in a saucepan. Cook over low heat 5 minutes or until butter melts. Cook over medium heat until bubbles appear on the surface. (It will not come to a rolling boil.) Remove from heat; gradually stir in sugar and vanilla. Beat at medium speed with an electric mixer until smooth and sugar dissolves, about 1 minute. Stir in pecans. **Makes** about 4 cups.

LEONE IVEY
EL PASO, TEXAS

Frozen Sangría
make ahead
PREP: 10 MIN., FREEZE: 24 HRS.

1 gal. sangría
1 (12-oz.) can frozen limeade, thawed
1 (2-liter) bottle lemon-lime soft drink
Garnishes: orange slices, lemon slices, lime slices

1. Place 1 (2-gal.) zip-top freezer bag inside another 2-gal. zip-top freezer bag. Combine first 3 ingredients in the inside bag. Seal both bags, and freeze 24 hours. (Double bagging is a precaution to avoid spills.)
2. Remove mixture from freezer 1 hour before serving, squeezing occasionally until slushy. Transfer mixture to a 2-gal. container. Garnish, if desired. **Makes** about 1½ gal.

PATRICIA LETTUNICH AND VALERIE DAVIS
FABENS, TEXAS

Super Steak and Sides

Sample this cooking pro's thick, juicy rib eye, soul-satisfying sides, and top-rated pecan pie.

There's no worry about when to turn the steaks, and no wondering what sides and dessert to serve with them when you make this impressive menu from Walter Royal. The executive chef at The Angus Barn restaurant in Raleigh, North Carolina, takes away the guesswork by sharing his tips.

Country Ham Mini Biscuits
PREP: 5 MIN., BAKE: 15 MIN.

1 (24-oz.) package frozen mini biscuits
    (24 biscuits)
1 (8-oz.) package thin-sliced country
    ham
Black Pepper Honey

1. Bake biscuits according to package directions.
2. Fill biscuits evenly with ham. Serve with Black Pepper Honey. **Makes** 24 appetizer servings.

Note: For testing purposes only, we used Mary B's Bite-Sized Butter Milk Tea Biscuits.

Black Pepper Honey:
PREP: 5 MIN.

½ cup honey
2 tsp. coarsely ground pepper
2 drops hot sauce

1. Stir together all ingredients in a small bowl until blended. **Makes** ½ cup.

Fantastic Dinner
Serves 6

Country Ham Mini Biscuits

Grilled Rib-eye Steaks

Sautéed Early Winter Greens

Smashed Rutabagas and Turnips
With Parmesan Cheese

Balsamic-Butter-Glazed
Baby Carrots

Pecan Pie

Walter's Ultimate Vanilla Ice Cream

Grilled Rib-eye Steaks
PREP: 5 MIN., STAND: 25 MIN., GRILL: 10 MIN.
Walter knows steak. He assures patrons that the thousands of pounds of beef served weekly at the restaurant are the very best. His grilling technique is to slowly cook steak over low temperatures for juicy results.

6 (1-inch-thick) boneless rib-eye steaks
3 tsp. steak seasoning
3 Tbsp. butter, softened

1. Let steaks stand at room temperature 15 to 20 minutes. Rub steaks evenly with steak seasoning.
2. Grill, covered with grill lid, over medium heat (300° to 350°) 2½ minutes. Using tongs, turn each steak at a 60-degree angle, and grill 2½ more minutes. Flip steaks, and grill 2½ minutes. Turn steaks at a 60-degree angle, and grill 2½ more minutes (medium-rare) or to desired degree of doneness.
3. Remove steaks from grill, and brush evenly with butter. Let stand 5 minutes. **Makes** 6 servings.

Note: For testing purposes only, we used McCormick Grill Mates Montreal Steak Seasoning.

Walter's Guide to Perfect Steaks

Rib eyes are Walter's choice for grilling individual steaks. For him, they have the best lean-to-fat distribution, producing excellent flavor and tenderness. Follow these steps for success with steaks at the grill.
■ Allow steak to stand at room temperature for 15 to 20 minutes before grilling for more even cooking.
■ Use tongs to turn and flip meat. Never pierce or prick with a fork because this allows all the natural juices to escape and causes the steak to be dry.
■ Walter's rib-eye recipe yields a medium-rare doneness. For rare rib eyes, grill 2 minutes; then rearrange on grill at a 60-degree angle to produce restaurant-style grill marks. Cook 2 more minutes. Flip steaks, and repeat the procedure. For medium doneness, grill 4 minutes each turn. For medium-well, allow about 5 minutes each turn.
■ Remove steaks to a warm plate, brush with butter, and let stand 5 minutes before serving to allow juices to evenly distribute through steak.

Sautéed Early Winter Greens

fast fixin's

PREP: 10 MIN., COOK: 15 MIN.

Three types of greens set this recipe apart.

4 Tbsp. butter
2 Tbsp. olive oil
3 garlic cloves, minced
½ (1-lb.) package fresh turnip greens, washed, trimmed, and chopped
½ (1-lb.) package fresh kale, washed, trimmed, and chopped
½ (1-lb.) package fresh mustard greens, washed, trimmed, and chopped
½ tsp. salt
¼ tsp. pepper

1. Melt butter with oil in a large Dutch oven over medium-high heat; add garlic, and cook, stirring often, 1 minute.
2. Add chopped turnip greens and remaining ingredients; cook, stirring often, 10 to 14 minutes or until greens are tender. Serve immediately. **Makes** 6 servings.

Note: Any combination of winter greens can be used in this recipe.

Smashed Rutabagas and Turnips With Parmesan Cheese

PREP: 15 MIN., COOK: 50 MIN.

1 lb. rutabagas, peeled and chopped
1 tsp. salt
6 cups water
1½ lb. turnips, peeled and chopped
¼ cup grated Parmesan cheese
6 Tbsp. butter
½ cup whipping cream
¾ tsp. salt
¼ tsp. pepper
2 Tbsp. bourbon (optional)

1. Combine rutabagas, 1 tsp. salt, and 6 cups water in a large Dutch oven; bring to a boil, and cook 25 minutes. Add turnips, and cook 20 more minutes or until vegetables are tender; drain.
2. Combine vegetables, cheese, and next 4 ingredients in a large mixing bowl; mash with a potato masher (or beat at medium speed with an electric mixer) to desired consistency. Stir in bourbon, if desired. **Makes** 6 servings.

Balsamic-Butter-Glazed Baby Carrots

PREP: 10 MIN., COOK: 30 MIN.

3 (1-lb.) bags baby carrots
6 cups water
½ cup balsamic vinegar
2 Tbsp. brown sugar
6 Tbsp. butter
2 tsp. minced fresh thyme
2 tsp. chopped fresh tarragon
¼ tsp. salt
¼ tsp. pepper

1. Combine carrots and 6 cups water in a Dutch oven. Bring to a boil over medium-high heat; reduce heat to low, and simmer 20 minutes or until carrots are crisp-tender. Drain and keep warm.
2. Cook vinegar in a small saucepan over medium-high heat 4 to 5 minutes or until reduced by half. Stir in brown sugar and butter until smooth.
3. Pour vinegar mixture over warm carrots, tossing to coat. Stir in thyme and next 3 ingredients. Serve immediately. **Makes** 6 servings.

Pecan Pie

PREP: 5 MIN., BAKE: 40 MIN.

This pie received our highest rating. It's delicious with Walter's ice cream recipe.

½ (15-oz.) package refrigerated piecrusts
3 large eggs
½ cup sugar
¼ tsp. salt
3 Tbsp. butter, melted
1 cup dark corn syrup
1 tsp. vanilla extract
2 cups pecan halves
Walter's Ultimate Vanilla Ice Cream (optional)
Garnish: fresh mint sprigs

1. Fit piecrust into a 9-inch pieplate according to package directions. Fold edges under, and crimp.
2. Whisk together eggs and next 5 ingredients until thoroughly blended. Stir in pecans. Pour mixture into piecrust.
3. Bake at 350° on lower rack 40 minutes or until pie is set, shielding edges with aluminum foil after 15 minutes. Cool completely on a wire rack. Serve with Walter's Ultimate Vanilla Ice Cream, if desired. Garnish, if desired. **Makes** 6 servings.

Walter's Ultimate Vanilla Ice Cream

freezeable • make ahead

PREP: 20 MIN., COOK: 5 MIN.,
STAND: 20 MIN., CHILL: 1 HR., FREEZE: 1 HR.

2 cups milk
6 large egg yolks
¾ cup sugar
⅛ tsp. salt
2 tsp. vanilla extract
1 qt. whipping cream

1. Microwave milk in a microwave-safe container at HIGH 1 minute.
2. Whisk together yolks and next 3 ingredients in a large bowl until thick and pale. Gradually whisk in warm milk. Pour into a heavy saucepan.
3. Cook milk mixture over very low heat, stirring constantly, 5 minutes or until mixture thickens and coats a spoon. Remove from heat; pour through a wire-mesh strainer into a bowl.
4. Fill a large bowl with ice. Place bowl containing milk mixture in ice, and let stand, stirring occasionally, 20 minutes.
5. Remove bowl from ice bath, and stir in cream. Cover and chill 1 hour.
6. Pour mixture into freezer container of a 1-gal. electric ice-cream maker, and freeze according to manufacturer's instructions. (Instructions and times may vary.) **Makes** 6 servings.

Six Bright Ideas

This year, Associate Foods Editor Shirley Harrington's letter to Santa includes a confession: "I was really good, except that I eavesdropped on my colleagues." With the best of intentions, she listened in on their holiday-happenings chatter, learned of their inner creativity, and nagged them to tell her too. She wanted their best holiday ideas to share with you. Happily, many obliged, and six were chosen to show off creations that bring joy to themselves and to their friends or guests. All in all, she thinks offering you their clever ideas was worth a stint on Santa's naughty list.

*Cheesecake
Christmas Trees*

Cheesecake Christmas Trees

PREP: 15 MIN.; STAND: 20 MIN.;
FREEZE: 1 HR., 15 MIN.

"A tray of these makes a great open house dessert," suggests Julia Pittard Coker, senior copy editor. "Or give one tree as a gift to each coworker." Place a tree on a dessert-size paper plate, include a plastic fork, and slide a cellophane bag over it. Tie with ribbon, and keep frozen until ready to give.

1 to 2 big peppermint candy sticks
1 (30-oz.) frozen New York-style
   cheesecake
1 (7.25-oz.) bottle chocolate fudge shell
   coating
1 (6.4-oz.) tube green easy-flow
   decorator icing
12 red candy-coated chocolate pieces

Classy Centerpiece

Designer/Illustrator Christopher Davis found almost everything he needed for this centerpiece at a supercenter store. Cover pots with textured spray paint, and let dry. Plug holes in pots with florist adhesive. Soak florist foam in water; cut to fit pots. Push a small cluster of tea roses and curly willow pieces through the loop on a tassel and into the foam. Tie with ribbon, cover foam with moss, and arrange on the dining table.

1. Measure ½ to ¾ inch from end of peppermint stick, and make a small cut using a sharp knife. Gently break peppermint stick at cut. Repeat procedure with remaining peppermint stick to make 12 pieces.
2. Remove cheesecake from box according to package directions. Let stand 5 minutes. (Do not thaw.) Carefully cut cheesecake into 12 wedges. Gently push 1 peppermint piece partially into curved edge of each cheesecake wedge to form tree trunks. Place wedges on a wire rack on a baking sheet, and freeze 10 minutes or until firm.
3. Remove pan from freezer; evenly coat tops of each cheesecake wedge with fudge shell coating, allowing excess to drip down sides and curved edge. Freeze 5 minutes.
4. Remove pan from freezer; squeeze icing on top of each wedge in a pattern using ribbon tip. Place 1 red candy piece at tip of each slice. Freeze at least 1 hour or up to 8 hours. Let stand 15 minutes before serving. **Makes** 12 servings.

Quick Mocha Latte
fast fixin's
PREP: 5 MIN.
We caught Mary Allen Perry, Associate Foods Editor, at the coffeepot making this special afternoon "de-stress-her." (Pictured on page 186)

1 (0.71-oz.) envelope instant cocoa mix
⅔ cup hot strong-brewed coffee
⅓ cup milk
Toppings: whipped topping, crushed
   chocolate-covered espresso beans

1. Pour instant cocoa mix into a large mug. Stir in hot coffee.
2. Microwave milk in a glass measuring cup at HIGH 30 seconds or until hot. Stir into cocoa mixture. Serve with desired toppings. **Makes** 1 serving.

Quick Mocha Latte

Decked-Out Water

Pretty, Easy Place Cards

Associate Photo Stylist Alan Henderson designed this simple tent place card from scraps of card stock. "Slide a tea rose and hypericum berry sprig through a hole punched near the top," he says. "Then push the stems into a florist's plastic water vial."

Decked-Out Water

make ahead

PREP: 5 MIN., CHILL: 1 HR.

This is a standard at Assistant Test Kitchens Director James Schend's dinner parties. "It's flavored water that's more refreshing than plain tap or bottled water," he says.

1 medium cucumber
12 cups water
3 thin orange slices
3 thin lemon slices
3 fresh, thin ginger slices
3 fresh flat-leaf parsley or cilantro sprigs
6 fresh or frozen cranberries, thawed
Garnish: fresh parsley or cilantro sprigs

1. Cut 2 thin lengthwise slices from cucumber. Reserve remaining for another use.
2. Stir together cucumber slices, 12 cups water, and next 5 ingredients in a pitcher; cover and chill 1 hour. Pour over ice in glasses before serving. Garnish, if desired. **Makes** 12 cups.

Matzo Toffee Brittle

PREP: 15 MIN., COOK: 8 MIN., BAKE: 15 MIN., STAND: 32 MIN., CHILL: 30 MIN.

"My neighbor Marion Usher always includes this recipe for her brittle when she offers it as a gift," says James H. Schwartz, Executive editor of our sister publication Coastal Living. "It's irresistible."

3½ sheets unsalted matzos
1 cup unsalted butter
1 cup firmly packed light brown sugar
1 cup semisweet chocolate morsels
⅓ cup finely chopped slivered almonds, toasted

1. Line a 15- x 10-inch jelly-roll pan with nonstick aluminum foil. Arrange matzos in prepared pan, breaking as necessary to fit and completely cover bottom of pan.
2. Bring butter and brown sugar to a boil in a small saucepan over medium-high heat, stirring occasionally. Boil, stirring constantly, 3 minutes. Carefully pour mixture evenly over matzos in pan, and spread over matzos.
3. Bake at 350° for 15 minutes. (Mixture will start to bubble at about 10 minutes. Continue to bake to 15 minutes.) Carefully remove pan from oven to a wire rack. (Mixture will still be bubbly.) Let stand 1 minute at room temperature or until no longer bubbly. Sprinkle top evenly with morsels; let stand 1 minute or until morsels soften. Spread morsels over brittle. Sprinkle with almonds; let stand at room temperature 30 minutes. Place pan in refrigerator; chill 30 minutes or until chocolate is firm. Break into about 20 pieces. Store in an airtight container up to 1 week in refrigerator. **Makes** about 20 pieces (about 1½ lb.).

Note: For testing purposes only, we used Manischewitz Unsalted Matzos.

Matzo Toffee Brittle

How to Wow

Four people cook and tell.
Here are their secrets to main-dish success.

The holidays are a terrific time to dazzle family and friends. Whether you're a fledgling or a pro in the kitchen, you need a main dish that you can prepare with confidence.

We assembled three fantastic entrées we think you'll love. Then we recruited four home cooks to test them and give us their thoughts. The ingredients aren't cheap, but they are worth the splurge.

Crown Pork Roast

freezeable • make ahead
PREP: 20 MIN.; BAKE: 2 HRS., 30 MIN.;
STAND: 15 MIN.

This roast makes a lot, so if you have leftovers, simply cut it into chops, and freeze in zip-top plastic freezer bags up to 3 months. Pull a bag out of the freezer, and thaw in the refrigerator overnight. You can then brown the chops in a skillet to warm them.

3 Tbsp. steak seasoning
1 (11-rib) crown pork roast, trimmed
    and tied
1 large apple
1 cup fresh kumquats
Garnishes: fresh thyme sprigs, flat-leaf
    parsley, small apples ,pears, and
    kumquats

1. Rub steak seasoning evenly over all sides of pork roast. Place roast in a roasting pan; position a large apple in center of roast to help hold its shape.
2. Bake pork roast at 350° for 2 hours. Top apple with 1 cup kumquats, and bake 30 more minutes or until a meat thermometer inserted between ribs 2 inches into meat registers 160°. Let pork roast stand 15 minutes or until thermometer registers 165° before slicing. Garnish, if desired.
Makes 8 to 10 servings.

Note: For testing purposes only, we used McCormick Grill Mates Montreal Steak Seasoning.
GENE MCCALL
BIRMINGHAM, ALABAMA

Sticky Ducks With Cornbread Dressing

PREP: 30 MIN.; CHILL: 8 HRS.;
BAKE: 2 HRS., 30 MIN.; STAND: 10 MIN.
We substituted a stuffing mix for home-made cornbread in Dolores's dressing. Purchase ducks in the frozen foods section of your supermarket.

2 (5-lb.) fresh ducks or thawed frozen
    ducks
1 cup balsamic vinaigrette
2 Tbsp. butter
6 green onions, chopped
½ cup chopped celery
1 (8-oz.) bag cornbread stuffing
1 (14.5-oz.) can chicken broth
½ cup chopped flat-leaf parsley
½ tsp. pepper
1 (12-oz.) jar molasses
1 (2-oz.) bottle hot sauce
Garnish: flat-leaf parsley

1. Remove giblet packages from ducks, and reserve for another use. Rinse ducks, and pat dry; remove excess fat and skin. Place 1 duck and ½ cup balsamic vinaigrette each in 2 large zip-top plastic freezer bags; seal and chill 8 hours, turning occasionally.
2. Remove ducks from vinaigrette, discarding vinaigrette. Pat ducks dry, and prick legs and thighs with a fork, avoiding the breast area.
3. Melt butter in a large skillet over medium heat; add chopped green onions and celery, and sauté until tender. Remove from heat. Stir in cornbread stuffing, broth, chopped parsley, and pepper. Stuff each duck with half of mixture, and tie ends of legs together with string; tuck wing tips under. Place ducks, breast sides up, in a roasting pan.
4. Stir together molasses and hot sauce. Brush ducks evenly with about 3 Tbsp. mixture.
5. Bake at 350° for 2 hours, brushing with remaining molasses mixture every 15 minutes during first 1½ hours of baking or until leg joints move easily. Cover loosely with aluminum foil, and bake 30 more minutes or until an instant-read thermometer inserted in

An apple inserted in the center of the roast before baking helps the roast keep its shape and lends moisture. Kumquats will be placed on top of the apple during baking for an elegant presentation.

Placing the meat thermometer at the right spot in the roast is essential for achieving the proper degree of doneness. Insert it 2 inches into the meat between the ribs.

thickest portion of thigh registers 210° and internal temperature in center of stuffing registers 190°. Let stand 10 minutes. Garnish, if desired. **Makes 6 servings.**

DOLORES VACCARO
PUEBLO, COLORADO

Sticky Chickens With Cornbread Dressing: Substitute 2 (4-lb.) whole chickens for ducks. Do not prick chickens. Proceed as directed. Bake at 350° for 1 hour and 45 minutes or until an instant-read thermometer inserted in thigh registers 180° and internal temperature in center of stuffing registers 190°.

So-Easy Paella

PREP: 20 MIN., COOK: 50 MIN.,
STAND: 10 MIN.

We streamlined this usually complicated dish by using a deli-roasted chicken, minced garlic from a jar, frozen vegetables, and packaged saffron rice. You can buy bags of mussels at your local seafood counter. Rinse them, and then pull off any remaining pieces of the stringlike beard. Discard any mussels that don't close when you tap them. If you can't find mussels, add an extra ½ lb. of shrimp.

1 lb. unpeeled, large fresh shrimp
1 (32-oz.) container chicken broth
½ lb. chorizo sausage, sliced
1 (10-oz.) package frozen diced onion, red and green bell pepper, and celery
2 tsp. minced garlic
1 (10-oz.) package saffron rice
½ tsp. freshly ground black pepper
3½ cups chopped cooked chicken
1 cup frozen small green peas
18 fresh mussels (about ¾ lb.)
2 lemons, cut into wedges

1. Peel shrimp, reserving shells; set shrimp aside.
2. Bring shrimp shells and chicken broth to a boil in a large saucepan over medium-high heat; reduce heat, and simmer 5 minutes. Remove from heat, and let stand 10 minutes. Pour mixture through a fine wire-mesh strainer into a bowl; discard shells.
3. Sauté sausage and frozen vegetables in a paella pan or large heavy skillet over medium heat until vegetables are tender; add garlic, and cook 1 minute. Stir in rice; cook, stirring to coat, 1 minute. Stir in shrimp broth and pepper; cover, reduce heat, and simmer 15 minutes.
4. Remove pan from heat; stir in shrimp and chicken. Sprinkle peas evenly over mixture; arrange mussels around outside of pan, hinge ends down.
5. Cook, covered, over medium-low heat 20 minutes or until liquid is absorbed and mussel shells are open. (Discard any unopened mussels.) Serve paella with lemon wedges. **Makes** 6 to 8 servings.

Note: For testing purposes only, we used McKenzie's Seasoning Blend for frozen diced onion, red and green bell pepper, and celery.

A Word From Our Testers

Crown Pork Roast
Chogie Fields said it took some convincing to get her butcher to prepare the roast by trimming and tying it, so be sure to call ahead.
Chogie: "I love the fact that you prep the roast, put it in the oven, and let it do its thing—I had time to do other things. Be sure to adjust the oven racks ahead so you'll have room for the roast. And you definitely need a meat thermometer for this one."

Sticky Ducks With Cornbread Dressing
Brent Warren served these succulent, tender birds to his family to rave reviews.
Brent: "I brushed on the molasses mixture every 30 minutes instead of every 15, and it still turned out beautifully. I'd like the stuffing to have a little more texture, though, so I might add cranberries and more celery the next time around."

So-Easy Paella
Tara Stewart and Mark Hardee double-teamed this one; Tara shopped and Mark cooked.
Tara: "The hardest part was figuring out that saffron rice is just the yellow rice that I buy all the time!"
Mark: "It's a rather simple dish to make, though you have to watch it toward the end so it doesn't dry out. It's a great entertaining dish—makes plenty to feed at least six people, and it's a good conversation piece because it's something you don't serve every day."

Company's Coming

Relax and enjoy these laid-back recipes when relaxing with family and friends.

Hosting guests during the holidays is a Southern tradition. But planning meals over a two- or three-day period is a challenge. "We know we're going to have one big blowout supper, so, in a funny way, that's the easiest part," explains Martha Foose, who with her husband, Donald Bender, owns the Mockingbird Bakery in Greenwood, Mississippi. "It's finding solutions for breakfast, lunch, and snacks that takes the most mental energy for me." Her secret to a low-stress experience is to keep it simple. One thing's for sure: Thanks to Martha, this family celebrates the season while enjoying great food.

Ambrosia Cocktail

PREP: 30 MIN., STAND: 30 MIN.
Place turbinado sugar in a saucer rather than a bowl. The thin layer of sugar will make the rim of the glass more attractive.

3 navel oranges, peeled and sectioned
1 red grapefruit, peeled and sectioned
½ fresh pineapple, peeled, cored, and cut into cubes
1½ Tbsp. orange liqueur or orange juice
¼ cup turbinado sugar
1 (750-milliliter) bottle sparkling rosé wine
½ cup frozen grated coconut, thawed and toasted
8 maraschino cherries

1. Toss together oranges, grapefruit, and pineapple; set aside.
2. Pour orange liqueur into a shallow saucer. Dip rims of 8 glasses in liqueur; dip rims in sugar, and let stand 30 minutes to dry completely.
3. Spoon fruit mixture into glasses. Add rosé wine, filling three-fourths full; top with grated coconut and cherries. Serve immediately. **Makes** 8 servings.

Note: For testing purposes only, we used Sugar In The Raw for turbinado sugar.

Delta Hot Chocolate

family favorite
PREP: 15 MIN., COOK: 25 MIN.
Martha likes to garnish individual servings with toasted marshmallows.

1 qt. milk
2 cups whipping cream
2 cinnamon sticks
⅛ tsp. freshly ground nutmeg
1 cup unsweetened cocoa
¾ cup sugar
1 Tbsp. vanilla extract
2 (3-oz.) bars bittersweet chocolate, chopped

1. Cook first 4 ingredients in a Dutch oven over medium-low heat, stirring occasionally, 15 to 20 minutes or just until milk begins to steam. (Do not boil.) Remove from heat. Remove and discard cinnamon sticks. Whisk in cocoa, sugar, and vanilla, whisking until blended.
2. Cook over low heat 5 minutes. Add chocolate, whisking until blended. Keep warm over low heat. **Makes** about 7 cups.

Pepper Jelly Danish

PREP: 25 MIN., BAKE: 18 MIN. PER BATCH
Martha uses a locally produced honey-infused pepper jelly; we've added 1 Tbsp. of honey to regular pepper jelly for a similar taste.

4 (8-oz.) cans refrigerated crescent rolls
1 (8-oz.) package cream cheese, softened
1 large egg, lightly beaten
⅓ cup pepper jelly
1 Tbsp. honey

1. Unroll 1 can crescent roll dough onto a lightly floured surface; divide into 2 pieces, separating at center perforation. Press each piece into a 7-inch square. Bring corners to center, partially overlapping each; gently press corners into centers using thumb, making a small indentation. Repeat process with remaining cans of crescent rolls. Transfer to lightly greased baking sheets.
2. Stir together cream cheese and egg; stir together pepper jelly and honey. Spoon 1 Tbsp. cream cheese mixture into center of each dough circle, and top with 2 tsp. pepper jelly mixture.
3. Bake in batches at 375° for 15 to 18 minutes or until golden brown. **Makes** 8 servings.

Cane Pole Kabobs

PREP: 25 MIN., SOAK: 30 MIN., GRILL: 11 MIN.

13 (12-inch) wooden or metal skewers
1 (16-oz.) package smoked sausage, cut into 2-inch pieces
1 (16-oz.) jar marinated cherry peppers, drained
2 medium-size sweet onions, quartered
1 cup barbecue sauce

1. Soak wooden skewers in water 30 minutes to prevent burning.
2. Thread sausage, peppers, and onion quarters evenly onto skewers.
3. Grill, covered with grill lid, over medium heat (300° to 350°) 4 to 6 minutes or until sausage is lightly browned.

Turn and grill 3 more minutes; brush with barbecue sauce, and grill 2 more minutes. Serve with additional barbecue sauce, if desired. **Makes** 8 servings.

Curried Pumpkin Soup

PREP: 25 MIN., COOK: 40 MIN.

For a more elegant touch, top this hearty soup with cooked shrimp or crabmeat.

1 large sweet onion
1 Tbsp. olive oil
1 Tbsp. minced garlic
1 Tbsp. minced fresh ginger
1 Tbsp. curry powder
⅛ tsp. ground red pepper
⅛ tsp. ground cumin
2 (15-oz.) cans unsweetened pumpkin
1 cup water
1 (32-oz.) container low-sodium fat-free chicken broth
1 (13.5-oz.) can lite coconut milk
2 Tbsp. fresh lime juice
2½ tsp. salt
Garnishes: sour cream, chopped fresh chives

1. Sauté onion in hot oil in a Dutch oven over medium-high heat 8 minutes or until tender. Add garlic and next 4 ingredients; sauté 1 minute. Add pumpkin, 1 cup water, and broth; bring to a boil. Reduce heat to medium; add coconut milk, lime juice, and salt, and simmer, stirring often, 25 minutes. Remove from heat; cool.
2. Process pumpkin mixture, in batches, in a blender or food processor until smooth, stopping to scrape down sides. Return pumpkin mixture to Dutch oven, and cook over medium heat until thoroughly heated. Garnish, if desired. **Makes** about 11½ cups.

Creamy Apple-and-Pecan Salad

PREP: 25 MIN., STAND: 10 MIN.

Martha uses this as a side at a sit-down lunch and as a stuffing for pitas for a more casual gathering.

1 cup water
½ cup dried cranberries
¼ cup golden raisins
½ cup mayonnaise
3 Tbsp. plain yogurt
2 Tbsp. sugar
2 tsp. grated lemon rind
1 Tbsp. fresh lemon juice
4 apples (1 Granny Smith and 3 Gala apples), cored and chopped
1 cup diced celery
½ cup chopped pecans, toasted

1. Bring 1 cup water to a boil in a medium saucepan. Remove from heat, and stir in dried cranberries and raisins. Let stand 10 minutes, and drain.
2. Stir together mayonnaise and next 4 ingredients in a large bowl. Stir in apples, celery, cranberries, and raisins. Cover and chill. Sprinkle apple mixture with pecans just before serving. **Makes** 8 servings.

Creamy Apple-and-Pecan Salad Pita Pockets: Cut 1 regular pita round in half. Stuff pita halves evenly with ¼ cup mixed salad greens and ½ cup Creamy Apple-and-Pecan Salad. **Makes** 2 servings. Prep: 5 min.

Mockingbird Pound Cake

PREP: 20 MIN.; BAKE: 1 HR., 5 MIN.; COOL: 15 MIN.

1 cup butter, softened
½ cup shortening
3 cups granulated sugar
6 large eggs
3 cups all-purpose flour
½ tsp. salt
½ tsp. baking powder
1 cup milk
1 tsp. almond extract
1 tsp. vanilla extract
Powdered sugar

1. Beat butter and shortening at medium speed with an electric mixer until creamy. Gradually add 3 cups granulated sugar, beating at medium speed until light and fluffy. Add eggs, 1 at a time, beating after each addition just until yellow disappears.
2. Combine flour, salt, and baking powder; add to butter mixture alternately with milk, beginning and ending with flour mixture. Beat at low speed just until blended after each addition, scraping bottom and sides of bowl as needed. Beat in extracts. Pour batter into a greased and floured 12-cup Bundt pan.
3. Bake at 325° for 1 hour and 5 minutes or until a wooden pick inserted in center comes out clean. Cool in pan on a wire rack 15 minutes. Remove from pan; cool completely on wire rack. Dust cake evenly with powdered sugar. **Makes** 10 to 12 servings.

Magi Olives

PREP: 15 MIN., CHILL: 8 HRS., STAND: 30 MIN.

Martha prefers a mix of green and black Spanish olives as well as Greek kalamatas. However, your favorite olives will work just fine. This can be made up to one week ahead and kept in the refrigerator.

5 cups assorted pitted olives
½ cup extra-virgin olive oil
1 Tbsp. grated lemon rind
1 Tbsp. fresh lemon juice
1 Tbsp. grated orange rind
2 Tbsp. fresh orange juice
1 Tbsp. minced garlic
1 tsp. fennel seeds
½ tsp. dried crushed red pepper
½ tsp. dried oregano

1. Stir together all ingredients in a large bowl.
2. Cover and chill at least 8 hours. Let stand 30 minutes at room temperature before serving. Serve olive mixture with a slotted spoon. **Makes** 5 cups.

Breakfast Goodies

Pamper yourself and your guests with something special for breakfast. We know the first meal of the day is good for the body, but setting aside the bran flakes for a more indulgent treat can be good for the soul. Make breakfast as simple as granola or as substantial as enchiladas. Either way, you'll start everyone off with a smile.

Breakfast Enchiladas

family favorite • make ahead

PREP: 10 MIN., CHILL: 8 HRS.,
STAND: 40 MIN., BAKE: 39 MIN.
Serve this make-ahead casserole with salsa.

2 cups diced cooked ham (about ¾ lb.)
½ cup chopped green onions
10 (8-inch) flour tortillas
2 cups (8 oz.) shredded Cheddar cheese, divided
6 large eggs
2 cups half-and-half
½ tsp. salt
¼ tsp. ground red pepper

1. Sprinkle ham and green onions evenly down the center of each tortilla; top each with 2 Tbsp. shredded cheese. Roll up tortillas, and place seam sides down in a lightly greased 13- x 9-inch baking dish.
2. Whisk together eggs and next 3 ingredients in a large bowl. Pour mixture evenly over tortillas.
3. Cover and chill at least 8 hours. Remove from refrigerator, and let stand 30 minutes at room temperature before baking.
4. Bake, covered, at 350° for 20 minutes; uncover and bake 15 more minutes. Sprinkle with remaining ¾ cup Cheddar cheese, and bake 3 to 4 more minutes or until cheese melts. Let stand 10 minutes before serving. **Makes** 8 to 10 servings.
DIANA COPPERNOLL
LINDEN, NORTH CAROLINA

Sausage-Cheese Muffins

PREP: 15 MIN., BAKE: 25 MIN.
(Pictured on page 186)

1 (1-lb.) package ground pork sausage
3 cups all-purpose baking mix
1½ cups (6 oz.) shredded Cheddar cheese
1 (10¾-oz.) can condensed cheese soup
¾ cup water

1. Cook sausage in a large skillet, stirring until it crumbles and is no longer pink. Drain and cool.
2. Combine sausage, baking mix, and shredded cheese in a large bowl; make a well in center of mixture.
3. Stir together soup and ¾ cup water; add to sausage mixture, stirring just until dry ingredients are moistened. Spoon into lightly greased muffin pans, filling to top of cups.
4. Bake at 375° for 20 to 25 minutes or until lightly browned. **Makes** 15 muffins.
KATHY POOLE
COLLIERVILLE, TENNESSEE

Early-Morning Granola

make ahead

PREP: 15 MIN., COOK: 5 MIN., BAKE: 25 MIN.,
COOL: 30 MIN.
Stock your pantry with this easy-to-make recipe. Store in an airtight container in a cool, dry place for up to a month.

3 cups uncooked regular oats
1 cup wheat germ
½ cup chopped pecans
½ cup sliced almonds
⅓ cup sunflower seeds
½ tsp. ground cinnamon
¼ cup honey
¼ cup maple syrup
2 Tbsp. brown sugar
2 Tbsp. vegetable oil
1 cup raisins
½ cup chopped dried apricots
½ cup chopped dried apples
Yogurt (optional)

1. Combine first 6 ingredients in a large bowl; stirring well.

2. Cook honey and next 3 ingredients in a large saucepan over low heat, stirring until sugar dissolves. Stir in oat mixture.
3. Spread mixture in a lightly greased aluminum foil-lined 15- x 10-inch jelly-roll pan.
4. Bake at 350° for 25 minutes or until golden, stirring every 5 minutes. Invert onto wax paper; let cool 30 minutes. Stir in dried fruits. Serve with yogurt, if desired. **Makes** 6 cups.
STACIE STANDIFER
MURFREESBORO, TENNESSEE

Turkey With a Twist

Start a new tradition with smoked turkey. Cookbook authors Karen Adler and Judith Fertig (known as the BBQ Queens) created this recipe, perfect for small gatherings. It reflects their personal style: Take a simple food and make it frilly. Once your friends and family try this moist, delicious turkey, they'll vote you queen for the day.

Brie-and-Basil-Stuffed Turkey Breast

PREP: 20 MIN., SOAK: 30 MIN., SMOKE: 2 HRS.
This stellar main dish can easily be doubled. Once the aroma wafts next door, you'll have extra guests waiting for samples. It's adapted from The BBQ Queens' Big Book of Barbecue *(Harvard Common Press, 2005).*

Wood chunks
1 (1½- to 2½-lb.) boneless turkey breast half, skinned
¼ tsp. salt
¼ tsp. pepper
1 (4-oz.) Brie wedge, rind removed
5 fresh basil leaves
3 oz. thinly sliced prosciutto *
Garnishes: fresh basil leaves, apple wedges, flat-leaf parsley sprigs

1. Soak wood chunks in water at least 30 minutes.

2. Sprinkle turkey breast evenly with salt and pepper. Cut a slit lengthwise in 1 side of breast half to form a pocket, cutting to, but not through, opposite side. Slice Brie wedge; place Brie and basil into pocket. Wrap prosciutto around turkey, closing pocket.

3. Prepare smoker according to manufacturer's directions. Bring internal temperature to 225° to 250°, and maintain temperature for 15 to 20 minutes. Drain wood chunks, and place on coals. Place turkey breast on upper cooking grate; cover with smoker lid.

4. Smoke turkey, maintaining temperature inside smoker between 225° and 250°, for 1½ to 2 hours or until a meat thermometer inserted into thickest portion registers 170°. Garnish, if desired. **Makes** 4 servings.

*Substitute thinly sliced country ham for prosciutto, if desired.

Best Green Beans Ever

Try out this seven-ingredient side dish. It comes from Caroline Harris of Lexington, Georgia, a finalist in our 2005 Cook-Off.

Green Beans With Mushrooms and Bacon

PREP: 20 MIN., COOK: 20 MIN.
We loved the dash of dried crushed red pepper—it made the flavor lively, not hot.

2 lb. fresh green beans, trimmed
8 bacon slices
3 cups sliced shiitake mushrooms (about 7 oz.)
¼ cup chopped shallots
⅛ to ¼ tsp. dried crushed red pepper
½ tsp. freshly ground black pepper
¼ tsp. salt

1. Cook beans in boiling salted water to cover in a Dutch oven over medium-high heat 4 minutes or until crisp-tender; drain. Plunge into ice water to stop the cooking process; drain and set aside.

2. Cook bacon in a large skillet over medium-low heat until crisp; remove bacon, and drain on paper towels, reserving 1½ Tbsp. drippings in skillet. Discard remaining drippings. Crumble bacon.

3. Sauté mushrooms and shallots in hot drippings over medium-high heat 5 minutes or until shallots are tender. Add green beans and crushed red pepper; sauté 1 to 2 minutes or until thoroughly heated. Stir in crumbled bacon, ½ tsp. black pepper, and ¼ tsp. salt. **Makes** 8 servings.

Asparagus With Mushrooms and Bacon: Substitute 2 lb. fresh asparagus for green beans. Snap off and discard tough ends of asparagus. Cut asparagus into 1½-inch pieces. Proceed with recipe as directed, cooking asparagus pieces for 2 to 4 minutes.

Sugar Snaps With Mushrooms and Bacon: Substitute 1½ lb. sugar snap peas, trimmed, for green beans. Proceed with recipe as directed.

Slice the turkey breast half lengthwise to create a pocket, and place the Brie and basil inside.

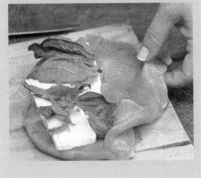

Secrets You'll Want To Know

Caroline offers this advice for making Green Beans With Mushrooms and Bacon.

"I usually use the common green beans," she says. Snap or break to remove the woody tip. You can buy haricots verts [ah-ree-koh-VEHR], a more slender and sweeter bean, for a good price at wholesale clubs during the holidays. Shorten the recipe cook time when using the skinnier beans. Don't use pole beans—they're tougher and require a longer cooking time. At peak freshness, look for a velvety skin and listen for a snap when a bean is broken in half.

Caroline suggests doing the first recipe step the day before serving. Pat beans dry with paper towels, and refrigerate in a zip-top plastic bag.

Use the mushroom cap only; discard the tough stem. Use a soft brush to clean caps. "Avoid rinsing them with water; they soak it up like sponges," Caroline explains.

Our Favorite Test Kitchens Secrets

We'll guide you through your holiday cooking.

Here's our gift to you: three classic recipes with step-by-step information to make them foolproof. Just follow these tips for fantastic results every time.

Butter Tips

- Soften butter at room temperature for about 30 minutes. Test the softness of butter by gently pressing the top of the stick with your index finger. If an indentation remains but the stick of butter still holds its shape, it's perfectly softened.
- Butter that's too cold overworks the dough when cut in and yields a tough biscuit. Likewise, butter that's too soft coats the flour and prevents the pea-size pellets from forming, thus yielding a flat biscuit.
- Perfectly softened butter combines with flour to form small pea-size pellets that distribute evenly throughout the dough and release steam during cooking. These steam pockets cause the biscuit to puff for a fluffy, tender product with melt-in-your-mouth butter flavor.

Too cold (left), perfectly softened (center), too soft (right)

Easy Homemade Biscuits

PREP: 10 MIN., BAKE: 11 MIN. *(Pictured on page 10)*

⅓ cup butter, softened and cubed *****
2¼ cups self-rising flour
1 cup buttermilk
3 Tbsp. butter, melted

1. Cut softened butter into flour with a pastry blender or 2 forks just until butter cubes are coated with flour. Using your hands, gently combine until mixture resembles small peas. Stir in buttermilk with a fork just until blended. (Mixture will be wet.)
2. Turn dough out onto a generously floured surface, and pat to ½-inch thickness. Cut dough with a well-floured 2-inch round cutter, and place on lightly greased baking sheets.
3. Bake at 450° for 9 to 11 minutes or until lightly browned. Remove from oven, and brush warm biscuits with melted butter. Serve immediately. **Makes** about 1½ dozen.

Note: For testing purposes only, we used White Lily Self Rising Flour.

*Substitute ⅓ cup shortening, if desired.

Easy Cheddar Biscuits: Add 1 cup shredded Cheddar cheese to butter and flour mixture just before adding buttermilk. Proceed as directed.

Tender, Flaky Goodness

Biscuits Step-by-Step
- Cut softened butter into flour with a pastry blender or two forks just until cubes are coated with flour (photo A).
- No spoon is required. Using your hands, gently combine the flour and butter mixture until it resembles small peas and the dough is crumbly. It's crucial to use your hands in this step, so you can feel the texture of the dough (photo B).
- Turn dough out onto a heavily floured surface (photo C). Use floured hands to pat dough to a ½-inch thickness (photo D). Don't use a rolling pin here; this will prevent the dough from being overworked.

More Biscuit Tricks
- When cutting out biscuits, don't twist the cutters. Simply press down, and pull straight up. Twisting compresses and seals the edges and prevents biscuits from rising.
- We prefer the texture of biscuits prepared with White Lily flour because it is a soft winter wheat flour and yields a more tender product.

Sides Perfection

Potatoes Step-by-Step

■ Evaporate the extra water absorbed by boiling peeled potatoes by putting the cooked and drained potatoes back on the stove for a few minutes over low heat. This allows steam to release and the potatoes to dry.

■ Use warm liquid instead of cold when mixing ingredients for the creamiest texture.

■ One of our favorite gadgets—the potato ricer—is the key to the fluffiest mashed potatoes (photo A). A potato masher works fine, too. Avoid using an electric mixer or food processor; these result in gummy mashed potatoes.

Gravy Step-by-Step

■ Prepare a roux by cooking melted butter and flour until golden brown, whisking constantly with a wire whisk. Slowly whisk warm stock or pan drippings into the roux to thicken (photo B).

■ Avoid lumpy gravy by thickening with a roux instead of cornstarch. Also, when cold liquid is added to the roux, it will seize, causing clumps. Instead, add warm liquid in small increments.

Roasted Garlic Mashed Potatoes

family favorite

PREP: 15 MIN., BAKE: 1 HR., COOL: 10 MIN., COOK: 35 MIN., STAND: 1 MIN.

1 garlic bulb
2½ lb. Yukon gold potatoes, peeled and cut into 2-inch pieces
½ cup whipping cream
⅓ cup sour cream
¼ cup butter, melted
1¼ tsp. salt
½ tsp. pepper

1. Cut off pointed end of garlic; place garlic on a piece of aluminum foil. Fold foil to seal.

2. Bake at 400° for 1 hour, and let cool 10 minutes. Squeeze pulp from garlic bulb; discard husk, and set pulp aside.

3. Bring potatoes and cold water to cover to a boil in a large Dutch oven; boil 25 minutes or until tender. Drain.

Place back in Dutch oven, and heat 3 to 5 minutes over low heat until potatoes are dry. Set aside.

4. Heat whipping cream in a small saucepan over low heat 4 minutes or just until warm; remove from heat, and stir in sour cream.

5. Press potatoes through a ricer into Dutch oven. Let stand 1 minute. Stir in roasted garlic pulp, melted butter, salt, and pepper until blended. Gradually stir in warm whipping cream mixture, stirring just until blended. Serve immediately. **Makes** 4 to 6 servings.

Make-Ahead Turkey Gravy

family favorite • make ahead

PREP: 15 MIN., COOK: 55 MIN.

This recipe uses a homemade stock. If you prefer pan drippings, substitute 2 cups pan drippings for the first 7 ingredients.

2 turkey necks
1 Tbsp. vegetable oil
1 medium onion, coarsely chopped
1 celery rib, coarsely chopped
5 cups low-sodium chicken broth
¼ cup loosely packed fresh flat-leaf parsley
1 fresh thyme sprig
3 Tbsp. butter
¼ cup all-purpose flour
¼ cup white wine
¼ tsp. rubbed sage
Salt and freshly ground pepper to taste

1. Brown turkey necks in hot oil in a large saucepan over medium-high heat 2 to 3 minutes on each side. Add onion and celery; sauté 5 minutes. Stir in broth, parsley, and thyme. Bring to a boil; reduce heat, and simmer, stirring occasionally, 30 minutes. Pour through a wire-mesh strainer; discard solids.

2. Melt butter in a large skillet over medium-low heat; whisk in flour until smooth. Cook, whisking constantly, 4 to 5 minutes or until mixture is golden. Gradually whisk in stock (or pan drippings), wine, and sage; bring to a boil over medium heat. Reduce heat; simmer, stirring occasionally, 5 to 10 minutes or until thickened. Stir in salt and pepper to taste. **Makes** about 2 cups.

Chicken and Dumplings

Associate Foods Editor Vicki Poellnitz's grandma, Faye Abercrombie, taught her to make chicken and dumplings as a preteen. Take time to teach someone you love how to cook them as well.

Chicken and Dumplings
family favorite
PREP: 15 MIN., COOK: 25 MIN.
We used a deli-roasted chicken for this recipe. One chicken yields about 3 cups.

1 (32-oz.) container low-sodium
    chicken broth
1 (14½-oz.) can low-sodium
    chicken broth
3 cups shredded cooked chicken
    (about 1½ lb.)
1 (10¾-oz.) can reduced-fat
    cream of celery soup
¼ tsp. poultry seasoning
1 (10.2-oz.) can refrigerated jumbo
    buttermilk biscuits

1. Stir together first 5 ingredients in a Dutch oven over medium-high heat; bring to a boil. Reduce heat to low; simmer, stirring occasionally, 15 minutes.
2. Place biscuits on a lightly floured surface. Roll or pat each biscuit to ⅛-inch thickness; cut into ½-inch-wide strips.
3. Return broth mixture to a low boil over medium-high heat. Drop strips, 1 at a time, into boiling broth. Reduce heat to low; simmer 10 minutes, stirring occasionally to prevent dumplings from sticking. **Makes** 4 to 6 servings.

JAN KIMBELL
VESTAVIA HILLS, ALABAMA

Chicken 'n' Sage Dumplings
family favorite
PREP: 20 MIN., COOK: 40 MIN.
Start with the convenience of frozen vegetables, all-purpose baking mix, and skinned and boned chicken breasts.

1½ lb. skinned and boned chicken
    breasts, cut into bite-size pieces
3 (14½-oz.) cans low-sodium
    chicken broth
3 cups water
½ medium onion, chopped
1½ tsp. chopped fresh thyme
1½ tsp. chopped fresh sage
1 tsp. salt
½ tsp. pepper
1 (16-oz.) package frozen mixed
    vegetables
3⅓ cups reduced-fat all-purpose
    baking mix
1⅓ cups buttermilk
½ tsp. poultry seasoning
¼ tsp. pepper
¼ tsp. salt

1. Bring first 8 ingredients to a boil in a large Dutch oven over medium-high heat; reduce heat to medium-low, and simmer, stirring occasionally, 20 minutes or until chicken is done. Add mixed vegetables, and bring to a boil over medium-high heat.
2. Stir together baking mix and next 4 ingredients until blended. Drop dough by rounded teaspoonfuls into slowly boiling mixture in Dutch oven. (Don't let dumplings touch.) Reduce heat to medium-low; cook, uncovered, 10 minutes, stirring occasionally to prevent dumplings from sticking. Cover and cook 10 more minutes. **Makes** 6 to 8 servings.

FRANKI HYDE MARTIN
PAULINE, SOUTH CAROLINA

South Louisiana Chicken and Dumplings
family favorite
PREP: 20 MIN., COOK: 35 MIN.

1 large sweet onion, chopped
1½ lb. skinned and boned chicken
    breasts, cubed
1½ tsp. Creole seasoning, divided
4 cups water
1 (14½-oz.) can low-sodium
    chicken broth
6 Tbsp. instant roux mix
1 cup chopped green onions
6 (8-inch) flour tortillas
Garnish: green onion curls

1. Microwave chopped onion in a small microwave-safe bowl at HIGH 2 minutes or until tender. Set aside.
2. Sprinkle chicken with 1 tsp. Creole seasoning. Sauté chicken in a lightly greased Dutch oven over medium-high heat 5 minutes or until lightly browned. Remove chicken using a slotted spoon.
3. Whisk together 4 cups water, broth, and roux mix. Pour mixture into Dutch oven, and stir to loosen particles from bottom. Bring to a boil over medium-high heat, whisking until smooth. Reduce heat to medium-low, and simmer 5 minutes. Stir in onion, chicken, and remaining ½ tsp. Creole seasoning. Cover and cook, stirring occasionally, 20 minutes. Stir in 1 cup green onions.
4. Stack tortillas; cut into 2- x 1-inch strips. Add strips, 1 at a time, making a single layer over top of mixture in Dutch oven; gently submerge strips. Return mixture to a low  boil; repeat with remaining strips. Cook 3 to 4 more minutes, stirring gently after 2 minutes. Garnish, if desired. **Makes** 4 to 6 servings.

Note: For testing purposes only, we used Tony Chachere's Creole Instant Roux Mix.

MARY PAT BROUSSARD
JACKSON, LOUISIANA

Deliciously Simple

If making bread isn't your bag, then try these quick, clever dress-ups—all use convenience products, such as canned crescent dough and egg roll wrappers. With these sweet and savory solutions, it will only look like you spent hours in the kitchen.

Cranberry-Stuffed Crescents
family favorite
PREP: 25 MIN., BAKE: 17 MIN.

1 (8-oz.) package cream cheese, softened
1 cup powdered sugar
1 egg yolk
4 (8-oz.) cans refrigerated crescent rolls
1 (16-oz.) can whole-berry cranberry sauce
½ cup finely chopped walnuts, toasted

1. Beat cream cheese at medium speed with an electric mixer until smooth. Gradually add sugar, beating until combined. Add egg yolk, beating until blended.
2. Separate crescent rolls into 32 triangles. Spoon 1 tsp. cream cheese mixture onto short end of each triangle. Top with 1 tsp. cranberry sauce, and sprinkle evenly with walnuts. Fold long ends over filling, tucking edges under. Place on lightly greased baking sheets.
3. Bake at 350° for 15 to 17 minutes or until golden. Serve warm. **Makes** 32 rolls.

LISA VARNER
GREENVILLE, SOUTH CAROLINA

Orange-Almond Stuffed Crescents: Stir 1½ tsp. grated orange rind into cranberry sauce. Substitute ½ cup toasted sliced almonds for walnuts. Prepare and assemble crescents as directed. Stir together 1 egg and 1 tsp. water; brush over unbaked crescents. Sprinkle with sliced almonds, if desired. Bake as directed. Stir together 1 cup powdered sugar and 2 Tbsp. orange juice; drizzle over baked crescents. Serve warm.

Sticky Crescent Rolls
family favorite
PREP: 20 MIN., BAKE: 15 MIN.

¼ cup granulated sugar
1 tsp. ground cinnamon
16 large marshmallows
3 Tbsp. butter, melted
2 (16-oz.) cans refrigerated crescent rolls
1 cup powdered sugar
2 Tbsp. milk
¼ cup pecans, toasted and chopped (optional)

1. Combine granulated sugar and cinnamon in a small bowl.
2. Dip marshmallows in melted butter, and roll in cinnamon mixture.
3. Separate crescent rolls into 16 triangles. Wrap 1 marshmallow with 1 triangle, pinching edges to seal. Repeat with remaining marshmallows and triangles. Place in lightly greased muffin pans.
4. Bake at 375° for 10 to 15 minutes or until golden.
5. Stir together powdered sugar and milk to form a smooth glaze. Drizzle over warm rolls; sprinkle with pecans, if desired. **Makes** 16 rolls.

LORI COOK
WICHITA FALLS, TEXAS

Crispy Parmesan Crackers
family favorite • fast fixin's
PREP: 5 MIN., BAKE: 10 MIN.
Look for egg roll wrappers in the produce area or refrigerated section of your grocery store.

¼ cup freshly grated Parmesan cheese
½ tsp. dried parsley flakes
¼ tsp. garlic powder
6 egg roll wrappers
3 Tbsp. butter or margarine, melted
Salt to taste

1. Combine first 3 ingredients; set aside.
2. Cut each egg roll wrapper into 4 strips lengthwise. Arrange strips on parchment paper-lined baking sheets. Brush strips with melted butter, and sprinkle with cheese mixture.
3. Bake at 425° for 8 to 10 minutes or until edges are golden brown. Sprinkle with salt to taste. **Makes** 2 dozen crackers.

Parmesan Breadsticks: Substitute 1 (11-oz.) can refrigerated breadsticks for egg roll wrappers. Roll each piece of dough into a 10-inch rope. Brush with melted butter, and sprinkle with cheese mixture. Bake at 375° for 11 to 13 minutes or until golden. **Makes** 1 dozen. Prep: 10 min., Bake: 13 min.

Comfort Food for Supper

Kick off a week of great meals with this tasty duo. Scoop casserole leftovers into individual portions, and freeze for another time.

Spinach Salad With Cider Dressing
fast fixin's
PREP: 10 MIN.

2 (6-oz.) packages fresh baby spinach
6 bacon slices, cooked and crumbled
3 hard-cooked eggs, chopped
Cider Dressing

1. Toss together first 3 ingredients in a large bowl; drizzle with Cider Dressing, and toss gently to coat. **Makes** 6 to 8 servings.

Cider Dressing:
make ahead
PREP: 5 MIN., CHILL: 30 MIN.

½ cup vegetable oil
⅓ cup sugar
1 green onion, chopped
3 Tbsp. cider vinegar
2 Tbsp. prepared mustard
½ tsp. celery seeds

1. Process all ingredients in a blender or food processor until smooth, stopping to scrape down sides. Cover and chill 30 minutes. **Makes** about 1 cup.

DELLA TAYLOR
JONESBOROUGH, TENNESSEE

Chicken Spaghetti
family favorite

PREP: 20 MIN., COOK: 15 MIN., BAKE: 20 MIN.

1 (16-oz.) package vermicelli
1 (2-lb.) whole deli-roasted chicken *
1 Tbsp. butter or margarine
1 (8-oz.) package sliced fresh
   mushrooms
1 large onion, chopped
1 large green bell pepper, chopped
½ cup chopped celery
1 (16-oz.) loaf pasteurized prepared
   cheese product, cubed
1 (10-oz.) can diced tomatoes and green
   chiles
1 cup frozen green peas
½ tsp. salt
½ tsp. ground black pepper
¼ cup Italian-style breadcrumbs
¼ cup Parmesan cheese

1. Prepare pasta according to package directions. Drain and set aside.
2. Remove chicken from bones; cut chicken into bite-size pieces, and set aside.
3. Melt butter in a large Dutch oven over medium heat. Add mushrooms and next 3 ingredients; sauté 8 minutes or until vegetables are tender.
4. Add chicken, cheese cubes, and next 4 ingredients to vegetable mixture, and cook over low heat until cheese is melted and all ingredients are combined. Add pasta, and toss to combine. Pour mixture into a lightly greased 13- x 9-inch baking dish. Sprinkle with breadcrumbs and Parmesan cheese.
5. Bake at 350° for 20 minutes or until bubbly. **Makes** 6 to 8 servings.

*Substitute 2 cups chopped cooked chicken, if desired.

KAREN ALLEN
NORMAN, OKLAHOMA

Cozy Soups

Take the chill out of winter by ladling up a satisfying supper.

Southwestern Chicken-and-Rice Soup With Tortilla Strips

PREP: 35 MIN., COOK: 28 MIN.

1 medium onion, chopped
1 large carrot, peeled and chopped
½ medium-size red bell pepper, chopped
1 Tbsp. vegetable oil
2 garlic cloves, minced
2 cups shredded cooked chicken
¾ cup uncooked white rice *
2 medium plum tomatoes, chopped
1 to 2 Tbsp. chopped pickled jalapeño
   slices
1 tsp. ground cumin
¼ tsp. black pepper
8 cups chicken broth
¼ cup loosely packed cilantro leaves,
   chopped
Juice of 1 lime (about 2 Tbsp.)
1 ripe avocado, chopped
Tortilla Strips

1. Sauté first 3 ingredients in hot oil in a large Dutch oven over medium heat 7 minutes or until vegetables are tender. Add garlic; sauté 1 minute.
2. Stir in chicken and next 5 ingredients. Stir in chicken broth. Bring to a boil, reduce heat, and simmer 20 minutes or until rice is tender. Stir in cilantro and lime juice. Serve with chopped avocado and Tortilla Strips. **Makes** about 6 servings.

*Substitute ¾ cup brown rice, if desired. Prepare recipe as directed, increasing simmer time to 45 minutes or until rice is tender.

WENDY OWENS
ATLANTA, GEORGIA

Tortilla Strips: Cut 6 (6-inch) corn tortillas into strips; place on a baking sheet coated with vegetable cooking spray. Spray cooking spray over tops of strips. Bake at 400° for 10 to 15 minutes or until crisp, stirring occasionally. Prep: 5 min., Bake: 15 min.

Turkey Gumbo

PREP: 25 MIN.; COOK: 1 HR., 10 MIN.

This dish is flavored with andouille sausage, the spicy smoked sausage that's a traditional ingredient in gumbo. If you can't find andouille sausage, your favorite spicy sausage will work just fine.

1 (16-oz.) package andouille sausage,
   sliced
3 Tbsp. vegetable oil
3 Tbsp. all-purpose flour
½ cup chopped onion
½ cup chopped celery
½ cup chopped green bell pepper
2 garlic cloves, minced
4 cups chicken broth
2 cups chopped cooked turkey
1 (14.5-oz.) can diced tomatoes
1 cup frozen whole kernel corn
1 cup frozen sliced okra
1 Tbsp. no-salt-added Cajun
   seasoning
½ tsp. dried thyme
¼ tsp. pepper
Hot cooked rice

1. Brown sausage over medium heat in a large Dutch oven; remove sausage, and drain on paper towels. Wipe Dutch oven clean with paper towels.
2. Stir together 3 Tbsp. vegetable oil and 3 Tbsp. flour in Dutch oven over medium heat, stirring constantly, 20 to 25 minutes or until roux is caramel colored.
3. Stir in chopped onion, celery, bell pepper, and minced garlic; cook, stirring often, 8 to 10 minutes or until vegetables are tender. Gradually stir in 4 cups chicken broth, and bring mixture to a boil; add browned sausage, chopped turkey, and next 6 ingredients. Reduce heat to low, and simmer, stirring occasionally, 30 minutes. Serve gumbo with hot cooked rice. **Makes** 8 servings.

Note: For testing purposes only, we used McCormick Gourmet Collection Cajun Seasoning.

from our kitchen

Don't toss out those limp carrots and celery stalks! Fresh fruits and vegetables past their prime can still be used to line a roasting pan, creating a colorful rack that adds terrific flavor to both the meat and pan juices. Browning the roast before baking caramelizes the surface of the meat and seals in the juices. The same ingredients used to marinate Apple-Bourbon Turkey Breast (page 250) help to create an exceptionally tender Pear-Glazed Pork Roast.

Tips and Tidbits

Finishing Touches

Toasting pecans with brown sugar and corn syrup creates a shimmering sweet glaze that tastes like the crunchy topping of a pecan pie. We like to keep these easy-to-make treats on hand during the holidays to use as a last-minute garnish. It's a simple recipe that transforms even a store-bought dessert into a work of art. The glaze on the pecans begins to melt soon after it comes in contact with a damp surface, so you'll want to add them as a garnish just before serving. They're also delicious in salads or stirred into softened ice cream.

Pecan Pie-Glazed Pecans (below, left) are best made in small batches. Timing is important—once the sugars begin to caramelize, the color of the glaze will darken quickly. As the glaze boils and thickens during baking, the bubbles become smaller and closer together. After 12 to 15 minutes, the glaze should form sticky threads when stirred, indicating it's thick enough to coat the pecans.

Pear-Glazed Pork Roast

PREP: 15 MIN., CHILL: 8 HRS., COOK: 5 MIN.,
BAKE: 45 MIN., STAND: 15 MIN.
(Pictured on page 1)

Apple-Bourbon Marinade (page 251)
1 (4-lb.) boneless pork loin roast
1½ tsp. salt
1 tsp. seasoned pepper
3 Tbsp. olive oil
Assorted sliced fruits and vegetables
½ (11.5-oz.) jar pear preserves
½ (10-oz.) jar pepper jelly

1. Pour Apple-Bourbon Marinade into a 2-gal. zip-top freezer bag; add pork loin roast. Seal bag, and chill at least 8 hours or up to 24 hours, turning occasionally.
2. Remove roast from bag, discarding marinade. Pat roast dry with paper towels; sprinkle evenly with salt and seasoned pepper. Brown roast on all sides in hot oil in a roasting pan over medium-high heat. Remove roast from pan.
3. Arrange sliced fruits and vegetables in a single layer in bottom of pan;

return roast to pan. Stir together pear preserves and pepper jelly; brush roast evenly with mixture.
4. Bake at 375° for 45 minutes or until a meat thermometer inserted into thickest portion registers 155°. Remove from oven, and let stand 15 minutes before slicing. Serve with pan juices.
Makes 8 servings.

Pecan Pie-Glazed Pecans: Stir together 2 cups pecan halves, ½ cup firmly packed light brown sugar, and 6 Tbsp. dark corn syrup in a small bowl. Spread mixture in a lightly greased aluminum foil-lined jelly-roll pan. Bake at 350° for 12 to 15 minutes or until glaze thickens, stirring every 4 minutes. Spread pecans in a single layer on wax paper; cool completely, separating pecans as they cool. (For the prettiest garnish, leave some in clusters.) Store in an airtight container at room temperature. **Makes** about 2 cups. Prep: 5 min., Bake:15 min.

Everyone loves apple pie, especially fresh from the oven on a chilly fall day. Ready to spoon into a crust whenever you get a craving, make-ahead Cranberry-Apple Pie Filling can be stored in an airtight container in the refrigerator up to one week or frozen up to one month. For great taste and texture, try combining two or three different types of apples, such as Granny Smith, Gala, and McIntosh.

Cranberry-Apple Pie Filling: Peel 12 large apples (about 6 lb.), and cut into wedges; toss with 1½ cups sugar and ⅓ cup all-purpose flour. Melt ½ cup butter in a large skillet over medium heat; add apple mixture to skillet, and sauté 10 to 15 minutes or until apples are tender. Stir in 1 cup sweetened dried cranberries; remove from heat, and let cool completely.

Cranberry-Apple Pie

PREP: 15 MIN., BAKE: 45 MIN.

Sparkling sugar can be found in specialty supermarkets, stores that carry cake-decorating supplies, or ordered online from **www.wilton.com.** *(Pictured on page 1)*

1 (15-oz.) package refrigerated
    piecrusts, divided
1 large egg, lightly beaten and divided
1 recipe Cranberry-Apple Pie Filling
    (recipe above)
¼ cup sparkling sugar

1. Fit 1 piecrust into a 9-inch pieplate according to package directions; trim off excess piecrust along edges. Brush edges of piecrust with egg. Spoon Cranberry-Apple Pie Filling into piecrust, mounding pie filling in center of pie.

2. Unroll remaining piecrust on a lightly floured surface. Brush piecrust lightly with egg; sprinkle evenly with sparkling sugar. Using the width of a ruler as a guide, cut the piecrust into 9 (1-inch-wide) strips. Arrange strips in a lattice design over filling; gently press ends of strips, sealing to bottom piecrust. Place pie on a baking sheet.

3. Bake pie at 400° for 45 minutes on lower oven rack, shielding with aluminum foil after 30 minutes to prevent excessive browning. Remove from oven, and let cool on a wire rack. **Makes** 8 servings.

The Sweet Side of Potatoes

Twice-Baked Sweet Potatoes *(Pictured on page 1)* are a fun twist on a holiday favorite. Peel small sweet potatoes (to avoid a greenish cast, buy mature sweet potatoes); rub with oil. Place on a lightly greased baking sheet. Bake at 350° for 45 minutes or until tender; cool completely. Carefully scoop out pulp, leaving ¼-inch-thick shells intact.

Mash together pulp with butter, brown sugar, cinnamon, and nutmeg to taste; spoon mixture evenly into shells. Bake, covered, at 350° for 20 minutes or until thoroughly heated. Uncover and top potatoes evenly with Buttercrunch Topping and miniature marshmallows; bake, uncovered, 10 more minutes.

Buttercrunch Topping: Stir together 3 cups crushed cornflakes cereal, 1½ cups chopped pecans, ½ cup firmly packed light brown sugar, and ¼ cup melted butter until blended. Store in freezer in a zip-top plastic freezer bag up to 3 months. Makes about 4 cups. Prep: 10 min. **Note:** This mixture is also delicious with winter squash and fruits such as apples; just sprinkle it on during the last 10 minutes of baking.

Festive Turnout

Molding hot cooked rice into individual servings is a fast way to turn an everyday side dish into something special*(Pictured on page 1)*. These drum-shaped delights, known as timbales, can be made with any type of rice—even the new ready-to-serve

microwaveable pouches. For this menu, we stirred sweetened dried cranberries, chopped parsley, green onions, and toasted pecans into hot cooked brown rice.

Prepare rice according to package directions or use one of your favorite recipes, and add desired stir-ins. Fill lightly greased 6-oz. custard cups or ramekins with hot rice, packing the mixture tightly into the cup with the back of a spoon; invert the cup onto a serving plate, unmolding rice. Rice timbales may be prepared up to a day ahead. Cover and chill the filled cups, and reheat them in the microwave just before unmolding.

december

Unforgettably Delicious

Great taste is just one of the reasons we love these spectacular cakes.

Here are the recipes we choose most often for our own celebrations, be they grand occasions or simple anniversaries of the heart. Of course, there's no reason to tell company how easy these spectacular cakes are to make.

Each versatile batter can be prepared in 20 minutes or less. The delicious frostings and fillings are just as quick, but when time is an issue, you can always bake and freeze the layers to assemble on another day. You'll find details on freezing cakes in this month's "From Our Kitchen" on page 308.

Lemon-Coconut Cake
PREP: 30 MIN., BAKE: 20 MIN.
(Pictured on cover)

1 cup butter, softened
2 cups sugar
4 large eggs, separated
3 cups all-purpose flour
1 Tbsp. baking powder
1 cup milk
1 tsp. vanilla extract
Lemon Filling
Cream Cheese Frosting
2 cups sweetened flaked coconut
Garnishes: fresh rosemary sprigs, gumdrops

1. Beat butter at medium speed with an electric mixer until fluffy; gradually add sugar, beating well. Add egg yolks, 1 at a time, beating until blended after each addition.
2. Combine flour and baking powder; add to butter mixture alternately with milk, beginning and ending with flour mixture. Beat at low speed until blended after each addition. Stir in vanilla.
3. Beat egg whites at high speed with electric mixer until stiff peaks form; fold one-third of egg whites into batter. Gently fold in remaining beaten egg whites just until blended. Spoon batter into 3 greased and floured 9-inch round cakepans.
4. Bake at 350° for 18 to 20 minutes or until a wooden pick inserted in center comes out clean. Cool in pans on wire racks 10 minutes; remove from pans, and cool completely on wire racks.
5. Spread Lemon Filling between layers. Spread Cream Cheese Frosting on top and sides of cake. Sprinkle top and sides with coconut. Garnish, if desired. **Makes** 12 servings.

Lemon Filling:
fast fixin's
PREP: 10 MIN., COOK: 5 MIN.

1 cup sugar
¼ cup cornstarch
1 cup boiling water
4 egg yolks, lightly beaten
2 tsp. grated lemon rind
⅓ cup fresh lemon juice
2 Tbsp. butter

1. Combine sugar and cornstarch in a medium saucepan; whisk in 1 cup boiling water. Cook over medium heat, whisking constantly, until sugar and cornstarch dissolve (about 2 minutes). Gradually whisk about one-fourth of hot sugar mixture into egg yolks; add to remaining hot sugar mixture in pan, whisking constantly. Whisk in lemon rind and juice.
2. Cook, whisking constantly, until mixture is thickened (about 2 to 3 minutes). Remove from heat. Whisk in butter; let cool completely, stirring occasionally. **Makes** about 1⅔ cups.

Cook's Notes

■ We like to use Lemon Filling in lots of different ways. For a quick teatime treat, serve it over cream cheese with a basket of vanilla wafers and gingersnaps. Spoon into small tart shells, spread on warm biscuits and scones, or dress up a pan of gingerbread.

■ It takes only a minute to squeeze fresh lemon juice, and the taste it delivers is definitely worth it. A Microplane® zester/grater, available in kitchen shops for around $12, makes grating the rind super easy. This handy gadget can also be used to finely shred hard cheeses and chocolate.

■ Don't stir Lemon Filling after refrigerating— just spoon onto cake layers, and spread. Once chilled and set, fillings made with cornstarch will break down and liquefy if stirred.

Cream Cheese Frosting:
fast fixin's
PREP: 10 MIN.

½ cup butter, softened
1 (8-oz.) package cream cheese, softened
1 (16-oz.) package powdered sugar
1 tsp. vanilla extract

1. Beat butter and cream cheese at medium speed with an electric mixer until creamy. Gradually add powdered sugar, beating at low speed until blended; stir in vanilla. **Makes** about 3 cups.

Pecan Pie Cake
family favorite
PREP: 15 MIN., BAKE: 25 MIN.

2 cups finely chopped pecans, toasted
1 recipe Pecan Pie Cake Batter
¾ cup dark corn syrup
1 recipe Pecan Pie Filling
Garnishes: raspberries, fresh mint sprigs

1. Sprinkle pecans evenly into 3 generously buttered 9-inch round cakepans; shake to coat bottoms and sides of pans. Spoon Pecan Pie Cake Batter evenly into prepared pans.
2. Bake at 350° for 25 minutes or until a wooden pick inserted in center comes out clean. Cool in pans on wire racks 10 minutes. Invert layers onto wax paper-lined wire racks. Brush tops and sides of layers evenly with corn syrup, and cool completely.
3. Place 1 cake layer, pecan side up, on a serving plate. Spread top with half of Pecan Pie Filling. Place second layer, pecan side up, on top; spread top of cake layer with remaining filling. Top with remaining layer, pecan side up. Garnish slices, if desired. **Makes** 12 servings.

Pecan Pie Cake Batter
fast fixin's
PREP: 20 MIN.

½ cup butter, softened
½ cup shortening
2 cups sugar
5 large eggs, separated
1 Tbsp. vanilla extract
2 cups all-purpose flour
1 tsp. baking soda
1 cup buttermilk
1 cup finely chopped pecans, toasted

1. Beat ½ cup butter and shortening at medium speed with an electric mixer until fluffy; gradually add sugar, beating well until blended. Add egg yolks, 1 at a time, beating just until blended after each addition. Stir in vanilla.
2. Combine flour and baking soda; add to butter mixture alternately with buttermilk, beginning and ending with flour mixture. Beat at low speed until blended after each addition. Stir in pecans.
3. Beat egg whites at medium speed until stiff peaks form; fold one-third of egg whites into batter. Gently fold in remaining beaten egg whites just until blended. Use immediately as directed in recipe. **Makes** about 6 cups.

Pecan Pie Filling
PREP: 7 MIN., COOK: 7 MIN., CHILL: 4 HRS.

½ cup firmly packed dark brown sugar
¾ cup dark corn syrup
⅓ cup cornstarch
4 egg yolks
1½ cups half-and-half
⅛ tsp. salt
3 Tbsp. butter
1 tsp. vanilla extract

1. Whisk together first 6 ingredients in a heavy 3-qt. saucepan until smooth. Bring mixture to a boil over medium heat, whisking constantly; boil 1 minute or until thickened. Remove from heat; whisk in butter and vanilla. Place a sheet of wax paper directly on surface of mixture to prevent a film from forming, and chill 4 hours. **Makes** about 3 cups.

Cook's Notes

Never fearing too much of a good thing, we love to create variations of our favorite recipes. When we tasted this twist on Pecan Pie Cake, we decided it was too wonderful not to share with our readers.

Caramel Cream Cake
family favorite
PREP: 20 MIN., BAKE: 25 MIN.
(Pictured on page 192)

1 cup finely chopped sweetened flaked coconut
1 recipe Pecan Pie Cake Batter (recipe at left)
1 recipe Pecan Pie Filling (recipe at left)
1 recipe Cream Cheese Frosting (recipe at left)
1 cup finely chopped pecans, toasted
1 cup sweetened flaked coconut, toasted
Garnishes: raspberries, fresh mint sprig

1. Stir 1 cup finely chopped coconut into Pecan Pie Cake Batter; spoon batter into 3 greased and floured 9-inch round cakepans.
2. Bake at 350° for 25 minutes or until a wooden pick inserted in center comes out clean. Cool in pans on wire racks 10 minutes; remove from pans, and cool completely on wire racks.
3. Spread Pecan Pie Filling between layers. Spread Cream Cheese Frosting on top and sides of cake. Sprinkle top and sides with toasted pecans and toasted coconut. Garnish, if desired. **Makes** 12 servings.

Chocolate-Mint Cake
family favorite

PREP: 25 MIN., BAKE: 30 MIN.

Adding hot water to the batter helps to create an exceptionally moist and tender cake. (Pictured on page 11)

1½ cups semisweet chocolate morsels
½ cup butter, softened
1 (16-oz.) package light brown sugar
3 large eggs
2 cups all-purpose flour
1 tsp. baking soda
½ tsp. salt
1 (8-oz.) container sour cream
1 cup hot water
2 tsp. vanilla extract
Peppermint Frosting
Chocolate Ganache

1. Melt chocolate morsels in a microwave-safe bowl at HIGH for 30-second intervals until melted (about 1½ minutes). Stir until smooth.
2. Beat butter and sugar at medium speed with an electric mixer about 5 minutes or until well blended. Add eggs, 1 at a time, beating just until blended after each addition. Add melted chocolate, beating just until blended.
3. Sift together flour, baking soda, and salt. Gradually add to chocolate mixture alternately with sour cream, beginning and ending with flour mixture. Beat at low speed just until blended after each addition. Gradually add 1 cup hot water in a slow, steady stream, beating at low speed just until blended. Stir in vanilla. Spoon batter evenly into 2 greased and floured 10-inch round cakepans.
4. Bake at 350° for 30 minutes or until a wooden pick inserted in center comes out clean. Cool in pans on wire racks 10 minutes; remove from pans, and let cool completely on wire racks. Spread Peppermint Frosting evenly between cake layers. Spread Chocolate Ganache evenly on top and sides of cake. **Makes** 16 servings.

Peppermint Frosting:
fast fixin's

PREP: 10 MIN.

Peppermint oil, available from cake-supply stores, has an intense, highly concentrated flavor like that found in the chocolate-covered peppermint patties we used to garnish our cake.

½ cup butter, softened
1 (16-oz.) package powdered sugar
⅓ cup milk
¼ tsp. peppermint oil

1. Beat butter at medium speed with an electric mixer until creamy; gradually add powdered sugar alternately with milk, beginning and ending with powdered sugar. Beat at low speed just until blended after each addition. Stir in peppermint oil. **Makes** about 3 cups.

Chocolate Ganache:
fast fixin's

PREP: 10 MIN., STAND: 20 MIN.

1 (12-oz.) package semisweet chocolate morsels
1½ cups whipping cream
3 Tbsp. butter

1. Microwave semisweet chocolate morsels and whipping cream in a 2-qt. microwave-safe bowl on MEDIUM (50% power) 2½ to 3 minutes or until chocolate begins to melt. Whisk until chocolate melts and mixture is smooth. Whisk in butter; let stand 20 minutes.
2. Beat at medium speed with an electric mixer 3 to 4 minutes or until soft peaks form. **Makes** about 2 cups.

Cream Cheese Pound Cake
family favorite

PREP: 15 MIN.; BAKE: 1 HR., 45 MIN.

1½ cups butter, softened
1 (8-oz.) package cream cheese, softened
3 cups sugar
6 large eggs
3 cups all-purpose flour
⅛ tsp. salt
1 Tbsp. vanilla extract

1. Beat butter and cream cheese at medium speed with an electric mixer until creamy. Gradually add sugar, beating until light and fluffy. Add eggs, 1 at a time, beating just until blended after each addition.
2. Combine flour and salt; gradually add to butter mixture, beating at low speed just until blended. Stir in vanilla. Spoon batter into a greased and floured 10-inch tube pan.
3. Bake at 300° for 1 hour and 45 minutes or until a long wooden pick inserted in center comes out clean. Cool in pan on a wire rack 15 minutes; remove from pan, and let cool completely on wire rack. **Makes** 12 servings.

Cook's Notes

■ Ganache is a rich frosting made with melted chocolate and whipping cream. The mixture, which thickens as it cools, should be warm enough to pour, yet thick enough to spread and coat the sides of a cake. Pour the ganache into the center of the cake; spread quickly, using a spatula to push the frosting over and down the sides of the cake.

■ Ganache can also be used as a filling for cakes, cookies, and tarts. After chilling for several hours, it becomes firm enough to shape into truffles.

■ Coarsely chopped chocolate-covered peppermint patties add a simple but striking garnish to Chocolate-Mint Cake. For quick, clean cuts, partially freeze the candy before chopping.

Party Punches

Stir up your get-togethers with fabulous beverages. Our assortment of thirst quenchers includes something for all ages. Sparkling Holiday Punch showcases pomegranate and blood orange juice for a new twist. Eggnog and hot chocolate are signature drinks of the season. Serve these delicious versions in your prettiest punch bowls, glasses, or mugs for extra glamour. Then raise your cup, and enjoy the occasion.

Classic Eggnog
make ahead
PREP: 15 MIN., COOK: 45 MIN., COOL: 1 HR., CHILL: 4 HRS.

1½ cups sugar
12 large eggs, lightly beaten
4 cups half-and-half
4 cups milk
¼ tsp. salt
½ cup bourbon
½ cup brandy
2 tsp. vanilla extract
2 cups whipping cream
½ tsp. ground nutmeg

1. Gradually add sugar to eggs in a large glass bowl, whisking until blended.
2. Stir together half-and-half, milk, and salt in a Dutch oven over medium-low heat. Cook, stirring occasionally, 12 to 15 minutes or just until mixture begins to bubble around edges of pan. (Do not boil.)
3. Gradually stir half of hot milk mixture into egg mixture. Stir egg mixture into remaining hot milk mixture in Dutch oven.
4. Cook mixture over medium-low heat, stirring constantly, until mixture slightly thickens and a thermometer registers 160° (about 25 to 30 minutes). Remove from heat, and stir 1 minute. Pour mixture through a fine wire-mesh strainer into a serving bowl. Stir in bourbon, brandy, and vanilla; let cool 1 hour. Cover and chill at least 4 hours.
5. Beat whipping cream at high speed with an electric mixer until soft peaks form. Fold whipped cream into chilled

eggnog, and sprinkle with nutmeg. **Makes** about 3 qt.

Eggnog With Coffee and Irish Cream: Prepare recipe as directed, substituting 4½ cups chilled strongly brewed coffee and 3 cups Irish cream liqueur for bourbon and brandy. Prepare and fold in the whipped cream as directed. Omit nutmeg. Garnish with additional whipped cream and thin chocolate mints, if desired. **Makes** about 1 gal.

Note: For testing purposes only, we used Baileys The Original Irish Cream and Andes Creme de Menthe Thins for chocolate mints.

Sparkling Holiday Punch
make ahead
PREP: 5 MIN., CHILL: 2 HRS.
This recipe uses blood oranges, which have dark red pulp and juice and are less acidic than traditional oranges. They are grown in Texas and California. The fruit is available December through May in the produce section of the supermarket; the juice may be found in the refrigerated section of gourmet food stores or supermarkets year-round.

3½ cups blood orange juice, chilled*
1 cup pomegranate juice, chilled
1 liter ginger ale, chilled
1 orange, thinly sliced

1. Stir together blood orange juice and pomegranate juice in a large serving bowl. Chill at least 2 hours or up to 24 hours.
2. Stir in ginger ale and orange slices. Serve immediately. **Makes** 8½ cups.

Note: For testing purposes only, we used Triple Sec orange liqueur.

*Substitute sweet red grapefruit juice, if desired.

Pomegranate-Orange Punch: Prepare recipe as directed, omitting ginger ale. Stir in ¾ cup chilled vodka, 1 cup chilled orange liqueur, and orange slices before serving. **Makes** 6¾ cups.

Hot Sangría

make ahead

PREP: 10 MIN., COOK: 35 MIN.
Keep warm in a slow cooker, if desired.

1¾ cups orange juice
1 cup apple cider
½ cup sugar
1 cinnamon stick, halved
4 whole cloves
3 Tbsp. raisins, chopped
1 (750-milliliter) bottle dry red wine
¼ cup brandy
1 orange, peeled and sliced
1 lemon, peeled and sliced
Garnishes: cinnamon sticks, orange rind
     curls

1. Bring first 6 ingredients to a boil in a large saucepan over medium-high heat. Reduce heat to medium-low, and cook, stirring occasionally, 10 to 15 minutes. Stir in red wine, and cook, stirring occasionally, 10 to 15 more minutes or until thoroughly heated.
2. Pour mixture through a fine wire-mesh strainer into a large saucepan; discard solids. Stir in brandy.
3. Cook over medium-low heat 2 to 3 minutes or until thoroughly heated. Remove from heat. Stir in orange and lemon slices. Serve immediately. Garnish, if desired. **Makes** 6 cups.

Hot Chocolate With White Chocolate Whipped Cream

fast fixin's

PREP: 5 MIN., COOK: 15 MIN.

4 cups milk
¼ cup firmly packed light brown
     sugar
⅛ tsp. salt
1 (4-oz.) package bittersweet chocolate
     baking squares, chopped into small
     pieces
½ cup whipping cream
2 tsp. vanilla extract
White Chocolate Whipped Cream
Garnish: chocolate shavings

1. Stir together milk and sugar in a medium saucepan over medium-low heat until smooth. Add salt, and cook 6 to 8 minutes or just until mixture

begins to bubble around edges of pan. (Do not boil.) Remove from heat.
2. Stir together chocolate and whipping cream in a medium saucepan over low heat, and cook, stirring constantly, 2 to 3 minutes or until chocolate is melted and mixture is smooth. Gradually add warm milk mixture to chocolate mixture, whisking until blended after each addition.
3. Cook mixture over medium-low heat, stirring frequently, 3 to 4 minutes or until thoroughly heated. Stir in vanilla. Serve warm with White Chocolate Whipped Cream. Garnish, if desired. **Makes** 5 cups.

Note: For testing purposes only, we used Triple Sec orange liqueur.

Hot Chocolate With Orange Liqueur: Prepare Hot Chocolate as directed, adding ½ cup orange liqueur with vanilla. Serve warm with White Chocolate Whipped Cream. Garnish with orange rind curls, if desired. **Makes** 5½ cups.

White Chocolate Whipped Cream:

make ahead

PREP: 10 MIN., CHILL: 2 HRS.
You can make this topping in advance. Prepare it early in the day, and store it in an airtight container in the refrigerator until you're ready to serve.

2 (1-oz.) white chocolate baking
     squares, chopped into small pieces
1 cup whipping cream, divided

1. Microwave chocolate and ¼ cup whipping cream in a microwave-safe bowl at HIGH 40 to 60 seconds or until chocolate is melted and mixture is blended and smooth, stirring every 20 seconds.
2. Stir remaining whipping cream into melted chocolate mixture, and chill 2 hours.
3. Beat chilled chocolate mixture at high speed with an electric mixer 2 to 3 minutes or until soft peaks form. **Makes** about 1 cup.

Stock Up for Easy Entertaining

During the Christmas season, keep the following drinks on hand for impromptu gatherings.

- ginger ale
- cranberry juice cocktail
- club soda
- frozen juice concentrates
- sparkling apple cider
- eggnog
- tea

Laid-back Breakfast

You might think of fancy dinner parties when you think of holiday entertaining, but less formal gatherings often offer the greatest enjoyment. Busy mom and volunteer Beth Morris, who lives with husband Andy in Trussville, Alabama, has a gift for easygoing entertaining.

A talented artist, Beth is as creative in the kitchen as she is in her home studio. Many of her recipes have been passed along from family and friends—those must-have favorites everyone loves. Here, she shares a few from her breakfast collection. All received rave reviews from our Foods staff. As an added bonus, most of the ingredients can be kept on hand in the pantry or freezer.

Don't pass up the Brown Sugar-Pecan Coffee Cake (page 290). It's equally spectacular served warm from the oven or left on the kitchen counter to season overnight. But, be forewarned, it's so delicious that it just may vanish into crumbs before company comes!

Breakfast Pizza
family favorite
PREP: 15 MIN., BAKE: 40 MIN., COOK: 10 MIN.
You can also bake this in a 12-inch deep-dish pizza pan or cakepan. (Pictured on page 187)

1 (8-oz.) can refrigerated crescent rolls
1 lb. hot ground pork sausage
1 (32-oz.) package frozen hash browns with onions and peppers
1 cup (4 oz.) shredded Cheddar cheese
4 large eggs
½ cup milk
1 tsp. salt
½ tsp. pepper

1. Unroll crescent roll dough; press on bottom and partially up sides of a 13- x 9-inch baking dish; press perforations to seal. Bake at 375° for 5 minutes.
2. Cook sausage in a large skillet over medium-high heat, stirring until sausage crumbles and is no longer pink. Drain well, and sprinkle evenly over crust.
3. Prepare hash browns according to package directions; spoon evenly over sausage. Sprinkle cheese evenly over hash browns. (Cover and chill up to 24 hours, if desired.) Whisk together eggs and next 3 ingredients; pour evenly over cheese.
4. Bake at 350° for 30 to 35 minutes or until set. **Makes** 8 servings.

Cheesy Baked Grits
family favorite
PREP: 15 MIN., BAKE: 50 MIN.
If you're lucky enough to have leftovers, they can be reheated in the microwave. (Pictured on page 187)

1 cup uncooked regular grits
1 (16-oz.) package pasteurized prepared cheese product, cubed
½ cup butter
6 large eggs
¼ cup milk
½ tsp. salt

1. Prepare grits according to package directions; remove from heat, and stir in cheese and butter until blended.

2. Whisk together eggs, milk, and salt. Gradually whisk about one-fourth of hot grits mixture into egg mixture; add to the remaining hot grits mixture, whisking constantly. Spoon mixture evenly into a lightly greased 13- x 9-inch baking dish.
3. Bake at 350° for 40 to 50 minutes or until set. **Makes** 8 servings.

Note: For testing purposes only, we used Velveeta for pasteurized prepared cheese product.

Toffee-Apple Dip
fast fixin's
PREP: 5 MIN.
One recipe makes enough dip for six large apples or pears. To prevent the cut fruit from turning brown, Beth soaks the slices for an hour in canned pineapple juice. We couldn't resist spreading this creamy mixture over the top of a chocolate sheet cake. It doesn't get as a firm as a traditional frosting, so store the cake in the refrigerator.

1 (8-oz.) package cream cheese, softened
1 (8-oz.) package toffee bits
¾ cup firmly packed light brown sugar
½ cup granulated sugar
1 tsp. vanilla extract

1. Stir together all ingredients until well blended. Serve immediately, or store in an airtight container in the refrigerator up to 5 days. **Makes** about 3 cups.

Note: For testing purposes only, we used Hershey's Heath Bits o' Brickle Toffee Bits.

Apple-Cinnamon Breakfast Cobbler
family favorite
PREP: 30 MIN., COOK: 5 MIN., BAKE: 1 HR.
Topped with ice cream, this makes a sweet follow-up to any meal.

2 cups sugar
2 cups water
½ cup shortening
1½ cups sifted self-rising flour
⅓ cup milk
2 cups finely chopped peeled apples
1 tsp. ground cinnamon
½ cup butter

1. Bring sugar and water to a boil in a medium saucepan over medium-high heat. Boil, stirring occasionally, 1 to 2 minutes or until sugar dissolves and mixture is clear; remove from heat, and set aside.
2. Cut shortening into flour with a pastry blender or 2 forks until crumbly; add milk, stirring just until dry ingredients are moistened.
3. Turn dough out onto a lightly floured surface; knead 2 or 3 times. Pat or roll dough into an 11- x 7-inch rectangle (about ¼ inch thick). Stir together apples and cinnamon; sprinkle evenly over dough. Roll up, jelly-roll fashion, starting at 1 long end; cut into 12 slices (each just less than 1 inch thick).
4. Melt butter in a 13- x 9-inch baking dish in a 350° oven; arrange dough slices, cut side down, in a single layer in melted butter; pour sugar syrup evenly over slices. (This will seem like too much liquid, but the dough will absorb it as it bakes.)
5. Bake at 350° for 1 hour or until center rolls are golden brown and syrup is absorbed. **Makes** 12 servings.

Brown Sugar-Pecan Coffee Cake
family favorite

PREP: 15 MIN., BAKE: 30 MIN.

We added pecans to Beth's original recipe; it's delicious either way.

2 cups all-purpose flour
2 cups firmly packed light brown sugar
¾ cup butter, cubed
1 cup sour cream
1 large egg, lightly beaten
1 tsp. baking soda
3 Tbsp. granulated sugar
1 tsp. ground cinnamon
1 cup chopped pecans

1. Stir together flour and brown sugar in a large bowl. Cut butter into flour mixture with a pastry blender or 2 forks until crumbly. Press 2¾ cups crumb mixture evenly on the bottom of a lightly greased 13- x 9-inch pan.
2. Stir together sour cream, egg, and baking soda; add to remaining crumb mixture, stirring just until dry ingredients are moistened. Stir together granulated sugar and cinnamon. Pour sour cream mixture over crumb crust in pan; sprinkle evenly with cinnamon mixture and pecans.
3. Bake at 350° for 25 to 30 minutes or until a wooden pick inserted into center comes out clean. **Makes** 12 servings.

healthy & light

Sensational Sweet Potatoes

Sweet potatoes are one of the healthiest and best-tasting vegetables. Not only do they provide the body with a wealth of nutrients, but they're also wonderful in both savory and sweet dishes. Loaded with vitamins A and C, sweet potatoes are a high-fiber, antioxidant-rich, cancer-fighting food.

Simple Sweet Potato Biscuits
fast fixin's

PREP: 15 MIN., BAKE: 10 MIN.

You can use either canned or freshly cooked and mashed sweet potatoes in this recipe. We preferred the texture of the freshly mashed potatoes, but we enjoyed the taste of both.

⅓ cup light butter
2¾ cups reduced-fat all-purpose baking mix
1 cup mashed sweet potato
½ cup 2% reduced-fat milk

1. Cut butter into baking mix with a pastry blender or 2 forks until mixture is crumbly. Whisk together sweet potato and milk; add to butter mixture, stirring with a fork just until dry ingredients are moistened.
2. Turn dough out onto a lightly floured surface; knead gently 4 or 5 times. (Dough will be moist.) Pat or roll dough to ½-inch thickness; cut with a 2-inch round cutter. Place biscuits on lightly greased baking sheets.
3. Bake at 450° for 10 minutes or until golden brown. **Makes** 2 dozen biscuits.

ANGELA JOHNSON
ATLANTA, GEORGIA

Per biscuit: Calories 73 (28% from fat); Fat 2.3g (sat 0.8g, mono 0.6g, poly 0.2g); Protein 1.4g; Carb 12.3g; Fiber 0.5g; Chol 4mg; Iron 0.6mg; Sodium 176mg; Calc 62mg

Easy Sweet Potato Casserole
family favorite

PREP: 10 MIN., BAKE: 40 MIN.

4 cups cooked, mashed sweet potato ✱
½ cup light butter, softened
½ cup fat-free milk
1 large egg
½ tsp. salt
½ tsp. vanilla extract
1 cup firmly packed brown sugar, divided
Vegetable cooking spray
½ cup all-purpose flour
3 Tbsp. cold light butter, cut into small pieces
⅓ cup finely chopped pecans

1. Beat first 6 ingredients and ½ cup brown sugar at medium speed with an electric mixer until smooth. Spoon potato mixture into a 13- x 9-inch baking dish coated with cooking spray.
2. Combine flour and remaining ½ cup brown sugar in a food processor; pulse to combine. Add chilled butter, and process about 45 seconds or until mixture resembles coarse meal. Stir in pecans; sprinkle over potato mixture.
3. Bake, covered, at 350° for 40 minutes or until topping is golden brown and potatoes are thoroughly heated. **Makes** 12 servings.

✱Substitute 4 to 5 cups canned mashed sweet potatoes such as Trappeys (15-oz. cans) or Princella (29-oz. can), if desired.

Per serving: Calories 250 (29% from fat); Fat 8.5g (sat 3.6g, mono 1.5g, poly 0.9g); Protein 3.2g; Carb 43g; Fiber 3.2g; Chol 32mg; Iron 1.5mg; Sodium 232mg; Calc 63mg

Stuffed Sweet Potatoes

family favorite

PREP: 15 MIN.; BAKE: 1 HR., 10 MIN.; COOL: 5 MIN.

Use the pumpkin pie spice blend for a quick and cost-effective way to enjoy the flavors of cinnamon, cardamom, ginger, allspice, and nutmeg.

4 small sweet potatoes (about 8 oz. each)
¼ cup firmly packed light brown sugar
3 Tbsp. light sour cream
1 tsp. grated orange rind
1 Tbsp. fresh orange juice
2 tsp. butter
1 tsp. pumpkin pie spice
2 Tbsp. chopped toasted pecans (optional)

1. Pierce sweet potatoes several times with a fork. Place on an aluminum foil-lined jelly-roll pan.
2. Bake at 350° for 1 hour or until tender; cool 5 minutes.
3. Cut a 1½-inch-wide strip from top of each baked potato. Carefully scoop out pulp into a medium bowl, leaving shells intact.
4. Mash together pulp, brown sugar, and next 5 ingredients. Spoon mixture evenly into shells. Place shells on jelly-roll pan.
5. Bake at 350° for 10 minutes or until thoroughly heated. Top evenly with toasted pecans, if desired. **Makes** 4 servings.

Per serving (not including pecans): Calories 217 (11% from fat); Fat 2.9g (sat 1.7g, mono 0.8g, poly 0.1g); Protein 2.8g; Carb 48g; Fiber 4.2g; Chol 9mg; Iron 0.7mg; Sodium 71mg; Calc 59mg

Spicy Roasted Sweet Potato Fries

family favorite

PREP: 15 MIN., BAKE: 30 MIN.

Make the crispiest fries by first preheating the pan with oil so when the potatoes are added, they'll sizzle and caramelize on the outside.

1 Tbsp. olive oil, divided
2 large sweet potatoes (about 1¼ lb.)
¼ tsp. salt
¼ tsp. chili powder
1 tsp. brown sugar

1. Brush an aluminum foil-lined jelly-roll pan with 2 tsp. olive oil. Heat pan in a 425° oven for 5 minutes.
2. Peel sweet potatoes, and cut into 3- x ½-inch strips. Combine strips, salt, chili powder, brown sugar, and remaining 1 tsp. oil in a large zip-top plastic freezer bag, tossing to coat.
3. Place strips in a single layer in prepared pan.
4. Bake at 425° for 30 minutes or until crisp, stirring every 10 minutes. **Makes** 4 servings.

CHAMBLISS KEITH
BIRMINGHAM, ALABAMA

Per serving: Calories 117 (27% from fat); Fat 3.5g (sat 0.5g, mono 2.5g, poly 0.4g); Protein 1.5g; Carb 20.3g; Fiber 2.8g; Chol 0mg; Iron 0.8mg; Sodium 183mg; Calc 31mg

Chipotle Sweet Potato Soup With Lemon Cream

PREP: 15 MIN., COOK: 35 MIN., STAND: 5 MIN.

4 medium-size sweet potatoes (about 2 lb.)
½ cup light sour cream
3 Tbsp. lemon juice (about 1 lemon)
2 tsp. light butter
1 cup diced sweet onion
1 (32-oz.) container low-sodium fat-free chicken broth
1 to 2 canned chipotle peppers in adobo sauce, finely chopped
2 Tbsp. minced fresh cilantro (optional)

1. Pierce sweet potatoes several times with a fork. Place in a large microwave-safe bowl; cover with damp paper towels. Microwave at HIGH 15 minutes or until tender, turning every 5 minutes. Let stand 5 minutes. Cut potatoes in half and scoop pulp into a medium bowl. Set aside.
2. Whisk together sour cream and lemon juice. Cover and chill.
3. Melt butter in a large saucepan over medium heat; add onion, and sauté 5 minutes or until tender. Stir in sweet potatoes and ½ container broth, and process mixture with a handheld immersion blender until smooth. Add chipotle peppers and remaining chicken broth, stirring until well blended.
4. Cover and simmer, stirring occasionally, over low heat 15 minutes. Ladle 1⅓ cups soup into each of 5 bowls. Top each serving of soup with 1 Tbsp. lemon cream mixture and, if desired, cilantro. **Makes** 5 servings.

Note: If you do not have a handheld immersion blender, use a blender or food processor to puree the soup in batches.

JANICE ELDER
CHARLOTTE, NORTH CAROLINA

Per serving (1⅓ cups soup and 1 Tbsp. lemon cream): Calories 184 (17% from fat); Fat 3.8g (sat 2.1g, mono 0.5g, poly 0.4g); Protein 7g; Carb 33.4g; Fiber 4.9g; Chol 10mg; Iron 1.4mg; Sodium 230mg; Calc 57mg

Fruit Salads With Style

Food gifts are always welcome. And don't rule out fruit just because it's winter. Apples, pears, oranges, grapefruit, and others are at their peak during cooler months. So add a fruit basket to your gift list. It looks lovely, is great to eat, and is good for you too. Best of all, you can use the produce in a variety of recipes from desserts to salads.

Cinnamon Apple Salad
fast fixin's • make ahead
PREP: 15 MIN., COOL: 10 MIN.
Dress this salad for the season by using Red Delicious or Granny Smith apples.

1 Golden Delicious apple, quartered and cored
2 tsp. water
2 tsp. ground cinnamon, divided
¼ cup raspberry vinegar
1 tsp. sugar
1 tsp. Dijon mustard
¼ tsp. salt
½ cup canola oil
1 (8- to 10-oz.) package gourmet mixed salad greens, thoroughly washed
½ (4-oz.) package crumbled goat cheese
3 Tbsp. walnuts, coarsely chopped

1. Cut apple quarters into ¼-inch slices. Microwave apple slices, 2 tsp. water, and 1 tsp. cinnamon in a microwave-safe bowl at HIGH 1 minute, stirring once. Cool 10 minutes.
2. Whisk together vinegar, sugar, mustard, salt, and remaining 1 tsp. cinnamon until well combined. Add canola oil in a slow, steady stream, whisking constantly.
3. Toss ½ cup vinaigrette with salad greens. Sprinkle salad evenly with goat cheese, walnuts, and apple mixture. Serve remaining vinaigrette with salad, if desired, or refrigerate up to 1 week. **Makes** 4 servings.

ANN FOSNIGHT
BOULDER, COLORADO

Holiday Cranberry Mold
make ahead
PREP: 25 MIN., COOK: 5 MIN., CHILL: 11 HRS.

1 (20-oz.) can crushed pineapple in juice
2 (6-oz.) packages raspberry-flavored gelatin
1 cup water
1 (16-oz.) can whole-berry cranberry sauce
1 cup finely chopped celery
2 cups pineapple juice
1 Tbsp. fresh lemon juice
1 (8-oz.) package cream cheese, softened
½ cup mayonnaise
½ cup finely chopped pecans
Green leaf lettuce
Mayonnaise (optional)

1. Drain pineapple well over a medium saucepan, reserving juice in pan. Stir together reserved juice (about 1 cup), gelatin, and 1 cup water, and bring to a boil, stirring until gelatin dissolves. Remove from heat; stir in cranberry sauce, next 3 ingredients, and crushed pineapple. Cover and chill 3 hours or until slightly set.
2. Beat cream cheese and mayonnaise at medium speed with an electric mixer until smooth. Stir in chopped pecans.
3. Spoon cream cheese mixture evenly into 8 lightly greased 1-cup molds. Top with gelatin mixture. Cover and chill 8 hours.
4. Gently run a sharp knife around edges of molds to loosen. Invert molds onto lettuce-lined salad plates; top each with a dollop of mayonnaise, if desired. **Makes** 8 servings.

SHIRLEY SCHMIDT
PASS CHRISTIAN, MISSISSIPPI

Jalapeño, Orange, and Cucumber Salad
make ahead
PREP: 20 MIN., CHILL: 1 HR.

2 cucumbers, peeled
4 to 5 large oranges, peeled and sectioned (about 4 cups)
½ cup thinly sliced red onion
2 Tbsp. fresh lime juice
2 tsp. paprika
½ tsp. salt
1 jalapeño pepper, seeded and minced
1 small head iceberg lettuce, chopped into 1-inch pieces *
Garnish: cilantro sprigs

1. Cut cucumbers in half lengthwise; remove seeds, and cut into thin slices.
2. Combine cucumbers, oranges, and next 5 ingredients; toss gently. Cover and chill 1 hour or until ready to serve.
3. Pour orange mixture over lettuce in a large bowl; toss gently. Garnish, if desired. **Makes** 4 cups.

*Substitute 1 (10-oz.) package salad greens with iceberg lettuce, thoroughly washed, if desired.

KELLI CONTRERAS
GRANITE FALLS, WASHINGTON

Dressed-Up Pot Pies

Pot pie may sound like the same old dish, but we've created a couple of recipes to update this dinner standby. Sausage Gumbo Pie With Garlic Bread Crust pairs iconic Southern foods, including gumbos, with a bread topping to make a savory dish. We also included a dish for the global table—Thai Shrimp Pot Pie With Sesame Wonton Wrappers, which showcases shrimp, coconut milk, and ginger. Try these mouthwatering choices, and you'll have new mealtime favorites.

Thai Shrimp Pot Pie With Sesame Won Ton Toppers

fast fixin's

PREP: 10 MIN., COOK: 15 MIN.

This elegant pot pie is not only quick to put together, but the personal size is also great for entertaining.

1 (8-oz.) package sliced baby portobello or button mushrooms
1 cup snow peas
1 red bell pepper, finely diced
1 Tbsp. grated fresh ginger
2 garlic cloves, minced
1 (13.5-oz.) can coconut milk
1 (14-oz.) can chicken broth
7 Tbsp. all-purpose flour
1 tsp. red curry paste
½ tsp. salt
1 pound uncooked medium-size fresh or frozen shrimp, peeled and tails removed
Sesame Won Ton Toppers
Garnish: sliced green onions

1. Stir-fry first 5 ingredients in a lightly greased Dutch oven over medium-high heat 4 to 5 minutes or until vegetables are softened. Stir in coconut milk. Whisk together broth and next 3 ingredients; stir into mushroom mixture. Cook, whisking constantly, 5 minutes or until thickened.

2. Stir in shrimp, and cook 5 minutes or just until shrimp turn pink. Spoon mixture evenly into 8 (10-oz.) ramekins or individual soufflé dishes. Top each ramekin with 3 Sesame Won Ton Toppers. Garnish, if desired. **Makes** 8 servings.

Note: Look for red curry paste at the supermarket on the aisle with the Asian foods.

Sesame Won Ton Toppers:

fast fixin's

PREP: 5 MIN., BAKE: 5 MIN.

24 won ton wrappers
2 Tbsp. butter, melted
1 Tbsp. sesame seeds
¼ tsp. salt

1. Brush 1 side of each won ton wrapper with butter; sprinkle evenly with sesame seeds and salt. Place on ungreased baking sheets.
2. Bake at 425° for 5 minutes or until golden brown. **Makes** 24 pieces.

Note: Won ton wrappers can be found in the refrigerated produce section of most large supermarkets.

Sausage Gumbo Pot Pie With Garlic Bread Crust

PREP: 15 MIN., COOK: 15 MIN., BAKE: 20 MIN., STAND: 10 MIN.

1 lb. smoked sausage, cut into ¼-inch-thick slices
1 medium-size green bell pepper, chopped
1 small onion, chopped
¼ cup instant roux mix
1 (10-oz.) can diced tomatoes and green chiles
1 (32-oz.) container chicken broth
1 (16-oz.) package frozen okra
1 cup quick-cooking rice, uncooked
½ tsp. Cajun seasoning
½ tsp. dried thyme
3 Tbsp. butter, melted
2 garlic cloves, minced
1 (12-oz.) French baguette, cut into ½-inch-thick slices
Garnish: finely chopped fresh parsley

1. Sauté first 3 ingredients in a Dutch oven over medium-high heat 8 minutes or until browned; stir in roux mix. Cook, stirring constantly, 2 minutes. Stir in tomatoes and next 5 ingredients, and bring to a boil. Remove from heat. Pour into a 13- x 9-inch baking dish.
2. Stir together butter and garlic; brush on 1 side of bread slices. Top sausage mixture with bread slices, buttered side up.
3. Bake, covered, at 425° for 10 minutes; uncover and bake 10 more minutes. Let stand 10 minutes before serving. Garnish, if desired. **Makes** 8 to 10 servings.

Note: For testing purposes only, we used Tony Chachere's Creole Instant Roux Mix found in the spice section of the supermarket.

Winning Won Tons

Thai Shrimp Pot Pie With Sesame Won Ton Toppers is easy to make. It has a 10-minute cook time, while the flaky toppers bake up in 5 minutes. Our step-by-steps show you how.

1 The sauce starts with a quick stir-fry of vegetables combined with chicken broth, coconut milk, and seasonings. Add the shrimp, and ladle into ramekins.

2 The crusts are made from won ton wrappers. Separate the wrappers you need, working quickly to prevent them from drying out. While you work, cover the wrappers with a damp cloth or paper towel to keep them moist.

3 Arrange the won ton wrappers on a pan. Brush with butter, and top with sesame seeds and salt; bake and place three on top of individual pot pies to serve.

Soup and Sandwiches for Supper

A toasted club and a satisfying soup make a perfect meal for the busiest time of year.

Stack up big flavor in a flash with these sandwiches. Pile toasted bread slices high with deli meats, crisp bacon, cheese, lettuce, and tomato. Cut sandwiches in quarters, and secure with wooden picks—plain or frilly—for eye appeal. Top it all off with a cup of Chunky Vegetable Soup, and you've got a terrific relaxed meal just right for tonight, a shopping day lunch, or a weekend supper.

Toasted Club Sandwiches
fast fixin's
PREP: 15 MIN.

¾ cup mayonnaise
2 Tbsp. yellow mustard
12 sourdough bread slices, toasted
8 (1-oz.) slices deli ham
8 (1-oz.) slices deli turkey breast
16 fully cooked bacon slices
8 (¾-oz.) Swiss cheese slices
16 plum tomato slices
4 iceberg lettuce leaves, halved

1. Stir together mayonnaise and mustard in a small bowl. Spread mayonnaise mixture evenly onto 1 side of bread slices. Layer 4 bread slices, mayonnaise sides up, with 1 slice ham, 1 slice turkey, 2 bacon slices, 1 Swiss cheese slice, 2 tomato slices, and ½ lettuce leaf. Top each with 1 bread slice, mayonnaise side down; layer with

remaining ham, turkey, bacon, cheese, tomato, and lettuce. Top with remaining 4 bread slices, mayonnaise sides down. Secure with wooden picks, if desired, and cut each sandwich into quarters. **Makes** 4 servings.

Note: For testing purposes only, we used Pepperidge Farm Sourdough Bread.

LOUISE JORDAN
YORK, SOUTH CAROLINA

Toasted Vegetable Club Sandwiches:
Omit ham, turkey, bacon, Swiss cheese slices, 16 tomato slices, and lettuce. Prepare sandwiches as directed, substituting 8 arugula leaves, 24 plum tomato slices, 24 avocado slices, 24 cucumber slices, and 8 (1-oz.) slices Provolone cheese. **Makes** 4 servings. Prep: 15 min.

Toasted Cuban-Style Club Sandwiches:
Omit ham, turkey, bacon, tomatoes, and lettuce. Prepare sandwiches as directed; substituting 8 (1-oz.) roasted pork slices, 8 (1-oz.) pastrami-seasoned turkey breast slices, and 16 sandwich-cut dill pickles. **Makes** 4 servings. Prep: 15 min.

Fix and Freeze

The recipe below makes almost 2 gal. of soup. Unless you're feeding a crowd you'll have extra, so freeze meal-size portions in zip-top plastic freezer bags. Fold top edge of freezer bag down, and place in a large glass measuring cup to stabilize the bag while filling. Seal the bag, removing as much air as possible; label and freeze up to 3 months. Thaw in the refrigerator.

Chunky Vegetable Soup
family favorite
PREP: 10 MIN., COOK: 35 MIN.

2 lb. ground chuck
1 small sweet onion, chopped
1 tsp. salt
½ tsp. pepper
3 (14-oz.) cans low-sodium beef broth
3 (29-oz.) cans mixed vegetables with potatoes, rinsed and drained
3 (14½-oz.) cans diced new potatoes, rinsed and drained
1 (15-oz.) can sweet peas with mushrooms and pearl onions, rinsed and drained
2 (26-oz.) jars tomato, herbs, and spices pasta sauce
1 (14½-oz.) can diced tomatoes with sweet onion

1. Cook ground chuck and onion, in batches, in a large Dutch oven over medium-high heat, stirring until meat crumbles and is no longer pink. Drain well, and return to Dutch oven. Stir in salt, pepper, and beef broth, and bring to a boil.

2. Stir in mixed vegetables and remaining ingredients. Bring to a boil; cover, reduce heat, and simmer at least 20 minutes or until thoroughly heated. **Makes** 35 cups (about 2 gal.).

Note: For testing purposes only, we used Classico Organic Tomato, Herbs & Spices Pasta Sauce.

GENEVA CHANEY
PELHAM, ALABAMA

top-rated menu
Entertain With Ease

In celebration of our 40th anniversary, we asked former Senior Foods Editor Jean Wickstrom Liles for her most memorable *Southern Living* recipe. Without hesitation, she singled out Shrimp Destin. "It started as a quick, delicious recipe served to me and my husband while visiting our friends, the Ponders, at their beach house in Destin, Florida, back in 1982," she says. According to Jean, who was part of our Foods team for 20 years, the recipe immediately took on a life of its own when she featured it in the magazine a few months later. It has since become one of our most requested recipes. Jean often pairs it with Asparagus With Curry Sauce for a stellar brunch or supper.

Shrimp Supper

Serves 4

Shrimp Destin over toast

Asparagus With Curry Sauce

Chocolate-Mint Cake (page 286)

Shrimp Destin

PREP: 25 MIN., COOK: 7 MIN.
Short on time? Purchase 1½ lb. already peeled and deveined shrimp, and you're ready to go.

2 lb. unpeeled, large fresh shrimp
½ cup butter
⅓ cup chopped green onions
1 Tbsp. minced garlic
¼ cup dry white wine
1 tsp. lemon juice
¼ tsp. fresh coarse ground pepper
⅛ tsp. salt
1 Tbsp. chopped fresh dill or 1 tsp. dried dillweed
1 Tbsp. chopped fresh parsley
4 (1.3-oz.) French rolls, split and toasted
Garnish: fresh parsley sprigs

1. Peel shrimp, and devein, if desired.
2. Melt butter in a large skillet over medium; add green onions and garlic, and sauté 2 minutes or until tender. Add shrimp, wine, and next 3 ingredients. Cook over medium heat, stirring occasionally, 5 minutes or until shrimp turn pink. Remove from heat; stir in dill and parsley.
3. Place toasted roll halves on 4 individual serving plates. Spoon shrimp mixture evenly over toasted rolls, and garnish, if desired. Serve immediately. **Makes** 4 servings.

FRANCES PONDER
DESTIN, FLORIDA

Asparagus With Curry Sauce
fast fixin's
PREP: 10 MIN., COOK: 6 MIN.

½ cup light or regular mayonnaise
1½ Tbsp. frozen orange juice concentrate, thawed
1 tsp. curry powder
1 lb. fresh asparagus

1. Stir together first 3 ingredients until blended. Cover and chill until ready to serve.
2. Snap off tough ends of asparagus. Peel asparagus, if desired.
3. Cook asparagus, covered, in boiling salted water to cover 6 minutes or until crisp-tender; drain. Plunge asparagus into ice water to stop the cooking process; drain.
4. Arrange asparagus on a serving platter; top with mayonnaise mixture. **Makes** 4 servings.

DALE SAFRIT
RALEIGH, NORTH CAROLINA

Cook's Notes

If fresh shrimp are not available, try frozen. They're versatile, easy to use, and economical. Frozen shrimp are just what the doctor ordered for everything from a quick stir-fry to an almost-instantaneous appetizer. You can buy them in a variety of forms—cooked or raw and either unpeeled, peeled with tail on, or fully peeled. Look for frozen shrimp at stores with good product turnover, and avoid bags with excess ice, particularly in clumps. This is a telltale sign the shrimp have been thawed and refrozen. In a Test Kitchens taste test, we found that the Celine brand, purchased from a warehouse club, consistently offered the best taste and texture.

Easy Enchiladas

They're fast to make and perfect to freeze.

A Tasty Tex-Mex Plate

Serves 6

Chicken-and-Spinach Enchiladas

Dressed-Up Refried Beans

Mexican rice

apple and pear slices with Toffee–Apple Dip
(page 290)

W hen you're in the mood for Tex-Mex, this is the dinner to make. From kitchen to table, it takes about an hour, and half of that is hands-off baking or cooking time. Make a few pans of enchiladas and keep them in the freezer for this busy month. Each recipe will bake from the frozen state to piping hot in just less than one hour.

Individual ramekins make easy work of portioning and serving refried beans.

Chicken-and-Spinach Enchiladas
freezeable • make ahead
PREP: 15 MIN., BAKE: 30 MIN., STAND: 5 MIN.

1 (10-oz.) package frozen chopped
   spinach, thawed
1 (16-oz.) jar medium salsa with cilantro,
   divided
2 (10-oz.) cans enchilada sauce
1 (8-oz.) package cream cheese *
2½ cups shredded or chopped roasted
   chicken
10 (7- to 8-inch) flour tortillas
1 (8-oz.) package shredded Mexican
   four-cheese blend
Toppings: shredded lettuce, guacamole,
   chopped fresh cilantro, chopped red
   onion, halved grape tomatoes

1. Drain spinach well, pressing between paper towels. Set aside.
2. Stir together ¼ cup salsa and enchilada sauce, and set aside.
3. Microwave cream cheese in a medium micowave-safe bowl at HIGH 1 minute or until very soft. Add spinach, chicken, and remaining salsa, and stir until blended.

4. Spoon a heaping ⅓ cup chicken mixture down center of each tortilla. Roll up tortillas, and place, seam sides down, in a lightly greased 13- x 9-inch baking dish. Pour enchilada sauce mixture evenly over top of rolled tortillas, and sprinkle with cheese.
5. Bake at 350° for 30 minutes or until bubbly. Let stand 5 minutes. Serve with desired toppings. **Makes** 6 servings.

Note: For testing purposes only, we used Tostitos Medium Salsa and Old El Paso Enchilada Sauce.

* Substitute ⅓-less-fat cream cheese, if desired.

CLAUDIA HON
VESTAVIA HILLS, ALABAMA

Dressed-Up Refried Beans
PREP: 10 MIN., BAKE: 30 MIN.
If desired, use full-fat refried beans and cheese instead of fat-free and reduced-fat products.

2 (16-oz.) cans fat-free refried
   beans
6 (¾-inch) reduced-fat Monterey Jack
   cheese cubes
6 pickled whole jalapeño peppers

1. Spoon refried beans evenly into 6 (6-oz.) lightly greased ramekins or custard cups. Top each with 1 cheese cube, pressing gently into center of beans. Top beans with 1 jalapeño pepper. Place ramekins on a baking sheet.
2. Bake at 350° for 30 minutes or until cheese is melted and beans are thoroughly heated. **Makes** 6 servings.

Note: If you prefer, spread beans into a lightly greased 8- x 8-inch baking dish. Top with cheese cubes, pressing gently into beans. Top each cheese cube with 1 jalapeño pepper. Bake as directed above.

Succulent Rib Roast

This traditional selection makes a meal extra special.

Make a special menu extraordinary by cooking splurge-worthy Perfect Prime Rib. It's impressive and easy; once the meat is in the oven, you're free to tend to other dishes. Top each slice with a dollop of Fluffy Horseradish Sauce. Serve tossed salad and steamed broccoli with diced red peppers to round out your meal. These recipes allow you and your friends to dine-in, restaurant style.

Perfect Prime Rib

PREP: 5 MIN.; COOK: 1 HR., 30 MIN.; STAND: 20 MIN.

1½ tsp. kosher salt
1 tsp. coarsely ground pepper
1 Tbsp. extra-virgin olive oil
1 (6-lb.) prime rib roast (about 3 ribs)
Fluffy Horseradish Sauce
Garnish: rosemary sprigs

1. Combine salt, pepper, and olive oil; rub evenly over roast. Place roast on a wire rack in an aluminum foil-lined roasting pan.
2. Bake at 450° for 45 minutes; reduce oven temperature to 350°, and bake 45 minutes or until a meat thermometer inserted in thickest portion registers 145° (medium rare) or to desired degree of doneness. Remove from oven, cover loosely with aluminum foil, and let stand 20 minutes before slicing. Serve with Fluffy Horseradish Sauce. Garnish, if desired. **Makes** 6 servings.

HOWARD GREEN
ATLANTA, GEORGIA

Fluffy Horseradish Sauce:
fast fixin's
PREP: 10 MIN.
This robust sauce is inspired by a recipe served with moist and tender beef at Lawry's The Prime Rib restaurants. With just four ingredients, it's easy to whip up while the roast is standing.

1 cup whipping cream
4 Tbsp. prepared horseradish
1 to 2 Tbsp. chopped fresh parsley
¼ tsp. garlic salt

1. Beat cream at medium-high speed with a heavy-duty stand mixer 1 minute or until stiff peaks form.
2. Fold in remaining ingredients. Serve immediately, or cover and refrigerate up to 8 hours. **Makes** about 2 cups.

Use a meat fork to hold the rib roast steady as you slice.

Choose Your Beverage

Perfect Prime Rib needs a special beverage. Serve one of the following wines selected by *Southern Living* wine expert and Executive Editor Scott Jones:
■ Greg Norman Estates, Limestone Coast Cabernet Merlot, Australia, $15
■ Covey Run, Merlot, Columbia Valley, Washington $9

Christmas All Through the House.

Celebrate the season with our creative menu ideas and tips for outdoor entertaining.

Ready, Set, Bake

Giggles and wonderful aromas fill the house when you and your kids bake cookies.

It's great fun to bake cookies and cupcakes with and for your kids during the holidays. Rebecca Kracke Gordon, Test Kitchens Professional, shows us how to work magic with her homemade cookie dough, store-bought refrigerated cookie dough, and a cake mix. Let the kids help measure ingredients and choose shapes and colors. Store decorated cookies between sheets of wax paper in an airtight container. The process will create a loving memory and sweet treats for everyone.

Wacky Reindeer Cupcakes
family favorite
PREP: 45 MIN., BAKE: 22 MIN.
Decorate these fun cupcakes as you go because the glaze hardens quickly.

1 (18.25-oz.) package white cake
   mix
3 large eggs
1¼ cups buttermilk
⅓ cup butter, melted
Snow White Glaze
Miniature colorful candy canes or
   pretzel sticks
Candy-coated chewy fruit candies

1. Beat first 4 ingredients at low speed with an electric mixer 30 seconds; beat at medium speed 2 minutes, stopping to scrape down sides of bowl. Place 24 paper baking cups in muffin pans; spoon batter evenly into paper cups, filling two-thirds full.
2. Bake at 350° for 18 to 22 minutes or until a wooden pick inserted in center comes out clean. Remove cupcakes from pans, and let cool completely on wire racks.

3. Spread 4 cupcakes evenly with Snow White Glaze. (Glaze will be thin.) Place on wax paper, and decorate with candy canes or pretzel sticks for antlers, and candy-coated chewy fruit candies for eyes and nose to resemble reindeer. Repeat until all cupcakes are decorated. Stir glaze if necessary. **Makes** 24 cupcakes.

Snow White Glaze:
fast fixin's
PREP: 5 MIN.

3 cups powdered sugar
¼ cup milk

1. Whisk together powdered sugar and milk until smooth. **Makes** about 1½ cups.

Note: For testing purposes only, we used Skittles bite-size candies.

Wreath Cupcakes: Frost cupcakes as directed. Omit miniature candy canes and fruit candies. Decorate cupcake edges with green candy sprinkles and red cinnamon candies to resemble wreaths.

Chocolate-Dipped Cookie Sticks

family favorite

PREP: 20 MIN., BAKE: 8 MIN. PER BATCH

¼ (18-oz.) package refrigerated sugar
   cookie dough
3 oz. chocolate candy coating, chopped
Assorted holiday candy sprinkles

1. Shape dough into 24 (2½-inch-long)
ropes (about ½ tsp. each), using your
hands, and place on parchment paper-
lined baking sheets.
2. Bake at 350° for 6 to 8 minutes or
until edges are lightly browned. Cool
completely on wire racks.
3. Microwave chocolate coating in a
microwave-safe bowl at HIGH 1½ minutes, stirring every 30 seconds, or until
melted.
4. Dip ends of cookies in melted chocolate, and roll in candy sprinkles. Place
on wax paper, and let stand until firm.
Makes 2 dozen.

Santa's Cookie Plate

family favorite

PREP: 45 MIN., BAKE: 8 MIN. PER BATCH

*Have fun with the vivid color and design of
these cookies.*

¼ (18-oz.) package refrigerated sugar
   cookie dough
Cream Cheese Frosting, divided
Assorted food coloring gel
Assorted colored sugars
Assorted edible glitter
Assorted colored sprinkles
Red cinnamon candies
Garnish: gumdrops

1. Roll dough to a ⅛-inch thickness on
a lightly floured surface. Cut with
desired cookie cutters, and place 2
inches apart on parchment paper-lined
baking sheets.
2. Bake at 350° for 6 to 8 minutes or
until lightly browned on edges. Cool
completely on wire racks.
3. Set aside ½ cup Cream Cheese
Frosting. Divide remaining frosting
evenly between 3 or 4 bowls; tint

desired colors with food coloring gel.
Spread cooled cookies with frosting,
and decorate with desired colored sugars, edible glitter, sprinkles, and cinnamon candies.
4. Attach cookies around edge of a
white 10-inch dinner plate with
reserved ½ cup frosting. Garnish, if
desired. **Makes** 15 (2-inch) cookies.

Cream Cheese Frosting:

family favorite • fast fixin's

PREP: 5 MIN.

½ cup butter, softened
1 (8-oz.) package cream cheese,
   softened
1 (3-oz.) package cream cheese,
   softened
1 (16-oz.) package powdered sugar

1. Beat together all ingredients at
medium-high speed with an electric
mixer until smooth. **Makes** about
3 cups.

Sugar Plum Thumbprints

family favorite

PREP: 15 MIN., CHILL: 30 MIN., BAKE: 12 MIN.
PER BATCH

*These cookies offer a burst of flavor from
colorful gumdrops.*

1 cup butter, softened
1 cup powdered sugar
1 tsp. vanilla extract
2 cups all-purpose flour
¼ tsp. salt
⅔ cup ready-to-spread cream cheese
   frosting
Gumdrops
Colored edible glitter
Powdered sugar

1. Beat butter at medium speed with an
electric mixer until creamy. Gradually
add 1 cup powdered sugar and vanilla,
beating well. Add flour and salt, mixing
until well combined. Cover and chill 30
minutes.

2. Roll dough into 48 (¾-inch) balls,
and place on parchment paper-lined
baking sheets. Press thumb in center of
each cookie to make an indention.
3. Bake at 350° for 10 to12 minutes or
until lightly browned on edges. Cool
completely on wire racks.
4. Dollop cream cheese frosting into
cookie indentions; top each cookie with
a gumdrop. Sprinkle with edible glitter,
and dust with powdered sugar. **Makes**
about 4 dozen.

Note: Edible glitter can be found at
crafts stores.

Winter Mittens

family favorite

PREP: 30 MIN., BAKE: 10 MIN. PER BATCH

*Busy cooks will love these festive treats that
are made with refrigerated sugar cookie
dough and canned frosting.*

½ (18-oz.) package refrigerated sugar
   cookie dough
1 (16-oz.) container ready-to-spread
   vanilla frosting
Blue food coloring gel
White edible glitter
Garnish: powdered sugar

1. Roll dough to a ⅛-inch thickness on
a lightly floured surface; cut with a (5-
x 3-inch) mitten cookie cutter, and
place on parchment paper-lined baking sheets.
2. Bake at 350° for 8 to 10 minutes or
until edges are lightly browned. Cool
completely on wire racks.
3. Tint half of frosting with blue food
coloring gel to desired shade. Spread
on cookies.
4. Spoon remaining half of frosting
into a 1-qt. zip-top plastic bag. (Do not
seal.) Snip a tiny hole in 1 corner of
bag, and pipe decorative design on
cookies. Sprinkle with edible glitter.
Garnish, if desired. **Makes** 8 cookies.

Peanut Butter Snowballs
family favorite
PREP: 25 MIN., BAKE: 15 MIN. PER BATCH,
COOL: 5 MIN. PER BATCH

1 cup butter, softened
⅔ cup granulated sugar
⅔ cup chunky peanut butter
2½ cups all-purpose flour
¼ tsp. salt
¾ cup powdered sugar, sifted
White edible glitter (optional)

1. Beat butter at medium speed with an electric mixer until creamy; gradually add granulated sugar, beating well. Stir in peanut butter until blended.
2. Combine flour and salt; gradually add to peanut butter mixture, beating until well blended.
3. Roll dough into 60 (1-inch) balls; place 1 inch apart on parchment paper-lined baking sheets.
4. Bake at 350° for 12 to 15 minutes. Cool on baking sheets on wire racks 5 minutes. Roll warm cookies in powdered sugar. Dust with edible glitter, if desired. **Makes** about 5 dozen.

Great Cheese Snacks

These tasty party starters require as little as five minutes prep time.

Whipped, flavored, or plain cream cheese is a popular holiday recipe ingredient. The familiar foil-wrapped block of spreadable goodness is the foundation for many of our favorite appetizers. Orange Blossom Cheese Spread and Tortilla Cheese Wrap-Ups require chill time, but the remaining recipes yield ready-to-serve results. If you're expecting guests or they take you by surprise, whip out the cream cheese to make an easy finger food such as Spicy Cranberry Spread.

Orange Blossom Cheese Spread
make ahead
PREP: 10 MIN., CHILL: 1 HR.

1 (8-oz.) package cream cheese, softened
2 cups (8 oz.) shredded sharp Cheddar cheese
½ cup orange marmalade
½ cup chopped pecans, toasted
¼ cup sweetened dried cranberries
¼ cup raisins
Gingersnaps

1. Beat first 3 ingredients at medium speed with an electric mixer until well blended. Stir in chopped pecans, cranberries, and raisins. Cover and chill at least 1 hour or up to 8 hours. Serve with gingersnaps. **Makes** 8 to 10 appetizer servings.
BRENDA D. SMITH
MCGAHEYSVILLE, VIRGINIA

Tortilla Cheese Wrap-Ups
make ahead
PREP: 15 MIN., CHILL: 2 HRS.

1 (3-oz.) package cream cheese, softened
1 Tbsp. chopped fresh cilantro
½ tsp. taco seasoning mix
3 (8-inch) flour tortillas
9 (¾-oz.) Cheddar cheese slices
18 wooden picks
Salsa

1. Combine first 3 ingredients until well blended. Spread about 2 Tbsp. cream cheese mixture evenly over each tortilla.
2. Top each tortilla with 3 slices of Cheddar cheese, cutting slices to fit. Roll up tortillas tightly, and wrap in plastic wrap; chill 2 hours.
3. Remove tortillas from plastic wrap, and cut into 1-inch slices, discarding end slices. Secure slices with wooden picks, and serve with salsa. **Makes** 6 to 8 appetizer servings (18 pieces).
DIANE BALDWIN
FRANKLIN, NORTH CAROLINA

Cheese Bites

PREP: 15 MIN., BAKE: 10 MIN., STAND: 10 MIN.

Use a piece of dental floss pulled taut to cut chilled cream cheese.

½ (8-oz.) package cream cheese
1 (16.3-oz.) can refrigerated flaky
    buttermilk biscuits
½ cup jalapeño pepper jelly*

1. Cut cream cheese into 24 pieces and let soften.
2. Separate each biscuit into thirds, making 3 rounds. Press biscuit rounds into bottom and up sides of 24 mini-muffin cups. Spoon about 1 tsp. jelly into center of each biscuit cup; top each with 1 cream cheese piece.
3. Bake at 425° for 8 to 10 minutes or until golden brown. Let stand 10 minutes before serving. **Makes** 12 appetizer servings.

*Substitute ½ cup mango chutney, if desired.

Brie Cheese Bites: Prepare recipe as directed, substituting 1 (8-oz.) Brie round, rind removed, for cream cheese. Bake as directed.

Mini-Phyllo Cheese Bites: Prepare recipe as directed, substituting 24 frozen mini phyllo pastry shells, thawed, for biscuits, and reducing jelly to ¼ cup. Spoon about ½ tsp. jelly into each shell; top each shell with 1 piece cream cheese. Bake as directed.

JULIE SEREEBUTRA
DALLAS, GEORGIA

Serve these delicious little bites to guests straight from the oven.

Chile-Cheese Quesadillas

fast fixin's

PREP: 15 MIN., COOK: 8 MIN.

Let guests share the fun of making a steady supply of warm chile cheese quesadillas.

1 (3-oz.) package cream cheese,
    softened
1 cup (4 oz.) shredded American cheese
1 cup (4 oz.) shredded Cheddar cheese
1 (4.5-oz.) can chopped green chiles
¼ tsp. garlic powder
⅛ tsp. ground red pepper
8 (8-inch) flour tortillas
Toppings: sour cream, salsa
Garnish: cilantro sprigs

1. Beat first 6 ingredients at medium speed with an electric mixer until well blended. Spread about ½ cup cheese mixture onto each of 4 tortillas, leaving a ½-inch border. Top with remaining tortillas.
2. Heat a lightly greased large nonstick skillet over medium-high heat just until hot. Cook quesadillas in 4 batches, 1 minute on each side or until filling melts and outside browns. Serve with toppings. Garnish, if desired. **Makes** 8 servings.

EVELYN DYKES
FIELDALE, VIRGINIA

Spicy Cranberry Spread

fast fixin's

PREP: 5 MIN.

1 (8-oz.) package cream cheese,
    softened
¾ cup Cranberry Pepper Jelly
Assorted crackers

1. Place cream cheese on a serving platter, and spoon ¾ cup Cranberry Pepper Jelly evenly over cheese. Serve with assorted crackers. **Makes** 8 to 10 servings.

Cranberry Pepper Jelly:

fast fixin's • make ahead

PREP: 5 MIN., COOK: 10 MIN.

You can share the remaining jelly as a gift.

1 (16-oz.) can whole-berry cranberry
    sauce
1 (10.5-oz.) jar hot jalapeño pepper jelly

1. Cook cranberry sauce and pepper jelly in a small saucepan over medium heat, stirring often, 10 minutes or until melted. Remove from heat; cool completely. Store in an airtight container in the refrigerator up to 1 week. **Makes** 2½ cups.

ELIZABETH HUNTEBRINKER
KANSAS CITY, MISSOURI

Cocktails by Candlelight

Host a happy hour with ease. Just fill your home with pretty candle arrangements and serve these signature sippers.

Somewhere between your 50th mad dash to the mall and baking cookies for Santa, you want to squeeze in socializing with your friends. Think you can't fit it into your schedule? Then this is the plan for you. It's quick, it's easy, and it offers all the basics—great atmosphere, casual time with friends, and delicious drinks. Let this be your countdown to throwing an impressive holiday cocktail party.

Get the Word Out
Make it easy on yourself and invite guests via email. Visit **www.evite.com** for help. Let your invitation read: "Stop by at six for cocktails and more. With music and munchies—it won't be a bore! Don't bring a thing—just your holiday cheer. It'll be casual and fun, so why not be here?"

Set the Scene
Round up several different shapes and sizes of candles—from tea lights to tapers.

Group them in vases, glass jars, and on top of small trays and pedestal stands. Add fresh greenery, berries, and flowers around your arrangements. Safety note: Never place greenery near a flame.
Quick tip: If you're using scented candles, be sure to stick with a single fragrance. so you don't want overwhelm your space—or your guests.

Make Room for Munchies
What's a cocktail party without great snacks? But you don't have to go to a lot of trouble. Simply set out your favorite crackers and cheeses, nuts, and chips. Fill several colorful bowls with different snacks, and arrange them all around your gathering area so your guests can mingle and munch in more than one spot.

Start Pouring

Shaken or stirred, these cocktail recipes are a cinch to make. Cut down your bartending duties by serving one or two specialty drinks, along with wine and Champagne.

Chocolate Martini
fast fixin's
PREP: 10 MIN.

⅓ cup chocolate liqueur
⅓ cup dark cream of cocao
⅔ cup half-and-half
¼ cup vodka
Crushed ice cubes

1. Stir together first 4 ingredients.
2. Fill half of cocktail shaker with ice. Add half of chocolate liqueur mixture, cover with lid, and shake 8 to 10 seconds until thoroughly chilled. Strain into chilled martini glasses. Repeat with remaining mixture. Serve immediately. **Makes** 4 servings.

Note: For testing purposes only, we used Godiva Liqueur for the chocolate liquer.

BECKY MOON
COLUMBIA, TENNESSEE

Smart Hostess Tips

■ Make sure you don't run out of ice—a common conundrum. The day before your get-together, fill extra ice cube trays, pick up a bag or two, or put your ice-maker to work overtime.
■ Offer guests nonalcoholic drinks as well. Set out soft drinks and juices. Serve hot cocoa and Hot Mulled Cider.
■ Always keep each candlewick trimmed to a quarter inch to minimize the flame's flicker and smoke.

To decorate your bar area, fill martini glasses with water, and place floating candles inside.

Chocolate Eggnog

fast fixin's

PREP: 15 MIN.

1 qt. refrigerated eggnog
1 qt. milk
1 (16-oz.) can chocolate syrup
½ cup light rum (optional)
1 cup whipping cream
2 Tbsp. powdered sugar
Unsweetened cocoa (optional)

1. Stir together first 3 ingredients and, if desired, rum in a punch bowl, stirring well.
2. Beat whipping cream at high speed with an electric mixer until foamy. Add powdered sugar, beating until medium peaks form. Dollop whipped cream over individual servings. Sift cocoa over whipped cream, if desired. **Makes** about 9½ cups.

SANDY RUSSELL
ORANGE PARK, FLORIDA

Champagne and Cranberries

fast fixin's

PREP: 5 MIN.
Cranberries will dance in the glass.

6 dried cranberries
¾ cup Champagne or sparkling wine, chilled

1. Place cranberries in Champagne flute. Pour Champagne over berries. Serve immediately. **Makes** 1 serving.

Hot Mulled Cider

family favorite

PREP: 15 MIN., COOK: 1 HR.

2 qt. apple cider
½ cup firmly packed light brown sugar
1 tsp. whole allspice
½ tsp. whole cloves
2 (3-inch) cinnamon sticks
1 orange, peeled and sliced

1. Stir together apple cider and brown sugar in a large Dutch oven. Tie allspice, cloves, and cinnamon sticks in a small piece of cheesecloth with kitchen twine. Add spice bag and orange slices to cider. Cook over low heat 1 hour. Remove spice bag and oranges before serving. **Makes** 7½ cups.

JOAN B. HENDERSON-LEESE
VICKSBURG, MISSISSIPPI

Cape Codder Punch

PREP: 10 MIN..

1 (48-oz.) bottle cranberry juice cocktail
1½ cups vodka
⅓ cup sweetened lime juice
1 (1-liter) bottle ginger ale, chilled
Ice cubes
Garnish: fresh cranberries and lime wedges on swizzle sticks

1. Stir together first 3 ingredients. Stir in ginger ale just before serving. Serve over ice. Garnish, if desired. **Makes** about 12 cups.

Note: For testing purposes only, we used Rose's West India Sweetened Lime Juice.

Sour Apple Martini

fast fixin's

PREP: 10 MIN.

4 very thin Granny Smith apple wedges
Cinnamon sugar
¾ cup vodka
¾ cup sour apple Schnapps
Crushed ice cubes

1. Rub rims of chilled martini glasses with apple slices. Place cinnamon sugar in a saucer; spin rim of each glass in cinnamon sugar. Attach 1 apple slice on rim of each glass.
2. Stir together vodka and Schnapps. Fill half of cocktail shaker with ice. Add half of vodka mixture, cover with lid, and shake 10 seconds or until thoroughly chilled. Strain into chilled glasses. Repeat with remaining vodka mixture. Serve immediately. **Makes** 4 servings.

Note: For testing purposes only, we used DeKuyper Pucker Sour Apple Schnapps.

For the Sour Apple Martini, rim the glass with cinnamon sugar, and garnish with an apple slice. Skewer cranberries and lime wedges to make a stirrer for Cape Codder Punch.

Your Party, Your Budget

Whether you host a seated dinner or a casual buffet, we have you covered. Use these mix-and-match menus for a party that suits your style.

When the party's at your house, try one of these festive menus. One takes longer to prepare and is a bit more lavish; the other saves both time and money. No matter which option you select, you'll be proud of the results.

Celebration Dinner

Serves 8

Sweet-and-Sour Tapenade

Herb-Crusted Pork Tenderloins

Cheesy Herbed Scalloped Potatoes

steamed sugar snap peas

Turtle Trifle

Easy Pasta Dinner

Serves 8

Sweet-and-Sour Tapenade

Pounded Pork Parmesan With Linguine

steamed sugar snap peas

Cappuccino-Frosted Brownies

Sweet-and-Sour Tapenade

fast fixin's

PREP: 15 MIN.

Raisins add a sweet note to this salty olive-and-caper spread.

1 (10-oz.) jar pitted kalamata olives (about 2 cups), drained
½ cup raisins
2 Tbsp. chopped fresh basil
1 garlic clove
1 Tbsp. drained capers
1 Tbsp. Dijon mustard
¼ cup olive oil
Garnish: fresh basil leaves
Pita chips

1. Pulse first 6 ingredients in a food processor or blender until coarsely chopped. Gradually add oil, processing just until mixture is well blended. Cover and chill until ready to serve. Garnish, if desired. Serve with pita chips. **Makes** 8 servings (about 1⅓ cups).

GILDA LESTER
WILMINGTON, NORTH CAROLINA

Herb-Crusted Pork Tenderloins

PREP: 10 MIN., CHILL: 4 HRS., BAKE: 40 MIN., STAND: 10 MIN.

Herbes de Provence is a combination of dried basil, fennel seeds, lavender, marjoram, rosemary, sage, summer savory, and thyme.

¼ cup firmly packed brown sugar
2 Tbsp. herbes de Provence or dried Italian seasoning
1 tsp. ground coriander
1 tsp. salt
¼ tsp. pepper
2 (1- to 1 ½-lb.) pork tenderloins, trimmed

1. Combine first 5 ingredients. Rub mixture evenly into pork. Place pork in a large shallow dish or large zip-top plastic freezer bag. Cover or seal, and chill 2 to 4 hours.
2. Place pork on a wire rack in a lightly greased shallow roasting pan.
3. Bake at 450° for 10 minutes. Reduce heat to 350°, and bake 20 to 30 minutes or until a meat thermometer inserted in thickest portion registers 155°. Remove from oven, and cover pork loosely with aluminum foil; let stand 10 minutes before serving. **Makes** 6 to 8 servings.

CATHY DWYER
FREEDOM, NEW HAMPSHIRE

Cheesy Herbed Scalloped Potatoes

family favorite

PREP: 20 MIN.; COOK: 10 MIN.;
BAKE: 1 HR., 30 MIN.

½ cup mayonnaise
2 Tbsp. all-purpose flour
½ tsp. salt
⅛ tsp. pepper
1½ cups milk
1 cup (4 oz.) shredded sharp Cheddar
    cheese
1 tsp. chopped fresh parsley
1 tsp. chopped fresh chives
1 tsp. chopped fresh thyme
4 cups (3 lb.) thinly sliced baking
    potatoes (about 4 large)
2 Tbsp. grated Parmesan cheese

1. Combine first 4 ingredients in a saucepan. Gradually add milk; cook, stirring constantly, over medium-low heat 8 to 10 minutes or until thickened. Remove from heat.

2. Add Cheddar cheese and herbs, stirring until cheese melts and is well blended.

3. Place half of potato slices evenly in a lightly greased 11- x 7-inch baking dish; pour half of cheese mixture over potatoes. Repeat layers with remaining half of potato slices and cheese mixture. Sprinkle evenly with Parmesan cheese.

4. Bake, covered, at 350° for 1 hour. Uncover, and bake 30 more minutes or until potatoes are golden brown and fork-tender. **Makes** 8 servings.

SHARON CLOR
FORT LAUDERDALE, FLORIDA

Turtle Trifle

make ahead

PREP: 20 MIN., CHILL: 1 HR.

Mascarpone is rich double or triple cream cheese made from cow's milk.

8 oz. mascarpone cheese, softened **＊**
1½ cups whipping cream
1½ tsp. vanilla extract
1 (2-lb.) frozen pecan pie, thawed and
    cut into 1-inch cubes
⅓ cup chocolate fudge topping
⅓ cup caramel topping
½ cup chopped pecans, toasted

1. Beat first 3 ingredients in a large bowl at medium speed with a heavy-duty electric stand mixer, using the whisk attachment, 2 to 3 minutes or until smooth and firm.

2. Place half of pie cubes in bottom of a 4-qt. trifle dish or tall, clear 4-qt. glass bowl. Spread half of whipped cream mixture over pie cubes. Drizzle with half each of chocolate fudge topping and caramel topping. Sprinkle with half of chopped pecans. Repeat layers.

3. Cover and chill at least 1 hour or up to 8 hours. **Makes** 10 servings.

Note: For testing purposes only, we used Edwards Georgia Pecan Pie, Smucker's Chocolate Fudge Topping, and Smucker's Caramel Flavored Topping.

＊ Substitute 1 (8-oz.) package cream cheese, if desired.

STACEY GRIFFITH
BATESVILLE, ARKANSAS

1-2-3 Decorate! Easy Ways to Style for Company

• Go stemless this year. Stemless wine glasses are easier to carry on a tray and a lot less likely to get knocked over. (photo 1)
• For a buffet centerpiece, think big and dramatic. Float green apples in tall clear-glass containers. Add white flowers with graceful stems, such as 'Casa Blanca' lilies, French tulips, or callas. (photo 2)
• For that simple, special touch, tie satin ribbons (in the same colors as your napkins and plates) around some larger serving pieces such as cake and trifle stands. (photo 3)

Pounded Pork Parmesan With Linguine

PREP: 15 MIN., FRY: 8 MIN., BAKE: 20 MIN.

This recipe easily doubles. Choose thin, boneless breakfast chops to use in this recipe.

1 (12-oz.) package linguine, uncooked
2 Tbsp. butter
4 boneless center cut pork chops (about 1¼ lb.)
½ cup all-purpose flour
¼ tsp. salt
¼ tsp. pepper
1 large egg, lightly beaten
1 cup Italian-seasoned breadcrumbs
½ cup olive oil
1 Tbsp. chopped fresh basil
1 (26-oz.) jar tomato-and-basil spaghetti sauce
2 cups (8 oz.) shredded mozzarella cheese
½ cup (2 oz.) grated Parmesan cheese
Garnish: chopped fresh basil

1. Prepare linguine according to package directions; drain. Toss with butter. Set aside, and keep warm.
2. Place pork between 2 sheets of heavy-duty plastic wrap, and flatten to ¼-inch thickness, using a rolling pin or the flat side of a meat mallet.
3. Combine flour, salt, and pepper in a shallow bowl. Dredge pork in flour mixture, dip in beaten egg, and dredge in breadcrumbs.
4. Sauté pork, in batches, in hot oil in a large skillet over medium-high heat 2 minutes on each side or until golden. Arrange pork in a single layer in a 13- x 9-inch baking dish.
5. Stir chopped fresh basil into spaghetti sauce. Top pork evenly with spaghetti sauce, mozzarella cheese, and Parmesan cheese.
6. Bake at 400° for 20 minutes or until cheese is melted and lightly browned. Garnish, if desired. Serve immediately with hot buttered linguine. **Makes** 4 servings.

WALTER C. LUND, SR.
MIAMI, FLORIDA

Cappuccino-Frosted Brownies

PREP: 20 MIN., BAKE: 35 MIN.

People line up when Copy Chief Paula Hunt Hughes brings these treats to the office. These brownies are so good that you'll want to make two batches.

4 (1-oz.) unsweetened chocolate baking squares
¾ cup butter
2 cups sugar
4 large eggs
1 cup all-purpose flour
1 tsp. vanilla extract
1 cup semisweet chocolate morsels
Cappuccino Buttercream Frosting
Garnish: chocolate shavings

1. Microwave chocolate squares and butter in a large microwave-safe bowl at HIGH 1½ minutes, stirring after 1 minute and then every 30 seconds or until melted. Stir until smooth. Stir in sugar. Add eggs, 1 at a time, beating with a spoon just until blended after each addition.
2. Stir in flour and vanilla, and then stir in chocolate morsels. Pour mixture into a lightly greased 13- x 9-inch pan.
3. Bake at 350° for 30 to 35 minutes or until a wooden pick inserted in center comes out clean. Cool completely on a wire rack.
4. Spread Cappuccino Buttercream Frosting evenly over top of cooled brownies. Garnish, if desired. Cut into squares. Cover and chill, if desired. **Makes** 10 to 12 servings.

Cappuccino Buttercream Frosting:
fast fixin's

PREP: 10 MIN., COOL: 10 MIN.

1 (1.16-oz.) envelope instant mocha cappuccino mix
¼ cup hot milk
½ cup butter, softened
1 (16-oz.) package powdered sugar

1. Dissolve cappuccino mix in hot milk in a small cup, stirring to combine; cool completely. Pour milk mixture into a mixing bowl; add butter, and beat at medium speed with an electric mixer until well combined.
2. Gradually add powdered sugar, beating until smooth and fluffy. **Makes** 1½ cups.

Note: For testing purposes only, we used Land O'Lakes Suisse Mocha Hot Cappuccino Mix.

PAULA HUNT HUGHES
HOMEWOOD, ALABAMA

Festive Touches

Monogramming your table linens is one way to give a party more panache. Bonus: You can use them year after year. We love chocolate brown and green napkins, with alternating colors of thread. Try "Merry Christmas," "Happy Holidays," or even "Bon Appétit!" On a square or rectangular tablecloth, monogram one side with tall letters that will greet guests with a happy holiday saying when they walk into the dining area.

Party With Peppermint

Our favorite Christmas confection does double holiday duty. Try these projects with your kids for some sweet time together.

The sassy swirls of peppermint have been inspiring Christmas smiles for hundreds of years—whether your first taste was a piece passed down a church pew from Grandpa on Christmas morning, or a lick of a candy cane that Santa left in your stocking. We've all enjoyed the frosty flavor for snacks and baking, but this striped sweet is great for decorating too. Try these family-friendly ideas for tradition with a twist. They're the seasonal solution to, "Mom, I'm bored."

For peppermints and other candies, you can visit **www.candydirect.com** or **www.hammondscandies.com.**

North Pole Cupcakes

family favorite • fast fixin's
PREP: 25 MIN.
These cool cupcakes are a specialty from the North Pole. Make some with your little elves, and don't forget to leave one for Santa.

1. Purchase 12 cupcakes with vanilla frosting from your grocery store or bakery. Top evenly with 3 cups miniature marshmallows; dust evenly with ⅓ cup powdered sugar.
2. Cut 12 (3- x 3- x 1½-inch) triangles from paper; write a message on each triangle. Attach triangles to 12 (3½-inch) peppermint sticks with ⅓ cup ready-to-spread vanilla frosting. Place a peppermint stick in center of each cupcake. Pipe a dollop of frosting on top of each peppermint stick to resemble snow. **Makes** 12 cupcakes.

Note: For testing purposes only, we used King Leo Peppermint Sticks.

Note: If you're short on time, omit message step, and decorate with marshmallows, powdered sugar, and a peppermint stick.

Perfect Peppermints

This winter wonderland is easy to assemble. Using a red tray for the base, add different size marshmallows for snow. Glue peppermint candies on plastic foam cones for trees. Complete the landscape with colorful peppermint lollipops.

Try a cute parfait. Start with tall glasses, and fill them about halfway with miniature marshmallows. Insert a candy cane, and place glass on a red-and-white cocktail napkin for a simple, seasonal presentation.

from our kitchen

Sweet Remembrances

We all look for unique but affordable ways to remember those special people who brighten our spirits throughout the year. Packaged in sets of two, with clear, snap-on lids, these festive tree-shaped foil pans are perfect for baking and delivering everything from cakes to casseroles. Made by Reynolds, the set sells for less than $3 in most supermarkets.

Christmas Tree Cake: One 18.25-oz. package of cake mix yields enough batter to fill both pans. Prepare and bake the cake mix according to package directions for 2 (8-inch) pans. A 16-oz. can of ready-to-spread vanilla frosting makes a quick topping for both cakes. Stir in a few drops of green food coloring, and microwave for 10 to 15 seconds or until the frosting begins to melt; stir until smooth. Pour and spread frosting evenly over the top of each cake; decorate as desired with holiday candies and cake sprinkles.

Other tree-shaped treats: The pans can also be used to shape and bake cookie dough, brownies, and breakfast rolls. They can even be used to mold a congealed salad.

Christmas Tree Cinnamon Rolls: When you need a really quick treat, pop open a can of ready-to-bake refrigerated cinnamon rolls. One (12.4-oz.) can of eight rolls fills one pan—just bake according to package directions. Or crumble and press 1 (18-oz.) package of refrigerated cookie dough evenly on the bottom of one lightly greased pan; bake at 375° for 20 to 22 minutes or until golden brown.

Tips and Tidbits
Cake Freezing Tips

For the freshest taste, it's best to bake and freeze unfrosted cake layers and pound cake. Cakes shrink when frozen and expand when thawed, which can cause the frosting to crack.

Place baked, completely cooled, unfrosted cake layers on baking sheets, and freeze until firm. Wrap each frozen layer in plastic wrap, and place in large zip-top plastic freezer bags; freeze up to 1 month. Thaw at room temperature, or try filling and frosting the cake layers while they're still partially frozen— it makes for super-easy spreading.

The Magic Is in the Mix

Over the years, our readers have shared hundreds of delicious recipes that start with a cake mix. You'll find their secrets for adding made-from-scratch flavor on **southernliving.com.** Some replace water with buttermilk, while some substitute sour cream for vegetable oil. Others call for using softened butter or cream cheese. Quick Italian Cream Cake, Holiday Lane Cake, and Easy Perfect Chocolate Cake are just a few of the many top-rated favorites we've included.

Tower of Treats

Transform your favorite brownie recipe into a chocolate lover's delight. We found the recipe for Chocolate Ganache (page 286) to be a perfect match for a 13- x 9-inch pan of brownies. Prepare the ganache as directed; pour over the top of baked, completely cooled brownies, spreading evenly to the sides of the pan. Sprinkle 2 cups coarsely chopped cookies or candy bars evenly over the ganache, and let stand until firm. Cut brownies into bars of graduated size, and stack as desired.

To package the brownies as a gift, place each stack on a piece of aluminum foil-covered cardboard; tie with decorative ribbon, and place inside a cellophane bag.

2006 cook-off winners

2006
Cook-Off Winners

Our annual event gets better every year.

What does it take to become a finalist in the $100,000 *Southern Living* Cook-Off? From our perspective, it boils down to one key ingredient: a creative, stellar, great-tasting recipe that works perfectly every time. This year, we sorted through thousands of entries to find the these 15 finalists, each of them a winner.

This year's event in Charleston, South Carolina, was truly exciting. The finalists prepared their recipes to be presented to the judges at the Culinary Institute of Charleston, a state-of-the-art professional cooking school. The next day, the contestants were featured in a stage show hosted by TV Food Network's Tyler Florence.

Grand Prize Winner

Maureen (Mo) Tischue and Christie Katona didn't set out to create a prize-winning recipe—Mo simply wanted to bake a better cinnamon roll. The Kent, Washington, massage therapist credits divine intervention with her decision to make a few cinnamon rolls from a batch of sweet potato dinner roll dough last Thanksgiving. She turned to Christie, a caterer and cookbook author, to help make them tastier.

Christie gave her a basic cinnamon roll recipe that turned out well with sweet potato worked into the dough. "Christie said, 'I think we could tweak this and do something with it,'" Mo says. "So we tweaked! They were so good, Christie suggested we enter the recipe in the Cook-Off." The resulting rolls are tender, gooey, and sweet.

Note: To enter the contest, you must use at least one sponsor's product.

YOUR BEST RECIPE

YOUR BEST RECIPE
Category Winner

Sweet Potato Cinnamon Rolls
PREP: 30 MIN., STAND: 5 MIN., RISE: 2 HRS., BAKE: 20 MIN., COOL: 30 MIN.
You can make this dough the night before and let it rise overnight in the refrigerator. Just in case some of the Glaze spills over, you might want to put an aluminum foil-lined baking sheet on the next rack below the pan while baking. (Pictured on page 13)

2 (¼-oz.) envelopes active dry yeast
½ cup warm water (100° to 110°)
1 tsp. DOMINO Granulated Sugar
5½ cups all-purpose flour
1 cup mashed sweet potatoes
1 egg, lightly beaten
1 cup buttermilk
½ cup DOMINO Granulated Sugar
¼ cup melted butter
2 Tbsp. grated orange rind
1½ tsp. salt
1 tsp. baking soda
CRISCO No-Stick Cooking Spray
Filling
Glaze

1. Pulse first 3 ingredients in a large capacity (11-cup) food processor 4 times or just until combined, using the metal blade. Remove metal blade, scraping yeast mixture into food processor bowl. Let stand 5 minutes.

2. Insert short plastic dough blade; add ½ cup flour to processor bowl, and process 2 minutes. Add mashed sweet potatoes, next 7 ingredients, and 4 cups flour; process 2 minutes. Add remaining 1 cup flour, and process 30 seconds or until a dough forms, coming together to hold a shape. (Dough will be sticky.)

3. Place dough in a large bowl coated with cooking spray. Cover with plastic wrap, and let rise in a warm place (85°), free from drafts, 1 hour to 1 hour and 30 minutes or until doubled in bulk.

4. Punch dough down. Turn dough out onto a well floured surface; roll into an 18- x 10-inch rectangle. Spread evenly with Filling, leaving a 1-inch border. Roll up dough, jelly-roll fashion, starting at 1 long side. Cut into 12 (1½-inch) slices; arrange in a lightly greased 13- x 9-inch pan. Cover with plastic wrap, and let rise in a warm place (85°), free from drafts, 30 minutes.

5. Bake rolls at 400° for 10 minutes. Remove rolls from oven; drizzle about ½ cup Glaze slowly over rolls, starting at 1 edge of pan and drizzling in a circular pattern; let Glaze soak in. Repeat with remaining Glaze.

6. Bake rolls 7 to 10 more minutes or until lightly browned and a wooden pick inserted in center comes out clean.

7. Remove rolls from oven, and invert onto an aluminum foil-lined baking sheet. Invert again, glaze side up, onto a serving platter. Let cool 20 to 30 minutes. Serve warm. **Makes** 12 rolls.

Filling:
PREP: 5 MIN.

¾ cup melted butter
2 cups firmly packed DOMINO Light
  Brown Sugar
1 cup chopped toasted pecans
2 Tbsp. ground cinnamon

1. Stir together all ingredients until blended. **Makes** 2½ cups.

Glaze:
PREP: 10 MIN., COOK: 5 MIN.

1 cup firmly packed DOMINO Light
  Brown Sugar
⅓ cup light corn syrup
¼ cup butter
½ cup whipping cream
1 tsp. vanilla extract

1. Stir together sugar, corn syrup, and butter in a small saucepan over medium heat. Bring to a light boil, stirring constantly. Remove from heat, and stir in cream and vanilla. **Makes** 1½ cups.

CHRISTIE KATONA
RENTON, WASHINGTON

MAUREEN TISCHUE
KENT, WASHINGTON

Judges' Notes

"When they brought the Sweet Potato Cinnamon rolls out to us, they were huge," says Head Judge and Senior Foods Writer Andria Scott Hurst. "They were light, fluffy pillows of goodness with nuts and cinnamon. They could have just floated away. The sweet potato flavor came through, and offered a great twist on a familiar favorite.

Mexi-Texi Bistec Pedazos on Roasted Corn and Garlic Chipotle-Cilantro Mashers

PREP: 30 MIN.; COOK: 2 HRS., 40 MIN.
(Pictured on page 13)

3 lb. BEEF Boneless Top Sirloin Roast,
  cut into 2- to 2½-inch pieces
1½ tsp. salt, divided
½ tsp. black pepper
3 Tbsp. CRISCO Vegetable Oil
¾ cup all-purpose flour
2 tsp. MCCORMICK Gourmet Collection
  Mexican Style Chili Powder
2 tsp. MCCORMICK Gourmet Collection
  Mexican Oregano Leaves
2 tsp. MCCORMICK Gourmet Collection
  Ground Cumin
½ tsp. MCCORMICK Gourmet Collection
  Chipotle Chile Pepper
1 cup warm water
2 cups beef broth
Roasted Corn and Garlic Chipotle-
  Cilantro Mashers
Sour cream (optional)
Chopped cilantro (optional)
Garnish: sliced avocado

1. Sprinkle roast evenly with ½ tsp. salt and ½ tsp. black pepper. Brown roast on all sides in hot oil in a Dutch oven over high heat.

2. Stir together flour, next 4 ingredients, and remaining 1 tsp. salt in a large bowl. Whisk in 1 cup warm water until smooth.

3. Add 2 cups beef broth to Dutch oven. Stir in flour mixture. Bring to a boil over high heat; cover tightly, reduce heat to low, and simmer 2 hours to 2 hours and 30 minutes or until meat is tender, stirring every 20 minutes.

4. Divide Roasted Corn and Garlic Chipotle-Cilantro Mashers evenly among 6 serving plates. Arrange roast equally on top of Mashers, and top with gravy mixture. Dollop each serving with sour cream, and sprinkle with chopped cilantro, if desired. Garnish, if desired. **Makes** 6 servings.

Roasted Corn and Garlic Chipotle-Cilantro Mashers:
PREP: 15 MIN., BAKE: 1 HR., COOK: 25 MIN.

1 garlic bulb
2 Tbsp. CRISCO Vegetable Oil, divided
3 medium ears fresh corn
2 lb. red potatoes, cut into 1½- to
  2-inch cubes
¾ cup sour cream
½ cup butter
½ cup milk
1½ tsp. salt
1 canned chipotle pepper in adobo
  sauce, finely chopped
1 tsp. adobo sauce from can
1 tsp. pepper
½ cup chopped cilantro

1. Cut off pointed end of garlic; place garlic on a piece of aluminum foil, and drizzle with 1 Tbsp. oil. Fold foil to seal. Brush corn with remaining 1 Tbsp. oil, and place on a baking sheet.

2. Bake garlic at 400° for 1 hour. After 15 minutes, place corn in oven, and bake, with garlic, 45 more minutes or until corn is golden brown. Squeeze pulp from garlic cloves, and set aside. Let corn cool completely.

3. Hold 1 corn cob upright on a cutting board, and carefully cut downward, cutting kernels from cob. Repeat with remaining 2 corn cobs. Discard cobs. Set corn aside.

4. Cook potatoes in boiling water to cover in a large saucepan until fork-tender (about 15 to 20 minutes). Drain and return to pan.

5. Whisk together reserved roasted garlic pulp, sour cream, and next 6 ingredients in a medium saucepan over medium heat until butter melts and mixture is thoroughly heated.

6. Mash potatoes slightly; add warm milk mixture to pan, and continue to mash just until blended (mixture should be coarsely mashed). Stir in chopped cilantro and reserved corn. **Makes** 6 servings.

LORIE ROACH
BUCKATUNNA, MISSISSIPPI

Fantastic Foolproof Smokey Jambalaya

PREP: 15 MIN., COOK: 10 MIN., BAKE: 1 HR.

1 cup peeled, uncooked, medium-size fresh or frozen WILD AMERICAN Shrimp
1 onion, finely chopped
1 green bell pepper, finely chopped
1 celery rib, finely chopped
1 cup diced smoked sausage
1 cup cubed PILGRIM'S PRIDE Boneless, Skinless Chicken Thighs
4 Tbsp. CRISCO Vegetable Oil
1½ cups uncooked MAHATMA Extra Long Grain White Rice
1 cup shredded smoked pork
2 (10½-oz.) cans beef broth
1 cup water
3 Tbsp. ZATARAIN'S Creole Seasoning
1 bay leaf
Garnish: green onion tops

1. If frozen, thaw shrimp according to package directions. Devein, if desired, and set aside.
2. Cook onion and next 4 ingredients in hot oil in a 4-qt. cast-iron Dutch oven over medium-high heat, stirring constantly, 10 minutes or until chicken is lightly browned. Stir in rice and next 5 ingredients.
3. Bake, covered, at 325° for 50 minutes. (Do not remove lid or stir.)
4. Remove from oven, and stir in shrimp. Bake, covered, 10 more minutes or just until shrimp turn pink. Garnish, if desired. **Makes** 4 to 6 servings.

DOUG WINGO
PONCHATOULA, LOUISIANA

HEALTHY AND GOOD FOR YOU

Grilled Sweet Chili Chicken With Mango-Cucumber Slaw

PREP: 15 MIN., GRILL: 12 MIN.
(Pictured on page 14)

½ cup sweet chili sauce
3 Tbsp. FLORIDA'S NATURAL Premium Brand Orange Juice
2 Tbsp. honey
1 Tbsp. lite soy sauce
1 tsp. minced jalapeño pepper *
1 tsp. minced fresh ginger
PAM Original No-Stick Cooking Spray
4 PILGRIM'S PRIDE Boneless, Skinless Chicken Breasts
Mango-Cucumber Slaw
2 Tbsp. chopped roasted USA-GROWN PEANUTS (optional)

1. Whisk together first 6 ingredients in a small bowl until blended. Remove and reserve half of sweet chili sauce mixture.
2. Coat cold cooking grate with cooking spray, and place on grill over medium heat (300° to 350°). Lightly spray chicken with cooking spray, and place on cooking grate. Grill chicken 6 minutes on each side or until done, basting with sweet chili sauce mixture during last few minutes on each side.
3. Divide Mango-Cucumber Slaw evenly among 4 serving plates, topping each with 1 chicken breast. Drizzle with reserved half of sweet chili sauce mixture, and, if desired, sprinkle with roasted peanuts. **Makes** 4 servings.

Note: For testing purposes only, we used Maggi Taste of Asia Thai Sweet Chili Sauce.

* Substitute 1 tsp. sambal oelek for minced jalapeño, if desired. Sambal oelek is an Indonesian chili sauce that can be found in the ethnic aisle of the supermarket.

Mango-Cucumber Slaw:

PREP: 20 MIN., CHILL: 1 HR.

3 cups thinly sliced napa cabbage
2 cups thinly sliced red cabbage
1 ripe mango, peeled and cut into thin strips
½ cucumber, peeled, seeded, and cut into thin strips
½ small sweet onion, thinly sliced
½ small red bell pepper, thinly sliced
1 carrot, shredded
¼ cup fresh cilantro leaves
3 Tbsp. rice vinegar
2 Tbsp. fresh lime juice
3 Tbsp. CRISCO Vegetable Oil
1 Tbsp. sweet chili sauce
2 tsp. DOMINO Granulated Sugar
1 tsp. toasted sesame oil

Judges' Notes

"The recipes in this category showed readers are really into finding ways of making healthier meals," Head Judge and Senior Foods Writer Andria Scott Hurst says. "The flavors were so bright in Grilled Sweet Chili Chicken With Mango-Cucumber Slaw—it was really fresh tasting, with wide appeal. All the judges liked this one."

1. Combine first 8 ingredients in a large bowl.
2. Whisk together vinegar and next 5 ingredients until sugar dissolves. Pour over cabbage mixture, and toss to coat. Cover and chill 1 hour. **Makes** about 7 cups.

EDWINA GADSBY
GREAT FALLS, MONTANA

Tex-Mex Fiesta Steak
PREP: 15 MIN., CHILL: 8 HRS., COOK: 2 MIN., GRILL: 12 MIN.

3 Tbsp. tequila
1 tsp. grated lime rind
3 Tbsp. fresh lime juice
1 Tbsp. olive oil
1¼ tsp. MCCORMICK Gourmet Collection Chipotle Chile Pepper
1 tsp. MCCORMICK Gourmet Collection Mexican Oregano Leaves
¾ tsp. freshly ground MCCORMICK Gourmet Collection Black Peppercorns
½ tsp. MCCORMICK Gourmet Collection Ground Cumin
½ tsp. kosher salt
2 tsp. minced garlic
4 (1-inch-thick) BEEF Top Sirloin Steaks (about 6 oz. each)
PAM Olive Oil No-Stick Cooking Spray
Guacamole Butter
Fiesta Black Bean Salsa

1. Stir together first 10 ingredients in a large bowl until blended. Trim fat from steaks; add steaks to marinade, turning to coat. Cover and chill 8 hours, turning occasionally, or, if desired, let stand at room temperature up to 2 hours.
2. Remove steaks from marinade. Bring marinade to a boil in a small saucepan over medium heat, and boil 2 minutes.
3. Heat a grill pan coated with cooking spray over medium-high heat. Grill steaks 5 to 6 minutes on each side or to desired degree of doneness, basting occasionally with marinade.
4. Remove steaks from grill pan, and place on a serving plate. Dollop each with Guacamole Butter. Spoon Fiesta Black Bean Salsa around steaks, and serve immediately with remaining Guacamole Butter. **Makes** 4 servings.

Guacamole Butter:
PREP: 10 MIN.

1 small avocado
2 green onions, chopped
2 Tbsp. chopped fresh cilantro
2 Tbsp. light sour cream
¼ tsp. kosher salt
Pinch of MCCORMICK Gourmet Collection Ground Cayenne Red Pepper

1. Peel and coarsely chop avocado, discarding pit.
2. Process avocado, green onions, and remaining ingredients in a food processor or blender until smooth, stopping to scrape down sides. Place mixture in a bowl; cover and chill until ready to serve. **Makes** about ½ cup.

Fiesta Black Bean Salsa:
PREP: 15 MIN.

1 (15-oz.) can black beans, rinsed and drained
1 cup frozen whole kernel corn, thawed
½ cup chopped red bell pepper
¼ cup chopped green onion
¼ cup chopped fresh cilantro
2 to 3 jalapeño peppers, seeded and minced
3 Tbsp. fresh lime juice
1 Tbsp. olive oil
1 tsp. minced garlic
½ tsp. kosher salt
½ tsp. freshly ground MCCORMICK Gourmet Collection Black Peppercorns

1. Stir together all ingredients in a large bowl. Cover and let stand at room temperature until ready to serve. **Makes** about 2¾ cups.

VIRGINIA ANTHONY
JACKSONVILLE, FLORIDA

Quick Collard Greens and Beans Risotto
PREP: 20 MIN., COOK: 30 MIN.

4 qt. water
1 Tbsp. salt
1 (16-oz.) package chopped fresh collard greens, thoroughly washed
1 cup chopped onion (about 1 large)
3 large garlic cloves, minced
1 Tbsp. ENOVA Oil
3 cups chicken broth
2 Tbsp. all-purpose flour
1 (15.5-oz.) can cannellini beans, rinsed and drained
½ tsp. salt
¼ tsp. freshly ground black pepper
1 (3.5-oz.) bag SUCCESS Brown Rice
½ tsp. dried crushed red pepper
¾ cup grated Parmesan cheese, divided
Garnish: ¼ cup chopped fresh parsley

1. Bring 4 qt. water to a boil in a large Dutch oven. Add 1 Tbsp. salt, and stir until dissolved. Add collard greens to Dutch oven, and cook 2 minutes or until wilted. Drain greens in a colander; rinse with cold water. Drain and pat dry with paper towels. Set aside.
2. Sauté onion and garlic in hot oil in Dutch oven over medium heat 3 to 4 minutes or until tender.
3. Whisk together chicken broth and flour; add to Dutch oven, and bring to a boil. Add cannellini beans, ½ tsp. salt, pepper, and collard greens. Simmer, uncovered, 5 minutes. Reduce heat to low, and stir in rice and red pepper. Simmer, stirring frequently, 10 minutes or until greens and rice are tender. Remove from heat, and stir in ½ cup Parmesan cheese.
4. Sprinkle each serving with remaining ¼ cup cheese, and garnish, if desired. Serve immediately. **Makes** 6 to 8 servings.

TRACY SCHUHMACHER
PENFIELD, NEW YORK

SOUTHERN DESSERTS

SOUTHERN DESSERTS
Category Winner

DOMINO SUGAR *Brand Winner*

Baby Sweet Potato Cakes With Pecans and Sticky Caramel Sauce
PREP: 25 MIN., BAKE: 15 MIN., COOL: 5 MIN.
(Pictured on page 15)

½ cup butter, softened
1 cup DOMINO Granulated Sugar
2 large eggs, at room temperature
1¼ cups all-purpose flour
1 tsp. baking soda
1 tsp. vanilla extract
½ tsp. salt
½ tsp. MCCORMICK Gourmet Collection Ground Ginger
½ tsp. MCCORMICK Gourmet Collection Saigon Cinnamon
1 (15-oz.) can sweet potatoes, drained and mashed
⅓ cup buttermilk
CRISCO Butter Flavor No-Stick Cooking Spray
½ cup chopped pecans, toasted
Sticky Caramel Sauce
Vanilla ice cream (optional)
Heavy cream (optional)

1. Beat butter and sugar at medium speed with an electric mixer until smooth. Add eggs, 1 at a time, beating until blended after each addition.
2. Combine flour and baking soda. Gradually add half of flour mixture to butter mixture, beating at low speed until blended, and stopping to scrape bottom and down sides of bowl. Add remaining half of flour mixture, and beat until blended. Add vanilla and next 5 ingredients, beating at medium speed until smooth. Spoon batter into 12 muffin cups coated with cooking spray, filling two-thirds full.

3. Bake at 350° for 15 minutes or until a wooden pick inserted in center comes out clean. Cool in pan on a wire rack 5 minutes. Remove warm cakes from pan, and sprinkle with toasted pecans. Top each cake with 2½ Tbsp. Sticky Caramel Sauce. Serve with vanilla ice cream or ice-cold heavy cream, if desired. **Makes** 12 cakes.

Sticky Caramel Sauce:
PREP: 10 MIN., COOK: 10 MIN.

½ cup butter
¾ cup firmly packed DOMINO Light Brown Sugar
1 cup heavy cream
½ tsp. instant coffee granules

1. Cook butter and sugar in a medium nonstick skillet over medium heat 2 to 3 minutes or until butter melts and sugar dissolves. Whisk in heavy cream and coffee granules. Bring mixture to a light boil, stirring constantly. Turn off heat, and let stand on cooktop until slightly cool, stirring often. **Makes** about 2 cups.

KAREN HARRIS
CASTLE ROCK, COLORADO

PHILADELPHIA CREAM CHEESE
Brand Winner

Caramel Macchiato Cheesecake With Caramel Sauce
PREP: 20 MIN.; BAKE: 1 HR., 10 MIN.; CHILL: 6 HRS.

1¾ cups crushed crisp, sweet cookies (about 27 cookies)
¼ cup butter, melted
PAM Original No-Stick Cooking Spray
4 (8-oz.) packages PHILADELPHIA Cream Cheese, softened
1 cup DOMINO Granulated Sugar
2 Tbsp. heavy cream
1¼ tsp. instant espresso
Caramel Sauce, divided
4 large eggs
Garnishes: Caramel Sauce, whipped cream, dark chocolate curls

1. Stir together crushed cookies and butter; press mixture on bottom and up sides of a 9-inch springform pan coated with cooking spray.
2. Bake at 350° for 10 minutes. Cool on a wire rack. Reduce oven temperature to 325°.
3. Beat cream cheese and sugar at medium speed with an electric mixer until blended. Add heavy cream, espresso, and 9 Tbsp. Caramel Sauce, beating at low speed until well blended. Add eggs, 1 at a time, beating just until yellow disappears after each addition. Pour batter into prepared crust. Cover and chill remaining Caramel Sauce until ready to serve.
4. Bake at 325° for 1 hour or until center is almost set. Remove cheesecake from oven; gently run a knife around edge of cheesecake to loosen from sides of pan. (Do not remove sides of pan.) Cool completely on a wire rack. Cover and chill 6 hours.
5. Release and remove sides of pan from cheesecake. Garnish, if desired, and serve with remaining Caramel Sauce. **Makes** 8 servings.

Note: For testing purposes only, we used Pepperidge Farm Bordeaux cookies.

Caramel Sauce:
PREP: 10 MIN., COOK: 35 MIN.

¼ cup light corn syrup
1⅓ cups DOMINO Granulated Sugar
1¼ cups warm water, divided
1 cup heavy cream
2 Tbsp. butter, softened
2 tsp. vanilla extract

1. Cook corn syrup, sugar, and 1 cup warm water in a medium saucepan over high heat, stirring constantly, 3 minutes or until sugar dissolves. Using a pastry brush dipped in water, brush down any sugar crystals on sides of pan.
2. Bring to a boil; reduce heat to medium, and simmer, stirring occasionally, 23 minutes or until mixture turns pale amber. Remove pan from heat;

carefully stir in remaining ¼ cup warm water. Stir in cream, butter, and vanilla.

3. Cook mixture over medium-low heat 5 to 6 minutes or until sauce thickens and a candy thermometer registers 220° to 222°. **Makes** 1¾ cups.

BRYAN THOMAS
KENT, WASHINGTON

Judges' Notes

Judge and Associate Foods Editor Shirley Harrington says, "The Sweet Potato Baby Cakes were just so unexpected and so delicious. It was wonderful to have individual servings—everyone likes to have their own little dessert. The coffee gave the caramel sauce full-bodied flavor that was just perfect, a great compliment to the sweetness of the cake and the ice cream that was served with it."

KEEBLER CLUB MULTI-GRAIN CRACKERS *Brand Winner*

Southern Peanut Butter Silk Delight

PREP: 30 MIN., BAKE: 8 MIN., FREEZE: 30 MIN., CHILL: 1 HR.

1¾ cups crushed KEEBLER CLUB Multi-Grain Crackers
⅓ cup DOMINO Granulated Sugar
⅓ cup melted butter
1 (4-oz.) milk chocolate candy bar, broken into small pieces
3 Tbsp. whipping cream, warmed
2 cups whipping cream, divided
1 (8-oz.) package PHILADELPHIA Cream Cheese, softened
½ cup DOMINO 10X Confectioners Sugar, sifted
1 cup Creamy USA-GROWN PEANUT Butter
1½ tsp. vanilla extract, divided
1 (4-oz.) white chocolate baking bar, melted
Ganache
1 cup chopped lightly salted cocktail USA-GROWN PEANUTS
¼ cup DOMINO 10X Confectioners Sugar
Garnishes: lightly salted USA-GROWN PEANUTS, chocolate curls

1. Combine crushed crackers, ⅓ cup sugar, and melted butter in a medium bowl. Press mixture on bottom and up sides of an ungreased 9-inch deep-dish pieplate.

2. Bake at 350° for 8 minutes or until golden brown. Let cool on a wire rack.

3. Stir together chocolate candy bar pieces and 3 Tbsp. warm whipping cream until chocolate is melted and smooth. Pour into cooled piecrust.

4. Beat ⅔ cup whipping cream at medium-high speed with an electric mixer until soft peaks form.

5. Beat together cream cheese and ½ cup confectioners sugar at medium speed with an electric mixer until blended. Add peanut butter, ⅓ cup whipping cream, 1 tsp. vanilla, and white chocolate, beating at medium speed until blended. Fold in whipped cream. Spread mixture evenly over milk chocolate layer in pieplate. Cover and freeze 30 minutes or until slightly firm.

6. Spread Ganache evenly over chocolate layer, and sprinkle with chopped nuts.

7. Beat remaining 1 cup whipping cream at high speed with an electric mixer until soft peaks form. Add ¼ cup confectioners sugar and remaining ½ tsp. vanilla, beating until stiff peaks form.

8. Spoon cream mixture into a 1-qt. zip-top plastic bag. (Do not seal.) Snip a tiny hole in 1 corner of bag, and pipe onto edges of pie by gently squeezing bag. Cover and chill at least 1 hour. Garnish, if desired. **Makes** 8 servings.

Ganache:
PREP: 5 MIN., COOK: 5 MIN.

½ cup whipping cream
¾ cup semisweet chocolate morsels

1. Bring whipping cream to a light boil over medium-high heat. Remove from heat, and pour over chocolate morsels in a medium bowl. Stir until smooth. **Makes** about 1 cup.

DIANE TITE
CHINA, MICHIGAN

SUPER-QUICK FAMILY FAVORITES

Spicy Braised Short Ribs With Peach Gravy and Green Rice

PREP: 20 MIN., COOK: 5 HRS. *(Pictured on page 12)*

1 (6-oz.) bag fresh baby spinach
1 (3-oz.) package JELL-O Brand Peach Flavor Gelatin
3 Tbsp. MCCORMICK Gourmet Collection Chipotle Chile Pepper
1 Tbsp. DOMINO Light or Dark Brown Sugar
2 tsp. kosher salt
4 lb. BEEF Short Ribs, trimmed
3 Tbsp. ENOVA Oil
1 red onion, sliced
3¼ cups beef broth, divided
3 Tbsp. lime juice
2 Tbsp. cornstarch
¼ cup cold water
¼ cup peach preserves
1 cup uncooked MAHATMA Basmati Rice
Garnish: assorted fresh herbs

> ### Judges' Notes
>
> Using peach Jell-O as part of the rub in Spicy Braised Short Ribs With Peach Gravy and Green Rice was "pure genius," Head Judge and Senior Writer Andria Scott Hurst says. "You got the hint of peach, but it wasn't sugary sweet like a dessert. And the fact that it is so hands off makes this dish really easy." Andria also reports that the short ribs were so tasty that she made them for dinner the Sunday following the Cook-Off.

1. Thoroughly wash spinach. Coarsely chip, and set aside.
2. Combine gelatin and next 3 ingredients in a small bowl. Rub mixture evenly over ribs.
3. Brown ribs, in batches, in hot oil in a large nonstick skillet over medium-high heat 5 minutes or until browned. Place ribs in a 6-qt. slow cooker; sprinkle with any remaining brown sugar mixture, and top with onion slices.
4. Stir together 1½ cups beef broth and 3 Tbsp. lime juice, and pour over ribs in slow cooker.
5. Cook, covered, on HIGH 4 to 5 hours or on LOW 8 to 10 hours. Remove ribs from slow cooker, and place on a heated plate. Cover with aluminum foil.
6. Skim fat from broth mixture in slow cooker. Pour broth mixture through a fine wire-mesh strainer into a small saucepan. Bring to a boil over medium-high heat.
7. Stir together cornstarch and cold water. Stir into boiling broth mixture; reduce heat, and simmer, stirring constantly, until mixture is thickened (about 2 minutes). Add peach preserves, and stir until preserves melt and are blended. Keep warm.
8. Bring remaining 1¾ cups beef broth to a boil in a medium saucepan over high heat. Stir in rice. Cover, reduce heat to low, and simmer 20 minutes or until broth is absorbed and rice is tender. Remove from heat, and stir in baby spinach.
9. Spoon rice mixture onto a serving platter. Arrange ribs around rice mixture, and pour peach gravy over top of ribs. Garnish, if desired. **Makes** 4 servings.

DIANE SPARROW
OSAGE, IOWA

Bacon-Wrapped Fried Chicken With White Barbecue Sauce

PREP: 15 MIN., COOK: 10 MIN.

½ cup mayonnaise
1 Tbsp. cider vinegar
1 Tbsp. lemon juice
2 Tbsp. barbecue seasoning
4 PILGRIM'S PRIDE Boneless, Skinless Chicken Breasts
4 bacon slices
1 cup Japanese breadcrumbs (panko)
2 Tbsp. butter

1. Stir together first 3 ingredients in a small bowl. Set aside.
2. Rub barbecue seasoning evenly onto each chicken breast. Wrap 1 bacon slice around 1 seasoned chicken breast, stretching bacon, as necessary, to cover most of surface of chicken; slightly flatten each breast with palm of hand. Secure bacon with a wooden pick. Firmly press chicken in breadcrumbs in a large shallow bowl. Repeat procedure with remaining chicken, bacon, and breadcrumbs.
3. Melt butter in a large nonstick skillet over medium-high heat. Cook chicken in skillet 4 to 5 minutes on each side or until deep golden brown and done. Remove from skillet, and let cool slightly. Remove wooden picks before serving, and serve with mayonnaise mixture. **Makes** 4 servings.

Note: For testing purposes only, we used McCormick Grill Mates Barbecue Seasoning.

NANCY MAUERER
BROOKLYN PARK, MINNESOTA

PARTY STARTERS

Sizzlin' Cuban Beefstro

PREP: 20 MIN., CHILL: 15 MIN., GRILL: 14 MIN.

4 (1-inch-thick) BEEF Flat Iron Steaks
    (about 8 oz. each)
¼ cup lite soy sauce
2 Tbsp. ENOVA Oil
1½ tsp. MCCORMICK Gourmet
    Collection Mexican Style Chili
    Powder
PAM Original No-Stick Cooking Spray
Black Bean-Pineapple Salsa
½ cup finely chopped red onion
2 Tbsp. chopped fresh cilantro
Garnishes: lime wedges, cilantro sprigs

1. Place first 4 ingredients in a large zip-top plastic freezer bag; seal and turn steaks to coat. Chill at least 15 minutes or up to 2 hours. Remove steaks from marinade, discarding marinade.
2. Coat cold cooking grate with cooking spray, and place on grill over medium heat (300° to 350°). Place steaks on cooking grate, and grill 5 to 7 minutes on each side or to desired degree of doneness. Serve steaks with Black Bean-Pineapple Salsa, chopped red onion, and chopped cilantro. Garnish, if desired. **Makes** 4 servings.

Black Bean-Pineapple Salsa:

PREP: 10 MIN., COOK: 5 MIN.

1 (15-oz.) can black beans, rinsed and
    drained
½ cup chopped fresh pineapple
1 serrano chile pepper or jalapeño
    pepper, seeded and finely chopped
2 Tbsp. seasoned rice wine vinegar
2 Tbsp. orange marmalade

1. Stir together all ingredients in a small saucepan until blended. Cook, stirring occasionally, over medium heat 4 to 5 minutes or until thoroughly heated. **Makes** about 2 cups.

LINDA MORTEN
KATY, TEXAS

Shrimp Bruschetta With Guacamole

PREP: 35 MIN., BAKE: 6 MIN., COOK: 10 MIN.,
BROIL: 2 MIN. *(Pictured on page 15)*

24 unpeeled, uncooked, large fresh or
    frozen WILD AMERICAN Shrimp
1 (16-oz.) French bread baguette
PAM Olive Oil No-Stick Cooking Spray
2 large avocados
2 tsp. fresh lime juice
½ tsp. salt
¼ tsp. MCCORMICK Gourmet Collection
    Ground Cumin
1 garlic clove, finely chopped
1 Tbsp. diced shallot
¼ cup medium salsa
½ cup chopped fresh cilantro
2 garlic cloves, finely chopped
¼ cup extra virgin olive oil
¾ cup freshly grated Manchego cheese
Garnish: 12 fresh cilantro sprigs

1. If frozen, thaw shrimp according to package directions. Peel shrimp, and, if desired, devein. Set aside.
2. Cut bread diagonally into 12 (½-inch-thick) slices, discarding ends. Coat both sides with cooking spray, and place on a baking sheet.
3. Bake at 375° for 5 to 6 minutes or until edges are crisp. Reserve bread on pan.
4. Peel and coarsely chop avocados, and place in a medium bowl. Add lime juice and next 6 ingredients, and gently combine, being careful to retain small avocado chunks. (Do not mash.) Chill until ready to serve.
5. Sauté garlic in hot oil in a medium skillet over medium heat 1 minute. Add shrimp, in batches, and cook 2 minutes on each side or just until shrimp turn pink. (Shrimp should be slightly undercooked.) Remove from pan, and place 2 shrimp on top of each baguette slice on baking sheet. Top each with 1 Tbsp. Manchego cheese.
6. Broil 5 inches from heat 1 to 2 minutes or until cheese melts. Remove from oven, and top each with 1 to 2 Tbsp. avocado mixture. Garnish, if desired. Serve immediately. **Makes** 12 servings.

OLGA ESQUIVEL-HOLMAN
WICHITA, KANSAS

Judges' Notes

"Everything was perfect about the Shrimp Bruschetta With Guacamole," Head Judge and Senior Writer Andria Scott Hurst says. "Even with all layers of ingredients on the bread, they didn't fall apart when you took a bite. And the bread was not soggy but totally crisp, despite the toppings. The flavor combos work really well. I would be happy to start any of my parties with these." Andria admits to being pleased with both of the other choices, Cuban Pork Flautas With Mojo-Mayo Dip and Chunky Tomato 'n' Grilled Corn Bisque. "I liked that you can make the Flautas ahead then cook them just before party time, and I found the bisque very flavorful. I'd serve it in small cups so my guests could eat it and move around at the same time."

Cuban Pork Flautas With Mojo Mayo Dip

PREP: 40 MIN., STAND: 30 MIN.,
CHILL: 30 MIN., COOK: 40 MIN.

10 to 12 garlic cloves, finely minced
½ cup minced onion
½ cup FLORIDA'S NATURAL Premium
    Brand Orange Juice
¼ cup fresh lime juice (about 3 limes)
¼ cup fresh lemon juice (about
    3 lemons)
1 tsp. dried oregano
1 tsp. salt
1 tsp. pepper
2 (17-oz.) packages fully cooked pork
    roast au jus
½ cup olive oil
1 cup mayonnaise
2 cups CRISCO Vegetable Oil
30 corn tortillas
Garnish: fresh mint sprigs

1. Stir together first 8 ingredients in a medium bowl. Let stand 30 minutes at room temperature.
2. Meanwhile, rinse au jus from pork roasts. Shred roasts using hands, and place in a large zip-top plastic freezer bag.
3. Heat olive oil in a small saucepan over medium heat just until warm (about 3 to 5 minutes). Remove from heat, and whisk warm oil into orange juice mixture until well blended.
4. Pour 1 cup orange juice mixture evenly over shredded pork in bag. Seal and chill 30 minutes. Stir together mayonnaise and remaining orange juice mixture until well blended. Cover and chill until ready to serve.
5. Heat vegetable oil to 350° to 375° in a large skillet over medium-high heat. Cook tortillas, in batches, 3 to 5 seconds on each side or until softened and pliable. Drain well on paper towels. Remove skillet from heat, reserving vegetable oil in skillet.
6. Spread 1 heaping Tbsp. marinated pork roast mixture down center of 1 softened tortilla. Roll up tightly, and secure with a wooden pick. (If the tortilla cracks when rolling, unroll, remove filling, and cook again in hot oil a few more seconds.) Repeat with remaining tortillas.
7. Reheat vegetable oil in skillet to 350° to 375° over medium-high heat. Fry pork wraps, in batches, 1 minute on each side or until golden brown. Drain on paper towels. Remove wooden picks, and serve with mayonnaise mixture. Garnish, if desired. **Makes** 10 to 15 appetizer servings.

JANA RUARK
AURORA, COLORADO

Chunky Tomato 'n' Grilled Corn Bisque

PREP: 15 MIN., COOK: 1 HR., GRILL: 12 MIN.,
STAND: 5 MIN. *(Pictured on page 14)*

4 Tbsp. butter, divided
2 Tbsp. olive oil
2 large shallots, chopped
2 garlic cloves, pressed
1 (6-oz.) can tomato paste
1 (28-oz.) can peeled whole tomatoes,
    undrained and chopped
2 Tbsp. DOMINO Granulated Sugar
1 Tbsp. MCCORMICK Gourmet
    Collection Mediterranean Basil
    Leaves
2 (14-oz.) cans chicken broth
½ tsp. salt
¼ tsp. pepper
1 cup whipping cream, divided
3 oz. blue cheese, crumbled
3 ears fresh corn, husks removed
CRISCO No-Stick Cooking Spray
Garnish: fresh basil sprigs

1. Melt 1 Tbsp. butter with oil in a Dutch oven over medium heat; add shallots, and sauté 3 to 5 minutes or until shallots are tender. Stir in garlic and tomato paste; sauté 1 minute. Add tomatoes, sugar, and basil, and sauté 3 minutes.
2. Add chicken broth, salt, and pepper. Cover and bring to a boil. Reduce heat to low; uncover and simmer, stirring often, 30 minutes. Stir in ¾ cup cream, and simmer, stirring often, 15 minutes.
3. Combine crumbled blue cheese and remaining 3 Tbsp. butter in a small microwave-safe bowl. Microwave at HIGH 25 seconds or until cheese melts. Whisk until well blended. Brush mixture evenly onto corn.
4. Coat a cold cooking grate with cooking spray; place on grill over medium-high heat (350° to 400°). Arrange corn on cooking grate, and grill 12 minutes, turning every 3 minutes or until done. Let stand 5 minutes. Hold each grilled cob upright on a cutting board, and carefully cut downward, cutting kernels from cob. Discard cobs. Stir kernels into soup.
5. Ladle soup into bowls, and drizzle evenly with remaining cream. Garnish, if desired. **Makes** 11 cups.

STEPHANIE BINGHAM
MOUNT PLEASANT, SOUTH CAROLINA

BRAND WINNERS

Coconut Orange Rolls

PREP: 30 MIN., STAND: 5 MIN., RISE: 3 HRS.,
BAKE: 30 MIN.

1 (¼-oz.) envelope active dry yeast
¼ cup warm water (100° to 110°)
1 cup DOMINO Granulated Sugar,
    divided
8 Tbsp. butter, melted and divided
1 tsp. salt
2 large eggs
½ cup sour cream
3 cups all-purpose flour
1 cup sweetened flaked coconut,
    toasted and divided
2 Tbsp. grated orange rind
CRISCO No-Stick Cooking Spray
Orange Glaze

1. Combine yeast and warm water (100° to 110°) in a 1-cup glass measuring cup; let stand 5 minutes.

2. Stir together yeast mixture, ¼ cup sugar, 6 Tbsp. melted butter, and next 3 ingredients in a large bowl. Gradually stir in flour, making a stiff dough. Cover and let rise in a warm place (85°), free from drafts, 2 hours or until doubled in bulk.

3. Combine ¾ cup coconut, orange rind, and remaining ¾ cup sugar in a small bowl.

4. Turn dough out onto a well-floured surface, and knead 15 or 16 times or until smooth and elastic. Divide dough in 2 equal portions. Roll 1 dough portion into a 12-inch circle; brush with 1 Tbsp. melted butter, and sprinkle with half of coconut mixture. Cut into 12 equal wedges. Repeat procedure with remaining dough portion.

5. Roll up wedges, starting at wide end, to form a crescent shape. Place rolls, point side down, in 3 rows in a 13- x 9-inch baking dish coated with cooking spray. Cover and let rise in a warm place (85°), free from drafts, 1 hour or until doubled in bulk.

6. Bake at 350° for 25 to 30 minutes or until golden. Remove from oven, and place on a wire rack. Spread Orange Glaze evenly over top of hot rolls in pan, and sprinkle with remaining ¼ cup coconut. Serve immediately. **Makes** 2 dozen.

Orange Glaze:
PREP: 5 MIN., COOK: 3 MIN.

¾ cup DOMINO Granulated Sugar
½ cup sour cream
2 Tbsp. FLORIDA'S NATURAL Premium Brand Orange Juice
¼ cup butter

1. Stir together all ingredients in a small saucepan. Bring mixture to a boil over medium heat, and cook, stirring constantly, 3 minutes or until blended. Remove from heat. **Makes** 1¾ cups.

MELVA SHERWOOD
VERMILION, OHIO

PAM No-Stick Cooking Spray
Brand Winner

Pork Tenderloin Medallions With Cherry-Apple Chutney
PREP: 15 MIN., BAKE: 25 MIN., COOK: 6 MIN.

1 (1½-lb.) pork tenderloin
½ tsp. coarse-grain salt
½ tsp. freshly ground pepper
PAM Original No-Stick Cooking Spray
2 Tbsp. unsalted butter
½ cup diced sweet onion
1½ cups peeled and diced Granny Smith apples
¾ cup cherry preserves
½ cup dried sweetened cherries
2 Tbsp. chili sauce
½ tsp. Worcestershire sauce
Garnish: fresh parsley sprigs

1. Pat pork tenderloin dry with paper towels, and sprinkle with salt and pepper. Coat a roasting rack with cooking spray, and place in a roasting pan coated with cooking spray. Place tenderloin on rack.

2. Bake, on middle oven rack, at 375° for 25 minutes or until a meat thermometer inserted into thickest portion registers 160°.

3. Melt butter in a small saucepan over medium-high heat; add onions, and sauté 3 minutes or until golden and tender. Reduce heat to medium, and stir in apples and next 4 ingredients. Cook, stirring occasionally, 3 minutes or until apples are slightly softened.

4. Cut pork diagonally into 1-inch-thick medallions, and arrange on a serving platter; spoon apple chutney over pork. Garnish, if desired. **Makes** 4 servings.

TERESA RALSTON
NEW ALBANY, OHIO

RAGU *Brand Winner*

Farfalle in Ragu Cream Sauce With Sun-dried Tomatoes
PREP: 15 MIN., COOK: 35 MIN.

1 (16-oz.) package farfalle pasta
¼ cup butter
2 garlic cloves, pressed
2 shallots, minced
½ cup vodka
1 cup chicken broth
1 cup RAGU Old World-Style Traditional Pasta Sauce
¼ cup chopped sun-dried tomatoes
Salt and pepper to taste
½ cup whipping cream
1 Tbsp. chopped fresh basil
Freshly grated Parmesan or Romano cheese (optional)

1. Prepare pasta according to package directions, using, if desired, 1 to 2 tsp. salt in water.

2. Melt butter in a large skillet over medium heat. Add garlic and shallots, and sauté 1 minute. Remove from heat, and stir in vodka. Return to heat, and cook 2 to 3 minutes or until liquid is reduced by half. Stir in broth, pasta sauce, and sun-dried tomatoes. Sprinkle with salt and pepper to taste.

3. Bring sauce to a low boil over medium heat; reduce heat to low, and simmer 15 to 18 minutes. Stir in whipping cream, and cook 4 to 5 more minutes. Stir in hot cooked pasta.

4. Place pasta mixture in a large serving platter or bowl, and sprinkle with basil and, if desired, freshly grated Parmesan cheese. **Makes** 4 servings.

MARY ANN MARIOTTI
PLAINFIELD, ILLINOIS

Peanuts, Peanut Butter, Peanut Products
Brand Winner

Over-the-Top Peanut Butter-White Chocolate Cream Cake

PREP: 30 MIN.; BAKE: 1 HR., 30 MIN.; COOL: 1 HR., 10 MIN.; CHILL: 2 HRS.

Filling
2 Tbsp. CRISCO All-Vegetable Shortening
2 Tbsp. all-purpose flour
2 cups all-purpose flour
¼ tsp. salt
¼ tsp. baking soda
12 Tbsp. unsalted butter, softened
6 oz. PHILADELPHIA Cream Cheese, softened
1 cup DOMINO Granulated Sugar
1 cup firmly packed DOMINO Brown Sugar
¾ cup Creamy USA-Grown PEANUT Butter
1½ tsp. vanilla extract
4 large eggs, at room temperature
¾ cup Dry-Roasted Unsalted USA-Grown PEANUTS, coarsely chopped and divided
Glaze

1. Set prepared Filling aside.
2. Grease a 12-cup Bundt pan with 2 Tbsp. Crisco shortening, and dust with 2 Tbsp. flour. Set pan aside.
3. Stir together 2 cups flour, salt, and baking soda in a medium bowl.
4. Beat butter and next 3 ingredients at medium speed with an electric mixer 3 minutes or until fluffy; scrape bottom and down sides of bowl. Beat in peanut butter and vanilla, stopping to scrape bottom and down sides of bowl. Add eggs, 1 at a time, beating until blended after each addition. Gradually add flour mixture, beating at low speed until blended. Stir in ¼ cup chopped peanuts.
5. Spoon one-third of peanut batter into prepared Bundt pan. Carefully spoon Filling onto center portion of batter. (Filling should not touch edges of pan as much as possible.) Spoon remaining batter over Filling.

6. Bake at 300° for 1 hour and 30 minutes or until a long wooden pick inserted in center of cake comes out clean. Cool in pan on a wire rack 10 minutes; remove from pan onto a wire rack, and cool 1 hour or until completely cool.
7. Drizzle Glaze evenly over top of cake, and sprinkle with remaining ½ cup chopped peanuts. Chill 2 hours. Serve chilled or at room temperature. **Makes** 16 servings.

Filling:
PREP: 10 MIN.

1 (6-oz.) package white chocolate baking squares
1½ (8-oz.) packages PHILADELPHIA Cream Cheese, softened
¼ cup DOMINO Granulated Sugar
½ tsp. vanilla extract

1. Microwave white chocolate in a medium microwave-safe bowl at HIGH 1½ minutes, stirring at 30-second intervals until melted.
2. Beat together melted white chocolate and remaining ingredients at low speed with an electric mixer until smooth. **Makes** 1½ cups.

Glaze:
PREP: 5 MIN.

1 (6-oz.) dark chocolate candy bar
⅓ cup whipping cream
½ tsp. vanilla extract

1. Microwave dark chocolate and whipping cream in a medium microwave-safe bowl at HIGH 1 minute, stirring after 30 seconds. Add vanilla, and stir until smooth. **Makes** ½ cup.

ANNA GINSBERG
AUSTIN, TEXAS

JELL-O *Brand Winner*

Fresh Coconut Cake With Pineapple Custard

PREP: 30 MIN.; BAKE: 30 MIN.; COOL: 1 HR., 10 MIN.; CHILL: 1 HR.

CRISCO All-Vegetable Shortening
All-purpose flour
1 cup butter, softened
4 large eggs, at room temperature
2 cups DOMINO Granulated Sugar
1 tsp. vanilla extract
2¾ cups sifted all-purpose flour
2 tsp. baking powder
½ tsp. salt
¼ cup FLORIDA'S NATURAL Premium Brand Orange Juice
1¼ cups coconut milk
2 (8-oz.) packages PHILADELPHIA Neufchatel Cheese, ⅓ Less Fat than Cream Cheese
1 (5.1-oz.) package JELL-O Vanilla Flavor Instant Pudding & Pie Filling
2 cups 2% reduced-fat milk
1 cup crushed pineapple, drained
1 (6-oz.) package frozen unsweetened grated coconut, thawed and divided
1 (16-oz.) container frozen whipped topping, thawed

1. Grease 2 (9-inch) round cakepans with shortening. Lightly flour pans.
2. Beat butter at medium speed with an electric mixer until creamy. Add eggs, 1 at a time, beating just until yellow disappears after each addition. Gradually add sugar, and beat until light and fluffy. Stir in vanilla.
3. Combine 2¾ cups flour, baking powder, and salt; add to butter mixture alternately with orange juice and coconut milk, beginning and ending with flour mixture. Beat at low speed just until blended after each addition, stopping to scrape bottom and down sides of bowl. Pour batter into prepared cakepans.
4. Bake at 350° for 30 minutes or until a wooden pick inserted in center comes out clean. Cool in pans on a wire rack 10 minutes. Remove from pans, and

cool on a wire rack 1 hour or until completely cool.

5. Cut each cooled layer in half lengthwise using a serrated knife. Chill layers 30 minutes.

6. Beat cream cheese at medium speed until fluffy. Add instant pudding and pie filling and milk, and beat at low speed until smooth.

7. Place pineapple in a wire-mesh strainer; press with paper towels to remove liquid. Stir pineapple and ½ cup grated coconut into cream cheese mixture. Chill 30 minutes or until firm.

8. Spread cream cheese mixture between cake layers. Spread whipped topping onto top and sides of cake; sprinkle top and sides with remaining 1 cup grated coconut. Chill until ready to serve. Store in refrigerator. **Makes** 8 servings.

LEA BECKETT
BELLEAIR, FLORIDA

VELVEETA Shells and Cheese
Brand Winner

Easy Queso Shells With Fresh Cilantro and Tomatoes

PREP: 15 MIN.

1 (12-oz.) package VELVEETA Shells & Cheese Dinner
1 (10-oz.) can diced tomatoes and green chiles
½ cup sour cream
¼ cup chopped fresh cilantro
PAM Original No-Stick Cooking Spray
1 cup shredded mild Cheddar cheese
Peeled tomato slices, fresh cilantro sprigs (optional)

1. Prepare package of shells and cheese according to package directions in a medium saucepan.

2. Process diced tomatoes in a food processor or blender until minced. Stir minced tomatoes into prepared shells and cheese in pan. Stir together sour cream and cilantro; add to shells and cheese mixture, stirring until well blended.

3. Coat a 2-qt. baking dish with cooking spray. Pour shells and cheese mixture into dish; sprinkle with Cheddar cheese.

4. Microwave mixture at HIGH 2 to 4 minutes or until cheese is melted. Top with tomato slices and cilantro sprigs, if desired. **Makes** 4 to 6 servings.

AMY WEEMS
GIDDINGS, TEXAS

ZATARAIN'S *Brand Winner*

Crab, Avocado, and Tomato Martini

PREP: 15 MIN.

¼ cup ZATARAIN'S Remoulade Sauce
¼ cup ZATARAIN'S Cocktail Sauce
2 Tbsp. gin
½ tsp. lemon pepper
½ garlic clove, chopped
¼ tsp. salt
1 medium-size avocado, peeled and chopped into ½-inch cubes
1 medium-size tomato, peeled, seeded, and chopped into ½-inch cubes
1 lb. fresh lump crabmeat, drained
12 ZATARAIN'S Stuffed Olives or Cocktail Onions

1. Process first 6 ingredients in a food processor or blender 15 seconds or until blended. Remove and reserve 3 Tbsp. remoulade sauce mixture. Stir together remaining remoulade sauce mixture, avocado, and tomato in a medium bowl.

2. Place half of crabmeat in 6 martini glasses. Top evenly with avocado mixture and remaining half of crabmeat. Drizzle each evenly with reserved 3 Tbsp. remoulade sauce mixture (about 1½ tsp. each). Spear 2 stuffed olives onto a wooden pick, and place in a glass; repeat with remaining stuffed olives. Serve immediately. **Makes** 6 servings.

HELEN CONWELL
FAIRHOPE, ALABAMA

OSCAR MEYER Ready-to-Serve Breakfast Meats *Brand Winner*

Bunco Blue Cheese Spread With Pecan-and-Bacon Topping

PREP: 15 MIN., CHILL: 8 HRS., COOK: 5 MIN.

½ cup butter, at room temperature
1 (8-oz.) package PHILADELPHIA Cream Cheese, at room temperature
1 (4-oz.) package crumbled blue cheese, at room temperature
¼ cup finely chopped green onions
⅛ tsp. MCCORMICK Gourmet Collection Ground Cayenne Red Pepper
⅛ tsp. MCCORMICK Gourmet Collection Garlic Powder
4 OSCAR MAYER Ready to Serve Bacon Slices, chopped
½ cup chopped pecans
1 tsp. DOMINO Dark Brown Sugar
PAM Original No-Stick Cooking Spray
Assorted crackers or crostini

1. Stir together first 3 ingredients in a medium bowl until blended. Stir in green onions, red pepper, and garlic powder, stirring until well blended.

2. Press cheese mixture into a 2-cup glass bowl or a mold lined with plastic wrap. Cover and chill at least 8 hours or up to 24 hours.

3. Combine chopped bacon, pecans, and brown sugar. Sauté bacon mixture in a large nonstick skillet coated with cooking spray over medium heat until pecans are toasted and bacon begins to crisp (about 5 minutes). Remove from heat, and let cool.

4. Invert cheese mixture onto a serving plate. Gently press pecan mixture onto top and sides of cheese. Serve with crackers or crostini. **Makes** 6 to 8 appetizer servings.

NANCY LEMOINE
BATON ROUGE, LOUISIANA

Kentucky Hot Brown Cornbread Skillet

PREP: 15 MIN., BAKE: 27 MIN., COOK: 10 MIN.

1 (6-oz.) package MARTHA WHITE Cotton Country or Buttermilk Cornbread Mix
½ cup canned French fried onions
½ cup milk
1 large egg, lightly beaten
¼ cup butter
3 Tbsp. all-purpose flour
2 cups milk
1 tsp. Worcestershire sauce
½ tsp. salt
¼ tsp. MCCORMICK Gourmet Collection Ground Cayenne Red Pepper
¼ tsp. freshly ground MCCORMICK Gourmet Collection Black Peppercorns
1½ cups freshly grated Parmesan cheese, divided
2 cups chopped cooked turkey
1 cup OSCAR MAYER Real Bacon Pieces, divided
1 large tomato, sliced *
Chopped fresh parsley, freshly grated Parmesan cheese (optional)

1. Generously grease a 10-inch cast-iron skillet; heat in a 425° oven 5 minutes.
2. Stir together cornbread mix and next 3 ingredients, and spoon evenly into hot skillet.
3. Bake at 425° for 8 to 10 minutes or just until light golden brown and set.
4. Melt butter in a medium saucepan over medium heat. Whisk in flour, and cook, whisking constantly, 1 minute. Gradually whisk in 2 cups milk and cook, whisking constantly, 3 to 5 minutes or until mixture is smooth and thickened. Stir in Worcestershire sauce, next 3 ingredients, and ½ cup Parmesan cheese until blended. Remove from heat, and keep warm.
5. Spoon turkey evenly over cooked cornbread mixture in skillet, and top with warm Parmesan sauce. Sprinkle with remaining 1 cup Parmesan cheese and ½ cup bacon pieces.
6. Bake at 425° for 8 to 12 minutes or until bubbly and lightly browned. Top with tomato slices and remaining ½ cup bacon pieces. Serve immediately. Sprinkle with parsley and Parmesan cheese, if desired. **Makes** 4 servings.

*Substitute 2 cups quartered grape tomatoes, if desired.

JANICE ELDER
CHARLOTTE, NORTH CAROLINA

More Brand-Winning Recipes

Crisco Oils, Shortening, and Cooking Sprays: Cuban Pork Flautas With Mojo Mayo Dip, page 318

Domino Sugar: Baby Sweet Potato Cakes With Pecans and Sticky Caramel Sauce, page 314

Enova Brand Oil: Quick Collard Greens and Beans Risotto, page 313

Keebler Club Multi-Grain Crackers : Southern Peanut Butter Silk Delight, page 315

Success/Mahatma Rice: Fantastic Foolproof Smokey Jambalya, page 312

McCormick Gourmet Collection: Mexi-Texi Bistec Pedazos on Roasted Corn and Garlic Chipotle-Cilantro Mashers, page 311

Philadelphia Cream Cheese: Caramel Macchiato Cheesecake With Caramel Sauce, page 314

Pilgrim's Pride Chicken: Grilled Sweet Chili Chicken With Mango-Cucumber Slaw, page 312

U.S. Beef: Spicy Braised Short Ribs With Peach Gravy and Green Rice, page 316

Wild American Shrimp: Shrimp Bruschetta With Guacaomole, page 317

merry Christmas menus

Christmas Entertaining

Enjoy some of our festive menus to make Christmas more special than ever.

Fancy Holiday Party

Invite friends to gather and share some great food and good cheer.

Southern-Style Christmas Dinner

Serves 8

Cran-Horseradish Sauce and Cream Cheese

Holiday Ham With Cumberland Sauce

Grits Dressing

Sweet Potato Hash Browns

Spicy Turnip Greens

Savannah Christmas Praline-Spice Cake

Southern ingredients shine in this upscale feast. Ham, hash browns, grits, and turnip greens get sophisticated twists in this mouthwatering menu.

Cran-Horseradish Sauce and Cream Cheese

PREP: 5 MIN., COOK: 8 MIN., CHILL: 1 HR.

This is cranberry sauce to write home about. It gets a surprise pungency from horseradish and a sweet splash of sugar. It's a beautiful jewel-toned appetizer when spooned over cream cheese. Or you may choose to give a gift jar of it to the cook.

1 (16-oz.) can whole-berry cranberry sauce
½ cup sugar
⅓ cup minced onion
2 Tbsp. prepared horseradish
½ tsp. salt
1 (8-oz.) package cream cheese
Garnishes: fresh rosemary sprigs, fresh cranberries

1. Stir together first 5 ingredients in a medium saucepan. Bring to a boil, stirring often. Remove from heat. Cover and chill 1 hour or up to 3 days.
2. When ready to serve, spoon Cran-Horseradish Sauce over cream cheese on a plate. Garnish, if desired. Serve with assorted crackers. **Makes** 8 servings.

Holiday Ham With Cumberland Sauce

PREP: 10 MIN.; BAKE: 2 HR., 30 MIN.; STAND: 15 MIN.

For a moist, juicy, herb-infused ham, bake it in an oven bag with rosemary sprigs. The sweet, tart English sauce highlights red currant jelly, citrus, and port wine, and spices up each slice of ham.

1 (7- to 10-lb.) fully cooked spiral-sliced ham half
8 to 10 fresh rosemary sprigs
1 oven cooking bag
Garnishes: fresh rosemary sprigs, fresh cranberries
Cumberland Sauce

1. Unwrap ham, and remove plastic disk covering bone. Tuck rosemary sprigs randomly between every 2 or 3 slices of ham. Place ham, cut side down, in an oven cooking bag; place in a 13- x 9-inch baking dish. Close bag with tie. Trim excess plastic to 2 inches. Cut 3 (½-inch) slits in top of bag. Bake at 275° on lowest rack for 2½ hours or until a meat thermometer inserted registers 140°.
2. Remove ham from oven; let stand in bag with juices 15 minutes. Remove ham from bag, and transfer to a carving board. Separate slices, and arrange on a serving platter. Garnish, if desired. Serve with Cumberland Sauce. **Makes** 10 servings.

Note: For testing purposes only, we used Smithfield spiral-sliced Honey Ham.

Cumberland Sauce:
fast fixin's • make ahead
PREP: 10 MIN., COOK: 15 MIN.

1 Tbsp. butter or margarine
¼ cup minced onion
1 (12-oz.) jar red currant jelly
1 Tbsp. grated orange rind
¼ cup orange juice
1 Tbsp. grated lemon rind
¼ cup lemon juice
1 Tbsp. Dijon mustard
1 cup port wine

1. Melt butter in a saucepan over medium heat; add onion, and sauté until tender. Add jelly and next 5 ingredients; cook over medium heat, stirring often, until jelly melts. Add wine; simmer, uncovered, 5 to 10 minutes. Serve warm. Cover and store in refrigerator up to 5 days. **Makes** 2 cups.

Grits Dressing
make ahead
PREP: 11 MIN.; COOK: 10 MIN.;
BAKE: 1 HR., 17 MIN.

There's no need for gravy here. This unique Southern dressing stands alone and sports crusty grits croutons and spicy sausage. Make the croutons and brown the sausage a day in advance.

3 (10½-oz.) cans condensed chicken
   broth, undiluted
1¼ cups uncooked quick-cooking grits
¾ cup freshly shredded Parmesan
   cheese
1 lb. ground hot pork sausage
5 celery ribs with leaves, finely chopped
4 garlic cloves, minced (about 1 Tbsp.)
1 large onion, chopped
⅓ cup butter or margarine,
   melted
1 large egg, lightly beaten
½ cup chopped fresh parsley

1. Bring broth to a boil in a large saucepan. Stir in grits, and return to a boil. Cover, reduce heat, and simmer 7 minutes or until grits are thickened, stirring twice. Stir in cheese. Remove from heat.

2. Spoon grits into a greased 13- x 9-inch baking dish. Cover and chill until firm. Unmold onto a large cutting board, sliding knife or spatula under grits to loosen them from dish. Cut grits into ¾-inch cubes. Place in a single layer on a large greased baking sheet or jelly-roll pan. Bake at 450° for 20 minutes; turn grits, and bake 10 to 12 more minutes or until crisp and browned.

3. Meanwhile, cook sausage in a large skillet, stirring until it crumbles and is no longer pink; drain.

4. Sauté celery, garlic, and onion in butter 5 minutes or until tender. Stir together onion mixture, sausage, and grits croutons, tossing gently. Drizzle egg over mixture; add parsley, stirring gently. Spoon dressing loosely into a greased 11- x 7-inch baking dish. Bake, uncovered, at 350° for 35 to 45 minutes or until browned. **Makes** 8 servings.

Note: For testing purposes only, we used Quaker grits.

Sweet Potato Hash Browns
PREP: 15 MIN., COOK: 33 MIN., CHILL: 8 HRS.
Sweet potatoes, honey, and rosemary blend beautifully in this rustic side dish. The key to success is chilling the partially cooked potatoes; this helps them keep their shape in the skillet.

4 large sweet potatoes, peeled and cut
   into ¾-inch pieces (3½ lbs.)
1½ Tbsp. chopped fresh rosemary
¾ tsp. salt
½ tsp. pepper
½ medium-size red onion,
   chopped
6 Tbsp. olive oil, divided
2 tsp. honey

1. Cook sweet potato in boiling water to cover 8 minutes or until barely fork tender (not soft); drain well. Spread potato in a single layer in a 13- x 9-inch pan. Cool; cover and chill at least 8 hours.

2. Stir together rosemary, salt, and pepper.

3. Sauté onion in 2 Tbsp. hot oil in a large nonstick skillet over medium-high heat until golden. Remove onion to a large bowl.

4. Increase heat to high. Add 2 Tbsp. oil to skillet, and heat oil until hot. Add half of sweet potato, and sauté 10 minutes or until well browned. Stir in half of rosemary mixture. Add sautéed potato to onion in bowl. Repeat procedure with remaining 2 Tbsp. oil, sweet potato, and rosemary mixture; add to potato and onion in bowl, drizzle with honey, and toss gently. Serve immediately. **Makes** 8 servings.

Spicy Turnip Greens
PREP: 9 MIN., COOK: 22 MIN.
Several convenience products make this recipe appealing, in addition to garlic, Worcestershire, and a hint of lemon. Water chestnuts lend a little crunch.

½ cup finely chopped onion
½ cup finely chopped celery
2 large garlic cloves, minced
2 Tbsp. butter or margarine, melted
2 (10-oz.) packages frozen chopped
   turnip greens
1 (8-oz.) can sliced water chestnuts,
   drained and chopped
1 (10¾-oz.) can cream of mushroom
   soup, undiluted
2 tsp. Worcestershire sauce
¼ tsp. grated lemon rind
6 to 8 drops of hot sauce
Salt and pepper to taste

1. Sauté first 3 ingredients in butter in a large saucepan until tender.

2. Cook turnip greens according to package directions; drain well. Add to saucepan. Stir in water chestnuts and remaining ingredients. Simmer, uncovered, 5 minutes, stirring occasionally. **Makes** 8 servings.

Savannah Christmas Praline-Spice Cake

PREP: 20 MIN., COOK: 10 MIN., BAKE: 22 MIN., STAND: 1 HR., FREEZE: 30 MIN., COOL: 10 MIN.

Two ingredients dress up canned frosting for this decadent layer cake. We offer you a double dose of candied nut garnishes, too. If you'd like to simplify, just choose one.

1 (18-oz.) package carrot cake mix *****
3 large eggs
1 cup water
⅓ cup vegetable oil
3 large carrots, grated
2 cups chopped pecans, toasted and divided
1 (8-oz.) can crushed pineapple, well drained
⅔ cup sugar
24 pecan halves
2 (16-oz.) containers homestyle cream cheese frosting
1 Tbsp. vanilla extract
Praline Crumbles

1. Grease 3 (8-inch) round cakepans. Line with wax paper; grease wax paper. Set pans aside.
2. Beat first 4 ingredients at low speed with an electric mixer 30 seconds. Beat at medium speed 2 minutes. Stir in carrot, 1 cup pecans, and pineapple. Pour batter evenly into pans.
3. Bake at 350° for 20 to 22 minutes or until a wooden pick inserted in center comes out clean. Cool in pans on wire racks 10 minutes. Remove from pans, and cool completely on wire racks. Wrap cake layers in nonstick aluminum foil. Freeze 30 minutes. (This step aids in frosting the finished product.)
4. Coat a sheet of wax paper with cooking spray; set aside.
5. Place sugar in a large heavy skillet. Cook over medium heat, stirring constantly with a wooden spoon, 5 to 10 minutes or until sugar melts and turns light brown. Remove from heat. Working quickly, drop pecan halves, a few at a time, into caramelized sugar turning to coat. Using a fork, remove pecans to greased wax paper. Cool completely; remove from wax paper,

and reserve for garnish.
6. Combine frosting, vanilla, and remaining 1 cup pecans in a bowl. Unwrap layers, and spread frosting between layers and on top and sides of cake. Let cake stand 1 hour before serving. Sprinkle Praline Crumbles over top of cake, and garnish rim of cake with candied pecans. **Makes** 1 (3-layer) cake.

Note: For testing purposes only, we used Betty Crocker carrot cake mix and Duncan Hines cream cheese frosting.

*Substitute 1 (18.25-oz.) package spice cake mix for the carrot cake mix, if desired. Increase the water to 1⅓ cups.

Praline Crumbles:
fast fixin's
PREP: 5 MIN.; COOK: 10 MIN.

1 Tbsp. butter
¼ cup sugar
½ cup chopped pecans

1. Melt butter in a medium skillet over low heat. Add sugar, reduce heat to medium-low, and cook until sugar melts. Stir in pecans; cook until pecans are coated and sugar turns light brown. Pour praline onto wax paper. Cool; break into coarse pieces. **Makes** about ½ cup.

Shortcut Solution: In a big hurry? You can frost this cake with plain frosting, minus the nuts and vanilla, and forgo making the garnishes.

Casual Holiday Gathering

Winter Harvest Supper

Serves 6

Butternut Squash Soup

Mustard-Crusted Pork Roast and Browned Potatoes

Cinnamon-Scented Cranapple Sauce

Green Bean Casserole With Fried Leeks

Cornmeal Streusel Apple Pie

Savor the holiday season with a celebration featuring nature's bountiful food gifts. Begin the feast with ginger-kissed bowls of butternut soup. Then, feast on a platter of mustard-crusted pork and roasted potatoes. Decorate each plate with glistening cranapple sauce. And for dessert, offer our dressed-up apple pie.

Butternut Squash Soup

PREP: 10 MIN., BAKE: 40 MIN., COOK: 35 MIN.

This velvety starter soup is a blend of puréed squash and carrots, cream, and a hint of ginger.

1 (3-lb.) butternut squash
¾ lb. carrots, scraped and cut into chunks (8 carrots)
2½ cups chicken broth
¾ cup orange juice
½ tsp. salt
½ tsp. ground ginger
½ cup whipping cream
2 Tbsp. finely chopped pecans, toasted
Ground nutmeg

1. Cut squash in half lengthwise; remove seeds. Place squash, cut sides down, in a shallow pan; add hot water to pan to a depth of ¾ inch. Cover with aluminum foil, and bake at 400° for 40 minutes or until tender; drain. Scoop out pulp; mash. Discard shell. Cook carrot in boiling water 25 minutes or until tender; drain and mash.

2. Combine squash, carrot, chicken broth, and next 3 ingredients in a bowl. Process half of mixture in a food processor or blender until smooth. Repeat procedure with remaining half of squash mixture.

3. Place puréed mixture in a large saucepan; bring to a simmer. Stir in cream; return to a simmer. Remove from heat. To serve, ladle into individual bowls. Sprinkle with pecans and nutmeg. **Makes** 8 cups.

Mustard-Crusted Pork Roast and Browned Potatoes

PREP: 15 MIN.; BAKE: 1 HR., 15 MIN.; STAND: 10 MIN.

A mustard-based glaze locks moisture in this pork roast. Rosemary potatoes roast alongside the pork, making a rustic side dish.

1 (4- to 5-lb.) boneless pork loin
   roast
¼ tsp. salt
¼ tsp. pepper
½ cup coarse-grained mustard
8 garlic cloves, minced
3 Tbsp. olive oil
3 Tbsp. balsamic vinegar
2 Tbsp. chopped fresh rosemary
2 lb. new potatoes
2 Tbsp. olive oil
1 Tbsp. chopped fresh rosemary
½ tsp. salt
½ tsp. pepper
Garnish: fresh rosemary sprigs

1. Place pork in a greased roasting pan. Rub with ¼ tsp. each of salt and pepper. Combine mustard and next 4 ingredients in a small bowl; spread evenly over pork.

2. Peel a crosswise strip around each potato with a vegetable peeler, if desired. Cut each potato in half lengthwise. Toss potatoes with 2 Tbsp. oil, 1 Tbsp. chopped rosemary, ½ tsp. salt, and ½ tsp. pepper. Add to roasting pan around pork. Insert meat thermometer into thickest part of roast.

3. Bake at 375° for 1 hour to 1 hour and 15 minutes or until thermometer registers 160°. Let stand 10 minutes. Transfer roast to a serving platter. Surround pork with potatoes. Garnish, if desired. **Makes** 8 servings.

Cinnamon-Scented Cranapple Sauce

PREP: 5 MIN., COOK: 45 MIN.

This jewel-toned cranberry sauce gets embellished with tart apple, cinnamon pears, and citrus. It's a wonderful match for pork roast or turkey.

1 (16-oz.) can whole-berry cranberry
   sauce
1 (15-oz.) can cinnamon-flavored pear
   halves, drained and chopped
1 (11-oz.) can mandarin orange
   segments, drained
1 Granny Smith apple, peeled and
   chopped
1 cup sugar
½ cup dried fruit mix

1. Combine all ingredients in a large saucepan; cook, uncovered, over medium-low heat 45 minutes or until thickened, stirring often. Remove sauce from heat; cover and chill.

2. Serve as an accompaniment with pork or turkey, or as a topping over vanilla ice cream, pound cake, or pancakes. **Makes** 3½ cups.

Note: If you can't find cinnamon-flavored pears, use regular canned pear halves, and add ½ tsp. ground cinnamon. For testing purposes only, we used Mariani Harvest Medley dried fruit mix.

Green Bean Casserole With Fried Leeks

PREP: 15 MIN., COOK: 26 MIN., BAKE: 5 MIN.

Remember the old green bean casserole made with convenience products: frozen or canned green beans, cream of mushroom soup, and French fried onions? Here it is again, only updated with some upscale ingredients.

2 Tbsp. butter or margarine
2 (8-oz.) packages sliced fresh
   mushrooms
1 tsp. dried thyme
2 shallots, finely chopped
½ cup Madeira
1 cup whipping cream
1¼ lb. fresh green beans, trimmed
Vegetable or peanut oil
2 large leeks, cleaned and thinly sliced
   crosswise
Salt

1. Melt butter in large heavy skillet over medium-high heat. Add mushrooms and thyme; sauté 5 minutes. Add shallots; sauté 3 minutes or until tender. Add Madeira, and cook over medium-high heat 3 minutes or until liquid evaporates. Add whipping cream, and cook 2 to 5 minutes or until slightly thickened. Remove from heat.

2. Meanwhile, cook beans in a small amount of boiling water 5 minutes or just until crisp-tender; drain. Add beans to mushroom mixture, and toss gently. Spoon into a greased 2-qt. gratin dish or shallow baking dish. Cover and keep warm.

3. Pour oil to a depth of 2 inches into a 3-qt. saucepan; heat to 350°. Fry leeks in 3 batches, 40 seconds each or until golden. Remove leeks with small metal strainer; drain on paper towels. Immediately sprinkle with salt. Sprinkle fried leeks over warm bean mixture. Bake, uncovered, at 400° for 5 minutes or until casserole is thoroughly heated. **Makes** 6 servings.

Cornmeal Streusel Apple Pie

PREP: 10 MIN.; BAKE: 1 HR., 15 MIN.

Dress up a store-bought fruit pie with our Southern cornmeal streusel. Your guests will all think that it's made from scratch.

½ cup chopped walnuts
½ cup firmly packed light brown sugar
3 Tbsp. all-purpose flour
3 Tbsp. yellow cornmeal
¾ tsp. ground cinnamon
¼ tsp. ground nutmeg
½ cup (2 oz.) shredded sharp Cheddar cheese
⅓ cup unsalted butter, slightly softened
1 (3-lb., 1-oz.) frozen deep-dish apple pie

1. Stir together first 6 ingredients in a medium bowl; stir in cheese. Gently work in butter with fingertips until mixture forms large crumbs. Cover and chill 30 minutes.
2. Meanwhile, remove frozen pie from aluminum pieplate, and place in an ungreased 10-inch deep-dish pieplate. Cut slits in top crust according to package directions. Bake, uncovered, at 375° for 50 minutes. Remove pie from oven.
3. Sprinkle cornmeal streusel over pie, mounding slightly in center. Bake, uncovered, 20 to 25 more minutes or until browned and bubbly. Cool in pieplate on a wire rack at least 30 minutes before serving. **Makes** 1 (10-inch) pie.

Note: For testing purposes only, we used Mrs. Smith's frozen deep-dish apple pie.

Homestyle Holiday Supper

Pot Pie Supper

Serves 6

Green Chile-Turkey Pot Pie

Lime-Marinated Tomatoes With Cilantro

Bakery brownies and cookies

Have some friends over during the holidays for relaxing and feasting on this easy meal. Turkey pot pie—what could be more inviting?

Green Chile-Turkey Pot Pie

PREP: 12 MIN., COOK: 15 MIN., BAKE: 30 MIN.

This one-dish pot pie is the ultimate in easy. You just spoon a cheesy biscuit topping over a turkey, bean, and green chile filling, and bake.

2 bunches green onions, chopped (about 1½ cups)
3 Tbsp. vegetable oil
2 (4.5-oz.) cans chopped green chiles, undrained
1 (2.25-oz.) can sliced ripe olives, drained
¼ cup all-purpose flour
1½ tsp. ground cumin
2 (16-oz.) cans pinto beans, rinsed and drained
1 (14-oz.) can chicken broth
2 cups chopped cooked turkey breast
1 cup all-purpose flour
1½ tsp. baking powder
2 cups (8 oz.) shredded Mexican four-cheese blend
⅔ cup milk
1 large egg, lightly beaten

1. Sauté green onions in oil in a Dutch oven over medium heat 1 minute. Add green chiles and next 3 ingredients; cook 2 minutes, stirring constantly. Stir in beans and broth; bring to a boil. Reduce heat, and simmer, stirring constantly, 5 to 7 minutes or until mixture is thickened. Stir in turkey. Pour into a greased 13- x 9-inch baking dish.
2. Combine 1 cup flour and baking powder in a small bowl. Add cheese, milk, and egg, stirring just until blended. Spread biscuit topping over filling, leaving a 1-inch border around edge.
3. Bake, uncovered, at 375° for 30 minutes or until topping is golden and pot pie is bubbly. **Makes** 6 servings.

Note: For testing purposes only, we used Sargento Mexican four-cheese blend.

Lime-Marinated Tomatoes With Cilantro

make ahead

PREP: 10 MIN., CHILL: 1 HR.

Here's an easy marinated tomato dish to pair with the pot pie. Plum tomatoes taste and look pretty good right through winter. If not, see the Note following the recipe.

6 plum tomatoes, cut into wedges
3 Tbsp. vegetable or olive oil
1½ to 2 Tbsp. fresh lime juice
1 Tbsp. chopped fresh cilantro
½ tsp. garlic salt
¼ tsp. grated lime rind
⅛ tsp. pepper

1. Place tomato wedges in a glass dish. Combine oil and remaining ingredients; stir well. Pour over tomato wedges. Cover and chill at least 1 hour. **Makes** 6 servings.

Note: If fresh tomatoes are not at their peak, substitute 2 (14½-ounce) cans tomato wedges, drained.

inspirations

berry fresh

We found out that you can turn blackberries into luscious ice cubes that will flavor a glass of water as they thaw. Try it to create a refreshing drink that looks—and tastes—like the essence of summer.

Blackberry Spritzer

1. Thread fresh blackberries on a 6-inch wooden skewer. Freeze 1 hour. Dip the rim of a glass in corn syrup, and roll in grated lime rind (about 1 lime). Place frozen blackberry skewer in prepared glass. Pour chilled sparkling water over skewer, and garnish with a mint sprig. **Makes** 1 per serving. Prep: 5 min., Freeze: 1 hr.

■ Don't have sparkling water on hand? These skewers work just as well in lemonade, iced tea, or any flavored fruit juice.

a bow tie affair

When it comes to summer meals, nothing beats quick, easy, light, and delicious. We've got all those covered—and more—with this five-ingredient pasta dish.

Tomato-Basil-Asparagus Pasta Salad

1. Cook 1 (16-oz.) package bow tie pasta according to package directions, adding 1 pound asparagus, cut into 2-inch pieces, during the last 2 minutes of cooking time. Drain and rinse under cool water. Stir together 1 cup bottled lemon vinaigrette (for testing purposes, we used Wish-Bone Lemon Garlic & Herb Vinaigrette) and 1 (1-oz.) package fresh basil, chopped; pour ¾ cup dressing mixture over pasta mixture. Stir in 1 pint grape tomatoes, halved, and salt and pepper to taste. Cover and chill 1 hour.
2. Toss pasta mixture with remaining ¼ cup dressing before serving. Garnish with fresh basil, if desired.
Makes 4 main-dish or 8 side-dish servings. Prep: 10 min., Cook: 14 min., Chill: 1 hr.

■ Add sliced grilled chicken, feta, blue cheese, or black olives for some tasty variations.
■ To save time, prep tomatoes, asparagus, and basil while pasta water comes to a boil.

red, white, blue— and delicious

Celebrating the Fourth is as easy as 1-2-3. You'll have this creamy, dreamy treat ready in a flash. Hail to the chef!

Strawberry-Blueberry Shortcake Ice-Cream Sandwiches

1. Combine 1 lb. fresh strawberries, sliced, with 2 cups fresh blueberries; sprinkle with 3 Tbsp. sugar, and toss. Let stand 10 minutes. Spoon evenly over 10 vanilla or chocolate miniature ice-cream sandwiches, and dollop with 1/2 (8-oz.) container thawed whipped topping.

Makes 10 servings. Prep: 10 min., Stand: 10 min.

Note: Add an additional lb. of fresh strawberries, sliced, for the blueberries.

spinach leaf + salad

We've whipped up a flavor combo guaranteed to wow the taste buds. No, it's not difficult. Pick up your favorite ready-made chicken salad at a local deli; then follow a few steps for a fresh take on a regional classic.

Strawberry-Chicken Salad Appetizers

1. Arrange 36 spinach leaves on a large serving platter.

2. Divide 1/2 lb. deli chicken salad evenly among spinach leaves (about 1/2 tsp. each). Sprinkle evenly with 3 Tbsp. chopped, toasted pecans; 1/2 cup slivered strawberries; and freshly ground pepper to taste.

Makes 18 appetizer servings. Prep: 20 min.

■ If desired, cover platter with plastic wrap, and chill for up to 30 minutes. Once removed from the refrigerator, serve within an hour.

■ To add a Southern touch and make them easier to manage, place each spinach leaf atop a cornbread cracker (we used Town House Bistro brand), and then serve within 1 hour.

best figs you've ever tasted

August brings the peak season for delectable figs. The unique taste of lemon figs—sweet with a little twang—anchors one of the best appetizers we've eaten. Serve them with a cool drink.

Lemon Figs With Pecans and Feta

1. Peel stem end back from 6 lemon figs. Slice each fig into quarters, cutting to—but not through—bottom, leaving figs intact. Place them on a foil-lined baking sheet; drizzle evenly with 1 Tbsp. olive oil. Broil 6 inches from heat 2 to 3 minutes or until edges begin to brown. Sprinkle evenly with 2 Tbsp. chopped toasted pecans and 2 Tbsp. crumbled feta cheese. Add salt and freshly ground pepper to taste. **Makes** 6 servings. Prep: 10 min., Broil: 3 min.

■ If you can't find lemon figs, look for Mission or Brown Turkey figs at your local grocery store or farmers market.

party peppers

Check out this serving idea for your next casual cookout.

Use hollowed-out red and green bell peppers as clever containers for the condiments. Assembled together, they form an eye-catching centerpiece. Here's how.

■ Cut about 1 inch from the top or side of each bell pepper; remove seeds and membrane, leaving a hollow shell. To prevent the peppers from rolling, cut a small sliver from the bottom or side of each to form a flat surface. Fill with different toppings, such as ketchup, mustard, mayonnaise, shredded cheese, chopped onions, pickle relish, sauerkraut, and slaw.

pb & good

Peanut butter was never so good—or good for you.

Peanut butter sandwiches take a bum rap. Because they're easy to make and easier to eat, some people think they just can't be healthy. We've come up with a version that proves those folks wrong. The monounsaturated fat in peanut butter and most nuts can, in fact, help lower cholesterol. Instead of heaping on lots of jelly, start with a wholesome bread and your favorite peanut butter, and then add nutritious ingredients such as the following.

- shredded carrots
- chopped apples
- sliced bananas
- chopped mixed nuts
- dried cranberries
- raisins
- low-fat granola cereal
- honey granola cereal

Tip: Don't like whole wheat bread? Consider using white wheat, a white bread with all the nutrients of wheat.

make your own

Try our easy base recipe for flavored vinegars. You can experiment with tastes or opt for some of our favorite combinations listed below. Either way, you'll be thrilled with the results.

Flavored Vinegars

1. Fill sterilized glass bottles with desired fresh herb sprigs, crushed garlic cloves, unpeeled fruit slices, orange rind, whole peppercorns, whole cloves, and/or cinnamon sticks. Bring about 2 to 3 cups of white vinegar (depending on bottle size) and 1/4 tsp. salt to a boil in a medium saucepan. Remove from heat, and pour into prepared bottles. Let stand 30 minutes at room temperature. Cover opening tightly with plastic wrap or bottle top; then refrigerate for at least a week before using.

- These combinations excel in salad dressings or served with olive oil on the side as bread dippers: rosemary-garlic vinegar, rosemary-pear-lemon vinegar, and lemon-garlic-thyme-peppercorn vinegar.

simply delicious

This effortless side dish starts with frozen mashed potatoes, but no one will believe it. That's because it tastes like twice-baked. The ingredient list is short, and it's ready in a snap.

Cheesy Ranch-and-Bacon Mashed Potatoes
1. Whisk together 1 (1-oz.) package Ranch dressing mix, 1 cup sour cream, and 1¾ cups milk in a large glass bowl. Stir in 1 (22-oz.) package frozen mashed potatoes. Microwave at HIGH 12 minutes, stirring every 4 minutes. Stir in 6 cooked and crumbled bacon slices and ½ cup shredded Cheddar cheese. Garnish with sliced green onions, if desired.
Makes 8 servings. Prep: 5 min., Cook: 12 min.

a special pairing

Try this tasty quesadilla with your favorite Cabernet Sauvignon for a fresh twist on wine and cheese.

Pecan-Havarti Quesadilla With Pear Preserves
1. Sprinkle 1 side of an 8-inch flour tortilla with ⅓ cup shredded Havarti cheese; top with 2 Tbsp. chopped, toasted pecans. Fold tortilla over filling. Coat a nonstick skillet with vegetable cooking spray; cook quesadilla over medium-high heat for 2 minutes on each side or until cheese melts. Remove from heat, slice into wedges, and serve with pear preserves. Pair it with a glass of Cabernet Sauvignon. **Makes** 2 servings. Prep: 5 min., Cook: 4 min.

■ This recipe can be easily doubled or tripled.
■ Our resident wine expert, Executive Editor Scott Jones, suggests Columbia Crest Cabernet Sauvignon.

shrimp julep

Free your imagination when you break out the silver. Check out this nifty idea for a traditional shrimp cocktail.

We used a julep cup from Kentucky, but we bet there's something in your china cabinet that would work every bit as beautifully.

■ To prepare our version, first fill the julep cup with crushed ice. Tuck a 2-oz. ramekin or sauce cup into ice; then fill with your favorite cocktail sauce. Arrange cooked shrimp around the rim of the cup. **Makes** 1 serving. Prep: 5 min.

dip into the holidays

December ushers in the ultimate season of sweets. This unusual but easy-to-make treat will turn your party's dessert tray into the most popular spot in the house.

Brittle Fondue
1. Microwave 1 (12-oz.) package semisweet chocolate morsels and ¾ cup whipping cream in a medium microwave-safe glass bowl at HIGH 1 minute, whisking once after 30 seconds. Whisk until smooth. Transfer mixture to fondue pot. Serve with peanut or pecan brittle. **Makes** 8 servings. Prep: 5 min.

■ While peanut brittle is readily available at most grocery stores, you might need to go to the Internet to order pecan brittle. Start your pecan brittle search with **www.lalagniappe.com, www.paulineshandmadebrittle.com,** or **www.lcandy.com.**

menu index

This index lists every menu by suggested occasion. Recipes in bold type are provided with the menu and accompaniments are in regular type.

menus with local flavor

Down-Home Supper
Serves 4
(page 39)
Chicken-fried Steak
Creamy Mashed Potatoes
greens
store-bought pound cake

Southern Tapas Night
Serves 6
(page 118)
Polenta Rounds With Black-eyed Pea Topping
Grits-Stuffed Greens
Smoky Hot-Buffalo Chicken Pizzas
Ice-cream Crêpes

Glorious Texas Hill Country Menu
Serves 8
(page 124)
Cold Marinated Shrimp and Avocados
Roast Pork Loin With Peach Glaze served with **Chunky Peach Chutney**
Green Bean-and-New Potato Salad
Marinated Cherry Tomatoes
Tequila Mojitos
bakery-bought decorated cookies

Seaside Supper
Serves 12
(page 146)
Shrimp Sullivan's Island
West Indies Salad
Bacon-Wrapped Scallops
Greek Snapper on the Grill with **Dot's Tartar Sauce**
Red Rice
Sweet-and-Sour Slaw

Breakfast in the Big Easy
Serves 6
(page 232)
Grillades Over Yellow Grits Wedges
Fruit With Orange-Ginger Dressing
Creamy Rice Pudding With Praline Sauce
Citrus-Mint Sipper

Outdoor Menu
Serves 6 to 8
(page 236)
Sun-dried Tomato Cheese Spread
Chesapeake Chowder
Maryland Crab Cakes With Creamy Caper-Dill Sauce
Roasted Sweet Potato Salad
caramel apples
spiced cider

Southwestern Supper
Serves 4 to 6
(page 238)
Pan-Seared Skirt Steak With Poblano Chiles and Onions
Traditional Frijoles
Tres Leches Cake
Horchata

Mexican Soup Supper
Serves 8 to 10
(page 264)
Chile con Queso
Guacamole Granada
Chicken Sopa
Spinach Salad With Poppy Seed Dressing
Chocolate Sheet Cake
Frozen Sangria

A Tasty Tex-Mex Plate
Serves 6
(page 296)
Chicken-and-Spinach Enchiladas
Dressed-Up Refried Beans
Mexican rice
apple and pear slices with **Toffee-Apple Dip** (page 290)

» menus for special occasions

New Year's Dinner
Serves 6
(page 33)
Cooktop Cassoulet
New Year's Lucky Peas over rice
Texas Cornbread Sticks

Romantic Dining
Serves 2
(page 52)
Baby Blue Salad
Beef Fillets With Cognac-Onion Sauce
roasted potatoes
pound cake with chocolate sauce

Cool Spring Menu
Serves 10 to 12
(page 96)
Raspberry Lemonade
Chicken Salad Croissants
Fresh Corn Salad
Chocolate Fondue with assorted fresh fruit

Special Occasion Menu
Serves 4
(page 112)
Crab Cakes With Lemon Rémoulade
mixed baby greens
green beans with grape tomatoes
So-Easy Chocolate Soufflés

All-day Garden Hop
Serves 8
(page 126)
Breakfast:
Veggie Frittata
sliced tomatoes
Banana-Nut Bread
juice or coffee

Lunch:
Barbecue Pork Sandwiches
mixed veggie-potato chips
soft drinks

Afternoon Hors d'Oeuvres:
wine and cheese

Dinner:
Shrimp Penne
green tossed salad
Peach-and-Blueberry Parfaits

Street Party
Serves 4
(page 152)
Pimiento Cheese-Stuffed Burgers
Marinated Green Beans
Egg-and-Olive Potato Salad
ice cream sandwiches

Gathering by the Sea
Serves 8 to 10
(page 250)
Overnight Marinated Shrimp
Apple-Bourbon Turkey Breast (double the recipe)
cornbread dressing
Cranberry-Key Lime Sauce
Easy Sweet Potato Casserole
Key Lime Pie

Memorable Meal
Serves 2
(page 255)
Cornish Hens With Savory-Sweet Stuffing
Tiny Green Beans Amandine
Basil-Thyme Crème Brûlée

An Elegant Evening Menu
Serves 8
(page 256)
Kir Royale
assorted cheeses, crackers, breads, and fruit
Champagne Salad With Pear-Goat Cheese Tarts
Apricot-Ginger Salmon
Citrus Sweet Potatoes
Sautéed Beans and Peppers
Easy Apple Tart With Ol' South Custard

Hanukkah Celebration
Serves 8
(page 260)
Beef Tenderloin
Steamed Brussels Sprouts
Lemon Chess Pie

Southern-Style Christmas Dinner
Serves 8
(page 324)
Cran-Horseradish Sauce and Cream Cheese
Holiday Ham With Cumberland Sauce
Grits Dressing
Sweet Potato Hash Browns
Spicy Turnip Greens
Savannah Christmas Praline-Spice Cake

Winter Harvest Supper
Serves 6
(page 326)
Butternut Squash Soup
Mustard-Crusted Pork Roast and Browned Potatoes
Cinnamon-Scented Cranapple Sauce
Green Bean Casserole With Fried Leeks
Cornmeal Streusel Apple Pie

>> menus for family

Family Fun Feast
Serves 8
(page 34)
Lemony Baked Fish Sticks with Quick-and-Easy Tartar Sauce
Parsleyed New Potatoes
Microwave Corn on the Cob
Cream Puffs With Chocolate Sauce

Supper Tonight
Serves 4
(page 56)
Blackened Salmon With Hash Browns and Green Onions
green salad with peppercorn-Ranch dressing
cherry vanilla ice cream drizzled with hot fudge and sprinkled with toasted slivered almonds

Catfish Fry
Serves 6 to 8
(page 78)
Classic Fried Catfish
Baked Beans
coleslaw from your favorite barbecue restaurant
Hush Puppies
Pound Cake Banana Pudding
(page 68)

Sloppy Joe Supper
Serves 6 to 8
(page 79)
Richard's Sloppy Joes
mixed salad greens with **Honey-Mustard Vinaigrette**
PB & Chocolate Pan Cookie

Morning Menu
Serves 8
(page 92)
Oatmeal Pancakes With Cider Sauce
Brown Sugared Turkey Bacon
Parmesan-Portobello Grits

Busy-Day Dinner #1
Serves 4
(page 97)
Slow-cooker Turkey Chili
orange wedges and green grapes
focaccia or cornbread crackers

Busy-Day Dinner #2
Serves 8
(page 97)
Chili-Cheese-Potato Tot Casserole
mixed green salad with peppercorn-Ranch dressing
hot dinner rolls with honey butter

Two Speedy Suppers
Serves 6
(page 110)
Zesty Pork Loin With Apricot-Pan Sauce
Potato-and-Carrot Amandine
mixed salad greens
—and—
Pork-and-Soba Noodle Bowl
orange slices
fortune cookies

Weekday Supper
Serves 6
(page 133)
Easy Shredded Beef Over Rice
Seasoned Green Beans
Texas toast or hot dinner rolls
Warm Cookie Sundaes

Midweek Beef Brisket Menu
Serves 6
(page 158)
Slow-cooker Beef Brisket
flour tortillas
Tomato-and-Corn Chip Salad
Honeydew-Orange Toss
lemonade

Weeknight Pork Roast Supper
Serves 6
(page 159)
Zesty Pork Roast With Vegetables
Herbed Rice
ice cream
iced tea

Home-Cooked Flavor
Serves 6
(page 198)
Tee's Corn Pudding
fried okra
Butterbeans and Bacon
sliced tomatoes
Skillet Cornbread
sweet tea

Sandwich Supper
Serves 4
(page 199)
Cumin-Dusted Catfish Sandwiches or Cumin-Dusted Shrimp Sandwiches
Sweet Potato Fries
coleslaw

Brunch on the Double
Serves 2
(page 210)
Sausage-Cheese Breakfast Cups
Mint-Topped Broiled Oranges
Spiced Coffee Cake

A School Day Menu
Serves 4 to 6
(page 218)
Baked Curry-Glazed Chicken
Fruity Couscous
Zucchini Toss
Delta Velvet Pudding Dessert

>> menus for family *(continued)*

Back-to-School Lunch
Serves 6
(page 219)
Festive Turkey Rollups
Crunchy Munchy Mix
S'more Cupcakes
lemonade

Family Meal
Serves 6 to 8
(page 240)
Easy Lasagna
Italian Salad
toasted garlic bread
Spumone, pistachio, or
 Neapolitan ice cream with hot
 fudge sauce

Chilly Day Dinner
Serves 5
(page 253)
**Italian Sausage With Tomato-
 Pepper Relish**
Parmesan Cheese Grits
garlic toast
tossed salad with Italian
 dressing
**Chocolate-and-Almond
 Macaroons** (page 262)

Pot Pie Supper
Serves 6
(page 328)
Green Chile-Turkey Pot Pie
**Lime-Marinated Tomatoes With
 Cilantro**
Bakery brownies and cookies

>> menus for grilling

Outdoor Gathering
Serves 6 to 8
(page 60)
**Bacon-Wrapped Mushrooms
 With Honey-Barbecue Sauce**
Spicy Flank Steak
**Herbed Salad With Grilled
 Balsamic Vegetables**
Corn-Arugula-Tomato Medley
grilled bread
Sour Cream Pound Cake

Easy-to-Make Menu
Serves 8
(page 100)
**Grilled Flank Steak With
 Guacamole Sauce**
Easy Grilled Vegetables
rice
flour tortillas

Summer Picnic
Serves 6
(page 154)
Smoky Ribs
**Pan-fried Okra, Onion, and
 Tomatoes**
Chili-Lime Grilled Corn
Grilled Parmesan-Garlic Bread
Caramel-Cashew Ice Cream

Dinner for Two
Serves 2
(page 193)
**Grilled Steak and Potatoes With
 Red Onion Relish**
buttered, steamed green beans
**Outrageous Peanut Butter
 Cookies**
iced tea

Festive Fall Menu
Serves 8
(page 204)
Brick-Grilled Cornish Hens
Lump Blue Crab Salad Wraps
Squash Casserole
**Bourbon-Chocolate Cake With
 Praline Frosting**

Dinner on the Grill
Serves 4
(page 216)
**Portobello Mushroom Burgers
 With Carrot-Cabbage Slaw**
**Grilled Sweet Potato Salad With
 Basil Vinaigrette**

≫ menus for company

Perfect Porch Appetizer Menu
Serves 15 to 20
(page 98)
Pickled Okra-Ham Rolls
Catfish Poppers With Spicy Dipping Sauce
Cindy's Cheese Wafers
Tomato Chutney Cheesecake
Chocolate Chess Tartlets
Streusel-Topped Lemon Shortbread Bars

Outdoor Lunch
Serves 6
(page 103)
Black Bean-and-Brown Rice Pitas
Couscous and Garbanzo Salad
Caramel Dip with apple slices
lemonade and iced tea

Party Menu
Serves 12
(page 108)
Beer 'Garitas (triple the recipe)
Smoky Hot Sauce, Tomatillo Sauce
tortilla chips
Smoked Lemon-Chipotle Chickens
Wheat Berry Tabbouleh
green salad with **Avocado-Ranch Dressing**
Lemon Chill With Raspberry Sauce

Easy Taco Bar
Serves 8
(page 115)
Slow-cooker Beef Tacos
favorite toppings
Mexican Slaw
Black Beans and Yellow Rice

Brunch for a Bunch
Serves 10 to 12
(page 120)
Blueberry-Honey Breakfast Shake (make 5 times) and orange juice
Southwest Brunch Casserole
fruit salad
biscuits

Summer Sampler
Serves 4 to 6
(page 131)
Honey-Chicken Salad
Shrimp Salad
tomato-and-cucumber salad with **Sugar-and-Vinegar Dressing**
cornbread madeleines
iced tea
Sour Cream Pound Cake with fresh peaches (page 134)

Lunch at the Lake
Serves 8
(page 148)
Layered Bean Dip
Papaya Gazpacho
Mango-Chicken Wraps
Texas Pecan-and-Avocado Salad
Cilantro Potato Salad
Cream-Filled Chocolate Chip Wafers

Easy Entertaining
Serves 8
(page 211)
Layered Spicy Black Bean Dip with chips
Smoky Ranch Dip with raw veggies
Simple Antipasto Platter

Pasta Party
Serves 6
(page 229)
Antipasto Platter
Linguine Alfredo
Caesar salad
Lemon Tortoni Dessert

Party Starters
Serves 12 to 24
(page 240)
Peppered Pork With Pecan Biscuits
Marinated Cheese
assorted veggie tray

Christmas Luncheon
Serves 6
(page 259)
Pineapple-Nut Cheese With Cranberry Chutney
Orange-Cranberry-Glazed Pork Tenderloin
Pecan Wild Rice
Mandarin-Almond Salad
Belgian Wassail

Fantastic Dinner
Serves 6
(page 266)
Country Ham Mini Biscuits
Grilled Rib-eye Steaks
Sautéed Early Winter Greens
Smashed Rutabagas and Turnips With Parmesan Cheese
Balsamic-Butter-Glazed Baby Carrots
Pecan Pie
Walter's Ultimate Vanilla Ice Cream

Shrimp Supper
Serves 4
(page 295)
Shrimp Destin over toast
Asparagus With Curry Sauce
Chocolate Mint Cake (page 286)

Celebration Dinner
Serves 8
(page 304)
Sweet-and-Sour Tapenade
Herb-Crusted Pork Tenderloins
Cheesy Herbed Scalloped Potatoes
steamed sugar snap peas
Turtle Trifle

Easy Pasta Dinner
Serves 8
(page 304)
Sweet-and-Sour Tapenade
Pounded Pork Parmesan With Linguine
steamed sugar snap peas
Cappuccino-Frosted Brownies

recipe title index

This index lists every recipe by food category and/or major ingredient.
All microwave recipe page numbers are preceded by an "M."

month-by-month index

This index alphabetically lists every food article and accompanying recipes by month. All microwave recipe page numbers are preceded by an "M."

general recipe index

This index lists every recipe by food category and/or major ingredient.
All microwave recipe page numbers are preceded by an "M."

Meatloaf *(continued)*

Sandwich, Italian Meatloaf, 217
Sauce, Meatloaf, 64
Simple Meatloaf, 217
Turkey Meatloaf, 223

MELONS

Honeydew-Orange Toss, 159
Margarita, Melon, 201

Watermelon

Cups, Watermelon, 150
Frozen Watermelon Dippers, 151
Margaritas, Watermelon-Mint, 151
Salsa, Watermelon, 151

MERINGUE

Meringue, 67, 68

MICROWAVE RECIPES

Appetizers

Mushrooms With Honey-Barbecue Sauce,
Bacon-Wrapped, M60
Scallops, Bacon-Wrapped, M146
Spinach-and-Artichoke Dip, Baked, M252

Desserts

Bars, Chocolate Chip Cheesecake, M226
Brittle Fondue, M335
Brownies, Cappuccino-Frosted, M306
Cake, Chocolate-Mint, M286
Carmelitas, Oatmeal, M263
Cheesecake, Double Chocolate, M48
Cookie Sticks, Chocolate-Dipped, M299
Crêpes, Ice-cream, M119
Cupcakes With Orange Buttercream Frosting,
Double Chocolate-Orange, M224
Filling, M320
Fondue, Chocolate, M96
Ganache, Chocolate, M205
Glaze, M320
Ice Cream, Walter's Ultimate Vanilla, M267
Macaroons, Chocolate-and-Almond, M262
Soufflés, So-Easy Chocolate, M112
Whipped Cream, White Chocolate, M288
Latte, Quick Mocha, M268

Main Dishes

Beef Fillets, Bacon-Wrapped, M90
Black Beans and Mexican Rice, Speedy, M209
Boarding House Meatloaf, M64
Chicken and Dumplings, South
Louisiana, M278
Chicken Couscous, Mediterranean, M30
Chicken Pot Pie, Savory, M222
Chicken Thighs, Oven-Fried Bacon-
Wrapped, M73
Pizzas, Smoky-Hot Buffalo Chicken, M119
Pork Loin With Apricot-Pan Sauce,
Zesty, M111
Taco Cups, Mini, M140
Turkey Rollups, Festive, M219
Noodles, Parsleyed, M230
Salad, Chicken BLT, M195
Salad, Cinnamon Apple, M292
Shells With Fresh Cilantro and Tomatoes, Easy
Queso, M321

Soups

Sweet Potato Soup With Lemon Cream,
Chipotle, M291
Tomato 'n' Grilled Corn Bisque,
Chunky, M318

Vegetables

Brussels Sprouts, Steamed, M261
Corn on the Cob, Microwave, M35
New Potatoes, Parsleyed, M35

Potatoes, Cheesy Ranch-and-Bacon
Mashed, M334
Sweet Potato Fries, M199

MUFFINS

Brown Sugar-Banana Muffins, 94
Hush Puppy Muffins, 120
Morning Glory Muffins, 45
Peanut Butter Chocolate Chip Muffins, Freezer-
Friendly, 94
Pizza Muffins, 94
Sausage-Cheese Muffins, 274

MUSHROOMS

Bacon-Wrapped Mushrooms With Honey-
Barbecue Sauce, M60

Main Dishes

Chicken and Mushrooms, Champagne, 74
Chicken, Southern-Stuffed Rosemary, 242
Lasagna, Turkey-Mushroom, 117
Pasta, Fresh Tomato-Mushroom-Basil, 154
Portobello Mushroom Burgers With Carrot-
Cabbage Slaw, 216
Steaks With Mushrooms, Broiled, 85
Sauce, Mushroom-Onion, 77
Sauce, Simple Mushroom, 77

Side Dishes

Asparagus With Mushrooms and Bacon, 275
Green Beans With Mushrooms and
Bacon, 275
Portobello Grits, Parmesan-, 93
Sugar Snaps With Mushrooms and
Bacon, 275

N

NOODLES

Casserole, Noodle-and-Spinach, 83
Parsleyed Noodles, M230
Pork Lo Mein, 208
Ranch Noodles, 41
Salad, Thai Noodle, 247
Slaw, Sweet-and-Sour, 147
Soba Noodle Bowl, Pork-and-, 111
Vegetable-Bacon Noodle Toss, 131

O

OATMEAL

Bread, Honey-Oatmeal Wheat, 70
Carmelitas, Oatmeal, M263
Cookies, Oatmeal-Chocolate Chip, 48
Granola, Early-Morning, 274
Pancakes With Cider Sauce, Oatmeal, 92

OKRA

Pan-fried Okra, Onion, and Tomatoes, 155
Pickled Okra-Ham Rolls, 98

OLIVES

Bites, Olive Cheese, 99
Burgers, Olive, 101
Magi Olives, 273
Pesto, Black Olive, 101
Salad, Egg-and-Olive Potato, 152
Tapenade, Sweet-and-Sour, 304

ONIONS

Caramelized Onion Macaroni and Cheese, 220
Frijoles, Traditional, 239
Frittata, Lightened Zucchini-Onion, 69
Frittata, Zucchini-Onion, 69

Green Onions

Salmon With Hash Browns and Green Onions,
Blackened, 57
Sauce, Beef Fillets With Cognac-Onion, 52
Spread, Cheesy Onion, 197
Pan-fried Okra, Onion, and Tomatoes, 155

Relish, Red Onion, 193
Shallots, Green Beans With Bacon and, 139
Skirt Steak With Poblano Chiles and Onions,
Pan-Seared, 238

Sweet

Bake, Sweet Onion, 91
Casserole, Chicken Cobbler, 41
Relish, Minted Onion, 91
Sauce, Beef-Onion, 77
Sauce, Mushroom-Onion, 77
Sauce, Onion, 76
Shrimp Sullivan's Island, 146
Vidalia Onion Cornbread, 38

ORANGES

Beverages

Frosty, Orange-Pineapple, 66
Punch, Pomegranate-Orange, 287
Smoothie, Orange-Pineapple, 227
Spritzer, Quick Cranberry-Orange, 37
Broiled Oranges, Mint-Topped, 210
Crescents, Orange-Almond Stuffed, 279
Cupcakes With Orange Buttercream Frosting,
Double Chocolate-Orange, M224
Dressing, Fruit With Orange-Ginger, 233
Frosting, Orange Buttercream, 224

Main Dishes

Chicken Thighs, Orange-Ginger Grilled, 90
Ham, Citrus-Glazed, 88
Pork Tenderloin, Orange-Cranberry-
Glazed, 259
Peas, Orange-Mint, 113
Rolls, Coconut Orange, 318

Salads

Avocado Salad, Orange-, 116
Jalapeño, Orange, and Cucumber Salad, 292
Mandarin-Almond Salad, 260

Sauces and Glaze

Cranberry-Orange Sauce, 251
Cumberland Sauce, 325
Orange Glaze, 319
Spread, Orange Blossom Cheese, 300
Toss, Honeydew-Orange, 159

P

PANCAKES

Oatmeal Pancakes With Cider Sauce, 92
Pecan Pancakes, 247

PAPAYA

Gazpacho, Papaya, 148

PASTAS. *See also* **Couscous, Lasagna,
Macaroni, Manicotti, Spaghetti.**

Alfredo, Broccoli-Pasta, 130
Baked Pasta, Three-Cheese, 82
Bow Tie Pasta, Chicken, 200
Bow Tie Pasta Toss, 208
Casserole, Italian Pasta, 232
Farfalle in Ragu Cream Sauce With Sun-dried
Tomatoes, 319
Late-Night Pasta Chez Frank, 82
Penne, Shrimp, 127
Penne With Oregano, Fresh Tomato, 200
Ravioli Casserole, Tex-Mex, 55
Salad, Niçoise, Pasta, 230
Salad, Tomato-Basil-Asparagus Pasta, 330

Shells

Bake, Herb-Topped Pasta, 222
Cheesy Pasta With Bell Peppers, 228
Chili Mac, Skillet, 228
Queso Shells With Fresh Cilantro and
Tomatoes, Easy, M321
Tomato-Mushroom-Basil Pasta, Fresh, 154

favorite recipes journal

Jot down your family's and your favorite recipes for quick and handy reference. And don't forget to include the dishes that drew rave reviews when company came for dinner.

RECIPE	SOURCE/PAGE	REMARKS